The Psychologist as Detective

An Introduction to Conducting Research in Psychology

RANDOLPH A. SMITH
Ouachita Baptist University

STEPHEN F. DAVIS
Emporia State University

PRENTICE HALL
Upper Saddle River, NJ 07458

Library of Congress Cataloging-in-Publication Data

Smith, Randolph A.,
    The psychologist as detective : an introduction to conducting
research in psychology / Randolph A. Smith, Stephen F. Davis.
      p.   cm.
    Includes bibliographical references and index.
    ISBN 0-02-412581-4
    1. Psychology—Research.   2. Psychology—Research—Methodology.
3. Psychology, Experimental.   I. Davis, Stephen F.   II. Title.
    BF76.5.S54   1996   96-20148
    150'.72—dc20   CIP

Editor-in-Chief: *Pete Janzow*
Acquisition Editor: *Nicole Signoretti*
Director of Production and Manufacturing: *Barbara Kittle*
Managing Editor: *Bonnie Biller*
Project Manager: *Shelly Kupperman*
Manufacturing Manager: *Nick Sklitsis*
Prepress and Manufacturing Buyer: *Tricia Kenny*
Creative Design Director: *Leslie Osher*
Interior/Cover Design: *Amy Rosen*
Cover Art: *Cathie Bleck Illustrations*
Photo Research: *Sherry Cohen*
Electronic Art Creation: *PH Formatting*
Marketing Manager: *Gina Sluss*

The figures shown on pp. 442–445 were taken from the following sources:
    p. 442 Title heading from "Causal Models and the Acquisition of Category Structure," M. R.
Waldmann, K. J. Holyoak, and A. Fratianne, 1995, in *Journal of Experimental Psychology
General, 124,* pp. 181–206. Copyright ©1995 by the American Psychological Association.
Reprinted with permission.
    p. 443 Women's Minds, Women's Bodies, Joan H. Rolling, ©1996 by Prentice Hall, Inc.
    pp. 444, 445 Classic and Contemporary Readings in Social Psychology, Erik J. Coats and
Robert S. Feldman, ©1996 by Prentice Hall, Inc.

 ©1997 by Prentice-Hall, Inc.
Simon & Schuster/A Viacom Company
Upper Saddle River, NJ 07458

Printed in the United States of America
10 9 8 7 6 5 4 3

ISBN 0-02-412581-4

PRENTICE-HALL INTERNATIONAL (UK) Limited, *London*
PRENTICE-HALL of Australia Pty. Limited, *Sydney*
PRENTICE-HALL Canada, Inc., *Toronto*
PRENTICE-HALL of India Private Limited, *New Delhi*
PRENTICE-HALL of Japan, Inc., *Tokyo*
SIMON & SCHUSTER Asia Pte. Ltd., *Singapore*
EDITORA PRENTICE-HALL do Brasil, Ltda., *Rio de Janeiro*

Dedication

To our students, who give us the inspiration for what we do.

To Chris, for believing in this idea.

Contents

CHAPTER 2

Research Ideas, Hypotheses, and Ethics   23

CHAPTER 3

Nonexperimental Methods for Acquiring Data   63

CHAPTER 4

The Basics of Experimentation I: Variables and Control   99

CHAPTER 5

The Basics of Experimentation II: Participants and Apparatus, Cross-Cultural Considerations, and Beginning the Research Report   139

CHAPTER 6

Statistics Review   168

CHAPTER 9

Designing, Conducting, Analyzing, and Interpreting Experiments with Multiple Independent Variables   275

CHAPTER 12

Assembling the Research Report   407

Preface

NOTE TO THE INSTRUCTOR

Margery Franklin (1990) quotes former Clark University professor and chair Heinz Werner's views on psychological research. Werner indicated:

> I got rather apprehensive at finding that students were frequently taught that there was only one acceptable way of conduct in the laboratory there has to be an hypothesis set up, or a set of hypotheses, and the main job of the experimenter is to prove or disprove the hypothesis. What is missed here is the function of the scientist as a discoverer and explorer of unknown lands. . . . Hypotheses . . . are essential elements of inquiry, but they are so, not as rigid propositions but as flexible parts of the process of searching; by the same token, conclusions drawn from the results are as much an end as a beginning. . . . Now . . . academic psychologists [are beginning] to see research not as a rigid exercise of rules of a game but as a problem solving procedure, a probing into unknown lands with plans which are not fixed but modifiable, with progress and retreat, with branching out into various directions or concentration on one.

Clearly Werner's views are as applicable in the 1990s as they were during the heyday of behaviorism; they reflect perfectly the intent of this text.

From our vantage point, research in psychology is like a detective case; hence, the title we have chosen, *The Psychologist as Detective*. A problem presents itself, clues are discovered, bits of evidence that compete for our attention must be evaluated and accepted or discarded, and, finally, a report or summary of the case (research) is prepared for consideration by our peers.

When presented in this light, the research process in psychology will, we believe, be an interesting and stimulating endeavor for students. In short, our goal is to attract students to psychological research because of its inherent interest.

To accomplish this goal several pedagogical features have been employed in this text:

1. To provide a sense of relevance and continuity, the theme of "psychologist as detective" runs throughout the text.

2. ***Interactive Style of Writing.*** Based on the belief that the experimental psychology-research methods text should be lively and engaging, we employ an interactive, conversational style of writing that we hope will help draw students into the material being presented.

3. ***The Psychological Detective Feature.*** The questions or situations posed by these sections that appear throughout each chapter will encourage students to engage in critical thinking exercises. These sections also serve as excellent stimulants for productive class discussions.

4. ***Marginal Definitions.*** Key definitions appear in the margin, close to the introduction of the term in the text.

5. ***Review Summaries.*** To help students master smaller chunks of material, each chapter contains several review summaries.

6. ***Study Breaks.*** Each Review Summary is followed by a Study Break that students can use to test their mastery of the material they have just completed. These study breaks should be especially helpful to your students when they prepare for quizzes and examinations.

7. ***Hands-On Activities.*** Each chapter concludes with a Hands-on Activities section that students are encouraged to become engaged in. It's like having a laboratory manual built into the text!

We hope that these special features will provide your students with a positive experience as they learn the fundamentals of research methodology in psychology.

NOTE TO THE STUDENT

Welcome to the world of psychological research! Because the two of us have taught this course for over forty-five years (combined!), we have seen the excitement that research can generate in student after student. As you will learn, conducting psychological research is very much like being a detective on a case.

Throughout this text we have tried to make it perfectly clear that research is something that *you* can (and should) become involved in. We hope you will enjoy reading about the student projects that we use as research examples throughout this text. Student research projects are making valuable contributions to our field. We hope to see *your* name among those making such contributions!

At this point we encourage you to stop *immediately* to review the list of pedagogical features highlighted in the "Note to the Instructor". . . Did you humor us by actually looking at that list? If not, please do so now. To make full use of this text, you need to become *actively* involved; these pedagogical features will help you. Active involvement means that you need to stop to think about **The Psychological Detective** sections immediately when you encounter them, refer to figures and tables when directed to do so, complete the **Study Breaks** when they appear, and attempt some of the **Hands-On Activities,** even if they are not assigned. Becoming actively involved in this course helps the material come alive; your grade and your future involvement in psychology will thank you.

ACKNOWLEDGMENTS

We would like to express our appreciation to the consultants who reviewed earlier versions of this text: Diane Mello-Goldner, Pine Manor College; Trey Buchanan, Wheaton College; David Johnson, John Brown University. Their comments were especially helpful as we prepared the final draft.

In many ways the final preparation of a text is only as good as the publisher. We could have asked for none better than Prentice Hall! Chief Psychology Editor Pete Janzow was always there to listen to our suggestions and concerns. His instincts concerning what will make a good book are impeccable. Assistant Psychology Editor Nicole Signoretti was always supportive of those features that we felt would result in a more lively and appealing text. Thanks, folks—It would not have worked without your concern and support!

We also thank our families (Corliss, Tyler, and Ben—RAS; Kathleen and Jennifer—SFD) for putting up with us during the preparation of this text. True friends and real supporters are few and far between!

R. A. S.
S. F. D.

The Science of Psychology

We purposely titled our text "The Psychologist as Detective" to convey the excitement and thrill that researchers have when they investigate questions that are at the core of what it means to be a psychological being. The parallels between conducting psychological research and working on a detective case are striking. First, you have to know the boundaries of your case (a research question is developed). Suspects are eliminated (the researcher exercises control over unwanted factors). Evidence is gathered (the researcher conducts the experiment and makes observations). A solution is proposed (the results of the research are analyzed and an interpretation is offered). The proposed solution is presented to the jury (researchers share their results and/or interpretations with their peers).

To help you become a good psychological detective, we have included several "Psychological Detective" sections in each chapter. Each of these sections asks you to stop, then think about and answer a question concerning psychological research. Please take full advantage of these sections; they were designed to help you think critically about psychological research. Critical thinking is vital to good detectives. We want you to become the best psychological detective possible. We begin our examination of psychological research by considering a research project that would intrigue even the best psychological detective.

You are sitting on the witness stand at a trial and the defense attorney begins questioning you. "How fast were the cars going when they smashed into each other?" You give your answer. Next the attorney asks, "Was there any broken glass?" You frantically search your memory for an answer. "If the cars involved *smashed* into each other, then surely there was broken glass?" You respond affirmatively. Elizabeth Loftus's (1979) provocative research on eyewitness testimony has shown that the types of questions asked of witnesses may influence their answers and that their testimony may not be valid.

In a research study investigating the questions above concerning the automobile accident, Loftus (1979) found that the estimated speeds reported by research participants who were asked about cars that "smashed into" each other were higher than speeds estimated by participants who were asked about cars that merely "hit" each other. Moreover, participants who were told that the cars smashed into each other reported the presence of more broken glass.

Such results prompted other researchers to ask questions about the credibility of witnesses. For example, Pamela Feist (1993), a student at Southwest State University (Marshall, MN) wondered whether the way witnesses are dressed influences the perception of their credibility. As you can see from Figure 1-1, she found that female witnesses were seen as more credible when dressed conservatively than when they were dressed fashionably. On the other hand, fashionably dressed men were seen as being slightly more credible witnesses than were conservatively dressed men.

For the time being we will not concern ourselves with *how* Feist gathered this information relating style of dress and witness credibility. Our concern at present is *why* she gathered this information. The answer really is quite straightforward—an interesting question in need of an answer had presented itself. Asking and then attempting to answer questions are at the heart of what psychologists do. In short, psychologists are in the business of acquiring new information.

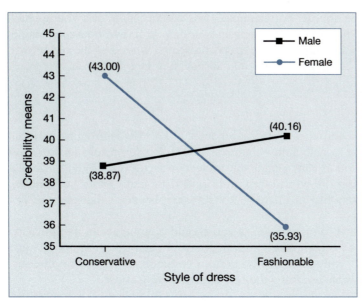

FIGURE 1-1. MEAN CREDIBILITY SCORES OF THE WITNESS IN CONSERVATIVE VERSUS FASHIONABLE DRESS AS RATED BY MALE AND FEMALE OBSERVERS.

Source: Figure 1 from *Effects of Style of Dress on Witness Credibility,* paper presented by P.S. Feist, May 1993, at annual meeting of the Midwestern Psychological Association, Chicago, IL. Used with permission of the author.

WAYS TO ACQUIRE KNOWLEDGE

Although the task of acquiring new knowledge may sound simple, it is actually more difficult than it appears. The difficulty is created because there is more than one way to acquire knowledge *and* because once knowledge is acquired, you need to ensure its truthfulness. Let's examine several ways that have been used to increase our store of knowledge. These techniques were suggested by the philosopher-scientist Charles S. Pierce, who in the 1880s was interested in helping establish psychology in the United States. As you will see, the **validity** of the knowledge produced by some of these methods is doubtful.

TENACITY

When we hear a statement repeated a sufficient number of times, we have a tendency to accept it as being true. Thus, **tenacity** refers to the continued presentation of a particular bit of information; no matter which way you turn, the same information seems to be present and you begin to believe it. According to the tenacity view of acquiring knowledge, you are expected to accept this

Validity The degree to which a knowledge claim is accurate.

Tenacity Acceptance of knowledge or information simply because it has been presented repeatedly.

definition

repeated message as being true. For example, consider the plight of a young child who has been *repeatedly* told that "a witch lives in the old brown house on Maple Street." Because this is the only message that is presented whenever the old brown house on Maple Street is discussed, the child accepts it as fact.

AUTHORITY

Much of our daily behavior relies on the acceptance of knowledge from authorities. For example, do *you* personally know that exposure to the sun results in skin cancer or do you put on lotion with a high sun protection factor (e.g., SPF 25) simply because you have taken the word of an authority? How many other authorities, such as ministers, automobile mechanics, stockbrokers, lawyers, and teachers, influence your daily life?

From watching television commercials you should now be aware that tenacity and authority may not be completely independent of each other. Think of how many times (tenacity) you saw that one certain commercial where the famous movie star (authority) was describing the bad effects of drug abuse.

Psychological Detective

Clearly, we are able to acquire new knowledge through tenacity and authority. However, this newly acquired knowledge may not be as valid as we would like. What problems can you identify with acquiring of knowledge through tenacity and authority? Write down your answers before reading further.

Tenacity and authority share two problems. First, you have no way of knowing if the knowledge you have gained is true or not. Merely because you are repeatedly told that the moon is made of green cheese does not make this statement true. The second problem concerns the inability (or unwillingness) of tenacity and authority to change in the face of contradictory evidence. When conflicting evidence is presented, individuals who have accepted knowledge based on tenacity or authority either ignore the evidence or find some way to discount it. For example, if you really believe that the moon is made of green cheese, and an astronaut reports bringing back a rock from the moon, you might decide that the astronaut had never been to the moon and that the claim that this rock came from the moon was an elaborate hoax.

Authority also depends on another factor—the credibility of the person presenting the information. The detective knows that the knowledge you acquire is only as good as the credibility of the authority who presents it. Any time of day or night you can see "authorities" dispensing great amounts of information as they try to convince you to buy any number of different products on television commercials. What credentials do these "authorities" have? How accurate is the information they are providing?

EXPERIENCE

Another way to gain knowledge is through direct experience. Surely if *you* experience something firsthand, there is no better or more accurate method for acquiring new information. Right? Unfortunately, this assumption is not always true. If you are colorblind or tone deaf, your perception of the world is altered and your knowledge base may not be accurate. Likewise, a theory that is developed under the effects of an hallucinogenic drug may not conform to reality very well. Even normal individuals under normal conditions may see the world differently. However, if others also agree that they have experienced the phenomenon under consideration, then its validity is increased.

REASON AND LOGIC

This approach is based on the premise that we can apply reason and logic to a situation in order to gain knowledge and understanding. Typically, we start with an assumption and then logically deduce consequences based upon this assumption. This process is frequently stated as a **logical syllogism.** For example, we may start with the assumption that "beautiful people are good." Then when we meet Claudia, who is an attractive person, we would say, "Beautiful people are good. Claudia is a beautiful person. Therefore Claudia is a good person." The fallacy of this logical syllogism should be apparent. We have no proof to support our original assumption that "beautiful people are good." Without such proof our conclusion cannot

Logical syllogism
A scheme of formal logic or argument consisting of a major premise, a minor premise, and a conclusion.

definition

be trusted. Before you say you are sure you would never fall prey to such faulty logic, we would like to point out that the "beautiful is good" stereotype is a thoroughly researched topic of social psychology; it is a bias with which many people seem to agree. For example, attractiveness has been shown to affect first impressions in job interviews (Mack & Rainey, 1990).

SCIENCE

Each of the techniques for acquiring knowledge that we have discussed so far has had a major problem(s) associated with it. Hence, psychologists seldom use these methods to add to our store of psychological knowledge. What method is preferred?

The year 1879 marks the beginning of modern psychological study. Although there are numerous other dates that could have been selected to mark the founding of psychology, 1879 was selected because it marked the establishment of a research laboratory at the University of Leipzig by Wilhelm Wundt. Wundt used the scientific method to gather new information. Over 100 years later psychologists continue to believe that the scientific approach is best suited for adding to our knowledge of psychological processes.

The key elements in the scientific approach are

1. objective measurements of the phenomenon under consideration
2. the ability to verify or confirm the measurements made by other individuals
3. self-correction of errors and faulty reasoning
4. exercising control to rule out the influence of unwanted factors.

We will discuss each of these characteristics in the next section. For now, we will simply say that the scientific method attempts to provide objective information that can be verified by anyone who wishes to repeat the observation in question.

Psychological Detective

Review the methods for acquiring knowledge that were presented. How does the scientific method avoid the problems that were associated with tenacity, authority, experience, and reason and logic? Write down your answers before reading further.

When the scientific method is used, a scientist makes observations and gathers new information. However, we don't have to accept the scientists' knowledge claims on faith (authority) or merely because they are repeatedly discussed and presented (tenacity). The methods and procedures the scientist uses to acquire knowledge are open to public scrutiny, and should individuals decide to question the scientist's information, they are able to test the conclusions themselves. Thus, the possibility of individual experiences also can be ruled out. In short, researchers can verify the knowledge claims made by science; the other methods do not afford us this opportunity.

COMPONENTS OF THE SCIENTIFIC METHOD

In this section the features that characterize the scientific method are described. We will have much more to say about these characteristics in subsequent chapters.

OBJECTIVITY

In conducting a research project the psychologist, just as the good detective, strives to be as objective as possible. For example, psychologists select the research participants in such a manner that biasing factors (such as age or gender) are avoided.

Researchers frequently make their measurements with instruments in order to be as objective as possible. We describe such measurements as being **empirical** because they are based on objectively quantifiable observations.

CONFIRMATION OF FINDINGS

Because the procedures and measurements are objective, we should be able to repeat them and *confirm* the original results. Confirmation of findings is important for establishing the validity of research. Psychologists use the term **replication** to refer to a research study that is conducted in exactly the same manner as a previous study. By conducting a replication study, the scientist hopes to confirm previous findings. Other studies may constitute a replication *with extension* whenever new information is generated at the same time that previous findings are being confirmed. For example, confirming the effects of a previously tested drug *and* also testing the effects of a different dosage would be a replication with extension.

Empirical Objectively quantifiable observations.

Replication An additional scientific study that is conducted in exactly the same manner as the original research project.

Control Two meanings: directly manipulating (a) a factor of interest in a research study to determine its effects or (b) other, unwanted variables that could influence the results of a research project.

definition

SELF-CORRECTION

Because scientific findings are open to public scrutiny and replication, errors and faulty reasoning that become apparent should lead to a change in the conclusions we reach. For example, some early American psychologists, such as James McKeen Cattell, once believed that intelligence was directly related to the quality of one's nervous system; the better the nervous system, the higher the intelligence (see Schultz & Schultz, 1996). To verify this predicted relationship Cattell attempted to demonstrate that college students with faster reaction times (therefore, having better nervous systems) earned higher grades in college. However, his observations failed to support the predicted relationship, and Cattell changed his view of intelligence and how it might be measured.

CONTROL

Probably no single term characterizes science better than **control.** Scientists go to great lengths to make sure that their conclusions accurately reflect the way nature operates.

Imagine that an industrial psychologist wants to determine whether providing new, brighter lighting will increase worker productivity. The new lighting is installed and the industrial psychologist arrives at the plant to monitor production and determine if productivity increases.

Psychological Detective

There is a problem with this research project that needs to be corrected. What is the nature of this problem and how can it be corrected? Give these questions some thought and write down your answers before reading further.

The main problem with this research project concerns the presence of the psychologist to check on production after the new lighting is installed. If the researcher was not present to observe production before the lighting changes were made, then he or she should not be present following the implementation of these changes. If production increases following the lighting changes, is the increase due to the new lighting or the presence of the researcher who is monitoring production? Unfortunately, there is no way of knowing. Control must be exercised to make sure that the only factor that could influence productivity is the change in lighting; other factors should not be allowed to exert an influence by varying also.

Our example of the research on the effects of lighting on worker productivity also illustrates another use of the term *control*. In addition to accounting for the effects of unwanted factors, control can also refer to the direct manipulation of the factor of major interest in the research project. Because the industrial psychologist was interested in the effects of lighting on productivity, a change in lighting was purposely created (*control* or direct manipulation of factors of major interest), whereas other, potentially influential but undesirable factors, such as the presence of the psychologist, were not allowed to change (control of unwanted factors).

When researchers implement control by directly manipulating the factor that is the central focus of their research, we say that an experiment has been performed. Because most psychologists believe that our most valid knowledge is produced by conducting an experiment, we will give this topic additional coverage in the next section.

The Psychological Experiment

In many respects you can view an experiment as an attempt to determine the cause-and-effect relations that exist in nature. Researchers are interested in determining those factors that result in or cause predictable events. In its most basic form the psychological experiment consists of three related factors: the independent variable, the dependent variable, and extraneous variables.

Independent Variable

The factor that is the major focus of the research and is directly manipulated by the researcher is known as the **independent variable (IV)**—

Independent variable (IV) A stimulus or aspect of the environment that the experimenter directly manipulates to determine its influences on behavior.

definition

"independent" because it can be independently manipulated by the investigator and "variable" because it is able to assume two or more values. The IV is the causal part of the relationship we seek to establish. Recall that lighting was the independent variable in our previous example. It had two values: the original level and the new, brighter level. Manipulation of the IV corresponds to one use of the term *control*.

DEPENDENT VARIABLE

The information or results (frequently called data; the singular is datum) that are recorded comprise the **dependent variable (DV)**. The DV is the *effect* half of the cause-and-effect relationship we are examining. In our example, level of productivity was the DV; it was measured under the two conditions of the IV. The term *dependent* is used because if the experiment is conducted properly, changes in DV scores will result from (depend on) the manipulation of the IV; the level of productivity will depend on the changes in lighting.

EXTRANEOUS VARIABLES

Extraneous variables are those factors, other than the independent variable, that can influence the dependent variable. Extraneous variables, such as the presence of the experimenter *only* during the new-lighting test period, can make our research data difficult, if not impossible, to interpret. Age, sex, educational level, socioeconomic status, time of day, temperature, and noise level are among the countless factors that could be extraneous variables. As we have seen, attention to extraneous variables represents another use of the term *control*.

ESTABLISHING CAUSE-AND-EFFECT RELATIONS

Why do psychologists hold experimental research in such high regard? The answer to this question involves the type of information that is acquired. Although we might be very objective in making our observations and even though these observations can be repeated, unless we have directly manipulated an independent variable, we cannot really learn anything about cause and effect in our research project. Only when we manipulate an independent variable and control potential extraneous variables are we able to infer a cause-and-effect relation.

What is so important about establishing a cause-and-effect relationship? Although objective, repeatable observations can tell you *about* an interesting phenomenon,

Dependent variable (DV) A response or behavior that is measured. Changes in the dependent variable should be directly related to manipulation of the independent variable.

Extraneous variable Undesired variables that may operate to influence the dependent variable and, thus, invalidate an experiment.

these observations cannot tell you *why* that phenomenon occurred. Only when we can give a cause-and-effect explanation do we begin to answer the *why* question.

For example, we might be interested in the effects of advertising on the purchasing behavior of junior high school students. We could carefully observe which magazines they read and monitor which television shows they watch in the hope that we might get a clue concerning what products they would buy. On the other hand, we could conduct an experiment in an attempt to isolate the influence of a relevant factor. Brian S. Mills (1993), a student at Missouri Western State College (St. Joseph, MO), conducted such an experiment. Brian was interested in whether the presence of a celebrity in an advertisement was an important influence in determining the desirability of products to junior high school students.

His independent variable was the person who was pictured with a product. Each advertisement was presented twice to each participant, once with the picture of a celebrity, such as Michael Jordan, and once with the picture of a noncelebrity. The participants rated each advertisement on the desirability of its product, such as basketballs. In all instances the junior high school students rated the products that were advertised by a celebrity as being more desirable.

Psychological Detective

Review Brian Mills's experiment that we just described. What extraneous variables did Brian control? Should he have controlled other extraneous variables? What was his dependent variable? Write down your answers to these questions before reading further.

One control for the effects of extraneous variables is presented in our description of Brian's research project. Other than the picture that was used, the advertisement was the same for celebrities and noncelebrities. If the advertisement had varied between the celebrity and the noncelebrity pictures, then Brian would not have known whether the rating differences he obtained were due to the different pictures, the different advertisements, or both. Other controls that he exercised included having all the experimental testing take place at one time in one room. Because the time of day and testing environment were the same for *all* participants, these factors could not cause some participants to answer in one manner and other participants to answer in another manner. Likewise, the experiment was conducted by one experimenter to avoid differences between experimenters affecting different participants in different ways. Finally, to help ensure objectivity, the participants completed their data sheets anonymously. Yes, control of extraneous variables is a *major* consideration when you conduct a psychological experiment.

The desirability ratings of the products served as Brian's dependent variable. By comparing the desirability ratings of advertisements having celebrity pictures to the ratings of advertisements without celebrity pictures, he was able to reach the conclusion that the presence of a celebrity does influence a product's desirability.

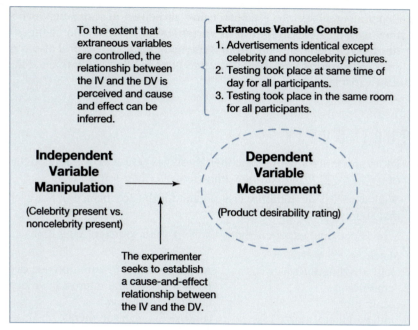

To the extent that extraneous variables are controlled, the relationship between the IV and the DV is perceived and cause and effect can be inferred.

Extraneous Variable Controls

1. Advertisements identical except celebrity and noncelebrity pictures.
2. Testing took place at same time of day for all participants.
3. Testing took place in the same room for all participants.

Independent Variable Manipulation

(Celebrity present vs. noncelebrity present)

Dependent Variable Measurement

(Product desirability rating)

The experimenter seeks to establish a cause-and-effect relationship between the IV and the DV.

FIGURE 1-2. DIAGRAM OF THE RELATIONSHIP OF THE IV, DV, AND EXTRANEOUS VARIABLE CONTROLS IN AN EXPERIMENT ON CELEBRITY PRESENCE IN ADVERTISING.

By controlling the extraneous variables, Brian established a cause-and-effect relationship between the nature of the advertisement (independent variable; celebrity present vs. celebrity absent) and product desirability (dependent variable). The greater our control of extraneous variables, the clearer our view of the cause-and-effect relationship between the independent variable and the dependent variable becomes. This arrangement of IV, DV, and extraneous variable control in Brian's experiment is diagrammed in Figure 1-2.

REVIEW SUMMARY

1. Psychologists engage in the process of acquiring new knowledge. Although knowledge can be gained through **tenacity** (repetition) from an authority, from experience, or by reason and logic, science is the preferred method.

2. The use of (a) objective (**empirical**) findings that can be (b) confirmed by others and (c) corrected, if necessary, by subsequent research are three characteristics of the scientific method.

3. **Control** also is a distinguishing characteristic of science. Control can refer to (a) procedures for dealing with undesired factors in an experiment, and/or (b) manipulation of the factor of main interest in an experiment.

4. Experimenters seek to establish cause-and-effect relations between variables they manipulate (**independent variables**) and behavioral changes (**dependent variables**) that result from those manipulations. Control also is exercised over **extraneous variables** (unwanted factors) that can influence the dependent variable.

STUDY BREAK

1. Radio announcers who repeat their messages *over and over* rely on the method of _____ to impart new knowledge to their listeners.

2. What aspect of an authority is important for the acceptance of knowledge from that source?

3. Why is personal experience not always a valid source of new knowledge?

4. Matching
   1. logical syllogism   A. conducting a research project over again
   2. empiricism   B. factor of central interest in an experiment
   3. replication   C. faulty reasoning
   4. independent variable   D. objective measurements
   5. dependent variable   E. results of an experiment

5. Explain what is meant by the "self-correcting nature of science."

6. Distinguish between the two meanings of the term *control*.

7. Explain the nature of the cause-and-effect relations that psychological research attempts to establish.

THE RESEARCH PROCESS

Although conducting experiments is a crucial aspect of research, it is not the only activity that is involved. There are a number of interrelated activities that comprise the research process. These activities are shown in Table 1-1. As you can see, one activity leads to the next one until we share our research information with others and the process starts all over again. We will briefly describe each of these steps below. Several of these topics will be covered in greater depth in subsequent chapters.

FINDING A PROBLEM

Each research project begins as a problem or a question for which we are seeking an answer. Pamela Feist (1993) wanted to know whether the style of dress affected the credibility of the testimony of a witness; Brian Mills (1993) wanted to know whether the presence of a celebrity photograph made the advertised product more desirable than a product with a noncelebrity photograph.

TABLE 1-1. COMPONENTS OF THE RESEARCH PROCESS

PROBLEM	You detect a gap in the knowledge base.
LITERATURE REVIEW	Consulting previous reports determines what has been found in the research area of interest.
THEORETICAL CONSIDERATIONS	The literature review highlights theories that point to relevant research projects.
HYPOTHESIS	The literature review also highlights hypotheses (statements of the relationship between variables in more restricted domains of the research area). Such hypotheses will assist in the development of the experimental hypothesis—the predicted outcome of your research project.
EXPERIMENTAL DESIGN	You develop the general plan for conducting the research project.
CONDUCT OF THE EXPERIMENT	You conduct the research project according to the experimental design.
DATA ANALYSIS AND STATISTICAL DECISIONS	Based upon the statistical analysis, you decide whether the independent variable exerted a significant effect upon the dependent variable.
DECISIONS IN TERMS OF PAST RESEARCH AND THEORY	The statistical results guide decisions concerning the relationship of the present research project to past research and theoretical considerations.
PREPARATION OF THE RESEARCH REPORT	You prepare a research report describing the rationale, conduct, and results of the experiment according to accepted American Psychological Association (APA) format.
SHARING YOUR RESULTS: PRESENTATION AND PUBLICATION	You share your research report with professional colleagues at a professional society meeting and/or by publication in a professional journal.
FINDING A NEW PROBLEM	Your research results highlight another gap in our knowledge base and the research process begins again.

REVIEWING THE LITERATURE

Once you have chosen the problem you plan to research, you must discover what we already know about the problem. Thus, the next step is to find out what research studies have already been conducted in this area. You may find that the exact experiment you have in mind has been conducted many times. Hence, a modification of your idea, not a replication, may be in order.

THEORETICAL CONSIDERATIONS

In the course of your literature review you will undoubtedly come across theories that have been developed in the area you have chosen to research. A **theory** is a formal statement of the

Theory A formal statement of the relationships among the independent and dependent variables in a given area of research.

definition

relationships among the relevant variables in a particular research area. Leon Festinger's (1957) cognitive dissonance theory is a good example of a psychological theory that has generated considerable research. Festinger proposed that tension is aroused when two beliefs, thoughts, or behaviors are psychologically inconsistent (dissonant). In turn, we are motivated to reduce this cognitive dissonance by altering our thoughts to make them more compatible. For example, (1) believing that high cholesterol is bad for your health and (2) eating pizza almost every day are inconsistent. The dissonance created by having this incompatible belief and behavior might be reduced by deciding that the reports on the harmful effects of cholesterol really are not correct *or* by eating pizza less often. Many researchers have tested predictions from Festinger's theory over the years.

All good theories share two common properties. First, they represent an attempt to organize a given body of scientific data. If a theory has not been developed in a particular area of research, we are faced with the task of having to consider the results of many separate experiments and how these results may or may not relate to each other.

The second property shared by theories is their ability to point the way to new research. By illuminating the relations among relevant variables, a good (i.e., testable) theory also suggests what might logically happen if these variables are manipulated in certain ways. You can think of a theory as being like a road map of your home state. The roads organize and show the relations among the towns and cities. By using this map and a bit of logic, you should be able to get from point A to point B. Thus, theories that you encounter while conducting a literature review will help point you to a relevant research project.

H YPOTHESIS

If a theory is like a road map of your home state, then you can think of a hypothesis as being like the map of a specific town in your state. The **hypothesis** attempts to state specific IV-DV relations within a selected portion of a larger, more comprehensive research area or theory. Within the general domain of cognitive dissonance theory, a number of studies have been concerned with *just* the arousal function of cognitive dissonance. The hypothesized arousal has been found to occur through increases in such physiological reactions as perspiration and heart rate (Losch & Cacioppo, 1990). Just as the map of your hometown may show you several ways to arrive at your destination, researchers may find that there is more than one route to their research objective. Hence, more than one hypothesis may be developed that will answer the research question. For example, you might predict that a reduction in arousal would result in a decrease in cognitive dissonance. This prediction was tested, and it has been shown that participants who consumed alcohol (arousal reduction) had reduced levels of cognitive dissonance (Steele, Southwick, & Critchlow, 1981).

As your own research project takes shape, you will develop a specific hypothesis. This hypothesis, frequently called the **research or exper-**

Hypothesis An attempt to organize certain data and specific independent and dependent variable relationships within a specific portion of a larger, more comprehensive theory.

definition

imental hypothesis, will be the *predicted* outcome of your research project. In stating this hypothesis you are stating a testable prediction about the relations between the independent and dependent variables in your experiment. Based on the scientific literature you have reviewed, your experimental hypothesis will be influenced by other hypotheses and theories that have been proposed in your area of interest. For example, your hypothesis might be "If potential customers are dressed in old, worn-out clothes, then they will not be waited on as quickly as customers dressed in better clothing."

It is important that you be able to directly test the experimental hypothesis that you propose. This requirement means that you must be able to objectively define all the variables you will be manipulating (IVs), recording (DVs), and controlling (extraneous variables).

Research or experimental hypothesis The experimenter's predicted outcome of a research project.

Experimental design The general plan for selecting participants, assigning participants to experimental conditions, controlling extraneous variables, and gathering data.

definition

EXPERIMENTAL DESIGN

Once your hypothesis has been formulated, you will need a general plan for conducting your research. This plan is called an **experimental design;** it specifies how your participants will be selected and assigned to groups, the type of extraneous variable control(s) that will be exercised, and how the data will be gathered.

CONDUCTING THE EXPERIMENT

The next step is to actually conduct the experiment. All your preparations and controls will be put to the test as you gather your experimental data.

DATA ANALYSIS AND STATISTICAL DECISIONS

Our experiment is not complete when the data are gathered; the next step is to analyze the data that were gathered. Based on the results of our data analysis, we will decide whether manipulating the IV had a significant effect on the DV. In short, our statistical decisions will tell us whether a cause-and-effect relationship has been uncovered. If our statistical test indicates that a significant difference exists between the groups we tested, then we can infer that our IV manipulation was the cause of the DV effect we recorded. We will have more to say about statistical significance later.

DECISIONS IN TERMS OF PAST RESEARCH AND THEORY

Once our statistical decisions are made, then we must interpret our results in light of past research and theory. Was our experimental hypothesis supported? Do our results agree with past research? How do they fit into the current theoretical structure in this research area? If our results do not fit perfectly, what changes need to be made in our interpretation and/or existing theory to accommodate them?

Experimenters want to be able to extend or generalize their experimental results as widely as they legitimately can. Will Pamela Feist's (1993) experimental results on the effect of eyewitnesses' dress generalize to other classes of participants besides college students? Will Brian Mills's (1993) data showing that celebrity photographs increase product desirability generalize to other products and other types of participants? These are the types of issues with which generalization deals.

PREPARING THE RESEARCH REPORT

Before we share the results of our research with the scientific community, we must prepare a written research report. This research report will be prepared according to the format prescribed by the American Psychological Association (APA). This format, often called APA format, is carefully detailed in the *Publication Manual of the American Psychological Association* (4th edition, 1994).

Although many specific details of APA format have evolved over the years, the basic structure of our research report was originally proposed by University of Wisconsin psychologist Joseph Jastrow in the early part of this century (Blumenthal, 1991). Jastrow's purpose in suggesting a standard format for all psychological papers was to make the communication of research results easier and more consistent. By having a standard form, researchers knew exactly what to include in their papers and readers knew where to look for specific experimental details, procedures, and results. We will have a great deal more to say about APA format throughout this book.

SHARING YOUR RESULTS: PRESENTATION AND PUBLICATION

Once you have conducted the experiment, analyzed the data, and prepared the research report, it is time to share your results. The two most popular ways to accomplish this objective are to (a) present an oral paper or a poster at a psychological convention, and/or (b) publish an article in a professional journal.

Even though many of you may be shaking your heads and saying, "I could never do that in a million years," we believe (and know, from experience) that such accomplishments are within the grasp of most motivated undergraduate psychology students. In fact, such opportunities, especially for presenting papers and posters at psychological conventions, have increased dramatically in recent years. Paramount among these opportunities is a growing number of state and regional student psychology conventions. These events, which are summarized in Table 1-2, feature student presentations exclusively. If there is not a student convention in your area, then you can consider presenting a paper in one of the Psi Chi (National Honor Society in Psychology) sessions at a regional convention. One of the six regional association meetings held each year (Eastern Psychological Association, Midwestern Psychological Association, Rocky Mountain Psychological Association, Southeastern Psychological Association, Southwestern Psychological Association, and Western Psychological Association) should be close enough to offer a potential forum for your research (see Table 1-3). In addition to the sessions at these regional meetings, Psi Chi sponsors student paper sessions at the national meetings of the American Psychological Association and the American Psychological Society. Finally, if none of these options is a viable opportunity for you to present your research, then you should consider starting a paper-reading/poster-presentation session on your own campus. Very successful, annual events of this nature have been started at several schools.

Although the opportunities for students to publish a journal article may be a bit more difficult to find than opportunities to present a paper at a convention, such opportunities do exist. For example, *Modern Psychological Studies* and *The Psi Chi Journal of Undergraduate Student Research* (see Table 1-4) are journals devoted to the publication of research conducted and reported *only* by undergraduate students. If your faculty advisor has made a significant contribution to the design and conduct of your project, then you may want to consider including your faculty ad-

---

TABLE 1-2. OPPORTUNITIES FOR UNDERGRADUATES TO PRESENT AND PUBLISH THEIR RESEARCH

STATE AND REGIONAL STUDENT CONFERENCES

Southeastern Undergraduate Psychology Research Conference

Arkansas Symposium for Psychology Students

ILLOWA Undergraduate Psychology Conference

Mid-America Undergraduate Psychology Research Conference

Great Plains Students' Psychology Convention

Michigan Undergraduate Psychology Paper Reading Conference

Minnesota Undergraduate Psychology Conference

Carolinas Psychology Conference

Delaware Valley Undergraduate Research Conference

Lehigh Valley Undergraduate Psychology Research Conference

University of Winnipeg Undergraduate Psychology Research Conference

Information concerning these conferences appears regularly in the *APA Monitor*. Faculty members who are APA members automatically receive the *APA Monitor*; ask them to loan you the copy that has this listing. The journal *Teaching of Psychology* also carries a comprehensive listing of undergraduate student conferences. For information about *Teaching of Psychology* contact

Dr. Randolph A. Smith, Editor
Teaching of Psychology
Department of Psychology
Ouachita Baptist University
Arkadelphia, AR 71998-0001

S. Gross, '1994 *The New Yorker Magazine, Inc.*

"Well, you don't look like an experimental psychologist to me."

Attending a psychological convention will convince you that experimental psychologists are a most diverse group. Although you may not feel like an experimental psychologist now, completing a research project or two will change that situation.

visor as a coauthor. The *Journal of Psychology and the Behavioral Sciences* is an annual journal that solicits manuscripts by students and faculty. Your faculty advisor also will be able to suggest other journals to which your paper might be submitted. Although undergraduates typically do not publish by themselves in the professional journals, collaborative papers featuring student and faculty authors are not uncommon.

TABLE 1-3. STUDENT SESSIONS SPONSORED BY PSI CHI (NATIONAL HONOR SOCIETY IN PSYCHOLOGY)

Psi Chi routinely features student paper and/or poster sessions at the following regional and national conferences:

Eastern Psychological Association	Rocky Mountain Psychological Association
Southeastern Psychological Association	Western Psychological Association
Midwestern Psychological Association	American Psychological Association
Southwestern Psychological Association	American Psychological Society

For information on Psi Chi and these sessions contact

Psi Chi National Office
407 East Fifth Street, Suite B
Chattanooga, TN 37043
(615) 756-2044

The dates and locations of these conferences are routinely published in the *American Psychologist*. (Faculty members who belong to the APA receive copies of this journal.)

TABLE 1-4. PUBLICATION OPPORTUNITIES FOR STUDENTS

Several journals publish papers authored by students. Write each journal to determine specific submission procedures.

1. *The Journal of Psychology and the Behavioral Sciences*
   Professor John Brandi, Faculty Editor
   Department of Psychology
   Fairleigh Dickinson University
   Madison, NJ 07904

2. *Modern Psychological Studies*
   Department of Psychology
   University of Tennessee at Chattanooga
   Chattanooga, TN 37043-2598

3. *Journal of Undergraduate Studies*
   Department of Psychology

   Pace University
   861 Bedford Rd.
   Pleasantville, NY 10570

4. *Der Zeitgeist, Student Journal for Psychology*
   Jens A. Schipull, Editor-in-Chief
   800 High Street, #B
   Bellingham, WA 98225

5. *The Psi Chi Journal of Student Research*
   Psi Chi National Office
   407 East Fifth Street, Suite B
   Chattanooga, TN 37043

The main point of this discussion is to encourage you to take advantage of the opportunities to share your research results with others. Much of the research you will read about in this book was conducted by students and then presented at a convention and/or published in a journal such as *Modern Psychological Studies*. If they can do it, so can you! Once you are involved in the research process, you will quickly find that it is a highly stimulating endeavor that never seems to end. There are always new problems to investigate.

FINDING A NEW PROBLEM

As you consider the relationship of your experimental results to past research and theory, and share your results with others who give you feedback, new research ideas will present themselves. Why didn't the results turn out exactly as predicted? Was some extraneous variable left uncontrolled? What would happen if this or that variable were manipulated in a different manner? The more deeply you immerse yourself in a research area, the more questions and problems you will find to research. As you can see from Table 1-1, we have now come full circle to the start of a new research project.

WHY IS THE RESEARCH METHODS COURSE IMPORTANT?

When students are asked, "Why are you taking a course in research methods?" the typical response(s) might be these:

"It's required for the major."

or

"I really don't know; I'll never conduct any research after this course."

As we go through this text, we hope to convince you that an understanding of research methods and data analysis can give you some real advantages in the field of psychology. Here are a few of those advantages:

1. ***Assisting You in Other Psychology Classes.*** Because psychology's knowledge base rests on a foundation of research, it only makes good sense that much of what is covered in your other psychology classes will consist of research examples. The more completely you understand research methodology, the better you will be able to master the material in your other classes. Although this point might make sense for courses such as learning or perception, even courses such as personality and abnormal psychology are based on research.

2. ***Conducting a Research Project after Graduation.*** Your authors learned a long time ago that it is smart to "never say never." This caution also applies to you as students of psychology. Consider the following example. In 1969 a very bright student took the research methods course with one of your authors. Although this student found the class sessions interesting and intellectually stimulating, she disliked the material and vowed that she would *never* have to think about research in psychology after the class was over. How wrong she was—her first job following graduation was conducting research for the Medical College of Virginia! If your career plans even remotely relate to the field of psychology, then the chances are quite good that you may have to conduct some type of research project as part of your job. Clearly, a course in research methods will provide a good understanding of what you will need to do in such instances.

3. ***Getting into Graduate School.*** There is no getting around the fact that a course in research methods or experimental psychology is viewed very positively by psychology graduate school admissions committees (Lawson, 1995; Purdy, Reinehr, & Swartz, 1989; Smith, 1985). Your having completed such a course tells the admissions committee that you have a good grasp of basic research methodology. Such knowledge is valued by graduate programs in psychology.

    Frequently the research methods course includes or is followed by the conducting of an original student research project. If you have such an opportunity, take advantage of it and then plan to present and/or publish your research findings (refer to our earlier discussion of the research process). Having presented and/or published a research report is also rated very highly by graduate school admissions committees (Keith-Spiegel, 1991; Purdy et al., 1989; Smith, 1985).

4. ***Becoming a Knowledgeable Consumer of Research.*** Our society is flooded with knowledge claims. Many of these claims deal with psychological re-

search and phenomena, such as the claims that a particular type of diet will improve your disposition, IQ tests are good (or bad), scientific tests have proven that this cola tastes best of all, or that this toothpaste fights cavities better than the rest. How do you know which of these claims to believe?

If you understand the research on which these claims are based and the "facts" that are being presented as supporting evidence (or that there is no supporting evidence), then you are in a position to make a more educated decision concerning such knowledge claims. The research methods course is designed to give you the basic foundation from which you can make educated decisions concerning knowledge claims you encounter in your everyday life.

REVIEW SUMMARY

1. The research process consists of several interrelated, sequential steps: The Problem, Literature Review, Theoretical Considerations, Hypothesis, Experimental Design, Conduct of the Experiment, Data Analysis and Statistical Decisions, Decisions in Terms of Past Research and Theory, Preparing the Research Report, Sharing Your Results, and Finding a New Problem.

2. A **theory** is a formal statement of relationships among variables in a particular research area, whereas a **hypothesis** attempts to state relationships among variables in a selected portion of a theory.

3. The **research or experimental hypothesis** is the experimenter's predicted outcome of a to-be-conducted experiment.

4. The **experimental design** specifies how (a) participants will be selected, (b) groups will be formed, (c) extraneous variables will be controlled, and (d) data will be gathered.

5. We encourage students to submit their research reports for presentation at professional society meetings and publication in journals.

6. The research methods course can (a) assist you in understanding research in other courses, (b) prepare you to conduct research after graduation, (c) increase your chances of being accepted to graduate school, and (d) make you a knowledgeable consumer of the results of psychological research.

STUDY BREAK

1. Briefly describe the steps involved in the research process.

2. Distinguish between a theory and a hypothesis.

3. What is the research or experimental hypothesis?

4. When Brian Mills dealt with such issues as how to select and assign his participants to groups, how long each participant would be allowed to view each

advertising piece, and the time of day his experiment would be conducted, he was dealing with _____ _____.

5. Other than fulfilling a requirement, what are (describe) the reasons for taking a research methods or experimental psychology course?

LOOKING AHEAD

In this chapter we provided you a general introduction to how psychologists gather data. Subsequent chapters will build on and expand this general introduction. In Chapter 2 we will examine how you can find a researchable problem. Once our sources of research problems have been identified, then we will discuss the formulation of a good research hypothesis. Finally, we will consider the ethics involved in the conduct of human and animal research.

HANDS-ON ACTIVITIES

1. **Acquiring Knowledge.**   It is one thing to read about the various ways of acquiring knowledge in books; it may be a totally different experience to encounter them firsthand. For this hands-on exercise you are to look for examples of tenacity, authority, experience, reason and logic, and science in the real world. How trustworthy are these sources? Do other people seem to believe them?

2. **Attending Conventions.**   As we discussed in this chapter, your growth and development as a psychologist is enhanced when you attend psychological conventions. Until you have conducted your own research to present at these conventions, your role will be that of spectator. As a spectator, you can learn a great deal about experimental psychology by listening very carefully to the papers that are presented and/or by carefully scrutinizing the posters you look at. Can you detect the flow of the research process in the presentation or poster? What are the independent and dependent variables? Which extraneous variables were controlled? Is the cause-and-effect conclusion believable?

3. **Your Professional Library.**   It is never too early to start your own professional library. For this reason we encourage you to keep all your psychology textbooks. It is difficult to imagine professionals who do not have the tools of their trade; books are among the tools the psychologist uses. Journals also are important tools for the psychologist; they keep you on top of current developments. Enhance your own professional library by subscribing to a journal. The journals that publish student research feature a wide variety of articles (a good approach for the beginning psychologist) and are reasonably priced. Write for information and then subscribe to the one that best fits your needs and interests.

CHAPTER 2

Research Ideas, Hypotheses, and Ethics

definition

Research idea
Identification of a gap in the knowledge base in an area of interest.

THE RESEARCH IDEA

The starting point for your project is a **research idea** or problem. You find a research idea when you identify a gap in the current knowledge base that interests you. For example, in Chapter 1 we saw that Pamela Feist was interested in whether style of dress was related to the credibility of eyewitnesses. She found that this information was not available and conducted research to correct this deficiency. In this section we will examine the characteristics of good research ideas and then explore several sources for research ideas.

CHARACTERISTICS OF GOOD RESEARCH IDEAS

All possible solutions to a detective case are not equally likely. Likewise, not all research ideas are equally good. Good ideas have certain characteristics that set them apart from less acceptable ideas and problems.

Testable. The most important characteristic of a good research idea is that it is testable. Can you imagine trying to conduct research on a phenomenon or topic that cannot be measured or tested? This situation would be like trying to answer the old question "How many angels can dance on the head of a pin?" Although you may be chuckling to yourself and saying, "That will never happen to me," remember our caution in Chapter 1 about never saying never.

Suppose, for example, you became interested in cognitive processes in animals. Although humans can describe their thoughts, a research project designed to measure cognitive abilities in animals directly is doomed to failure before it starts. At present, the best one can do in this situation is to provide an indirect measure of animal cognition. This is the approach that Richard Burns and his students at Southeast Missouri State University have taken (Burns & Gordon, 1988; Burns & Sanders, 1987). They trained rats in tasks, such as running fast or slow in a maze, that require numerical ability to master. The extent to which the task is solved indicates the numerical ability of the animal and provides a reflection of cognitive ability. The point we are making is that although some research problems, such as the number of angels dancing on the head of a pin, may never be testable, others such as animal cognition may lend themselves to evaluation through indirect tests. Moreover, just because a problem is not presently testable does not mean it will always remain in that category. You may have to wait for technology to catch up with your ideas. For example, synapses and neurotransmitters in the nervous system were proposed long before they were directly seen and verified.

Likelihood of Success. If you stop to think about it, each research project that is conducted is a contest to unlock the secrets of nature. (If all of nature's secrets were already known, there would be no need for research.) Given that our view of nature is not complete, we must try to arrange our research project to be as close to reality as possible (Medewar, 1979). The closer our project comes to approximating reality, the greater the likelihood of successfully unlocking some of the secrets of nature. Sometimes our view of nature is not very clear and our research does not work very well—consider the following example.

In the 1980s a new chemical compound, denatonium saccharide, claimed to be the most bitter substance in existence, was placed on the market. Because denatonium saccharide offered intriguing practical applications such as being an additive for plastic telephone and/or computer cable coverings and garbage bags to discourage destructive animal pests, one of your authors and several of his students began to conduct research on this noxious chemical. Our view of nature was that denatonium saccharide was incredibly bitter and that *all* creatures great and small would react to it as such. To verify this prediction we began testing the aversiveness of denatonium saccharide with a variety of animals ranging from rats, grasshopper mice, and gerbils, to prairie dogs. Test after test yielded the same results: Our animal subjects did *not* behave toward denatonium saccharide as especially bitter or aversive (Davis, Grover, Erickson, Miller, & Bowman, 1987; Langley, Theis, Davis, Richard, & Grover, 1987). Following an experiment in which human participants rated denatonium saccharide as significantly more bitter than a comparable solution of quinine (Davis, Grover, & Erickson, 1987), our view of nature changed. Denatonium saccharide is a *very* strong bitter as far as humans are concerned; when animal subjects are tested, however, it is not seen in the same light. Had we not changed our view of nature, we might still be conducting experiment after experiment wondering why our animal subjects were not behaving as they were "supposed" to.

Hence, in addition to testability, a second characteristic of the good research idea is that your chances for success are increased when your view of nature approximates reality as closely possible.

Psychological Detective

Other than by trial and error, how can we find out about the proposed nature of the factors in our chosen research area? Give this question some thought and write down your answer before reading further.

Examining past research is your best bet. Those variables that were effective in previous studies are likely to be the ones that will work in your experiment. We will have more to say about that topic presently.

SOURCES OF RESEARCH IDEAS

There appear to be two general sources of research ideas: nonsystematic and systematic. We will discuss each source in some detail.

Nonsystematic sources Sources for research ideas that present themselves in an unpredictable manner; a concerted attempt to locate researchable ideas has not been made.

Serendipity Situations where we look for one phenomenon but find something else.

Nonsystematic Sources. **Nonsystematic sources** include those occurrences that give us the illusion that a research idea has dropped out of the sky. These sources are nonsystematic in that we have not made any concerted effort to locate researchable ideas; they present themselves to us in a somewhat unpredictable manner. Even though we refer to these sources as nonsystematic, we are not implying that the researcher is unfamiliar with the research area. In all instances good researchers are familiar with the published literature and previous research findings. We do not seem to generate meaningful research ideas in areas with which we are not familiar.

Among the major nonsystematic sources of research ideas are inspiration, serendipity, and everyday occurrences.

Inspiration. Some research ideas may appear to be the product of a blind flash of genius; in the twinkle of an eye an inspired research idea is born. Perhaps the most famous example of inspiration in science is Albert Einstein (Koestler, 1964). Ideas just seemed to pop into his mind, especially when he was sailing. Although such ideas just seem to appear, it is often the case that the researcher has been thinking about this research area for some time. We see only the end product, the idea, not the thinking that preceded its appearance.

Serendipity. **Serendipity** refers to those situations where we look for one phenomenon but find another. Serendipity often serves as an excellent source for research ideas.

Consider the following scenario in which B. F. Skinner described his reaction to the malfunctioning of a pellet dispenser in an operant conditioning chamber (commonly called a Skinner box). His initial reaction is predictable; he saw the malfunction as a nuisance and wanted to eliminate it. However, with the eyes of an insightful researcher he saw beyond his temporary frustration with the broken equipment to a more important possibility. By disconnecting the pellet dispenser he could study extinction. All of the subsequent research conducted on extinction and the various schedules of reinforcement that were developed indicate that Skinner capitalized on this chance happening. It was truly a serendipitous occurrence.

As you begin to complicate an apparatus, you necessarily invoke a fourth principle of scientific practice: Apparatuses sometimes break down. I had only to wait for the food magazine to jam to get an extinction curve. At first I treated this as a defect and hastened to remedy the difficulty. But eventually, of course, I deliberately disconnected the magazine. I can easily recall the excitement of that first complete extinction curve. I had made contact with Pavlov at last! . . . I am not saying that I would have not got around to extinction curves without a breakdown in the apparatus. . . . But it is no exaggeration to say that some of the most interesting and surprising results have turned up first because of similar accidents. (Skinner, 1961, p. 86)

Everyday Occurrences. You do not have to be working in a laboratory to come in contact with good research ideas. Frequently, our daily encounters provide some of the best possibilities for research. Another incident from the life of B. F. Skinner provides an excellent example of this source for a research project.

When we decided to have another child, my wife and I decided that it was time to apply a little labor-saving invention and design to the problems of the nursery. We began by going over the disheartening schedule of the young mother, step by step. We asked only one question: Is this practice important for the physical and psychological health of the baby?

When it was not, we marked it for elimination. Then the "gadgeteering" began. . . . We tackled first the problem of warmth. The usual solution is to wrap the baby in half-a-dozen layers of cloth—shirt, nightdress, sheet, blankets. This is never completely successful. Why not, we thought, dispense with clothing altogether—except for the diaper, which serves another purpose—and warm the space in which the baby lives? This should be a simple technical problem in the modern home. Our solution is a closed compartment about as spacious as a standard crib [see Figure 2-1]. The walls are insulated, and one side, which can be raised like a window, is a large pane of safety glass. . . . our baby daughter

FIGURE 2-1.   SKINNER'S AIR CRIB.

Source: Folk/Monkmeyer Press

has now been living [in this apparatus] for eleven months. Her remarkable good health and happiness and my wife's welcome leisure have exceeded our most optimistic predictions. (Skinner, 1961, p. 420)

This description of the original Air Crib appeared in 1945. Subsequently, the Air Crib was commercially produced and several hundred infants were raised in them. Thus an everyday problem led to an interesting, if not unusual, research problem for B. F. Skinner.

It also is clear that your ability to see a potential research project as you go through your daily activities depends on some knowledge of your field of interest. Because your authors are not well versed in archaeology, we do not see possible sites for excavations and discoveries as we travel. Conversely, an archaeologist would find it difficult to propose meaningful research problems in psychology.

Systematic Sources. Study and knowledge of a specific topic form the foundation for **systematic sources** of research ideas. Research ideas developed from systematic sources tend to be carefully organized and logically thought out. The results of past research, theories, and classroom lectures are the most common examples of systematic sources for research ideas.

Past Research. As you read the results of past research, you gradually form a picture of the knowledge that has been accumulated in a research area. Perhaps this picture will highlight our lack of knowledge, such as the influence

"The curse of mad scientist's block"

Unlike this poor fellow, psychologists find potential research ideas all around them.

of dress on eyewitness credibility. On the other hand, you may find that there are contradictory reports in the literature; one research project supports the occurrence of a particular phenomenon, whereas other reports cast doubt on its validity. Perhaps your research project will be the one that isolates the variable(s) responsible for these discrepant findings! Your consideration of past research may also indicate that a particular experiment has been conducted only once and is in need of replication, or you may find that a particular project has been conducted numerous times and needs not replication but new research. In each of these instances our review of past research has prompted a research project.

One specific type of past research that can serve as an excellent source of research ideas deserves special mention. The failure to replicate a previous finding creates an intriguing situation for the psychological detective. What features of the initial research resulted in the occurrence of the phenomenon under investigation? What was different about the replication that caused the results to turn out to be different? Only continued research will answer these questions.

Theory. As we noted in Chapter 1, the two main functions of a theory are to organize data and guide further research. The guidance function of a theory provides an endless panorama of projects for researchers who take the time and trouble to master the theory and understand its implications.

Consider, for example, *social facilitation* theory. According to Robert Zajonc (1965), the presence of other people serves to arouse one's performance. In turn, this increased arousal energizes the most dominant response. If you are a skilled pianist, then the presence of others at a recital will likely yield a stellar performance; playing well is the dominant response in this situation. If you are just learning to play the piano, mistakes may be your dominant response and the presence of others may result in an embarrassing performance. Based on this theory, over 300 social facilitation studies involving thousands of participants have been conducted (Guerin, 1986). Theory truly does guide research!

Classroom Lectures. Many excellent research projects are the result of a classroom lecture. Your instructor describes research in an area that sparks your interest and ultimately this interest leads to the development and conduct of a research project. Although lectures may not seem to be strictly nonsystematic or systematic sources of research ideas, we chose to include them as systematic sources because they often include an organized review of the relevant literature.

For example, after hearing a lecture on conditioned taste aversion, one of our students, Susan Nash, became interested in the topic. Subsequently, she did a term paper and conducted her senior research project in this area. Moreover, several of the research projects she conducted as a graduate student dealt with the process by which taste aversions are acquired. Yes, one lecture can contain a wealth of potential research ideas; it will pay rich dividends to pay close attention to lectures and keep careful notes when you see potential topics for research.

SURVEYING THE PSYCHOLOGICAL LITERATURE

The importance of being aware of past research has already presented itself several times in this chapter. However, simply telling someone to go look up the past research in an area may present a seemingly insurmountable task. Michael Mahoney (1987) summarized the state of affairs as follows:

> The modern scientist sometimes feels overwhelmed by the size and growth rate of the technical literatures relevant to his or her work. It has been estimated, for example, that there are over 40,000 current scientific journals publishing 2 new articles per minute (2,880 per day and over one million per year). . . . These figures—which are, indeed, overwhelming—do not include books, newsletters, or technical monographs.
>
> Given the sizeable and growing number of active journals, one should not be surprised by the emergence and popularity of services that summarize, abstract, scan, and otherwise condense the literature into more feasible dimensions. No one would be able to "keep up" without the aid of such services. (p. 165)

Given the vast amount of literature that we may be dealing with, an organized strategy is needed. Table 2-1 summarizes the procedures you should follow in reviewing the literature in a particular area. The steps are as follows:

1. **Selection of Index Terms.** The key to conducting a search of the literature is to begin with terms that will help you access the relevant articles in your chosen area. Whether we are working with a computer database (see Step 2) or going through paper abstracts (see Step 3), the terms we choose will be our guides.

    An excellent starting place for selecting terms is the *Thesaurus of Psychological Index Terms* (Walker, 1994). The first edition of the *Thesaurus of Psychological Index Terms* was based on the 800 terms used in *Psychological Abstracts* prior to 1973. These terms were expanded to include terms that

---

TABLE 2-1. STEPS IN CONDUCTING A SEARCH OF THE LITERATURE

1. **Selection of Index Terms.** Select relevant terms for your area of interest from the *Thesaurus of Psychological Index Terms.*

2. **Computerized Search of the Literature.** Use the selected index terms to access a computerized database, such as PsycLIT, for articles published from 1974 to the present.

3. **Manual Search of the Literature.** Use index terms to access pre-1974 publications in *Psychological Abstracts.*

4. **Obtaining Relevant Publications.** Use a combination of reading and note taking, photocopying, interlibrary loan, and writing for reprints to obtain needed materials.

5. **Integrating the Results of the Literature Search.** Develop a plan that will facilitate the integration and usefulness of the results of the literature search.

---

described interrelationships and related categories. Each edition of the *Thesaurus of Psychological Index Terms* is updated to include the addition of new terms. For example, let's assume that you have an interest in child abuse. Figure 2-2 shows a page from the *Thesaurus* that contains relevant terms for the general topic of child abuse. You select *battered child syndrome* and *child neglect* as your key terms.

2. *Computerized Searches of the Literature.* Once you have selected your key terms, the next step is to use them to access a database. For publications in psychology and related areas dating from 1974, it is becoming increasingly more common for colleges and universities to offer the PsycLIT service on CD-ROM. PsycLIT provides the author(s), title, journal, volume, page numbers, and an abstract of each article published from 1974 to the present. All you need to do is enter your index terms from the *Thesaurus* and let the computer do the rest. (An example of a PsycLIT printout is shown in Figure 2-3.) Once you have determined the number of entries in your chosen area, you can limit or expand your choices as you see fit. Because easy-to-follow instructions are provided, running the PsycLIT computer will pose no problems for you. Your librarian can assist when you need to change the CD-ROM disk and with any problems you may encounter. If you are interested in just the most recent literature, you might also ask your librarian about PsycFIRST. PsycFIRST maintains only the last three years of PsycLIT and is handy for a quick scan of the most current literature.

If your library does not yet have such a computerized system, do not despair. Your librarian should be able to help you find a nearby library that can (for a minimal fee) accommodate your needs. As we will see in the next section, you can also conduct a manual search of the literature.

3. *Manual Searches of the Literature.* For material published prior to 1974 and those cases where a computerized search is not available, you will need to conduct a manual search of the literature. *Psychological Abstracts* is a monthly journal that provides essentially the same information that the PsycLIT computer search yields. Because the index terms used in the *Thesaurus* were

FIGURE 2-2. A PAGE FROM THE *THESAURUS OF PSYCHOLOGICAL INDEX TERMS.*

Source: Reprinted with permission of the American Psychological Association, publisher of *Psychological Abstracts* and the *Thesaurus of Psychological Index Terms* (7th Edition), all rights reserved.

Chi Square Test	RELATIONSHIP SECTION	Childhood Development

Chi Square Test — (cont'd)
B   Nonparametric Statistical Tests [67]
R   Statistical Significance [73]

Chicanos
   Use Mexican Americans

Chickens [67]
PN 1438   SC 08630
B   Birds [67]

Child Abuse [71]
PN 4139   SC 08650
SN   Abuse of children or adolescents in a family, institutional, or other setting.
B   Crime [67]
     Family Violence [82]
N   Battered Child Syndrome [73]
R   Anatomically Detailed Dolls [91]
     Child Neglect [88]
     Child Welfare [88]
     Emotional Abuse [91]
     Failure to Thrive [88]
     Patient Abuse [91]
     Pedophilia [73]
     Physical Abuse [91]
     ↓ Sexual Abuse [88]

Child Advocacy
   Use Advocacy

Child Attitudes [88]
PN 643   SC 08658
SN   Attitudes of, not toward, children.
B   Attitudes [67]
R   ↓ Children [67]

Child Behavior Checklist [94]
PN 0   SC 08659
B   Nonprojective Personality Measures [73]

Child Care [91]
PN 129   SC 08660
SN   Care of children of any age in any setting.
UF   Babysitting
N   Child Day Care [73]
     Child Self Care [88]
R   ↓ Childrearing Practices [67]
     Foster Care [78]

Child Care Workers [78]
PN 588   SC 08663
SN   Mental health, educational, or social services personnel providing day care or residential care for children.
R   Child Day Care [73]
     Day Care Centers [73]
     ↓ Nonprofessional Personnel [82]
     ↓ Service Personnel [91]

Child Custody [82]
PN 654   SC 08665
SN   Legal guardianship of a child.
B   Legal Processes [73]
R   Child Support [88]
     Child Visitation [88]
     Divorce [73]
     Guardianship [88]
     Joint Custody [88]
     ↓ Living Arrangements [91]
     Mediation [88]
     ↓ Parental Absence [73]

Child Day Care [73]
PN 1016   SC 08670

Child Day Care — (cont'd)
SN   Day care that provides for a child's physical needs and often his/her developmental or educational needs. Kinds of day care include day care centers and school-based programs.
UF   Day Care (Child)
B   Child Care [91]
R   Child Care Workers [78]
     Child Self Care [88]
     Child Welfare [88]
     Day Care Centers [73]
     Quality of Care [88]

Child Discipline [73]
PN 484   SC 08680
UF   Discipline (Child)
B   Childrearing Practices [67]
     Family Relations [67]
N   Parental Permissiveness [73]
R   ↓ Parent Child Relations [67]
     Parental Role [73]

Child Guidance Clinics [73]
PN 207   SC 08690
SN   Facilities which exist for the diagnosis and treatment of behavioral and emotional disorders in childhood.
UF   Child Psychiatric Clinics
B   Clinics [67]
R   ↓ Community Facilities [73]
     Community Mental Health Centers [73]
     ↓ Mental Health Programs [73]
     ↓ Mental Health Services [78]
     Psychiatric Clinics [73]

Child Neglect [88]
PN 344   SC 08695
SN   Failure of parents or caretakers to provide basic care and emotional support necessary for normal development.
B   Antisocial Behavior [71]
R   ↓ Child Abuse [71]
     Child Welfare [88]
     Emotional Abuse [91]
     Failure to Thrive [88]

Child Psychiatric Clinics
   Use Child Guidance Clinics

Child Psychiatry [67]
PN 1224   SC 08710
SN   Branch of psychiatry devoted to the study and treatment of behavioral, mental, and emotional disorders of children. Use a more specific term if possible.
B   Psychiatry [67]
R   Orthopsychiatry [73]

Child Psychology [67]
PN 316   SC 08720
SN   Branch of developmental psychology devoted to the study of behavior, adjustment, and development and the treatment of behavioral, mental, and emotional disorders of children. Use a more specific term if possible.
B   Developmental Psychology [73]

Child Psychotherapy [67]
PN 1433   SC 08730
B   Psychotherapy [67]
N   Play Therapy [73]
R   Adolescent Psychotherapy [94]
     Reality Therapy [73]

Child Self Care [88]
PN 48   SC 08733

Child Self Care — (cont'd)
SN   Responsibility for personal care without adult supervision usually before or after the school day. Primarily used for children under age 14.
UF   Latchkey Children
B   Child Care [91]
R   Child Day Care [73]
     Child Welfare [88]
     Self Care Skills [78]

Child Support [88]
PN 24   SC 08735
SN   Legal obligation of parents or guardians to contribute to the economic maintenance of their children including provision of education, clothing, and food.
R   Child Custody [82]
     Divorce [73]
     Joint Custody [88]
     ↓ Marital Separation [73]

Child Visitation [88]
PN 66   SC 08737
SN   The right of or court-granted permission to parents, grandparents, or guardians to visit children.
UF   Visitation Rights
B   Legal Processes [73]
R   Child Custody [82]

Child Welfare [88]
PN 225   SC 08738
R   ↓ Adoption (Child) [67]
     Advocacy [85]
     ↓ Child Abuse [71]
     Child Day Care [73]
     Child Neglect [88]
     Child Self Care [88]
     Foster Care [78]
     Social Casework [67]
     ↓ Social Services [82]

Childbirth
   Use Birth

Childbirth (Natural)
   Use Natural Childbirth

Childbirth Training [78]
PN 154   SC 08746
B   Prenatal Care [91]
R   ↓ Birth [67]
     Labor (Childbirth) [73]
     Natural Childbirth [78]
     ↓ Obstetrics [78]
     ↓ Pregnancy [67]

Childhood [94]
PN 56869   SC 08750
SN   Mandatory age identifier used for ages 0–12. Where appropriate, more specific index terms (e.g., INFANTS, PRESCHOOL AGE CHILDREN) are used in addition to this age identifier. The other two age identifiers are ADOLESCENCE and ADULTHOOD.
R   ↓ Children [67]
     ↓ Infants [67]
     Neonates [67]

Childhood Development [67]
PN 5122   SC 08760
SN   Process of physical, cognitive, personality, and psychosocial growth occurring from birth through age 12. Use a more specific term if possible.
B   Human Development [67]
N   ↓ Early Childhood Development [73]
R   Adolescent Development [73]

```
TI: Elderly people with learning disabilities in hospital: A
    psychiatric study.
AU: Sansom,-D.-T.; Singh,-I.; Jawed,-S.-H.; Mukherjee,-T.
IN: Chelmsley Hosp, Birmingham, England
JN: Journal-of-Intellectual-Disability-Research; 1994 Feb Vol
    38(1) 45-52
AB: In a study of 124 hospital residents (aged 60-94 yrs) with
    a learning disability, Diagnostic and Statistical Manual of
    Mental Disorders-III-Revised (DSM-III-R) diagnostic criteria
    were used to determine the prevalence of dementia (12.9%),
    mood disorder (8.9%), and schizophrenia (6.5%). Ss were cate-
    gorized according to the age groups 60-69 yrs, 70-79 yrs, and
    80 yrs and older. The figure for the prevalence of dementia
    corresponds with the prevalence figures of previous studies,
    but the figures for mood disorder and schizophrenia were
    higher. Mood disorder was more common in the age group 60-69
    yrs; dementia was more common in the age group 70-79 yrs.
    There were no significant differences in the prevalence of
    schizophrenia with age. (PsycLIT Database Copyright 1994
    American Psychological Assn, all rights reserved).
```

FIGURE 2-3.   A PRINTOUT FROM PSYCLIT.

taken from *Psychological Abstracts,* it will be an easy task to use this resource to locate relevant articles. Once you have the index terms from your computerized search, you can go straight to the *Psychological Abstracts* index.

Let's assume that you have completed your PsycLIT search on child abuse from 1974 through the present. Now you need to consult the literature prior to 1974. Figure 2-4 presents a subject index page from a 1973 issue of *Psychological Abstracts.* As you can see, our key terms *battered child syndrome* and *child neglect* are listed. The numbers at the end of each subject listing identify abstracts in that issue that might be of interest to us. Although there are no abstracts for *battered child syndrome,* there are several for *child neglect.* Now, you have to locate abstracts 40709, 41206, and 41314 to determine whether they describe literature you need to consult in greater depth and detail.

The items you locate in a search of the *Psychological Abstracts* also indicate the number of references each publication contains. These references should be consulted to determine whether you have overlooked any relevant works in your search. Once you have seen which authors repeatedly publish in your area of interest, you should use those authors' names as key terms to make both your PsycLIT and *Psychological Abstracts* searches as thorough as possible.

FIGURE 2-4. AN INDEX PAGE FROM *PSYCHOLOGICAL ABSTRACTS*.

Source: Reprinted with permission of the American Psychological Association, publisher of *Psychological Abstracts* and the *Thesaurus of Psychological Index Terms* (7th Edition), all rights reserved.

Bonding (Emotional) [See Attachment Behavior]
Bone Disorders [See Osteoporosis]
Bone Marrow—Chapters: 41546
Books [See Textbooks]
Borderline States—Serials: 40488, 40648, 41285, 41359 Chapters: 40653
Boys [See Human Males]
Braille—Serials: 42136, 42143
Brain [See Also Brain Stem, Cerebellum, Forebrain, Mesencephalon]—Serials: 39898, 40162, 41520 Books: 39744, 39792, 39793, 42332 Chapters: 39677, 39803, 40614
Brain Ablation [See Brain Lesions]
Brain Concussion—Serials: 41080, 41130
Brain Damage [See Also Brain Concussion]—Serials: 40607, 41080, 41097, 41107, 41130, 41749
Brain Damaged—Serials: 39397, 39400, 41057, 41060, 41066, 41070, 41077, 41081, 41083, 41094, 41103, 41105, 41113, 41114, 41122, 41123, 41127, 41129, 41363, 41527, 41724, 41725, 41732, 41817 Chapters: 41141
Brain Disorders [See Aphasia, Brain Damage, Cerebrovascular Accidents, Encephalopathies, Epilepsy, Epileptic Seizures, Organic Brain Syndromes, Parkinsons Disease]
Brain Injuries [See Brain Damage]
Brain Lesions—Serials: 39763, 39781, 39782 Chapters: 39806, 39812, 39816, 39823, 39830
Brain Mapping [See Stereotaxic Atlas]
Brain Maps [See Stereotaxic Atlas]
Brain Metabolism [See Neurochemistry]
Brain Stem—Serials: 41098 Chapters: 39802
Brain Stimulation [See Electrical Brain Stimulation]
Brand Names—Serials: 42270
Brand Preferences—Serials: 42257
Brazil—Serials: 40105, 40761, 41770
Breast Neoplasms—Serials: 41111, 41355, 41558
Breathing [See Respiration]
Breeding (Animal) [See Animal Breeding]
Brief Psychotherapy—Serials: 41215, 41240, 41243, 41253, 41364 Books: 41266 Chapters: 41369
Brief Reactive Psychosis [See Acute Psychosis]
Bright Light Therapy [See Phototherapy]
Bromocriptine—Serials: 39916, 41771
Brothers—Serials: 42049
Budgets [See Costs and Cost Analysis]
Bulgaria—Serials: 40196
Bulimia—Serials: 40922 Chapters: 40925
Burnout [See Occupational Stress]
Burns—Chapters: 41002
Business—Serials: 41813
Business and Industrial Personnel [See Blue Collar Workers, Secretarial Personnel, Service Personnel, Skilled Industrial Workers, Technical Personnel, White Collar Workers]
Business Organizations—Serials: 39970, 42223, 42256, 42271
Business Students—Serials: 42094, 42104
Buying [See Consumer Behavior]

Caffeine—Serials: 39887, 40798
Calcium—Serials: 39924
Calcium Channel Blockers [See Channel Blockers]
Calculus [See Mathematics]
Calories—Serials: 39683, 39684

Canada—Serials: 40064, 40806, 41172, 41560, 41648, 41831, 42363, 42366 Chapters: 40513, 41622, 41856
Cancers [See Neoplasms]
Candidates (Political) [See Political Candidates]
Cannabis—Serials: 40801
Capgras Syndrome—Serials: 40607
Capital Punishment—Serials: 40838, 40842, 40843
Capsaicin—Serials: 39897, 39913
Carbamazepine—Serials: 41404, 41522
Carbohydrate Metabolism [See Glucose Metabolism]
Carbohydrates [See Sugars]
Carcinomas [See Neoplasms]
Cardiac Disorders [See Heart Disorders]
Cardiac Rate [See Heart Rate]
Cardiography [See Electrocardiography]
Cardiovascular Disorders [See Also Cerebrovascular Disorders, Heart Disorders, Hypertension]—Serials: 42185
Cardiovascular Reactivity—Serials: 39858, 39860, 39862, 39863, 39872, 40767
Cardiovascular System—Serials: 39903, 39938
Career Aspirations [See Occupational Aspirations]
Career Change—Serials: 42213
Career Choice [See Occupational Choice]
Career Counseling [See Occupational Guidance]
Career Development—Serials: 41909, 41930, 42181 Books: 41863
Career Goals [See Occupational Aspirations]
Career Guidance [See Occupational Guidance]
Career Transitions [See Career Development]
Careers [See Occupations]
Caregiver Burden—Serials: 39467, 40528, 41663, 41664, 41666, 41673, 41674, 41678, 41683
Caregivers—Serials: 41660, 41661, 41662, 41663, 41665, 41667, 41668, 41669, 41671, 41672, 41673, 41675, 41676, 41677 Chapters: 39732
Carotid Arteries—Serials: 41119
Cartoons (Humor)—Serials: 39320
Case History [See Patient History]
Case Management [See Also Discharge Planning]—Serials: 41582, 41602, 41603, 41629, 41643, 41780, 41842, 41881 Chapters: 41208
Caseworkers [See Social Workers]
Caste System—Serials: 40198 Chapters: 42171
Castration—Chapters: 40305
CAT Scan [See Tomography]
Catabolites [See Metabolites]
Catamnesis [See Posttreatment Followup]
Catatonia—Serials: 40526, 40529
Catecholamines [See Also Dopamine, Norepinephrine]—Serials: 39870
Categorizing [See Classification (Cognitive Process)]
Catharsis—Chapters: 40476
Caucasians [See Whites]
Caudate Nucleus—Serials: 39911
Causal Analysis—Books: 40056
Cells (Biology) [See Chromosomes, Neurons]
Central Nervous System [See Also Spinal Cord]—Serials: 39914
Central Nervous System Disorders [See Also Chorea, Dysarthria]—Serials: 41096, 41102, 41118
Central Tendency Measures [See Mean]
Cerebellar Cortex [See Cerebellum]
Cerebellar Nuclei [See Cerebellum]

Cerebellopontile Angle [See Cerebellum]
Cerebellum [See Also Purkinje Cells]—Serials: 39770, 39782
Cerebral Atrophy—Serials: 40518, 41107
Cerebral Blood Flow—Serials: 39771, 39778, 40612, 41074, 41092, 41118
Cerebral Cortex [See Also Corpus Callosum, Frontal Lobe, Left Brain, Limbic System, Occipital Lobe, Parietal Lobe, Right Brain, Temporal Lobe]—Serials: 39770, 39771, 39788, 39790, 39847, 41076, 42327 Chapters: 39798, 39805, 39814
Cerebral Dominance [See Also Lateral Dominance]—Serials: 39787
Cerebral Ischemia—Serials: 41100, 41119
Cerebral Lesions [See Brain Lesions]
Cerebral Vascular Disorders [See Cerebrovascular Disorders]
Cerebrovascular Accidents—Serials: 41047, 41048, 41049, 41051, 41063, 41078, 41081, 41089, 41093, 41098, 41724 Chapters: 41053, 41207
Cerebrovascular Disorders [See Also Cerebral Ischemia, Cerebrovascular Accidents]—Serials: 40957, 41119
Certification (Professional) [See Professional Certification]
Chance (Fortune) [See Statistical Probability]
Change (Organizational) [See Organizational Change]
Change (Social) [See Social Change]
Channel Blockers—Serials: 39924, 41443
Character [See Personality]
Character Development [See Personality Development]
Character Disorders [See Personality Disorders]
Character Formation [See Personality Development]
Charitable Behavior—Serials: 40406
Chemical Elements [See Calcium]
Chemicals—Serials: 39899, 40939
Chemistry [See Biochemistry]
Chemotherapy [See Drug Therapy]
Chess—Serials: 39556
Chicanos [See Mexican Americans]
Child Abuse—Serials: 39352, 40659, 40670, 40679, 40684, 40701, 40706, 40709, 40806, 40836, 41471, 41836, 41897, 41939 Books: 40711, 40712, 40715, 40716, 41177 Chapters: 40718, 40719, 40720, 40723, 40724, 40725, 40726, 40727, 40728, 40731, 40732, 40733, 40734, 40737, 40738, 40740, 40741, 40746, 40750, 40751, 40752, 40755, 40757, 40759, 40824, 40874, 41192, 42359
Child Advocacy [See Advocacy]
Child Attitudes—Serials: 39352, 40051, 40064, 40093, 40932
Child Behavior Checklist—Serials: 39337, 40501
Child Care—Serials: 39998, 42013
Child Care Workers—Serials: 42211
Child Neglect—Serials: 40709, 40806, 41314
Child Psychiatry—Serials: 40570, 41710 Chapters: 40517, 41205
Child Psychology—Chapters: 41190
Child Welfare—Serials: 41648, 41886, 42363, 42366
Childbirth [See Birth]
Childhood Development [See Also Early Childhood Development]—Serials: 40087, 40296, 40794, 41681, 42154 Chapters: 40557, 40937, 41655, 41658
Childhood Memories [See Early Memories]
Childhood Play Behavior—Serials: 39411, 39472, 40087, 40100, 40857, 40862, 41298, 41996

We cannot emphasize too strongly the importance of conducting a pre-1974 search of the *Psychological Abstracts*. It is tempting to limit your search to the ease and convenience of computer automation. However, unless you are thorough and conduct the hand search of the pre-1974 literature, you will not know if the project you have in mind has already been conducted.

4. ***Obtaining the Relevant Publications.*** Once you have assembled a listing of books and journal articles relevant to your area of interest, it is time to acquire copies. There are several techniques for going about this task; you will probably find that a combination of these strategies works best. First, find out what is available in your own library and plan to spend time reading this material and/or make photocopies for later use.

There are two options for obtaining items that are not available in your library. You can order them through the *interlibrary loan* department or in the case of journal articles you can write directly to the author to request a *reprint(s)*. Most interlibrary loan services are reasonably fast and efficient. However, there may be a small fee for providing copies of journal articles.

Writing for reprints has an added advantage; it allows you to request additional, related articles that the author may have published. With the advent of electronic mail (E-mail) and the Internet, the task of communicating with researchers in your area of interest has become much easier. This form of communication is fast and convenient. Most authors are pleased to comply with such requests and there is no charge for reprints. Your literature search is likely to uncover publications that are several years, even decades, old. Because authors are supplied with a large number of reprints when an article is published, the chances are good that they will have copies of their older articles. Don't hesitate to ask. Concerned about addresses for authors? The PsycLIT search or the abstract in *Psychological Abstracts* lists the institutional affiliation of the author(s). Hence, you should be able to look up the institutional address in any number of the guide books to colleges and universities that can be found in your library. If you have only the author's name, then consult your faculty members to see if they have a membership directory for the APA and/or the American Psychological Society. There is a good chance that the author(s) you are trying to locate will be a member of one or both of these associations. If so, you can get the institutional and E-mail addresses from a current membership directory.

5. ***Integrating the Results of the Literature Search.*** Once you have assembled the journal articles, book chapters, and books relevant to your research area, you will need to make sense of this material. This task can be formidable, indeed; it will help if you have a plan.

Our students have found the following procedure to be quite effective. You also may find it useful in organizing the results of your literature search. As you read each article, keep good, but succinct, notes on each of the following aspects. Because most journal articles are presented in the following sequence, your task will not be difficult. We will have more to say about how you actually write the results of your research in Chapters 5 and 12. For now, you need to master the task of summarizing what others have already written and published.

Reference Information. List the complete citation (in APA format; see Chapter 12) for the article you are abstracting. This information will facilitate completion of the reference section of your research report.

Introduction. Why was the project undertaken? What theory does this research seek to support?

Method. Use the following sections to describe how the project was conducted:

> *Participants.* Describe the participants who were tested. List such specifics as species, number, age, and sex.
>
> *Apparatus.* Describe the equipment that was used. Note any deviations from the standard apparatus, as well as any unusual features.
>
> *Procedure.* Describe the conditions under which the participants were tested.

Results. Which statistical tests were used? What were the results of these statistical tests?

Discussion. What conclusions did the author(s) reach? How do these conclusions relate to theory and past research? Describe any criticisms of the research that occurred to you as you read the article.

Once you have completed taking notes on these sections, you should condense them so that all this information will fit on one side of a sheet of paper. As you prepare these single sheets, be sure always to use the same sequence of headings that you followed in making your notes. An example of a completed sheet is shown in Figure 2-5.

Once you have prepared all your relevant literature in this manner, it is an easy task to lay out the pages on a table and make comparisons and contrasts. Because the same type of information is found in the same location on each page, comparisons of the various aspects and details are greatly facilitated. Additionally, the use of a single sheet for each reference allows you to arrange and rearrange the references to suit your various needs: alphabetically to create a reference list, into separate stacks to represent positive and negative findings, and so forth.

As you have probably realized, the format we are suggesting is modeled after the accepted APA format for preparing papers. We will cover the APA format for preparing research papers in considerable depth in this book. The experience you get in summarizing the results of your literature search will help you as you prepare a full-length APA format paper. At this point, we are now ready to do something with the results of our literature survey.

FORMULATING THE RESEARCH HYPOTHESIS

Once you have completed your literature review, your own research begins to take shape. The next task is to develop a research hypothesis.

Recall from Chapter 1 that the hypothesis is an attempt to organize data and independent and dependent variable relationships within a specific portion of a larger,

FIGURE 2-5.   SAMPLE OF THE SUMMARY OF A JOURNAL ARTICLE.

Wann, D. L., & Dolan, T. J. (1994). Spectators' evaluations of rival and fellow fans. The Psychological Record, 44, 351-358.

Introduction

Even though "sports fans are biased in their evaluations and attributions concerning their team" (p. 351), no research has examined the evaluations spectators make of other spectators. Hence the present experiment was conducted to examine spectators' evaluations of home team and rival fans.

Method

Participants - One hundred three undergraduate psychology students received extra credit for participation.

Instruments - A questionnaire packet consisting of an information sheet, Sports Spectator Identification Scale, a five-paragraph scenario describing the behavior of a home team or rival spectator at an important basketball game, and several questions concerning the general behavior of the spectator described in the scenario was given to each participant.

Procedure - The questionnaire packet was completed after an informed consent document was completed and returned. One-half of the participants read the home team fan scenario, while the remainder of the participants read the rival team fan scenario. The determination of which scenario was read was determined randomly.

Results

Analysis of variance was used to analyze the data. The results of these analyses indicated that the home team fan was rated more positively than the rival team fan by participants who were highly identified with the home team. This pattern of results was not shown by lesser identified fans. Of particular note was the finding that the highly identified participants did not rate the rival team fan more negatively than did the lesser identified participants; they just rated the home team fan positively.

Discussion and Evaluation

These results support the authors' initial predictions that participants would give more positive evaluations of fans rooting for the same team and more negative evaluations of fans rooting for a different team. Wann and Dolan's prediction that such evaluations would be shown only by fans who were highly identified with their team also was supported. These predictions were seen to be in accord with social identity theory. The study appeared to be well conducted. The fact that the study was not conducted at a sporting event limits its applicability.

more comprehensive research area or theory. Thus, hypotheses that have been supported by experimental research can make important contributions to our knowledge base.

Because we have yet to conduct our research project, the **research or experimental hypothesis** is our *prediction* about the relationship that exists between the independent variable that we are going to manipulate and the dependent variable that will be recorded. If our research hypothesis is supported by the results of our experiment, then it has the potential to make a contribution to theory; you have some grounds on which to infer a cause-and-effect relationship. In order to understand the nature of the research hypothesis, we will examine some of its general characteristics.

CHARACTERISTICS OF THE RESEARCH HYPOTHESIS

For the detective and the psychologist, all acceptable research hypotheses share certain characteristics—they are stated in a certain manner, they involve a certain type of reasoning, and they are presented in a certain format.

Types of Statements. Because our research hypothesis is nothing more than a statement of what we believe will occur when an experiment is conducted, we must carefully consider the statements used in constructing it.

Synthetic, Analytic, and Contradictory Statements. A statement can be one of three types: synthetic, analytic, or contradictory.

Synthetic statements are those statements that can be *either true or false*. The statement "Abused children have lower self-esteem" is synthetic because although there is a chance that it is true, there also is a chance that it is false.

Analytic statements are those statements that are *always true*. For example, "I am making an 'A' *or* I am not making an 'A'" is an analytic statement; it is always true. You are either making an "A" or you are not making an "A," no other possibilities exist.

Contradictory statements are those statements that are *always false*. For example, "I am making an 'A' *and* I am not making an 'A'" is a contradictory statement; it is always false. You cannot make an "A" and not make an "A" at the same time.

Research or experimental hypothesis The experimenter's predicted outcome of a research project.

Synthetic statement Statements that can be *either true or false.*

Analytic statement Statements that are *always true.*

Contradictory statement Statements that are *always false.*

definition

Psychological Detective

Review the three different types of statements that were just presented. Which one is best suited for use in our research hypothesis? Why? Write down your answers before reading further.

definition	**General implication form** Statement of the research hypothesis in an "if . . . then" form.

When an experiment is conducted, we are attempting to *establish* the existence of a cause-and-effect relationship. At the outset of the experiment we do not know whether our prediction is correct or not. Therefore, synthetic statements, which can be true or false, must constitute our research hypothesis. If the research hypothesis is comprised of analytic or contradictory statements, there is no need (or way) to conduct research on that topic. We already know what the outcome will be by merely reading the statements.

General Implication Form. The research hypothesis must be able to be stated in **general implication,** "if . . . then," form. The "if" portion of such statements refers to the independent variable manipulation(s) that are going to be made, whereas the "then" portion of the statement refers to the dependent variable changes one expects to observe. An example of a general implication form statement would be the following:

> *If* students in one group of third graders are given an M&M each time they spell a word correctly, *then* their spelling performance will be better than that of a group of third-graders who do not receive an M&M for each correctly spelled word.

If you have read articles in the psychological journals, you are probably saying to yourself, "I don't recall seeing many statements in general implication form." You are probably correct; most researchers do not formally state their research hypothesis in strict general implication form. For example, the hypothesis about the third-graders and their spelling performance might have been stated thusly:

> Third-graders who receive an M&M each time they spell a word correctly will spell better than third-graders who do not receive an M&M for each correctly spelled word.

Regardless of how the research hypothesis is stated, it must be restateable in general implication form. If it cannot be stated in this manner, then there is a problem with either our independent variable manipulation or the dependent variable we have chosen to measure.

Psychological Detective

Read the last general implication statement again. What independent variable is being manipulated? What is the dependent variable? In addition to being stated in general implication form, is this statement synthetic, analytic, or contradictory? Write down your answers to these questions before reading further.

Whether or not the students receive an M&M after correctly spelling a word is the independent variable. The spelling performance of the two groups of third-graders is the dependent variable. Because this statement has the potential to be true *or* false, it is synthetic.

The use of synthetic statements that are presented in general implication form highlights two additional, but related, characteristics of the research hypothesis. The **principle of falsifiability,** the first characteristic, means that when an experiment does not turn out as you predicted, then this result is seen as evidence that your hypothesis is false. After the experiment, if the two groups of third-graders do not differ in spelling ability, then you must conclude that you made a bad prediction; your research hypothesis was not an accurate portrayal of nature.

Because we use synthetic statements for our research hypothesis, our results will *never* prove its truth absolutely; this is the second characteristic of the research hypothesis. Assume that we had found that third-graders who received M&Ms spelled better than third-graders who did not receive M&Ms. Later we decide to replicate our experiment. Just because we obtained positive results the first time we conducted the experiment does not prove that our research hypothesis is unquestionably true and that we will always obtain positive results. When we conduct a replication, or any experiment for that matter, our hypothesis contains a synthetic statement that is either true or false. Thus, a research hypothesis may never be absolutely proved; it simply has yet to be disproved. Certainly, as the number of experiments that support the research hypothesis increase, our confidence in the research hypothesis increases.

Types of Reasoning. In stating our research hypothesis, we also must be aware of the type of reasoning or logic we use. As we will see, inductive and deductive reasoning involve different processes.

Inductive Logic. **Inductive logic** involves reasoning from specific cases to general principles. Inductive logic is the process that is involved in the construction of theories; the results of several independent experiments are considered simultaneously and general theoretical principles designed to account for the behavior in question are derived.

For example, John Darley and Bibb Latané (1968) were intrigued by a famous incident that occurred in 1964 in the Queens section of New York. A young woman named Kitty Genovese was stabbed to death. Given the number of murders that take place each year in any large city, this event may not seem especially noteworthy. However, an especially horrifying aspect of this murder was that the killer attacked the young woman on *three* separate occasions in the course of half an hour and that 38 people saw the attacks or heard the young woman's screams. The killer was frightened off twice when people turned their lights on or called from their windows. However, on both occasions he resumed his attack. None of the people who witnessed the attack came to the victim's aid and no one called the police while she was being attacked. Why?

Principle of falsifiability Results not in accord with the research hypothesis are taken as evidence that this hypothesis is false.

Inductive logic Reasoning that proceeds from specific cases to general conclusions or theories.

definition

Darley and Latané (1968) reported the results of several experiments they had conducted and then theorized that when individuals are alone, they are more likely to give assistance than when others are present. The finding that groups of bystanders are less likely than individuals to aid a person in trouble is known as the bystander effect. The development of this principle is an example of the use of inductive reasoning; several specific results were combined to formulate a more general principle.

definition

Deductive logic
Reasoning that proceeds from general theories to specific cases.

Deductive Logic. **Deductive logic** is the converse of inductive logic; we reason from general principles to specific conclusions or predictions. Deductive logic is the reasoning process we are using in formulating our research hypothesis. By conducting a search of the literature, we have assembled a large amount of data and considered several theories. From this *general* pool of information we seek to develop our research hypothesis, a statement about the relationship between a *specific* independent variable and a *specific* dependent variable. For example, based on previous research on the bystander effect, the following deductive statement might be made:

If a person pretends to have a seizure on a subway, then that person will receive less assistance when there are more bystanders present.

Psychological Detective

Read the above statement once again. Is this statement acceptable as a research hypothesis?   Write your answer for this question before reading further.

Yes, this statement would appear to be acceptable as a research hypothesis. It is a synthetic statement that is stated in general implication form. Moreover, deductive logic is involved as we have gone from a general body of knowledge (about the bystander effect) to make a specific prediction concerning a specific independent variable (number of bystanders present) and a specific dependent variable (receiving assistance).

Certainly we are not maintaining that deductive and inductive reasoning are totally separate processes. They can, and do, interact with each other. As you can see from Figure 2-6, the conduct of several initial experiments in a particular research area may lead to the development of a theory in that area (inductive reasoning). In turn, an examination of that theory and past research may suggest a specific research project (deductive reasoning) that needs to be conducted. The results of that project may result in modification of the theory (inductive reasoning), which prompts the conduct of several additional research projects (deductive reasoning),

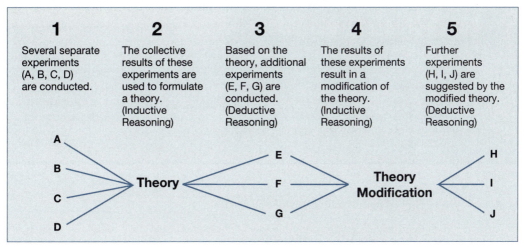

1	2	3	4	5
Several separate experiments (A, B, C, D) are conducted.	The collective results of these experiments are used to formulate a theory. (Inductive Reasoning)	Based on the theory, additional experiments (E, F, G) are conducted. (Deductive Reasoning)	The results of these experiments result in a modification of the theory. (Inductive Reasoning)	Further experiments (H, I, J) are suggested by the modified theory. (Deductive Reasoning)

FIGURE 2-6.   THE RELATIONSHIP BETWEEN DEDUCTIVE AND INDUCTIVE REASONING.

and so forth. Clearly, the research process we described in Chapter 1 is based upon the interplay between these two types of logical reasoning.

Directional versus Nondirectional Research Hypotheses. Finally, we must consider whether we are going to predict the direction of the outcome of our experiment in our research hypothesis. In a **directional research hypothesis** we specify the outcome of the experiment.

For example, if we test two groups, we could entertain one of the following directional hypotheses:

Group A will score significantly higher than Group B.

or

Group B will score significantly higher than Group A.

In either case, we are directly specifying the direction that we predict the outcome of our experiment will take. (Please note that although we can entertain either of these directional hypotheses, we cannot consider both of them at the same time.)

On the other hand, a **nondirectional research hypothesis** does not predict the exact directional outcome of an experiment; it simply predicts that the groups we are testing will differ. Using our two-group example once again, a nondirectional hypothesis would indicate that

Group A's scores will differ significantly from Group B's.

For this hypothesis to be supported, Group A can score either significantly higher or significantly lower than Group B.

Directional research hypothesis
Prediction of the specific outcome of an experiment.

Nondirectional research hypothesis
A specific prediction concerning the outcome of an experiment is not made.

definition

Psychological Detective

Review the differences between directional and nondirectional hypotheses. How would you write a directional research hypothesis for the M&Ms and third-grade spelling experiment we described earlier? How would you write a nondirectional hypothesis for this same experiment? Write down your two hypotheses before reading further.

A directional hypothesis might read as follows:

> If students in one group of third-graders are given an M&M each time they spell a word correctly, then *their spelling performance will be better* than that of a group of third-graders who do not receive an M&M for each correctly spelled word.

Of course, you might predict that receiving M&Ms would cause spelling performance to decrease and fall below that of the group that did not receive the M&Ms. In either instance, a directional hypothesis is being used.

A nondirectional hypothesis would read as follows:

> If students in one group of third-graders are given an M&M each time they spell a word correctly, then *their spelling performance will differ* from that of a group of third-graders who do not receive an M&M for each correctly spelled word.

In this instance, we are simply predicting that the two groups will differ.

Which type of hypothesis, directional or nondirectional, should you choose? If you are *absolutely certain* of your prediction, then you may want to use a directional hypothesis. For reasons that we will discuss later, your chances of finding a statistically significant result are increased when you use a directional hypothesis. However, if you adopt a directional hypothesis, there is no changing your mind. When the results turn out exactly opposite to your prediction, the only thing you can say is that you were wrong and that nature doesn't operate as you thought it did. Because nature has a way of playing cruel tricks on our predictions, most researchers take a more conservative approach and state a nondirectional research hypothesis. Even though it may be slightly more difficult to achieve statistical significance, there is less potential disappointment with the outcome of the research project when a nondirectional hypothesis is used.

REVIEW SUMMARY

1. The starting point for the research project is the **research idea** or identification of a gap in our current knowledge base.
2. Good research ideas should be testable and have a high likelihood of success (closely approximate nature).

3. **Nonsystematic sources** of research ideas give the impression that the idea simply appeared with little or no forethought. Inspiration, **serendipity** (looking for one phenomenon, but finding another), and everyday occurrences are the major nonsystematic sources of research ideas.

4. Formal study and knowledge of a topic form the basis for **systematic sources** of research ideas. Past research and theories are the two main systematic sources of research ideas.

5. An organized approach is required to conduct a survey of the psychological literature. Such a search typically begins with the selection of index terms from the *Thesaurus of Psychological Index Terms*. Once these terms have been selected, they are used to access a computer database, such as PsycLIT, and/or the *Psychological Abstracts*. After the relevant literature has been identified and copies acquired, it must be integrated in a meaningful manner.

6. Once the literature review is complete, the researcher is ready to develop a **research or experimental hypothesis**—the *predicted* outcome of the experiment.

7. The research hypothesis contains **synthetic statements** that can be either true or false and is stated in **general implication form** ("if . . . then").

8. The **principle of falsifiability** indicates that when an experiment does not turn out as predicted, the truthfulness of the research hypothesis is discredited. Because a research hypothesis is composed of synthetic statements, it can never be absolutely proved, it can only be disproved.

9. The development of the research hypothesis involves the use of **deductive logic** in which one reasons from general principles to specific cases.

10. A **directional research hypothesis** is used when the *specific* direction or nature of the outcome of an experiment is predicted. When the experimenter does not predict the specific nature of the group differences, only that they will differ, a **nondirectional research hypothesis** is used.

STUDY BREAK

1. Matching
   1. research idea
   2. serendipity
   3. *Psychological Abstracts*
   4. PsycLIT
   5. experimental hypothesis
   6. synthetic statement
   7. analytic statement

   A. look for one thing, find another
   B. articles from 1974 to present
   C. identification of a gap in the knowledge base
   D. articles prior to 1974
   E. always true
   F. either true or false
   G. experimenter's predicted answer to research

2. Good research ideas must be _____ and have a high _____ _____ _____.

3. Distinguish between nonsystematic and systematic sources of research ideas. What are the specific ways each general source may be shown?

4. Describe the steps involved in conducting a good review of the psychological literature.

5. What advantages does requesting reprints offer?

6. Why are synthetic statements used in the experimental hypothesis?

7. Describe general implication form. Be thorough.

8. What is meant by the "principle of falsifiability"?

9. The construction of theories involves _____ logic; the development of the experimental hypothesis involves _____ logic.

10. When you are absolutely sure of the outcome of an experiment, you might use a _____ experimental hypothesis; otherwise, it is safer to use a _____ experimental hypothesis.

ETHICS IN PSYCHOLOGICAL RESEARCH

Although it may appear that we are ready to begin our research project once we have developed our research hypothesis, this simply is not the case. We still have one major issue to deal with before we finalize our research design and start gathering data; the ethical nature of the research must be considered. The days of beating a confession out of a suspect with a rubber hose are gone for the detective. Likewise, psychologists must ask and answer such questions as "Are we putting our participants at risk?" "Is our experimental treatment harmful?" "Is the information we will gather from our experiment worth the potential risk and harm that is involved?" Despite older views to the contrary, science does not operate in a moral vacuum (Kimmel, 1988).

Under the 1974 National Health Research Act, the United States government demands assurance that federally funded projects have been reviewed and approved by a group of the proposing scientist's peers and that informed consent concerning research participation is given by human participants. Since that time, seeking approval for a project from a Human Subjects Review Panel, an Animal Care and Utilization Committee, or an Institutional Review Board has become standard practice.

What has prompted such concern with ethics? Although we could cite many unethical practices, we will describe three that created major concern: the medical atrocities of World War II, the Tuskegee syphilis project, and Stanley Milgram's obedience studies of the 1960s.

During World War II Nazi doctors conducted a lengthy series of experiments on civilian prisoners of war to determine the effects of various viruses, toxic agents, and drugs. The prisoners had no choice concerning whether they wanted to participate. After World War II many of these doctors were tried in courts for the unethical practices they had inflicted on their unwilling participants. Many were found guilty and either hanged or given long prison sentences. The Nuremberg War Tribunal was responsible for the development of a code of medical and research ethics (Sasson & Nelson, 1969). Among other things, the Nuremberg Code stressed a consideration of the following ethical aspects of research:

1. Participants should consent to participate in research.
2. Participants should be fully informed of the nature of the research project.
3. Risks should be avoided whenever possible.
4. Participants should be protected against risks to the greatest extent possible.
5. Projects should be conducted by scientifically qualified personnel.
6. Participants have the right to discontinue participation at any time.

As we will see, the Nuremberg Code has had a major impact upon the APA code of ethics to which psychologists adhere.

The Tuskegee syphilis study (Jones, 1981) was begun in 1932 and continued into the early 1970s. The purpose of the study was to observe the course of the syphilis disease in untreated individuals. To accomplish this goal 399 African-American men who were infected with syphilis were recruited as participants. They were told that they were being treated for syphilis by the United States Public Health Service (USPHS). They were *not* told the real purpose of the study, nor were they *ever* given any treatment for syphilis. Moreover, local physicians were told not to treat these men for syphilis and the participants were told that their USPHS treatment would be discontinued if they sought any sort of additional treatment for the disease. Although information about the course of syphilis may have been gained from this project, it was done at the physical expense and lives of the unknowing participants.

Psychological Detective

Review the points of research concern from the Nuremberg Code. Which of these principles did the Tuskegee syphilis study violate? How were these principles violated? Write down your answers to these questions before reading further.

It would appear that with the exception of the principle concerning the conduct of the project by a qualified scientist, *all* of the principles of the Nuremberg Code were violated. The men did not consent to participate, nor were they fully informed about the project. The participants were not protected against risks and they certainly did not appear to have the right to decline to participate.

In Milgram's (1963) obedience-to-authority study, each participant was assigned the role of "teacher" in what was portrayed as a "learning experiment." Another "participant" (actually an accomplice of the experimenter) was assigned to the role of "learner." The teacher's task was to teach the learner a series of words. The teacher was told that the purpose of the experiment was to determine the effects of punishment on memory. Every time the learner, who was in an adjacent room, made a mistake, the teacher was to correct the learner by administering an electric shock. Even though no shocks were actually administered, the teacher (true participant) did not know it, and the learner always acted as if shock had been administered.

Once the experimental session began, the learner purposely made mistakes so that the teacher would have to administer shocks. With each mistake the teacher was instructed by the experimenter to increase the voltage level of the shock. As the mistakes (and voltage level) increased, the learner began to moan and complain and finally refused to answer any questions. The experimenter told the teacher to treat no response as a mistake and continue administering shocks. The session was concluded when the teacher (participant) refused to administer any more shocks. Contrary to Milgram's initial prediction, the participants administered *many* shocks at what they assumed were *very high* voltage levels.

Although this research contributed to our understanding of obedience to authority, it was not without ethical problems. For example, rather than protecting the rights of the participants, the experimenter purposely made them feel discomfort and emotional distress by ordering them to continue administering the electrical shocks (Baumrind, 1964). Moreover, Milgram (1964) was not prepared for the amount of emotional upset his participants experienced. Even though this high level of discomfort was noted, the decision was made to continue the research. To Milgram's credit, all participants received a debriefing session after the experiment was completed. During this session the purpose of the experiment was explained and the "learner" talked with the real participant. Subsequently, all participants received a follow-up report describing the results of the experiment. It is noteworthy that such debriefing and follow-up procedures were not required in the early 1960s.

APA Principles in the Conduct of Research with Humans

Experiments such as the Tuskegee syphilis project and Milgram's study have led to the development of ethical guidelines by the APA. The original APA code of ethics was adopted and published in 1973; it was revised in 1982.

The 10 APA "Ethical Principles in the Conduct of Research with Human Subjects" are shown in Table 2-2. Those principles dealing with (a) placing the participants "at risk" or "at minimal risk" (Principle B) and informing them of such risks (Principle G), (b) securing "informed consent" from the participants (Principle D), and (c) using "deception" in research (Principle E) have proved to be controversial.

Psychological Detective

Why have these principles proved to be controversial in the conduct of psychological re- search? Give this question some thought and write down an answer before read- ing further.

Much psychological research, especially in the area of social psychology, has involved the use of deception. Researchers believe that in many cases honest and unbiased responses can be obtained only when the participants are unaware of the true nature of the research. Hence, researchers have found it difficult to give their participants a complete and accurate description of the experiment and secure in- formed consent before the research is conducted. Such difficulties have caused many critics to wonder whether deception in research is necessary.

Is Deception in Research Necessary? Ideally, the researcher should be able to explain the purpose of a research project to the participants and enlist their cooper-

---

TABLE 2-2. APA PRINCIPLES FOR THE ETHICAL TREATMENT OF HUMAN SUBJECTS

PRINCIPLE A	In planning a study, the investigator has the responsibility to make a careful evaluation of its ethical acceptability. To the extent that the weighing of scientific and human values suggests a compromise of any principle, the investigator incurs a correspondingly serious obligation to seek ethical advice and to observe stringent safeguards to protect the rights of human participants.
PRINCIPLE B	Considering whether a participant in a planned study will be a "subject at risk" or "subject at minimal risk," according to recognized standards, is of primary ethical concern to the investigator.
PRINCIPLE C	The investigator always retains the responsibility for insuring ethical practice in research. The investigator is also responsible for the ethical treatment of research participants by collaborators, assistants, students, and employees, all of whom, however, incur similar responsibilities.
PRINCIPLE D	Except in minimal-risk research, the investigator establishes a clear and fair agreement with the research participants, prior to their participation, that clarifies the obligations and responsibilities of each. The investigator has the obligation to honor all promises and commitments included in that agreement. The investigator informs the participants of all aspects of the research that might reasonably be expected to influence willingness to participate and explains all other aspects of the research about which the participants inquire. Failure to make full disclosure prior to obtaining informed consent requires additional safeguards to protect the welfare and dignity of the research participants. Research with children or with participants who have impairments that would limit understanding and/or communication requires special safeguarding procedures. *(continued)*

TABLE 2-2. APA PRINCIPLES FOR THE ETHICAL TREATMENT OF HUMAN SUBJECTS (continued)

PRINCIPLE E	Methodological requirements of a study may make the use of concealment or deception necessary. Before conducting such a study, the investigator has a special responsibility to (1) determine whether the use of such techniques is justified by the study s prospective scientific, educational, or applied value; (2) determine whether alternative procedures are available that do not use concealment or deception; and (3) ensure that the participants are provided with sufficient explanation as soon as possible.
PRINCIPLE F	The investigator respects the individual s freedom to decline to participate in or to withdraw from the research at any time. The obligation to protect this freedom requires careful thought and consideration when the investigator is in a position of authority or influence over the participant. Such positions of authority include, but are not limited to, situations in which research participation is required as part of employment or in which the participant is a student, client, or employee of the investigator.
PRINCIPLE G	The investigator protects the participant from physical and mental discomfort, harm, and danger that may arise from research procedures. If risks of such consequences exist, the investigator informs the participant of that fact. Research procedures likely to cause serious or lasting harm to a participant are not used unless the failure to use these procedures might expose the participant to risk of greater harm or unless the research has great potential benefit and fully informed and voluntary consent is obtained from each participant. The participant should be informed of procedures for contacting the investigator within a reasonable time period following participation should stress, potential harm, or related questions or concerns arise.
PRINCIPLE H	After the data are collected, the investigator provides the participant with information about the nature of the study and attempts to remove any misconceptions that may have arisen. When scientific or humane values justify denying or withholding this information, the investigator incurs a special responsibility to monitor the research and to ensure that there are no damaging consequences for the participant.
PRINCIPLE I	Where research procedures result in undesirable consequences for the individual participant, the investigator has the responsibility to detect and remove or correct these consequences, including long-term effects.
PRINCIPLE J	Information about the research participant obtained during the course of an investigation is confidential unless otherwise agreed upon in advance. When the possibility exists that others may obtain access to such information, this possibility, together with plans for protecting confidentiality, is explained to the participant as part of the procedure for obtaining informed consent.

Source: This material has been adapted from *Ethical Principles in the Conduct of Research with Human Participants* (pp. 92-93) by the American Psychological Association, 1982, Washington, DC: APA. Copyright ©1982 by the American Psychological Association. Reprinted with permission. APA cautions that the 1990 *Ethical Principles of Psychologists* are no longer current and that the guidelines and information provided in the 1973 and 1982 *Ethical Principles in the Conduct of Research with Human Participants* are not enforceable as such by the APA Ethics Code of 1992, but may be of educative value to psychologists, courts, and professional bodies.

ation. However, providing a *complete* explanation or description of the project may influence the participants' responses. Consider, for example, the research conducted by either Pamela Feist (1993) on style of dress and eyewitness testimony or Brian Mills (1993) on the use of celebrity and noncelebrity photographs in advertisements. Had the participants known they were to evaluate the style of dress or the type of individual pictured in an advertisement, then their responses could easily have been influenced by what they believed their responses were supposed to be. As we will see, it is very important in psychological research with human participants to try to ensure that the participants are not responding simply because (a) they have "figured out" the experiment and know how they are supposed to act or (b) they think the experimenter expects them to respond in a certain manner (see Rosenthal, 1966, 1985).

Hence, it is arguable that deception may be justified in some cases if our results are to be unbiased or uncontaminated by knowledge of the experiment and the expectancies that such knowledge may bring. If deception is employed, how does the researcher deal with obtaining informed consent for participation?

Informed Consent. Principle D indicates that the participants should give informed consent regarding their participation in a research project. This informed consent frequently takes the form of a statement concerning the research that the participants sign before taking part in the research project. An example of an informed consent form is shown in Figure 2-7. As you can see, this document gives the participants a *general* description of the project they are going to participate in and informs them that no penalties will be invoked if they choose not to participate. Also, it is clearly stated that the participants have the right to withdraw their participation at any time they desire.

Although the objectives of Principle D may not seem difficult to satisfy, there is one group of participants that creates special problems—children. For example, if you want to conduct a project using first-graders, your research proposal would initially have to be approved by a college or university committee. (We will discuss the Institutional Review Board at the end of this chapter.) Once this approval is granted, then you will need to contact the school system for approval. This approval may need to be granted at several levels—superintendent, principal, and teacher. Each of these individuals will scrutinize your proposal thoroughly to safeguard the rights of the children. Once these hurdles have been successfully cleared, then permission from the parent or legal guardian must be secured. The parent or legal guardian is the individual who will sign the informed consent form.

The more general the statement of the research project, the more room there is for the possible use of deception or for not completely explaining the project. For example, the informed consent document shown in Figure 2-7 does not explicitly tell the participants that they are taking part in a study that will examine the relationship between interpersonal flexibility, self-esteem, and fear of death (Hayes, Miller, & Davis, 1993).

By deceiving participants about the true purpose of an experiment or not providing complete information about the experiment, the experimenter may take the chance of placing some participants "at risk." Who is to say that completing a par-

---

Informed Consent Document

Read this consent form. If you have any questions ask the experimenter and he/she will answer the question.

The Department of Psychology supports the practice of protection for human participants participating in research and related activities. The following information is provided so that you can decide whether you wish to participate in the present study. You should be aware that even if you agree to participate, you are free to withdraw at any time, and that if you do withdraw from the study, you will not be subjected to reprimand or any other form of reproach.

In order to help determine the relationship between numerous personality characteristics you are being asked to complete several questionnaires. These questionnaires will be completed anonymously.

"I have read the above statement and have been fully advised of the procedures to be used in this project. I have been given sufficient opportunity to ask any questions I had concerning the procedures and possible risks involved. I understand the potential risks involved and I assume them voluntarily. I likewise understand that I can withdraw from the study at any time without being subjected to reproach."

_____   _____
Subject and/or authorized representative   Date

FIGURE 2-7.   AN EXAMPLE OF AN INFORMED CONSENT FORM.

ticular survey or questionnaire will not provoke an intense emotional reaction in a given participant? Perhaps one of the participants in an investigation of child abuse was sexually molested as a preschooler and completing your questionnaire will reawaken those terrifying memories.

Participants at Risk and Participants at Minimal Risk. Participants at risk are participants who, by virtue of their participation in the research project, are placed under some emotional or physical risk. Certainly, the participants in the Tuskegee syphilis study and Milgram's obedience studies were participants at risk. Securing informed consent from participants at risk is a mandatory condition.

Participants at minimal risk are participants who will experience no harmful effects through taking part in the research project. For example, you might want to determine how many people purchase a particular brand of cola after being given a sample as compared to the number of people who do not receive a sample and buy the cola. In this situation the participants are at minimal risk; your recording of their purchases will not influence their physical or emotional well-being. Although desirable, it is not mandatory to secure informed consent from participants at minimal risk.

Participants at risk
By participating in an experiment, the participants are placed under some type of physical or emotional risk.

Participants at minimal risk
Participation in an experiment does *not* place the participants under physical or emotional risk.

definition

But what about those participants at risk who are participating in a study involving deception? How do we satisfy the ethical guidelines in such a case?

First, the participants should be told about *all* aspects of the research that are potentially harmful. If deception is used, the participants should not be deceived about some potentially harmful aspect of the research. For example, it would not be acceptable to tell participants that they will be taking a vitamin tablet when the drug they are to consume is a hallucinogen. When participants are informed about all potentially harmful aspects of a research project, then they are able to give valid informed consent about participating.

The second procedure used to satisfy the ethical guidelines when deception is used is to thoroughly debrief the participants once the experiment is completed. We turn to the topic of debriefing next.

Debriefing session
The nature and purpose(s) of an experiment are explained at its conclusion.

The Debriefing Session. The **debriefing session,** usually the final step in the conduct of the research project, involves explaining to the participants the nature and purpose(s) of the project. Debriefing can be very important and should not be taken lightly by the researcher. Eliot Aronson and J. M. Carlsmith (1968) proposed several excellent guidelines for effective debriefing. They are summarized as follows:

1. The researcher's integrity as a scientist must be conveyed to the participants. The researcher's personal belief in the scientific method is the foundation for explaining why deception was necessary and how it was employed in the research project that was just completed.

2. If deception was used, the researcher should reassure the participants that it was not wrong or a reflection on their integrity or intelligence to feel that they have been tricked or fooled. Such feelings indicate that the deception used in the project was effective.

3. Because it is usually the last step in the conduct of the research project, there may be a tendency to try to rush through the debriefing session. This approach is not advisable. The participants have a lot to digest and try to understand; therefore, the debriefing session should progress slowly. The explanations should be clear and understandable.

4. The researcher should be sensitive to indications that the participants' discomfort is not being alleviated by the debriefing session and strive to correct this situation. The goal of the debriefing session is to return the participants to the same (or as close to the same) state they were in at the beginning of the project.

5. The researcher should repeat all guarantees of confidentiality and anonymity that were made at the beginning of the project. For such assurances to be seen as believable, the researcher must have clearly established his or her integrity as a scientist.

6. Do not try to satisfy debriefing requirements by saying that you will send an explanation and the results of the project at a later date. For maximum effectiveness, the debriefing session should be conducted immediately following the experimental session; there are no "easier" ways to satisfy this obligation.

Thus, the main purpose of the debriefing session is to explain the nature of the experiment, remove or alleviate any undesirable consequences the participants may be experiencing, and generally try to return them to the same state of mind they were in prior to the experiment. The debriefing session also can provide the experimenter with valuable feedback concerning the conduct of the experiment from the participants' viewpoint. Was the IV manipulation successful? If deception was used, was it successful? Were the instructions clear? The answers to these and other relevant questions can be obtained during the debriefing session.

THE ETHICAL USE OF ANIMALS IN PSYCHOLOGICAL RESEARCH

Up to this point our ethical considerations have dealt with research in which humans are the participants. Since Willard S. Small used the first rat maze at Clark University in 1900, considerable psychological research has involved the use of animals. The use of animals in psychological research has created considerable controversy, debate, and even violence in recent years. Supporters of animal research point to the numerous accomplishments and scientific breakthroughs that are based on the results of animal studies (Kalat, 1992; Miller, 1985). For example, such medical procedures as blood transfusions, anesthesia, pain killers, antibiotics, insulin, vaccines, chemotherapy, CPR, coronary bypass surgery, and reconstructive surgery are based on animal studies. For nearly 100 years psychologists have used animals in studies of learning, psychopathology, brain and nervous system functioning, and physiology. It is undeniable that animal research has yielded *numerous* important and beneficial results.

However, animal activist critics argue that the price we have paid for such progress is too high. They point to problems with housing conditions, as well as the pain and suffering that research animals endure, and insist that such treatment must stop (Miller & Williams, 1983; Reagan, 1983; Singer, 1975).

Although the debate between the researchers and the animal activists is likely to continue for some time, our present concern is with the ethical conduct of animal research. In addition to the concern over the ethics of human experiments, the 1960s also witnessed an increase in the concern for the ethical treatment of animals. For example, the Animal Welfare Act of 1966 was national legislation specifically passed to protect research animals. The APA has also developed a list of guidelines for the use of animals. The complete list of these principles is shown in Table 2-3. We will briefly summarize them here:

I. *Justification of Research.* The research should have a clear scientific purpose.

II. *Personnel.* Only trained personnel who are familiar with the animal care guidelines should be involved with the research. All procedures must conform to appropriate federal guidelines.

III. *Care and Housing of Animals.* Animal housing areas must comply with current regulations.

TABLE 2-3. APA PRINCIPLES FOR THE ETHICAL TREATMENT OF ANIMAL SUBJECTS

I. JUSTIFICATION OF THE RESEARCH

A. Research should be undertaken with a clear scientific purpose. There should be a reasonable expectation that the research will a) increase knowledge of the processes underlying the evolution, development, maintenance, alteration, control, or biological significance of behavior; b) increase understanding of the species under study; or c) provide results that benefit the health or welfare of humans or other animals.

B. The scientific purpose of the research should be of sufficient potential significance to justify the use of animals. Psychologists should act on the assumption that procedures that would produce pain in humans will also do so in other animals.

C. The species chosen for study should be best suited to answer the question(s) posed. The psychologist should always consider the possibility of using other species, nonanimal alternatives, or procedures that minimize the number of animals in research, and should be familiar with the appropriate literature.

D. Research on animals may not be conducted until the protocol has been reviewed by the institutional animal care and use committee (IACUC) to ensure that the procedures are appropriate and humane.

E. The psychologist should monitor the research and the animals' welfare throughout the course of an investigation to ensure continued justification for the research.

II. PERSONNEL

A. Psychologists should ensure that personnel involved in their research with animals be familiar with these guidelines.

B. Animal use procedures must conform with federal regulations regarding personnel, supervision, record keeping, and veterinary care.[1]

C. Behavior is both the focus of study of many experiments as well as a primary source of information about the animal's health and well-being. It is therefore necessary that psychologists and their assistants be informed about the behavioral characteristics of their animal subjects, so as to be aware of normal, species-specific behaviors and unusual behaviors that could forewarn of health problems.

D. Psychologists should ensure that all individuals who use animals under their supervision receive explicit instruction in experimental methods and in the care, maintenance, and handling of the species being studied. Responsibilities and activities of all individuals dealing with animals should be consistent with their respective competencies, training, and experience in either the laboratory or the field setting.

III. CARE AND HOUSING OF ANIMALS

The concept of "psychological well-being" of animals is of current concern and debate and is included in Federal Regulations (United States Department of Agriculture [USDA], 1991). As a scientific and professional organization, APA recognizes the complexities of defining psychological well-being. Procedures appropriate for a particular species may well be inappropriate for others. Hence, APA does not presently stipulate specific guidelines regarding the maintenance of

(continued)

TABLE 2-3. APA PRINCIPLES FOR THE ETHICAL TREATMENT OF ANIMAL SUBJECTS (continued)

psychological well-being of research animals. Psychologists familiar with the species should be best qualified professionally to judge measures such as enrichment to maintain or improve psychological well-being of those species.

A. The facilities housing animals should meet or exceed current regulations and guidelines (USDA, 1990, 1991) and are required to be inspected twice a year (USDA, 1989).

B. All procedures carried out on animals are to be reviewed by a local IACUC to ensure that the procedures are appropriate and humane. The committee should have representation from within the institution and from the local community. In the event that it is not possible to constitute an appropriate local IACUC, psychologists are encouraged to seek advice from a corresponding committee of a cooperative institution.

C. Responsibilities for the conditions under which animals are kept, both within and outside of the context of active experimentation or teaching, rests with the psychologist under the supervision of the IACUC (where required by federal regulations) and with individuals appointed by the institution to oversee animal care. Animals are to be provided with humane care and healthful conditions during their stay in the facility. In addition to the federal requirements to provide for the psychological well-being of nonhuman primates used in research, psychologists are encouraged to consider enriching the environments of their laboratory animals and should keep abreast of literature on well-being and enrichment for the species with which they work.

IV. ACQUISITION OF ANIMALS

A. Animals not bred in the psychologist's facility are to be acquired lawfully. The USDA and local ordinances should be consulted for information regarding regulations and approved suppliers.

B. Psychologists should make every effort to ensure that those responsible for transporting the animals to the facility provide adequate food, water, ventilation, space, and impose no unnecessary stress on the animals.

C. Animals taken from the wild should be trapped in a humane manner and in accordance with applicable federal, state, and local regulations.

D. Endangered species or taxa should be used only with full attention to required permits and ethical concerns. Information and permit applications can be obtained from the Fish and Wildlife Service, Office of Management Authority, U.S. Dept. of the Interior, 4401 N. Fairfax Dr., Rm. 432, Arlington, VA 22043, 703-358-2104. Similar caution should be used in work with threatened species or taxa.

V. EXPERIMENTAL PROCEDURES

Humane consideration for the well-being of the animal should be incorporated into the design and conduct of all procedures involving animals, while keeping in mind the primary goal of experimental procedures—the acquisition of sound, replicable data. The conduct of all procedures is governed by Guideline I.

TABLE 2-3. APA PRINCIPLES FOR THE ETHICAL TREATMENT OF ANIMAL SUBJECTS (continued)

A. Behavioral studies that involve no aversive stimulation or overt sign of distress to the animal are acceptable. This includes observational and other noninvasive forms of data collection.

B. When alternative behavioral procedures are available, those that minimize discomfort to the animal should be used. When using aversive conditions, psychologists should adjust the parameters of stimulation to levels that appear minimal, though compatible with the aims of the research. Psychologists are encouraged to test painful stimuli on themselves, whenever reasonable. Whenever consistent with the goals of the research, consideration should be given to providing the animals with control of the potentially aversive stimulation.

C. Procedures in which the animal is anesthetized and insensitive to pain throughout the procedure and is euthanized before regaining consciousness are generally acceptable.

D. Procedures involving more than momentary or slight aversive stimulation, which are not relieved by medication or other acceptable methods, should be undertaken only when the objectives of the research cannot be achieved by other methods.

E. Experimental procedures that require prolonged aversive conditions or produce tissue damage or metabolic disturbances require greater justification and surveillance. This includes prolonged exposure to extreme environmental conditions, experimentally induced prey killing, or infliction of physical trauma or tissue damage. An animal observed to be a state of severe distress or chronic pain that cannot be alleviated and is not essential to the purposes of the research should be euthanized immediately.

F. Procedures that use restraint must conform to federal regulations and guidelines.

G. Procedures involving the use of paralytic agents without reduction in pain sensation require particular prudence and humane concern. Use of muscle relaxants or paralytics alone during surgery, without general anesthesia, is unacceptable and shall not be used.

H. Surgical procedures, because of their invasive nature, require close supervision and attention to humane considerations by the psychologist. Aseptic (methods that minimize risks of infection) techniques must be used on laboratory animals whenever possible.

    1. All surgical procedures and anesthetization should be conducted under the direct supervision of a person who is competent in the use of the procedures.

    2. If the surgical procedure is likely to cause greater discomfort than that attending anesthetization, and unless there is specific justification for acting otherwise, animals should be maintained under anesthesia until the procedure is ended.

    3. Sound postoperative monitoring and care, which may include the use of analgesics and antibiotics, should be provided to

(continued)

TABLE 2-3. APA PRINCIPLES FOR THE ETHICAL TREATMENT OF ANIMAL SUBJECTS (continued)

minimize discomfort and to prevent infection and other untoward consequences of the procedure.

4. Animals cannot be subjected to successive surgical procedures unless these are required by the nature of the research, the nature of the surgery, or for the well-being of the animal. Multiple surgeries on the same animal must receive special approval from the IACUC.

I. When the use of an animal is no longer required by an experimental protocol or procedure, in order to minimize the number of animals used in research, alternatives to euthanasia should be considered. Such uses should be compatible with the goals of research and the welfare of the animal. Care should be taken that such an action does not expose the animal to multiple surgeries.

J. The return of wild-caught animals to the field can carry substantial risks, both to the formerly captive animals and to the ecosystem. Animals reared in the laboratory should not be released because, in most cases, they cannot survive or they may survive by disrupting the natural ecology.

K. When euthanasia appears to be the appropriate alternative, either as a requirement of the research or because it constitutes the most humane form of disposition of an animal at the conclusion of the research:

1. Euthanasia shall be accomplished in a humane manner, appropriate for the species, and in such a way as to ensure immediate death, and in accordance with procedures outlined in the latest version of the "American Veterinary Medical Association (AVMA) Panel on Euthanasia."[2]

2. Disposal of euthanized animals should be accomplished in a manner that is in accord with all relevant legislation, consistent with health, environmental, and aesthetic concerns, and approved by the IACUC. No animal shall be discarded until its death is verified.

VI. FIELD RESEARCH   Field research, because of its potential to damage sensitive ecosystems and ethologies, should be subject to IACUC approval. Field research, if strictly observational, may not require IACUC approval (USDA, 1989, pg. 36126).

A. Psychologists conducting field research should disturb their populations as little as possible—consistent with the goals of the research. Every effort should be made to minimize potential harmful effects of the study on the population and on other plant and animal species in the area.

B. Research conducted in populated areas should be done with respect for the property and privacy of the inhabitants of the area.

C. Particular justification is required for the study of endangered species. Such research on endangered species should not be conducted unless IACUC approval has been obtained and all requisite permits are obtained (see above, III D).

TABLE 2-3. APA PRINCIPLES FOR THE ETHICAL TREATMENT OF ANIMAL SUBJECTS (continued)

VII. EDUCATIONAL USE OF ANIMALS	APA has adopted separate guidelines for the educational use of animals in precollege education, including the use of animals in science fairs and demonstrations. For a copy of APA's "Ethical Guidelines for the Teaching of Psychology in the Secondary Schools," write to: High School Teacher Affiliate Program, Education Directorate, APA, 750 First St., NE, Washington, DC 20002-4242.

  A. Psychologists are encouraged to include instruction and discussion of the ethics and values of animal research in all courses that involve or discuss the use of animals.

  B. Animals may be used for educational purposes only after review by a committee appropriate to the institution.

  C. Some procedures that can be justified for research purposes may not be justified for educational purposes. Consideration should always be given to the possibility of using nonanimal alternatives.

  D. Classroom demonstrations involving live animals can be valuable as instructional aids in addition to videotapes, films, or other alternatives. Careful consideration should be given to the question of whether this type of demonstration is warranted by the anticipated instructional gains.

NOTES

[1]U.S. Department of Agriculture. (1989, August 21). Animal welfare; Final rules. *Federal Register*.
U.S. Department of Agriculture, (1990, July 16). Animal welfare; Guinea pigs, hamsters, and rabbits. *Federal Register*.
U.S. Department of Agriculture. (1991, February 15). Animal welfare; Standards; Final rule. *Federal Register*.
[2]Write to: AVMA, 1931 N. Meacham Road, Suite 100, Schaumburg, IL 60173, or call (708) 925-8070.
Source: From *Guidelines for Ethical Conduct in the Care and Use of Animals* (pp. 3-10) by the American Psychological Association, 1983, Washington, DC: APA. Copyright ©1983 by the American Psychological Association. Adapted with permission.

    IV. *Acquisition of Animals.* If animals are not bred in the laboratory, they must be acquired in a lawful, humane manner.

    V. *Experimental Procedures.* "Humane consideration for the well-being of the animal should be incorporated into the design and conduct of all procedures involving animals, while keeping in mind the primary goal of experimental procedures—the acquisition of sound, replicable data."

    VI. *Field Research.* Field research must be approved by the appropriate review board. Investigators should take special precautions to disturb their research population(s) and the environment as little as possible.

    VII. *Educational Use of Animals.* The educational use of animals also must be approved by the appropriate review board. Instruction in the ethics of animal research is encouraged.

Now that we have considered the ethical treatment of human and animal participants, let's examine the group that decides whether the proposed research should or should not be conducted. For the detective, the jury will make such decisions. In the case of the psychologist, our attention turns to the Institutional Review Board (IRB).

THE INSTITUTIONAL REVIEW BOARD

At some institutions the review panel for the use of human participants may be the Human Subjects Review Panel, whereas the Animal Care and Utilization Committee reviews proposals for animal research. At other institutions the IRB reviews both types of proposals. Although the exact name of the group may vary from institution to institution, its composition and functions are quite similar.

The typical IRB is composed of a cross-section of individuals. For example, if we examine a college or university IRB, we might find that it consists of faculty members from history, biology, education, psychology, and economics. Additionally, there will probably be one or two individuals from the community who are not associated with the institution. A veterinarian must be a member of the panel that reviews animal research proposals.

The task of this group is not to decide on the scientific merits of the proposed research; the scientist proposing the research is the expert in that area. The IRB's responsibility is to examine the proposed procedures, any psychological tests or questionnaires that will be used, the informed consent document, plans for debriefing the participants, the use of pain in animal research, procedures for disposing of animals humanely, and so forth. If participants are placed at risk, will they be made aware of this risk before the experiment is conducted? Do participants have the ability to terminate participation at any time? Will debriefing counteract the effects of deception if it has been used? Is it possible that a particular questionnaire or survey may evoke a strong emotional reaction? In short, the IRB serves to ensure that research participants, whether they are humans or animals, are treated according to the established ethical guidelines.

THE EXPERIMENTER'S RESPONSIBILITY

Ultimately the experimenter is the single individual who is accountable for the ethical conduct of the research project. In accepting this responsibility, the researcher carefully weighs the *benefits* and *costs* of the project and then decides whether it should be conducted. The new knowledge produced by the project represents the benefit. What about costs? Such factors as time and expense clearly are costs and must be considered. Whether the participants will be placed at risk is a major cost to be dealt with.

Students doing research as part of the requirements of a course also are responsible for conducting their projects in an ethical manner. Applications to use participants must be submitted to and approved by the appropriate IRB. In most cases such submissions are signed by the supervising faculty member.

ETHICAL OBLIGATIONS ONCE THE RESEARCH IS COMPLETED

The experimenter's ethical responsibilities do not end when the data are collected and the participants are debriefed. Experimenters are responsible for presenting the results of their research in an ethical manner. The two main problems encountered in this regard are plagiarism and fabrication of data.

Plagiarism. **Plagiarism** refers to the use of someone else's work without giving credit to the original author. Certainly, plagiarism is an obvious violation of the ethical standards of psychologists. Although it is difficult to believe that plagiarism occurs among established professionals, it does (Broad, 1980).

Unfortunately, plagiarism is not an uncommon occurrence in colleges and universities. Although some students may view plagiarism as an easy way to complete an assignment or term paper, many students have told us that no one had ever explained plagiarism to them. The Department of Psychology at Bishop's University (1994) has clearly summarized what you need to do to avoid plagiarism. The following is suggested:

> **Plagiarism** Using someone else's work without giving credit to the original source.

definition

1. Any part of your paper which contains the exact words of an author must appear in quotation marks, with the author's name, and the date of publication and page number of the source attached.

2. Material should not be adapted with only minor changes, such as combining sentences, omitting phrases, changing a few words, or inverting sentence order.

3. If what you have to say is substantially your own words, but the facts or ideas are taken from a particular author, then omit the quotation marks and reference with a bracketed citation such as (Jones, 1949).

4. Always acknowledge "secondary sources."

5. Every statement of fact, and every idea or opinion not your own must be referenced unless the item is part of common knowledge.

6. Do not hand in for credit a paper which is the same or similar to one you have handed in elsewhere.

7. It is permissible to ask someone to criticize a completed paper before you submit it, and to bring to your attention errors in logic, grammar, punctuation, spelling, and expression. However, it is not permissible to have another person re-write any portion of your paper, or to have another person translate into English for you a paper which you have written in another language.

8. Keep rough notes and drafts of your work, and photocopies of material not available in your college or university library.

In our experience, Guideline 2 is most problematic for students. If you reread this guideline, you will find that even paraphrasing an author's words is considered plagiarism. It is a good idea to read your sources thoroughly but to put them away when you write so that you are not tempted to copy or paraphrase.

Why would a scientist engage in plagiarism? Although the specific reason(s) will vary from individual to individual, the pressure to publish one's research findings probably represents the single greatest cause (Mahoney, 1987). Because one's job security (tenure) and/or salary increases are often directly tied to the publication record, research and publication may become the central focus in the professional career. In one's haste to prepare articles and build an impressive publication record, it may seem easier and quicker to "borrow" a paragraph here and a paragraph there, especially if writing is not an easy and enjoyable task.

> **definition**
>
> **Fabrication of data**
> Those instances where the experimenter either deliberately alters or creates research data.

Fabrication of Data. **Fabrication of data** refers to those instances where the experimenter either deliberately changes or alters data that were already gathered or simply makes up data to suit his or her needs. As with plagiarism, fabrication of data is an obvious ethical violation.

What would cause a scientist to fabricate data? Again, we can point to the pressure to "publish or perish." Remember that we use synthetic statements in our research hypothesis; hence, there is always a chance that a project will not turn out as we predicted. When the data do not turn out as we had hoped, there may be a temptation to "fix" the data in order to bring them in line with our predictions and theory. Certainly, it is much easier (and quicker) to change a few numbers here and there than it is to redo an entire experiment. It does not seem to be a very great step to go from changing a few numbers to eliminating the experiment altogether and fabricating all the data.

The consequences of having false information in the body of scientific knowledge should be obvious to you. By falsifying a research finding, other researchers are unknowingly encouraged to conduct projects on a topic that is doomed to failure! The expenditures in time, effort, participants, and money can be enormous. As considerable research is supported by federal grants, the costs to the taxpayers can be substantial and fruitless.

Now, we do not want to leave you with the impression that plagiarism and fabrication of data characterize all or even many scientists; they do not. Most scientists enjoy designing and conducting their own research projects to see if they can unlock nature's secrets. However, it takes only a few unethical individuals to give science a bad name. We hope you will not be among the ranks of the unethical.

REVIEW SUMMARY

1. It is the responsibility of the experimenter to ensure that a research project is conducted in an ethical manner.
2. The World War II atrocities perpetrated by Nazi doctors, the Tuskegee syphilis project, and psychological research such as Milgram's obedience studies have increased ethical concerns and awareness.

3. The American Psychological Association (APA) has developed a set of 10 ethical principles for the conduct of research with human participants.

4. Although the researcher should try to avoid it, the use of deception may be justified in order to yield unbiased responses.

5. Informed consent is a signed statement indicating that participants understand the nature of the experiment and agree to participate in it.

6. **Participants at risk** are individuals whose participation in an experiment places them under some emotional and/or physical risk. **Participants at minimal risk** are individuals whose participation in an experiment results in no harmful consequences.

7. The nature and purpose of the experiment are explained to the participants during the **debriefing session.** Although the debriefing session was designed to counteract any negative effects of research participation, it also can provide the experimenter with valuable information about the research procedures that were employed.

8. Ethical guidelines have also been developed for the conduct of research using animals.

9. The Institutional Review Board (IRB) is a group of the researcher's scientific and nonscientific peers who evaluate research proposals for adherence to ethical guidelines and procedures.

10. Researchers have a responsibility to present their findings in an ethical manner. **Plagiarism** (the use of another's work without giving proper credit) and **fabrication of data** are the chief ethical infractions encountered in the presentation of research results.

STUDY BREAK

1. Describe the three projects that raised concern about the ethical conduct of research.

2. What aspects of the research endeavor did the Nuremberg Code stress?

3. In what types of research situations might the use of deception be justified? If deception is used, how can the need to provide "informed consent" be satisfied?

4. Distinguish between "at risk" and "at minimal risk."

5. How do Aronson and Carlsmith characterize an effective debriefing session?

6. Describe the guidelines for the ethical use of animals in psychological research.

7. What is an IRB? Describe the composition of the typical IRB. What responsibility does an IRB have?

8. With regard to the conduct of research, what is the ethical responsibility of the experimenter?

9. Distinguish between plagiarism and fabrication of data. What sets of pressures are responsible for these unethical actions?

LOOKING AHEAD

Now that the sources of research problems, conduct of an effective literature review, and development of an experimental hypothesis have been accomplished, we turn our attention to actual techniques for gathering data. In the next chapter you will learn about nonexperimental research methods. These descriptive and observational techniques provide ways to gather data in situations where it may not be possible or desirable to conduct a scientific experiment.

HANDS-ON ACTIVITIES

1. **The Research Idea.**   Propose a research idea. Explain whether your idea was influenced by nonsystematic sources (which one[s]), systematic sources (which one[s]), or both sources.

2. **Searching the Literature.**   Refine the research idea you created for Question 1 such that you can go to the *Thesaurus of Psychological Index Terms* or *Psychological Abstracts* and select relevant index terms. Now, conduct a PsycLIT or *Psychological Abstracts* search of the literature for the past two years.

3. **The Experimental Hypothesis.**   With your research idea (Activity 1) and the results of your literature search (Activity 2) in hand, prepare an experimental hypothesis. Be sure to state it in general implication form. Circle the synthetic statement(s) that are used in your experimental hypothesis. Does your experimental hypothesis involve inductive or deductive logic? Explain.

4. **Nondirectional and Directional Hypotheses.**   Change the directionality of the experimental hypothesis you proposed for Activity 3. In other words, if you originally wrote a directional hypothesis, change it to a nondirectional one, and vice versa.

5. **Ethics in Human Research.**   Survey an entire issue of a psychological journal that deals with human research. (Some good choices are *Journal of Personality and Social Psychology* and *Journal of Experimental Psychology: Memory and Cognition.*) How many of the articles published in that issue described ethical procedures such as IRB approval and informed consent and debriefing procedures? What other steps were taken to protect the participants' rights?

6. **Ethics in Animal Research.**   Survey an entire issue of a psychological journal that deals with animal research. (Some good choices are *Animal Learning & Behavior, Journal of Experimental Psychology: Animal Behavior Processes,* and *Journal of Comparative Psychology.*) What percentage of the articles report the implementation of ethical practices in accordance with the APA guidelines? Describe the steps taken to conform with these guidelines. Be thorough in your analysis of this last question. Describe any procedures that should have been described but were not.

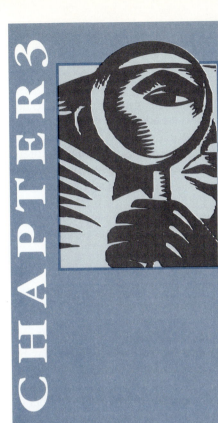

CHAPTER 3

Nonexperimental Methods for Acquiring Data

DESCRIPTIVE METHODS

Not all research projects can use the experimental method; hence, other methods for gathering data have been developed. We examine several of these methods and compare them to the experimental method in this chapter. Because these methods do not involve the manipulation of an independent variable, they are called **descriptive research methods;** when we use them, we can only speculate about causation that may be involved.

ARCHIVAL AND PREVIOUSLY RECORDED SOURCES OF DATA

In some instances researchers may not gather their own data; they may find that their research question can be answered by using data recorded by other individuals for other purposes. In some instances the records and data you need to consult are stored in a central location. For example, public health and census data may be analyzed years later to answer questions about socioeconomic status, religion, and/or political party affiliation. Similarly, the Archives of the History of American Psychology were established at the University of Akron in 1974 for the conduct of research on the history of psychology. Although the letters, documents, and photographs contained in this collection were originally produced for numerous reasons, they are now used by researchers interested in answering questions about the history of our discipline.

Not all sources of previously recorded data are conveniently stored in an archive or library for our use. For example, if you are interested in differences in sexual preoccupation between men and women, you might choose to examine graffiti on the walls of public restrooms. Likewise, observing the settings of radio dials in automobiles can provide interesting information concerning musical preferences of different groups of individuals.

Psychological Detective

The use of archival and previously recorded data is certainly in line with being a psychological detective. You are putting together bits and pieces of data to answer research questions. Unfortunately, there are several problems associated with this approach to gathering information. Consider conducting this type of research and see what problems you can discover. Write down your answers before reading further.

Potential Problems. There are several problems associated with using archival and previously recorded sources of data. First, unless you are dealing with the papers and documents of a few clearly identified individuals, you will not know exactly who left the data you are investigating. Not knowing the participants who comprise your sample will make it most difficult to generalize your results. Consider the graffiti example. You may choose to record graffiti from restrooms on your campus. Who created this graffiti? Was it created by a representative sample of students? Although common sense may tell you that the sample of graffiti writers is not representative of students on your campus, let alone college students in general, you do not know. Your ability to make statements other than those that merely describe your data is severely limited.

Second, the participants may have been selective in what they chose to write. Clearly, this consideration may be important in our graffiti example where we are evaluating the presence of sexual comments. What is chosen to be recorded may drastically influence our conclusions in other instances. For example, until recently what we knew about Wilhelm Wundt, the founder of scientific psychology, was provided by E. B. Titchener who originally translated Wundt's books and papers from German into English. Unfortunately, Titchener chose to misrepresent Wundt on several occasions; hence, our impression of Wundt may be severely distorted (Schultz & Schultz, 1996). Fortunately, Wundt's original writings are still available for retranslation and examination. Even if his works are retranslated, we will still be faced with the possible problem that Wundt may have omitted things from his own writings that he did not want to share with others. Whenever archival or previously recorded sources are used, this problem of *selective deposit* may not be avoided.

A third problem with this type of data concerns the survival of such records. In our study of graffiti it will be important to know something about the cleaning schedule for the restroom(s) we are observing. Are they scrubbed clean each day or is the graffiti allowed to accumulate? In this example the data in which you are interested will probably not have a very high survival rate. Printed materials may not fare much better. During the 1920s John Watson and his call to behaviorism made psychology immensely popular in the United States; the number of journal articles and books written during this period attest to its popularity. It was only recently, however, that researchers discovered a very popular magazine, *Psychology: Health, Happiness, and Success* that was published from 1923 to 1938 (Benjamin, 1992). Why the mystery surrounding this once popular magazine? The problem had to do with the type of paper on which the magazine was printed. The high acid content of the paper led to rapid disintegration of these magazines; hence, only a precious few have survived.

Comparisons with the Experimental Method. Certainly, valuable information can be gained from archival and prerecorded sources. However, we must be aware of the problems of a nonrepresentative sample, data that are purposely not recorded, and data that have been lost. A comparison of using this technique with conducting an experiment reveals other weaknesses in addition to these limitations. Because we examined data and/or documents that were produced at another time under potentially unknown circumstances, we are not able to exercise any control with regard to gathering these data. Hence, we are unable to make any type of cause-and-effect statement; the best we can do is speculate about what might have occurred.

Because of the potential problems and lack of control, this type of data gathering is used when no other possibilities exist. In the next section we examine methods in which we observe the phenomenon of interest firsthand.

OBSERVATIONAL TECHNIQUES

Even though the techniques described in this section involve the direct observation of the phenomenon or behavior of interest, they do not involve the direct manipulation of any variables by the experimenter. Being able to specify which responses are to be observed is as close to control as we come with these methods. Among the most common observational techniques are case studies, naturalistic observation, and the use of surveys or questionnaires.

Case Studies. When we conduct case studies, we intensively observe and record the behavior of a single (possibly two) participant(s) over an extended period of time. Because there are no guidelines for conducting a case study, the procedures employed, behaviors observed, and reports produced may vary substantially.

Frequently, case studies are used in clinical settings to help formulate hypotheses and ideas for further research. For example, the French physician Paul Broca (1824–1880) reported the case study of a patient who was unable to say anything except the word "tan." Based on his lengthy observations, Broca hypothesized that the center controlling the production of speech was located in the frontal lobe of the left hemisphere of the brain and that this area was damaged in the patient's brain. An autopsy indicated that Broca's hypothesis was correct. This case study provided the inspiration for numerous subsequent studies that provided considerable information concerning the neurological system that is responsible for the comprehension and production of speech. Other examples of case studies might involve the observation of a rare animal in the wild or at a zoological park, a specific type of mental patient in a hospital, or a gifted child at school.

Although case studies often provide interesting data, their results are applicable only to the individual participant who was observed. In other words, the researcher should not generalize beyond the participant who was studied when the case study method is used. Additionally, because no variables are manipulated, use of the case study method precludes establishing cause-and-effect relations.

Naturalistic Observation. **Naturalistic observation** involves seeking answers to research questions by observing behavior in the real world. For example, each spring animal psychologists interested in the behavior of migrating sandhill cranes conceal themselves in camouflage blinds to observe the roosting behavior of these birds on the Platte River in central Nebraska. Likewise, a researcher who is interested in the behavior of preschool children might be found at a day-care center observing the children.

The possibilities for conducting studies using naturalistic observation are limited only by our insight into a potential area of research. Regardless of the situation that is chosen, we have two goals in using naturalis-

Naturalistic observation Seeking answers to research questions by observing behavior in the real world.

definition

tic observation. The first goal should be obvious from the name of the technique: One objective is to describe behavior as it occurs in the *natural* setting without the artificiality of the laboratory. If the goal of research is to understand behavior in the real world, what better place to gather research data than in a natural setting? The second goal of naturalistic observation is to describe the variables that are present and the relationships among them. Returning to our sandhill crane example, naturalistic observation may provide clues concerning why the birds migrate at a particular time of the year and those factors that seem to determine the length of stay in a certain area.

In a naturalistic observation study, it is important that the researcher not interfere with or intervene in the behavior being studied. For example, in our study of preschoolers the observer should be as inconspicuous as possible. For this reason, the use of one-way mirrors that allow researchers to observe without being observed has become popular.

Psychological Detective

Why should the researcher be concealed or unobtrusive in a study using naturalistic observa-tion? Give this question some thought and write down your answer(s) before reading further.

The main reason the researcher must be unobtrusive in studies using naturalistic observation is to avoid influencing or changing the behavior of the participants being observed. The presence of an observer is not part of the natural setting for sandhill cranes or preschoolers; they may well behave differently in the presence of observers.

The **reactance** or **reactivity effect** refers to the biasing of the participants' responses because they know they are being observed. Perhaps the most famous example of a reactivity effect occurred in a study conducted at the Western Electric Company's Hawthorne plant in Chicago, Illinois, in the late 1930s (Roethlisberger & Dickson, 1939). The purpose of the research was to determine the effects of factors such as working hours and lighting on productivity. When productivity of the test participants was compared to that of the general plant, an unusual finding emerged. The test participants produced at a higher rate, often under test conditions that were inferior to those normally experienced. For example, even though the room lighting was reduced well below normal levels, productivity remained high. What caused these individuals to produce at such a high rate? The answer was simple: Because these workers knew they were research participants and that they were being observed, their productivity increased. Thus, the knowledge that one is participating in an experiment and is being observed may result in dramatic changes in behavior. Because of the location of the

Reactance or reactivity effect The finding that participants respond differently when they know they are being observed.

definition

Hawthorne effect
Another name for
reactance or
reactivity effect.

original study, this reactivity phenomenon is often referred to as the **Hawthorne effect.** Having considered the general nature of naturalistic observation, we will examine a specific observational project more closely.

Melissa Fowler and Kyndal Mashburn, students at Missouri Southern State College, in Joplin, MO, conducted an interesting study that used naturalistic observation. Melissa and Kyndal were interested in "whether the style of art-work affected viewing time" (Fowler & Mashburn, 1993, p. 2). To answer this research question they observed the viewing time of individuals who visited the art gallery on their campus. They selected a sample of art that included realistic and abstract pieces, as well as two-dimensional and three-dimensional pieces from the gallery's exhibition of wall hangings and sculptures. The participants of the study were sixteen college students (nine women, seven men) who were selected at random as they entered the gallery. In order to be as inconspicuous as possible and avoid a reactance effect, the observer sat at a centrally located table that provided a good view of the gallery and pretended to do homework. Once a participant was selected, the observer recorded the sex, approximate age, and total amount of time the participant viewed each designated piece of artwork. The results of this study indicated that although there was no difference in viewing time for two-dimensional and three-dimensional art, the participants spent significantly more time viewing the abstract art than they spent viewing the realistic art. Fowler and Mashburn (1993) caution against the temptation to infer that the greater viewing time reflects a preference for abstract art that can be generalized to all patrons of art galleries. They point out that the art gallery in which they conducted their study is in close proximity to the art department; hence, it is reasonable to assume that the majority of their participants were art majors. Is there a difference in the viewing time for abstract art between a knowledgeable art major and a casual patron? Without such information, it is not possible to make a generalized statement concerning the popularity of one type of art over the other. Unfortunately, when naturalistic observation is used, this type of information cannot be obtained.

As you may have surmised by now, the main drawback with the use of naturalistic observation is, once again, the inability to make cause-and-effect statements. Because we do not manipulate any variables when this technique is used, such conclusions are not possible.

Why use naturalistic observation if it does not allow us to make cause-and-effect statements? The first reason is quite straightforward: Naturalistic observation may be the *only* technique available to us to study a particular type of behavior. Psychologists who are interested in reactions to natural disasters, such as earthquakes, tornadoes, and fires, cannot ethically create such life-threatening situations just to study behavior. These investigators must make their observations when such events occur naturally.

A second reason for using naturalistic observation is as an adjunct to the experimental method. For example, naturalistic observation might be used before an experiment is conducted to give us an indication of the relevant variables involved in the situation. Once you have an idea about which variables are (and are not) important, then systematic, controlled studies of these variables can be conducted in the laboratory setting. Once laboratory experiments have been conducted, then you may want to return to the natural setting to see whether the insights gained in the laboratory are indeed mirrored in real life. Hence, psychologists may use naturalistic observation before *and* after an experimental research project to acquire further information concerning relevant variables.

Participant Observation.   When naturalistic observation is employed, researchers attempt to be as unobtrusive as possible. When **participant observation** is used, the researcher abandons his or her concealment and becomes part of the group that is studied. Yes, the participant observer is just like the detective who goes undercover to acquire information.

This research technique is often used when the goal of the research project is to learn something about a specific culture or socioeconomic group. The investigator assumes the role of a member of the group and makes observations from this vantage point.

Participant observation is not limited to the study of human behavior; it can also be implemented in animal studies. The study of gorillas in the Ghombe Stream Reserve in Africa by Jane Goodall is a good example of the use of this technique with nonhumans. Goodall spent enough time observing the gorillas each day that she was finally treated more as a member of the gorilla group than as an outside observer. Such acceptance facilitated her observations.

Psychological Detective

The participant observer technique has considerable appeal as a research technique; the researcher is actually a part of the situation under study. What better way to acquire the desired information! Despite such appeal, this procedure has its drawbacks and weaknesses. Think through this approach to research and list several weaknesses before reading further.

There are two drawbacks to the use of participant observation. First, an extended period of time may be required before the participant observer is accepted as a member of the group that is under study. Has such an extended period been budgeted into the overall design of the project in terms of both cost and time? Moreover, just being part of the situation does not guarantee that the observer will be accepted. If such acceptance is not granted, the amount of information that can be acquired is severely limited. If the observer is accepted and becomes part of the group, then a loss of objectivity may result. Thus, time, finances, acceptance, and objectivity may pose severe problems for participant observer research.

As with the other observation techniques, the ability to make cause-and-effect statements is the second problem with participant observer research. Even though the participant observer may be close to the source of relevant information, no attempts are made to manipulate independent variables or control extraneous variables. Hence, the results of such projects must remain descriptions; they are not cause-and-effect statements.

In this section we have examined three observational research strategies—case studies, naturalistic observation, and participant observation. Once you have decided which type of observational research you will be conducting, then you will have to decide which behaviors to observe and how to record your observations.

CHOOSING BEHAVIORS AND RECORDING TECHNIQUES

Time Sampling and Situation Sampling. It is one thing to say you are going to conduct an observational study, but it is another task to actually complete such a project. Just because the researcher does not manipulate the variables does not mean that a great deal of planning has not taken place. Several important decisions must be made before making the first observations. Let's examine several of these decisions.

It seems simple enough to indicate that all behaviors will be observed; hence, everything of interest will be captured. Saying may be quite different from (and much easier than) doing, however. For example, observing and recording *all* behaviors may necessitate using video equipment, which may, in turn, make the observer identifiable. A participant observer with a video camera would probably not be especially effective. Likewise, had Melissa Fowler and Kyndal Mashburn used video equipment in their naturalistic study in the art gallery, their obvious presence could have influenced the behavior of their participants. Hence, they chose to concentrate their observations on only one behavior, viewing time.

Because they did not observe at exactly the same time each day, Fowler and Mashburn employed a procedure known as time sampling. **Time sampling** involves making observations at different time periods in order to obtain a more representative sampling of the behavior of interest. The selection of time periods may be determined randomly or in a more systematic manner. Moreover, the use of time sampling may apply to the same or different participants. If you are observing a group of preschoolers, then using the time-sampling technique will allow you to describe the behavior of interest over a wide range of times in the same children.

On the other hand, using time sampling may purposely result in the observation of different participants. Perhaps different types of art lovers attend art galleries at different times during the day. Hence, conducting the observations at different times of the day ensures that a particular type of patron will not be overrepresented in the sample.

As we saw, the Fowler and Mashburn study was limited in its ability to make generalizations beyond the art gallery in which the research was conducted. Had the investigators used the technique of situation sampling, this limitation would have been reduced. **Situation sampling** involves observing the same behavior in several different situations. This

Time sampling
Making observations at different time periods.

Situation sampling
Observing the same behavior in different situations.

technique offers the researcher two advantages. First, by sampling behavior in several different situations, you are able to determine whether the behavior in question changes as a function of the context in which it is observed. For example, a researcher might use situation sampling to determine if the amount of personal space we prefer differs from one situation to another.

The second advantage of the situation sampling technique involves the fact that different participants are likely to be observed in the different situations that are observed. Because different individuals are observed, our ability to generalize any behavioral consistencies we notice across the various situations is increased. If Fowler and Mashburn had made their observations at several different galleries and obtained the same results at each gallery, then the findings could not be attributed to a specific group of individuals observed in one gallery.

Qualitative and Quantitative Decisions. Even if you have decided to time sample and/or situation sample, there is still another major decision to be made before you actually conduct your research project. We need to decide if we plan to present the results of our research project in a qualitative or quantitative manner. If you choose the qualitative approach, then your report will consist of a description of the behavior in question and the conclusions prompted by this description. When the qualitative approach is used, the observer typically produces a narrative record. Such records can be in the form of written or tape-recorded notes that are made during or after the behavior has been observed. Video recordings also are frequently made. If notes are written or tape-recorded after the behavior has occurred, they should be recorded as soon as possible. In all instances the language and terms used should be as clear and precise as possible; the observer should avoid making speculative comments.

If your research plans call for a quantitative or numerical approach, then you will need to know how you are going to measure the behavior under investigation and how these measurements will be analyzed. In order to answer the "how-to-measure" question we must consider which scale of measurement we will use. A **scale of measurement** consists of the rules by which symbols are assigned to behaviors or events. There are four scales (or sets of rules) of measurement: nominal, ordinal, interval, and ratio.

The **nominal scale** of measurement involves assigning behaviors and/or events to one of a set of categories. For example, people attending a holiday party could be categorized as (a) drinking alcoholic beverages, (b) drinking nonalcoholic beverages, or (c) not drinking any beverage. A checklist on which the observer records tally marks representing behavioral frequency is often used to record nominal data.

When we use the **ordinal scale** of measurement, we rank order the behaviors and/or events under investigation and can indicate that a particular event or behavior is greater or less than another event or behavior. However, when ordinal measurements are used, there is no way to tell how far apart the ranks are. For example, a researcher interested in studying the relationship between test-taking time and grade earned might record

Scale of Measurement A set of rules for assigning symbols to behaviors and/or events.

Nominal scale Assignment of behaviors and/or events to categories.

Ordinal scale Rank ordering of behaviors and/or events. No assumption of equality of ranks.

definition

Interval scale Rank ordering of behaviors and/or events with an assumption of equality of intervals. No true zero.

Ratio scale Rank ordering of behaviors and/or events, equality of intervals, and a true zero.

Interobserver reliability The extent to which observers agree.

which papers are turned in first, second, third, and so on. The researcher will be able to rank order the papers according to when they are completed but will not know if the first paper was turned in one minute or twenty minutes before the second paper.

When we use **interval scale** measurements, the events and/or behaviors can be rank-ordered *and* the distance separating adjacent behaviors and/or events is equal. For example, the difference between a score of 16 and a score of 17 on the American College Test (ACT) is equal to the difference between a score of 19 and a score of 20 on the same test. The interval scale lacks a true zero point. If, for example, an individual scores 0 on the ACT, we would not say that this person was *completely* senseless.

The **ratio scale** combines all the attributes of the interval scale with the presence of a true zero point; thus, behaviors can be ranked, the difference between ranks is equal, and there is a true zero. The measurement of height or weight would be examples of ratio measurements.

The choice of which scale of measurement you employ will influence the type of summary results you can report, as well as the type of statistical analyses you are able to perform on your data. We will have more to say about these statistical issues in Chapters 4 and 6.

USING MORE THAN ONE OBSERVER: INTEROBSERVER RELIABILITY

Another consideration we must deal with in the case of observational research is whether one or more observers will be used. As the good detective knows, there are two main reasons for using more than one observer: A bit of behavior may be missed or overlooked by one observer, and there may be some disagreement concerning exactly what was seen and how it should be rated or categorized. More than one observer may be needed even when videotape is used to preserve the complete behavioral sequence; someone has to watch the videotape and rate or categorize the behavior contained there.

When two individuals observe the same behavior, it is possible to see how well their observations agree. The extent to which the observers agree is called **interobserver reliability.** Low interobserver reliability indicates that the observers disagree about the behavior(s) they observed; high interobserver reliability indicates agreement. Such factors as fatigue, boredom, emotional and physical state, and experience can influence interobserver reliability. If both observers are well rested, interested in their task, in good physical and emotional health, then high interobserver reliability should be obtained. An observer's physical, emotional, and attitudinal state can be detected and dealt with easily. Additionally, the need for training observers should be considered. The importance of thorough training, especially when complex and/or subtle behaviors are being observed, cannot be stressed too much. Such training should include clear, precise definitions of the behavior(s) to be observed. Concrete examples of positive and negative instances of the behavior in question should be provided if at all possible.

How is interobserver reliability measured? One popular technique involves determining the number of agreements between the two observers and the number of opportunities the observers had to agree. Once these numbers have been determined, they are used in the following formula:

$$\frac{\text{no. of times observers agree}}{\text{no. of opportunities to agree}} \times 100 = \text{percentage of agreement}$$

The final calculation indicates the percentage of agreement. For example, assume that two researchers are interested in studying interpersonal dynamics. They observe whether a person makes eye contact when another person approaches. Out of a total of 125 instances, the two observers *agree* that eye contact was or was not made on 113 of these occasions. Thus, their percentage of agreement is 90.40%.

$$\frac{113 \text{ (times the observers agree)}}{125 \text{ (opportunities to agree)}} \times 100 = 90.40\%$$

Even though a descriptive research project may require considerable time and effort, it is still unable to provide cause-and-effect statements. In the next section we consider an approach that directly examines the relationship between two variables. Possibly this approach will yield more satisfying results.

CORRELATIONAL STUDIES

In its basic form a **correlational study** involves the measurement and determination of the relationship between two variables. In order to understand the intent and purpose of a correlational study, we need to review some basic facts about correlations.

One of three basic patterns may emerge when a correlation is calculated. The two variables may be **positively correlated;** as one variable increases, scores on the other variable also increase. For example, a student who makes a low score on Test 1 also scores low on Test 2, whereas a student who scores high on Test 1 also scores high on Test 2. Likewise, height and weight are positively related; the taller a person is, the more he or she weighs. Figure 3-1A graphically depicts a positive correlation. Note that low scores on Variable 1 are paired with low scores on Variable 2, and vice versa. When increases in one variable are accompanied by *consistent* increases in the second variable, a **perfect positive correlation** exists. For example, if a score of 55 on Variable 1 is paired with a score of 45 on Variable 2, then a score of 60 might be paired with a score of 55 on Variable 2. Hence, a score of 61 on Variable 1 would be paired with a score of 57 on Variable 2; for every increase of one unit in Variable 1,

Correlational study
Determination of the relationship between two variables.

Positive correlation
As scores on one variable increase, scores on the second variable also increase.

Perfect positive correlation
Increases in scores on one variable are accompanied by a consistent increase in the scores on the second variable.

definition

FIGURE 3-1

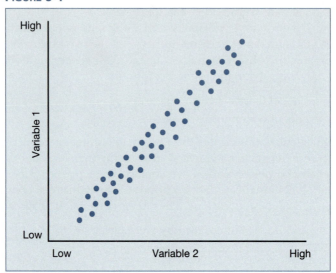

A.   A POSITIVE CORRELATION.

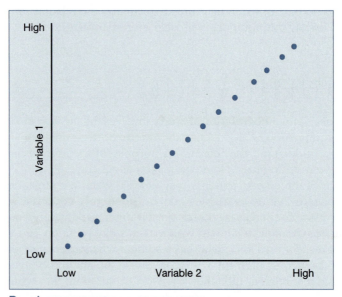

B.   A PERFECT POSITIVE CORRELATION.

Negative correlation
As scores on one variable increase, scores on the second variable decrease.

there is a consistent increase of two units on Variable 2. A perfect positive correlation is shown in Figure 3-1B. A perfect positive correlation has a value of +1.00, whereas positive correlations in general range from .01 to .99.

Two variables may also be negatively related. **A negative correlation** indicates that an *increase* in one variable is accompanied by a *de-*

FIGURE 3-2

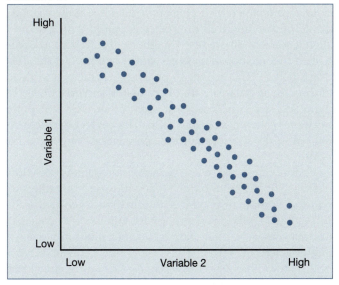

A. A NEGATIVE CORRELATION.

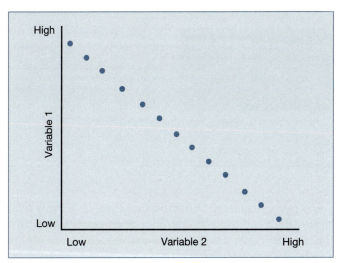

B. A PERFECT NEGATIVE CORRELATION.

crease in the second variable. For example, drinking water on a hot day and thirst are negatively related; the more water consumed, the less intense the thirst. Likewise, increasing self-esteem scores might be accompanied by decreasing anxiety scores. Thus, an individual who scores high on a self-esteem scale would have a low score on an anxiety scale, whereas an individual who scores low on the self-esteem scale would score high on the anxiety scale. Figure 3-2A depicts a negative correlation; low scores on Variable 1 are paired with high scores on Variable 2, and

Perfect negative correlation Increases in scores on one variable are accompanied by a consistent decrease in the scores on the second variable.

Zero correlation The two variables under consideration are not related.

vice versa. A **perfect negative correlation** exists when increases in one variable are accompanied by a *consistent* decrease in the second variable. For example, if a score of 28 on Test 1 is paired with a score of 70 on Test 2, then a score of 30 on Test 1 might be paired with a score of 64 on Test 2. Given this relationship, what would you predict the Test 2 score will be for a person who scores 33 on Test 1? If there is a consistent decrease of three units on Test 2 for every unit of increase on Test 1, then a person who scores 33 on Test 1 will score 55 on Test 2. A perfect negative correlation is shown in Figure 3-2B. The perfect negative correlation has a value of –1.00, whereas negative correlations in general range from –.01 to –.99.

After considering positive and negative correlations, an important use of correlations should be apparent: They are used to make predictions. For example, you probably took an entrance examination, such as the ACT or the Scholastic Aptitude Test (SAT), when you applied for admission to college. Previous research has shown that scores on such entrance examinations are positively correlated with first-semester grades in college. Thus, your entrance exam score is used to predict how you will perform in your college classes. Obviously, the closer a correlation comes to being perfect, the better our predictions will be.

Psychological Detective

We have seen that correlations can range from –1.00 (perfect negative) to +1.00 (perfect positive). What has happened when we obtain a zero correlation? Write down your answer as completely as possible before reading further.

For all intents and purposes a zero correlation may not be exactly 0.00. For example, a correlation of 0.03 will be considered a **zero correlation** by most researchers. Such correlations indicate that the two variables under consideration are not related. High scores on one variable may be paired with low, high, or intermediate scores on the second variable, and vice versa. In short, knowing what the score on Variable 1 is does *not* help us predict what the score on Variable 2 will be. An example of a zero correlation is diagrammed in Figure 3-3.

It is important to remember that a correlation tells us only the extent to which two variables are related. Because these two variables are not under our direct control, we are still unable to make cause-and-effect statements. In short, *correlations do not imply causation*. It is possible that a third variable is involved. A rather farfetched example illustrates this point quite well. In an introductory statistics class, one of your authors was told about a correlational study that investi-

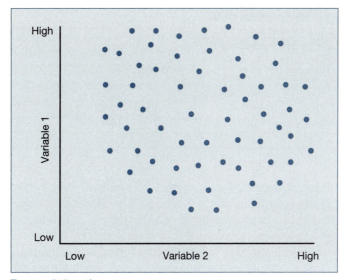

FIGURE 3-3. A ZERO CORRELATION.

gated the relationship between the number of telephone poles erected in Australia each year for the 10 years following World War II and the yearly birth rate in the United States during the same time period. The result was a very high, positive correlation. The point of the example was to illustrate that correlation does not imply causation. It also illustrates the likely presence of a third variable. It is arguable that the increasingly better worldwide economic conditions that followed World War II encouraged both industrial development (the increase in telephone poles in Australia) and the desire to have a family (the higher birth rate in the United States).

Now that we have reviewed the nature and types of correlations, let's examine an example of correlational research. Michael Vitacco and Sean Schmidt, students at the University of Wisconsin at Oshkosh, were interested in studying the relationship between death anxiety and level of self-esteem. Their review of the literature indicated that this relationship had been studied almost exclusively in college students. Hence, they included a sample of male college students (age range 18–30) *and* a sample of male blue-collar workers (truck drivers)–(age range 31–60) in their study. All participants completed the Rosenberg Self-Esteem Scale and Templer's Death Anxiety Scale. Subsequently, the scores on these two scales were correlated. The results of this study (Vitacco & Schmidt, 1993), which were presented in a Psi Chi session at the Midwestern Psychological Association convention, indicated that the correlation between death anxiety and self-esteem was 0.14 for the college men and 0.28 for the blue-collar men. Although neither of these correlations is especially large, the fact that they are both positive suggests that higher self-esteem scores *may* be associated with higher death anxiety, whereas lower self-esteem scores *may* be associated with lower death anxiety.

Psychological Detective

As Vitacco and Schmidt noted, one encounters some potential problems in interpreting the results of this study. What are these potential problems and how might a future research project correct them? Give these questions some thought and write down your answers before reading further.

Vitacco and Schmidt indicated that a potential problem with the project concerns the nature of the groups that were evaluated. The group of college men was much younger (18–30 years) than the group of blue-collar men (31–60 years). Also, there may be a difference in educational level between the two groups; one would anticipate that the college men have received more formal schooling than have the blue-collar men. How can these problems be corrected? The addition of two samples, a group of older college men and a group of younger blue-collar men, would strengthen this study. Then, comparisons of the correlations between self-esteem and death anxiety could be made for younger and older participants, as well as for college and blue-collar men. We would, however, still have to contend with the problem of differences in educational levels.

As we have seen, correlational studies are used when data on two variables are available but we cannot manipulate either variable. Although we can determine the degree of relationship that exists between these two variables, we are not able to offer a cause-and-effect statement concerning these two variables.

In the next section we will examine another procedure in which the relevant variables are carefully selected and examined. What makes this procedure unique is that the variables are selected after the fact and the experimenter has no control over their administration.

Ex Post Facto Studies

Are we unable to conduct experimental research on variables that we cannot control or manipulate? No, we can conduct research on such variables but must be cautious in drawing conclusions. When we work with IVs that we cannot manipulate, we are conducting an **ex post facto study.** *Ex post facto* is a Latin phrase meaning "after the fact." When we conduct an ex post facto study, we are using an IV "after the fact"—it has already varied before we arrived on the scene. A great deal of detective work would seem to fall into this category. Because the experimenter has no control over administering the independent variable, let alone determining who receives this variable and under what conditions it is administered, the ex post facto study clearly qualifies as a descriptive research technique. However, it does have some properties in common with experimental methods.

definition

Ex post facto study The variable(s) to be studied are selected after they have occurred.

For example, a current hot research topic is sex differences—how or why men and women behave differently. We do not have control over sex as an IV; we cannot manipulate it. You cannot bring a research participant into the lab and randomly assign "it" to either a male or female group. Participants come to the lab with their sex predetermined. All we can do with such IVs is categorize, classify, or measure our participants with regard to the characteristic in question. As we will see in Chapter 4, these nonmanipulable variables are often called subject variables. Many interesting psychological factors fall into this subject variable category: personality styles or traits, socioeconomic status, childhood experiences, brain structure or organization, and so on.

Let's look at an example of student research using an ex post facto approach. Sara Plair (1994), of Southern Arkansas University in Magnolia, AR, asked 36 male and 54 female college students about their reactions following their first act of sexual intercourse. Plair found that men had more positive attitudes than women. Men scored higher on reported pleasure, satisfaction, and excitement, whereas women were higher in reported sadness, guilt, exploitation, tension, embarrassment, fear, and pain. At first glance, these results seem predictable from society's differential attitudes toward male and female sexuality. On the other hand, notice that women reported more pain than men. Perhaps the difference in the attitudes of men and women toward their first act of intercourse is based simply on physical sensations: Men find it pleasurable and women find that it hurts. Or perhaps the answer is as simple as sexual gratification. Men are probably more likely to experience orgasm during their first intercourse than are women. Although we are able to report the sex differences, we can't be sure of their origin.

Psychological Detective

What causes Plair's research to fall into the ex post facto category? Write down your answer to this question before reading further.

Because Plair had no control over when the first act of sexual intercourse occurred and the individuals who engaged in this behavior, this project is an example of ex post facto research. In the next section research employing surveys, questionnaires, tests, and inventories will be considered. Such research is quite popular.

REVIEW SUMMARY

1. **Descriptive research methods** are non-experimental procedures for acquiring information. They do not involve the manipulation of variables.

2. Some researchers make use of archival and previously recorded sources of data. Although the use of such data avoids biasing participants' responses, this approach suffers from lack of generalizability, selective deposit, and selective survival.

3. Although observational techniques do not involve the direct manipulation of variables, they do allow the researcher to directly observe the behavior(s) of interest.

4. Case studies involve the intensive observation of a single participant over an extended period of time. They are often used in clinical settings.

5. **Naturalistic observation** involves directly observing behaviors in the natural environment. In these studies the observer should remain unobtrusive in order to avoid a **reactance** or **reactivity effect** on the part of the participants.

6. When the **participant observation** approach is used the observer actually becomes a member of the group that is under study. An extensive time commitment may be required to conduct this type of study.

7. Because the observer may not be able to observe all behaviors at all times, decisions concerning which behaviors to observe, as well as when and where to observe them, must be made.

8. **Time sampling** involves making observations at different time periods, whereas **situation sampling** involves observing the same behavior(s) in several different situations.

9. The use of more than one observer may be desirable to avoid missing important observations and to help resolve disagreements concerning what was or was not observed. **Interobserver reliability** refers to the degree to which the observers agree.

10. A **correlational study** involves the measurement and determination of the relationship between two variables.

11. Two variables are **positively correlated** when an increase in one variable is accompanied by an increase in the other variable. A **perfect positive correlation exists** when increases in one variable are accompanied by consistent (proportional) increases in the second variable.

12. Two variables are **negatively correlated** when an increase in one variable is accompanied by a decrease in the other variable. A **perfect negative correlation** exists when increases in one variable are accompanied by consistent (proportional) decreases in the second variable.

13. A **zero correlation** exists when a change in one variable is unrelated to changes in the second variable.

14. In an **ex post facto** study the variable(s) have been experienced before they are examined by the researcher. Thus, control and variable manipulation cannot be accomplished when this type of research is conducted.

STUDY BREAK

1. What is the reactance effect? How is it avoided by the use of archival sources of data?

2.   Describe the problems associated with the use of archival data.

3.   Matching

1. case study   *C*
2. naturalistic observation *A*
3. Hawthorne effect *D*
4. participant observation *E*
5. measurement *B*

A. behavior is observed in the real world
B. establishes a set of rules to assign symbols to events
C. behavior of a single individual is observed over a lengthy period of time
D. observing participants influences their behavior
E. experimenter joins the group being studied

4.   Why are time sampling and situation sampling employed? *generality*

5.   Indicate which scale of measurement each of the following situations describes.

A. The number of burglaries and homicides committed in a two-week period. *nominal*
B. Scores on a 100-point test. *r*
C. The order of finishing in a track meet. *or*
D. How many people drive Toyotas, Hondas, and Mazdas in your hometown. *nom*
E. The amount of electricity required to run various appliances in your kitchen. *ra*
F. A feature article in the Sunday paper describes the ten wealthiest people in the United States. *ordinal*

non ord Interval ratio

6.   What is interobserver reliability? How is it calculated? *Extent of researchers agreement*
agreement
X of ben   × 100

7.   Distinguish among positive, zero, and negative correlations.

8.   What is an ex post facto study?

SURVEYS, QUESTIONNAIRES, TESTS, AND INVENTORIES

Surveys, questionnaires, tests, and inventories are frequently used to assess attitudes, thoughts, and emotions or feelings. Because the researcher typically does not manipulate variables in this type of study, these procedures also can be classified as descriptive research.

One reason surveys and questionnaires are popular is that they appear to be quite simple to conduct; when you want to know how a group of individuals feel about a particular issue, all you have to do is ask them or give them a test. As we will see, appearances can be quite deceptive; it is not as easy to use this technique as it appears. First, we must decide whose attitudes, opinions, and/or feelings we will measure. This consideration brings us to the topic of sampling.

SAMPLING

Assume that you want to determine which of two new titles for the college newspaper—*The Wilderbeast* (named after your school mascot) or *The Observer*—appeals most to the student body. You ask the 36 students in your senior-level biopsychology course and find that 24 prefer *The Observer* and 12 prefer *The Wilderbeast*. You report your findings to the publications advisory board and recommend that *The Observer* be chosen as the new title.

Psychological Detective

Should the publications advisory board accept your recommendation? Are there some reasons to question your findings? Give these questions some thought and write down your answers before reading further.

Population The complete set of individuals or events.

Sample A group that is selected to represent the population.

Random sample A sample in which every member of the population has an equal likelihood of being included.

Random sampling without replacement Once chosen, a score, event, or participant cannot be returned to the population to be selected again.

Random sampling with replacement Once chosen, a score, event, or participant can be returned to the population to be selected again.

The publications advisory board should not accept your recommendation. The main problem with your data concerns the students you surveyed. Is your senior-level biopsychology class representative of the entire campus? The answer to this question must be a resounding no; only senior-level psychology majors take this class. Moreover, a quick check of the class roster indicates that the majority (67%) of the students in your class are women. Clearly, you should have selected a group of students more representative of the general student body at your college.

We shall designate the general student body as the **population** or complete set of individuals or events that we want to represent. The group that is selected to represent the population is called the **sample.** When every member of the population has an equal likelihood of being selected for inclusion in the sample, a **random sample** has been created.

How would you obtain a random sample of students on your campus to take the newspaper title survey? Computer technology has made this task quite simple; you simply indicate the size of the sample you desire, and the computer can be programmed to randomly select a sample of that size from the names of all currently enrolled students. Because a name is not eligible to be chosen again once it has been selected, this technique is called **random sampling without replacement.** If the chosen item can be returned to the population and is eligible to be selected again, the procedure is termed **random sampling with replacement.** Because psychologists do not want the same participant to appear more than once in a group, random sampling without replacement is the preferred technique for creating a random research sample.

A sample of 80 students has been randomly selected from the entire student body by the computer and you are examining the printout. Even though this sample was selected randomly, it also has some apparent problems. Just by chance the majority of the students selected are freshmen and sophomores. Moreover, the majority of this sample are men. The views on the two newspaper titles held by this group of randomly selected students may not be much better than our original sample. What can be done to produce an even more representative sample?

There are two techniques that we can use to increase the representativeness of our sample. The first procedure is quite simple: We can select a larger sample. Generally speaking, the larger the sample, the more representative it will be of the population. If we randomly selected 240 students, this larger sample would be more representative of the general student body than our original sample of 80 students. Although larger samples may be more like the population from which they are drawn, there is a potential drawback. Larger samples mean that more participants will need to be tested. In our project dealing with the two newspaper titles the testing of additional participants may not present any major problems. However, if we were administering a lengthy questionnaire or paying participants for their participation, increasing the number of participants may create unmanageable time and/or financial obstacles.

If simply increasing the sample size does not offer a good solution to the problem of achieving a representative sample, the researcher may want to use the technique of stratified random sampling. **Stratified random sampling** involves dividing the population into subpopulations or strata and then drawing a random sample from one or more of these strata. For example, one logical subdivision of a college student body would be by classes: freshmen, sophomores, juniors, and seniors. A random sample could then be drawn from each class. How many students will be included in each stratum? One option would be for each stratum to contain an equal number of participants. Thus, in our newspaper title project we might include 20 participants from each academic classification. A second option would be to sample each stratum in proportion to its representation in the population. If freshmen comprise 30% of the student body, then our random sample would contain 30% of freshmen. What about the number of men and women sampled in each stratum? We could have equal numbers or we could sample in proportion to the percent of men and women in each stratum. As you have probably surmised, the use of stratified random sampling indicates that you have considerable knowledge of the population in which you are interested. Once you have this knowledge, you can create a sample that is quite representative of the population of interest. A word of caution is in order, however. Although it may be tempting to specify a number of characteristics that your sample must possess, this process can be carried too far. If your sample becomes too highly specified, then you will be able to generalize or extend your results only to a population having those very specific characteristics.

Once the size and nature of our sample have been decided, the type of instrument we will use must be carefully evaluated. We first consider surveys and questionnaires, then we turn our attention to tests and inventories.

Stratified random sampling Random samples are drawn from specific subpopulations or strata of the general population.

definition

SURVEYS AND QUESTIONNAIRES

Because we have all been asked to complete a survey at one time or another, we have probably been part of a random sample. Surveys typically request our opinion on some topic or issue that is of interest to the researcher.

SURVEY RESEARCH CENTER

ELEVATOR

UP

UNDECIDED

DOWN

Copyright ©Harley Schwadron from The Cartoon Bank, Inc.

Types of Surveys. The purpose of your research project will determine the type of survey you choose to administer. If you seek to determine what percentage of the population has a certain characteristic, holds a certain opinion, or engages in a particular behavior, then you will use a **descriptive survey.** The Gallup Poll that evaluates voter preferences and the Nielsen television ratings are examples of descriptive surveys. When this type of survey is used, no attempt is made to determine what the relevant variables are and how they may be related. The end product is the description of a particular characteristic or behavior of a sample with the hope that this finding is representative of the population from which the sample was drawn.

The **analytic survey** seeks to determine what the relevant variables are and how they might be related. Assume, for example, that a psychologist is interested in studying bungee jumping. A descriptive survey might be administered to determine what proportion of a particular socioeconomic group engages in this behavior. Once participants and nonparticipants have been identified, an analytic survey could be administered to determine what differences exist between these two groups. Perhaps there is an age or educational difference. What about gender or group membership? To address the issues you are interested in, the questions for the analytic survey will have to be chosen carefully before the survey is administered. In fact, it will probably be necessary to do some pilot testing of the analytic survey before it is used in a full-scale investigation. **Pilot testing** refers to testing and evaluating that is done in advance of the complete research project. During this preliminary stage a small number of participants are tested and the researcher may even use in-depth interviews to help determine the type of questions that should appear on the final survey instrument.

Developing a Good Survey or Questionnaire. A good survey or questionnaire, one that measures the attitudes and opinions of interest in an unbiased manner, is not developed overnight; considerable time and effort typically go into its construction. Once you have decided exactly what information your research project seeks to ascertain, there are several steps that should be followed in order to develop a good survey or questionnaire. These steps are summarized in Table 3-1.

Descriptive survey
Seeks to determine the percentage of the population that has a certain characteristic, holds a particular opinion, or engages in a particular behavior.

Analytic survey
Seeks to determine the relevant variables and how they are related.

Pilot testing
Preliminary, exploratory testing that is done prior to the complete research project.

definition

TABLE 3-1. STEPS IN DEVELOPING A GOOD SURVEY OR QUESTIONNAIRE	
STEP 1	Decide what type of instrument to use. How will the information be gathered?
STEP 2	Identify the types of questions to use.
STEP 3	Write the items: They should be clear, short, and specific.
STEP 4	Pilot test and seek opinions from knowledgeable others.
STEP 5	Determine the relevant demographic data to be collected.
STEP 6	Determine administration procedures and develop instructions.

The first step is to determine how the information you seek is to be obtained. Will you use a mail survey? Will your project involve the use of a questionnaire that is administered during a regular class session at your college or university? Will trained interviewers administer your questionnaire in person, or will a telephone interview be conducted? Decisions such as these will have a major impact on the type of survey or questionnaire you will develop.

Once a decision concerning the type of instrument to be developed has been made, specific attention can be given to the *nature* of the questions that will be used and the type of responses that can be made to these questions. Among the types of questions that are frequently used in surveys and questionnaires are the following:

1. ***Yes-No Questions*** The respondent answers "yes" or "no" to the items.

   EXAMPLE

   The thought of death seldom enters my mind.
   (*Source:* Templer's Death Anxiety Scale; Templer, 1970)

2. ***Forced Alternative Questions*** The respondent is forced to select between two alternative responses.

   EXAMPLE

   A.　　There are institutions in our society that have considerable control over me.

   B.　　Little in this world controls me. I usually do what I decide to do.
   (*Source:* Reid-Ware Three-Factor Locus of Control Scale; Reid & Ware, 1973)

3. ***Multiple-Choice Questions*** The respondent must select the most suitable response from among several alternatives.

   EXAMPLE

   Compared to the average student:

   A.　　I give much more effort.

   B.　　I give an average amount of effort.

   C.　　I give less effort.
   (*Source:* Modified Jenkins Activity Scale; Krantz, Glass & Snyder, 1974)

4. ***Likert-type Scales*** The individual answers a question by selecting a response alternative from a designated scale. A typical scale might be the following: (5) strongly agree, (4) agree, (3) undecided, (2) disagree, or (1) strongly disagree.

EXAMPLE

I enjoy social gatherings just to be with people.

A.	**B.**	**C.**	**D.**	**E.**
not at all characteristic of me	not very	slightly	fairly	very much characteristic of me

(*Source:* Texas Social Behavior Inventory; Helmreich & Stapp, 1974)

5. ***Open-ended Questions*** A question is asked to which the respondent is required to construct his or her own answer.

EXAMPLE

How would you summarize your chief problems in your own words?

(*Source:* Mooney Problem Check List; Mooney, 1950)

Clearly, the questions you choose to use on your survey or questionnaire will directly influence the type of data you will gather and be able to analyze when your project is completed. If you choose the yes-no format, then you will be able to calculate the frequency or percentage of such responses for each question (nominal scale of measurement). The use of a Likert-type scale allows you to calculate an average or mean response to each question (interval scale of measurement). Should you choose to use open-ended questions, you will have to decide how to code or quantify the responses or you will have to establish a procedure for preparing a summary description of each participant's answers.

The third step is to actually write the items for your survey or questionnaire. As a general rule, these questions should be clear, short, and specific; use familiar vocabulary; and be at the reading level of the individuals you intend to test. In preparing your items, you should avoid questions that might constrain the respondents' answers. For example, you might ask your participants to rate the effectiveness of the president of the United States in dealing with "crises." Assuming that the president has dealt with several crises, it may not be clear whether the question is referring to one particular type of crisis or another. Hence, the respondents will have to interpret the item as best they can; their interpretation may not coincide with your intended meaning. Also, questions that might bias the respondents' answers should be avoided. A negatively worded question may result in a preponderance of negative answers, whereas a positively worded question may result in a preponderance of positive answers.

Psychological Detective

 Consider this yes-no question: "Do you agree that wealthy professional athletes are overpaid?" What is wrong with this question and how can it be improved? Write your answers before reading further.

By indicating that professional athletes are wealthy, you have created a mental set that suggests that they may be overpaid. Thus, your respondents may be biased to answer yes. Also, using the word "agree" in the question may encourage yes answers. If the question is rewritten as follows, it is less likely to bias the respondents' answers: "Are professional athletes overpaid?"

> **Demographic data**
> Information about participant's characteristics such as age, gender, income, and academic major.
>
> definition

The next step is to pilot test your survey or questionnaire. It is important to ask others, especially those who have expertise in your area of research interest, to review your items. They may be able to detect biases and unintended wordings that you had not considered. It will also be helpful at this preliminary stage to administer your questionnaire to several individuals and then discuss the questions with them. Often there is nothing comparable to the insights of a participant who has actually completed a testing instrument. Such insights can be invaluable as you revise your questions. In fact, you may find it necessary to pretest and revise your survey in this manner several times before a final draft is achieved.

The fifth step involves a consideration of the other relevant information that you want your participants to provide. Frequently such information falls under the heading of **demographic data,** which may include such items as age, sex, annual income, size of community, academic major, and academic classification. Although the need for this step may seem obvious, it is important to review these items very carefully to ensure that you have not forgotten to request a vital bit of information. We cannot begin to tell you how many survey projects designed to evaluate male-female differences were less than successful because they failed to include an item that requested the participant's sex.

The final step is to clearly specify the procedures that will be followed when the survey or questionnaire is administered. If the survey is self-administering, what constitutes the printed instructions? Are they clear, concise, and easy to follow? Who will distribute and collect the informed consent forms and deal with questions that may arise? If your survey or questionnaire is not self-administering, then an instruction script must be written. The wording of this set of instructions must be clear and easily understood. Whether these instructions are presented in a face-to-face interview, over the telephone, or in front of a large class of students, they must be thoroughly practiced and rehearsed by the individuals who will be giving them. The researcher in charge of the project must be sure that all interviewers present the instructions in the same manner on all occasions. Likewise, questions raised by the participants must also be dealt with in a consistent manner.

As we saw, the final step in creating a good survey involves a determination of the administration procedures. Because these choices are crucial to the success of this type of research, we will examine the three basic options—mail surveys, personal interviews, and telephone interviews—in more detail.

Mail Surveys Most likely you have been asked to complete a survey you received in the mail. This popular technique is used to gather data on issues that range from our opinions on environmental problems to the type of food we purchase.

One advantage of sending surveys through the mail is that the researcher does not have to be present while the survey is being completed. Thus, surveys can be sent to a much larger number of participants than a single researcher could ever hope to contact in person.

Although it is possible to put a survey in the hands of a large number of respondents, there are several disadvantages associated with this research strategy. First, the researcher cannot be sure who actually completes the survey. Possibly the intended respondent was too busy to complete the survey and asked a family member or friend to finish it. Hence, the time and trouble that was spent in creating a random sample from the population of interest may be severely jeopardized.

Even if the intended respondent completes the survey, there is no guarantee that the questions were answered in the same order in which they appeared on the survey. If the order of answering questions is relevant to the project, then this drawback may be a major obstacle to the use of mail surveys.

The low return rate associated with the use of mail surveys highlights another problem. In addition to disappointment and frustration, low return rates suggest a potential bias in the researcher's sample. What type of individuals returned the surveys? How did they differ from those individuals who did not return the surveys? Were they the least (most) busy? Were they the least (most) opinionated? We really do not know, and as the response rate drops lower, the possibility of having a biased sample increases. What constitutes a *good* response rate to a mail survey? Because it is not uncommon to have a response rate of 25%–30% to a mail survey, response rates of 50% and higher are considered to be quite acceptable.

Psychological Detective

Assume that you are planning to conduct a mail survey project. You are concerned about the possibility of having a low response rate and want to do everything possible to ensure the return of your surveys. What can you do to increase your response rate? Give this question some thought and write down your answers before reading further.

Researchers have developed several strategies designed to increase the response rates of mail surveys. Some of these techniques are:

1. The initial mailing should include a letter that *clearly* summarizes the nature and importance of the research project, how the respondents were selected, and the fact that all responses are confidential. A prepaid envelope for the return of the completed survey should also be included.

2. It may be necessary to send an additional mailing(s) to your respondents. Because the original survey may have been misplaced or lost, it is important to include a replacement. One extra mailing may not be sufficient, you may find it necessary to send two or three requests before you achieve an acceptable response rate. These extra mailings are typically sent at two- to three-week intervals.

The use of mail surveys is not accepted by all researchers. Low response rates, incomplete surveys, and unclear answers are among the reasons that cause some researchers to use direct interviews to obtain data. These interviews may be done in person or over the telephone.

Personal Interviews. When a survey is administered by a trained interviewer in a respondent's home, the response rate climbs dramatically. It is not uncommon to have a 90% completion rate under these circumstances. In addition to simply increasing the response rate, the trained interviewer is able to cut down on the number of unusable surveys by clarifying ambiguous questions, making sure that all questions are answered in the proper sequence, and generally assisting with any problems that the respondents may experience.

Although this technique offers some advantages when compared to the mail survey, there are drawbacks. First, the potential for considerable expenditure of time *and* money exists. Time has to be devoted to the training of the interviewers. Once trained, the observers will have to be paid for their time on the job. Second, the fact that the survey is being administered by an individual introduces the possibility of interviewer bias. Some interviewers may present some questions in a more positive (or negative) manner than do other interviewers. Only careful and extensive training of all interviewers to present all items in a consistent, neutral manner can overcome this potential difficulty. Finally, the prospect of administering surveys in the home is becoming less appealing and feasible. In many instances no one is at home during the day, and an increasing number of people are not willing to sacrifice their leisure evening hours to complete a survey. Additionally, the rising crime rates in many urban areas have served to discourage face-to-face interviewing. In its place many investigators have turned to telephone interviewing.

Telephone Interviews. In addition to overcoming several of the problems associated with personal interviews and mail surveys, telephone interviewing offers several other advantages. For example, the development of random-digit dialing allows researchers to establish a random sample with ease: The desired number of calls is specified and the computer does the rest. It is noteworthy that a random sample generated in this manner will contain both listed and unlisted telephone numbers because the digits in each number are selected randomly. With 95% of all households in the United States currently having telephones, previous concerns about creating a biased sample consisting of only households having telephones seems largely unfounded.

Computer technology has increased the desirability of conducting telephone interviews in other ways. For example, it is now possible to enter the participant's responses directly as they are being made. Hence, the data are stored directly in the computer and are ready for analysis at any time.

Despite these apparent advantages, telephone interviews do have potential drawbacks. Even though technology has assisted telephone researchers, it also has provided an obstacle. Many households are now equipped with answering machines that allow incoming calls to be screened. Hence, potential respondents may be lost because they refused to answer the phone. Even if the call is answered, it is easier to say no to an unseen interviewer on the telephone than to a person at your front door. These two situations lower the response rate and raise the possibility that a biased sample is being created.

The use of the telephone also prohibits the use of visual aids that might serve to clarify certain questions. Because the telephone interviewer cannot see the respondent, it is also not possible to evaluate nonverbal cues such as facial expressions, gestures, and posture. Such cues might suggest that a certain question was not completely understood or that an answer is in need of clarification.

Not being in face-to-face contact with the respondent also makes it more difficult to establish rapport. Hence, telephone respondents may not be as willing to participate in the survey. This potential lack of willingness has led to the use of shorter survey instruments.

Although surveys and questionnaires are popular research tools with many investigators, there are other ways to gather data. Since the late 1800s when Sir Francis Galton (1822-1911) attempted to evaluate people's ability or intelligence by measuring physical attributes, such as reaction time or visual acuity, psychologists have developed a large number of tests and inventories for a wide variety of purposes.

TESTS AND INVENTORIES

Unlike surveys and questionnaires, which are designed to evaluate opinions on some topic or issue, tests and inventories are designed to assess a specific attribute, ability, or characteristic possessed by the individual being tested. In this section we look at the characteristics of good tests and inventories and then discuss three general types of tests and inventories: achievement, aptitude, and personality.

Characteristics of Good Tests and Inventories. Unlike surveys and questionnaires, the researcher is less likely to be directly involved with the development of a test or inventory. Because their development and pilot testing has already taken place, you will need to scrutinize the reports concerning the development of each test or inventory you are considering. A good test or inventory should possess two characteristics: It should be valid and it should be reliable.

Validity. A test or inventory has **validity** when it actually measures what it is supposed to measure. If your research calls for a test that measures spelling achievement, you want the instrument you select to measure that accomplishment, not another accomplishment, such as mathematical proficiency.

There are several ways to establish the validity of a test or inventory. **Content validity** indicates that the test items actually represent the type of material they are supposed to. A panel of expert judges is often used to assess the content validity of test items. Although the more subjective evaluation of such judges may not lend itself to a great deal of quantification, their degree of agreement, known as **interrater reliability,** can be calculated. Interrater reliability is similar to interobserver reliability. The main difference is that interrater reliability measures agreement between

Validity The extent to which a test or inventory measures what it is supposed to measure.

Content validity The extent to which test items actually represent the type of material they are supposed to.

Interrater reliability Degree of agreement among judges concerning the content validity of test or inventory items.

judgments concerning a test item, whereas interobserver measures agreement between observations of behavior.

Concurrent validity can be established when we already have another measure of the desired trait or outcome and can compare the score on the test or inventory under consideration with this other measure. For example, the scores made by a group of patients on a test designed to measure aggression might be compared with a diagnosis of their aggressive tendencies made by a clinical psychologist. If the test and the clinical psychologist rate the aggressiveness of the patients in a similar manner, then concurrent validity for the test has been established. Often our second measure may not be immediately accessible. When the test score is to be compared with an outcome that will occur in the future, the researcher is attempting to establish the **criterion validity** of the test. Thus, criterion validity refers to the ability of the test or inventory to predict the outcome or criterion. For example, it is the desired outcome that the SAT and ACT predict performance in college. To the extent that these tests are successful, their criterion validity has been established.

Reliability. Once we have determined that a particular test is valid, we will also want to make sure that it is reliable. **Reliability** refers to the extent that the test or inventory is consistent in its evaluation of the same individuals over repeated administrations. For example, if we have developed a test to measure aptitude for social work, we would want individuals who score high (or low) on our test on its first administration to make essentially the same score when the test is administered again. The greater the similarity between scores produced by the same individuals on repeated administrations, the greater the reliability of the test or inventory.

Reliability is typically assessed through the test-retest or split-half procedures. When the **test-retest procedure** is used, the test is simply given a second time and the scores from the two tests are compared; the greater the similarity, the higher the reliability.

Concurrent validity Degree to which the score on a test or inventory corresponds with another measure of the designated trait.

Criterion validity Is established by comparing the score on a test or inventory with a future score on another test or inventory.

Reliability Extent to which a test or inventory is consistent in its evaluation of the same individuals.

Test-retest procedure Determination of reliability by repeatedly administering a test to the same participants.

Psychological Detective

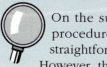

On the surface, the test-retest procedure appears to be quite straightforward and reasonable. However, there may be a problem with establishing reliability in this manner. Give this situation some thought and briefly describe any potential problems you detect before reading further.

The main problem with the test-retest procedure concerns the fact that the participants are repeatedly administered the same test or inventory. Having already taken

Split-half technique
Determination of reliability by dividing the test or inventory into two subtests and then comparing the scores made on the two halves.

Achievement test
Designed to evaluate an individual's level of mastery or competence.

Aptitude test
Designed to assess an individual's potential ability or skill in a particular job.

the test or inventory may result in the individuals' remembering the questions and/or answers the next time the instrument is administered. Therefore, their answers may be biased by the previous administration. If a lengthy time period is allowed to elapse between administrations, the participants might forget the question and answers and this familiarity problem might be overcome. However, this lengthy time period may influence reliability in yet another manner. An extended time period allows the participants to have numerous experiences and learning opportunities between administrations. These experiences may influence their scores when the test or inventory is given again. Hence, the reliability measure may become influenced by the experiences that intervened between the two testing sessions.

It is possible to overcome the problems of test familiarity and lengthy time periods separating administrations by using the split-half approach. The **split-half technique** of establishing reliability involves dividing a test or inventory into two halves or subtests and then administering them to the same individuals on different occasions or by administering the entire test and then splitting it into two halves. Because the questions that comprise the two subtests were drawn from the same test, it is assumed that they are highly related to each other if the test is reliable. Typically, the questions that comprise these two subtests are selected randomly or in some predetermined manner, such as odd-even. The higher the degree of correspondence between scores on the two subtests, the greater the reliability of the overall test from which they were selected.

Having determined that a test or inventory should be valid and reliable, we now examine several types of these instruments that are currently used for research and/or predictive purposes.

Types of Tests and Inventories. **Achievement tests** are given when an evaluation of an individual's level of mastery or competence is desired. For example, doctors must pass a series of medical board examinations before they are allowed to practice medicine, and lawyers must pass the bar examination before they are allowed to practice law. The score that distinguishes passing from failing determines the minimum level of achievement that must be attained. You can probably think of many other achievement tests you have taken during your life.

At many colleges and universities the counseling center or career development office offers students the opportunity to take an aptitude test to assist them in selecting a major or making a career choice. An **aptitude test** is used to assess an individual's ability or skill in a particular situation or job. For example, the Purdue Pegboard Test is often administered to determine one's aptitude for jobs that require manual dexterity. According to Anastasi (1988), "This test provides a measure of two types of activity, one requiring gross movements of hands, fingers, and arms, and the other involving tip-of-the-finger dexterity needed in small assembly work" (p. 461). Similarly, if you are planning to attend graduate school, you will probably be required to take the Graduate Record Examination (GRE). For most graduate schools, the two most important scores on the GRE are those of the verbal and quantitative subtests. These scores are used as measures of your aptitude to successfully complete verbal and quantitative courses on the graduate level.

The **personality test** or **inventory** measures a specific aspect of an individual's motivational state, interpersonal capability, or personality. The use of a personality inventory in research is exemplified by a project reported by Constance L. Meyer, a student at Xavier University in Cincinnati, OH (Meyer, 1993). The purpose of this study was to examine the relationship between the level of self-esteem reported by a sample of adults and the type of parental discipline they received as children. A total of 137 students (87 women, 50 men) volunteered to serve as participants. Each student completed a shortened (18-item) version of Coopersmith's Self-Esteem Inventory. Additionally, all participants also completed a parental discipline survey that sought to determine how often they were rewarded and punished between the ages of 6 and 13. In agreement with previous research (e.g., Gussmann & Harder, 1990), Meyer's (1993) results showed that self-esteem was negatively related to the amount of self-reported punishment; as the amount of self-reported punishment increased, the level of self-esteem decreased. It is interesting to note that Meyer used two types of instruments in her research; she used a personality inventory to evaluate the level of self-esteem, and she used a survey to determine the amount of punishment and reward that had been experienced.

Having completed our review of surveys, questionnaires, tests, and inventories, we conclude this section with a consideration of the types of research strategies that these instruments are used in. The main strategies used by researchers are the single-strata, cross-sectional, and longitudinal approaches.

RESEARCH STRATEGIES USING SURVEYS, QUESTIONNAIRES, TESTS, AND INVENTORIES

Even though you have chosen your sample, completed your survey or questionnaire, or selected your test or inventory and have prepared your instructions, you simply cannot rush out to start testing participants. Some thought needs to be given to the research question and how your project can best be conducted in order to answer that question. There are three basic approaches you can adopt: single-strata, cross-sectional, and longitudinal.

The **single-strata approach** seeks to acquire data from a single, specified segment of the population. For example, a particular Gallup Poll may be interested only in the voting preferences of blue-collar workers. Hence, a sample composed only of individuals from this stratum would be administered a voter-preference survey. This approach typically seeks to answer a rather specific research question.

When the single-strata approach is broadened to include samples from more than one stratum, a cross-sectional approach is being employed. **Cross-sectional research** involves the comparison of two or more groups of participants during the same,

definition

Longitudinal research project Obtaining research data from the same group of participants over an extended period of time.

Cohort A group of individuals born during the same time period.

rather limited, time span. For example, a researcher may want to compare voter preferences of different age groups. To acquire this information, random samples of 21-, 31-, 41-, 51-, 61-, and 71-year-old voters are obtained and their responses to a voter-preference survey are compared.

Perhaps the researcher wants to obtain information from a group of participants over an extended period of time. In this instance a **longitudinal research project** would be conducted. A random sample from the population of interest would be obtained; then this sample might be given an initial survey or test to complete. The same participants would then be contacted periodically to determine what, if any, changes had occurred during the ensuing time in the behavior of interest. This group of individuals that is born in the same time period and repeatedly surveyed or tested is called a **cohort.** For example, a researcher might be interested in the changes in the degree of support for environmental conservation that occur as individuals grow older. To evaluate such changes a group of grade school children is randomly selected. Every five years all members of this cohort are contacted and administered an environmental conservation survey. These research strategies are compared in Table 3-2.

TABLE 3-2. SINGLE-STRATA, CROSS-SECTIONAL, AND LONGITUDINAL RESEARCH STRATEGIES

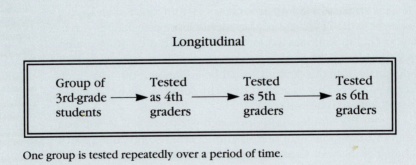

Single Strata

| 1st-graders |
| 2nd-graders |
| 3rd-graders |
| 4th-graders |
| 5th-graders |
| 6th-graders |

A group is selected from one stratum.

Cross–Sectional

1st-graders	→ sample
2nd-graders	→ sample
3rd-graders	→ sample
4th-graders	→ sample
5th-graders	→ sample
6th-graders	→ sample

A sample is selected from each stratum.

Longitudinal

Group of 3rd-grade students → Tested as 4th graders → Tested as 5th graders → Tested as 6th graders

One group is tested repeatedly over a period of time.

REVIEW SUMMARY

1. Surveys, questionnaires, tests, and inventories are used to assess attitudes, thoughts, and emotions or feelings. Research using these instruments does not typically involve the manipulation of variables.

2. The **sample** of individuals who complete a survey, questionnaire, test, or inventory should be representative of the **population** from which it is drawn.

3. When a **random sample** is selected, every member of the population has an equal likelihood of being selected. When **random sampling without replacement** is used, an item cannot be returned to the population once it has been selected. When **random sampling with replacement** is used, selected items can be returned to the population to be selected again.

4. **Stratified random sampling** involves dividing the population into subpopulations or stratum and then drawing random samples from these stratum.

5. **Descriptive surveys** seek to determine the percentage of a population that has a certain characteristic, holds a certain opinion, or engages in a particular behavior. **Analytic surveys** seek to determine the variables that are relevant in a situation and their relationship.

6. The steps to be completed in developing a good survey or questionnaire include consideration of the type of instrument to be developed, determining the types of questions to be used, writing the items, pilot testing, determining the relevant demographic data to be collected, and deciding on administration procedures.

7. **Demographic data** include relevant information, such as gender, age, income, and educational level, about the participants.

8. Mail surveys can be sent to a large number of potential respondents. However, the researcher cannot be sure who actually completed the survey or in what order the questions were completed. Low response rates for mail surveys can be dealt with by stressing the importance of the project and by sending additional mailings.

9. Personal interviews yield a higher rate of completed surveys but are costly in terms of time and money. The increase in the number of working families and the escalating crime rate in urban areas have made the use of personal interviews less desirable.

10. Telephone interviews allow the researcher to reach a large number of respondents more efficiently than personal interviews and mail surveys. However, answering machines and the inability to see nonverbal cues are drawbacks to this approach.

11. Tests and inventories should be **valid** (measure what they are supposed to measure) and **reliable** (be consistent in their evaluation).

12. Validity may be established by the **content, concurrent,** and **criterion** methods.

13. The **test-retest** and **split-half** procedures are used to establish reliability.

14. **Achievement tests** evaluate level of mastery or competence. Aptitude tests assess an individual's ability or skill in a particular situation or job. A **personality test** or **inventory** measures a specific aspect of the individual's motivational state, interpersonal capability, or personality.

15. Surveys, questionnaires, tests, and inventories may be administered to (a) a **single strata** of a specified population, (b) samples from more than one strata in a **cross-sectional** project, or (c) a single group of participants over an extended time period in a **longitudinal** study.

STUDY BREAK

1. The general group of interest is the _____. The group that is selected to represent the general group is a _____.

2. What is random sampling? With replacement? Without replacement?

3. What is stratified random sampling and why is it used?

4. Matching
   1. descriptive survey
   2. analytic survey
   3. pilot testing
   4. demographic data
   5. cohort
   6. concurrent validity
   7. criterion validity

   5 A. defines participants born in the same time period
   7 B. affects ability to predict the outcome
   4 C. may include age, sex, and annual income
   1 D. indicates the percentage having a certain characteristic
   6 E. compares scores on two separate measures
   2 F. tries to determine what the relevant variables are
   3 G. does testing or evaluating in advance of the complete research project

5. Describe the steps involved in creating a good survey.

6. How can the low return rate of mail surveys be improved?

7. Why is the use of personal interviews declining?

8. Distinguish between achievement and aptitude tests.

9. Distinguish among the single-strata, cross-sectional, and longitudinal approaches to research.

LOOKING AHEAD

In this chapter we have considered approaches to gathering research data that did not include the direct manipulation of an IV by the researcher. Hence, these approaches do not qualify as true experiments. In the next chapter we begin our consideration of experiments. First we carefully examine the variables involved in an experiment; then we consider procedures involved in the control of these variables.

H A N D S - O N A C T I V I T I E S

1. **Archival Research.**   Archival research can be done in your college library. For example, try answering the question "Is psychology the science of the college student?" by consulting the journals in your library that publish research using human participants. Pick one or two of these journals and check all the articles that were published during a one- or two-year period. What percentage of these articles used college student participants? What percentage used non–college student participants?

2. **Case Study.**   Select an elderly member of your community; this individual can be a grandparent, friend at church, someone at a senior citizen center, and so on. Plan to interview this individual several times over an extended period of time (i.e., four or five weeks). Your objective is to produce a case study of the individual you select. What unique trends characterize his or her life? What recurrent aspirations, motives, and/or problems are expressed? In short, you want to be as complete as possible in your description of this individual.

3. **Naturalistic Observation.**   Select a specific animal or group of animals at the local zoo or nearby wildlife refuge and observe the behaviors that occur during a set period of time (e.g., one or two hours). Establish different categories for the behaviors you observe. Once you have established these categories, conduct a second observation session. Did your categories help with the second observation? What conclusions did you draw about the behavior(s) you observed? How valid are these conclusions? Was your observation unobtrusive? Explain. Was time sampling or situation sampling involved? Explain.

4. **Sampling at College.**   Most colleges and universities publish an annual student directory. The student directory can be used to select a random sample. Once you have obtained the student directory, you will need to determine the following:

   a.   The size of the sample you want to select. We recommend a sample of 40 students.

   b.   The method of random selection that will be used. The table of random numbers is among the most convenient. Ask one of your faculty members to loan you a table of random numbers and give you a few pointers concerning its use.

Now you are ready to randomly select your sample of 40 students. Once you have completed that task, answer the following questions. How many were men? Women? How many were first-, second-, third-, and fourth-year students? Once you have randomly selected your sample of 40 students, randomly assign them to two groups of 20 students. Once these two groups have been formed, answer the same questions that were asked about the sample you selected. Would stratified random sampling have produced a more representative sample and groups? Explain.

CHAPTER 4

The Basics of Experimentation I: Variables and Control

Even though potentially valuable information can be gained through the use of the methods described in Chapter 3, these methods suffer because the experimenter cannot make cause-and-effect statements. In this chapter we begin to examine methods and procedures that allow us to make cause-and-effect inferences. We begin by carefully examining the three types of variables that the researcher deals with: independent, dependent, and extraneous variables. Recall from Chapter 2 that independent variables are directly manipulated by the experimenter, dependent variables change in response to the independent variable manipulation, and that extraneous variables can distort or invalidate our experimental results. Once we have discussed these variables and made their relation to the experiment clear, we will consider the procedures that have been developed to keep unwanted, extraneous variables from influencing the results of our experiment.

THE NATURE OF VARIABLES

Variable An event or behavior that can assume two or more values.

Before jumping into a discussion of independent variables, let's look at the nature of variables in general. A **variable** is an event or behavior that can assume at least two values. For example, temperature is a variable; it can assume a wide range of values. The same could be said for height, weight, lighting conditions, the noise level in an urban area, and your responses to a test; each of these events can assume two or more values or levels.

So, when variables involved in a psychological experiment are discussed, we are talking about events or behaviors that have assumed at least two values. If the independent variable has only one level, we would have nothing to compare its effectiveness with. Assume that you want to demonstrate that a new brand of toothpaste is the best on the market. You have a group of participants try the new toothpaste and then rate its effectiveness. Even though the entire group rates the toothpaste in question as "great," you still cannot claim that it is best; you do not have ratings from other groups using different brands.

Just as the independent variable must have at least two values, the dependent variable also must be able to assume two or more values. Your toothpaste study would be meaningless if the only response the participants can make is "great"; more than one response alternative is needed.

The same logic applies in the case of extraneous variables. If two or more values are not present, then the event in question is not an extraneous variable. If all the participants in our toothpaste study are women, then we do not have to be concerned with sex differences between the groups that are tested. (This point will be important later in the Control section of this chapter.)

Notice that our concern about extraneous variables is quite different from our concern about independent and dependent variables. Whereas we were concerned that the independent and dependent variables have or are able to assume two or more values, we seek to avoid those instances where extraneous variables can assume two or more values. In short, we seek to reduce extraneous variables to a nonvariable status.

OPERATIONALLY DEFINING VARIABLES

As you will recall from Chapter 2, we suggested that replication of past research can be a valuable source of research ideas. Let's assume that you have located a piece of research that needs replication. You carefully read how the experiment was conducted and find that "each participant was given a reward following every correct response." Assume that this sentence is the only information you have concerning the "reward" and "response" involved in the experiment. If we asked ten different researchers what reward they would use and what response they would record, how many different responses would you get? With this limited and vague information, chances are good that we would get as many different answers as people we ask. How valid will your replication be? If you use a totally different reward and a totally different response, have you even conducted a replication?

Problems and concerns such as these led a 1920s Harvard University physicist, Percy W. Bridgman, to propose a way to obtain clearer communication among researchers and thus achieve greater standardization and uniformity in experimental methodology (Schultz & Schultz, 1996). Bridgman's suggestion was simple: Researchers should define their variables in terms of the operations needed to produce them (Bridgman, 1927). If you define your variables in this manner, then other scientists can replicate your research by following the definitions you have given for the variables involved. Such definitions are called **operational definitions.** Operational definitions have been a cornerstone of psychological research for nearly three quarters of a century because they allow researchers to communicate clearly and effectively with each other.

To illustrate the use of operational definitions, let's return to the "reward" and "response" situation we described above. If we define reward as "a 45-mg Noyes Formula A food pellet," then other researchers can replicate our research by ordering a supply of 45-mg Formula A pellets from the P. J. Noyes Company. Likewise, if we define the response as "making a bar press in an operant conditioning chamber (Lafayette Model 81335)," then our research setup can be replicated by purchasing a similar piece of equipment from the Lafayette Instrument Company.

The experimenter must be able to clearly convey such information about all the variables involved in a research project. Hence, it is crucial that operational definitions be given for independent, dependent, and extraneous variables.

Operational definition Defining the independent, dependent, and extraneous variables in terms of the operations needed to produce them.

Independent variable A variable that is directly manipulated by the experimenter to determine its influence on behavior.

INDEPENDENT VARIABLES

As you saw in Chapter 2, **independent variables** (IVs) are those variables that are purposely manipulated by the experimenter.

The IV constitutes the reason that the research is being conducted; the experimenter is interested in determining what effect the IV has. The term *independent* is used because the IV does not depend on other variables; it stands alone. A few examples of IVs that have been used in psychological research are sleep deprivation, temperature, noise level, drug type (or dosage level), removal of a portion of the brain, and psychological context. Rather than attempting to list all possible IVs, it is easier to indicate that they tend to cluster in several general categories.

TYPES OF IVs

Physiological. When the participants in an experiment are subjected to conditions that alter or change their normal biological state, a **physiological IV** is being employed. For example, Susan Nash (1983), a student at Emporia State University in Emporia, KS, obtained several pregnant rats from an animal supplier. Upon arrival at the laboratory, half of the rats were randomly assigned to receive an alcohol-water mixture during gestation; the remainder received plain tap water. The alcohol-exposed mothers were switched to plain tap water when the pups were born. Thus, some rat pups were exposed to alcohol during gestation, whereas others were not. Susan tested all the pups for alcohol preference when they were adults and found that those animals that were exposed to alcohol (the physiological IV) during gestation drank more alcohol as adults. Susan received the 1983 J. P. Guilford–Psi Chi National Undergraduate Research Award for this experiment. Just as alcohol exposure was the physiological IV in Susan's experiment, the administration of a new drug to determine whether it is successful in alleviating schizophrenic symptoms also represents the use of a physiological IV.

Experience. When the effects of amount or type of previous training or learning are the central focus of the research, an **experience IV** is being employed. A study conducted by Robert Waterman, a student at Texas Lutheran University in Seguin, TX, illustrates the use of experience as an IV. Waterman (1993) predicted that experience playing a video game that involved rotating two-dimensional spatial figures would increase scores on a test of spatial ability. Initially all the participants completed the test of spatial ability, then half the participants played the video game Tetris for 45 minutes twice a week for two weeks. All participants then retook the spatial ability test. The results indicated that the video-game experience did not increase spatial ability scores. (It is important to keep in mind the fact that even though research may not always yield the results you predict or anticipate, it always provides valuable information.)

Stimulus. Some IVs fall into the category of **stimulus or environmental** variables. When this type of IV is used, some aspect of the environment is being manipulated.

Linda Grunchla, Mary Rose Hegarty, Amy Himmegar, and Renee Hollett (students at Southern Illinois University—Edwardsville, IL) conducted a study under the direction of Dr. Mark Hostetter in which a stimulus IV was used (Grunchla, Hegarty,

Himmegar, Hollett, & Hostetter, 1993). In an attempt to determine whether the type of auditory background influences reading comprehension, these researchers randomly assigned 65 undergraduate students to four groups. One group listened to light rock vocals while reading an assigned passage; two other groups listened to rap music and television audio background, respectively, while reading the passage. The fourth group read the passage in silence. The results indicated that the television audio background significantly impaired reading comprehension when compared to silence and light rock vocals. Rap music was no more advantageous to comprehension than was silence. In this experiment, the type of auditory background experienced by the participants was a stimulus IV.

Participant. It is common to find **participant characteristics**, such as age, sex, personality traits, or academic major, being treated as if they were IVs.

Psychological Detective

Although many researchers may treat participant characteristics as if they are IVs, they really are not. Why? Give this question some thought and write your answers down before reading further.

To be considered an IV, the behavior or event in question must be directly manipulated by the experimenter. Although experimenters can manipulate physiological, experience, and stimulus IVs, they are not able to directly manipulate participant characteristics. Thus, experimenters do not consider them to be true IVs. The experimenter does not create the participants' gender or cause participants to be a certain age. Thus, participant characteristics or variables are best viewed as classification, *not* manipulation, variables. The categories for participant variables are created before the experiment is conducted, and the experimenter simply assigns the participants to these categories on the basis of the characteristics they display.

Participant characteristics
Aspects of the participant, such as age, sex, and/or personality traits, that are treated as if they are IVs.

Dependent variable
A response or behavior that is measured. It is desired that changes in the dependent variable be directly related to manipulation of the independent variable.

DEPENDENT VARIABLES

The **dependent variable** (DV) changes as a function of the levels of the IV; thus, the DV truly *depends on* the IV. The DV consists of the data or results of our experiment. As with all aspects of psychological research, the experimenter must give the DV appropriate consideration when the experiment is being formulated. Such considerations as selecting the appropriate DV, deciding exactly which measure of the DV will be used, and whether to record more than one DV must be dealt with.

definition

Selecting the DV

Because **psychology** often is defined as the **science of** *behavior*, the **DV** typically consists of **some type of behavior or response**. However, when the IV is administered, it is likely that several responses will occur. Which one should be selected as the DV? One answer to this question is to look carefully at the experimental hypothesis. Assuming that you have stated your **hypothesis** in general implication (**"if ... then,"** see Chapter 2) form, the "then" portion of the hypothesis will give you an idea of the general nature of your DV. For example, Robert Waterman (1993) might have proposed the following experimental hypothesis in his study of the effects of playing video games:

> If one group of participants receives practice on a video game that requires two-dimensional rotation, then their scores on a test of spatial ability will be higher than the scores of participants who do not receive such practice.

In this case the DV is clearly specified as "scores on a test of spatial abilities." What if his hypothesis were more general and indicated only that the "spatial abilities" of the video-game players would be superior to those of the non-video-game players? Where could he find information to help him choose a specific DV? Hopefully, you are already a step ahead of us and have said that our literature review (see Chapter 2) can provide valuable guidelines. If a particular response has been used successfully as a DV in previous research, then chances are good that it will be a good choice again. Another reason for using a DV that has been used previously is that you will have a comparison for your own results. Although totally different DVs may provide exciting new information, the ability to relate the results of different experiments is made more difficult.

Recording or Measuring the DV

Once you have selected the DV, you will have to decide exactly how it will be measured or recorded. Several possibilities exist.

Correctness. Consider that you are conducting an experiment to determine whether a rote memory or guided imagery method of teaching classical conditioning is best. Quite likely your measure of success will be how the students in the two groups perform on a test covering this material. You will evaluate the effectiveness of the two teaching methods based on whether the answers to the test (your DV) are correct or incorrect.

Rate or Frequency. If you are studying the lever-pressing performance of a rat or pigeon in an operant conditioning chamber (Skinner box), then your DV is likely to be the rate of responding that is shown. Rate of responding determines how rapidly responses are made during a specified time period. Your data will be plotted in the form of a cumulative record with steeper slopes representing higher rates (i.e., large numbers of responses being made in shorter periods of time). Figure 4-1 shows some different rates of responding.

If you are studying the number of interactions made by children during free play at a kindergarten, you may want to record frequency, rather than the rate of responding. Hence, your DV would simply be the number of responses that are shown during a specified time period without any concern for how rapidly the responses are made.

Degree or Amount. Often the DV is not measured in terms of correctness or rate/frequency but in terms of degree or amount. An experiment conducted by Kristine Martin, Sue Farruggia, and Kyle Yeske (1993), students at Saint Mary's College of Minnesota, illustrates this type of DV measurement. These students were interested in evaluating changes in anxiety produced by exposing participants to high-stress conditions. College students completed Spielberger's State-Trait Anxiety Inventory before a normal class session (low-stress condition) *and* before a classroom examination (high-stress condition). The results of this experiment indicated that trait anxiety (more permanent emotional arousal) did not differ between the two situations, but that state anxiety (temporary emotional arousal) was significantly higher before the classroom examination than before the regular class session. In this situation, the measurement of anxiety (the DV) was in terms of degree or amount.

Latency or Duration. In many situations, such as studies of learning and memory, how quickly a response is made (latency) and/or how long the response lasts (duration) are of particular interest. If

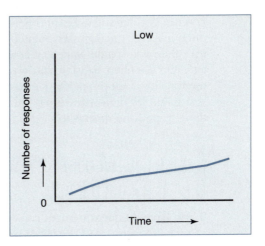

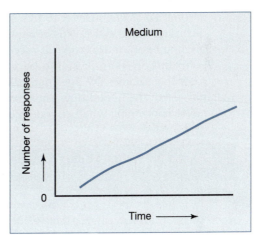

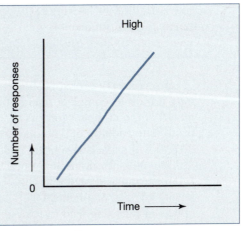

FIGURE 4-1. DIFFERENT RATES OF RESPONDING.

you are conducting an experiment on reversed eye-hand coordination (this task often involves tracing a six-pointed star pattern by looking at its reflection in a mirror), then you would want to record the latency (in seconds) taken to complete the task. On the other hand, if you were interested in the effect(s) of different types of reinforcement on the performance of a boring task, such as sealing envelopes, then you might be more concerned with how long (duration) the participants will continue to perform this task.

SHOULD MORE THAN ONE DV BE RECORDED?

If you have the measurement capabilities, there is nothing to prohibit the recording of more than one DV. Possibly additional data will strengthen your knowledge claim in the same way it might strengthen a detective's case. Should you record additional DVs? The answer to this question really boils down to deciding whether recording additional DVs is going to add appreciably to your understanding of the phenomenon under study. If recording an additional DV(s) makes a meaningful contribution, then it should be given serious consideration. If measuring and recording another DV does not make a substantive contribution, then it is probably not worth the added time and trouble. Often previous research can be used as a guide concerning whether you should consider recording more than one DV.

Psychological Detective

Consider the reversed eye-hand coordination (mirror-tracing) experiment mentioned above. In this experiment the time taken to complete a tracing (a latency DV) was recorded. Is this DV sufficient to give you a good, complete picture of the performance of this task; should another DV also be recorded? Give this question some thought and write down your answer before reading further.

A second DV probably should be recorded. The latency DV indicates *only* how long it took to complete tracing the star pattern. Hence, the experimenter has no record of the number of errors (going beyond the boundaries of the figure) that are made. The addition of a second DV that measures the number of errors (a frequency DV) will make a significant contribution to this experiment.

The need for more than one DV was seen in an experiment conducted by Sara L. Armstrong and Matthew Huss (students at Emporia State University) and their faculty advisor, Stephen Davis. These researchers were interested in the behavioral effects of ingesting lead (a toxic metal commonly found in the environment). Two groups of rats served as participants; one group was exposed to lead in their drinking water, whereas the other group drank plain tap water. Subsequently, both groups were tested for aggressiveness. The number of aggressive responses (a frequency DV) and the total time of aggression (a duration DV) were recorded for each participant. What additional information was gained by recording these two DVs? If both DVs were not recorded, the experimenters could not determine whether differences between the groups were due to the number of responses, the average duration of each response, or both factors. The results indicated that the lead-exposed animals made significantly more *and* significantly longer aggressive responses (Davis, Armstrong, & Huss, 1993).

CHARACTERISTICS OF A GOOD DV

Although considerable thought may go into deciding exactly how the DV will be measured and recorded and whether more than one DV should be recorded, the experimenter still has no guarantee that a good DV(s) has been selected. What constitutes a good DV? In Chapter 3 we saw that a good test or inventory must be valid and reliable. Because tests and inventories are designed to *measure or evaluate* some aspect of the participant, it should come as no surprise that the DV in an experiment shares the same characteristics. In other words, the DV is valid when it measures what the experimental hypothesis says it should measure. For example, assume that you are interested in studying intelligence as a function of differences in regional diet. You believe that the basic diet consumed by people living in different regions of the United States results in differences in intelligence. You devise a new intelligence test and set off to test your hypothesis. As the results of your project start to take shape, you notice that the scores from the Northeast are higher than those from other sections of the country; your hypothesis appears to be supported. However, a closer inspection of the results indicates that only certain questions are missed by participants not living in the Northeast. Are all the questions fair and unbiased, or do some favor northeasterners? How many individuals from Arizona are familiar with blueberries or subways? Thus, your DV (scores on the intelligence test) may have a regional bias and may not be measuring the participants' intelligence consistently from region to region. A good DV must be directly related to the IV and measure the effects of the IV manipulation as the experimental hypothesis predicts it will.

A good DV also is reliable. If the scores on an intelligence test are used as the DV, then we would expect to see similar scores when the test is again administered under the same IV conditions (test-retest procedure; see Chapter 3).

Although it appears that the IV and the DV are the only important variables in the development and conduct of an experiment, there is a third category of variables that the experimenter must be *acutely* aware of. We turn our attention to extraneous variables.

EXTRANEOUS VARIABLES ⸻

As we saw in Chapter 1, **extraneous variables** are those factors that can have an *unintended* influence on the results of our experiment. In order to have clear and accurate results, it is impera-

Extraneous variables Variables that may unintentionally operate to influence the dependent variable.

definition

tive that extraneous variables be controlled. The types of control employed by psychologists will be presented later in this chapter; in this section we examine two main types of extraneous variables, nuisance variables and confounders.

NUISANCE VARIABLES

Nuisance variables are either characteristics of the participants or unintended influences of the experimental situation that make the effects of the IV more difficult to see or determine. It is important to understand that nuisance variables influence *all* groups in an experiment; their influence is not limited just to one specific group. When they are present, nuisance variables result in greater variability in the DV; the scores *within* each group spread out more. For example, assume that you are interested in studying reading comprehension. Can you think of a participant characteristic that might be related to reading comprehension? How about intelligence or IQ?

Figure 4-2, Part A, shows the spread of the reading comprehension scores within a group when there are not wide differences in intelligence among the participants within the group. In this instance a nuisance variable is *not* operating. You can see how the majority of the comprehension scores are similar and cluster in the middle of the distribution; there are relatively few extremely low and extremely high scores. Figure 4-2, Part B, shows the distribution of comprehension scores when there are wide differences in intelligence (i.e., a nuisance variable is present). Notice that the scores are more spread out; there are fewer scores in the middle of the distribution and more scores in the extremes.

How does a nuisance variable influence the results of an experiment? To answer that question we need to add another group of participants to our example and conduct a simple experiment. Imagine that in our experiment, we are evaluating two methods for teaching reading comprehension—the standard method and a new method. Look at Figure 4-3, Part A. Here we are comparing two groups that have not been influenced by the nuisance variable; the difference between these two groups is pronounced. Let's add the effects of a nuisance variable to each group and then compare the groups. As you can see in Figure 4-3, Part B, when

Psychological Detective

For each example indicate the nuisance variable and its effect. Write your answers before reading further.

1. An experimenter is measures reaction time in participants ranging in age from 12 to 78 years.

2. The ability of participants to recall a list of words is being studied in a room that is located by the elevator shaft.

3. The laboratory where participants are tested for manual dexterity has frequent, unpredictable changes in temperature.

the scores spread out more, there is greater overlap and the difference between the groups is not as distinct and clear as when the nuisance variable was not present. When a nuisance variable is present, our view is clouded; we are unable to see clearly the difference the IV may have created between the groups in our experiment. Notice that when the nuisance variable was added (Fig. 4-3, Part B), the *only* thing that happened was that the scores spread out in both extremes of each distribution—the relative location of the distributions did not change. *Nuisance variables increase the spread of scores within a distribution; they do not cause a distribution to change its location.*

In the first situation, the wide age range is the nuisance variable. The younger participants should display faster reaction times than the older participants. Thus the scores will spread into both ends of the distribution. The change in noise level

FIGURE 4-2.

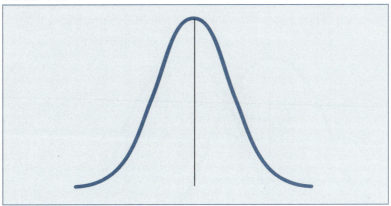

A. The spread of scores within a group when a nuisance variable is not operating.

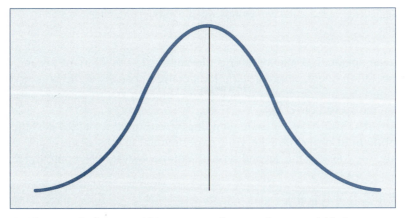

B. The spread of scores within a group when a nuisance variable is operating.

FIGURE 4-3.

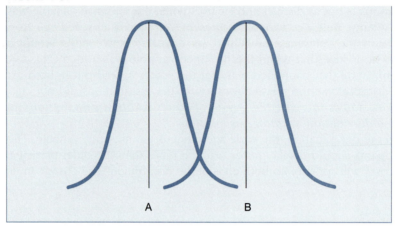

A. A comparison of two groups when a nuisance variable is not operating.

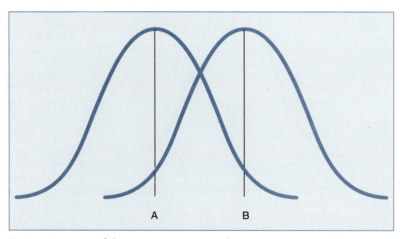

B. A comparison of the same two groups when a nuisance variable is operating.

due to the operation of the elevator is the nuisance variable in the second example, whereas the frequent, unpredictable temperature changes is the nuisance variable in the third example; in both examples the change in environmental conditions will increase the spread of scores.

Now that you have an understanding of nuisance variables and the need to control them in order to make your experimental results as clear and distinct as possible, we consider the second type of extraneous variable, confounders.

CONFOUNDERS

Whereas a nuisance variable influences all participants in an experiment and causes the scores to spread out within the groups, a confounder influences the difference *between* groups. Figure 4-4, Part A, shows the relationship of two groups without the influence of a confounder; two possible effects of a confounder are shown in Figure 4-4, Parts B and C. Thus, a **confounder** can unintentionally cause groups to move closer together (Fig. 4-4, Part B) or farther apart (Fig. 4-4, Part C).

Confounder
Extraneous variables that can cause the difference *between* groups to change.

definition

Psychological Detective

Review Figure 4-4 and the information we have presented about confounders. The effect of a confounder is similar to that of another major component of the experiment. What role does a confounder appear to play in an experiment? How is the presence of a confounder detrimental to the experiment? Give these questions some thought and write down your answers before reading further.

The only other component of an experiment that can influence the difference between groups is the IV. Thus, a confounder affects the outcome of an experiment in the same manner as the IV. Just as other likely interpretations can damage a detective's case beyond repair, the presence of a confounder is devastating to research; the results of an experiment are completely invalidated. Why? There are two variables that may have caused the groups to differ: the IV you manipulated *and* the unwanted confounder. You have no way to determine which of these two variables caused the differences you observed. When an experiment is confounded, the best course of action is to discontinue the research and profit from your mistake. The confounder can be controlled in the next experiment.

To illustrate how a confounder works, we will use our reading comprehension study once again. We have first- and second-graders available to serve as participants. All the first-graders are assigned to the standard method for teaching reading comprehension, whereas all the second-graders are assigned to the new method. The experiment is conducted and we find that the comprehension scores for students using the new method are substantially better than those of students using the standard method (see Figure 4-4, Part C). What would have happened if the second-graders had been assigned to the standard method and the first-graders to the new method? We might have seen results like those of Figure 4-4, Part B. Why did these two sets of results occur? In each instance it is arguable that preexisting differences in reading comprehension between the two groups acted as an IV. Assuming that second-graders have superior reading comprehension, it seems reasonable to suggest that the new method seemed even more effective when the second-graders used it (i.e., the difference between the groups was exaggerated). However, when the second-graders used the standard method, their superior ability (rather than the method) increased the scores and moved the groups closer together (i.e., group differences decreased). Certainly, all of this commentary is only

FIGURE 4-4.

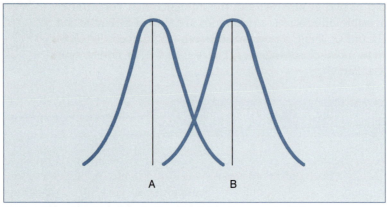

A. The difference (A = Standard method; B = New method) between two groups with no confounder operating.

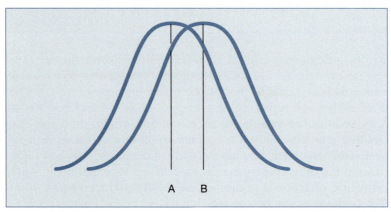

B. The difference between two groups when a confounder is present and has moved the groups closer together.

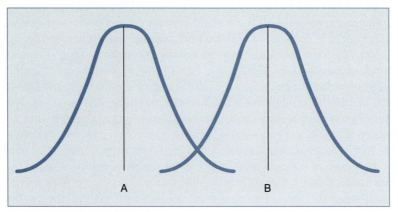

C. The difference between two groups when a confounder is present and has moved the groups farther apart.

speculation on our part. It is just as likely that the IV created the group differences that we observed. The main point is that we really do not know what caused the differences—the IV (type of method used) or the confounder (grade level).

The presence of a confounder is often very difficult to spot. It may take several knowledgeable individuals scrutinizing an experiment from every possible angle to determine whether a confounder is present. If a confounder is detected *before* the experiment is conducted, then it can be dealt with and the experiment can proceed. Techniques for controlling confounders and reducing the effects of nuisance variables are presented in the next section.

REVIEW SUMMARY

1. A **variable** is an event or behavior that can assume at least two levels.
2. **Independent variables** (IVs) are purposely manipulated by the experimenter and form the core or purpose of the experiment. **Physiological IVs** refer to changes in the biological state of the participants, whereas **experience IVs** refer to manipulations of previous experience or learning. **Stimulus IVs** are manipulations in some aspect of the environment.
3. Whereas participant characteristics such as age, gender, and/or personality traits are often treated as IVs, technically they are not IVs because they are not directly manipulated by the experimenter.
4. The **dependent variable** (DV) changes as a function of changes in the IV. The experimental hypothesis can provide possible guidelines concerning the selection of the DV. Past research also can assist the experimenter in selecting the DV.
5. The DV can be recorded in terms of correctness, rate or frequency, degree or amount, and latency or duration. If additional information will be gained, the experimenter should consider recording more than one DV. A good DV is directly related to the IV (valid) and reliable.
6. **Extraneous variables** are those factors that can have an unintended influence on the results of an experiment. **Nuisance variables** are extraneous variables that increase the variability of scores *within* groups, whereas **confounders** are extraneous variables that influence the differences *between* groups. The presence of nuisance variables makes the results of an experiment less clear; the presence of a confounder invalidates the experiment.

STUDY BREAK

1. An event or behavior that can assume at least two values is a_____ .
2. Matching
    1. DV
    2. extraneous variable

    A. change in normal biological state
    B. manipulation of environment

3. physiological IV
4. experience IV
5. stimulus IV
6. participant variable

C. can damage the experiment and its results
D. age
E. changes as a function of changes in IV
F. amount of previous learning

3. Describe the four ways to measure or record a DV.

4. You should record more than one DV under what conditions?

5. Distinguish between nuisance variables and confounders. Which is more damaging to the experiment? Why?

CONTROLLING EXTRANEOUS VARIABLES

definition

Randomization
A control technique that ensures that each participant has an equal chance of being assigned to any group in an experiment.

The experimenter must exercise control over both nuisance variables and confounders so that the results of the experiment are as clear (minimal influence of nuisance variables) and meaningful (no confounders present) as possible. When you are dealing with a variable that can be clearly specified and quantified (e.g., gender, age, educational level, temperature, lighting intensity, or noise level), then one of the five basic control techniques should be applicable. These five basic control techniques—randomization, elimination, constancy, balancing, and counterbalancing—are described in the next section.

BASIC CONTROL TECHNIQUES

As we discuss the basic control techniques, it is important to keep in mind that their goals are to (a) reduce the effects of nuisance variables as much as possible and (b) produce groups that are equivalent prior to the introduction of the IV, thereby eliminating confounders.

Randomization. We begin our discussion of control with randomization because it is the most widely used technique. **Randomization** is a control technique that guarantees that each participant has an equal chance of being assigned to any group in the experiment. The logic behind the use of randomization is as follows. Because all participants have an equal likelihood of being selected for each group in an experiment, any unique characteristics associated with the participants should be equally distributed across all groups that are formed. Consider level of motivation, for example. Although it may not be feasible to measure each participant's level of motivation, this variable can still be controlled by randomly forming the groups in our experiment. Just by chance we would expect that *each* group would have some participants who are highly motivated, some participants who are moderately motivated, and some participants who are barely motivated. Thus, the groups should be equated with regard to the average level of motivation, as well as the myriad of other unknown and unsuspected extraneous variables that might be present. Because we are never fully aware of the variables that randomization controls and thus do not know whether these variables are distributed evenly to all groups, we cannot be sure that this control technique is effective. It *is* possible that all the highly motivated participants will be randomly assigned to the same group.

Psychological Detective

Even though it is the most widely used control procedure, randomization has one major drawback. What is this drawback? Give this question some thought and write down an answer before reading further.

To answer this question, you need to consider what is being controlled when randomization is employed. If you find yourself having some difficulty specifying exactly what is controlled by randomization, then you are on the right track. Randomization is used as a control technique for all variables that *might* be present that the experimenter is unaware of. If the experimenter is unaware of exactly which variables are being controlled and how effective the control is, then it should come as no surprise that the experimenter is never *completely* sure how effective randomization has been.

Elimination. When the extraneous variable(s) is(are) known, our approach can be more direct. For example, we might choose to completely remove or **eliminate the unwanted variable**. Sounds easy, but in practice you may find it quite difficult to *completely* remove a variable.

Let's consider two experiments. In the first experiment, one group of participants is always tested between 8:00 A.M. and 9:00 A.M. at the peak of rush-hour traffic; the noise is deafening. By 9:00 A.M., when the second group is tested, traffic noise is *much lower*. In this experiment, noise functions as a confounder; the first group experiences excessive noise, but the second one does not. In the second situation, an experiment is being conducted in the basement of the oldest building on campus. It's winter and the unpredictable, bone-jarring rattle of the heating pipes frequently interrupts the experiment at unexpected times. In this situation noise serves as a nuisance variable; its unpredictable application ensures that all participants may be influenced. Whether noise functions as a confounder (first experiment) or a nuisance variable (second experiment), let's see if elimination can be used to control it. To completely eliminate noise, we would have to conduct our experiment inside a specially constructed chamber where there are *no* sounds other than those you make yourself. Such an environment is known as an anechoic chamber, and it is so quiet inside that you can actually hear your own heart beating! Yes, it may be most difficult to *completely* eliminate an extraneous variable such as noise. In the case of an extraneous variable such as lighting conditions, it may not be practical to completely eliminate the extraneous variable; few experiments are conducted in absolute darkness.

Elimination
A control technique whereby extraneous variables are completely removed from an experiment.

definition

definition

Constancy
A control technique by which an extraneous variable is reduced to a single value that is experienced by all participants.

When the extraneous variable in question consists of an entire category of events, such as noise, temperature, or lighting condition, it may be difficult to eliminate. However, if the extraneous variable is a specific occurrence within one of these more general categories, such as temperatures above 80 degrees, then it may be possible to eliminate that aspect of the variable. In this situation, however, the interest of the experimenter is not just on eliminating a variable but also on producing and maintaining a constant condition under which the participants in the experiment are tested.

Constancy. When it is difficult or impossible to completely eliminate an extraneous variable, the experimenter may choose to exercise control by creating a uniform or constant condition that is experienced by all participants. **Constancy** has become a standard control technique for many researchers. For example, experimental testing may take place in the same room, with the same lighting and temperature levels, at the same time of day each day that the experiment is conducted. In this instance the location of the experiment, the temperature level, the lighting level, and the time of day have not been eliminated but, rather, have assumed a constant value.

Psychological Detective

Juan and Nancy are interested in determining which of two methods of teaching psychological statistics is best. Two statistics classes are available: Juan teaches one method to one class, while Nancy teaches the second method to the other class. This experiment is confounded because Juan and Nancy each taught one of the classes and it is impossible to tell whether differences between the classes are due to the method or the teacher. How would you use constancy to control this extraneous variable? Give this question some thought and write down your answer before reading further.

The easiest approach would be to have only one of the experimenters, Juan or Nancy, teach both classes. Thus, the extraneous variable, teacher, is the same for both classes and the experiment is no longer confounded.

By making sure that the experimental testing conditions do not vary unpredictably, constancy also is used to control for nuisance variables. When the testing conditions are the same from testing session to testing session, there is greater likelihood that the scores within the groups will not spread out as much. Constancy can also control nuisance variable effects that are produced by participant variables such as age, gender, and educational level. Recall that wide variations in such participant variables may result in greater spread of scores within the groups. If the technique of stratified random sampling (see Chapter 3) is employed, then the variability among the participants' scores should be smaller because the participants are more homogeneous. In such instances constancy is created by randomly sampling only a certain type of participant, such as first-year college women between the ages of 18 and 19.

Although constancy can be an effective control technique, there are situations where the extraneous variable(s) cannot be reduced to a single value that is experienced by all participants in the experiment. What can be done in those instances where the extraneous variable assumes two or more values? The answer may lie in the control technique known as balancing.

Balancing. Balancing represents a logical extension of control through constancy. Thus, the groups in our experiment are said to be balanced or equivalent when each group experiences all extraneous variables in the same manner or to the same degree.

In the simplest example of balancing we would test two groups; one group (the experimental group) would receive the IV, while the second group (the control or comparison group) would be treated identically but would not receive the IV. If the groups were balanced or equated with regard to extraneous variables, then we could tentatively conclude that differences between them were caused by the IV. This general situation is diagrammed in Table 4-1.

When the potential extraneous variables, such as various personality differences in human participants, are unknown, randomization is used to form balanced groups and we assume that the respective extraneous variables have been distributed equally to all groups. When the extraneous variables, such as sex of the experimenter, are known, then the experimenter can be more systematic in the use of balancing.

Psychological Detective

Let's assume that all the students included in Juan and Nancy's experiment cannot be taught by one teacher; two are needed. How could balancing be used to remove the potential confounding due to a different teacher teaching each of the new methods? Give this question some thought and write down your answer (a diagram will do fine) before reading further.

As you can see in Table 4-2, an easy solution to their problem is to have Juan and Nancy each teach half the students under *each* method. Thus, the two teachers appear equally under each teaching method and the classes are balanced with regard to that potential confounding variable. This teaching example illustrates the simplest situation in which balancing is used to control one extraneous variable. Balancing can be used with several extraneous variables (see Table 4-1); the only requirement is that each extraneous variable appear to the same extent in each group.

Balancing A control procedure that achieves group equality by distributing extraneous variables equally to all groups.

definition

TABLE 4-1. BALANCED EXTRANEOUS VARIABLES	
When the extraneous variables are experienced in the same manner, the groups are said to be balanced.	
GROUP 1	GROUP 2
Treatment	Treatment
Ext. Var. 1	Ext. Var. 1
Ext. Var. 2	Ext. Var. 2
Ext. Var. 3	Ext. Var. 3
Ext. Var. 4	Ext. Var. 4

TABLE 4-2. USING BALANCING TO ELIMINATE CONFOUNDING IN TEACHING TWO METHODS OF PSYCHOLOGICAL STATISTICS	
JUAN	NANCY
25 students → Method 1	25 students → Method 1
25 students → Method 2	25 students → Method 2

Although elimination, constancy, and balancing offer the experimenter powerful control techniques, they are not able to deal with all control problems. In the next section we examine one of these problem situations, sequencing or order, and how to control it through counterbalancing.

Counterbalancing. In some experiments participants are required to participate in more than one experimental condition. For example, you might want to conduct a "cola taste test" to determine which of two brands of cola is most preferred. As you set up your tasting booth at the local mall, you are sure you have taken all the right precautions: The tasting cups are all the same, the two colas will be poured from identical containers, the participants will consume the same amount of Cola A and Cola B (in that order), and the participants will be blindfolded during the test so color differences will not influence their choice. Yes, your control seems to be perfect. Is it?

Psychological Detective

Review the experiment we have just described and write down your answers to the following questions before reading further. What control procedures are being used? There is a problem that has been overlooked that needs to be controlled. What is this problem and how might it be controlled?

Constancy is achieved by ensuring that (a) the tasting cups are the same, (b) the colas are poured from similar containers, and (c) all participants consume the same amount of each cola. By blindfolding the participants, you have *eliminated* any problems that may be caused by differences in the visual appearance of the two colas. These are all relevant control procedures. The problem we overlooked concerns the sequence or order for sampling the two colas. If Cola A is always sampled before Cola B and one cola is liked more, you cannot be sure the preference is due to its great flavor or the fact that the colas were always sampled in the same order and this order may have influenced the participant's reactions. The technique used when a sequence or order effect must be controlled is known as **counterbalancing.** There are two types of counterbalancing, within-subject and within-group. **Within-subject counterbalancing** attempts to control the sequence effect within each participant, whereas **within-group counterbalancing** attempts to control this problem by presenting different sequences to different participants.

Counterbalancing
A procedure for controlling order effects by presenting different treatment sequences.

Within-subject counterbalancing
Presentation of different treatment sequences to the same participant.

Within-group counterbalancing
Presentation of different treatment sequences to different participants.

definition

Within-Subject Counterbalancing. Returning to the problem of sequence in our cola challenge, we could deal with this problem by having each participant sample the two colas in the following sequence: ABBA. By using within-subject counterbalancing, *each* participant will taste Cola A once before *and* once after tasting Cola B. Thus, the experience of having tasted Cola A first is counterbalanced by tasting Cola A last. If we had tested three colas and used within-subject counterbalancing, the sequence for each participant would have been ABCCBA.

Although it may be relatively easy to implement within-subject counterbalancing, there is one major drawback to its use: Each participant is required to experience each condition more than once. In some situations the experimenter may not want or be able to present the treatments more than once to each participant. For example, you may not have sufficient time to conduct your cola challenge and allow each participant the opportunity to sample each brand of cola more than once. In such instances within-group counterbalancing may offer a better control alternative.

Within-Group Counterbalancing. Another way to deal with the cola challenge sequencing problem is to randomly assign half the participants to experience the two colas in the Cola A → Cola B sequence and the remaining half of the participants to receive the Cola B → Cola A sequence. The preference of participants who tasted Cola A before Cola B could be compared with the preference of the participants who tasted Cola B first.

Assuming that we tested six participants, the within-subject counterbalanced presentation of the two colas would be diagrammed as shown in Table 4-3. As you can see, three participants receive the A → B sequence, whereas three participants receive the B → A sequence. This basic diagram illustrates the three requirements of within-subject counterbalancing:

1. ***Each treatment must be presented to each participant an equal number of times.*** In this example each participant tastes Cola A once and Cola B once.

TABLE 4-3. COUNTERBALANCING FOR THE TWO-COLA CHALLENGE WHEN SIX PARTICIPANTS ARE TESTED		
	TASTING 1	**TASTING 2**
Participant 1	A	B
Participant 2	A	B
Participant 3	A	B
Participant 4	B	A
Participant 5	B	A
Participant 6	B	A

2. **Each treatment must occur an equal number of times at each testing or practice session.** Notice that Cola A is sampled three times at Tasting 1 and three times at Tasting 2.

3. **Each treatment must precede and follow each of the other treatments an equal number of times.** In this example Cola A is tasted first three times and is tasted second three times.

Counterbalancing is not limited to two-treatment sequences. For example, let's assume that your cola challenge involves three colas instead of two. The counterbalancing that will be needed in that situation is diagrammed in Table 4-4A. Carefully examine this diagram. Does it satisfy the requirements for counterbalancing? It appears that all the requirements have been met. Each cola is tasted an equal number of times (six), is tasted an equal number of times (twice) at each tasting session, and precedes and follows each of the other colas an equal number of times (twice). It is important to note that if we want to test more participants, they will have to be added in multiples of six. The addition of any other number of participants violates the rules of counterbalancing by creating a situation where one cola is tasted more than the others, appears more often at one tasting session(s) than the others, and/or does not precede and follow the other colas an equal number of times. Try adding only one or two participants to Table 4-4A to see if you can satisfy the requirements for counterbalancing.

Table 4-4 also illustrates another consideration that must be taken into account when counterbalancing is used. When only a few treatments are used, the number of different sequences that will have to be administered remains relatively small and counterbalancing is manageable. When we tested two colas, only two sequences were involved (see Table 4-3); however, the addition of only one more cola resulted in the addition of 4 sequences (see Table 4-4, Part A). If we added an additional cola to our challenge (Colas A, B, C, and D), we would now have to administer a total of 24 different sequences (see Table 4-4, Part B) and our experiment would be much more complex to conduct! Our minimum number of participants would be 24 and if we wanted to test more than 1 participant per sequence, participants would have to be added in multiples of 24.

TABLE 4-4. COUNTERBALANCING FOR THE THREE- AND FOUR-COLA CHALLENGES

A. COUNTERBALANCING FOR THE THREE-COLA CHALLENGE WHEN SIX PARTICIPANTS ARE TESTED

	Tasting Session		
	1	*2*	*3*
Participant 1	A	B	C
Participant 2	A	C	B
Participant 3	B	A	C
Participant 4	B	C	A
Participant 5	C	A	B
Participant 6	C	B	A

B. COUNTERBALANCING FOR THE FOUR-COLA CHALLENGE

	Tasting Session			
	1	*2*	*3*	*4*
Participant 1	A	B	C	D
Participant 2	A	B	D	C
Participant 3	A	C	B	D
Participant 4	A	C	D	B
Participant 5	A	D	B	C
Participant 6	A	D	C	B
Participant 7	B	A	C	D
Participant 8	B	A	D	C
Participant 9	B	C	A	D
Participant 10	B	C	D	A
Participant 11	B	D	A	C
Participant 12	B	D	C	A
Participant 13	C	A	B	D
Participant 14	C	A	D	B
Participant 15	C	B	A	D
Participant 16	C	B	D	A
Participant 17	C	D	A	B
Participant 18	C	D	B	A
Participant 19	D	A	B	C
Participant 20	D	A	C	B
Participant 21	D	B	A	C
Participant 22	D	B	C	A
Participant 23	D	C	A	B
Participant 24	D	C	B	A

How do you know how many sequences will be required? Do you have to write down all the possible sequences to find out how many there are? No. You can calculate the total number of sequences by using the formula $n!$ (n factorial). All that is required is to take the number of treatments (n) and then factor or break that number down into its component parts and then multiply these factors or components. Thus,

$$2! \text{ would be } 2 \times 1 = 2$$
$$3! \text{ would be } 3 \times 2 \times 1 = 6, \text{ and}$$
$$4! \text{ would be } 4 \times 3 \times 2 \times 1 = 24,$$

Complete counterbalancing
All possible treatment sequences are presented.

Incomplete counterbalancing
Only a portion of all possible sequences are presented.

and so forth. When you can administer all possible sequences, **complete counterbalancing** is being used. Although complete counterbalancing offers the best control for sequence or order effects, often it cannot be attained when several treatments are included in the experiment. As we just saw, the use of four colas would require a minimum of 24 participants ($4! = 4 \times 3 \times 2 \times 1 = 24$) for complete counterbalancing. Testing five colas would increase the number of sequences (and the minimum number of participants) to 120 ($5! = 5 \times 4 \times 3 \times 2 \times 1 = 120$). In situations requiring a large number of participants to implement complete counterbalancing, either you can reduce the number of treatments until your time, financial, and participant resources allow complete counterbalancing, or you can complete the experiment without completely counterbalancing.

Incomplete counterbalancing refers to the use of some, but not all, of the possible sequences. Which sequences are to be used and which ones are to be excluded? Some experimenters randomly select the sequences they will employ. Once the number of participants to be tested has been determined, the experimenter randomly selects an equal number of sequences. For example, Table 4-5 illustrates the random selection of sequences for conducting the cola challenge with four colas and only 12 participants. Although random selection appears to be an easy approach to the use of incomplete counterbalancing, there is a problem. If you examine Table 4-5 carefully, you will see that although each participant receives each

TABLE 4-5. RANDOMLY SELECTED TESTING SEQUENCES FOR THE FOUR-COLA CHALLENGE USING 12 PARTICIPANTS

	TESTING SESSION			
	1	*2*	*3*	*4*
Participant 1	A	B	C	D
Participant 2	A	B	D	C
Participant 3	A	C	D	B
Participant 4	A	D	C	B
Participant 5	B	A	C	D
Participant 6	B	C	D	A
Participant 7	B	C	A	D
Participant 8	C	A	B	D
Participant 9	C	B	A	D
Participant 10	C	D	B	A
Participant 11	D	B	C	A
Participant 12	D	C	B	A

treatment an equal number of times, the other requirements for counterbalancing are not satisfied. Each treatment does not appear an equal number of times at each testing or practice session, and each treatment does not precede and follow each of the other treatments an equal number of times.

There are two approaches that can be adopted to resolve this problem, although neither one is completely satisfactory. We could randomly determine the treatment sequence for the first participant and then systematically rotate the sequence for the remaining participants. This approach is diagrammed in Table 4-6. Thus, the first participant would taste the colas in the order B, D, A, C, while the second participant would experience them in the order D, A, C, B. We would continue systematically rotating the sequence until each cola appears once in each row and each column. To test a total of 12 participants, 3 participants would be assigned to each of the four sequences. By ensuring that each treatment appears an equal number of times at each testing session, this approach comes close to satisfying the conditions for counterbalancing. It does not, however, ensure that the treatments precede and follow each other an equal number of times. A more complex procedure, the Latin square technique, is used to address this issue. Because of its complexity, this procedure is seldom used. If you are interested in reading about its use, Rosenthal and Rosnow (1991) offer a nice presentation of its particulars.

Now that we have examined the mechanics involved in implementing complete and incomplete counterbalancing, let's see exactly what it can and cannot control. To simply say that counterbalancing controls for sequence or order effects does not tell the entire story. Although counterbalancing controls for sequence or order effects, as you will see, it also controls for carryover effects. It cannot, however, control for differential carryover.

Sequence or Order Effects. **Sequence or order effects** are produced by the participant's being exposed to the sequential presentation of the treatments. For example, assume that we are testing reaction time to three types of dashboard warning lights: red (R), green (G), and flashing white (FW). As soon as the warning light comes on, the participant is to turn the engine off. To completely counterbalance this experiment would require six sequences and at least six participants ($3! = 3 \times 2 \times 1 = 6$). If we found that the reaction time to the

> **Sequence or order effects** The position of a treatment in a series determines, in part, the participants' response.

TABLE 4-6. AN INCOMPLETE COUNTERBALANCING APPROACH

This approach involves randomly determining the sequence for the first participlant and then systematically rotating the treatments for the following sequences.

	TESTING SEQUENCE			
	1	*2*	*3*	*4*
Participant 1	B	D	A	C
Participant 2	D	A	C	B
Participant 3	A	C	B	D
Participant 4	C	B	D	A

Carryover effect
The effects of one treatment persist or carryover and influence responding to the next treatment.

first warning light, regardless of type, was 10 seconds, and that improvements of 4 and 3 seconds were made to the second and third lights, respectively, we would be dealing with a sequence or order effect. This example is diagrammed in Table 4-7. As you can see, the sequence or order effect depends on *where* in the sequential presentation of treatments the participant's performance is evaluated, *not* which treatment is experienced.

Sequence or order effects will be experienced equally by all participants in counterbalanced situations because each treatment appears an equal number of times at each testing session. This consideration points to a major flaw in the use of randomized, incomplete counterbalancing: The treatments may not be presented an equal number of times at each testing session (see Table 4-5). Thus, sequence or order effects are not controlled in this situation.

Carryover Effects. When a **carryover effect** is present, the effects of one treatment persist to influence the participant's response to the next treatment. For example, let's assume that experiencing the green (G) warning light before the red (R) light always causes participants to *decrease* their reaction time by two seconds. Conversely, experiencing R before G causes participants to *increase* their reaction time by two seconds. Experiencing the flashing white (FW) warning light either before or after G has no effect on reaction time. However, experiencing R before FW increases reaction time three seconds, and experiencing FW before R reduces reaction three seconds. In the R → G/G → R and R → FW/FW → R transitions, the previous treatment influences the participant's response to the subsequent treatment in a consistent and predictable manner. These effects are diagrammed in Table 4-8. Note that counterbalancing includes an equal number of each type of transition (e.g., R → G, G → R, R → FW, etc.). Thus the opposing carryover effects cancel each other.

TABLE 4-7. EXAMPLE OF SEQUENCE OR ORDER EFFECTS IN A COUNTERBALANCED EXPERIMENT

The performance increase shown in parentheses below each sequence indicates the effect of testing at that particular point in the sequence. Thus, second and third testings result in increases of 4 and 3, respectively, regardless of the experimental task.

	ORDER OF TASK PRESENTATION		
Performance Increase →	A (0	B 4	C 3)
	A (0	C 4	B 3)
	B (0	A 4	C 3)
	B (0	C 4	A 3)
	C (0	A 4	B 3)
	C (0	B 4	A 3)

TABLE 4-8. EXAMPLE OF CARRYOVER EFFECTS IN A COUNTERBALANCED EXPERIMENT

Carryover effects occur when a specific preceding treatment influences the performance in a subsequent treatment. In this example experiencing Treatment G prior to Treatment R results in a decrease of 2 (i.e., –2), whereas experiencing Treatment R prior to Treatment G results in an increase of 2 (i.e., +2). Experiencing Treatment G prior to FW or Treatment FW prior to G, does not produce a unique effect. However, experiencing Treatment R prior to FW results in an increase of 3, whereas experiencing Treatment FW prior to R results in a decrease of 3.

	SEQUENCE OF TREATMENTS		
	G	R	FW
Effect on Performance →	(0	–2	+3)
	G	FW	R
	(0	0	–3)
	R	G	FW
	(0	+2	0)
	R	FW	G
	(0	+3	0)
	FW	G	R
	(0	0	–2)
	FW	R	G
	(0	–3	+2)

Differential Carryover. Although counterbalancing can control many things, it offers no protection against differential carryover. **Differential carryover** occurs when the response to one treatment depends on *which* treatment is experienced previously. Consider an experiment investigating the effects of reward magnitude on reading comprehension in second-grade children. Each child reads three similar passages. After each passage is completed, a series of questions is asked. Each correct answer is rewarded by a certain number of M&Ms (the IV). In the (A) low-reward condition one M&M is received after each correct answer; three and five M&Ms are received in the (B) medium-reward and (C) high-reward treatments, respectively.

Although this experiment might be viewed as another six-sequence example (see Table 4-4A) of counterbalancing, the effects may not be symmetrical as in the carryover example we just considered. The participant who receives the A → B → C sequence may be motivated to do well at all testing sessions because the reward progressively increases from session to session. What about the student who receives the B → C → A sequence? In this case the reward rises from three M&Ms (Session 1) to five M&Ms (Session 2), but then is reduced to one M&M (Session 3). Will the decrease from five M&Ms to one M&M produce a unique effect, such as the student's refusing to participate, that the other transitions do not produce? If so, differential carryover has occurred and counterbalancing is not an effective control procedure. Some possible effects of differential carryover in the M&M study are shown in Table 4-9. As you can see, the drastic decrease in performance produced by the C (five M&Ms)-to-A(one M&M) transition is not canceled out by a comparable increase resulting from the A-to-C transition.

Differential carryover
The response to one treatment depends on *which* treatment was administered previously.

definition

TABLE 4-9. EXAMPLE OF DIFFERENTIAL CARRYOVER IN A COUNTERBALANCED EXPERIMENT

Differential carryover occurs when performance depends on which specific sequence occurs. In the example below experiencing Treatment A prior to Treatment B results in an increase of 6 (i.e., +6), whereas all other sequences result in an increase of 2 (i.e., +2).

	SEQUENCE OF TREATMENTS		
	A (one M&M)	B (three M&Ms)	C (five M&Ms)
Effect on Performance →	(0	+6	+2)
	A	C	B
	(0	+2	+2)
	B	A	C
	(0	+2	+2)
	B	C	A
	(0	+2	+2)
	C	A	B
	(0	+2	+6)
	C	B	A
	(0	+2	+2)

The potential for differential transfer exists whenever counterbalancing is employed. The experimenter must be sensitive to this possibility. A thorough review of the relevant literature can help sensitize you to the possibility of differential carryover. If this threat exists, it is advisable to employ a research procedure that does not involve presenting more than one treatment to each participant.

REVIEW SUMMARY

1. Randomization controls for extraneous variables by distributing them equally to all groups.

2. When **elimination** is used as a control technique, the experimenter seeks to completely remove the extraneous variable from the experiment.

3. **Constancy** controls an extraneous variable by creating a constant or uniform condition with regard to that variable.

4. **Balancing** achieves control of extraneous variables by ensuring that all groups receive the extraneous variables to the same extent.

5. **Counterbalancing** controls for sequence or order effects when participants receive more than one treatment. **Within-subject counterbalancing** involves the administration of more than one treatment sequence to each participant, whereas **within-group counterbalancing** involves the administration of a different treatment sequence to each participant.

6. The total number of treatment sequences can be determined by $n!$. When all sequences are administered, **complete counterbalancing** is being em-

ployed. **Incomplete counterbalancing** involves the administration of fewer than the total number of possible sequences.

7. The random selection of treatment sequences, systematic rotation, or the Latin square approaches can be used when incomplete counterbalancing is implemented.

8. Counterbalancing can control for **sequence or order** and **carryover** effects. It cannot control for **differential carryover** where the response to one treatment depends on *which* treatment was experienced previously.

STUDY BREAK

1. Matching

    1. randomization
    2. elimination
    3. constancy
    4. balancing
    5. counterbalancing

    A. complete removal of the extraneous variable
    B. extraneous variable is reduced to a single value
    C. most widely used control procedure
    D. used to control for order effects
    E. extraneous variable is distributed equally to all groups

2. Briefly describe the logic involved in the use of randomization as a control technique

3. Distinguish between within-subject and within-group counterbalancing.

4. What can *n*! be used for? What is 4!

5. What are the requirements for complete counterbalancing?

6. What is incomplete counterbalancing? What is the Latin square procedure?

7. Distinguish between carryover and differential carryover.

    In the following sections we highlight two potential extraneous variables that often go overlooked: the experimenter and the participant. As the science of psychology has matured, increasing attention has been given to these factors.

THE EXPERIMENTER AS AN EXTRANEOUS VARIABLE

Just as the characteristics of the detective can influence the responses of the suspects who are questioned, several aspects of the experimenter can influence the responses of the participant (Rosenthal, 1976). First we explore physiological and psychological experimenter effects; then we will consider experimenter expectancies.

EXPERIMENTER CHARACTERISTICS

Physiological. Physiological experimenter characteristics refer to such attributes as age, gender, and race. Each of these variables has been shown to have an influence on participants' responses. For example, Robert Rosenthal (1977) has shown that male experimenters are more friendly to their participants than female experimenters are.

Even though constancy is achieved by having one experimenter conduct the research project, it is possible that the experimenter will influence the participants in a unique manner. Perhaps the friendliness of a male experimenter will encourage *all* participants to perform at a very high level, thus making the differences between the treatment groups less evident. Hence, problems can arise when one attempts to compare the results of similar research projects conducted by different experimenters. If these projects yield different results, you cannot be sure if the differences are attributable to differences in the IV or to effects created by the different experimenters.

Psychological. Psychological attributes of the experimenter that can influence the results of an experiment include personality characteristics such as hostility, anxiety, and introversion or extraversion. An experiment conducted by an experimenter who is highly anxious is likely to yield different results than an experiment conducted by a confident, self-assured experimenter. The same can be said for other personality characteristics.

EXPERIMENTER EXPECTANCIES

In addition to physiological and psychological characteristics, the experimenter's expectations concerning the participants' behavior can, and do, affect performance. The experimenter's expectations cause him or her to behave toward the participants in such a manner that the *expected* response is, indeed, more likely shown. The experimenter is literally a cause of the desired or expected response. Are experimenter expectancies best categorized as nuisance variables or confounders? If experimenter expectancy is operating in your experiment, you cannot tell whether your results are due to the influence of the IV or experimenter expectancy; hence they are best labeled as confounders.

Such effects have been demonstrated in both human and animal experiments. One of the most widely cited studies of the effects of human experimenter expectancy involved the IQ scores of grade-school children (Rosenthal & Jacobson, 1968). At the start of the school year all children in the classes that were studied were given an IQ test. Then, several children in each class were *randomly* selected and the respective teachers told that these children were "intellectual bloomers." Several months later when all the children retook the IQ test, the IQ scores of the intellectual bloomers had increased more than those of the other children. Because the intellectual bloomers were *randomly* selected, it is doubtful that they were intellectually superior. However, they were perceived in this manner and were treated differently by the teachers. In turn, these students responded in accordance with the teachers' expectations.

Experimenter expectancy is not limited just to studies of humans; even rats will perform in accordance with what the experimenter anticipates. Rosenthal and Fode (1963) told half the students in a class that the rats they were going to train were "maze bright"; the remainder of the students were told that their rats were "maze dull." In actuality, there were no differences among the rats at the start of the project. The results were consistent with the students' expectations: The "smart" rats learned the maze better and more quickly than did the "dumb" rats. Because the rats did not differ at the start of training, this study clearly highlights the strong effects that experimenter expectancies can have on participants' performance. Because Rosenthal and his colleagues were among the first to systematically study experimenter expectations, the results of such expectations are often called **Rosenthal effects.**

> **Rosenthal effect**
> The experimenter's preconceived idea of appropriate responding influences the treatment of participants and their behavior.

CONTROLLING EXPERIMENTER EFFECTS

Physiological and Psychological Effects. The reason that experimenters have traditionally paid little attention to these variables may be clear by now: They are difficult to control. For example, to achieve constancy, all these characteristics would have to be measured in all potential experimenters and then the choice of experimenters would be determined by the level of each factor that was desired—a difficult, if not impossible, task. Likewise, we've already seen that balancing can be used to avoid confounding due to the sex of the experimenter. Although this control technique equates the groups for experimenter sex, it does not simultaneously control for other physiological and psychological characteristics. At present the best approach to such variables is to understand their potential influence on an experiment, be sensitive to their presence, exercise those controls that can be implemented, and replicate your research. A thorough literature review will help make you aware of the relevant variables in your area of research interest.

Experimenter Expectancies. There are several things that can be done to reduce, possibly eliminate, experimenter expectancies. First, the instructions that the

Single-blind experiment
An experiment in which the experimenter (*or* participants) is unaware of the treatment the participants are receiving.

experimenter gives to the participants should be carefully prepared so their manner of presentation will not influence the participants' responses. Likewise, any instructions concerning scoring the participants' responses should be as objective and concrete as possible and established before the experiment is started. If these instructions are subjective, then there is room for experimenter expectancies to dictate how they will be scored.

A second method for controlling experimenter expectancies involves the use of instrumentation and automation. For example, instructions to participants may be tape-recorded prior to experimental testing in order to reduce any influences the experimenter might have. In many instances, potential influences of the experimenter are eliminated through the use of printed instructions and/or computer displays. Also, automated equipment can be used to ensure the accurate recording and storage of response data. In some instances the participants' responses are entered directly at a computer terminal and thus are stored and ready for analysis at any time.

A third method for minimizing experimenter expectancies is to conduct a single-blind experiment. The **single-blind experiment** keeps the experimenter in the dark regarding which participants are receiving which treatment(s). (As we will see, this procedure can be used to control participant effects as well.) For example, suppose you are conducting an experiment testing the effects of different descriptions of an individual's degree of altruism on the amount of warmth that individual is perceived as possessing. Quite likely the different written descriptions will be printed such that they all have the same appearance (constancy). If these different descriptions have the same demographic cover sheet, then all materials will appear to be identical. If another experimenter is in charge of determining which participants read which descriptions and arranging the order in which the testing materials will be distributed to the participants, then the experimenter who actually conducts the research sessions will not know which descriptions are being read by which participants at any session and therefore experimenter expectancies cannot influence the participants' responses. The single-blind procedure can also be used effectively when the IV consists of some type of chemical compound, whether it be in tablet or injection form. If all tablets or injections have the same physical appearance, the experimenter will be unaware of which participants are receiving the active compound and which participants are receiving a placebo. The experimenter truly does not know what treatment condition is being administered in single-blind experiments of this nature.

PARTICIPANT PERCEPTIONS AS EXTRANEOUS VARIABLES

Just as the experimenter can unintentionally influence the results of an experiment, so can the participant. As you will see, there are numerous aspects of the participants' perception of the research project that can operate as extraneous variables.

Reprinted from *The Chronicle of Higher Education*. By permission of Mischa Richter and Harold Bakker.

"Haven't we met in a previous experiment?"

It is important that participants not communicate about the nature of a psychological experiment.

DEMAND CHARACTERISTICS AND GOOD PARTICIPANTS

If you have ever served as a participant in a psychological experiment, you know that most participants believe that they are supposed to behave in a certain manner. As we have seen, the cues that participants use to guide their behavior may come from the experimenter; they may also be part of the experimental context and/or IV manipulation. When these cues are used to determine what the experimenter's hypothesis is and how participants are supposed to act, they are referred to as the **demand characteristics** of the experiment (Orne, 1962). In short, participants in psychological research attempt to figure out how they are supposed to respond and then behave in this manner. The desire to cooperate and act as the participants believe the experimenter wants them to is called the **good participant effect** (Rosenthal & Rosnow, 1991).

Jennifer Weiss and Kim Gilbert (students at Belmont University in Nashville, TN) were interested in studying the relationship between cheating in college and Type A behavior (Weiss, Gilbert, Giordano, & Davis, 1993). Their research can be categorized as a correlational study because they sought only to determine the relationship between two variables rather than directly

Demand characteristics Features of the experiment that inadvertently lead participants to respond in a particular manner.

Good participant effect Tendency of participants to behave as they perceive the experimenter wants them to behave.

definition

manipulating variables (see Chapter 3). They hypothesized that competitive, hard-driven, workaholic Type A individuals would show higher cheating rates than the more laid-back Type B individuals. Jennifer and Kim informed the participants in their study only that they would be completing a personality inventory and a cheating survey. Had the exact nature of their hypothesis been divulged, then the demand characteristics would have been quite strong and the participants might have tried to decide which group they were in and how they were expected to respond. (As it turned out, Jennifer and Kim demonstrated that Type A individuals have *lower* cheating rates than Type B individuals.)

Psychological Detective

Although experimenters have an ethical responsibility (see Chapter 2) to inform the participants about the general nature of the experiment, we have just seen that they usually do not want to reveal the exact nature of their experimental hypothesis. To do so can introduce strong demand characteristics that could influence the participants' behavior. Do demand characteristics operate as nuisance variables or as confounders? Give this question some thought and write down your answer before reading further.

Depending on how the demand characteristics are perceived, they can operate either as a confounder or as a nuisance variable. If it is very clear to the participants which group they are in and how that group is expected to act, then the demand characteristics are functioning as a confounder. When the experiment is completed, the experimenter will not be able to tell if the differences *between* the groups were due to the effects of the IV or the demand characteristics. If, however, the participants perceive the demand characteristics but are not sure which group they are in, then the demand characteristics may function as a nuisance variable. In this situation we would expect the demand characteristics to produce both increases and decreases in responding *within* all groups. Thus, the scores of all groups would spread out more.

RESPONSE BIAS

There are several factors that can produce a response bias on the part of research participants. Here we examine such influences as yea-saying and response set.

Yea-Saying. You most likely know individuals who seem to agree with everything, even if agreeing means that they contradict themselves. We may never know whether these individuals agree because they truly believe what they are saying or they are simply making a socially desirable response at the moment. Clearly, these individuals, known as **yea-sayers**, who say yes to all questions, pose a threat to psychological research. (In-

Yea-sayers
Participants who tend to answer yes to all questions.

dividuals who always respond negatively to all questions are known as **nay-sayers.**) Contradicting one's own statements by answering yes (or no) to all items on a psychological inventory or test seriously threatens the validity of that participant's score.

Response Set. Sometimes the experimental context or situation in which the research is being conducted can cause participants to respond in a certain manner or have a **response set.** The effects of response set can be likened to going for a job interview: you take your cues from the interviewer and the surroundings. In some cases you will need to be highly professional, whereas in other interview situations you can be a bit more relaxed.

Consider the two following descriptions of an experimenter and the testing room in which the research is being conducted. In the first instance the experimenter is wearing a tie and a white laboratory coat. The experiment is being conducted in a nicely carpeted room that has pleasing furnishings, several bookcases, and attractive plants; it looks more like an office than a research room. The second experimenter is dressed in jeans, a sweatshirt, and tennis shoes. In this case the research is being conducted in a classroom in a less-than-well-kept building. Have you already developed a response set for each of these situations? Will you be more formal, and perhaps give more in-depth answers, in the first situation? Even though the second situation may help put you at ease, does it seem less than scientific? Notice that our descriptions of these two situations did not make reference to the physiological or psychological characteristics of the experimenters or to the type of experiment that is being conducted. Hence, we are dealing with an effect that occurs in addition to experimenter and demand effects.

Likewise, the nature of the questions themselves may create a response set. For example, how questions are worded or their placement in the sequence of questions may prompt a certain type of response; it may seem that a socially desirable answer is being called for. Also, it may seem that a particular alternative is called for. In such cases a position bias is developed. Clearly, response set can be a major influence on the participant's response.

CONTROLLING PARTICIPANT EFFECTS

As we have seen, there are aspects of the participant that can affect the results of our research. Although such factors are rather difficult to control, several techniques have been developed.

Demand Characteristics. You will recall that one technique used to control for experimenter expectancies is to keep the experimenter in the dark by conducting a single-blind experiment. This same approach can be applied to the control of demand characteristics, only this time the participants will be unaware of such features as the experimental hypothesis, the true nature of the experiment, or which group they happen to be in.

Double-blind experiment
An experiment in which *both* the experimenter and the participants are unaware of which treatment the participants are receiving.

It takes only a moment's thought to reach the conclusion that these two approaches can be combined; we can conduct an experiment in which *both* the experimenter and the participants are unaware of which treatment is being administered to which participants. Such experiments are known as **double-blind experiments.**

Regardless of whether a single- or a double-blind experiment is conducted, it is likely that the participants will attempt to guess what the purpose of the experiment is and how they should respond. It is difficult to conceal the fact that they are participating in an experiment, and the information provided them prior to signing the informed consent document (see Chapter 2) may give the participants a general idea concerning the nature of the experiment.

Psychological Detective

Let's assume that you conduct a single- or a double-blind experiment and leave your participants to their own devices to guess what the experiment is about. In this case you may be introducing an extraneous variable into your research project. What general type of extraneous variable may be introduced under these circumstances and what effect might it have? Give this question some thought before reading further.

It is almost certain that all participants will not correctly guess the true nature of the experiment and which group they are in. Those participants who make correct guesses may show improved performance; those participants who make incorrect guesses may have inferior performance. If the ability to correctly guess the nature of the experiment and which group one is in is comparable in all groups, then the scores within all groups will spread out. You have introduced a *nuisance variable*, that will make it more difficult to see the differences that develop between the groups. Is there any way to avoid this problem? The answer is yes.

Another technique that can be used to control for demand characteristics is to give *all* participants incorrect information concerning the nature of the experiment. In short, the experimenter purposely deceives all the participants, thus disguising the true nature of the experiment and keeping the participants from guessing how they are supposed to respond. Although this procedure can be effective, it suffers from two drawbacks. First, we have already seen that the use of deception raises ethical problems with regard to the conduct of research. If deception is employed, a good IRB (see Chapter 2) will be careful to make sure that it is a justifiable and necessary procedure. The second problem is that the information used to deceive the participants may result in erroneous guesses about the nature of the experiment; the participants are then responding to the demand characteristics created by the deception. Clearly, demand characteristics may be very difficult to control.

Yea-Saying. The most typical control for yea-saying (and nay-saying) is to rewrite some of the items so that a negative response represents agreement (control for yea-saying) or a positive response represents disagreement (control for nay-saying). Once some of the items have been rewritten, a decision concerning the order for presenting items needs to be made. All the rewritten items should not be presented as a group. One presentation strategy is to randomize the complete list, thereby presenting the original and rewritten items in an undetermined sequence. This approach works quite well with longer lists. If the list is smaller, within-subject counterbalancing can be used.

Response Set. The best safeguard against response set is to review all questions that are asked or items to be completed to see if there is a socially desired response that is implied in any manner. The answer given or response made should reflect the participant's own feelings, attitudes, or motives. Checking for response set offers excellent opportunities for pilot testing and interviewing of participants to determine if the questions and/or behavioral tasks create a particular response set. Additionally, the nature of the experimental situation or context should be carefully examined to avoid the presence of undesired cues.

R E V I E W   S U M M A R Y

1. Experimenter characteristics can affect the results of an experiment. Physiological experimenter characteristics include such aspects as age, gender, and race. Psychological experimenter attributes include such personality characteristics as hostility, anxiety, and introversion or extraversion.

2. Experimenter expectancies can produce behaviors in the experimenter that cause participants to make the desired response. Such experimenter expectancy effects are often called **Rosenthal effects.**

3. Because of their potential abundance, experimenter characteristics are difficult to control.

4. Experimenter expectancies can be controlled through the use of objective instructions and response-scoring procedures, as well as instrumentation and automation. A **single-blind experiment,** in which the experimenter does not know which participants are receiving which treatments, also can be used to control experimenter expectancies.

5. **Demand characteristics** refer to those aspects of the experiment that may provide the participants with cues concerning the experimenter's hypothesis and how they are supposed to act. Demand characteristics can be controlled through the use of single-blind and **double-blind experiments** (where both the experimenter and the participants do not know which treatment the participants are to receive).

6. The desire to cooperate and act in accordance with the experimenter's expectation is called the **good participant effect.**

7. Response bias is caused by several factors. **Yea-saying** refers to the tendency to answer yes to all questions; **nay- saying** refers to the tendency to answer no to all questions. Yea- and nay-saying are controlled by writing some items such that a negative response represents agreement (control for yea-saying) and a positive response represents disagreement (control for nay-saying).

8. When the experimental situation or context prompts a certain response, a **response set** has been created. The best safeguards against response set are careful scrutiny of the experimental situation, thorough review of all questions, pilot testing, and interviewing of participants.

STUDY BREAK

1. Explain how the experimenter can be an extraneous variable.

2. Matching

   1. age, gender, race   A. psychological experimenter effects
   2. hostility or anxiety   B. experimenter expectancies
   3. Rosenthal effects   C. physiological experimenter effects
   4. single-blind experiment   D. control for demand characteristics and
   5. double-blind experiment   experimenter expectancies
                                   E. control for experimenter expectancies

3. How is a Rosenthal effect created?

4. Explain how instrumentation and automation can control experimenter expectancies.

5. What is the relationship between demand characteristics and the good participant effect?

6. Rewriting items in a questionnaire so that a negative response represents agreement is a control for _____.

LOOKING AHEAD

In this chapter we have explored the nature of variables in general and have seen the importance of selecting appropriate independent and dependent variables. The potentially damaging effects of nuisance variables and confounders has led to the development of procedures for their control.

We continue our examination of the basics of experimentation in the next chapter. There we will discuss the selection of appropriate types and numbers of participants and the actual collection of research data.

HANDS-ON ACTIVITIES

1. **Types of IVs.**   Find separate published articles that contain examples of each of the different types of true IVs (physiological, experience, stimulus). Find an example of a published article in which a participant characteristic is treated as an IV.

2. **Measuring the DV.**   For each type of IV identified in Activity 1, describe the DV and indicate what type it is (correctness, rate or frequency, degree or amount, latency or duration). Do the examples you have found meet the requirements for a good DV? Explain. Was more than one DV used in any of the experiments you examined? Was the use of more than one DV justified? Explain.

3. **Detecting Nuisance Variables.**   Carefully examine each of the articles used in Activities 1 and 2 for the presence of potential nuisance variables. Thoroughly describe each nuisance variable that is identified.

4. **Detecting Confounders.**   Want to try your hand at detecting confounders? Below are descriptions of various experimental setups. Read each one carefully to see if you can determine what the confounder is.

   A.   Mechelle is a hard-working graduate student. In addition to studying for her classes, she conducts research on human memory. Her current project is quite complex and involves the testing of four different groups of participants. To accommodate her busy schedule, Mechelle decides to test two groups of participants early in the morning; the remaining two groups are scheduled for late in the afternoon.

   B.   A new, fast-acting drug to cure schizophrenia has been developed and needs to be tested. Thirty diagnosed schizophrenics volunteer to be participants. Fifteen of these volunteers are randomly assigned to receive the drug; the remaining 15 patients comprise a comparison group that does not receive the drug. After a week all patients in the experiment are given a test to measure their level of schizophrenia.

5. **Exercising Control.**   You will need to consult the journal articles you used in Activities 1, 2, and 3 once again. This time you should examine the articles for the use of the control techniques described in this chapter (i.e., randomization, elimination, constancy, balancing, or counterbalancing).

6. **The Experimenter as an Extraneous Variable.**   Once again examine the same four articles you used for Activities 1, 2, 3, and 5. This time determine if there are any instances in which the experimenter might have acted as an extraneous variable. Be sure to consider physiological attributes, psychological attributes, and experimenter expectancies. Describe each problem area that is detected and indicate how it should have been controlled.

7. **Controlling Subject Perceptions.**   We promise this is the last time you will use the set of four articles you've been dissecting in Activities 1, 2, 3, 5, and 6. (However, this thorough dissection should indicate to you how careful and painstaking good research should be.) This time you are to examine the articles for any instances where the participants' perceptions may have influenced the outcome of the experiment. In other words, you are looking for the presence of demand characteristics and response bias. If such problems are detected, what should have been done to control them? If you do not detect any of these problems, explain the steps the researcher(s) took to avoid them.

CHAPTER 5

The Basics of Experimentation II: Participants and Apparatus, Cross-Cultural Considerations, and Beginning the Research Report

In the previous chapters we dealt with such topics as sources of research ideas, conducting a literature review, formulating the research hypothesis, the role of ethics in research, and the nature of variables and their control. In this chapter we continue our discussion of research basics by considering the type and number of participants to be used, the type of apparatus or testing equipment that will be employed, and the procedure by which the experiment will be conducted. Finally, we begin our discussion of how to prepare the research report according to acceptable APA format.

Participants

Both the type and the number of participants to be used are important considerations in the formulation of an experiment. These aspects are discussed in this section.

Type of Participants

definition

Precedent
An established pattern.

A moment's reflection will indicate that there is a wealth of potential organisms that can serve as participants in a psychological experiment. For example, animal researchers might choose from bumblebees, flies, dolphins, chimpanzees, elephants, and rats. Likewise, researchers dealing with humans might choose as their participants infants, young adults, the aged, the gifted, the handicapped, or the maladaptive. The range of participants for your research project may be overwhelming. Which one represents the best choice? There are three guidelines that can help you answer this question: precedent, availability, and the nature of the problem.

Precedent. If your literature review indicates that a particular type of participant has been used successfully in prior research projects in your area of interest, then you may want to consider using this type of participant. For example, when Willard S. Small (1901) conducted the first rat study in the United States, he began a **precedent,** or established pattern, that continues to this day. Likewise, the precedent for using college students (especially those enrolled in introductory psychology) has a venerable history. For example, research in the area of human memory and cognitive processes relies heavily on research conducted with college students. How strong is this reliance? We selected a recent copy of the *Journal of Experimental Psychology: Learning, Memory and Cognition* (Vol. 20, No. 5, September 1994) at random and examined it. There were 17 articles published in this issue. Of these 17 articles, 15 reported results from experiments that used college students exclusively as participants, 1 reported using aged adults *and* college students, and the remaining 1 reported the results of several computer simulations. It is noteworthy that in 12 of the 15 articles using college students, the participants were drawn from a subject pool or participated in order to receive partial course credit.

Psychological Detective

Such precedents for the selection of participants have their advantages and disadvantages. Before reading further, consider what such advantages and disadvantages might be and write them down.

The fact that a particular type of participant has been used repeatedly in psychological research ensures that a body of knowledge has been accumulated. Researchers can take advantage of this wealth of knowledge as they plan their own research. Already validated procedures can be implemented without expending hours of exploratory testing and designing new equipment. Being able to draw upon this body of already proven techniques means that the *likelihood of success* (see Chapter 2) is increased.

However, the continual use of one type or species of participant can limit the generalizability of the information that is gathered. For example, although the study of self-esteem in college students may tell us about this trait in that group, it may not tell us much about self-esteem in the general population. Likewise, although the choice to use white rats in an experiment may be prompted by the extensive literature on this animal that already exists, additional rat studies may not provide any useful information about other species.

Availability. The continued use of white rats and college students also stems from another source, their availability. White rats are relatively inexpensive, at least compared to many other animals, and are easy to maintain. Likewise, college students, especially those students enrolled in introductory psychology classes, constitute an easily accessible population from which participants can be drawn. For example, in their study of voter reaction to marital infidelity on the part of political candidates, Linda Hurt, Sandra Palmer, Mark Sereg, and Laura Stephens (1993) used 102 undergraduates at Southern Illinois University at Edwardsville as the participants. Likewise, in her study of the variables affecting mate selection, Melanie Van Dyke (1993), a student at Saint Louis University, recruited 116 students enrolled in a general psychology course to serve as participants. In addition to their availability, college students are inexpensive participants because they are not usually paid for their participation. At some institutions participation in a research project(s) may be a course requirement, thus ensuring the ready availability of research participants.

Clearly, availability of one type of participant may preclude the use of others. In turn, we have seen that the development of a large body of knowledge about a particular type of participant can result in pressures to use that participant in future research projects. Obviously, the problem can easily become circular. The precedent for using one type of participant is established and leads to the development of an extensive literature concerning that type of participant, which further encourages the use of that type of participant.

Precocial Able to display considerable independent behavior immediately after birth.

Type of Research Project. Often the nature of your research project will determine the type of participant you decide to use. For example, if you are interested in studying the visual ability of birds of prey, you are limited to studying such birds as eagles, vultures, hawks, and owls; ducks, geese, and songbirds are not predators. Likewise, if you want to study hallucinations and delusions, then you have limited your choice of potential participants to humans who are able to communicate.

Consider the research project conducted by Jennifer Messina, a student at Dartmouth College in Hanover, NH. She was interested in studying opiate addiction in fetuses and newborns (Messina, 1993). Because of obvious ethical reasons, her research had to be conducted with animals. She could not randomly assign pregnant women and newborn infants to two groups and then administer drugs to one of these groups. A review of the literature showed that tolerance to morphine in rats *does not* develop during the first two postnatal weeks of life. Thus, the effects of *prenatal* exposure to an opiate, such as morphine, might be difficult to demonstrate in rats. The effect of drugs experienced prenatally would have worn off by the time tolerance could be observed. Also, the helplessness of newborn rat pups makes it difficult to observe typical withdrawal symptoms, such as twitching, "wet dog" shakes, and irritability. Hence, a more **precocial** (able to display considerable independent behavior immediately after birth) subject than the laboratory rat was needed. Jennifer chose to use guinea pigs. The results of her study indicated that unlike rats, the infant guinea pigs displayed withdrawal symptoms attributable to the prenatal morphine exposure.

Number of Participants

Once you have decided what type of participant to use in your research project, you must then determine how many participants you are going to test. In making this decision, there are numerous factors that must be taken into account. Some of these factors include:

1. *Finances.* How much will it cost to test each participant? Animals must be purchased and cared for. It may be necessary to pay humans for their participation. Does the person who actually conducts the experiment need to be paid? If so, this cost also must be considered; it will rise as additional participants are tested.

2. *Time.* As additional participants are tested, time requirements will increase, especially if participants are tested individually.

3. *Availability.* The sheer number of participants that are available may influence the number that you choose to use in your experiment.

In addition to these more practical considerations, there is another factor that enters into our determination of the number of participants we will use. This factor is the amount of variability we expect to be present within each group. The less within-group variability (i.e., the more homogeneous the participants), the fewer participants we will need. Conversely, the greater the within-group variability (i.e., the more heterogeneous the participants), the greater the number of participants we will need.

What is the reasoning behind these statements about variability and the number of participants to be tested in an experiment? In thinking about this question, you may want to review the material on distractors (see Chapter 4). Write down your answer before reading further.

When a distractor, in this case the heterogeneous nature of the participants, is present the scores within each group spread out considerably and the amount of group overlap is increased. The extremely high and extremely low scores make it more difficult to see differences between the groups. One way to deemphasize these extreme scores is to test more participants. By increasing the number of scores (i.e., participants), we increase the number of scores that cluster in the center of the distribution and, therefore, decrease the impact of the extreme scores. When distractors are not present (i.e., the groups are more homogeneous), there are fewer extreme scores and the differences between the groups can be seen more clearly.

As you saw in Chapter 4, another way to create more homogeneous groups is to use stratified random sampling. By sampling a more specific type of participant, we remove extremes from our sample. We will have more to say about the number of observations and variability in the next chapter.

Your literature review also can, and should, be used as a guideline concerning the number of participants you will use in your experiment. If previous studies have successfully employed a certain number of participants, then you can assume that you will need to test a comparable number if you are conducting research in the same area. For example, based on a review of the relevant literature, Julie D. Arb, Kyle Wood, and Jennifer O'Loughlin (1994), students at Emporia State University, chose to use nine rats per group in their experiment relating chronic cadmium ingestion and aggressive responding. However, if you are conducting a project in an area that has not received much research attention, then you will want to test as many participants as possible given your financial, time, and availability constraints.

APPARATUS

While you are deciding on the number and type of participants to be used in your research, you also need to consider the type of apparatus, if any, you will be using. Apparatus can be used for both presenting the IV and recording the DV.

IV PRESENTATION

Often the nature of the IV will influence the type of apparatus one chooses to use. For example, Angela Schmeising and Nicole Englert, students at Southwest State

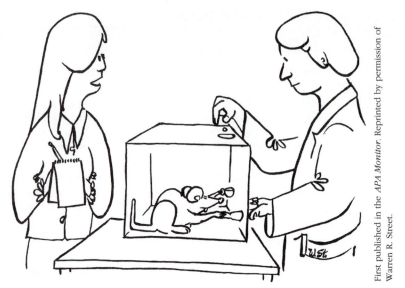

First published in the *APA Monitor*. Reprinted by permission of Warren R. Street.

"Besides operant equipment, Professor, have the federal cutbacks hurt you?"

Although large research laboratories may require extensive funds and elaborate equipment, you can conduct meaningful research on a limited budget with little or no fancy equipment.

University in Marshall, MI, were interested in studying the effects of annoying noise on social interaction in pairs of participants (Schmeising & Englert, 1993). Static from a television station that was not broadcasting was selected as the type of noise to be presented. These sounds were tape-recorded and then presented to the pairs of experimental participants. Pairs who were not exposed to the noise condition were tested in a normally quiet room. The results of this study indicated that participants in the quiet condition interacted over twice as much as did participants in the noisy condition.

The possible ways that the IV can be presented are limited by the type of IV that you are manipulating, by finances, and by your own ingenuity. Clearly, the presentation of certain types of IVs requires specialized equipment. For example, the administration of a particular type of light wave will require a specialized projector. On the other hand, the presentation of food to a hungry rat that has learned to press a lever does not have to involve the purchase of an expensive Skinner box and/or food-pellet dispenser. We have seen very effective, handmade Skinner boxes and food-delivery systems! For example, a sturdy cardboard box works just fine in place of a commercial Skinner box. What about the lever? No problem. Anything that protrudes into the box that the rat can learn to press or touch will work fine. In fact, some students have simply drawn a circle on one wall and required that it be touched before food is delivered. A piece of plastic tubing can serve as the food-delivery system. Simply fasten the tubing to the outside of the box such that one end is at the top and the other end enters the box near the bottom and is situated over a small dish. Dropping a piece of food down the tube results in a reinforcer being delivered into the food dish in the box. Some creative thought at this stage of planning can often save substantial amounts of money.

DV Recording

Whereas recording evidence at the scene of a crime may be a major concern to the detective, recording the DV is such a fundamental task that it often is overlooked by the psychologist. However, there are problems and options to be addressed. Consider the social interaction experiment conducted by Schmeising and Englert (1993). Their first DV recording decision concerned the general manner by which social interaction would be measured. First they operationally defined social interaction as the time that the participants engaged in interacting (talking). Their next decision concerned how this measurement would be made. They chose to use stopwatches. Both experimenters independently recorded the time of interaction. Then these two times were averaged to yield a single score for each pair of participants that was tested. Certainly, more sophisticated equipment could have been used in this experiment. For example, each session could have been videotaped and then scored at a later time. This procedure would have allowed the experimenters to measure additional DVs, such as the number of words spoken and/or the amount of personal space present.

Psychological Detective

Although technologically sophisticated equipment can be beneficial to conducting research, there are potential drawbacks associated with its use. Give this issue some thought and write down some of the drawbacks you see before reading further.

Whether presenting the IV or recording the DV, the experimenter should not become a slave to the equipment that is available. Just because you have access to a certain piece of equipment does not mean that it *must* be used. If a handheld stopwatch provides better (or equivalent) data than an elaborate computer setup, then the less elaborate equipment is to be preferred. If researchers begin to rely too heavily on their equipment, then the choice of research problems may start to be dictated by the equipment, not by the researchers' creativity. In such situations there is more concern for the IV(s) that can be presented by the equipment than there is for the problem that is being investigated. Also, the presence of elaborate pieces of equipment assumes that the researcher has sufficient funds to provide appropriate maintenance for such equipment. Consider the problems your research would face if it depended on a particular piece of equipment that was broken and you had no funds to pay for its repair.

OTHER CONSIDERATIONS

Just because you have selected the type and number of participants to be tested and have secured the equipment to be used in your research, your preparations are far from complete. As you will recall from Chapters 2, 3, and 4, such factors as the general procedure that will be used in conducting experimental sessions, the instructions, if any, that are given, the distribution and collection of informed consent documents to human participants, and the conduct of the debriefing sessions must be carefully planned. Because these topics were covered previously, we simply remind you of their importance at this point. The best way to test their effectiveness is to conduct a pilot study and interview the participants.

REVIEW SUMMARY

1. **Precedent,** availability, and the nature of the problem are factors that influence the choice of participants to be used in psychological research.

2. The number of participants used in a research project will be determined by financial considerations, time constraints, and participant availability.

3. The use of homogeneous groups of participants allows the experimenter to use smaller groups, whereas heterogeneous groups dictate the use of more participants.

4. Automated equipment can be used for IV presentation and DV recording, but often quality data can be recorded with less-sophisticated equipment.

STUDY BREAK

1. Explain the relationship between precedent and the type of participant used in a research project.

2. Why are white rats and college students the favorite participants in psychological research?

3. Describe the factors that will influence the number of participants you use in a research project.

4. How is the literature review related to the number of participants used in a research project?

5. Describe the concern the experimenter must be aware of when using automated equipment to present the IV and/or the DV.

THE INTERFACE BETWEEN RESEARCH AND CULTURE

The recent and continuing explosion in information technology, coupled with the availability of inexpensive air travel, highlights the diverse, multicultured nature of our planet. For example, it is common to see live reports on the television evening news from countries on the other side of the world. In our own country the "information superhighway" instantly links diverse peoples in the farthest reaches of the United States.

As we complete the material on the basics of experimentation, it is important to keep such cultural differences in mind; they may influence how research is conceptualized, conducted, analyzed, and interpreted. To this end, cross-cultural psychology has grown dramatically in recent years. The goal of **cross-cultural psychology** is to determine whether research results and psychological phenomena are universal (found in individuals from different cultures) or specific to the culture in which they were reported. Before we examine cross-cultural research, a definition of culture is needed.

Psychological Detective

Rather than simply giving you a definition of culture, we would like you to spend a few minutes on this topic. Before reading further, write down those aspects or features that you believe should be included in a definition of culture.

You probably began thinking about culture with the word "similar." After all, it's the similarities that help define our own culture and distinguish it from other cultures. If you then started listing the important aspects that serve to distinguish cultures, you're on the right track. Among the important features that differentiate one culture from another are attitudes, values, and behaviors. Moreover, these culture-defining attitudes, values, and behaviors must be long-lasting or enduring. This enduring quality indicates that these attitudes, values, and behaviors are communicated or transmitted from one generation to the next. Putting these considerations together, we can tentatively define **culture** as the lasting values, attitudes, and behaviors that a group of people share and transmit to subsequent generations. It is important to note that our definition does not imply that race and nationality are synonymous with culture. Individuals can be of the same race or nationality and *not* share the same culture. Carrying this thought one step further, we can see that several cultures

definition

Etic Cross-cultural finding.

Emic Culture-specific finding.

Ethnocentric Other cultures are viewed as an extension of one's own culture.

may exist within the same country or even in the same large city. Now, let's see how culture is related to what we consider to be truth.

CULTURE, KNOWLEDGE, AND TRUTH

A finding that occurs across cultures is called an **etic.** You can think of an etic as a universal truth or principle. The finding that reinforcement increases the probability of the response it follows appears to be an etic; it occurs in all cultures. In contrast, an **emic** is a finding that is linked to a specific culture. The value placed on independence and individuality is an emic; it varies from culture to culture. Emics represent truths that are relative, whereas etics represent absolute truths. Given the great diversity of cultures, it should not surprise you to find that the number of emics is considerably greater than the number of etics.

Psychological Detective

At this point you may be wondering how this discussion relates to a course in experimental psychology. Give this issue some thought and write down your answers before reading further.

If the goal of your research project is to discover the effects of IV manipulations *only* within a certain culture, then this discussion may have little relevance. However, few researchers purposely set their research sights on only a single culture (also see Chapter 10). In fact, the question of culture may never enter the researcher's mind as a study is taking shape. Similarly, when the data are analyzed and conclusions reached, cultural considerations may not be addressed. The result is a project that one *assumes* is not culture dependent. In short, researchers often become very **ethnocentric**—they view other cultures as an extension of their own. Hence, they interpret research results in accord with the values, attitudes, and behaviors that define their own culture and assume that these findings are applicable in other cultures as well. In Chapter 10 we will have more to say about the generalizability of research findings when we consider the internal and external validity of our research.

THE EFFECT OF CULTURE ON RESEARCH

If you step back from your own culture and try to put research in a more international perspective, it is clear that culture influences all aspects of the research process. We will consider cultural effects on the choice of the research problem, the nature of the experimental hypothesis, and the selection of the IV and the recording of the DV. In order to solve their respective problems, the detective and the research psychologist need a broad base of information that includes cultural information.

Choice of the Research Problem. In some cases there may be no doubt that the choice of your research problem is culture dependent. For example, let's assume that you are interested in studying the nature of crowd interactions at a rock concert. Whereas this topic may represent a meaningful project in the United States, it has much less relevance to a psychologist conducting research in the bush country of Australia. In this example, culture clearly dictates the nature of the research project; some problems are important in one culture, but not in another.

Nature of the Experimental Hypothesis. Once you have selected a problem that is relevant beyond your own culture, then you must deal with the experimental hypothesis. For example, even though the study of factors that determine one's personal space is relevant in a number of cultures, the creation of an experimental hypothesis that applies to all cultures will be most difficult. In some cultures very little personal space is the norm, whereas considerable personal space is expected in other cultures. Such cultural differences may lead to very different hypotheses.

Selection of the IV and the DV. Culture also can influence the selection of the IV and the DV. In technologically advanced cultures such as the United States, Japan, or Great Britain, IV presentation may be accomplished via a computer. Likewise, DV measurement and recording also may be done by computer. Because such technology is not available in all cultures, the choice of the IV and the procedure for recording the DV may differ considerably. For example, handheld stopwatches, not digital electronic timers, may be used to record the time required to complete an experimental task. Similarly, the participants may read the stimulus items in booklet form, rather than having them presented at set intervals on a video screen by a computer. In fact, stimuli that have high (or low) meaning in one culture may not have the same meaning in another culture.

METHODOLOGY AND ANALYSIS ISSUES

In either conducting or evaluating cross-cultural research, a number of methodological issues will necessitate careful and thorough consideration. Among these issues are the participants and sampling procedures used, the survey or questionnaire employed, and the effects of cultural response set on data analysis.

Participants and Sampling Procedures. The basic question here is whether the sample of participants is representative of the culture from which they were drawn. Are sophomore college students representative of culture in the United States? What steps have been taken to ensure that the sample is representative of the culture in question? For example, extreme differences may exist between samples drawn from large urban centers and those drawn from rural areas.

Assuming that you can satisfy the requirement that a sample is representative of its culture, you are likely to be faced with an equally difficult task: being able to ensure that samples from two or more cultures are equivalent before the research is conducted. We have stressed, and will continue to stress, the importance of establishing group equivalence before an IV is administered. Only when group equivalence is demonstrated can we have confidence in saying that our IV has had an effect in producing the observed differences.

Psychological Detective

Let's assume that you are reading research reports from three different cultures. All three investigations used freshman-level college students as participants. Can you assume that the requirement of group equivalence between these studies has been satisfied through the use of this common type of participant? Write your answer and reason(s) for this answer before reading further.

Even though the same *type* of participant was used, freshman college students, you cannot assume that the groups were equivalent before the research was conducted. Before this assumption can be made, you must be able to demonstrate that the same type of student attends college in all three cultures. Perhaps the collegiate experience in one culture is quite different from the collegiate experience in another culture and therefore attracts students who differ from those in the culture with which it is being compared. For example, economics may dictate that only the wealthy attend college in some cultures. In short, assessing group equivalence will not be an easy task for cross-cultural research.

Type of Survey or Questionnaire Used. Although an existing survey or questionnaire may work in a few instances, most likely the researcher will not be able to use it for research in a different culture. Aside from the potential problems faced in translating the instrument into another language is the very real problem of whether the other cultures to be tested value the concept that is to be measured or evaluated. If they do not, then the survey or questionnaire is worthless.

Even if you determine that the concept or trait in question is valued in other cultures, there remains the problem of making sure that the *specific items* are equivalent when the survey or questionnaire is prepared for use in other cultures. Just translating the items into another language may not be sufficient. For example, a question about riding the subway that is appropriate for an industrialized society may have no meaning in less-developed cultures or in parts of the industrialized society. Clearly, the same comment can be made for questions dealing with customs, values, and beliefs.

Cultural Response Set. In Chapter 4 you learned that research participants may begin an experiment with a preexisting response set; some participants may be yea-sayers and others are nay-sayers. We have the same general concern, only on a larger scale, when conducting cross-cultural research.

> **Cultural response set** Tendency of a particular culture to respond in a certain manner.

In this instance it is the response of the entire culture, not individual participants, that concerns us. A **cultural response set,** or tendency of a particular culture to respond in a certain manner, may be operative. How often have individuals in another culture answered questions on a Likert-type rating scale like those commonly used in the United States? What reaction(s) will they have to being tested by such a scale? Just because you use such scales effectively in your research does not mean that participants in other cultures will find them easy to understand and answer. The same comments can be made about any survey or questionnaire that is used. Both the type of questionnaire (Likert-type scale, true-false, multiple-choice, etc.) and the nature of the items themselves may intensify an already existing cultural response set.

How do you know if a cultural response set is present? If differences exist among the groups tested in various cultures, a cultural response set may be operating.

Psychological Detective

The presence of a cultural response set is one possible cause for the differences among groups from various cultures. What other factor might cause such differences? What problem is created if you cannot distinguish between these two causes? Reflect on these questions and write your answers before reading further.

If you indicated that the influence of a manipulated IV or differences in the specific trait being measured could also be responsible for the differences among groups, you are absolutely correct. If you then indicated that the research would be confounded (see Chapter 4) if the researcher could not distinguish whether the scores on a questionnaire were caused by the trait or IV or the cultural response set, then you are correct again. Remember that our research results are worthless when a confounder is present. Hence, it is vitally important that cultural response set be accounted for whenever you are conducting or evaluating cross-cultural research.

The purpose of this section was not to teach all the fine points of cross-cultural research; it would take an entire book to accomplish that goal. Rather, we wanted to make you aware of these issues and problems before we began our discussion of statistics and research designs. Being acquainted with the issues involved in cross-cultural research will make you a better consumer of psychological research, regardless of where it is conducted.

REVIEW SUMMARY

1. The goal of **cross-cultural psychology** is to determine whether research findings are culture specific (i.e., **emics**) or universal (i.e., **etics**).

2. Culture can influence the choice of a research problem, the nature of the experimental hypothesis, and the selection of the IV and the DV.

3. In conducting or comparing cross-cultural research, the cultural representativeness of the participants and the sampling procedures used to acquire the participants must be carefully evaluated.

4. The appropriateness of a survey or questionnaire for cross-cultural research must be evaluated. Once the general trait or concept has been accepted, then the specific items must be examined and deemed acceptable for cross-cultural use.

5. The presence of a **cultural response set** must be considered in the conduct of cross-cultural research.

STUDY BREAK

1. Distinguish between emics and etics.

2. Why is the goal of cross-cultural research incompatible with ethnocentrism?

3. In what ways can culture affect the conduct of psychological research?

4. What is a cultural response set and how is it dealt with?

THE APA FORMAT PAPER

We have come to the point where you are about to collect your research data. In the following chapters we will present a statistics review and then begin an evaluation of various research designs and types of data analysis. Before we turn our attention to those topics, we begin our consideration of the preparation of your research report. Have you ever seen or heard of a detective who did not have to write reports? Although several styles exist for the preparation of scientific papers, psychologists have developed their own format to meet their specific needs. Because the American Psychological Association (APA) originally developed this style, it is often referred to as **APA format.**

APA format
Accepted American Psychological Association (APA) form for preparing reports of psychological research.

In this chapter we look at those sections of the research report that can be completed at this point in the experimental process. Additional sections of the report must wait until your experiment is completed; we will detail them in subsequent chapters.

What Is APA Format?

In Chapter 1 we saw that in the 1920s University of Wisconsin psychologist Joseph Jastrow found a need to bring uniformity to the publication of research articles in our field. The lack of a set model or pattern had resulted in published research reports that were nearly impossible to compare. In addition to the fact that there was no prescribed order for the presentation of information, there also was no consistent manner for describing one's methodology, procedure, and/or data analysis. In short, the order and manner of presentation varied from one article to the next. The development of the APA format for preparing papers was an attempt to bring order to this state of chaos.

The particular form for preparing APA format papers is found in the fourth edition of the *Publication Manual of the American Psychological Association* (American Psychological Association, 1994). The APA *Publication Manual* has changed and evolved since it was first published in 1952. Many of the changes that have occurred over the years, as well as much of the actual format itself, were implemented to assist printers—after all, APA format was adopted to help make the *publication* of journal articles more uniform. For example, you will notice in Figure 5-1 that two or three descriptive words appear at the top of each page to the left of each page number. These words are called the manuscript page header. Should the pages become separated, they can be reassembled because the manuscript page header tells you which pages go with which pages. Although many earlier APA format matters had the printer in mind, the latest edition of the APA *Publication Manual* clearly shows the influence and importance of the computer. For example, the requirement of large 1 1/2-inch margins has been replaced by more computer friendly 1-inch margins. Likewise, the reference section, which used to require cumbersome three-space indentations, now allows you to use the tab key on your computer or word processor.

In addition to being computer friendly, the general layout of the APA format paper is designed to be reader friendly. For example, the use of separate, specifically designated sections allows the reader to know exactly which part of the project is being dealt with. You are introduced to the first four in this chapter.

Sections of the APA Format Paper

The major components of an APA format paper are, in order,

1. Title page
2. Abstract
3. Introduction
4. Method section
5. Results section
6. Discussion section
7. References
8. Author note
9. Tables (if any)
10. Figures (if any)

```
                                    Cheating in College      1
         Running head: CHEATING AND TYPE A




                  Cheating in College and the Type A Personality:

                              A Reevaluation

                    Stephen F. Davis and Maureen C. Pierce

                         Emporia State University

              Lonnie R. Yandell, Paul S. Arnow, and Ann Loree

                              Belmont University
```

FIGURE 5-1   THE TITLE PAGE OF AN APA FORMAT PAPER

In this chapter we consider the title page, abstract, introduction, and method section. A complete APA format paper will be presented and discussed in Chapter 12.

Title Page. A sample title page is shown in Figure 5-1. The important features are the manuscript page header, page number, running head, author(s), and affiliation(s). As we saw, the **manuscript page header** consists of the first two or three words of the title and is used to identify pages of a particular manuscript should they become separated. It appears in the upper-right-hand portion of each page two lines above the 1-in. margin. The page header appears either five spaces to the left of the page number or two lines above the page number. Neither the page number nor the

Manuscript page header The first two or three words of the report's title. Appears five spaces to the left of the page number on each page of the research report.

page header should extend beyond the margin on the right side of the page. The manuscript page header and page number appear on *all* pages of the paper, *except* the figures.

Two lines below the manuscript page header, flush against the left margin we find the running head. The **running head** is a condensed title that will be printed at the top of alternate pages when your paper is published in a journal. When you type the running head on the title page, it is in all-capital letters. Also, note that the *h* in running head is not capitalized. The running head "should be a maximum of 50 characters, including letters, punctuation, and spaces between words" (APA *Publication Manual*, 1994, p. 8).

The title of the paper, which is centered, may begin six or eight lines below the page number. The first word and all major words of the title are capitalized. Your title should summarize clearly and simply the nature of the research you are reporting, but it should not be overly long. The recommended length for the title is 10 to 12 words. If your title is too long to fit on one line, then it can be presented on two lines.

The name(s) of the author(s) is(are) double-spaced below the title. The author's institutional affiliation is double-spaced below the author's name. If there is more than one author, the authors should be listed in order of importance of their contributions to the research project. If authors are from the same institution, they may be listed on one line.

Abstract. Figure 5-2 shows an abstract page. Note, once again, the placement of the manuscript page header and page number. The word "Abstract" is centered and appears two lines below the page number. (A centered section title in which the first letters of major words are capitalized is designated as a **Level 1 heading.**)

Running head
A condensed title that is printed at the top of alternate pages of a published article.

Level 1 heading
A centered section title in which the first letters of major words are capitalized. Occupies a line by itself.

Abstract A brief description of the research that is presented in an APA format paper.

Psychological Detective

Put yourself in the place of someone who has just picked up the journal issue containing your article. You are skimming through the journal to see if you might be interested in reading this or that article. What feature of the article will you use as a guide in deciding whether to read a particular article in its entirety? What information would you utilize in making this decision? Write down your answers before proceeding.

Of course, the title of this section answers the first question; you will use the abstract as a guide to determine whether you want to read the complete article. The **abstract** of an experimental report consists of a brief (960 characters, approximately 120 words), one-paragraph description of the research presented in your paper. In order to help you make an educated decision about pursuing an article in depth, the paragraph that comprises the abstract should include a description of the intent

Cheating in College 2

Abstract

College students completed a Type A/B survey, a learning/grade orientation questionnaire, and an academic dishonesty questionnaire. Responses to these instruments replicated previous reports by showing that (a) learning orientation and Type A characteristics were positively related and (b) grade orientation and Type B characteristics were positively related. Type A participants showed higher cheating rates on a word-forming task only when they were placed under conditions that precluded their control.

FIGURE 5-2 THE ABSTRACT PAGE OF AN APA FORMAT PAPER

and conduct (including participants and method) of your project, the results you obtained, and the project's implications and/or applications. Clearly, complete preparation of the abstract will have to wait until you complete your project and analyze your data. However, you can start putting down some tentative ideas at this point in the procedure. Also, it is important to note that the abstract is typed in block form; there is no indentation on the first line.

definition

Introduction First major section of the APA format paper. Contains the thesis statement, review of relevant literature, and experimental hypothesis.

Introduction. Your **introduction** section begins on page 3 of your report. Notice that the word "Introduction" does not appear as the Level 1 heading that begins this section. Rather, you repeat the title from page 1.

Be sure that the title is exactly the same in both places. Figure 5-3A shows the first page of an Introduction section; the concluding page of the introduction section is shown in Figure 5-3B.

The first paragraph of the Introduction section should contain your thesis statement. The **thesis statement** should indicate the general topic in which you are interested and your general view of the relationship of the relevant variables in that area. In Figure 5-3A we can see that the general area of interest is cheat-

> **Thesis statement** A statement of the general research topic of interest and the perceived relationship of the relevant variables in that area.
>
> *definition*

FIGURE 5-3A

The first page of the Introduction section of an APA format paper.

```
                                    Cheating in College      3
              Cheating in College and the Type A Personality:

                            A Reevaluation
        Type A individuals have been described as aggressive,
   hostile, easily aroused, competitive, and achievement oriented
   (Matthews, 1982). The competitiveness and achievement
   orientation of Type A students often translates into the
   attainment of higher grades compared to those of the Type B
   counterparts. Perry, Kane, Bernesser, and Spicker (1990)
   questioned the achievements made by Type A students and
   speculated that their higher grades may not necessarily be the
   result of direct, sustained efforts to master learning; the
   methods used by Type A students may be linked to academic
   dishonesty.
        Recent studies (Huss et al., 1993; Wiess, Gilbert,
   Giordano, & Davis, 1993) examined this contention and reported
   that Type A students were more learning-oriented and reported
   cheating less on examinations than did Type B students, who
   were grade oriented and reported cheating more often. It is
   noteworthy that students determine their preparation for an
   examination; hence, they are able to exert control over their
   academic success in such situations.
        What about those situations where Type A students cannot
   directly control their achievement success? The present project
   was based on the premise that Type A students will be more
   likely than Type B students to resort to dishonest means or
   methods to succeed if they feel they lack the ability to
   control their destiny and the opportunity to use such methods
```

```
                                           Cheating in College    4
exists. More specifically, students were exposed to a
word-forming task and allowed to report the number of words they
successfully constructed. Providing the participants with an
exceptionally high standard of comparison should place the Type
A students in an apparently uncontrollable situation and result
in the reporting of more word formations than actually occurred.
     A second purpose of the present experiment was to replicate
the self-report data concerning learning-/grade-orientation and
cheating on examinations difference between Type As and Bs
reported by Huss et al. (1993) and Weiss et al. (1993). Despite
displaying higher levels of cheating on tasks involving lack of
control, the Type A students should report higher grade-
orientation scores than Type B students, but should not differ
appreciably in self-reported cheating rates.
```

FIGURE 5-3B

The final page of the Introduction section of an APA format paper.

ing in college. Moreover, there seems to be a relationship between the relevant variables, Type A characteristics and cheating.

Once you have presented the thesis statement, the remainder of the introduction serves to report the results of previous research that supports and/or refutes your thesis statement. This material represents the outcome of your literature review. Careful thought should be given to its presentation; good organization and a logical flow of ideas are important ingredients. The introduction is similar to telling a story to someone who may not be familiar with what you are talking about; you must be clear and not make unwarranted assumptions. First, you establish the big picture. Then, you begin to fill in the details. Your ultimate goal is to lead the reader to a description of what you plan to do in your experiment. This description usually appears at the end of the Introduction section. It is here that you will state your experimental hypothesis. We like to use the analogy of a funnel to describe the Introduction section. Like the introduction, the funnel starts off broad, then narrows to a specific focus. At the end the focus is very specific and in the case of the Introduction section leads to a logical experimental question, your experiment.

The more general thesis statement and literature review should support your specific experimental hypothesis. Remember that even though you may not directly state it in this manner, the experimental hypothesis must ultimately be stateable in general implication form.

Although we cannot teach you *how* to write in the limited space available, we can give you a few pointers that will assist you as you prepare your Introduction section. First, the use of unbiased language is imperative. **Unbiased language** is language that does not state or imply a prejudice toward any individual or group. According to the APA *Publication Manual* (1994):

Unbiased language Language that does not display prejudice toward an individual or group.

> APA is committed both to science and to the fair treatment of individuals and groups, and policy requires authors of APA publications to avoid perpetuating demeaning attitudes and biased assumptions about people in their writing. Constructions that might imply bias against persons on the basis of gender, sexual orientation, racial or ethnic group, disability, or age should be avoided. Scientific writing should be free of implied or irrelevant evaluation of the group or groups being studied.
>
> Long-standing cultural practice can exert a powerful influence over even the most conscientious author. Just as you have learned to check what you write for spelling, grammar, and wordiness, practice reading over your work for bias. You can test your writing for implied evaluation by reading it while (a) substituting your own group for the group or groups you are discussing or (b) imagining you are a member of the group you are discussing (Maggio, 1991). (p. 46)

Second, as you can see from Figures 5-3A and 5-3B, when citing references in the text of an APA format paper, you use the last name of the author(s) and the year of publication. Such citations can take one of two forms. In the first form, the authors are either the subject or the object in a sentence in the text. In such cases only the date of the publication appears in parentheses. An example of this type of citation takes the following form:

Smith and Davis (1995) reported that . . .

In the second form of citation the reference is cited only as support for a statement you have made. In this instance the author(s) *and* the year of publication are included inside the parentheses. An example of this type of citation takes the following form:

Recent research (Smith & Davis, 1995) showed that . . .

There are two additional considerations for such references. When there are multiple authors, the name of the last author is preceded by the ampersand (&) sign, *not* the word "and." When more than one study is cited within parentheses, the references are to be arranged alphabetically by the first author's last name.

Psychological Detective

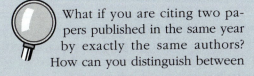

What if you are citing two papers published in the same year by exactly the same authors? How can you distinguish between these papers when you are citing them in the research report? Give this question some thought and write down an answer before reading further.

Reporting papers published in the same year is handled easily by placing a lowercase *a* or *b* after the date of each reference in question. Thus, if you had two 1994 references by Smith and Jones, you would cite them as follows:

Smith and Jones (1994a, 1994b)

or

(Smith & Jones, 1994a, 1994b)

The *a* and *b* designations will also appear as part of the complete citation of the article in the reference section (see Chapter 12).

Once you have presented your thesis statement, reviewed the relevant literature, and stated your experimental hypothesis, you are ready to tell the readers how you conducted your research. We turn to this topic next.

Method Section. The objective of the method section is to provide sufficient detail about your experiment to enable readers to evaluate its appropriateness and/or replicate your study should they desire. The method section is typically divided into three subsections: participants, apparatus (also designated materials or testing instruments), and procedure. Figure 5-4 shows the first subsection of the method section: participants. Note that "Method" is a Level 1 section head. You do not begin the method section on a new sheet if there is room on the previous page. There is no break between the introduction, method, results, and discussion sections of an APA format paper. You begin on a new sheet of paper only if a heading falls on the last line of a page; if it does, move it to the next page and begin the section there.

Participants. The subsection on participants answers three questions: Who participated in the study? How many participants were there? How were the participants selected? As you can see in Figure 5-4, a total of 168 undergraduate students (90 women, 78 men) participated in the study. These participants were enrolled in five separate classes, which were randomly assigned to either the experimental or the control condition of the experiment. In short, your description needs to be detailed enough to allow another investigator to replicate your samples. In addition to providing such demographic and selection information, you need to indicate any special arrangements, such as the receipt of extra credit for participation and/or the payment participants might have received. If any participants failed to complete the experiment, this fact must be mentioned, as must the reasons for their failing to complete the experiment.

If your experiment involves the use of animals, specify the number, species, and sex, as well as any other relevant physical characteristics, and the name of the supplier. Also, describe the housing conditions and routine care the animals received. The following description of animal participants, from the paper on cadmium ingestion and aggressive responding by Arb et al. (1994), is a good example of the type of information to include: "Eighteen male Holtzman rats served as subjects. The animals were 40 days old at the beginning of the experiment and 120 days old at the time of aggression testing. All animals were individually caged in suspended, wire-mesh cages with food and fluids available on a free-feeding basis."

Cheating in College   5

Method

<u>Participants</u>

One hundred sixty-eight undergraduate students (90 women, 78 men) enrolled in 5 classes at a medium size, regional state university volunteered to serve as participants. Two classes were randomly assigned to the Experimental condition; the three remaining classes constituted the Control condition.

<u>Testing Instruments</u>

The Modified Jenkins Activity Survey (JAS; Krantz, Glass, & Snyder, 1974), a 21-item questionnaire, was used to assess Type A characteristics. The LOGO II, a 32-item Likert-type scale, was used to assess learning and grade orientation (Eison & Pollio, 1989). In addition, each participant completed a cheating survey that questioned (1) past history of cheating in high school, (2) cheating in college, (3) fear of being caught, (4) importance of grades as a result of cheating, (5) the influence of strict penalties, (6) effective penalties, and (7) reasons for cheating. A demographic sheet requesting age, sex, and major, was also completed.

FIGURE 5-4   THE FIRST TWO SUBSECTIONS OF THE METHOD SECTION

Apparatus, Materials, or Testing Instruments. Figure 5-4 also shows the Apparatus (Testing Instruments) subsection of the method section. The equipment used in the experiment and its function(s) are briefly described in this subsection. If your equipment was commercially produced, mention the name of the manufacturer and the model number of the equipment. If your equipment was custom made, provide a more detailed description. In the case of complex equipment, you may want to include a diagram. If you report any physical measurements, such as height, weight, and/or distance, you must report them in metric units. For example, you will see the use of meters (m) and centimeters (cm) instead of inches, feet, and yards. The APA *Publication Manual* contains extensive sections describing the use of metric measurements and their correct abbreviations.

In some instances you will not use a piece of equipment; rather, you will use materials. In this case, this subsection will carry the designation "Materials." For example, in a study of eyewitness testimony, Dirk Dickens, Alice Ishigame, David Subacz, Stephanie Sponsel, Matthew Strader, and Judith Foy (1992), students at Loyola Marymount University in Los Angeles, CA, indicated in this section that "the stimulus materials consisted of slides, three of which were critical, depicting a theft scene" (p. 16).

Cheating in College   6

Procedure

    All testing took place during regularly scheduled class sessions. Following completion of an informed consent document, questionnaire booklets consisting of the JAS and LOGO II (counterbalanced to preclude order effects) and the demographic sheet were distributed to all participants. Although no time limits were imposed, all booklets were completed within 20 minutes.

    Following completion of these booklets the participants were exposed to a word-forming task which consisted of displaying five series of letters on separate 8 1/2" by 11" sheets of white typing paper. The letters were printed in upper case, black lettering that could be seen easily from all parts of the room. The five series (as used by Perry et al., 1990) were SGADBEE, ODIFICL, ETKPLAD, KLOITWN, and NAIGEVC. Each word series sheet was taped to the chalkboard and the participants allowed to view it for 30 seconds before it was removed. The strict time limit was imposed to create a pressured situation. Prior to scoring their own papers, the participants in the two experimental classes were told that the typical college student scores an average of 26.5 words per sheet. Based on research by Cooper and Peterson (1980), this score was inflated and was not characteristic of scores typically obtained by students. The participants in the three control classes were not given the "typical score" information. Following completion of the final word series, scoring instructions were presented and the

FIGURE 5-5 THE PROCEDURE SUBSECTION OF THE METHOD SECTION

As you saw in Figure 5-4, when your research involves a psychological test, questionnaire, or inventory, you may list this subsection as "Testing Instrument(s)." However, when you use a piece of laboratory equipment, you should label this subsection as "Apparatus." Emporia State University students Kyle Wood, Matthew Huss, Julie Hathaway, and Sharon Roberts (1995) provided an example of an apparatus description in their investigation of the role of odor cues in animal maze learning. They described their principal piece of equipment, a rat runway, as follows:

A single straight runway (11.4 cm wide × 12.7 cm high) served as the experimental apparatus. A gray startbox (28.1 cm) and a black goalbox (30.5 cm) were separated from the black run section (91.4 cm) by guillotine doors. Run and goal-approach

```
                                      Cheating in College      7
participants scored their own word-forming papers.
     Participants then completed the self-report cheating survey.
As all testing items were completed anonymously, they were
collected in the order that the students were seated in the
classroom to facilitate collation of the respective instruments
and data.
```

FIGURE 5-5   (continued)

latencies produced by a series of photoelectric cells (located 15.2, 92.4, and 116.8 cm, respectively, beyond the start door) were recorded on each trial by digital electric timers (Layfayette Model 54030). A plastic receptacle mounted into the end wall of the goalbox served as the goalcup. To ensure that conspecific odors were confined to the apparatus, a thin sheet of transparent plastic covered the entire top of the runway.

Procedure. The procedure section (see Figure 5-5) summarizes how you conducted the experiment. In addition to describing the steps that you followed, you need to include a description of the experimental manipulations and controls (see Chapter 4), such as randomization, balancing, constancy, and/or counterbalancing, that you employed. Summarize any instructions you used, unless they are unusual and/or complex. In the latter instance, you may want to present the instructions word for word.

If the experiment is involved and has several stages or phases, the procedure section can become lengthy (see Figure 5-5). In contrast, the procedure involved in the administration of a questionnaire may be straightforward and brief. For example, in their study of irrational beliefs Emporia State University students David Weintraub, Mindi Higgins, Megan Beishline, Debra Matchinsky, and Maureen Pierce (1994) indicated that

> All testing took place during regularly scheduled class sessions. The participants initially completed an informed consent document. After these forms were collected, a booklet containing a demographic sheet (requesting age, sex, academic classification, and major) and the testing instruments was distributed to each participant. The participants were instructed to complete the booklet according to the instructions printed on the first page of each item. Although no time limit was imposed, all participants completed the questionnaire booklet within twenty minutes.

Headings. Notice that the APA format paper uses a different type of heading for each section of the report. The major sections of the report, such as the introduction, method, results, and discussion, are introduced by a Level 1 heading. Subsections within these main sections are introduced by lower-level headings. For exam-

definition

Level 3 heading
A section title that is left-margin justified, underlined, and has the first letter of each major word capitalized. Occupies a line by itself.

Level 4 heading
A section title that is indented five spaces, underlined, has only the first word capitalized, and ends with a period. Does not occupy a separate line.

ple, the participants, apparatus, and procedure subsections of the method section are generally introduced by a Level 3 heading. **Level 3 headings** are left-margin justified, are underlined, have the first letter of each major word capitalized, and occupy a line by themselves. Should you need to further subdivide these subsections, a Level 4 heading would be used. **Level 4 headings** are indented five spaces, underlined, have only the first letter of the first word capitalized, and end with a period. You begin typing two spaces following the period that concludes a Level 4 heading.

Table 5-1 summarizes the five types of section heads used in APA format articles. Level 1 and Level 3 headings are the ones most frequently used in preparing a research report that describes a single experiment (see Table 5-1). As we have seen, however, the description of a single experiment may require the use of Level 4 headings when the participants, apparatus, and procedure subsections are further subdivided (see Table 5-1). Likewise, when you are presenting more than one experiment, you will use Level 1, 3, and 4 headings as shown in Table 5-1.

In summary, the intent of the method section is aptly summarized as follows:

The Method section describes in detail how the study was conducted. Such a description enables the reader to evaluate the appropriateness of your methods and the reliability and the validity of your results. It also permits experienced investigators to replicate the study if they so desire. (American Psychological Association, 1994, p. 12)

REVIEW SUMMARY

1. Psychologists have developed their own style, **APA format,** for the preparation of scientific reports.
2. The major sections of an APA paper include the title page, **abstract, introduction, method, results, discussion,** references, author note, tables, and figures.
3. The specific sections of the APA format paper are designated by various headings.
4. The **manuscript page header** appears on each page and is used to identify pages of a manuscript.
5. The **running head,** which appears on the title page of the manuscript, is a condensation of the title. It is printed on the pages of the published journal article.
6. The **abstract** provides a brief (100-120 words) summary of the contents of the paper.
7. The **introduction** includes a **thesis statement,** literature review, and statement of the experimental hypothesis.
8. The use of biased language in the research report is to be avoided.

TABLE 5-1. LEVELS AND LOCATIONS OF HEADINGS USED IN AN APA FORMAT PAPER

3.32 Selecting the Levels of Headings

Not every article requires all levels of headings. Use the guidelines that follow to determine the level, position, and arrangement of headings. Note that each subheading must have at least one counterpart at the same level within a section (see section 3.30); for brevity, the examples that follow do not include counterparts.

One level. For a short article, one level of heading may be sufficient. In such cases, use only centered uppercase and lowercase headings (Level 1).

Two levels. For many articles in APA journals, two levels of headings meet the requirements. Use Level 1 and Level 3 headings:

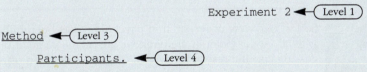

Method ◄— (Level 1)

Procedure ◄— (Level 3)

If the material subordinate to the Level 1 headings is short or if many Level 3 headings are necessary, indented, underlined paragraph headings (Level 4) may be more appropriate than Level 3 headings. (An indented, underlined paragraph heading—a Level 4 heading—should cover all material between it and the next heading, regardless of the heading level of the next heading.)

Three levels. For some articles, three levels of headings are needed. Use Level 1, Level 3, and Level 4 headings.

In a *single-experiment study,* these three levels of headings may look like this:

Method ◄— (Level 1)

Apparatus and Procedure ◄— (Level 3)

Pretraining period. ◄— (Level 4)

In a *multiexperiment study,* these three levels of headings may look like this:

Experiment 2 ◄— (Level 1)

Method ◄— (Level 3)

Participants. ◄— (Level 4)

Four levels. For some articles, particularly multiexperiment studies, monographs, and lengthy literature reviews, four levels of headings are needed. Use heading Levels 1 through 4:

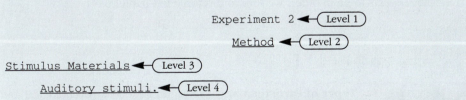

Experiment 2 ◄— (Level 1)

Method ◄— (Level 2)

Stimulus Materials ◄— (Level 3)

Auditory stimuli. ◄— (Level 4)

Five levels. If the article requires five levels of headings, subordinate all four levels above by introducing a Level 5 heading A CENTERED UPPERCASE HEADING above the other four (as shown in section 3.31).

9. The method section contains a thorough description of the participants, apparatus or materials, and procedure.

10. Level 1 and Level 3 headings are most commonly used with experimental reports. For more complex papers, **Level 4** headings may need to be added.

STUDY BREAK

1. What is meant by the term *APA format*? Why was it developed?

2. Matching

1. manuscript page header
2. running head
3. Level 1 heading
4. Level 3 heading
5. Level 4 heading
6. thesis statement

A. indicates the general topic you are interested in
B. centered, upper- and lower-case letters
C. first two or three words of the title
D. left margin, underlined, upper- and lower-case letters
E. condensed title
F. indented five spaces, underlined, only first word is capitalized, ends with period

3. What information should be presented in the abstract?

4. What is meant by "avoiding bias in your language" when writing an APA format paper?

5. Describe the information that is contained in the method section. What is the intent of this material?

LOOKING AHEAD

So far, our view of research in psychology has been rather general. At this point in the book we are on the verge of discussing specific research designs. (Our consideration of research designs begins in Chapter 7.) Because statistics and data analysis are integral components of the various research designs, a brief statistical refresher appears to be in order. We turn to this topic in Chapter 6.

HANDS-ON ACTIVITIES

1. Types of Participants.   Select an issue of a psychological journal that publishes human experimental research (e.g., *Memory and Cognition* or *Journal of Experimental Psychology: Human Learning, Memory, and Cognition*). Examine the articles in this issue to determine the type of participants used. How many projects used college students? Does it appear that participants are selected on the basis of precedent and/or availability? As you answer these questions, cite specific studies you reviewed.

2. **Apparatus.**   Survey the articles in an issue of *Journal of Experimental Psychology: Animal Behavior Processes* and *Journal of Experimental Psychology: Human Learning, Memory, and Cognition* to determine the type of apparatus employed. Beyond simply saying that some pieces of equipment are more suited to animal research, whereas others are more suited to human research, what generalizations can you make concerning differences in the equipment used by animal researchers and the equipment used by human researchers? Be as thorough as possible and take such factors as cost, availability, and specific use (e.g., IV presentation, DV recording) into account. Can you determine how the cost of the apparatus is being covered?

3. **Cross-Cultural Research.**   For this exercise you will interview psychology faculty at your school. (If you are at a small school, you may want to include all faculty engaged in research, regardless of department. If you are at a very large school, you may want to limit your interviews to those faculty members who are engaged in human research.) The purpose of the interview is to determine how aware researchers are of the importance of, and need for, cross-cultural research. Although we are not going to give you all the questions to ask during the interviews, we do want to get you started. Here are some questions you might want to use after you have described the purpose of your interview. You should be able to add your own questions (to determine, for example, how long the individuals have been conducting research and/or the nature of their research) to this list.

    A. How would you define culture?

    B. How is psychological research related to culture?

    C. Are current psychological researchers ethnocentric? Explain. More so than in previous years? Explain.

    D. What steps should be taken to make psychological research less culture specific?

    Once your interviews are completed, you should attempt to synthesize and integrate the results. What consistent patterns have emerged?

4. **Summarizing an APA Format Article.**   In Chapter 2 you learned how to conduct a search of the psychological literature. The final step in that search was to prepare a single-page summary of each article acquired in the literature search. This exercise asks you to prepare the first two sections of such a summary. To complete the exercise, you need to select an article of interest. At the top of the page list the full citation of the article you have selected (see Figure 2-5 if you need some help with the citation and format of the summary). Next, prepare a brief *Introduction* section. This description should address such issues as the general topic of the research, the relevant past findings, what the present research proposes to do, and the experimental hypothesis. The *method* section is summarized next. Be sure to include complete information about the (a) participants (who, how selected, dropouts, etc.), (b) apparatus (type and use), and (c) procedure (type of research, i.e., experimental, correlational, observation; variables involved, how conducted, any extraneous variable; special controls). You should strive to keep your summary to one-half of a single-spaced, typewritten page. Remember, there are other sections to be added to the summary. We will cover them in later chapters.

CHAPTER 6

Statistics Review

The detective is not alone in gathering data to help solve a case; psychologists, too, gather data. The topic of measurement has surfaced repeatedly during our discussion of psychological research methods. In later chapters we will be examining several statistical methods used to determine if the results of an experiment are meaningful. As we have seen, the term *significant* is used to describe those instances where the statistical results are likely to have been caused by our manipulation of the IV.

To better understand the nature of statistical significance, a closer look at statistics is in order. **Statistics** is a branch of mathematics that involves the collection, analysis, and interpretation of data. Various statistical techniques are used to aid the researcher in several ways during the decision-making processes encountered when conducting research.

The two main branches of statistics assist your decisions in different ways. **Descriptive statistics** are used to summarize any set of numbers so you can understand and talk about them more intelligibly. **Inferential statistics** are used to analyze data after an experiment is conducted to determine whether your independent variable had a significant effect.

DESCRIPTIVE STATISTICS

We use descriptive statistics when we want to summarize a set or distribution of numbers so that their essential characteristics can be communicated. One of these essential characteristics is a measure of the typical or representative score, called a measure of central tendency. The mode, median, and mean are the measures of central tendency used by psychologists. A second essential characteristic that we need to know about a distribution is how much variability or spread exists in the scores. However, before we discuss these measures of central tendency and variability, we need to examine the measurements on which they are based.

SCALES OF MEASUREMENT

We can define **measurement** as the assignment of symbols to events according to a set of rules. Your grade on a test is a symbol that stands for your performance; it was assigned according to a particular set of rules (the instructor's grading standards). The *particular* set of rules used in assigning a symbol to the event in question is known as a **scale of measurement.** The four scales of measurement that are of interest to psychologists are nominal, ordinal, interval, and ratio scales. How you choose to measure the DV (i.e., which scale of measurement you use) will directly determine the type of statistical test you can use to evaluate your data once a research project is completed.

Nominal Scale. The **nominal scale** is a simple classification system. For example, if you were categorizing the furniture in a classroom as tables *or* chairs, you are using a nominal scale of measurement. Likewise,

Statistics Branch of mathematics that involves the collection, analysis, and interpretation of data.

Descriptive statistics Procedures used to summarize any set of data.

Inferential statistics Procedures used to analyze data after an experiment is completed. Used to determine if the independent variable has a significant effect.

Measurement The assignment of symbols to events according to a set of rules.

Scale of measurement A set of measurement rules.

Nominal scale A scale of measurement where events are assigned to categories.

recording responses to an item on a questionnaire as "agree," "undecided," or "disagree" reflects the use of a nominal scale of measurement. The items being evaluated are assigned to mutually exclusive categories.

Ordinal Scale. When the events in question can be rank ordered, an **ordinal scale** of measurement is being used. Notice that we indicated *only* that the events under consideration could be rank ordered; we did not indicate that the intervals separating the units were comparable. Although we can rank the winners in a track meet (i.e., first, second, third, fourth), this rank ordering does not tell us anything concerning how far apart the winners were. Perhaps it was almost a dead heat for first and second; maybe the winner was far ahead of the second-place finisher.

Interval Scale. When the events in question can be rank ordered *and* equal intervals separate adjacent events, an **interval scale** is being used. For example, the temperatures on a Fahrenheit thermometer form an interval scale; rank ordering has been achieved *and* the difference between any two adjacent temperatures is the same, one degree. Notice that the interval scale does not have a true zero point, however. When you reach the "zero" point on a Fahrenheit thermometer, does temperature cease to exist? No, it's just *very* cold. Likewise, scores on tests such as the SAT and ACT are interval scale measures.

Ordinal scale
A scale of measurement that permits events to be rank ordered.

Interval scale
A scale of measurement that permits rank ordering of events with the assumption of equal intervals between adjacent events.

Ratio scale A scale of measurement that permits rank ordering of events with the assumptions of equal intervals between adjacent events and a true zero point.

Psychological Detective

Assume that you are on a college admissions committee and that you are reviewing applications. Each applicant's ACT score forms an integral part of your review. You have just come across an applicant who scored 0 on the verbal subtest. What does this score tell you? Formulate an answer to this question before reading further.

The score of 0 should not be interpreted as meaning that this individual has *absolutely* no verbal ability. Because ACT scores are interval scale measurements, there is no true zero. Hence, a score of 0 should be interpreted as meaning that the individual is *very low* in that ability. The same could be said for 0 scores on the wide variety of tests, questionnaires, and personality inventories that are routinely used in personality research. The presence of a true zero is characteristic only of the ratio scale of measurement.

Ratio Scale. The **ratio scale** of measurement takes the interval scale one step further. Just as the interval scale, the ratio scale permits the rank ordering of scores with the assumption of equal intervals between them, *but* it also assumes the presence of a true zero point. Physical measurements, such as the amplitude or intensity of sound or light, are ratio measurements. These measurements can be rank ordered and there are equal intervals between adjacent scores. However, when a sensitive measuring device reads 0, there is nothing there. The ratio scale also allows you to make ratio comparisons, such as twice as much or half as much.

Our discussion of scales of measurement has progressed from the nominal scale, which provides the least amount of information, to the ratio scale, which provides the greatest amount of information. When changes in the DV are evaluated, psychologists try to use a scale of measurement that will provide the most information; frequently, an interval scale is selected because psychologists often do not use measurements that have a true zero. We now turn to the topic of central tendency. Keep in mind that the scales of measurement directly determine which measure of central tendency will be used.

MEASURES OF CENTRAL TENDENCY

definition

Mode The score in a distribution that occurs most often.

Median The number that divides a distribution in half.

Measures of central tendency, such as the mode, median, and mean, tell us about the typical score in a distribution.

Mode. The **mode** is the number or event that occurs most frequently in a distribution. If students reported the following work hours

12, 15, 20, 20, 20,

the mode would be 20.

Mode = 20.

Although the mode can be calculated for any scale of measurement, it is the only measure of central tendency that can be calculated for nominal data.

Median. The **median** is the number or score that divides the distribution into equal halves. To be able to calculate the median, you must first rank order the scores. Thus, if you started with the following scores

56, 15, 12, 20, 17,

you would need to rank order them as follows:

12, 15, 17, 20, 56.

Now, it's an easy task to determine that 17 is the median (mdn):

mdn = 17

What if you have an even number of scores, as in the following distribution?

1, 2, 3, 4, 5, 6

In this case the median lies halfway between the two middle scores (3 and 4). Thus, the median would be 3.5, halfway between 3 and 4. The median can be calculated for ordinal, interval, and ratio data.

Mean. The **mean** is defined as the arithmetic average. To find the mean we add all the scores in the distribution and then divide by the number of scores we added. For example, assume we start with

12, 15, 18, 19, 16.

We use the Greek letter sigma, Σ, to indicate the sum. If X stands for the numbers in our distribution, then ΣX means to add the numbers in our distribution. Thus, $\Sigma X = 80$. If N stands for the number of scores in the distribution, then the mean would equal $\Sigma X / N$. For the above example, $16 = 80/5$. The sum of these numbers is 80 and the mean is 16 (80/5). The mean is symbolized by $\overline{X}$ (X bar). Thus, $\overline{X} = 16$. The mean can be calculated for interval and ratio data, but it is not normally calculated for nominal and ordinal data because it makes little sense.

Choosing a Measure of Central Tendency. Which measure of central tendency should you choose? The answer to that question depends on the type of information you are seeking. If you want to know which score occurred most often, then the mode is the choice. However, the mode may not be very representative of the other scores in your distribution. Consider the following distribution:

1, 2, 3, 4, 5, 11, 11

In this case the mode is 11. Because *all* the other scores are considerably smaller, the mode does not accurately describe the typical score.

The median may be a better choice to serve as the representative score because it takes into account all the data in the distribution. However, there are drawbacks with this choice. The median treats all scores alike; differences in magnitude are not taken into account. Thus, the median for *both* of the following distributions will be 14:

Distribution 1: 11, 12, 13, **14,** 15, 16, 17   **mdn = 14**
Distribution 2: 7, 8, 9, **14,** 23, 24, 25   **mdn = 14**

When we calculate the mean, however, the *value* of each number is taken into account. Although the medians for the two distributions above are the same, the means are not:

Distribution 1: 11, 12, 13, 14, 15, 16, 17
$\Sigma X = 98$ $\overline{X} = 98/7$ $\overline{X} = 14.00$
Distribution 2: 7, 8, 9, 14, 23, 24, 25
$\Sigma X = 110$ $\overline{X} = 110/7$ $\overline{X} = 15.71$

The fact that the mean of Distribution 2 is larger than that of Distribution 1 indicates that the value of each individual score has been taken into account.

Because the mean takes the value of each score into account, it usually provides a more accurate picture of the typical score and is the measure of central tendency favored by psychologists. However, there are instances when the mean may be misleading. Consider the following distribution of charitable donations:

Charitable Donations: $1, 1, 1, 5, 10, 10, 100

mode = $1

mdn = $5

mean = $128/7 $\overline{X}$ = $18.29

If you wanted to report the "typical" gift, would it be the mode? Probably not. Even though $1.00 is the most frequent donation, this amount is *substantially* smaller than the other donations, and more people made contributions over $1.00 than made the $1.00 contribution. What about the median? Five dollars appears to be more representative of the typical donation; there are an equal number of higher and lower donations. Would the mean be better? In this example the mean is substantially inflated by one large ($100.00) donation; the mean is $18.29 even though six of the seven donations are $10.00 or under. Although reporting the mean in this case may look good on a report of giving, it does not reflect the typical donation.

The lesson to be learned from this example is that when you have only a limited number of scores in your distribution, the mean may be inflated (or deflated) by extremely large (or extremely small) scores. The median may be a better choice as your measure of central tendency in such instances. As the number of scores in your distribution increases, the influence of extremely large (or extremely small) scores on the mean decreases. Look what happens if we collect two additional $5.00 donations:

Charitable Donations: $1, 1, 1, 5, 5, 5, 10, 10, 100

mode = $1 *and* $5

mdn = $5

mean = $138/9 $\overline{X}$ = $15.33

Note we now have two values ($1 and $5) for the mode (i.e., a bimodal distribution). The median stays the same ($5). However, the mean has decreased from $18.29 to $15.33; the addition of only two additional scores moved it closer to the median.

GRAPHING YOUR RESULTS

Once you have calculated a measure of central tendency, you can convey this information to others. If you have only one set of scores, the task is simple: You write down the value as part of your paper or report.

What if you are dealing with several groups or sets of numbers? Now the task is complicated and the inclusion of several numbers in a paragraph of text might be confusing. In such cases a graph or figure can be used to your advantage; a picture may well be worth a thousand words. It is not uncommon to see a detective use a chart or graph to help make a point. You may choose one of several types of graphs.

Pie chart Graphical representation of the percentage allocated to each alternative as a slice of a circular pie.

Pie Chart. If you are dealing with percentages that total 100%, then the familiar **pie chart** may be a good choice. The pie chart depicts the percentage represented by each alternative as a slice of a circular pie. The larger the slice, the greater the percentage. Ronald Hinkley and Andrew Kohut (1993) used a pie chart (see Figure 6-1) when they reported the results of the following question that was asked of East Germans: "Overall do you strongly approve, approve, disapprove, or strongly disapprove of the political and economic changes that have taken place in Germany over the past year or so?" From Figure 6-1 we can see that the mode is "Approve," as 90% of the respondents answered in this manner.

Histogram. We use the **histogram** to present our data in terms of frequencies per category. When we study a *quantitative variable,* we construct a histogram. The levels or categories of a quantitative variable must be arranged in a numerical order. For example, we may choose to arrange our categories from smallest to largest, or vice versa. Figure 6-2 shows a histogram for the age categories of participants in a developmental psychology research project.

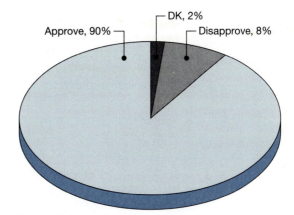

FIGURE 6-1   A pie chart representing the percentage of East Germans who responded "approve," "disapprove," or "don't know" to the question "Overall do you strongly approve, approve, disapprove, or strongly disapprove of the political and economic changes that have taken place in Germany over the past year or so?"
Source: From "Polling and democracy in the Former USSR and Eastern Europe" by R. H. Hinkley and A. Kohut, 1993. *The Public Perspective, 4,* pp. 15–18, fig. 5. © *The Public Perspective,* a publication of the Roper Center for Public Opinion Research, University of CT, Storrs. Reprinted by permission.

> **Histogram** A graph in which the frequency for each category of a quantitative variable is represented as a vertical column that touches the adjacent column.

FIGURE 6-2   HISTOGRAM DEPICTING THE FREQUENCY OF PARTICIPANTS IN VARIOUS AGE CATEGORIES IN A DEVELOPMENTAL PSYCHOLOGY RESEARCH PROJECT
Note that the sides of adjacent columns touch.

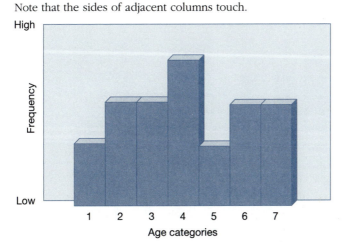

definition

Bar graph A graph in which the frequency for each category of a qualitative variable is represented as a vertical column. The columns of a bar graph do not touch.

Bar Graph. The **bar graph** also presents data in terms of frequencies per category. However, we are using *qualitative categories* when a bar graph is constructed. Qualitative categories are ones that cannot be numerically ordered. For example, single, married, divorced, and remarried are qualitative categories; there is no way to numerically order them.

FIGURE 6-3   BAR GRAPH DEPICTING THE SPORTS AND FITNESS PREFERENCES OF MEN AND BOYS (A) AND WOMEN AND GIRLS (B) WHO ARE FREQUENT PARTICIPANTS IN SUCH ACTIVITIES   Because a qualitative variable is depicted, the bars do not touch.

Source: The American Enterprise, September/October 1993, p. 101.

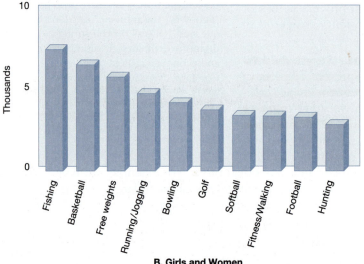

A. Boys and Men

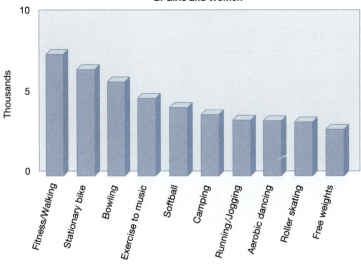

B. Girls and Women

Figure 6-3 shows a bar graph for the sports and fitness preferences of men and boys (Part A) and women and girls (Part B) who are frequent participants in such activities. Placing a space between the bars lets the reader know that qualitative categories are being reported. You can see at a glance that the number per category *and* type of activities differ drastically between the two groups. Think of how many words it would take to write about these results rather than present them as a graph!

Frequency Polygon. If we mark the middle of the crosspiece of each bar in a histogram with a dot, (see Figure 6-4A) connect the dots, and remove the bars, we have constructed a **frequency polygon** (see Figure 6-4pB). The frequency

FIGURE 6-4   THE FREQUENCY POLYGON IS CONSTRUCTED BY PLACING A DOT IN THE CENTER OF EACH BAR OF A HISTOGRAM AND CONNECTING THE DOTS (PART A) AND REMOVING THE BARS (PART B)

The frequency polygon, like the histogram, displays the frequency of each score or number.

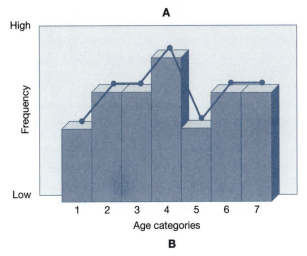

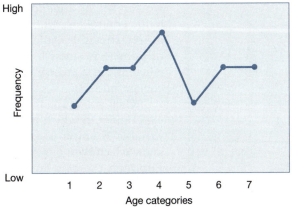

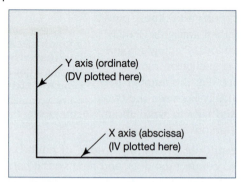

FIGURE 6-5   THE ORDINATE OR Y AXIS AND ABSCISSA OR X AXIS   The ordinate should be about 2/3 the size of the abscissa to portray the data as clearly as possible.

Ordinate The vertical or Y axis of a graph.

Abscissa The horizontal or X axis of a graph.

polygon, like the histogram, displays the frequency of each number or score. The only difference between the two is the use of bars in the histogram and the use of connected dots in the frequency polygon.

Line Graph. The results of psychological experiments are often presented as a line graph. In constructing a line graph, we start with two axes or dimensions. The vertical or Y axis is known as the **ordinate;** the horizontal or X axis is known as the **abscissa** (see Figure 6-5). Our scores or data (the DV) are plotted on the ordinate. The values of the variable we are manipulating (the IV) are plotted on the abscissa.

How tall should the Y axis be? How long should the X axis be? A good rule of thumb is for the Y axis to be approximately two thirds as tall as the X axis is long (see Figures 6-5 and 6-6). Other configurations will give a distorted picture of the data. For example, if the ordinate is considerably shorter, differences between groups or treatments will be obscured (see Figure 6-7A), whereas lengthening the ordinate tends to exaggerate differences (see Figure 6-7B).

In Figure 6-6 we have plotted the results of a hypothetical experiment in which the effects of different levels of stress on making correct landing decisions by air traffic controllers was evaluated. As you can see, as stress increased, the number of correct responses increased. What if we had tested two different groups of participants, college students and air traffic controllers? How would we display the results of both groups on the same graph? No problem. All we need to do is add the data points for the second group and a legend or box that identifies the groups (see Figure 6-8). Now, we can see at a glance that the air traffic controllers, whose occupation is very stressful, make more correct responses as stress level increases, whereas the converse is true for the college students.

When you graph the results of an experiment in which more than one variable is employed, how do you know which IV to plot on the abscissa? Although there is no fixed rule, a good guideline is to plot the variable

FIGURE 6-6   RESULTS OF A HYPOTHETICAL EXPERIMENT INVESTIGATING THE EFFECTS OF STRESS ON CORRECT RESPONDING IN AIR TRAFFIC CONTROLLERS

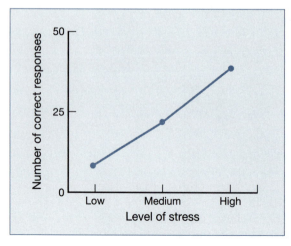

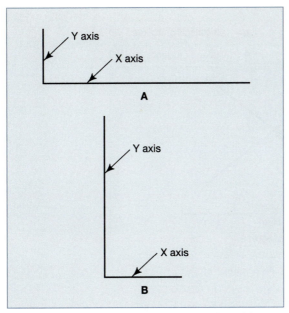

FIGURE 6-7   ALTERING THE X (ABSCISSA) OR Y
(ORDINATE) AXIS CAN DISTORT THE RESULTS OF AN
EXPERIMENT   A. If the ordinate is considerably shorter
than the abscissa, significant effects can be obscured.
B. If the ordinate is considerably longer than the
abscissa, very small effects can be exaggerated.

having the greatest number of levels on the abscissa. Thus, in Figure 6-8 the
three levels of stress were plotted on the abscissa, rather than the two levels of
participants.

Psychological Detective

Why would you want to plot the
IV with the greatest number of
levels on the abscissa? Give this
question some thought and write down
your answer before reading further.

By plotting the variable with the greater number of levels on the abscissa, you reduce the number of lines that will appear on your graph. The fewer the number
of lines, the less difficulty you will have in interpreting your graph. For example,
had we plotted the type of participants in our stress experiment on the abscissa,
then Figure 6-8 would have had three lines, one for each level of stress. We will
discuss the accepted APA format for preparing graphs and tables in Chapter 12.

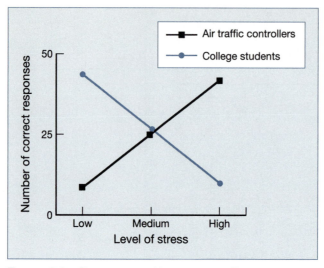

FIGURE 6-8 RESULTS OF A HYPOTHETICAL EXPERIMENT INVESTIGATING THE EFFECTS OF STRESS ON CORRECT RESPONDING IN AIR TRAFFIC CONTROLLERS *AND* COLLEGE STUDENTS

STATISTICS

At this point, it is important to note that this text is *not* a statistics text—we assume that you have already taken a statistics course. Therefore, we will not review formulas for all the various statistical calculations and tests that you will encounter in this book. You can find those formulas in your statistics book (which we hope you kept after taking your statistics course). Your calculating skills may be a little rusty, but all statistical formulas merely require addition, subtraction, multiplication, division, and finding square roots—not all that challenging for a college student!

By the same token, most psychologists (and probably psychology students) rarely use hand computation techniques for statistics after their initial statistics course; the vast majority use a computer package of some sort to analyze data they collect. Of course, these computer packages vary widely. You may have access to a large and powerful statistics package owned by your school or department—some standard packages are SPSS, SAS, and BMD. These programs may be run on a large schoolwide computer or they may be resident on PCs in the department. Alternatively, you may have access to a smaller statistics program—some schools even have students buy a statistics software program when they take the statistics course. These programs are much too numerous to list; some representative examples are MYSTAT, STATSTAR, or StataQuest. In any case, you are likely to have access to a computerized statistical analysis program. We cannot begin to give instructions about how to operate the particular program you might have access to—there are simply too many programs. However, we will attempt to give you some general hints about how to interpret the output you receive from such programs.

Throughout the chapters that deal with statistics, we will show you statistical output from one large computer package (SPSS) and one small package (MYSTAT)

and present interpretations from those packages. There should be enough similarity among statistical packages to allow for a high degree of generalization from our examples to the specific package you may use.

MEASURES OF VARIABILITY

Although measures of central tendency and graphs convey considerable information, there is still more that we can learn about the numbers we have gathered. We also need to know about the variability in our data.

Your last psychology test was just returned; your score is 64. What does that number tell you? By itself it may not mean very much. You ask your professor for additional information and find that the class mean was 56. You feel better because you were above the mean. However, after a few moments of reflection you realize that you still need more information. How were the other scores grouped? Were they all clustered close to the mean or did they spread out considerably? The amount of **variability** or spread in the other scores will have a bearing on the standing of your score. If most of the other scores are very close to the mean, then your score will be among the highest in the class. If the other scores are spread out widely around the mean, then your score will not be one of the strongest. Obviously, a measure of variability is needed to provide a complete picture of these data. The range and standard deviation are two measures of variability that are frequently reported by psychologists.

Range. The **range** is the easiest measure of variability to calculate; you rank order the scores in your distribution and then subtract the smallest score from the largest to find the range. Consider the following distribution:

1, 1, 1, 1, 5, 6, 6, 8, 25

When we subtract 1 (smallest score) from 25 (largest score), we find that the range is 24:

Range: 25 − 1 = 24

However, other than telling us the difference between the largest and smallest scores, the range does not provide much information. Knowing that the range is 24 does not tell us about the distribution of the scores we just considered. Consider Figure 6-9. The range is the same for Part A and Part B; however, the spread of the scores differs drastically between these two distributions. Most of the scores are clustered in the center of the first distribution (Figure 6-9A), whereas the scores are spread out more evenly in the second distribution (Figure 6-9B). We must turn to another measure, the standard deviation, to provide the additional information about how the scores are distributed.

Variance and Standard Deviation. In order to obtain the standard deviation, we must first calculate the variance. You can think of the **variance** as a single number

Variability The extent to which scores spread out around the mean.

Range A measure of variability that is computed by subtracting the smallest score from the largest score.

Variance A single number that represents the total amount of variation in a distribution.

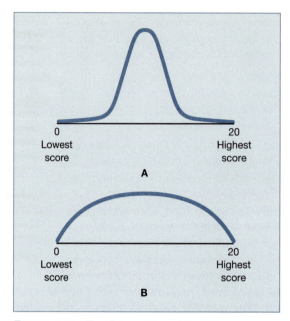

0
Lowest
score

20
Highest
score

A

0
Lowest
score

20
Highest
score

B

FIGURE 6-9   THE RANGE DOES NOT PROVIDE MUCH INFORMATION ABOUT THE DISTRIBUTION UNDER CONSIDERATION   Even though the range is the same, these two distributions differ drastically.

that represents the total amount of variability in the distribution. The larger the number, the greater the total spread of the scores. The variance and standard deviation are based on how much each score in the distribution deviates from the mean.

When an experiment is conducted, a sample of participants is used to provide information (an estimate) about an entire population. As an example we will calculate the variance of the set of nine numbers found on page 181. Once the variance is calculated, it is easy to determine the standard deviation.

Now we are ready to use the variance to find the standard deviation.

Interpreting the Standard Deviation. To find the **standard deviation** all we have to do is take the square root of the variance.

$$\text{standard deviation (SD)} = \sqrt{\text{variance}}$$
$$= \sqrt{58.25}$$
$$= 7.63$$

As with variance, the larger the standard deviation, the greater the variability or spread of scores.

The SPSS printout listing the mean, variance, and standard deviation for the nine scores we used when we calculated the range is shown in Table 6-1. As you can see, the computer informs us that we entered nine numbers. The mean of these nine numbers is 6.00, whereas the variance is 58.25 and the standard deviation is 7.63. Because the printout for descriptive statistics, such as the mean, variance, and standard deviation, differs very little between small and large computer programs, we will present only the SPSS results at this point.

Now that we have calculated the standard deviation, what does it tell us? To answer that question we must consider the normal distribution (also called the normal curve). The concept of the **normal distribution** is based on the finding that as we increase the number of scores in our sample, many distributions of interest to psychologists become symmetri-

TABLE 6-1. SPSS PRINTOUT SHOWING MEAN, STANDARD DEVIATION, AND VARIANCE

Number of valid observations (listwise) = 9.00

Variable	Mean	Std Dev	Variance	Range	Valid N
SCORE	6.00	7.63	58.25	24.00	9

cal or bell shaped. (Sometimes the normal distribution is called the bell curve.) The majority of the scores cluster around the measure of central tendency with fewer and fewer scores occurring as we move away from it. Thus, the normal distribution is the symmetrical or bell-shaped distribution of scores. As you can see from Figure 6-10, the mean, median, and mode of a normal distribution all have the same value.

Normal distributions and standard deviations are related in interesting ways. For example, distances from the mean of a normal distribution can be measured in standard deviation (SD) units. Consider a distribution with a $\overline{X}$ of 56 and SD of 4; a score of 60 can be described as falling one SD above the mean (+1 SD), whereas a score of 48 is two SDs below the mean (–2 SDs), and so on. As you can see from Figure 6-11, 34.13% of all the scores in *all* normal distributions occur between the mean and one standard deviation *above* the mean. Likewise, 34.13% of all the scores in a distribution occur between the mean and one standard deviation *below* the mean. Another 13.59% of the scores occur between one and two standard deviations *above* the mean; another 13.59% of the scores occur between one and two standard deviations *below* the mean. Thus, slightly over 95% of all the scores in a normal distribution occur between two standard deviations below the mean and two standard deviations above the mean. Exactly 2.28% of the scores occur *beyond* two standard deviations *above* the mean; another 2.28% of the scores occur beyond two standard deviations *below* the mean. It is important to remember that these percentages hold true for all normal distributions.

FIGURE 6-10   A SYMMETRICAL OR BELL-SHAPED NORMAL DISTRIBUTION   Note that the mean, median, and mode coincide in a normal distribution.

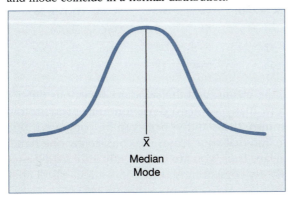

$\overline{X}$
Median
Mode

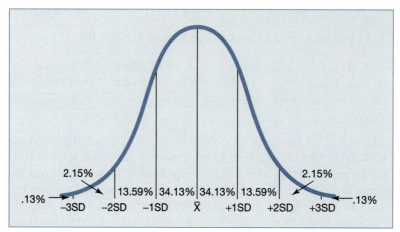

FIGURE 6-11 THE RELATIONSHIP OF STANDARD DEVIATIONS AND THE NORMAL DISTRIBUTION.

Now, let's return to your test score of 64. You know that the mean of the class is 56. If the instructor also tells you that the standard deviation is 4, what would your reaction be? Your score of 64 would be two standard deviations above the mean; you should feel pretty good. Your score of 64 puts you in the top 2.28% of the class (50% of the scores below the mean + 34.13% from the mean to one standard deviation above the mean + 13.59% that occur between one and two standard deviations above the mean)! (See Figure 6-12A.)

What if your instructor had told you that the standard deviation was 20? Now your score of 64 does not stand up as well as it did when the standard deviation was 4. You are above the mean but a long way from being even one standard deviation above the mean (see Figure 6-12B).

Because the percentage of the scores that occurs from the mean to the various standard deviation units is the same for *all* normal distributions, we can compare scores from different distributions by discussing them in terms of standard deviations above or below the mean. Consider the following scores:

TEST #	YOUR SCORE	$\overline{X}$	SD	RELATIONSHIP OF YOUR SCORE TO THE $\overline{X}$
1	46	41	5	One SD above
2	72	63	4	Over 2 SDs above
3	93	71	15	Over 1 SD above

Even though your scores, the means, and the standard deviations differ considerably, we can determine how many standard deviation units away from the mean each of your scores is. In turn, these differences can be compared. When these comparisons are made, we find that your scores are consistently one standard deviation or more above the mean. Thus, you are consistently in *at least* the top 15.87% of the class (50% + 34.13%). By comparing scores from various distributions in this

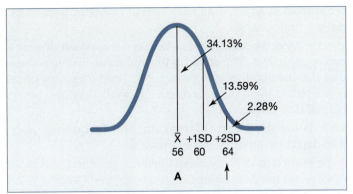

A. A score of 64 is exceptionally good when the mean is 56 and the standard deviation is 4.

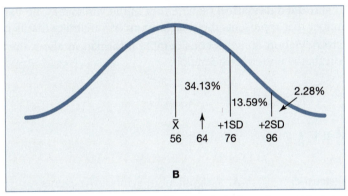

B. The same score is not as highly regarded when the standard deviation is 20.

FIGURE 6-12

manner, we are able to see patterns and suggest what might occur in the future. However, another type of descriptive statistic, the correlation coefficient, is often used for predictive purposes. We turn to this topic next.

REVIEW SUMMARY

1. **Statistics** involves the collection, analysis, and interpretation of data.
2. **Measurement** is the assignment of symbols to events according to a set of rules. A **scale of measurement** is a particular set of measurement rules.
3. A **nominal scale** is a simple classification system, whereas events can be rank ordered when an **ordinal scale** is used. Equal intervals separate rank-ordered events in an **interval scale.** The addition of a true zero to an interval scale results in a **ratio scale.**

4. **Descriptive statistics,** which summarize sets of numbers, include measures of central tendency and variability.

5. The **mode** is the most frequent score, whereas the **median** divides a distribution into two equal halves. The **mean** is the arithmetic average. Depending on the nature of the distribution, one or more of these measures of central tendency may not reflect the typical score equally well. They are, however, identical in a normal distribution.

6. Graphs, such as the **pie chart, histogram,** and **frequency polygon,** are often used to depict frequencies or percentages.

7. The line graph is used to depict experimental results. The DV is plotted on the vertical (Y) axis, and the IV is plotted on the horizontal (X) axis. A 2:3 relationship of Y to X axes produces a representative figure.

8. Measures of **variability** include the **range** (difference between high and low scores) and **standard deviation** (square root of the variance). The **variance** is a single number that represents the total amount of variability that is present.

9. The standard deviation conveys considerable information about the **normal distribution** that is under consideration.

STUDY BREAK

1. Matching
   1. inferential statistics G
   2. descriptive statistics E
   3. measurement A
   4. nominal scale C
   5. ordinal scale B
   6. interval scale F
   7. ratio scale D

   A. assignment of symbols to events
   B. rank order
   C. putting events into categories
   D. equal intervals plus a true zero
   E. used to summarize a set of numbers
   F. equal intervals
   G. used to analyze data after an experiment

2. The number that occurs most often is the _____, whereas the number that divides a distribution of scores in half is the _____.

3. When you are dealing with a normal distribution of scores, which measure of central tendency is preferred? Why?

4. When is a pie chart used? When is a histogram used?

5. You are constructing a line graph to depict the results of an experiment you just completed. What is the ordinate? What is the abscissa? What will be plotted on each of them?

6. Why does the range not convey much information about variability?

7. What is variance and how is it related to the standard deviation?

8. How does the standard deviation relate to the normal curve?

CORRELATION

Just as in the successful completion of a detective case, prediction plays an important role in psychology. Nowhere is this aspect of psychology more apparent than in high school and college. You probably took a college entrance examination while you were in high school. Based on the results of this exam, a prediction about your grades in college might be made. Similarly, should you plan to go on for graduate training after you complete your undergraduate degree, you probably will take another entrance examination. Depending upon your area of interest, you might take the Graduate Record Examination (GRE), the Law School Aptitude Test (LSAT), the Medical School Aptitude Test (MCAT), or some similar test.

Such predictions are based on the calculation of a correlation coefficient. The basic ideas of correlation were developed by Sir Francis Galton (1822–1911). Galton, who was independently wealthy, devoted his time to studying and investigating those things that interested him. According to E. G. Boring (1950), the eminent historian of psychology, Galton "was a free-lance and a gentleman scientist. He was forever seeing new relationships and working them out, either on paper or in practice. No field was beyond his possible interest, no domain was marked off in advance as being out of his province" (p. 461).

A **correlation coefficient** is a single number that represents the degree of relationship (i.e., "co-relation") between two variables. A correlation coefficient can range in value from –1.00 to +1.00.

> **definition**
>
> **Correlation coefficient** A single number representing the degree of relationship between two variables.

A correlation coefficient of –1.00 indicates that there is a *perfect negative relationship* between the two variables of interest. That is, whenever we see an increase of one unit in one variable, there is always a proportional decrease in the other variable. Consider the following scores on Tests X and Y:

	TEST X	TEST Y
Student 1	49	63
Student 2	50	61
Student 3	51	59
Student 4	52	57
Student 5	53	55

For each unit of increase in a score on Test X, there is a corresponding *decrease* of two units in the score on Test Y. Given this information, you are able to predict that if Student 6 scores 54 on Test X, the score on Test Y will be 53.

As you saw in Chapter 3, a zero correlation means that there is *little or no relationship* between the two variables. As scores on one variable increase, scores on the other variable may increase, decrease, or be the same. Hence, we are not able to predict how you will do on Test Y by knowing your score on Test X. A correlation coefficient does not have to be exactly 0.00 to be considered a zero correlation. The inability to make predictions is the key consideration. Two sets of scores having a zero correlation might look like this:

	TEST X	TEST Y
Student 1	58	28
Student 2	59	97
Student 3	60	63
Student 4	61	60
Student 5	62	50

In this case the correlation between Test X and Test Y is 0.04. A correlation that small tells you that you will not be able to predict Test Y scores by knowing Test X scores; you are dealing with a zero correlation.

A correlation coefficient of +1.00 indicates that there is a *perfect positive relationship* between the two sets of scores. That is, when we see an increase of one unit in one variable, we always see a proportional increase in the other variable. Consider the following scores on Tests X and Y:

	TEST X	TEST Y
Student 1	25	40
Student 2	26	41
Student 3	27	42
Student 4	28	43
Student 5	29	44

In this example there is an increase of one unit in the score on Test Y for every unit increase on Test X. The perfect positive correlation leads you to predict that if Student 6 scores 30 on Test X, then his/her score on Test Y will be 45.

THE PEARSON PRODUCT-MOMENT CORRELATION COEFFICIENT

The most common measure of correlation is the Pearson product-moment correlation coefficient (r). The Pearson product-moment correlation coefficient is named for Karl Pearson (1857–1936), who developed it. Pearson was one of Galton's students. This type of correlation coefficient is calculated when both the X variable and the Y variable are interval or ratio scale measurements and the data appear to be linear. Other correlation coefficients can be calculated when one or both of the variables are not interval or ratio scale measurements.

Examples of MYSTAT printouts for perfect positive and perfect negative correlations are shown in Table 6-2. As you can see, the correlation of Tests X and Y with themselves is always 1.00; however, the correlation of Test X with Test Y is –1.00 (Table 6-2A) when the relation is perfect negative and 1.00 (Table 6-2B) when the relation is perfect positive. MYSTAT does not provide a probability for

TABLE 6-2. MYSTAT PRINTOUT FOR: (A) PERFECT NEGATIVE CORRELATION, AND (B) PERFECT POSITIVE CORRELATION

```
A. Perfect Negative Correlation
   PEARSON CORRELATION MATRIX
                        TEST_X        TEST_Y
        TEST_X          1.000
        TEST_Y         -1.000        1.000
   NUMBER OF OBSERVATIONS: 5

B. Perfect Positive Correlation
   PEARSON CORRELATION MATRIX
                        TEST_X        TEST_Y
        TEST_X          1.000
        TEST_Y          1.000        1.000
   NUMBER OF OBSERVATIONS: 5
```

correlations. So, you would have to consult a table of correlation probabilities to determine if a particular correlation is significant.

Review the scatter diagrams in Chapter 3 (Figures 3-1, 3-2, and 3-3); they will help you visualize the various correlations we discussed. Perfect positive and perfect negative correlations always fall on a straight line, whereas nonperfect correlations do not. For positive correlations the trend of the points is from lower left to upper right, whereas the trend is from upper left to lower right for negative correlations. There is no consistent pattern for a 0.00 correlation.

Although descriptive statistics can tell us a great deal about the data we have collected, they cannot tell us everything. For example, when we conduct an experiment, descriptive statistics cannot tell us if the IV we manipulated had a significant effect on the behavior of the participants we tested or if the results we obtained would have occurred by chance. To make such determinations we must conduct an inferential statistical test.

INFERENTIAL STATISTICS

Once an experiment has been conducted, a statistical test is performed on the data that have been gathered. The results of this test will help you decide if the IV was effective or not. In other words, we shall decide if our statistical result is significant or not.

Courtesy of Sidney Harris.

Unlike the warning on this truck, psychologists view data and statistical procedures as tools to help answer research questions.

WHAT IS SIGNIFICANT?

The results of an inferential statistical test tell us whether the results of an experiment would occur frequently or rarely *by chance*. Small inferential statistics occur frequently *by chance*, whereas large ones occur rarely by chance. If the result occurs often by chance, we say that it is not significant and conclude that our IV did not affect the DV. However, if the result of our inferential statistical test occurs rarely by chance (i.e., it is significant), then we conclude that some factor other than chance is operative. If we have conducted our experiment properly and exercised good control (see Chapters 4 & 5), then our significant statistical result gives us reason to believe that the IV we manipulated was effective.

When do we consider that an event occurs rarely by chance? Traditionally psychologists say that any event that occurs by chance alone 5 times or fewer in 100 occasions is a rare event. Thus, you will see frequent mention of the ".05 level of significance" in journal articles. This statement means that a result is considered significant if it would occur 5 or fewer times by chance in 100 replications of the experiment. As the experimenter, you decide on the level of significance before the experiment is conducted.

You will encounter several significance tests in later chapters in this book. For the present we will use the *t* test to illustrate the use of a significance test.

THE *t* TEST

Assume that we are interested in determining if using a new textbook will improve scores in introductory psychology. We randomly select 16 students from an introductory psychology class. In turn, we randomly assign these students to one of two groups of 8 students each. Because we formed the groups randomly at the start of the experiment, we assume that they are comparable before they are exposed to the IV.

The students in Group A use the new textbook, while the students in Group B use the old textbook. Because the textbook used by Group A has no relation to, or effect on, the textbook used by the students in Group B, these groups are *independent* of each other. Finally, all students take two quizzes during the course. We add the scores for the two quizzes for each student and then compare the scores of the two groups to see if the new textbook was superior to the old textbook. The scores for the two groups appear below:

GROUP A (OLD TEXTBOOK)	GROUP B (NEW TEXTBOOK)
17	17
18	18
15	17
15	17
13	15
14	16
14	16
14	16
$\Sigma X = 120$	$\Sigma Y = 132$
$\overline{X} = 15.00$	$\overline{Y} = 16.50$

Do you think the new textbook is more effective? Just looking at the differences between the groups suggests that it might be; the mean score of Group B is higher than that of Group A. On the other hand, there is considerable overlap between the two groups; several of the students using the old textbook scored as well as some students using the new textbook. Is the difference we obtained large enough to be genuine, or is it just a chance happening? Merely looking at the results will not answer that question.

The *t* test is an inferential statistical test used to evaluate the difference between the means of *two groups* (see Chapter 7 for research designs using two groups). Because the two groups in our study method experiment were independent, we will be using an independent-groups *t* test. (The related-groups *t* test is discussed in Chapter 7.) The MYSTAT printout for our *t* test is shown in Table 6-3. You can see that our *t* value is 2.201 and that the probability of this *t* value is .045. Because the probability of this result occurring by chance is less than five times in one hundred, we can conclude that the two groups differ significantly.

t **Test** An inferential statistical test used to evaluate the difference between two means.

definition

TABLE 6-3. MYSTAT PRINTOUT FOR INDEPENDENT-GROUPS t TEST.

INDEPENDENT SAMPLES T TEST ON QUIZSCOR GROUPED BY TEXT$			
GROUP	N	MEAN	SD
old	8	15.000	1.690
new	8	16.500	0.926
POOLED VARIANCES T =	2.201 DF =	14 PROB =	.045

If your computer program does not provide the probability of your result as part of the printout, then *you* will have to make this determination yourself. Here's how. Recall that our t value is 2.201. Once we have obtained our t value, several steps must be followed in order to interpret its meaning:

1. Determine the degrees of freedom (df) involved. (Because some statistical packages may not automatically print the degrees of freedom for you, it is important to keep this formula handy.) For our study method problem:

$$df = (N_A - 1) + (N_B - 1)$$
$$= (8 - 1) + (8 - 1)$$
$$= 14$$

2. The degrees of freedom (we will discuss the meaning of degrees of freedom after we have completed the problem) are used to enter a t table (See Table A-1 in the Appendix). This table contains t values that occur by chance. We will compare our t value to these chance values. To be significant, the calculated t must be equal to or larger than the one in Table A-1.

3. We enter the t table on the row for 14 degrees of freedom. Reading across this row we find that a value of 2.145 occurs by chance 5% of the time (.05 level of significance). Because our value of 2.201 is larger than 2.145 (the .05 value in the table for 14 df), we can conclude that our result is significant. The type of study method had a significant effect on examination scores. This result is one that occurs fewer than five times in one hundred by chance. Had we chosen a different level of significance, such as once in one hundred occurrences (.01), the table value would have been 2.977 and we would conclude that our result is not significant. In many instances your computer program will print the probability of your t statistic automatically and you will not have to consult the t table.

Although it is easy to follow a formula to calculate the degrees of freedom, the meaning of this term may not be clear, even if you have already had an introductory statistics course. We will try to help you understand its meaning. By **degrees of freedom** we mean the ability of a number in a given set to assume any value. This ability is influenced by the restrictions that are imposed on the set of numbers. For every restriction, one number is determined and will assume a fixed or specified value. For example, assume that we have a set of 10 numbers and that we know the sum

Degrees of freedom The ability of a number in a specified set to assume any value.

of these numbers to be 100. Knowing that the sum is 100 is a restriction; hence, one of the numbers will be determined or fixed. In Example 1 below, the last number must be 15 because the total of the first 9 numbers (which can assume any value) is 85. In Example 2, the first 9 numbers have assumed different values. What is the value of the last number?

NUMBERS	1	2	3	4	5	6	7	8	9	10	SUM
Example 1	6	12	11	4	9	9	14	3	17	15	100
Example 2	21	2	9	7	3	18	6	4	5	?	100

As in the first example, the first 9 numbers can assume any value. In this example the sum of the first 9 numbers is 75. That means that the value of the last number is fixed at 25.

ONE-TAIL VERSUS TWO-TAIL TESTS OF SIGNIFICANCE

Recall from Chapter 2 that you state your experimental hypothesis in either a directional or a nondirectional manner. If the directional form is used, then you are specifying exactly how (i.e., the direction) the results will turn out. For the example we have been considering, the experimental hypothesis, stated in general implication form (see Chapter 2), might be as follows:

> If students are taught using a new textbook, then their quiz scores will be higher than those of students who use the old textbook.

Because we predict that the scores of students using the new textbook will be higher than those of students using the old textbook, we have a directional hypothesis. If we simply indicate that we expect a difference between the two groups and do not specify the exact nature of that difference, then we are using a nondirectional hypothesis.

Now, how do directional and nondirectional hypotheses relate to the *t* test? If you remember discussing one-tail and two-tail tests of significance in your statistics class, you're on the right track! A one-tail *t* test evaluates the probability of only one type of outcome, whereas the two-tail *t* test evaluates the probability of both possible outcomes. If you've associated directional hypotheses with one-tail tests, and nondirectional hypotheses with two-tail tests, you're right again.

Figure 6-13 depicts the relationship between the type of experimental hypothesis, directional versus nondirectional, and the type of *t* test, one-tail versus two-tail, used. As you can see, the region of rejection is large and only in one tail of the distribution when a one-tail test is conducted (Figure 6-13A). The probability of the result occurring by chance alone is split in half and distributed equally to the two tails of the distribution when a two-tail test is conducted (Figure 6-13B).

Although the calculations for a one-tail test of significance and a two-tail test of significance are the same, you would consult different columns in the *t* table. For the old-and-new text example we conducted a two-tail test of significance; 2.145 was our critical value at the .05 level of significance. Hence, a *t* value equal to or greater than

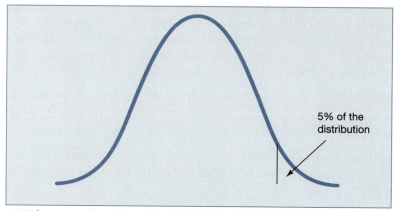

5% of the
distribution

A. With a one-tail test the region of rejection of the null hypothesis is located in one tail of the distribution. Directional hypotheses, such as A > B, are associated with one-tail tests.

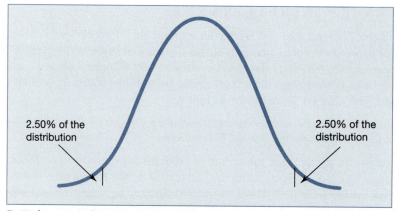

2.50% of the
distribution

2.50% of the
distribution

B. With a two-tail test the region of rejection of the null hypothesis is distributed evenly to both tails of the distribution. Nondirectional hypotheses, such as A ≠ B (A does not equal B), are associated with two-tail tests.

FIGURE 6-13   REGIONS OF REJECTION FOR (A) A ONE-TAIL TEST AND (B) A TWO-TAIL TEST

2.145 is significant (see Table A-1 in the Appendix). Had we done a one-tail test, our critical value at the .05 level of significance would have been 1.761 (see Table A-1).

Because a lower value is required for significance with a one-tail test of significance, it is somewhat easier to have a significant result. If this is the case, why don't experimenters *always* state directional experimental hypotheses? The main reason is that researchers don't always know exactly how an experiment will turn out. If we could predict the outcome of each experiment before it was conducted, there would be no need to do the experiment. If you state a directional hypothesis only to find the opposite result, you have to reject your hypothesis. Had you stated a nondirectional hypothesis, your experiment would have confirmed your predictions. When we conduct a *t* test, we are usually interested in either outcome; what if students actually perform worse with the new textbook?

THE LOGIC OF SIGNIFICANCE TESTING

Remember, we consider the result of an experiment to be statistically significant when it occurs rarely by chance. In such instances we assume that our IV produced the results.

However, typically our ultimate interest is not in the samples we have tested in an experiment but in what these samples tell us about the population from which they were drawn. In short, we want to generalize from our samples to the larger population.

We have diagrammed this logic in Figure 6-14. First, samples are randomly drawn from a specified population (Figure 6-14A). We assume that random selection has produced two equivalent groups: Any differences are due solely to chance factors. In Figure 6-14B we see the results of our experiment; the manipulation of the IV caused the groups to be significantly different. At this point generalization begins. Based on the significant difference that exists between the groups, we infer what would happen if our treatments were administered to all individuals in the population. In Figure 6-14C we have generalized from the results of our research using two samples to the entire population (see Chapter 10 for more on generalization). We are inferring that two separate groups would be created in the population due to the administration of our IV.

WHEN STATISTICS GO ASTRAY: TYPE I AND TYPE II ERRORS

Unfortunately, not all our inferences will be correct. Recall that we have determined that an experimental result is significant when it occurs rarely by chance (i.e., 5 times or less in 100). There always is the chance that your experiment represents one of those 5 times in 100 when the results did occur *by chance*. Hence, the null hypothesis is true and you will make an error in accepting your experimental hypothesis. We call this faulty decision a **Type I error** (alpha, α). The experimenter directly controls the probability of making a Type I error by setting the significance level. For example, you are less likely to make a Type I error with a significance level of .01 than with a significance level of .05.

However, the more extreme or critical you make the significance level (e.g., going from .05 to .01) to avoid a Type I error, the more likely you are to make a Type II or beta (β) error. A **Type II error** involves rejecting a *true* experimental hypothesis. Unlike Type I errors, Type II errors are not under the direct control of the experimenter. We can indirectly cut down on Type II errors by implementing techniques that will cause our groups to differ as much as possible. For example, the use of a strong IV and larger groups of participants are two techniques that will help avert Type II errors.

Type I error
Accepting the experimental hypothesis when the null hypothesis is true.

Type II error
Accepting the null hypothesis when the experimental hypothesis is true.

definition

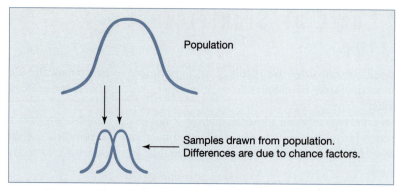

A. Random samples are drawn from a population.

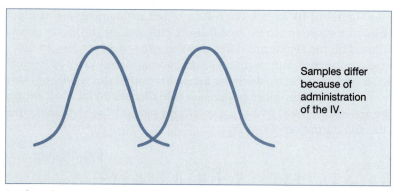

B. The administration of the IV causes the samples to differ significantly.

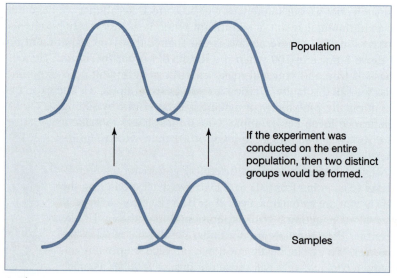

C. The experimenter generalizes the results of the experiment to the general population.

We will have more to say about Type I and Type II errors in subsequent chapters. They are summarized below:

| | | TRUE STATE OF AFFAIRS | |
		EXPERIMENTAL HYPOTHESIS IS TRUE	NULL HYPOTHESIS IS TRUE
	EXPERIMENTAL HYPOTHESIS IS TRUE	Correct Decision	Type I (α) Error
YOUR DECISION	NULL HYPOTHESIS IS TRUE	Type II (β) Error	Correct Decision

You should keep in mind that the typical practice is to set the alpha level at .05.

EFFECT SIZE

Before concluding this chapter, we want to introduce you to a statistical concept and procedure that currently is gaining in popularity and frequency of usage. **Effect size** is a statistical measure that conveys information concerning the magnitude of the effect produced by the IV. Doesn't obtaining significance with an inferential test give us the same information? After all, significance indicates the IV had an effect and that's what we are concerned with. So, why do we need anything else?

> **Effect size** The magnitude or size of the experimental treatment.

Unfortunately, a significant statistical test tells us only that the IV had an effect; it does not tell us about the size of the significant effect. Moreover, whether an effect is significant or not may depend on factors other than the IV. For example, you just saw that you are more likely to obtain significance (i.e., avoid a Type II error) when larger samples are used even though the influence of the IV remains the same. The APA *Publication Manual* (1994) indicates that "Neither of the two types of probability values [your selected alpha level and the probability level associated with the inferential statistic you calculate] reflects the importance or magnitude of an effect because both depend on sample size" (p. 18).

Such considerations have encouraged researchers to report effect size in addition to inferential statistics that are used. In fact, some statisticians (e.g., Kirk, 1996) can envision a time when the reporting of effect size will be more common than significance testing. Indeed, the latest edition of the APA *Publication Manual* (1994) says "You are encouraged to provide effect-size information" (p. 18).

There are several different ways to calculate effect size. Here are two that should give you no problems; others will be introduced in subsequent chapters.

Cohen's *d* (Cohen, 1977) is computed easily when two groups are used and a *t* test is calculated. In these cases:

$$d = \frac{t(N_1 + N_2)}{\sqrt{df}\sqrt{N_1 N_2}}$$

or, when the two samples are equal sized:

$$d = \frac{2t}{\sqrt{df}}$$

Cohen (1977) indicates that $d = .20$ to $.50$ is a small-effect size, $d = .50$ to $.80$ is a medium-effect size; and, d values greater than $.80$ reflect large-effect sizes.

A second technique for determining effect size is appropriate when you calculate a Pearson product-moment correlation (r): r^2 gives us an estimation of the proportion of the variance accounted for by the correlation in question (Rosenthal & Rosnow, 1984). For example, even though $r = .30$ is significant $(p < .01)$ with 90 pairs of scores, this correlation accounts for only 9% $(.30^2 = .09 = 9\%)$ of the variance. This is a rather small-effect size, indeed!

Review Summary

1. A **correlation coefficient** is a single number that represents the degree of relationship between two variables. Many predictions are based on correlations.

2. A perfect negative correlation (-1.00) exists when an increase of one unit in one variable is always accompanied by a proportional decrease in the other variable. A perfect positive correlation $(+1.00)$ exists when an increase of one unit is always accompanied by a proportional increase in the other variable. A correlation of 0.00 indicates that there is no relationship between the variables under consideration.

3. The Pearson product-moment correlation coefficient is calculated when both variables are interval scale measurements.

4. **Inferential statistics** help the experimenter decide if the IV was effective. A significant inferential statistic is one that occurs rarely by chance.

5. The **t test** is an inferential statistic that is used to test the differences between two groups.

6. When significance is achieved, the experimenter hopes to be able to extend the results of the experiment to the more general population.

7. A one-tail t test is conducted when a directional hypothesis is stated, whereas a two-tail t test is conducted when a nondirectional hypothesis is stated.

8. Even though lower critical values are associated with one-tail tests, making it easier to attain significance, most experimental hypotheses are nondirectional because the researchers do not know exactly how the research will turn out.

9. Sometimes the results of an inferential statistical test produce an incorrect decision. An experimental hypothesis may be incorrectly accepted (**Type I error**) or incorrectly rejected (**Type II error**).

STUDY BREAK

$H_0 = H_1$

1. Matching
   1. correlation coefficient *F*
   2. perfect negative correlation *H*
   3. perfect positive correlation *I*
   4. significant *B*
   5. inferential statistics *D*
   6. Type I error *C*
   7. Type II error *G*
   8. one-tail test *E*
   9. two-tail test *A*

   A. nondirectional hypothesis
   B. result occurs infrequently by chance
   C. rejecting a true null hypothesis
   D. tests conducted to determine if IV was effective
   E. directional hypothesis
   F. represents the degree of relationship between two variables
   G. rejecting a true experimental hypothesis
   H. −1.00
   I. +1.00

2. Explain the difference between a positive correlation and a perfect positive correlation.
3. What does a zero correlation signify?
4. Explain the logic involved when an independent-groups *t* test is conducted.
5. What is meant by "level of significance?" How is the level of significance determined?
6. If it is easier to obtain a significant result with a one-tail test, why would an experimenter ever state a nondirectional experimental hypothesis and be forced to use a two-tail test?

LOOKING AHEAD

So far we have considered sources of researchable problems (Chapter 1), developed an experimental hypothesis (Chapter 2), scrutinized our experiment for possible nuisance variables and/or confounders (Chapter 4), and implemented control procedures to deal with these extraneous variables (Chapters 4 and 5). Now we are ready to combine all of these elements in an experimental design. In Chapter 7 experimental designs involving the use of two groups of participants are considered. More complex designs will be considered in subsequent chapters.

HANDS-ON ACTIVITIES

1. **Which Measure of Central Tendency is Best?**   For each of the following indicate which measure of central tendency you would use and why.

   A.   You are studying turn-signal behavior in a large urban area. You observe cars at a busy intersection and record whether they used their turn signals properly, did not use their turn signals, or used their turn signals after they had entered the intersection.

B. The list of the "Top 25" basketball teams was just published in the newspaper.

C. Your college is studying retention of students during their four-year college programs. One component of the research involves calculating the number of first-, second-, third-, and fourth-year students.

D. Having an off-campus job while attending college continues to increase in frequency. The director of student life is interested in how many hours the typical student works off-campus each week. A random sample of 100 students is obtained and each student is asked to report the number of hours worked during the preceding week.

2. **Settle a Dispute by Calculating and Graphing the Means.** The Office of Institutional Research at your school is trying to settle a dispute: Faculty members believe that the number of hours worked at off-campus jobs decreases the longer one is in school—advanced courses are more challenging and more time must be devoted to studying. The director of student life holds the opposing view: She believes that students work more hours at off-campus jobs during the course of their college years because the debt increases and the need for cash is greater. To help resolve this dispute ten first-, second-, third-, and fourth-year students are randomly selected from the student body. All students report the number of hours they worked off-campus during the preceding week. The data are as follows:

First-Year: 6, 8, 10, 11, 14, 14, 4, 6, 8, 7

Second-Year: 7, 7, 10, 10, 8, 11, 16, 16, 8, 11

Third-Year: 8, 9, 12, 12, 11, 10, 11, 9, 18, 18

Fourth-Year: 12, 12, 15, 16, 18, 20, 20, 11, 8, 11

For these data do the following:

A. Calculate the mean number of hours worked by each type of student.

B. Graph these figures as a histogram.

C. Graph these figures as a frequency polygon.

D. Based on the means in Part A, explain who is correct, the faculty or the director of student life.

E. Explain the nature of the correlation between academic classification and hours worked.

3. **Are the Differences Significant?** You read the report on academic classification and hours worked off-campus prepared by the Office of Institutional Research. You wonder whether fourth-year students work significantly more than first-year students. Answer your question by conducting a *t* test.

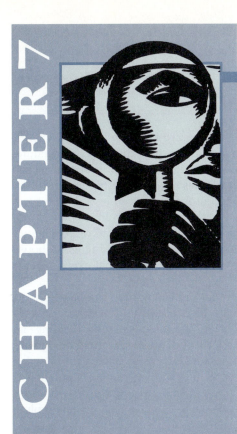

CHAPTER 7

Designing, Conducting, Analyzing, and Interpreting Experiments with Two Groups

EXPERIMENTAL DESIGN: THE BASIC BUILDING BLOCK

Now that the preliminaries are out of the way, we are ready to begin an experiment. Or are we? Although we have chosen a problem, read the relevant literature, developed a hypothesis, selected our variables, instituted control procedures, and considered the participants, we are still not ready to start the experiment. Before we can actually begin, we must select a blueprint for the experiment. If you were about to design a house, you would be faced with an overwhelming variety of potential plans—you would have many choices and selections ahead of you. Fortunately, selecting a blueprint for your experiment is simpler than designing a house because there are a relatively small number of standard choices that experimenters are likely to use in designing experiments.

Selecting a blueprint for your experiment is just as important as doing so for a house. Can you imagine what a house would look like if you began building it without any plans? The result would be a disaster. The same is true of "building" an experiment. We refer to the research blueprint as our **experimental design.** In Chapter 1 you learned that an experimental design is the general plan for selecting participants, assigning those participants to experimental conditions, controlling extraneous variables, and gathering data. If you begin your experiment without a proper design, your experiment may "collapse" just as a house built without a blueprint might do. How can an experiment "collapse"? We have seen students begin experiments without any direction only to end up with data that fit no known procedure for statistical analysis. We also have seen students collect data that have no bearing on their original question. Thus, we hope not only that you will use this text during your current course but also that you will keep the book and consult it as you design research projects in the future.

In this chapter we will begin developing a series of questions in a flowchart to help you select the correct design for your experiment. As Charles Brewer, distinguished professor of psychology at Furman University, is fond of saying, "If you do not know where you are going, the likelihood that you will get there borders on randomness." If you don't design your experiment well, the probability that it will answer your research question(s) is slim.

When you were a child and played with Legos or Tinkertoys, you probably got a beginner's set first. This set was small and simplistic, but with it you learned the basics of building. As you got older, you could use larger sets that allowed you to build and create more complicated objects. Building these complicated objects was fairly easy because you had started with the beginner set.

The parallel between children's building sets and experimental design is striking. In both cases the beginner's set helps us learn about the processes involved so that we can use the advanced set later; the basic set forms the backbone of the more advanced set. In both cases combining simple models increases the possibilities for building, although more complex models must still conform to the basic rules of building.

Experimental design The general plan for selecting participants, assigning participants to experimental conditions, controlling extraneous variables, and gathering data.

definition

THE TWO-GROUP DESIGN

In this chapter we examine the most basic experimental design, the two-group design, and its variations. This design is the simplest possible one that can yield a valid experiment. In research situations, we typically follow the **principle of parsimony** (also known as Ockham's [or Occam's] razor). William of Ockham (a fourteenth century philosopher) became famous for his dictum "Let us never introduce more than is required for an explanation" (McInerny, 1970, p. 370). In research, we apply the principle of parsimony to research questions, just as detectives apply the principle of parsimony to their investigations: Don't needlessly complicate the question that you are asking. The two-group design is the most parsimonious design available.

How Many IVs? The first question (see Figure 7-1) we must ask ourselves in order to select the appropriate design for our experiment is "How many **independent variables (IVs)** will our experiment have?" In this chapter and the next, we will deal with

Principle of parsimony
The belief that explanations of phenomena and events should remain simple until the simple explanations are no longer valid.

Independent variable (IV)
A stimulus or aspect of the environment that is directly manipulated by the experimenter to determine its influences on behavior.

FIGURE 7-1   EXPERIMENTAL DESIGN QUESTIONS

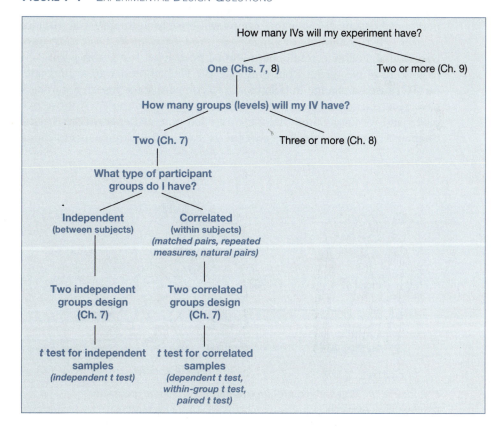

definition

Extraneous variables Undesired variables that may operate to influence the dependent variable and, thus, invalidate an experiment.

Levels Differing amounts or types of an IV used in an experiment (*also known as treatment conditions*).

experimental designs that have one independent variable. We covered the concept of IVs in Chapter 4. You will remember that an IV is a stimulus or aspect of the environment that is directly manipulated by the experimenter to determine its influences on behavior. Thus, the experimenter wishes to study what effect(s) the IV has on the behavior of an organism. If you want to determine how anxiety affects test performance, for example, anxiety would be your IV. If you wish to study the effects of different therapies on depression, the different therapies would be your IV. The simplest experimental design has only one IV. We will look at research designs with more than one IV in Chapter 9.

Only a minority of the published research studies use one IV. Does that mean that experiments with one IV are somehow poor or deficient? No, there is nothing wrong with a one-IV design; however, such a design may be viewed as simple and may not yield all the answers an experimenter desires. However, simple is not necessarily bad! Inexperienced researchers or researchers who are beginning to investigate new areas often prefer single-IV designs because they are easier to conduct than multiple-IV designs and it is simpler to institute the proper control procedures. Also, the results of several one-IV experiments, when combined in one report, can describe complex phenomena.

How Many Groups? Assuming we have chosen to use a single-IV design, we then come to our second question (see Figure 7-1) in determining the proper experimental design: "How many groups will I use to test my IV?" In this chapter, the answer is two. Although an experiment can have a single IV, it must have at least two groups. Follow carefully here—some people get lost at this point. Why do we have to have two groups but only one IV? The simplest way to find out whether our IV caused a change in behavior is to compare some research participants who have received our IV to some who have not received the IV. If those two groups differ, and we are assured that we controlled potential **extraneous variables** (see Chapter 4), then we conclude that the IV caused the participants to differ. So, the

CONTROL GROUP   OUT OF CONTROL GROUP.

Fortunately, we deal with control groups and *experimental* groups in psychological research!

way that we have two groups with only one IV is to make the two groups differ in the amount or the type of the IV that they receive. Note carefully that the last statement is *not* the same as saying that the groups have different IVs.

The most common manner of creating two groups with one IV is to present some amount or type of IV to one group and to withhold that IV from the second group. Thus, the *presence* of the IV is contrasted with the *absence* of the IV. These differing amounts of the IV are referred to as the **levels** (also known as treatment conditions) of the IV. Thus, in the common two-group design, one level of the IV is none (its absence) and the other is some amount (its presence). Notice that the presence and absence of an IV is conceptualized as two differing levels of the same IV rather than as two different IVs. Now let's return to our earlier examples.

Psychological Detective

If you were interested in the effects of anxiety on test performance or the effects of therapy on depression, how would you implement an experimental design so that you could compare the presence of the IV to the absence of the IV? Record your answer before going on.

In the first example, you would need to compare anxious test-takers (first level) to nonanxious test-takers (second level); in the second, you would compare depressed people receiving therapy (first level) to depressed people who were not receiving therapy (second level).

In this presence-absence situation, the group of participants receiving the IV is typically referred to as the **experimental group.** It is as if we were conducting the experiment on them. The group that does not receive the IV is known as the **control group.** The members of this group serve a control function because they give us an indication of how people or animals behave under "normal" conditions—that is, without being exposed to our IV. They also serve as a comparison group for the experimental group. We will use statistics to compare performance scores on the **dependent variable (DV)** for the two groups to determine whether or not the IV has had an effect. When our two groups differ significantly, we assume that the difference is due to the IV. If the groups do not differ significantly, we conclude that our IV had no effect.

Let's look at a research example using the two-group design. Nancy Cathey (1992), a student at Ouachita Baptist University in Arkadelphia, AR, was interested in the effects of caffeine on rats' ability to learn. Cathey's IV was caffeine exposure. Thus, her experimental group of rats received caffeine and the control group did

Experimental group In a two-group design, the group of participants that receives the IV.

Control group In a two-group design, the group of participants that does not receive the IV.

Dependent variable (DV) A response or behavior that is measured. It is desired that changes in the dependent variable be directly related to manipulation of the independent variable.

INDEPENDENT VARIABLE (CAFFEINE)

EXPERIMENTAL GROUP   CONTROL GROUP

Received caffeine	Received no caffeine

FIGURE 7-2   THE BASIC TWO-GROUP DESIGN

not receive any caffeine. Cathey randomly selected four female rats for breeding purposes. After breeding, two of the rats were randomly chosen to have caffeine in their drinking water; two had no caffeine. After the rat pups were born, those that had been exposed prenatally to caffeine continued to receive caffeine in their drinking water. When Cathey tested the baby rats on maze learning and bar pressing, she found that the caffeine-exposed rats learned more slowly than those that had not experienced caffeine. This basic two-group design is depicted in Figure 7-2. Block diagrams such as the one seen in Figure 7-2 are commonly used to graphically portray the design of an experiment. Note that the IV (caffeine) heads the entire block, with the two levels of the IV comprising the two subdivisions of the block. We will use this building block notation throughout the three chapters concerning experimental design so that you can conceptualize the various designs more easily.

Assigning Participants to Groups. We have yet another question to face before we can select our experimental design: We must decide how we plan to assign our research participants to groups. (Before the most recent edition of the *Publication Manual of the American Psychological Association* [1994], research participants were referred to as subjects. You are likely to read and hear this term for many years before the psychological language becomes standardized—it's hard to teach old psychologists new tricks!)

Random Assignment to Groups. As you saw in Chapter 4, an often-used approach for assigning participants to groups is **random assignment.** Given that we are dealing with only two groups, we could flip a coin and assign participants to one group or the other on the basis of heads or tails. As long as we flip a fair coin, our participants would have a 50-50 chance of ending up in either group. Remember that random assignment is *not* the same as **random selection,** which we also learned about in Chapter 4. Random assignment is concerned with control procedures in the experiment, whereas random selection influences the generality of the results. We will examine both of these issues more closely in Chapter 10.

When we randomly assign our participants to groups, we have created what are known as **independent groups.** This term simply means that the participants in one group have *absolutely* no ties or links to the participants in the other group—in other words, they are independent of each other. If you tried to relate or pair a participant in one group to one in the other group, there would be no logical way to do so. When we wish to compare the performance of participants in these two groups, we are making what is known as a **between-subjects comparison.** We are interested in the difference *between* these two groups of participants who have no ties or links to each other.

Terminology in experimental design can sometimes be confusing—for some reason, it has never been standardized. So, you may hear different people refer to "independent groups designs," "randomized groups designs," or "between-subjects designs." All these names refer to the same basic strategy of randomly assigning participants to groups. The key to avoiding confusion is to understand the principle behind the strategy of random assignment; when you understand the basic ideas, the names will make sense. As you can see in Figure 7-1, when we have one IV with two levels and participants that are assigned to groups randomly, our experiment fits the two independent groups design.

Random assignment is important in experimental design as a control factor. When we randomly assign our research participants to groups, we can usually assume that our two groups will now be equal on a variety of variables (Spatz, 1993). Many of these variables could be extraneous variables and might confound our experiment if they are left uncontrolled (see Chapter 4). Random assignment is one of those statistical procedures that is supposed to work—in the long run. However, there are no guarantees that it will create the expected outcome if we select a small sample. For example, we would not be surprised to flip a coin 10 times and get 7 or 8 heads. On the other hand, if we flipped a coin 100 times, we would be quite surprised if we obtained 70 or 80 heads.

Thus, when we randomly assign participants to groups, we expect the two groups to be equated on a variety of variables that could affect the experiment's outcome. Think back to Nancy Cathey's (1992) experiment dealing with caffeine and rats' ability to learn. When we described her experiment, we were careful to point out that of the four mother rats, two were *randomly* assigned to receive caffeine and the other two were *randomly* assigned to a group that did not get caffeine. What if she had picked the two smartest rats to be the control group? Putting the smart rats in the control group would cause the rats' intelligence to vary systematically with the IV (that is, smart rats would get no caffeine, but dumb rats would). Such assignment to groups would result in a **confounded experiment.** If the results showed that the caffeine-exposed rats performed more poorly on the learning tasks, we would not be able to draw a definite conclusion about why that happened. They may have performed poorly because they had dumb mothers, because they had been exposed to caffeine, or because of the combination of the two factors. Unfortunately, with a confounded experiment, there is no way to determine which conclusion is appropriate. If Cathey had conducted her experiment in this manner, she would have wasted her time.

Let us remind you of one more benefit of random assignment. In Chapter 4 you learned that random assignment is the only technique we have that will help us control unknown extraneous variables. For example, in Cathey's caffeine experiment, what extraneous variables might affect rats' learning? We have already identified the mothers' intelligence as a possibility. However, we have no way of measuring rat intelligence (Wechsler and Binet were more interested in measuring people's intelligence!). Other variables that we do not even consider could also play a role in the rats' performance. This was the reason that Cathey

Confounded experiment An experiment in which an extraneous variable varies systematically with the IV; makes drawing a cause-and-effect relationship impossible.

definition

was careful to randomly assign her mother rats to experimental and control groups. This random assignment should equate any differences between the two groups.

Psychological Detective

Can you think of a possible flaw in Cathey's reasoning behind random assignment? Write an answer before reading further.

Random assignment is a technique that should work in the long run. Because Cathey assigned only two rats to each group, we should not be surprised if random assignment did not make the groups perfectly equal. If you thought of this potential problem, congratulations! What can we do when we conduct an experiment with small numbers of participants?

Non-Random Assignment to Groups. In the previous section, we saw a potential pitfall of random assignment—the groups may not turn out equal after all. If we begin our experiment with unequal groups, we have a problem. Remember that random assignment should create equal groups in the long run. In other words, as our participant groups get larger, we can place more confidence in random assignment achieving what we want it to.

Suppose we are faced with a situation where we have few potential research participants and we are worried that random assignment may not create equal groups. What can we do? In this type of situation, we can use a non-random method of assigning participants to groups. What we will do is either capitalize on an existing relationship between participants or create a relationship between them. In this manner, we know something important about our participants before the experiment and will use **correlated assignment** (also known as matched or paired assignment) to create equal groups. There are three common ways that we can use correlated assignment.

1. Matched Pairs. To create **matched pairs,** we must measure our participants on a variable (other than our IV) that could affect performance on our experiment's DV. Typically we measure a variable that could result in confounding if not controlled. After we have measured this variable, we create pairs of participants that are equal on this variable. After we have created our matched pairs, we then randomly assign participants from these pairs to the different treatment conditions.

If this description seems confusing, an example should help clarify matters. Imagine that we wanted to replicate Cathey's caffeine study because we were worried that random assignment may not have created equal groups. Suppose we knew that dark-colored rats tend to be faster learners than light-colored rats (a totally fictitious supposition, but it makes a good example). In our rat colony, we have two dark rats and two light rats. If we flip a coin, both dark rats might end up in one group and both light rats in the other group. Therefore, we decide to use matched assignment to groups. First, we create our matched pairs. The first pair consists of the two dark rats and the second pair is the two light rats. With our two dark rats, we flip a coin to determine which rat is assigned to the experimental group and which to the control group. Then we repeat the procedure for our second pair (the light rats). After this matched assignment is completed, we have an experimental group with one dark and one light rat and a control group with one dark and one light rat. We have used matched assignment to create equal groups before our experiment begins.

> **Repeated measures**
> An experimental procedure in which research participants are tested or measured more than once.
>
> definition

Psychological Detective

In what way is matched assignment guaranteed to create equal groups when random assignment is not? Write your answer now.

The beauty of matched assignment is that we have measured our participants on a specific variable that could affect their performance in our experiment and have equated them on that variable. When we use random assignment, we are leaving this equating process to chance. Remember, we must match on a variable that could affect the outcome of our experiment. In the fictitious example we just used, you would need to be certain that rats' hair color was linked to their intelligence. If you cannot measure your participants on a variable that is relevant to their performance in your experiment, then you should not use matched assignment. If you match your participants on a variable that is *not* relevant to their performance, then you have actually hurt your chances of finding a significant difference in your experiment (see "Statistical Issues" in the "Advantages of Correlated Group Designs" section later in this chapter).

2.   Repeated Measures. In **repeated measures,** we use the ultimate in matched pairs—we simply measure the same participants in both treatment conditions of our experiment. The matched pairs here are perfectly equal because they consist of the same people or animals tested across the entire experiment. No extraneous variables should be able to confound this situation because any difference between the participants' performance in the two treatment conditions should be due to the IV. In this type of experiment, participants serve as their own controls.

Psychological Detective

Why is it not possible to use repeated measures in all experiments? Write down two reasons before reading further.

Thinking about using repeated measures for our groups forces us to consider some practical factors.

a. Can we remove the effects of the IV? Cathey could not use repeated measures in her experiment because she could not remove the effects of the caffeine on the rats. Think about it carefully—even though she could have weaned the rat pups away from caffeine, she would not have removed its permanent effects. If the caffeine had made a physiological change in the pups, taking it away from them would not remove its effects.

b. Can we measure our DV more than once? To this point, we have not focused on the dependent variable in this chapter because it has little to do with the choice of an experimental design. However, when you consider using repeated measures, the DV is highly important. When you use repeated measures, the DV is measured multiple times (at least twice). In some cases, it is simply not possible to use the same DV more than once. In Cathey's experiment, once the rats had learned to bar press, *learning* the bar-press task could not be used again as a DV. In other cases, we may be able to use a similar DV, but we must be cautious. To use repeated measures on maze learning in Cathey's experiment, we would need two different mazes, one for testing animals with the effects of caffeine and one for testing without its effects. If we use two different forms of our DV, we must ensure that they are comparable. Although we could use two mazes, they would have to be equally difficult, which might be difficult to determine. The same would be true of many different DVs—tests, word lists, puzzles, computer programs, and so on. If we cannot assure comparability of two measures of the same DV, then we should not use repeated measures designs.

c. Can our participants cope with repeated testing? This question relates at least to some degree to the ethics of research, which we covered in Chapter 2. Although no specific ethical principles speak to the use of repeated measures, we should realize that requiring extended participation in our experiment might affect participants' willingness to take part in the research. Also, in extreme cases, extended time in a strenuous or taxing experiment could raise concerns for physical or emotional well-being. Another of our worries in this area is whether human participants will agree to devote the amount of time that we request of them in a repeated measures design.

It is important that we think about these practical considerations when weighing the possibility of a repeated measures design. Although repeated measures designs are one of our better control techniques, there are some experimental questions that simply do not allow the use of such a design.

3.   Natural pairs. **Natural pairs** is essentially a cross between matched pairs and repeated measures. In this technique, we create pairs of participants from naturally occurring pairs (e.g., biologically or socially related). For example, psychologists who study intelligence often use twins (natural pairs) as their research participants. This approach is simi-

Natural pairs
Research participants in a two-group design who are naturally related in some way (e.g., a biological or social relationship).

definition

lar to using the same participant more than once (repeated measures) but allows you to compose your pairs more easily than through matching. Thus, when you see an experiment that uses siblings, parents and children, husbands and wives, litter mates, or some biological relationship between its participants, that experiment has used natural pairs.

In summary, whenever there is a relationship between participants in different groups, we are using a correlated groups design. By looking at Figure 7-1, you can see that planning an experiment with (a) one IV, that has (b) two levels, in which you plan to use (c) correlated assignment of participants to groups results in the two correlated groups design. We can create an experiment that uses correlated groups by creating matched pairs, using repeated measures, or using naturally occurring pairs. Such experiments use correlated participants. This label implies that there is a relationship between the participants in our various groups. In contrast to independent groups, there is a logical pairing of participants in correlated groups. Obviously, a single individual's scores would be related even in the different treatment conditions. In similar fashion, participants who have been matched on some variable or who share some relationship would have scores that are related. When we wish to compare the performance of such participants, we are making what has traditionally been known as a **within-subjects comparison.** We are essentially comparing scores within the same participants (subjects). Although such comparisons are literally true only for repeated measures designs, matched or natural pairs are the same with regard to the matching variable.

Let's look at a student example of a two correlated groups design. A major problem in drug treatment of individuals with psychological problems is medication compliance—actually getting the people to take their medication. It is impossible to manage the symptoms of a disorder if people don't take their medication. Kristen Bender and her colleagues (1993) from the University of the Pacific in Stockton, CA wanted to determine whether they could improve medication compliance in outpatient schizophrenics. They gave eight clients a questionnaire that assessed their knowledge about medication side effects and the importance of compliance with medication instructions. The clients then received training that focused on obtaining accurate information about antipsychotic medications, administering medication, and identifying medication side effects. After the training the clients completed the questionnaire again. The researchers found that clients experienced significant knowledge gain from the training.

Because it used repeated measures, Bender et al.'s experiment is a good example of a correlated groups design. The clients were given an assessment (often known as a pretest) before receiving the training, they received the training, and then they completed the assessment again (known as a posttest). In this experiment, the IV was the training and the DV was the knowledge the clients had about the medication and its effects. Some of the particularly important participant (subject) variables that were controlled by the use of repeated measures were clients' ages (perhaps younger or older clients know more about medication), severity of schizophrenia (perhaps more disordered clients have trouble remembering details about medication), and clients' intelligence (could certainly affect knowledge or memory about medication). All these extraneous variables (and others) were controlled because the *same* clients took both the pretest and posttest.

What if Bender and her colleagues had wanted to use matched pairs rather than repeated measures? Remember that matching should occur on a relevant variable—one that could be an extraneous variable if left unchecked. Suppose that these eight clients varied widely in the severity of their schizophrenia. The researchers might have wanted to create matched pairs based on that severity, thinking that the severity of the disorder would likely affect scores on the assessment. Again, other variables could be used for matching as long as the researchers felt certain that the variables were related to the clients' scores on the assessment.

Could Bender and her colleagues have run this experiment using natural pairs? Based on the information given you, there is no indication that natural pairs of clients existed. If the eight clients were four sets of twins, then this would be ideally suited for natural pairs. It seems unlikely that there was any factor that made these clients natural pairs, so if pairing was important to the researchers, they would have needed to create pairs by matching on some variable.

REVIEW SUMMARY

1. Psychologists plan their experiments beforehand using an **experimental design,** which serves as a blueprint for the experiment.

2. The **two-group design** is used for experimental situations in which you have one **IV** that has two levels or conditions.

3. Two-group designs often use an **experimental group,** which receives the IV, and a **control group,** which does not receive the IV.

4. **Independent groups** of research participants are formed by **randomly assigning** the participants to groups.

5. **Correlated groups** of research participants are formed by creating **matched pairs,** using **natural pairs,** or by measuring the participants more than once (**repeated measures**).

STUDY BREAK

1. Why can't we conduct a valid experiment with only one group?

2. The differing amounts of your IV are known as the _____ of the IV.

3. How are independent groups and correlated groups different? Why is this difference important to experimental design questions?

4. Matching
   1. random assignment D
   2. natural pairs A
   3. repeated measures B
   4. matched pairs C

   A. brother and sister
   B. take the same test each month
   C. two people with the same IQs
   D. flipping a coin

5. In what type of situation do we need to be most careful about using random assignment as a control technique?

6. You are planning an experiment that could use either independent groups or correlated groups. Under what conditions should you use a correlated groups design? When is it acceptable to use random assignment?

COMPARING THE TWO-GROUP DESIGNS

Looking at Figure 7-1 again, you can see that the two independent groups design and the two correlated groups design are quite similar. Both designs describe experimental situations in which you use one IV with two groups. The only difference comes in how you assign your participants to groups. If you simply assign on a random basis, you would use the two independent groups design. On the other hand, if you match your participants on some variable, if you test your participants twice, or if your participants share some relationship, then you would use the two correlated groups design.

Choosing a Two-Group Design. Now that you have two experimental designs that can handle very similar experimental situations, how can you choose between them? Should you use independent groups or should you use correlated groups of some sort?

You may remember that we said that random assignment is supposed to "work" (i.e., create equal groups) in the long run. Therefore, if you are using large groups of participants, random assignment should equate your groups adequately. The next question, of course, is how large is large? Unfortunately, there is no specific answer to this question—the answer may vary from researcher to researcher. If you are using twenty or more participants per group, you can feel fairly safe that randomization will create equal groups. On the other hand, if you are using five or fewer participants in a group, randomization may not work. Part of the answer to the question of numbers boils down to what you feel comfortable with, what your research director feels comfortable with, or what you think you could defend to someone. In Cathey's study, she felt justified in using independent groups because she had four mother rats (thus, she expected many rat pups [she ended up with 39]) to divide into two groups. In Bender et al.'s study of schizophrenic clients, they probably decided to use repeated measures in part because they had only eight clients to participate in the experiment. Whatever you decide, it is critical to remember that the larger your samples, the more likely random assignment is to create equal groups.

Advantages of Correlated Groups Designs. There are two primary advantages correlated groups designs provide for researchers: control and statistical issues. Both advantages are important to you as an experimenter.

Control Issues. One basic assumption that we make before beginning our experiment is that the participants in our groups are equal with respect to the DV. When our groups are equal before the experiment begins and we observe differences be-

Between-groups variability
Variability in DV scores that is due to the effects of the IV.

Error variability
Variability in DV scores that is due to factors other than the IV—individual differences, measurement error, and extraneous variation (also known as within-groups variability).

tween our groups on the DV after the experiment, then we can attribute those differences to the IV. Although randomization is designed to equate our groups, the three methods for creating correlated groups designs give us greater certainty of equality; we have exerted control to create equal groups. Thus, in correlated designs, we have some "proof" that our participants are equated beforehand. This equality helps us reduce some of the error variation in our experiment, which brings us to the statistical issues.

Statistical issues. Correlated groups designs can actually benefit us statistically because they can help reduce error variation. You might be wondering, "What is error variation anyhow?" In an experiment that involves one IV, you essentially have two sources of variability in your data. One source of variation is your IV—scores on the DV should vary due to the two different treatment groups you have in your experiment. This source of variation, referred to as **between-groups variability,** is what you are attempting to measure in the experiment. There are other sources of variation in the DV, such as individual differences, measurement errors, and extraneous variation—these are known collectively as **error variability.** As you might guess, our goal in an experiment is to *maximize* the between-groups variability and *minimize* the error or within-groups variability.

Why is it important to reduce error variability? Although formulas for different statistical tests vary widely, they can be reduced to the following general formula:

$$\text{statistic} = \frac{\text{between-groups variability}}{\text{error variability}}$$

Remember that the probability of a result occurring by chance goes down as the value of your statistic increases. Thus, larger statistical values are more likely to show significant differences in your experiment. Your knowledge of math tells you that there are two ways to increase the value of your statistic: increase the between-groups variability or decrease the error variability. (Increasing between-groups variability is a function of your IV [see Chapter 4] and will not be discussed here.)

Psychological Detective

Can you figure out why using a correlated groups design can help reduce error variability? Write an answer at this point.

Earlier in this section we listed individual differences as one source of error variability. Correlated groups designs help reduce this source of error. If in our treatment groups we use the same participants or participants who share some important characteristic, either naturally or through matching, those participants will exhibit smaller individual differences between the groups than will randomly chosen participants. Imagine how dissimilar to you another participant would be if we chose that person at random. Imagine how similar to you another participant would be if that person was related to you, had the same intelligence as you, or (in the most obvious situation) was you! So, the bottom line is that if we use a correlated design, error variability due to individual differences should decrease, our statistic should increase, and we should have a greater chance of finding a significant difference due to our IV.

Why did we use the hedge word *should* three times in the preceding sentence? Remember, when we discussed matched pairs earlier, we said matching on an irrelevant variable could actually hurt your chances of finding a significant difference. If you match on an irrelevant variable, then the between-groups differences do not decrease. This leaves your error variability the same as if you had used an independent groups design, which results in identical statistical test results. When we use a statistical test for a correlated groups design, we lose some of the degrees of freedom we would have if we conducted the same experiment with an independent groups design. In the two correlated groups situation, the degrees of freedom are equal to $N - 1$, where N represents the number of *pairs* of participants. In the two independent groups situation, the degrees of freedom are $N - 2$, where N represents the *total* number of participants.

Suppose you ran an experiment with 10 participants in each group. How many degrees of freedom would you have if this were an independent groups design? A correlated groups design? Did you determine 18 for the independent groups design and 9 for the correlated groups design? Using the t table in the back of the book (see Table A-1), you will see that the critical t value at the .05 level with 18 df is 2.101, whereas it is 2.262 with 9 df.

The critical t values above make it seem that it would be easier to reject the null hypothesis in the independent samples situation (critical $t = 2.101$) than in the correlated groups situation (critical $t = 2.262$). Yet we said earlier that the correlated groups situation could benefit us statistically. What's going on?

The numbers above *do* support the first sentence of the paragraph—it *would* be easier to find a t of 2.101 than of 2.262. However, you must remember that a correlated groups design reduces the error variability and results in a larger statistic. Typically, the statistic is increased enough to make up for the lost degrees of freedom. Remember that this reasoning is based on the assumption that you have matched on a relevant variable. Matching on an irrelevant variable does not reduce the error variability and will not increase the statistic—in which case the lost degrees of freedom actually hurt your chances of finding significance. We will show you an actual statistical example of this point at the end of the statistical interpretation section later in this chapter.

Advantages of Independent Groups Designs. The chief advantage of independent groups designs is their simplicity. Once you have planned your experiment, choosing your participants is quite easy—you merely get a large number of participants and randomly assign them to groups. You don't need to worry about measuring your participants on some variable and then matching them; you don't need to worry about whether each participant can serve in all conditions of your experiment; you don't need to worry about establishing or determining a relationship between your participants—these concerns are relevant to correlated groups designs.

Does the statistical advantage of correlated groups designs render independent groups designs useless? We cannot argue over the statistical advantage—it is real. However, as you can tell by reviewing the critical *t* values mentioned earlier, the advantage is not overwhelming. As the number of experimental participants increases, the difference becomes smaller and smaller. For example, the significant *t* value with 60 *df* is 2.00, and with 30 *df* it is only 2.04. If you expect your IV to have a powerful effect, then the statistical advantage of a correlated groups design will be overwhelmed.

One final point should be made in favor of independent groups designs. Remember that in some situations it is simply impossible to use a correlated groups design. Some circumstances do not allow repeated measures (as we pointed out earlier in the chapter), some participants variables cannot be matched, and some participants cannot be related in any way to other participants.

So what is the elusive bottom line? What should we conclude about using independent groups designs versus correlated groups designs? As you might guess, there is no simple, all-purpose answer. A correlated groups design provides you with additional control and a somewhat greater chance of finding statistical significance. On the other hand, independent groups designs are simpler to set up and conduct and can overcome the statistical advantages of correlated groups designs if you use large samples. What is our recommendation? If you have large numbers of participants and expect your IV to have a large effect, you are quite safe with an independent groups design. Alternatively, if you have only a small number of experimental participants and you expect your IV to have a small effect, the advantages of a correlated groups design would be important to you. For all those in-between cases, you need to weigh the alternatives and choose the type of design that seems to have the greatest advantage.

VARIATIONS ON THE TWO-GROUP DESIGN

To this point, we have described the two-group design as if all two-group designs are identical. This is not the case. Let's look at two variations on this theme.

Comparing Different Amounts of an IV. Earlier we said that the most common use of two-group designs was to compare a group of participants receiving the IV (experimental group) to a group that does not receive the IV (control group). Although this is the most common type of two-group design, it is not the only type. The presence-absence manipulation of an IV allows you to determine whether or not the IV has an effect. For example, Cathey (1992) was able to determine that caffeine hinders rats' learning; Bender et al. (1993) found that their training program increased schizophrenics' knowledge about medications. An analogous situation to using the presence-absence manipulation in detective work is trying to sort out the clues that relate to the guilt or innocence of a single suspect.

However, a presence-absence IV manipulation does not allow you to determine the precise effects of the IV. Cathey did *not* discover whether her dosage of caffeine caused a large or small disruption in learning, only that it disrupted learning. Bender et al. did not determine whether their training program was the best possible program, only that it increased knowledge.

Typically, after we determine that a particular IV has an effect, we would like to have more specific information about that effect. Can we produce the effect with more (or less) of the IV? Will a different IV produce a stronger (or weaker) effect? What is the optimum amount (or type) of the IV? These are just a few of the possible questions that remain after determining that the IV had an effect. Thus, we can follow up on our IV presence-absence experiment with a new two-group experiment that compares different amounts or types of the IV to determine their effectiveness. Similarly, a detective may have two suspects and be faced with the task of sorting the evidence to decide which suspect is more likely the guilty party.

On the other hand, some IVs simply cannot be contrasted through presence-absence manipulations. For example, Travis McNeal (1994), of Harding University in Searcy, AR, was interested in whether the amount of sleep affects dream recall. In his experiment, McNeal wanted to assess the effects of sleep (IV) on dream recall (DV). This question would make no sense in an IV presence-absence situation—how could people recall dreams if they had not slept? Instead, McNeal compared differing amounts of his IV. Based on participants' answers to a survey, he formed "high sleep" and "low sleep" groups. When he compared these two groups' degree of dream recall, he found no difference. Thus, the amount of sleep had no effect on dream recall in McNeal's experiment.

The key point to notice when we conduct an experiment contrasting different amounts of our IV is that we no longer have a true control group. In other words, there is no group that receives a zero amount of the IV. Again, we are not trying to determine whether the IV has an effect—we already know that it does. We are merely attempting to find a difference between differing types or amounts of our IV.

Dealing with Measured IVs. To this point every time we have mentioned IVs in this text, we have emphasized that they are factors that are *directly manipulated* by the experimenter. Technically, this statement is correct only for a **true experiment.** In a true experiment, the experimenter has total control over the IV and can assign participants to IV conditions. In other words, the experimenter can manipulate the IV. Cathey (1992) was able to assign her mother rats to either the caffeine group or the no-caffeine group. If I wish to assess the effects of two different reading programs on children's ability to learn to read, I can assign nonreading children to either program.

As you saw in Chapter 4, there are many IVs (participant IVs) that psychologists wish to study that we cannot directly manipulate but that we measure instead. For example, Chris Jagels (1993), a student at Santa Clara University in Santa Clara, CA, examined first-year students' adjustment to college as a function of the extraversion-introversion personality dimension. Recall from Chapter 3 that because he was *not* able to directly manipulate ex-

True experiment An experiment in which the experimenter directly manipulates the IV.

Ex post facto research A research approach in which the experimenter cannot directly manipulate the IV but can only classify, categorize, or measure the IV because it is predetermined in the participants (e.g., IV = sex).

traversion-introversion, Chris was conducting **ex post facto research.** In the context of the present chapter, he used a two-group design. The only difference he uncovered between the groups was that extraverts had higher social adjustment scores than introverts. He found no differences for either academic or personal-emotional adjustment. Based on what we know about introverts and extraverts, Jagels's social adjustment finding is not surprising. We can even develop hypotheses about how the extraverts probably developed more friendships and so on. However, we must again be cautious in our interpretation. It is conceivable that this result has nothing at all to do with college. Perhaps extraverts are better adjusted socially than introverts in *any* situation. Perhaps the test that Jagels used is confounded with extraversion, or perhaps it simply scores extraverted behaviors as more socially adjusted. In any case, although we do know from Jagels's research that extraverts scored higher than introverts in social adjustment during their first college quarter, we are not certain *why* they scored higher.

The drawback of ex post facto research is certainly a serious one. Conducting an experiment without being able to draw a cause-and-effect conclusion is limiting. Why would we want to conduct ex post facto research if we cannot draw definitive conclusions from it? As we mentioned earlier, some of the most interesting psychological variables do not lend themselves to any type of research other than ex post facto. If you wish to study the genesis of female-male differences, you have no option other than doing ex post facto studies. Also, as psychologists continue to do ex post facto research, they do make progress. Attempting to specify the determinants of intelligence involves ex post facto research—surely you remember the famous heredity-versus-environment debate over IQ. What we *think* we know today is that both factors affect IQ: Psychologists believe that heredity sets the limits of your possible IQ (i.e., your possible minimum and maximum IQs) and that your environment determines where you fall within that range (Weinberg, 1989). Thus, it seems clear that we should not abandon ex post facto research despite its major drawback. We do, however, need to remember to be extremely cautious in drawing conclusions from ex post facto studies. Detectives, of course, are always faced with ex post facto evidence—it is impossible to manipulate the variables *after* a crime has been committed.

REVIEW SUMMARY

1. **Correlated groups designs** provide more control because they guarantee equality of the two groups.
2. Correlated groups designs generally reduce error variability and are more likely to achieve statistically significant results.
3. An advantage of **independent groups designs** is that they are simple to conduct. With large numbers of research participants, they are also strong designs.
4. Two-group designs are often used to compare different amounts (or types) of IVs.

5. Some IVs cannot be manipulated, so we must resort to measuring them and conducting **ex post facto research,** which cannot demonstrate cause-and-effect relationships.

STUDY BREAK

1. Why is it important that our two groups are equal before the experiment begins?

2. The variability in DV scores that can be attributed to our experimental treatments is called _____ _____; variability from other sources is labeled _____ _____.

3. Compare and contrast the advantages and disadvantages of independent and correlated groups designs.

4. Other than the drug and sleep IV examples given in the chapter, give two examples of IVs for which you might wish to compare differing amounts.

5. List three original examples of IVs that you would have to study with ex post facto experiments.

STATISTICAL ANALYSIS: WHAT DO YOUR DATA SHOW? _____

After you have used your experimental design to conduct an experiment and gather data, you are ready to use your statistical tools to analyze the data. Let's pause for a moment to see how your experimental design and statistical tests are integrated.

THE RELATIONSHIP BETWEEN EXPERIMENTAL DESIGN AND STATISTICS

At the beginning of this chapter we compared experimental design to a blueprint and said that you needed a design to know where you were headed. When you have carefully planned your experiment and chosen the correct experimental design, you will also have accomplished another big step. Selecting the appropriate experimental design determines the particular statistical test you will use to analyze your data. Because experimental design and statistics are intimately linked, you should determine your experimental design *before* you begin collecting data to ensure that there will be an appropriate statistical test you can use to analyze your data. Remember, you don't want to be a professor's classroom example of a student who collected data only to find out there was no way to analyze the data!

ANALYZING TWO-GROUP DESIGNS

In this chapter we have looked at one-IV, two-group designs. You may remember from your statistics course, as well as Chapter 6, that this type of experimental design requires a *t* test to analyze the resulting data. You may also remember learning about two different types of *t* tests in your statistics class. For a two independent groups design, you would use a *t* test for independent samples (also known as an independent *t* test) to analyze your data. For a two correlated groups design, you would analyze your data with a *t* test for correlated samples (also called a dependent *t* test, a within-groups *t* test, or a paired *t* test).

Let's make certain that the relationship between experimental design and statistics is clear. A *t* test is indicated as the appropriate statistical test because you conducted an experiment with one IV that has two levels (treatment conditions). The decision of which *t* test to use is based on how you assigned your participants to their groups. If you used random assignment, then you will use the *t* test for independent samples. If you used repeated measures, matched pairs, or natural pairs, then you would use the *t* test for correlated samples.

CALCULATING YOUR STATISTICS

In Chapter 6 we provided the computer analysis of a *t* test. The research example involved a comparison of quiz scores from students using two different introductory psychology texts. In this chapter, we will examine those data more completely with computerized statistical packages. To help set the stage for the remainder of the chapter, let's review some details of the hypothetical experiment behind the data. We wondered whether the text that students use actually makes any difference in their learning. We decided to compare the text we currently use to a new text. We chose 16 students from an introductory class to participate, randomly assigning 8 to use the new text and 8 to use the old text.

Psychological Detective

 Which statistical test would you use to analyze data from this experiment and why? Write down your answer before reading further.

The simplest way to answer these questions is to use our chart in Figure 7-1. There is only one IV, the textbook being used. That IV has two levels, the old text and the new text. We randomly assigned the participants to their groups. Thus, this design represents a two independent groups design and should be analyzed with an independent *t* test.

INTERPRETATION: MAKING SENSE OF YOUR STATISTICS

We hope that your statistics instructor taught you an important lesson about statistics: Statistics are not something to be feared and avoided; they are a tool to help you understand the data from your experiment. Because of today's focus on computerized statistical analyses, calculating statistics is becoming secondary to interpreting them. Just as having a sewing machine or washing machine is useless if you don't know how to operate it, statistics are useless if you don't know how to interpret them. Detectives must learn the skills necessary to interpret the reports they receive from the police scientific labs also. We will focus on two types of interpretation in this section: interpreting computer statistical output and translating statistical information into experimental outcomes.

INTERPRETING COMPUTER STATISTICAL OUTPUT

Again, there may be hundreds of computer packages available for analyzing data. Thus, it would be impossible (and inefficient) to show output from every different package and teach you how to interpret each one. Remember that we will show you statistical output from both SPSS and MYSTAT and present interpretations of analyses from those packages. We believe that the similarity among statistical packages will allow you to generalize from our examples to the specific package that you may use. (Computerized statistical packages vary widely in the number of decimal places they report for statistical results. To be consistent with APA format, we will round the computerized output and use only two decimal places in the text.)

t **test for Independent Samples.** Let's return to our statistical example from Chapter 6. Remember, we randomly assigned students to one of two groups, a new textbook group and an old textbook group. We gave them two quizzes and obtained the total quiz scores you saw in Chapter 6. If we analyze these data using our two computer packages, what does the output look like? We presented abbreviated versions of the output in Chapter 6 for simplicity's sake. The complete printout from SPSS is shown in Table 7-1, the output from MYSTAT is given in Table 7-2.

SPSS Results. The first information that we usually wish to examine after running a statistical analysis is the descriptive statistics. The descriptive statistics are on the left side of the printout as you look at it, in an area marked off by a vertical line to the right. We see that GROUP 1 (defined at the top of the printout as "Old Text") had eight cases, a mean combined on the two quizzes of 15.0, a standard deviation of 1.69 quiz points, and a standard error of .60 quiz points. GROUP 2 (the "New Text"

TABLE 7-1. SPSS OUTPUT FOR *t* TEST FOR INDEPENDENT GROUPS

```
t-tests for independent samples of GROUP

GROUP 1 - GROUP EQ 1: Old Text
GROUP 2 - GROUP EQ 2: New Text
```

Variable	Number of cases	Mean	Standard Deviation	Standard Error	F Value
QUIZSCOR Score on 2 quizzes					
GROUP 1	8	15.0000	1.690	.598	
					3.33
GROUP 2	8	16.5000	.926	.327	

TABLE 7-2. MYSTAT OUTPUT FOR *t* TEST FOR INDEPENDENT GROUPS

```
INDEPENDENT SAMPLES T-TEST ON QUIZSCOR    GROUPED BY   TEXT$
        GROUP         N          MEAN        SD
old                   8         15.000      1.690
new                   8         16.500      0.926
SEPARATE VARIANCES T =     2.201 DF =      10.9 PROB = .052
   POOLED VARIANCES T =     2.201 DF =       14 PROB = .045
```

group) had eight cases, a combined mean of 16.5, a standard deviation of .93, and a standard error of .33. Be cautious at this point—an old saying we learned regarding computers is "garbage in, garbage out." This simply means that if you enter incorrect numbers into a computer, you will get incorrect numbers out of the computer. You should always verify any numbers you enter into the computer and, as much as possible, double-check its output. "Wait a minute," you may be saying, "what's the use of using a computer if I have to check its work?" We're not suggesting that you check up on the computer but that you check up on yourself! For example, suppose the computer information for GROUP 1 or GROUP 2 showed the number of cases to be seven. You would know that the computer didn't read one number—perhaps you entered only seven scores, perhaps you mislabeled one score. With only eight scores, it is simple enough to calculate the mean for each group yourself. Why should you do that? If you find the same mean that the computer displays, you can be reasonably certain that you entered the data correctly and, therefore, can go on to interpret your statistics.

The second set of statistics provided between vertical lines contains only two entries: "F Value" and "2-tail Prob." These represent the results of a test known as

2-Tail Prob.	Pooled Variance estimate			Separate Variance Estimate		
	t Value	Degrees of Freedom	2-tail Prob.	t Value	Degrees of Freedom	2-tail Prob.
.135	-2.20	14	.045	-2.20	10.85	.050

F_{max}, a statistic used to test the assumption of **homogeneity of variance** for the two groups (Kirk, 1968). Homogeneity of variance simply means that the variability of the scores of the two groups is similar. To use a *t* test, we must assume that the variances are similar. In this particular example, our assumption is justified because the probability of chance for the *F* value is .135, well above the standard .05 cutoff. Because we have homogeneity of variance, we will use the third "block" of information ("Pooled Variance estimate") to interpret our test.

In the second set of information, if our *p* value was less than .05, we would have found **heterogeneity of variance,** meaning that the variability of the scores of the two groups was not comparable. Thus, we would be violating an assumption for using the *t* test. Fortunately, statisticians have developed a procedure that allows us to interpret our statistics despite heterogeneity. In such a case, we would use the fourth block of information ("Separate Variance Estimate") rather than the third block. If the variances of the two groups are equivalent, we can pool or combine those estimates. However, if the variances are not equivalent, we must keep them separate. Again, in our current example, because the F_{max} statistic is *not* significant (*p* = .135), we will use the statistical results under the "Pooled Variance estimate" heading.

Looking at the third set of information, we find that our *t* value (calculated by the computer) is –2.20. We have 14 degrees of freedom ($N_1 + N_2 - 2$). Rather than having to locate these values in a *t* table to determine significance, we can use the significance level provided by the computer: the 2-tail probability is .045. Thus, the probability that two means as different as these could have come from the same populations by chance is less than 5 in 100. This probability is less than the magical .05 cutoff, so we conclude that these two means are significantly different.

Homogeneity of variance
The assumption that the variances are equal for two (or more) groups you plan to compare statistically.

Heterogeneity of variance
Occurs when we do not have homogeneity of variance; this means that our two (or more) groups' variances are not equivalent.

definition

MYSTAT Results. Again, we want to look first for our descriptive statistics. Table 7-2 shows us that the "old" group (representing the old text) had eight students in it, a mean of 15.0 (on the two quizzes), and a standard deviation of 1.69; the "new" group of eight students had a mean score of 16.5 with a standard deviation of 0.93.

In MYSTAT, no information about the F_{max} statistic is provided. This is an interesting omission given that both the pooled variance estimate and the separate variance estimate are provided. Generally speaking, t tests are **robust** with regard to the assumption of homogeneity (Kirk, 1968). A robust test is one that can tolerate violations of its assumptions and still provide accurate answers. Kirk (1968) notes that the test is so robust that the homogeneity assumption is often not even tested. Therefore, when reading a set of MYSTAT results for a t test for independent groups, we will attend to the "POOLED VARIANCES T." (Be sure to note that all the MYSTAT printed information is capitalized. You should refer to this test as a t test, however.)

Looking at the "POOLED VARIANCES T" information, we find a computed value for t of 2.20 with 14 degrees of freedom, yielding a probability of chance ("PROB") equal to .045. Fortunately, then, the information from our two different statistical packages is in agreement (the difference of sign for the t values simply reflects a difference in which mean is subtracted from the other mean). Our statistical conclusion, of course, will be identical to that from the SPSS analysis. This probability of chance (.045) is low enough ($p < .05$) that we are willing to conclude that the observed difference between our two means is *not* due to chance. This decision completes the process of interpreting the computer output. Our next task is describing our statistical information in terms of the experiment we conducted.

Translating Statistics into Words. Think back to the logic of an experiment: We start an experiment with two equal groups and treat them identically (for control purposes) with one exception (our IV); we measure the two groups (on our DV) in order to compare them. At this point, based on our statistical analyses, we know that we have a significant difference (i.e., not due to chance) between our two means. If two equal groups began the experiment and they are now unequal, to what can we attribute that difference? If our controls have been adequate, our only choice is to assume that the difference between the groups is due to the IV.

Looking at our example, we have decided that the groups using two different textbooks showed a significant difference on the quiz scores. Many students stop at this point, thinking that they have drawn a complete conclusion from their experiment.

Psychological Detective

Why would this conclusion be incomplete? Write down your answer *and* a complete conclusion before proceeding.

Saying that the quiz scores from the two texts differ is an incomplete conclusion because it specifies only a difference, not the *direction* of that difference.

Whenever we compare treatments and find a difference, we want to know which group has performed better. In a two-group experiment, this interpretation is quite simple. Because we have only two groups and we have concluded that they differed significantly, we can further conclude that the group with the higher mean score has outscored the group with the lower mean score (remember that high scores do not always indicate superior performance).

To fully interpret the results from this experiment, we examine our descriptive statistics and find that the new-text group had a mean of 16.5, whereas the old-text group averaged 15.0. Thus, we can conclude that students using the new book made higher quiz scores than those students who used the old book. Notice that this statement includes both the notion of a difference *and* the direction of that difference.

When we draw conclusions from our research, we want to communicate those results clearly and concisely in our experimental report. To accomplish these two objectives, we use both words and numbers in our communication. This communication pattern is part of the APA style for preparing research reports that we considered in Chapter 5 and will complete in Chapter 12 (APA, 1994). We will introduce the form for statistical results here. Bear in mind that you are trying to communicate—to tell what you found in words and provide statistical information to document those words. For example, if you were writing an interpretation of the results from our sample experiment, you might write something like the following:

> Students who used the new textbook ($\underline{M}$ = 16.5, $\underline{SD}$ = 1.69) scored significantly higher, $\underline{t}$(14) = -2.20, $\underline{p}$ = .045, on their quizzes than students who used the old textbook ($\underline{M}$ = 15.0, $\underline{SD}$ = 0.93). The effect size, estimated with Cohen's $\underline{d}$, was 1.18.

Notice that the words alone give a clear account of the findings—a person who has never taken a statistics course could understand this conclusion. The inferential statistics regarding the test findings are provided to document the conclusion. The descriptive statistics ($\underline{M}$ = mean, $\underline{SD}$ = standard deviation) are provided for each group to allow the reader to see how the groups actually performed and to see how variable the data were. This standard format allows us to communicate our statistical results clearly and concisely.

***t* test for Correlated Samples.**   Remember that we have covered two different two-group designs in this chapter. Now we will examine the SPSS and MYSTAT computer output for analysis of the two correlated groups design. Our experiment concerning the textbooks was an example of the two independent groups design, which would *not* require a *t* test for correlated samples.

Psychological Detective

How could this experiment be modified so that it used correlated groups rather than independent groups? Write your answer before going on.

You should remember that there are three methods for creating correlated groups: matched pairs, repeated measures, or natural pairs. If your modified experiment used one of these techniques, you made a correct change. As an example, let's assume that we were worried about intelligence of our students confounding our experiment. To better equate the students in our two groups, we decided to use the matched pairs approach. After obtaining the students' permission (for ethical reasons), we obtained copies of their entrance exam scores (either ACT or SAT) from the Registrar's Office. We used these scores to form eight matched pairs (i.e., two students with identical scores) and randomly assigned one student from each pair to the new-text group and one to the old-text group. Before beginning our experiment, we know that the mean entrance exam scores are identical for the two groups, thus removing intelligence as a potential confounding variable.

Next, we conduct our experiment. The 16 students take the introductory psychology course, with 8 using the new book and 8 using the old book. During the course, the students took two quizzes. Given this hypothetical example, the scores from Chapter 6 would now represent paired quiz scores rather than independent scores. After analyzing the data with our two computer packages, we find the SPSS output in Table 7-3 and the MYSTAT output in Table 7-4. (Please note that it is *not* legitimate to analyze the same data with two different statistical tests. We are doing so in this chapter merely for example's sake. If you tested real-world data multiple times, you would increase the probability of making a Type I error [see Chapter 6].)

SPSS Results. Look at Table 7-3. As usual, we first look for the descriptive statistics. Again, we find them on the left side of the printout. Of course, because we used the same data, we have the same descriptive statistics as for the independent samples test. The students using the new textbook produced a mean combined quiz score of 16.5 with a standard deviation of 0.93 and a standard error of 0.33. The students who studied with the old text had mean quiz scores of 15.0 with a standard deviation of 1.69 and a standard error of 0.60. Note that there are 8 *pairs* of scores rather than 16 individual scores. This difference between the two *t* tests will be important when we consider the degrees of freedom.

The second block of information shows us the size of the difference between the two means, as well as its standard deviation and standard error. This informa-

TABLE 7-3. SPSS OUTPUT FOR *t* TEST FOR CORRELATED GROUPS

```
t-tests for paired samples

Variable      Number                                    (Difference)
           of cases    Mean   Standard   Standard        Mean
                              Deviation    Error
-------------------------------------------------------------------
OT    Scores with Old Text
                    15.0000    1.690       .598
           8                                           -1.5000
                    16.5000     .926       .327
NT    Scores with New Text
```

tion is rarely used. The third block gives you some information about the relationship between the pairs of participants (or same participant for repeated measures). Here you can determine whether or not the paired scores were correlated. Remember that we want them to be correlated so that we will gain the additional control available by using the correlated groups design. As you can see in this example, the scores were highly positively correlated (see Chapter 3). In our example, this result implies that if one student of the pair scored high (or low) on the quizzes, the other student of the pair also scored high (or low).

In the fourth block we find the results of our inferential test. We obtained a *t* value of –4.58 with 7 degrees of freedom.

Psychological Detective

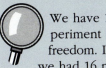

We have 16 students in our experiment but only 7 degrees of freedom. In our earlier example, we had 16 participants and 14 degrees of freedom. What is the difference in this case? Write your answer down before proceeding.

You may remember that our degrees of freedom for correlated samples cases are equal to the number of pairs of participants minus one. If this is fuzzy in your memory, refer to "Statistical Issues," discussed earlier in the chapter.

The computer tells us that the probability of a *t* of –4.58 with 7 *df* is .003. With such a low probability of chance for our results, we would conclude that there is a significant difference between the two textbooks. In other words, we believe that it is highly unlikely that the difference between our groups could have occurred by chance and that, instead, the difference must be due to our IV.

MYSTAT Results. We find the MYSTAT results in Table 7-4. You will find something interesting when you look for the descriptive statistics in the MYSTAT print-

Standard Deviation	Standard Error	Corr.	2-tail Prob.	t Value	Degrees of Freedom	2-tail Prob.
.926	.327	.913	.002	-4.58	7	.003

TABLE 7-4. MYSTAT OUTPUT FOR *t* TEST FOR CORRELATED GROUPS

```
PAIRED SAMPLES T-TEST ON NEWTEXT VS OLDTEXT WITH 8 CASES

MEAN DIFFERENCE =        1.500
SD DIFFERENCE=           0.926
T =          4.583 DF     7 PROB. = .003
```

TABLE 7-5. DESCRIPTIVE STATISTICS FROM MYSTAT

a. TOTAL OBSERVATIONS: 8

		OLDTEXT	NEWTEXT
	N OF CASES	8	8
	MINIMUM	13.000	15.000
	MAXIMUM	18.000	18.000
	MEAN	15.000	16.500
	STANDARD DEV	1.690	0.926

b. PEARSON CORRELATION MATRIX

		OLDTEXT	NEWTEXT
	OLDTEXT	1.000	
	NEWTEXT	0.913	1.000

NUMBER OF OBSERVATIONS: 8

out of a *t* test for correlated groups—there are none! Also, no information is provided regarding the correlation coefficient. This may happen with programs in other statistics packages as well. If you are working with such a package, don't despair. There is usually a simple program or routine within the package that will give you the descriptive statistics. In MYSTAT, we can run the STATS routine to obtain the descriptive statistics you see in Table 7-5a. Of course, you see the values from the two groups that we have obtained previously: The new-text group had mean quiz scores of 16.5 with a standard deviation of 0.93, and the old-text group averaged 15.0 with a standard deviation of 1.69.

Referring to Table 7-4 again, we find the results of the *t* test for correlated groups. As you would expect, we obtained the same results as with SPSS. The *t* value is 4.58, we have 7 *df*, and the probability of chance is again .003. So, again we find a significant difference between the performance of students who studied with the new textbooks and those who used the old textbooks. You will notice that no information is provided regarding the correlation between the two sets of scores—here, again, you would need to run a separate procedure if you wished to obtain that information. We ran the PEARSON routine to obtain the correlation information in Table 7-5b.

Translating Statistics into Words. Our experimental logic is exactly the same for this experiment as it was for the independent samples case. The only difference is that with our matched participants, we feel more certain that the two groups are equal before the experiment begins. We still treat our groups equally (control) with the one exception (our IV) and measure their performance (our DV) so that we can compare them statistically.

To translate our statistics into words, it is important to say more than the fact that we found a significant difference. We must know what form or direction that significant difference takes. With the *t* test for correlated samples, we are again comparing two groups, so it is a simple matter of looking at the group means to determine which group outperformed the other. Of course, because we are using the same data, our results are identical: The new group had mean quiz scores of 16.5 compared to 15.0 for the old group.

Psychological Detective

How would you write the results of this experiment in words and numbers for your experimental report? Write a sample sentence before you go further.

Did you find yourself flipping back in the book to look at our earlier conclusion? If so, that's a good strategy because this conclusion should be quite similar to the earlier conclusion. In fact, you could almost copy the earlier conclusion as long as you made three important changes. Did you catch those changes? Here's an adaptation of our earlier conclusion:

Students who used the new textbook ($\underline{M}$ = 16.5, $\underline{SD}$ = 0.93) scored significantly higher, $\underline{t}(7)$ = 4.58, $\underline{p}$ = .003, on their quizzes than students who used the old textbook ($\underline{M}$ = 15.0, $\underline{SD}$ = 1.69). The effect size, estimated with Cohen's $\underline{d}$, was 3.46.

As you can see, four numbers in the sentences changed: We had fewer degrees of freedom, our *t* value was larger, our probability of chance was lower and our effect size was larger. In this *purely hypothetical* example in which we analyzed the same data twice (a clear violation of assumptions if you were to do this in the real world), you can see the advantage of correlated groups designs. Although we lost degrees of freedom, the probability that our results were due to chance actually decreased and our effect size increased. Again, we gained these advantages because our matching of the participants helped to decrease the variability in the data.

You can see a vivid illustration of what we gained through matching by examining Table 7-6. In this example, we have used the same data from Chapter 6 but shuffled the scores for the second group before we ran a *t* test for correlated samples. Such a situation would occur if you matched your participants on an irrelevant variable (remember that we mentioned this possibility earlier in the chapter). As you can see by comparing Tables 7-6 and 7-3, the descriptive statistics remained the same because the scores in each group did not change. However, in Table 7-6, the correlation between

TABLE 7-6. SPSS OUTPUT FOR *t* TEST FOR CORRELATED GROUPS (SHUFFLED DATA)

Variable	Number of cases	Mean	Standard Deviation	Standard Error	(Difference) Mean
NM	Scores with New Text				
		16.5000	.926	.327	
	8				1.5000
		15.0000	1.690	.598	
OM	Scores with Old Text				

the two sets of scores is now .00. Because there is no correlation between our scores, the *t* value is 2.20, essentially the same as it was in our *t* test for independent groups (see Table 7-1). The marked change comes when we compare the inferential statistics in Table 7-3 and 7-6. The original analysis showed a *t* of 4.58 with *p* = .003. In contrast, with no correlation between the pairs of scores, the new analysis shows a *t* of 2.20 with *p* = .06. Thus, these results did not remain significant when the correlation between the participants disappeared. Again, the key point to remember is that when using a correlated groups design, the groups should actually be correlated.

THE CONTINUING RESEARCH PROBLEM

Research is a cyclical, ongoing process. It would be rare for a psychologist to conduct a single research project and stop at that point because that one project had answered all the questions about the particular topic. Instead, one experiment usually answers some of your questions, does not answer others, and raises new ones for your consideration. As you have studied the work of famous psychologists, you may have noticed that many of them established a research area early in their careers and continued working in that area for the duration of their professional lives. We're not trying to say that the research area you choose as an undergraduate will shape your future as a psychologist (although it could!). Rather, we are merely pointing out that one good experiment often leads to another.

We want to show you how research is an ongoing process as we move through the next two chapters with our continuing research problem. We sketched out a research problem in Chapter 6 (comparing how a new textbook and an old textbook affect student performance) and asked you to help us solve the problem through experimentation. We will continue to examine this problem throughout the next two chapters so that you can see how different questions we ask about the same problem may require different research designs. This research problem is purely hypothetical, but it has an applied slant to it. We hope the continuing research

Standard Deviation	Standard Error	Corr.	2-tail Prob.	t Value	Degrees of Freedom	2-tail Prob.
1.927	.681	.000	1.000	2.20	7	.064

problem helps you see how a single question can be asked in many different ways *and* that a single question often leads to many new questions.

To make certain you understood the logical series of steps we took in choosing a design, let's review those steps, paying particular attention to our experimental design questions shown in Figure 7-1:

1.   After reviewing relevant research literature, we chose our IV (textbook) and our DV (score on two combined quizzes).

2.   Because we were conducting a preliminary investigation into the effects of textbooks on student performance, we decided to test only one IV (the textbook).

3.   Because we wanted to determine only whether or not a textbook can affect student performance, we chose to use only two levels of the IV (new textbook vs. old textbook).

4a. If we have a large number of participants available, then we can use random assignment, which yields independent groups. In this case, we would use the two independent groups design and analyze the data with a *t* test for independent groups.

4b. If we expect to have a small number of participants and need to exert the maximum degree of control, we choose to use a design with repeated measures or matched groups, thus resulting in correlated groups. Therefore, we would use a two correlated groups design for the experiment and analyze the data with a *t* test for correlated groups.

5.   We concluded that the new textbook led to higher quiz scores than the old text.

REVIEW SUMMARY

1. The statistical test you use for analyzing your experimental data is related to the experimental design you chose.
2. When you have one IV with two groups and use randomly assigned research participants, the appropriate statistical test is the *t* test for independent samples.

3. When you have one IV with two groups and use matched pairs, natural pairs, or repeated measures with your participants, the appropriate statistical test is the *t* test for correlated samples.

4. Computer printouts of statistics typically give descriptive statistics (including means and standard deviations) and inferential statistics.

5. To communicate statistical results of an experiment, we use APA format for clarity and conciseness.

6. Research is a cyclical, ongoing process. Most experimental questions can be tested with different designs.

S TUDY B REAK

1. Which statistical test would you use if you compared the stereotyping of a group of female executives to a group of male executives? Explain your reasoning.

2. Which statistical test would you use if you compared the stereotyping of a group of male executives before and after the Equal Rights Amendment passed through Congress? Explain your reasoning.

3. What information do we usually look for first on a computer printout? Why?

4. If the variability of our two groups is similar, we have _____; if the variability of the groups is dissimilar, we have _____.

5. When we write a report of our experimental results, we explain the results in _____ and _____.

6. Interpret the following statistics:

   Group A ($M = 75$); Group B ($M = 70$); $t(14) = 2.53$, $p < .05$

7. Why do we describe research as a cyclical, ongoing process? Give an example of how this cycling might take place.

L OOKING A HEAD

In this chapter we have examined the notion of planning an experiment by selecting a research design. In particular we examined the basic building block designs with one IV and two groups. In the next chapter we will enlarge this basic design by adding more groups to our one IV. This enlarged design will give us the capability to ask more penetrating questions about the effects of our IV and to obtain more specific information about those effects.

H ANDS - O N A CTIVITIES

You have probably read and heard a great deal about the Type A personality or behavior pattern. No doubt you covered this topic in your introductory psychology course. Did you indulge in a little self-analysis trying to figure out whether you are a Type A or Type B person? In this section we'll give you a chance to find out which behavior pattern you fit and then give you an opportunity to conduct some research dealing with the Type A concept.

Table 7-7 provides a modified version of the Jenkins Activity Survey (Krantz, Glass, & Snyder, 1974). This version is a shorter form that was designed particularly for students. This survey will help you determine how closely your behavior pattern matches the Type A pattern. After completing the survey, use the scoring key provided in Table 7-8. If you score high on the scale, your behavior matches that of a Type A individual—driven, time urgent, and competitive. Although early research linked Type A behavior to coronary problems, subsequent research indicates that only hostile Type A behavior is associated with coronary problems. If you scored low on the scale, your behavior is more like that of a Type B individual—laid back, easy-going, and casual about life.

As you might guess, there is a great deal of research about Type A behavior and its relationships to other factors. There is no way we could survey this literature in our limited space, but you can go to your library and use *PsycLIT* or *Psychological Abstracts* to get an idea of some of the various topics that have been studied with respect to Type A behavior.

We want to give you the chance to use the Jenkins Scale in two research projects that fit the designs from Chapter 7. These research projects are not meant to be original, pioneering work; rather, they are meant to give you a chance to get your hands "dirty" with some data collection and analysis. Referring back to Figure 7-1, you will remember that we dealt with one-IV, two-group designs in this chapter.

1. **Two Independent Groups Designs.**   How could you devise an experiment with two independent groups revolving around the Jenkins Survey? Of course, there are a myriad of possibilities. One interesting idea about Type A scores is that they could be used as either an IV or a DV! We could administer the Jenkins to people and use it to classify them as either Type A or B and use that classification as our IV. On the other hand, we could pick an IV that divides people into two groups, administer the Jenkins, and then determine whether Jenkins scores differ between the two groups. For this research, we will choose the latter approach.

    One basic question we could ask about the Type A behavior pattern is whether it shows any sex differences. That is, do men and women differ in their scores on the Jenkins Survey? It would be a simple matter for you to randomly select 10 to 20 men and a like number of women and have them complete the Jenkins Survey. After collecting the data, use an independent *t* test to compare the scores.

Psychological Detective

Why can't you randomly assign your participants to groups in the research just described?   What type of research would this project involve? Write your answers before proceeding.

Of course, any time you use sex as an IV, you cannot randomly assign participants to groups—people come predetermined as women or men. Because the participants are already categorized in their groups, this would be an ex post facto

TABLE 7-7. MODIFIED JENKINS ACTIVITY SURVEY

1. How would your husband or wife (or closest friend) rate you?
   a. definitely hard-driving and competitive
   b. probably hard-driving and competitive
   c. probably relaxed and easy-going
   d. definitely relaxed and easy-going

2. How would you rate yourself?
   a. definitely hard-driving and competitive
   b. probably hard-driving and competitive
   c. probably relaxed and easy-going
   d. definitely relaxed and easy-going

3. How do you consider yourself compared to the average student?
   a. more responsible
   b. as responsible
   c. less responsible

4. Compared to the average student,
   a. I give much more effort
   b. I give the same amount of effort
   c. I give less effort

5. College has
   a. stirred me into action
   b. not stirred me into action

6. Compared to the average student,
   a. I am more precise
   b. I am as precise
   c. I am less precise

7. Compared to the average student,
   a. I approach life more seriously
   b. I approach life as seriously
   c. I approach life less seriously

8. How would most people rate you?
   a. definitely hard-driving and competitive
   b. probably hard-driving and competitive
   c. probably relaxed and easy-going
   d. definitely relaxed and easy-going

9. How would you rate yourself?
   a. definitely *not* having less energy than most people
   b. probably *not* having less energy than most people
   c. probably having less energy than most people
   d. definitely having less energy than most people

10. I frequently set deadlines for myself in courses or other things.
    a. yes   b. no   c. sometimes

11. Do you maintain a regular study schedule during vacations such as Thanksgiving, Christmas, and Easter?
    a. yes   b. no   c. sometimes

TABLE 7-7. MODIFIED JENKINS ACTIVITY SURVEY (continued)

12. I hurry even when there is plenty of time.
   a. yes   **b.** once in a while   **c.** sometimes

13. I have been told I eat too fast.
   a. often   **b.** once in a while   **c.** sometimes

14. How would you rate yourself?
   a. I eat more rapidly than most people
   b. I eat as rapidly as most people
   c. I eat less rapidly than most people

15. I hurry a speaker to the point.
   a. frequently
   b. once in a while
   c. never

16. How would most people rate you?
   a. definitely *not* doing most things in a hurry
   b. probably *not* doing most things in a hurry
   c. probably doing most things in a hurry
   d. definitely doing most things in a hurry

17. Compared to the average student,
   a. I hurry much less
   b. I hurry as much
   c. I hurry much more

18. How often are there deadlines in your courses?
   a. frequently   **b.** once in a while   **c.** never

19. Everyday life is filled with challenges to be met.
   a. yes   **b.** no   **c.** sometimes

20. I have held an office in an activity group or held a part-time job when in school.
   a. frequently   **b.** once in a while   **c.** never

21. I stay in the library at night while studying until closing.
   a. frequently   **b.** once in a while   **c.** never

Source: From "Helplessness, Stress Level, and the Coronary-Prone Behavior Pattern," by D. S. Krantz, D. C. Glass, and M. L. Snyder, 1974, *Journal of Experimental Social Psychology, 10,* pp. 284–300.

design. We have mentioned the problems involved with making cause-and-effect statements from ex post facto research. Is this a severe problem in this particular research? We don't think so . . . as long as you're careful about any conclusion you draw. If you view this as an investigative and descriptive study, there should be no problem. Thus, if either men or women end up having significantly higher Jenkins scores, you should simply note that the women (or men) scored higher. However, you should *not* conclude that being a woman (or a man) causes one to score high on the Jenkins or to exhibit Type A characteristics.

2. Two Correlated Groups Design.   To conduct a correlated groups design, you must use a within-subjects manipulation—matched pairs, repeated measures, or natural pairs. Natural pairs is probably out because finding twins would be too dif-

TABLE 7-8. SCORING AND NORMS FOR MODIFIED JENKINS ACTIVITY SURVEY

Give yourself one point for each answer that matches the following key:

1. a or b	**2.** a or b	**3.** a	**4.** a
5. a	**6.** a	**7.** a	**8.** a or b
9. a or b	**10.** a	**11.** a	**12.** a
13. a	**14.** a	**15.** a	**16.** c or d
17. c	**18.** a	**19.** a	**20.** a
21. a			

Score	Classification
13+	A+
9–12	A–
8	borderline
4–7	B–
0–3	B+

Source: From "Helplessness, Stress Level, and the Coronary-Prone Behavior Pattern," by D. S. Krantz, D. C. Glass, and M. L. Snyder, 1974, *Journal of Experimental Social Psychology, 10,* pp. 284–300.

ficult. Matching would be a good possibility, but you would need to know what matching variable to use. Because so many variables have been related to Type A behavior, it is difficult to know which variable would be a good matching variable. Therefore, let's use repeated measures. Also, because we have used an ex post facto variable (sex) previously, let's choose a situation that uses a different variable.

With repeated measures, we could attempt to answer the question of whether Type A behavior is consistent over time. In other words, is Type A behavior more likely a trait (consistent) or a state (variable over time)? We will tackle this question by comparing students who have no tests in a week to students who have two or al tests in a week could increase the degree of Type A behavior.

Begin this research by randomly selecting a group of about 30 students. We cannot directly control their testing during a semester, so we will use random assignment by assigning half to the high-stress condition (2+ tests in a week) first and the other half to the low-stress condition (no tests in a week) first. Ask your participants to tell you their testing schedules for the next month. Choose an appropriate week to test each participant. After they have all been measured, reverse their conditions and test them in the opposite condition (i.e., high-stress → low stress and low stress → high stress). When you have tested each participant in each condition (repeated measures), compare the scores with a *t* test for correlated samples.

What did you find? Does one's environment affect Type A behavior? If the Jenkins scores are higher during the heavy testing weeks, then it seems that environmental conditions can affect Type A behavior patterns. On the other hand, if the Type A scores are comparable in both conditions, then Type A would seem to be a stable traitlike condition.

CHAPTER 8

Designing, Conducting, Analyzing, and Interpreting Experiments with More than Two Groups

Experimental Design: Adding to the Basic Building Block

In Chapter 7 we learned many concepts and principles about **experimental design** that are basic to planning *any* experiment, not merely the basic two-group experiment. When we come to one of those topics in this chapter, we will briefly review it and refer you back to Chapter 7 for the original discussion.

Experimental design The general plan for selecting participants, assigning participants to experimental conditions, controlling extraneous variables, and gathering data.

Independent variable A stimulus or aspect of the environment that is directly manipulated by the experimenter to determine its influence on behavior.

In this chapter we will add to our basic building block design. Consider our previous analogy: As a child you quickly mastered the beginner's set of Legos or Tinkertoys. You learned to build everything there was to build with that small set and wanted to go beyond the simple objects that were possible to build larger, more exciting creations. To satisfy this desire, you got a larger set of building materials that you could combine with the starter set in order to build more complicated objects. Despite the fact you were using a larger set of materials, the basic principles you learned with your starter set still applied.

Experimental design works in much the same way. Researchers typically want to move beyond the two-group designs so that they can ask more complicated and interesting questions. Fortunately, they don't have to start from scratch—that's why we referred to the two-group design as the basic building block design in the previous chapter. Every experimental design is based on the two-group design. Although the questions you ask may become more complicated or sophisticated, your experimental design principles will remain constant. In the same way, when they are faced with a more difficult case, detectives still use the basic investigative procedures they have learned.

It is still appropriate to think of your experimental design as the blueprint of your experiment. We hope this analogy convinces you of the need for having an experimental design. Although you *might* be able to get by without a blueprint if you're building a doghouse, it is unlikely you would want to build *your* house without a blueprint. Think of building a small house as being equivalent to using the two-group design from Chapter 7. If you need a blueprint to build a house, imagine how much more you would need a blueprint to build an apartment building or a skyscraper. We will work toward the skyscrapers of experimental design in Chapter 9.

The Multiple-Group Design

Here, we will consider an extension of the two-group design. Turn back to Figure 7-2 for just a moment. What would be the next logical step to add to this design so that we could ask (and answer) slightly more complex questions?

How Many IVs? The first question that we ask when considering any experimental design is the same: "How many **independent variables** will I use in my exper-

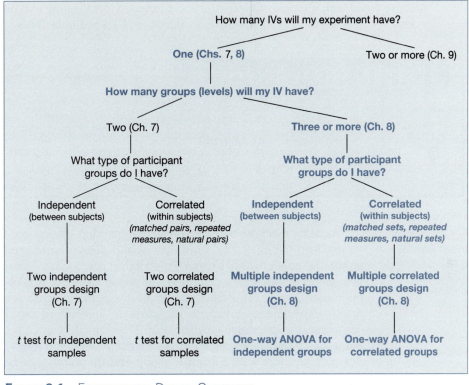

FIGURE 8-1   EXPERIMENTAL DESIGN QUESTIONS

iment?" (see Figure 8-1). In this chapter, we will continue to consider experiments that use only one IV. We should remember that although one-IV experiments may be simpler than experiments that use multiple IVs, they are not inferior in any way.

Many students who are designing their first research study decide to "throw in everything except the kitchen sink" as an IV. A well-designed experiment with one IV is vastly preferable to a sloppy experiment with many variables "thrown together." Remember the **principle of parsimony** from Chapter 7—if a one-IV experiment can answer your questions, use it and don't complicate things needlessly.

How Many Groups?   Once we have chosen to conduct a one-IV experiment, our second question (see Figure 8-1) revolves around how many groups we will use to test the IV. This question marks the difference between the multiple-group design and the two-group design. As their names imply, a two-group design compares two **levels** of an IV whereas a multiple-group design compares three or more levels of a single IV. Thus, we could compare three, four, five, or even more differing amounts or types of an IV. This experimental situation is similar to that experienced by a de-

Principle of parsimony The belief that explanations of phenomena and events should remain simple until the simple explanations are no longer valid.

Levels Differing amounts or types of an IV used in an experiment (*also known as treatment conditions*).

definition

tective faced with multiple suspects. Instead of merely investigating two people, the detective must conduct simultaneous investigations of several individuals.

Psychological Detective

In Chapter 7 we learned that the most common type of two-group design uses experimental and control groups. How will the multiple-group design differ from that common two-group design? Give this question some serious thought and record your answer before proceeding.

Treatment groups
Groups of participants that receive the IV.

Actually, there are two answers to that question—if you got either, pat yourself on the back. (1) A multiple-group design *can* have a control group. But rather than having an experimental and a control group, a multiple-group design with a control group would also have two or more experimental groups. This combination allows us to condense several two-group experiments into one experiment. Instead of conducting a two-group experiment to determine whether your IV has an effect and a second two-group experiment to determine the optimum amount of your IV, you could conduct a multiple-group experiment with a control group and the number of **treatment groups** you would like to assess. (2) A multiple-group design does not have to have a control group. If you already know that your IV has an effect, you can simply compare as many treatment groups as you would like in your multiple-group design. Did you figure out either of these answers to the Psychological Detective question?

Let's look at a research example using the multiple-group design. Lori Yarbrough (1993), of Harding University, wanted to determine whether the color of paper on which a survey was printed affected the return rate of the survey. She sent surveys printed on white, pink, or gold paper to college students. Why does this experiment fit the multiple-group design? First, it has only one IV—the color of the survey's paper. Second, the IV has more than two levels—it has three, based on the three different colored surveys. Thus, as you can see in Figure 8-1, with one IV and three levels, this experiment requires the use of a multiple-group design. We can draw the block diagram depicted in Figure 8-2 to portray this experimental design. If you compare Figures 7-2 and 8-2, you can easily see how the multiple group design is an extension of the two-group design.

All three groups in Figure 8-2 are experimental groups. Does this experiment use a control group? No, all three groups of participants represent different types of the IV—there is no way for a survey to be printed on paper with no color. In this experiment, Yarbrough was interested in the various differences among all three groups based on their differing colors of surveys. Of the 284 surveys Yarbrough sent to college students, 92 were returned. She found that there was no difference in the rate of return of the surveys based on their color. In statistical terminology, then, Yarbrough found results that support the null hypothesis (i.e., that there is no

INDEPENDENT VARIABLE (COLOR OF SURVEY PAPER)

EXPERIMENTAL GROUP 1	EXPERIMENTAL GROUP 2	EXPERIMENTAL GROUP 3
White	Pink	Gold

FIGURE 8-2   THE MULTIPLE-GROUP DESIGN USED BY YARBROUGH (1993).

difference between the groups). This is a perfect example, though, of why support for the null hypothesis is not the same as *proving* the null hypothesis. Did Yarbrough *prove* that color does not affect the return rate of surveys? No, she merely demonstrated that there was no difference for the colors she used and for her groups of participants. What about using different colors? What about using different research participants—designers, artists, or children, for example? File away this clue for future exploration—in Chapter 10 we will talk about how to generalize our results beyond the specific participants in our experiment.

Psychological Detective

Suppose you wished to test more than three colors of surveys. Could you use a multiple-group design in such a case? Why or why not? If so, what would happen to the block design in Figure 8-2? Write your answer before moving on.

Yes, the multiple-group design could be used if there were four or five colors of surveys to be assessed. In fact, it could be used if there were 10, 20, or 100 colors. The only requirement for using the multiple-group design is an experiment with one IV and more than two groups (see Figure 8-1). Practically speaking, it is rare that multiple-group designs are used with more than four or five groups. If we did use such a design with more than three groups, we would merely extend our block diagram, as shown in Figure 8-3.

Assigning Participants to Groups. After we decide to conduct a multiple-group experiment, we must decide about assignment of research participants to groups (see Figure 8-1). Just as in Chapter 7, we must choose between using **independent groups** or using **correlated groups.**

Independent groups Groups of participants that are formed by random assignment.

Correlated groups Groups of research participants that are related in some way, through matching, repeated measures, or natural sets.

definition

FIGURE 8-3   HYPOTHETICAL MULTIPLE-GROUP DESIGN WITH FIVE GROUPS

INDEPENDENT VARIABLE (COLOR OF SURVEY PAPER)

EXPL GROUP 1	EXPL GROUP 2	EXPL GROUP 3	EXPL GROUP 4	EXPL GROUP 5
Color A	Color B	Color C	Color D	Color E

cathy®

by Cathy Guisewite

Cathy ©Cathy Guisewite. Reprinted with permission of Universal Press Syndicate. All rights reserved.

Is Cathy using random assignment or random selection in this cartoon? You may want to look back at Chapters 3 and 4. Write your answer before reading further.

Because she is tasting chocolate Santas in a non-systematic way (rather than assigning Santas to groups), Cathy s gluttony illustrates random selection.

Random Assignment to Groups. Remember that in **random assignment** each participant has an equal chance of being assigned to any group. In her experiment on the color of surveys and their return rates, Yarbrough (1993) used random assignment when she sent the original 284 surveys—all 284 students had a 1 in 3 chance of receiving a white, pink, or gold survey. When we use large groups of participants, random assignment should create groups that are equal on potential extraneous variables such as personality, age, and sex. Recall from Chapter 7 that random assignment allows us to control extraneous variables about which we are unaware. Thus, random assignment serves as an important **control procedure.** For example, we would not want to send all the pink surveys only to women or to only men. We want to spread the different levels of the IV across all types of participants in order to avoid a **confounded experiment.** Suppose we sent all pink surveys to women and all gold surveys to men (or vice versa). When we tabulated our results, we would not be able to draw a clear conclusion about the effects of survey color because color was confounded with participant sex.

Random assignment results in participants who have no relationship to participants in other groups; in other words, the groups are independent of each other. We are interested in comparing differences between the various independent groups. As you can see in Figure 8-1, when we use random assignment in this design, we end up with a multiple independent groups design.

Non-Random Assignment to Groups. In the multiple-group design, we have the same concern about random assignment that we did with the two-group design: What if the random assignment does not work and we begin our experiment with unequal groups? We know that random assignment *should* create equal groups, but that it is most likely to work in the long run—that is, when we have many participants. If we have few participants or if we expect only small differences due to our IV, we may want more control than random assignment affords us. In such situations, we often resort to using nonrandom methods of assigning participants to groups and thus end up with correlated groups. Let's examine our three ways of creating correlated groups and see how they differ from Chapter 7.

> **Matching variable**
> A potential extraneous variable on which we measure our research participants and from which we form sets of participants who are equal on the variable.

1. Matched Sets. Matched pairs are not appropriate for the multiple-group design because we have at least three groups, so we must use matched sets. The principle of forming matched sets is the same as forming matched pairs. Before our experiment, we measure our participants on some variable that will affect their performance on the DV. Then we create sets of participants who are essentially the same on this measured variable, often known as the **matching variable.** The size of the sets will, of course, depend on how many levels our IV has. If our IV has five levels, for example, then each set would have five participants equated on the matching variable. After we create our matched sets, we then randomly assign the participants within each set to the different groups (treatments).

Returning to Yarbrough's experiment, suppose we did believe that participant sex would be an extraneous variable because we were using pink surveys. To ensure equality of her groups on sex, Yarbrough could have used sets of three participants who were matched on sex, with each participant then randomly assigned to one of the three groups. In this manner, she would have assured that the distribution of participant sex was uniform across all three groups. If all three of her groups had the same sex composition (regardless of whether it was 50-50), then participant sex could not be an extraneous variable.

One final caution is in order. We must remember that the potential extraneous variable must actually affect performance on the DV or else we have hurt our chances of finding a significant difference.

2. Repeated Measures. Other than the fact that participants perform in three or more conditions rather than only two, repeated measures in the multiple-group design is identical to repeated measures in the two-group design. When you use repeated measures in the multiple-group design, each participant must take part in all the various treatment conditions. Thus, for Yarbrough to have used repeated measures, each student would have received a white, a pink, *and* a gold survey.

Psychological Detective

Can you see any possible flaws in conducting Yarbrough's experiment using a repeated measures design? (Hint: Consider some of the practical issues from Chapter 7 about using repeated measures.) Jot down your ideas before proceeding.

Several problems could occur if we attempted the survey color experiment with a repeated measures design. Would you send one person the same survey three different times, each printed on a different color of paper? This would not seem to make any sense. The students might become suspicious about the differing colors; they would probably trash the new copies if they had responded to the first one; or they might return a later copy, not because of its color but because they felt guilty or wanted to stop the surveys from coming or for some other reason. What about sending three different surveys, each printed in a different color? Again, this could be problematic. Could we logically assume that returned surveys were returned because of the color? Not necessarily, because different surveys would have to cover different topics. Students would be more likely to return a survey that dealt with a topic they considered more important or interesting. Thus, we might be measuring the response rate to different survey topics rather than to different-colored surveys! It seems that this experiment simply would not work well as a repeated measures design. Remember that we mentioned this possible problem in Chapter 7—not all experiments can be conducted using repeated measures.

3. Natural Sets. Using natural sets is analogous to using natural pairs except that our sets must include more than two research participants. Using multiple groups takes away our ability to use some interesting natural pairs such as twins or husbands and wives, but other possibilities for using natural sets do exist. For example, many animal researchers will use litter mates as natural sets, assuming that their shared heredity makes them more similar than randomly selected animals. In a similar fashion, if your research participants were siblings from families with three (or more) children, natural sets would be a possibility. Most natural pairs or sets involve biological relationships.

We create multiple correlated groups designs when we use matched sets, repeated measures, or natural sets. The critical distinction is that the participants in these types of groups are related to each other in some way—we are comparing differences *within* groups (or within subjects, to use the old terminology). On the other hand, in independent groups designs, the participants have no common relationship. Thus, we compare differences *between* differing groups of subjects.

Roland Johnson and Emily Branscum (1993), of California State University in Stanislaus, CA, conducted an experiment that used a multiple correlated groups design. They were interested in measuring habituation in rats exposed to a novel environment. When animals are exposed to a new environment, many species show lower rates of activity and exploration and higher rates of defecation. This reaction is termed neophobia and is usually interpreted as evidence of fear or caution in the new situation (Tarpy, 1982). Johnson and Branscum conducted an open-field test with eight rats over three days. In the open-field test, rats are put in a novel environment and their movements are tracked over time to determine whether the activity level increases. By measuring the rats over three days, Johnson and Branscum could compare data for a novel trial (Day 1) to two habituation trials (Days 2 and 3).

Why does the Johnson and Branscum experiment exemplify a correlated groups design? Which particular correlated groups technique did they use? Why do you think they used a correlated groups design? Write your answers before reading further.

In this experiment, the IV is time, defined as days. Thus, there are three levels of the IV. Each rat was measured on each day, so the correlated groups were a result of using repeated measures. Johnson and Branscum probably used a correlated groups design because they had only eight rats to run through their experiment. Placing eight rats into three groups would result in very small groups, which raises a serious problem with the assumption that the groups were equivalent before the experiment began. By using each rat as its own control across the three days, the question of group equality was answered. The use of repeated measures helped control many subject variables that *might* have affected the rats' performance in the open-field test—factors such as activity level, intelligence, and sex.

Johnson and Branscum (1993) found that the rats showed increased ambulatory behavior (moving around the environment) over the three days. The rats defecated less across the days, but not significantly so. In this particular study, then, ambulatory behavior seemed to be a better measure of habituation in rats to a new environment.

Could Johnson and Branscum have used either of the other two methods of producing a correlated groups design? Yes, they could have created matched sets by observing and measuring the rats' activity levels before the experiment. After this measurement, they could have created a matched set of the three most active rats and then assigned one to each of the three groups, and so on until matching the three least-active rats and randomly assigning them to the groups. On the other hand, they could have used natural sets by using sets of three rats from the same litter and randomly assigning one to each of the three groups. However, note how inefficient using either matched or natural sets would have been. More rats would have been required in order to have samples that were not tiny. Also, the experimenters would have ignored some of the rats' behavior. Without using repeated measures, only one group would have been measured on Day 1, a second group only on Day 2, and a third group only on Day 3. It was much simpler and efficient to use one group of rats that was measured across each day. It is important to evaluate your experiment thoroughly beforehand to decide which experimental design will be the best choice for your research project.

COMPARING THE MULTIPLE-GROUP DESIGN TO THE TWO-GROUP DESIGN

The multiple-group design is highly similar to the two-group design. As a matter of fact, all you have to do to change your two-group design into a multiple-group design is to add another level to your IV. Given this high degree of similarity, how would we compare these two designs?

In choosing a design for your experiment, your paramount concern is your experimental question. Does your question require only two groups to find an answer, or does it necessitate three or more groups? This question almost seems like a "no brainer," but it cannot be taken for granted. Following the principle of parsimony from Chapter 7, we want to select the simplest design possible that will answer our question.

In Chapter 7 we provided you with an ideal situation for a two-group design—an experiment in which we merely wish to determine whether or not our IV has an effect. Often such an experiment is not necessary because that information already exists in the literature. You should never conduct an experiment to determine whether a particular IV has an effect or not without first conducting a thorough literature search (see Chapter 2). If you find no answer in a library search, then you should consider conducting a two-group (presence vs. absence) study. If, however, you find the answer to that basic question and wish to go further, then a multiple-group design might be appropriate.

Of course, a multiple-group design is appropriate only when you have three or more levels of the IV that you wish to test. If there are only two levels that interest you, do *not* add another level simply to use a more complicated design. Always test your hypothesis with the simplest possible design. If you add a level to your IV just for fun, it will cost you time and energy—you will have to run more participants through your experiment, your control procedures become somewhat more complex, and you have increased the complexity of your statistical procedures.

After all these considerations, what do you do when you face a situation in which either a two-group design or a multiple-group design is appropriate? Although this answer may sound odd, you should think about your (future) results. What will they look like? What will they mean? Most critically, what will the addition of any group(s) beyond the basic two tell you? If the information that you expect to find by adding a group or groups is important and meaningful, then by all means add the group(s). If, however, you're not really certain what you might learn by adding to the two groups, then you may be complicating your life needlessly to do so.

Think back to the two student examples cited in this chapter. Did they learn important information by adding an extra group to their two groups? Yarbrough (1993) found that survey response rate did not differ with three different colors of paper (white, pink, and gold). Most people would probably wish for more levels in this experiment rather than for fewer! In fact, we would guess that one of your first thoughts when you read about Yarbrough's experiment earlier was, "Gee, I wonder about _____" (fill in the blank with your favorite color). You may believe that her experiment was not a fair test of the question about return rates of surveys based on their color, especially if you disagree with her color choices. So it does appear that Yarbrough made a wise decision in using a multiple-group design rather than a two-group design. In fact, it might have been more informative had she used an even larger multiple-group design.

Johnson and Branscum (1993) measured their rats' habituation to a novel environment over a three-day period. Again, they probably benefited by using a multiple-group design. Think back to your experiences with new environments. It is possible that habituation does not take place quickly enough to be discernible by the second day.

Psychological Detective

Suppose Johnson and Branscum wanted to use a larger multiple-group design—say measuring rats' habituation over seven days rather than three. Would it be possible to use such a large multiple-group design? If so, how might their experimental question change with the larger design? Jot down your answer before reading further.

Could you use a multiple-group design with seven groups or measurements? Sure you could. The only limitation would be a practical consideration—could you get enough participants to take part (for matched sets or natural sets), or can the participants cope with being measured so many times (for repeated measures)? The Johnson and Branscum experiment used repeated measures, so our concern would be for the experimental participants. In this case, all that would happen to the rats is that they would be placed in a different environment from their cages more often. They are not required to do anything; the experimenters must observe them. So this experiment would be no problem to run over seven days; it would simply require more of the experimenters' time. It is likely, though, that Johnson and Branscum would have been asking a different question had they observed the rats for a week. It seems that they would have been interested in how long it takes for rats to completely habituate to a new environment or when the habituation process levels off and ends. Their shorter experiment was more likely designed simply to answer the question of whether or not habituation occurs in rats.

In summary, the multiple-group and two-group designs are quite similar. However, there are important differences between them that you should consider when choosing an experimental design for your research project.

COMPARING MULTIPLE-GROUP DESIGNS

As you might guess, our comparison of the multiple independent groups design to the multiple correlated groups design is going to be fairly similar to our comparison of the two-group designs in Chapter 7. However, practical considerations become somewhat more important in the multiple-group designs, so our conclusions will be somewhat different.

Choosing a Multiple-Group Design. Again, your first consideration in choosing an experimental design should always be your experimental question. Once you have decided on an experiment with one IV and three or more groups, you must determine whether you can use independent or correlated groups. If only one of those choices is viable, then you have no further considerations to make. If, however, you could use either independent or correlated groups, you must make that decision before proceeding.

Control Issues. As in Chapter 7 and the two-group designs, your decision to use the multiple independent groups design versus the multiple correlated groups design revolves around control issues. The multiple independent groups design uses the control technique of randomly assigning participants to groups. If you have a large number of research participants (at least 10 per group), you can be fairly confident that random assignment will create equal groups. Multiple correlated groups designs use the control techniques of matching, repeated measures, or natural pairs to assure equality of groups and to reduce error variability. Look back at the equation that represents the general formula for a statistical test in Chapter 7 on page 214. Reducing the error variability in the denominator of the equation will result in a larger computed statistical value, thereby making it easier to reject the null hypothesis. You may remember from Chapter 7 that using a correlated design reduces your degrees of freedom, which makes it somewhat more difficult to achieve statistical significance and reject the null hypothesis. However, the reduced error variability typically more than offsets the loss of degrees of freedom. Therefore, correlated designs are often stronger tests for finding statistical significance.

Practical Considerations. Matters of practicality become quite important when we contemplate using a multiple correlated groups design. Let's think about each type of correlated design in turn. If we intend to use *matched sets,* we must consider the potential difficulty of finding three (or more) participants to match on the extraneous variable we choose. Suppose we conduct a learning experiment and thus wish to match our participants on IQ. How difficult will it be to find three, four, five, or more participants (depending on the number of levels we use) with the same IQ? If we cannot find enough to make a complete set of matches, then we cannot use those participants in our experiment. Therefore, we may lose potential research participants through the requirement of large matched sets. We may be limited in our use of *natural sets* by set size also. How much chance would you have of running an experiment on triplets, quadruplets, or quintuplets? Using animal littermates is probably the most common use of natural sets in multiple-group designs. When we use *repeated measures* in a multiple-group design, we are requiring each participant to be measured at least three times. This requirement necessitates more time for each participant or multiple trips to the laboratory, conditions the participants may not be willing to meet. We hope this message is clear: If you intend to use a multiple correlated groups design, plan it very carefully so that these basic practical considerations do not sabotage your experiment.

What about practical considerations in multiple independent groups designs? The multiple independent groups design is simpler than the correlated version. The practical factor you must take into account is the large number of research participants you will need to make random assignment feasible *and* to fill the multiple groups. If participants are not available in large numbers, you need to consider using a correlated design.

Drawing a definite conclusion about running independent versus correlated multiple-group designs is not simple. The correlated designs have some statistical advantages, but they also require you to take into account several practical matters that may make using such a design difficult. Independent designs are simple to implement, but they force you to recruit or obtain many research participants to assure equality of your groups. The best advice we can provide is to remind you that each experiment presents you with unique problems, opportunities, and questions. You need to be aware of the factors we have presented and to weigh those carefully in conjunction with your experimental question when you choose a specific research design for your experiment.

VARIATIONS ON THE MULTIPLE-GROUP DESIGN

In Chapter 7 we discussed two variations on the two-group design. Those same two variations are also possible with the multiple-group design.

Comparing Different Amounts of an IV. This "variation" on the multiple-group design is not actually a variation at all—it is part of the basic design. Because the smallest possible multiple-group design would consist of three treatment groups, every multiple-group design must compare different amounts (or types) of an IV. Even if a multiple-group design has a control group, there are at least two different treatment groups in addition.

If we already know that a particular IV has an effect, then we can use a multiple-group design to help us define that effect. In this type of experiment, we often add an important control in order to account for a possible **placebo effect.** For example, is it possible that some of the effects of coffee on our alertness are due to what we *expect* the coffee to do? If so, a proper control group would consist of people who drink decaffeinated coffee. These participants would be blind to the fact that their coffee does not contain caffeine. This group, without any caffeine, would show us whether there are any placebo effects of coffee.

Placebo effect
An experimental effect that is due to expectation or suggestion rather than the IV.

Dealing with Measured IVs. All the research examples we have cited in this chapter deal with manipulated IVs. It is also possible to use measured IVs in a multiple-group design. In Chapter 7 you learned that research that we conduct with a measured rather than manipulated IV is termed **ex post facto research.** We cannot draw cause-and-effect relationships from such an experiment because we do not directly control and manipulate the IV ourselves. Still, an ex post facto design can yield interesting information. Let's look at a student example of an ex post facto design with a measured IV.

Keith Sanford (1993), from Seattle Pacific University in Seattle, WA, used an ex post facto approach in his study of the effects of styles of romantic attachment on several variables such as loneli-

ex post facto research A research approach in which the experimenter cannot directly manipulate the IV but can only classify, categorize, or measure the IV because it is predetermined in the participants (e.g., IV = sex).

definition

ness and dating frequency. Collins and Read (1990) had previously developed the Adult Attachment Questionnaire, which Sanford used to classify his participants' attachment style as secure, anxious, or avoidant. Why does this experimental design fit the multiple-group format? Does it have one IV? Yes, romantic attachment. Does it have three or more levels of that one IV? Yes, the secure, anxious, or avoidant attachment styles. These attachment styles were his measured IV—he could not assign students to one of the different styles; he could only measure which style they exhibited.

Sanford found that the avoidant group was the most lonely, the secure group was the least lonely, and the anxious group was moderately lonely. Secure individuals dated more frequently and were more likely to be dating steadily in comparison with the other two groups. Participants in the avoidant group were more likely to have experienced parental divorce than the other groups. Notice that the multiple-group design allowed Sanford to detect a difference between one group versus the two other groups *and* a difference that occurred among all three groups. These types of findings show the advantage of the multiple-group design over the two-group design. Remember these various types of differences because we will return to them in the statistical analysis section of the chapter.

REVIEW SUMMARY

1. Psychologists plan their experiments beforehand using an **experimental design,** which serves as a blueprint for the experiment.
2. You use the **multiple-group design** for experimental situations in which you have one **IV** that has three or more levels or conditions. A **control** group may or may not be used.
3. You form **independent groups** of research participants by **randomly assigning** them to treatment groups.
4. You form **correlated groups** of research participants by creating matched sets, using natural sets, or measuring each participant more than once (repeated measures).
5. *Multiple correlated groups designs* provide extra advantages for experimental control relative to *multiple independent groups designs.*
6. Practical considerations in dealing with research participants make the multiple correlated groups designs considerably more complicated than multiple independent groups designs.
7. Measured IVs can be used in multiple-group designs, resulting in **ex post facto studies.**

STUDY BREAK

1. Why is the two-group design the building block for the multiple-group design?
2. The simplest possible multiple-group design would have _____ IV(s) and _____ treatment group(s).

3. What advantage(s) can you see in using a multiple-group design rather than a two-group design?

4. Devise an experimental question that could be answered with a multiple-group design that you could not answer with a two-group design.

5. Why are matched sets, repeated measures, and natural sets all considered *correlated groups* designs?

6. What is the real limit on the number of groups that can be included in a multiple-group design? What is the practical limit?

7. Make a list of the factors you would consider in choosing between a multiple-group design and a two-group design.

8. Correlated groups designs are often advantageous to use because they _____
_____.

9. Why are practical considerations of using a multiple correlated groups design more demanding than for using a two correlated groups design or a multiple independent groups design?

10. If we wished to compare personality traits of firstborn, lastborn, and only children, what type of design would we use? Would this represent a true experiment or an ex post facto study? Why?

STATISTICAL ANALYSIS: WHAT DO YOUR DATA SHOW? _____

We will remind you from the previous chapter that experimental design and statistical analysis are intimately linked. You *must* go through the decision-making process we have outlined before you begin your experiment in order to avoid the possibility that you will run your experiment and collect your data only to find out that there is not a statistical test that can be used to analyze your data.

ANALYZING MULTIPLE-GROUP DESIGNS

In this chapter we have looked at designs that have one IV with three (or more) groups. In your introductory statistics course you probably learned that these multiple-group designs are analyzed with the analysis of variance (ANOVA) statistical procedure. As you will see, ANOVA will also be used to analyze our designs that include more than one IV (see Chapter 9), so we need some way to distinguish between these types of ANOVA. In this chapter, we are looking at an ANOVA for one IV, typically referred to as one-way ANOVA.

You remember that we have looked at both independent multiple groups and correlated multiple groups designs in this chapter. We need two different types of one-way ANOVA to analyze these two types of designs, just as we needed different *t* tests in Chapter 7. As you can see from Figure 8-1, when we assign our participants to multiple groups randomly, we will analyze our data with a one-way ANOVA for independent groups (also known as a completely randomized ANOVA). On the other hand, if we use matched sets, natural sets, or repeated measures, we will use a one-way ANOVA for correlated groups (also known as repeated measures ANOVA) to evaluate our data.

CALCULATING YOUR STATISTICS

In Chapter 7 we featured the statistical analysis of data from an experiment designed to compare quiz scores of students using two different textbooks for an introductory psychology class (also see Chapter 6). That example, of course, cannot serve as a data analysis example for Chapter 8 because it represents a two-group design.

Psychological Detective

Suppose we have already conducted the sample experiment covered in Chapters 6 and 7. How could we conduct a similar experiment within a multiple-group design? Write a short description of your experiment before proceeding.

The *most* similar experiment would be one in which students in the introductory class used one of three different textbooks rather than two texts. Suppose that we decide to investigate further because we found (in Chapter 7) that a new textbook seemed to lead to better student learning than our old text. After examining many texts, we choose the three best books (in our opinion) to determine whether there is a difference among any of them regarding student learning. We order enough free copies of the texts so that we can provide them free of charge to our student participants. We have 24 students in the class, so we use the random assignment procedure to create equal groups. We mix the textbooks in a large box and randomly pass them out to the students in the class. To be certain that none of the three texts is given an unfair advantage in class, we make sure that class lectures and quizzes cover only points that are contained in all three books. So, all students hear the same lectures and take the same quizzes but use one of three possible texts. Our DV will be the students' total quiz scores on two 10-point quizzes. You can see the students' quiz score totals in Table 8-1. Let's discuss the basis behind the analysis of variance procedure before we look at our statistical analyses.

Between-groups variability Variability in DV scores that is due to the effects of the IV.

Error variability Variability in DV scores that is due to factors other than the IV—individual differences, measurement error, and extraneous variation.

RATIONALE OF ANOVA

We expect that you learned something about ANOVA in your statistics course. If not, we introduced a highly related concept in Chapter 7, "Control Issues," so you may wish to refer back to that section. You will remem-

TABLE 8-1. STUDENTS' QUIZ TOTALS FOR HYPOTHETICAL TEXTBOOK EXPERIMENT

TEXT 1	TEXT 2	TEXT 3
17	17	13
18	18	15
15	17	14
15	17	15
13	15	14
14	16	14
14	16	13
14	16	13
Mean = 15.00	Mean = 16.50	Mean = 13.88

ber the variability in your data can be divided into two sources—**between-groups variability** and **error variability** (also known as **within-groups variability**). The between-groups variability represents the variation in the DV that is due to the IV, whereas the error variability is due to factors such as individual differences, errors in measurement, and extraneous variation. Look at Table 8-2, which is a slightly altered version of Table 8-1.

TABLE 8-2. STUDENTS' QUIZ TOTALS FOR HYPOTHETICAL TEXTBOOK EXPERIMENT

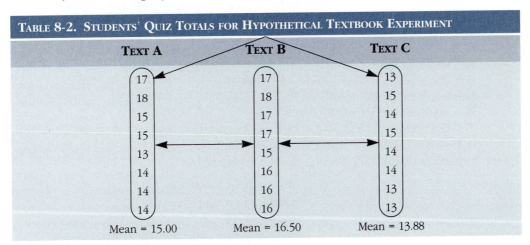

TEXT A	TEXT B	TEXT C
17	17	13
18	18	15
15	17	14
15	17	15
13	15	14
14	16	14
14	16	13
14	16	13
Mean = 15.00	Mean = 16.50	Mean = 13.88

Psychological Detective

What type of variability do you think is represented by the arrows in Table 8-2? What type of variability do you think is shown in the circled columns? Write your answers before going on. If you have trouble with these questions, reread the paragraph above.

The variability *between* the groups' quiz scores represents the variability caused by the IV (the different texts). Therefore, the arrows represent the between-groups variability. If the quiz scores differ among the three groups, we assume that the texts have made the difference. On the other hand, error variability should occur among the participants *within* each particular group, thus its name within-groups variability. This is the variability represented by the circled columns.

Wait a minute, you may say. What we have just described as within-groups variability—individual differences, measurement errors, extraneous variation—can occur between the groups just as easily as within the groups. We do hope that this thought occurred to you because it represents very good thinking on your part. This point is correct and is well taken. You may remember the general formula for statistical tests that we gave you in Chapter 7.

$$\text{statistic} = \frac{\text{between-groups variability}}{\text{error variability}}$$

The fact that we can find error between our groups as well as within our groups forces us to alter this formula to the general formula shown below for ANOVA. The *F* symbol is used for ANOVA in honor of Sir Ronald A. Fisher (1890–1962), who developed the ANOVA (Spatz, 1993).

$$F = \frac{\text{variability due to IV} + \text{error variability}}{\text{error variability}}$$

If our IV has a strong treatment effect and creates much more variability than all the error variability, we should find that the numerator of this equation is considerably larger than the denominator (see Figure 8-4a). The result, then, would be a large *F* ratio. If, on the other hand, the IV has absolutely no effect, there would be no variability due to the IV, meaning we would add 0 for that factor in the equation. In such a case, our *F* ratio should be close to 1.00 because the error variability between groups should approximately equal the error variability within groups. This situation is depicted in Figure 8-4b.

The notion that has evolved for the ANOVA is that we are comparing the ratio of between-groups variability to within-groups variability. Thus, the *F* ratio is conceptualized (and computed) as in the formula below.

$$F = \frac{\text{between-groups variability}}{\text{within-groups variability}}$$

A simple way to think of this is that you are dividing the treatment effect by the error. When the IV has a significant effect on the DV, the *F* ratio will be large; when the IV has no effect or only a small effect, the *F* ratio will be small (near 1.00). You may wish to put a bookmark at this page—we will refer back to it shortly.

INTERPRETATION: MAKING SENSE OF YOUR STATISTICS

With the addition of a third group, our experimental design has become slightly more complicated than the two-group design of Chapter 7. As you will see, adding

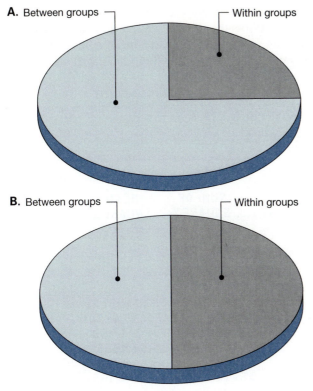

A. Between groups — ┐   ┌ — Within groups

B. Between groups — ┐   ┌ — Within groups

FIGURE 8-4   POSSIBLE DISTRIBUTIONS OF VARIABILITY IN AN EXPERIMENT

a third group (or more) creates an interesting statistical problem for us so that we often need to compute an extra statistical test to explore significant findings. As in Chapter 7, these next two sections will focus on interpreting computer output and on translating that output into English.

INTERPRETING COMPUTER STATISTICAL OUTPUT

Once again we will look at output from SPSS and from MYSTAT. The goal is not to teach these two specific packages but to give you experience with more than one type of output so that you can better generalize your knowledge to the particular statistical package that is available to you. The first set of SPSS results is shown in Table 8-3; the MYSTAT results appear in Table 8-4.

One-Way ANOVA for Independent Samples. We are examining results from a one-way ANOVA because we have one IV with three groups. We used the ANOVA for independent samples because we randomly assigned our students to the three different textbook conditions. The DV scores represent the students' summed performance on two 10-point quizzes.

SPSS Results. As usual, we look for information about descriptive statistics first. For the ONEWAY analysis, SPSS prints the descriptive statistics at the lower portion of Table 8-3A. We can see that Group 1 (Text 1) had a mean quiz score of 15.00 out of 20, Group 2 (Text 2) had a mean of 16.50, and Group 3 (Text 3) scored 13.88 on the

TABLE 8-3. SPSS OUTPUT FOR ONE-WAY ANOVA FOR INDEPENDENT SAMPLES

```
- - - - - - - - - - - - - - O N E W A Y - - - - - - - - - - - - - - -
A.        Variable   QZSCORES
     By Variable   TEXT

                                   ANALYSIS OF VARIANCE
                            SUM OF      MEAN        F        F
              SOURCE   D.F.  SQUARES   SQUARES   RATIO    PROB.

    BETWEEN GROUPS    2    27.7500   13.8750   9.4372   .0012

    WITHIN GROUPS    21    30.8750    1.4702

    TOTAL            23    58.6250
```

GROUP	COUNT	MEAN	STANDARD DEVIATION	STANDARD ERROR
Grp 1	8	15.0000	1.6903	.5976
Grp 2	8	16.5000	.9258	.3273
Grp 3	8	13.8750	.8345	.2950
TOTAL	24	15.1250	1.5965	.3259

```
B.        Variable   QZSCORES
     By Variable   TEXT

    MULTIPLE RANGE TEST

    SCHEFFE PROCEDURE
    RANGES FOR THE 0.050 LEVEL -

             3.72        3.72

    THE RANGES ABOVE ARE TABLE RANGES.
    THE VALUE ACTUALLY COMPARED WITH MEAN (J) - MEAN (I) IS..
          0.8574 * RANGE * DSQRT (1/N(I) + 1/N(J))

       (*) DENOTES PAIRS OF GROUPS SIGNIFICANTLY
            DIFFERENT AT THE 0.050 LEVEL

                              G G G
                              r r r
                              p p p

       Mean          Group    3 1 2

       13.8750       Grp 3
       15.0000       Grp 1
       16.5000       Grp 2        *
```

average. So, we do see numerical differences among these means, but we do not know if the differences are large enough to be significant until we examine the inferential statistics. We also see that for each group, SPSS prints the standard deviation and standard error (Group 1's quiz scores are more variable than the other two

- - - - - - - - - - - - - - - O N E W A Y - - - - - - - - - - - - - - - -

MINIMUM	MAXIMUM	95 PCT CONF INT FOR MEAN
13.0000	18.0000	13.5869 TO 16.4131
15.0000	18.0000	15.7260 TO 17.2740
13.0000	15.0000	13.1773 TO 14.5727
13.0000	18.0000	14.4508 TO 15.7992

groups'), the low (minimum) and high (maximum) scores, and 95% confidence intervals. You may remember from statistics that confidence intervals provide a range of scores between which μ (the true population mean) should fall. Thus, we are 95% confident that the interval of 13.18 to 14.57 contains the population mean for all students using Text 3. Before going on, remember that we recommended to make sure you have entered your data correctly in the computer by checking the means using a calculator. It will take only a few minutes but will spare you from using an incorrect set of results if you somehow goofed when you put the numbers in the computer.

The inferential statistics are printed immediately above the descriptive statistics. We see the heading "ONEWAY," which lets us know that we have actually computed a one-way ANOVA. The subheading shows us that we have analyzed "Variable QZSCORES By Variable TEXT." This simply means that we have analyzed our DV (QZSCORES, the quiz scores) by our IV (TEXT, the three texts).

The output from ANOVA is typically referred to as a **source table.** In looking at the table, you will see "SOURCE" printed in the upper-left corner. Source tables get their name because they isolate and highlight the different sources of variation in the data. In the one-way ANOVA table, you see two sources of variation: between groups and within groups. Do you remember what these two terms refer to? Between groups is synonymous with our treatment (IV) effect and within groups is our error variance.

The **sum of squares** is the sum of the squared deviations around the mean, which is used to represent the variability of the DV in the experiment (Kirk, 1968). We use ANOVA to divide (partition) the variability into its respective components, the between-groups and within-groups variability. In Table 8-3A, you see that the total sum of squares (variability in the entire experiment) is 58.63, which is partitioned into between-groups sum of squares (27.75) and within-groups sum of squares (30.88). The between-groups sum of squares added to the within-group sum of squares should always be equal to the total sum of squares (27.75 + 30.88 = 58.63).

If we formed a ratio of the between-groups variability and the within-groups variability based on the sums of squares, we would obtain a ratio of approximately 1.00. However, we cannot use the sums of squares for this ratio because each sum of squares is based on a different number of deviations (Keppel, Saufley, & Tokunaga, 1992). Think about this for a moment—there are only three groups that can contribute to the between-groups variability, but there are many participants who can contribute to the within-groups variability. Thus, to put them on an equal footing, we need to transform our sums of squares to **mean squares.** We make this transformation by dividing each sum of squares by its respective degrees of freedom. Because we have three groups, our between-groups degrees of freedom are 2 (number of groups minus one). Because we have 24 participants, our within-groups degrees of freedom are 21 (number of participants minus the number of groups). Our total degrees of freedom are equal to the total number of participants minus one, 23 in this case. As with the sums of squares, the between-groups degrees of freedom

---

Source table A table that contains the results of ANOVA. "Source" refers to the source of the different types of variation.

Sum of squares The amount of variability in the DV attributable to each source.

Mean square The "averaged" variability for each source; computed by dividing each source's sum of squares by its degrees of freedom.

definition

added to the within-groups degrees of freedom must equal the total degrees of freedom (2 + 21 = 23). Again, our mean squares are equal to each sum of squares divided by its degrees of freedom. Thus, our between-groups mean square is 13.88 (27.75/2) and our within-groups mean square is 1.47 (30.88/21).

TABLE 8-4. MYSTAT OUTPUT FOR ONE-WAY ANOVA FOR INDEPENDENT SAMPLES

A. THE FOLLOWING RESULTS ARE FOR:
                TEXT   =   1.000

TOTAL OBSERVATIONS: 8

Q_SCORES

        N OF CASES   8
        MINIMUM   13.000
        MAXIMUM   18.000
        MEAN   15.000
        STANDARD DEV   1.690

THE FOLLOWING RESULTS ARE FOR:
                TEXT   =   2.000

TOTAL OBSERVATIONS: 8

Q_SCORES

        N OF CASES   8
        MINIMUM   15.000
        MAXIMUM   18.000
        MEAN   16.500
        STANDARD DEV   0.926

THE FOLLOWING RESULTS ARE FOR:
                TEXT   =   3.000

TOTAL OBSERVATIONS: 8

Q_SCORES

        N OF CASES   8
        MINIMUM   13.000
        MAXIMUM   15.000
        MEAN   13.875
        STANDARD DEV   0.835

B.   ANALYSIS OF VARIANCE

SOURCE	SUM-OF-SQUARES	DF	MEAN-SQUARE	F-RATIO	P
TEXT	27.750	2	13.875	9.437	0.001

We should note at this point that a mean square is analogous to an estimate of the **variance,** which you may remember from statistics as the square of the standard deviation (σ^2). Once we have the mean squares, we can then create our distribution of variation. Rather than drawing pie charts like those shown in Figure 8-4, we compute an F ratio to compare the two sources of variation. Referring to the bookmark we advised you to use a few pages back, we find that the F ratio is equal to the between-groups variability divided by the within-groups variability. Because we are using mean squares as our estimates of variability, the equation for our F ratio becomes

$$F = \frac{\text{mean square between groups}}{\text{mean square within groups}}$$

Thus, our F ratio as shown in Table 8-3A, 9.44, was derived by dividing 13.88 by 1.47. This means that the variability between our groups is almost nine-and-a-half times larger than the variability within the groups. Or, perhaps more clearly, the variability due to the IV is almost nine-and-a-half times larger than the variability due to error. If we drew a pie chart for these results, it would look like Figure 8-5.

Finally, we come to the bottom line (or so we think!). Did the texts have a significant effect? Beside the "F RATIO," you see the "F PROB" entry of .0012. This probability of chance is certainly lower than .05, so we did find a significant difference. The difference in the quiz scores among the three groups probably did not occur by chance. Although the computer printed the probability of chance for you, you should know how to use a printed F table just in case. This activity is somewhat different than using a printed t table because in ANOVA we have two values for degrees of freedom. In this case, our degrees of freedom are 2 (between groups, in the numerator) and 21 (within groups, in the denominator). When we look in the F table (see Table A-2), one line will show the numerator df and the other line will show the denominator df. In this case, you must find 2 on the numerator line and 21 on the denominator line and locate the intersection of those two numbers. At that point you will see 3.47 as the .05 cutoff and 5.78 as the .01 cutoff. Because our F value of 9.44 is larger than either number, the probability that it could have occurred by chance is less than .01. Thus, if you were using a table rather than the computer output, you would have written $p < .01$.

With the two-group design, we would be finished with our computer output at this point and could go on to interpreting our statistics in words. However, this is not true with the multiple-group design when we find a significant difference. With significant findings in a two-group design,

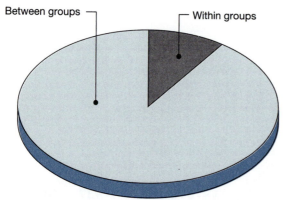

Between groups   Within groups

FIGURE 8-5   DISTRIBUTION OF VARIABILITY FOR DIFFERENT TEXTS EXPERIMENT

we merely choose the higher mean and conclude that it is significantly higher than the other mean. In this case, however, we have three means. We know there is significance among our means because of our significant F ratio, but which one(s) is (are) different from which one(s)? From a significant F ratio, we cannot tell.

To discern where the significance lies in a multiple-group experiment, we must do additional statistical tests known as **post hoc comparisons** (also known as follow-up tests). These tests allow us to determine which groups differ significantly from each other once we have determined that there is overall significance (by finding a significant F ratio). Many different post hoc tests exist, and there is much debate over these tests that is beyond the scope of this text. Simply remember that you will need to conduct post hoc tests if you find overall significance in a one-way ANOVA.

SPSS allows for several different post hoc comparisons. In Table 8-3B, you see the results of a post hoc test known as the Scheffé (shə-FAY). The Scheffé is known as a conservative test (Norusis, 1988), meaning that any difference detected between means with this test is a highly reliable difference—you can be sure that it will hold up to scrutiny. In looking at Table 8-3B, we see that Group 2 and Group 3 are significantly different at the .05 level according to the Scheffé test. This result means that the students with a quiz mean of 16.5 performed significantly better than the students with a quiz mean of 13.88. No other groups differed significantly from each other.

MYSTAT Results. MYSTAT's ANOVA routine does not automatically produce descriptive statistics, so you must use the STATS procedure to obtain the descriptive information shown in Table 8-4A. The STATS procedure gives us almost the same information as SPSS did, except it does not include the standard errors or 95% confidence intervals. We see that the students using Text 1 had a mean quiz score of 15.00 with a standard deviation of 1.69, and scores ranging from 13 to 18. The students with Text 2 produced scores from 15 to 18, with a mean of 16.50 and standard deviation of .93. The mean for the Text 3 students was 13.88 with a standard deviation of .84, and their scores ranged from 13 to 15. As we would expect, the descriptive statistics of Tables 8-4A and 8-3A agree.

Moving on to the inferential statistics in Table 8-4B, the source table is printed under the ANALYSIS OF VARIANCE heading. When you compare this source table to the SPSS source table in Table 8-3A, you see that they are basically the same. Notice that MYSTAT prints the name of your actual IV (TEXT) rather than BETWEEN GROUPS, as SPSS did. Again, we hope that you are learning general principles about computer printouts rather than specific words or terms for which you will blindly search. If you understand the general principles, interchanging BETWEEN GROUPS with TEXT (or the name of some other IV) should not be problematical for you—we're simply seeing two different ways of getting at the same thing (much like having slightly different names for the same test). In a similar fashion, MYSTAT uses the label ERROR whereas SPSS used WITHIN GROUPS, but both terms mean the same thing. There are two additional differences in the programs: (1) the programs switch the locations of the sum of squares and degrees of freedom columns and (2) MYSTAT does not print the information for TOTAL sum of squares and degrees of freedom (but it can be derived by adding the TEXT and ERROR information). The important bottom line is that given the same data, the two programs, find the same results.

In examining the MYSTAT results, we find that we have an F ratio of 9.44 with 2 and 21 degrees of freedom, yielding a chance probability of .001. Therefore, we know that some group(s) of students performed differently from another group or groups. As we noted earlier, this overall significant F does not tell us which groups are different. We must use post hoc comparisons to determine where the significance lies. Unfortunately, MYSTAT does not include post hoc comparisons in the program. To arrive at a final answer, then, you would need to check with your instructor or your statistics text about how to compute post hoc comparisons by hand. Once you have the ANOVA computed for you, it is a simple matter to calculate the post hoc tests.

Let us digress here for a moment. At this point you may be ready to dismiss MYSTAT as an inferior statistical program because it does not contain post hoc comparison tests. Remember from Chapter 7 that we are comparing apples and oranges when we compare the printouts from these two programs. We are using SPSS to represent the large, expensive (hundreds of dollars) computer packages designed to handle virtually any statistical test. We are using MYSTAT, on the other hand, to represent the small, inexpensive (less than $30) statistical packages that you can buy on one disk and load onto your own personal computer. It is standard for these smaller packages to leave some analyses out—they simply cannot afford, nor do they have the space, to put *everything* on a single disk. We are not trying to sell SPSS or downgrade MYSTAT in this text (nor are we trying to plug them); we are simply using them as typical examples.

Translating Statistics into Words. Let us remind you, as we did in Chapter 7, that the results of any statistical test are only as good as your experimental procedures. In other words, if you have conducted a sloppy experiment, your statistical results will be meaningless. When we draw the conclusion that our IV has caused a difference in the DV scores, we are assuming that we conducted a well-controlled experiment and removed extraneous variables from the scene. If you find that extraneous variables have confounded your experiment, you should not interpret your statistics because they are now meaningless. This is the same reason that detectives learn specific ways to collect evidence in the field. If they collect contaminated evidence, all the lab tests in the world cannot yield a definitive conclusion.

Based on our inferential statistics, we can conclude that the particular textbook that students use in introductory psychology is important because students did better on their quizzes with some book(s) than with other book(s).

Psychological Detective

Although this conclusion is technically correct, it is a poor conclusion. Why? How would you revise this conclusion to make it better? Write a new conclusion before going on.

This conclusion is poor because it is incomplete. Reread the sentence and decide what you learn from it. All you know is that students who used some book (or books) performed better on quizzes than students who used some other book (or books). Thus, you know that books can make a difference but, as a teacher, you wouldn't know which book is best to choose for your students. To write a good conclusion, we must go back to our inferential statistics. In Table 8-3, we find that students using Text 2 had a mean of 16.50 on their two quizzes, students using Text 1 had a mean of 15.00 on the quizzes, and students using Text 3 scored 13.88. The significant F ratio let us know that there is significance *somewhere* among those means. The Scheffé post hoc comparison tests informed us that the difference between Groups 2 and 3 was significant. To interpret this difference, we must examine our descriptive statistics. When we examine the means, we are able to conclude that students using Text 2 performed significantly better on their quizzes than the students using Text 3. *No other means showed significant differences.*

We must determine how to communicate our statistical findings in APA format. We will use a combination of words and numbers. There are many different ways to write this set of findings in an experimental report. Here is one example:

> The effect of different texts on quiz scores was significant, $\underline{F}(2, 21) = 9.44$, $\underline{p} = .001$. The proportion of variance accounted for by the text effect (η^2) was .47. Scheffé tests indicated that students using Text 2 ($\underline{M} = 16.50$, $\underline{SD} = .93$) made higher quiz scores (20 points possible) than students using Text 3 ($\underline{M} = 13.88$, $\underline{SD} = .83$). Students using Text 1 ($\underline{M} = 15.00$, $\underline{SD} = 1.69$) did not differ from the other groups.

The words alone should convey the meaning of our results. Could someone with no statistical background read and understand these sentences if we removed the numbers? We think so. The inferential test results document our finding to readers with a statistical background. The descriptive statistics allow the reader to observe exactly how the groups performed and how variable that performance was. The effect size information reported here, η^2, is similar to r^2 because it tells you the proportion of variance in the DV (quiz scores) accounted for by the IV (texts). ($\eta^2 = df_1 F / [df_1 F + df_2]$ according to the APA *Publication Manual* [1994, p. 18].) The reader has an expectation about what information will be given because we write our results in this standard APA format. You will find this type of communication in results sections in experimental articles. As you read more results sections, this type of communication will become familiar to you.

One-way ANOVA for correlated samples. Now we will look at the computer output for the one-way ANOVA for correlated samples. The sample experiment about texts and quiz scores we have used so far in the chapter fits the multiple-group design for independent samples and thus is not appropriate to analyze with the one-way ANOVA for correlated samples.

Psychological Detective

How could the experiment concerning the three textbooks be modified so that it used correlated groups rather than independent groups? Record your answer now before you read on.

To be correct, you should have proposed the use of matched sets, natural sets, or repeated measures in your modified experiment. The best choices would involve matched sets or repeated measures; we don't think that natural sets is feasible in this situation—you're not using littermates, and finding sets of triplets in a class is most unlikely! To use repeated measures, *each* student will have to use all three different texts. With only two quizzes being given, this procedure would be impossible.

If you choose matched sets, you must decide on a matching variable. Motivation would probably affect quiz scores because you are dealing with learning course material. Therefore, it would be a logical choice for matching. You could form sets of three participants matched on motivational test scores and then randomly assign one member of each set to a different group. In this manner you would be guaranteed equally motivated groups.

After measuring the students' level of motivation, forming matched sets, and assigning the students to groups, you are ready to begin the experiment. The 24 students each receive one of the three introductory psychology texts and study from it for two quizzes. Because we are using matched sets, we know for certain that the motivational level of the three groups is equated. Given this hypothetical example, the scores in Table 8-1 would now represent sets of quiz scores from matched students. (Remember that in the real world, it is not legitimate to analyze the same data with two different statistical tests. This is a textbook, certainly not the real world, and we are doing this as an example only.)

SPSS Results. You can see the SPSS results for the one-way ANOVA for correlated samples in Table 8-5. People who use SPSS on a regular basis often complain about running SPSS for repeated measures or matched participants because you cannot run such an analysis directly. Instead, such an ANOVA must be run through the MANOVA (multivariate analysis of variance) procedure. Still, the analysis can be run. Using the MANOVA program results in some output that we will ignore, but this is not unusual in many statistical packages.

As usual, we are first interested in obtaining descriptive statistics. MANOVA's descriptive output is shown in Table 8-5A. As you can see, we obtain the mean, standard deviation, sample size, and 95% confidence interval for each group. The descriptive statistics for the three groups match what we have previously seen in Tables 8-3A and 8-4A. This is logical. Although we are now using a correlated samples analysis, nothing has changed about the samples themselves. So, we see the same means, standard deviations, and confidence intervals that we have seen before.

Table 8-5B contains the inferential statistics. Notice that at the top of the page, SPSS tells us that TEXT is a within-subject effect. You may remember the term *within subjects* from Chapter 7. This merely tells us that we are using TEXT as an IV in a correlated manner (matched sets, repeated measures, or natural sets) rather than *between subjects,* in an independent groups manner. (Despite the fact that APA format now specifies the use of the term *participants* rather than *subjects* in experimental writing, it is likely that in statistics you will see and hear the term *subjects* used for quite some time.)

The other information that we see in Table 8-5B is our source table. Once again, the entries in this particular source table vary slightly from the tables we've looked at earlier. Although you may begin to believe that this is some sinister plot hatched just

TABLE 8-5. SPSS Output for One-Way ANOVA for Correlated Samples (MANOVA)

A.

Cell Means and Standard Deviations

Variable .. TEXT1

	Mean	Std. Dev.	N	95 percent Conf. Interval
For entire sample	15.000	1.690	8	13.587 16.413

Variable .. TEXT2

	Mean	Std. Dev.	N	95 percent Conf. Interval
For entire sample	16.500	.926	8	15.726 17.274

Variable .. TEXT3

	Mean	Std. Dev.	N	95 percent Conf. Interval
For entire sample	13.875	.835	8	13.177 14.573

B.

* * * * * A N A L Y S I S   O F   V A R I A N C E - - D E S I G N   1 * * * * * *

Tests involving 'TEXT' Within-Subject Effect.

AVERAGED Tests of Significance for TEXT using UNIQUE sums of squares

Source of Variation	SS	DF	MS	F	Sig of F
WITHIN CELLS	10.25	14	.73		
TEXT	27.75	2	13.88	18.95	.000

265

Asymptotic Refers to tails of distributions that approach the baseline but never touch the baseline.

to confuse you, you need to focus on the basic information, remembering that terms are used slightly differently in different situations. Here, our two sources of variance are labeled WITHIN CELLS and TEXT. Because you know that we are comparing different texts as our IV, it should be clear that TEXT represents the effect of our IV and WITHIN CELLS represents our source of error variation (refer back to Table 8-2 to see our within-cell variation pictorially represented by the circles). SPSS prints the IV effect on the bottom line of this source table, unlike any other source table we've seen. When we look at the source table, we find that the F ratio for the comparison of the quiz scores for different texts is 18.95, with 2 and 14 degrees of freedom, which results in a probability of chance of .000 according to the computer. This is an example of one of our pet peeves with computerized statistical programs. When you studied distributions in your statistics class, what did you learn about the tails of those distributions? We hope you learned that the tails of distributions are **asymptotic**—that is, the tails extend into infinity and never touch the baseline. This fact means that the probability of a statistic is *never* .000, no matter how large the statistic gets—there is always some small amount of probability under the tails of the distribution. Unfortunately, people who design statistics software apparently don't think about this issue, so they have the computer print a probability of .000, implying that there is no uncertainty. In light of this problem, we advise you to list $p < .001$ if you ever find such a result on your computer program.

Pardon the digression, but you know how pet peeves are! Back to the statistics. The overall effect of the texts is significant, which leads us to wonder which texts differ from each other.

Unfortunately, SPSS provides no post hoc comparison tests with MANOVA. Therefore, as with some procedures on some statistical packages, you would have to resort to comparing these three means by hand. Because this is not a statistics textbook, we will not go into detail about such computations—guidelines can be found in many advanced statistics texts (e.g., Kirk, 1968). As with the multiple-group design for independent samples, we used a Scheffé test for post hoc comparisons. We found that Group 2 was significantly different ($p < .05$) from both Group 1 and Group 3. However, Groups 1 and 3 did not perform significantly differently.

MYSTAT Results. Technically, MYSTAT does not contain a procedure for computing a one-way ANOVA for correlated groups. However, the program can be "tricked" into computing the analysis if you treat the subjects as a second IV and compute an ANOVA with two IVs (as we will discuss in Chapter 9). Rather than going into much detail about Chapter 9 procedures at this point, let us present the source table and discuss it briefly. The source table is shown in Table 8-6. As you can see, the DV is the quiz scores. The source table looks different because it shows the effects of two IVs—TEXT and SUBJECT. We will ignore the SUBJECT information because it does not provide anything we wish to know; it merely allowed us to use MYSTAT for a procedure that was not intentionally designed into the program.

When we look at the information for TEXT (the three different textbooks) and ERROR, we see that it is identical to that shown in Table 8-5b in the SPSS output (although ERROR was labeled WITHIN CELLS in SPSS). Thus, we have an F ratio of 18.95 with 2 and 14 degrees of freedom, yielding a probability of chance of less

TABLE 8-6. MYSTAT OUTPUT FOR ONE-WAY ANOVA FOR CORRELATED SAMPLES

ANALYSIS OF VARIANCE

SOURCE	SUM-OF-SQUARES	DF	MEAN-SQUARE	F-RATIO	P
TEXT	27.750	2	13.875	18.951	0.000
SUBJECT	20.625	7	2.946	4.024	0.013
ERROR	10.250	14	0.732		

Note: The output shown was actually computed using the syntax for a two-way ANOVA in MYSTAT. Subjects (participants) were treated as a separate IV, which partitions their variance separately. Procedures for programming MYSTAT were provided by C. H. Null through M. Levy (personal communication, March 16, 1993).

than .001 (remember that we cannot achieve a probability of chance equal to .000!). Once again, post hoc comparisons are not possible in MYSTAT, leaving us to compute them by hand. Given that we begin with the same means and source table information, our hand calculations would provide the same information that we summarized in the SPSS section. Group 2 was significantly different from both Group 1 and Group 3. However, Groups 1 and 3 did not perform significantly differently.

Translating Statistics into Words. Our experimental logic is no different from that for the independent-samples ANOVA. The only difference is that we used a somewhat more stringent control procedure in this design—we matched participants rather than assigning them to groups randomly. Again, this increases our confidence that our groups are equal before the experiment begins and it should decrease our error variance.

Our conclusions should combine our numbers with words to give the reader a clear indication of what we found. Remember to include information both about any difference that was found as well as the directionality of such a difference.

Psychological Detective

How would you write the results of this experiment in words and numbers for an experimental report? Write a sample conclu-sion before you go any further. (Hint: This conclusion will differ from the conclusion earlier in this chapter.)

Although the conclusion for the correlated-samples test is similar to that for the independent groups test, it is different in some important ways. We hope you figured out those important differences. Here's a sample conclusion:

The effect of three different texts on students' quiz scores was significant, $\underline{F}(2, 14) = 18.95$, $\underline{p} < .001$. The proportion of variance accounted for by the text effect (η^2) was .73. Scheffé tests showed that students who used Text 2 ($\underline{M} = 16.50$,

SD = .93) performed better on the quizzes (20 possible points) than either students who used Text 1 (M = 15.00, SD = 1.69) or students who used Text 3 (M = 13.88, SD = .83). Students using Texts 1 and 3 did not differ significantly.

Did your conclusion look something like this? Remember, the exact wording may not necessarily match—the important thing is that you have all the critical details covered.

Psychological Detective

There are five important differences between this conclusion and the conclusion for the independent groups ANOVA. Can you find them? Write your answers before you go on.

The *first* difference comes in the degrees of freedom. There are fewer degrees of freedom for the correlated groups ANOVA than for the independent samples case. *Second,* the *F* value for the correlated groups test is larger than for the independent situation. The larger *F* value is a result of reducing the variability in the denominator of the *F* equation. This difference in *F* values leads to the *third* difference, which is the probability of chance. Despite the fact that there are fewer degrees of freedom for the correlated samples case, its probability of chance is somewhat lower. *Fourth,* the proportion of variance accounted for by the text effect (η^2) was considerably larger. *Fifth,* the post hoc test results are different. In the independent groups situation, only Groups 2 and 3 were significantly different. In the correlated groups situation, however, Group 2 is shown to have outperformed both Group 1 and Group 3.

These last two differences most clearly show the advantage of a correlated groups design. Because matching the participants beforehand reduced some of the error variability, we were able to label a smaller difference (between Groups 1 and 2) as significant, which is something we could not do with the independent groups test. Thus, the conclusion from the correlated group design yields the clearest finding. Teachers should consider using Text 2 because the students using it scored higher on their quizzes than students using Text 1 or Text 3. We cannot promise that correlated groups designs will always allow you to find a difference that independent groups designs will not show. However, we can tell you that the correlated groups designs do increase your odds of detecting small significant differences because such designs reduce error variance.

THE CONTINUING RESEARCH PROBLEM

In Chapters 6 and 7 we began our continuing research project by looking at students' quiz scores as a function of whether they used an old textbook or a new textbook. Students' scores were significantly higher when they used the new text.

Because of these impressive results, we decided to pursue this research further and, in this chapter, compared three different new texts to each other. Based on our results, Text 2 seems to lead to better scores on quizzes than either of the other texts. Therefore, we decide to adopt Text 2 for the introductory psychology class.

Is our research project complete at this point? As you might guess, new editions of texts come out constantly. This research problem could go on forever! In all seriousness, you might have wondered about our choice of the two chapter quizzes—which chapters we chose, whether performance on both quizzes was similar for all texts, and so on. As we begin to ask more complicated questions, we must move to more complex designs to handle those questions. As we move to Chapter 9, we will be able to continue our research problem with an experiment using more than one IV at a time.

Let's review the logical steps we took in conducting this experiment. Refer back to Figure 8-1 to take note of our experimental design questions.

1.   After conducting a preliminary experiment (Chapter 7) and determining that students performed better after reading a new textbook, we decided to further test the effects of different texts (IV) on student quiz scores (DV).

2.   We chose to test only one IV (textbooks) because our research is still preliminary.

3.   We tested three different texts because all seemed to be good texts for introductory psychology.

4a.   With large numbers of students, we used random assignment to the three groups and, thus, a multiple independent groups design. We used a one-way ANOVA for independent groups and found that Text 2 produced higher quiz scores than Text 3. Quiz scores from Text 1 were intermediate and not different from the other texts.

4b.   With smaller numbers of students, we chose to form matched sets based on level of motivation. Thus, we used a multiple within-group design and a one-way ANOVA for correlated groups. Text 2 produced higher quiz scores than either Text 1 or Text 3.

5.   We concluded (hypothetically) that Text 2 was the best text for us to use in introductory psychology.

REVIEW SUMMARY

1. When your experimental design consists of one IV with three or more groups and you have randomly assigned participants to groups, the proper statistical analysis is a one-way ANOVA for independent groups.

2. When your experimental design has one IV with more than two groups and you have used matched sets, natural sets, or repeated measures, you should analyze your data with a one-way ANOVA for correlated groups.

3. ANOVA partitions the variability in your DV into **between-groups variance** (due to the IV) and **within-groups variance** (due to sources of error). We then compute a ratio between these two sources of variation known as the F ratio.

4. ANOVA results are typically shown in a source table, which lists each source of variance and displays the F ratio for the effect of the IV.

5. A significant F ratio merely indicates that there is a significant difference somewhere among your various groups. **Post hoc comparisons** are necessary to determine which groups differ from each other.

6. Within-subject analyses (correlated groups) are often somewhat more difficult to run on statistical computer packages.

7. Using APA format for our statistical results allows us to convey our findings in both words and numbers in a clear and concise manner.

8. Previous experiments often lead to further questions and new experiments. The multiple-group design is an ideal design to follow up on the results from a two-group experiment.

STUDY BREAK

1. Suppose you wish to compare the ACT or SAT scores of the freshman, sophomore, junior, and senior classes at your school to determine whether differences exist among those students. Draw a block diagram of this design. What design and statistical test would you use for this research?

2. You wonder whether students who take the ACT or SAT three times are able to significantly improve their scores. You select a sample of such students and obtain their three scores. What type of experimental design does this question represent? Draw a block diagram of it. What statistical test would you use to analyze the data?

3. When we look at our F ratio and its probability in a multiple-group design, why can't we examine the descriptive statistics directly to reach a conclusion about our experiment?

4. The variability that is due to our IV is termed the _____ _____ variance, whereas the variability due to individual differences and error is the _____ _____ variance.

5. Suppose you conducted the experiment summarized in Question 2 and found the following statistics: $F(2, 24) = 4.07$, $p < .05$. Based on this information, what could you conclude?

6. What additional information do you need in Question 5 to draw a full and complete conclusion?

7. In the continuing research problem from this chapter, why was it important to have the (hypothetical) knowledge from the similar study in Chapter 7?

8. You decide to test how people's moods vary by the four seasons. What type of experimental design would you use for this research project? Why?

9. You choose to test people's preferences for fast food hamburgers—you have McDonald's, Burger King, Wendy's, and White Castle franchises in your town. What type of experimental design would you use for this research project? Why?

LOOKING AHEAD

In this chapter, we have furthered our knowledge about research design and how it fits with particular experimental questions. Specifically, we looked at an extension of the basic building block design by using one IV and three or more groups. In the next chapter, we will make a significant alteration in our basic design by adding a second IV. This expanded design will give us the ability to ask much more sophisticated questions about behavior because most behaviors are affected by more than one variable at a time.

HANDS-ON ACTIVITIES

When you took your introductory psychology course and studied social psychology, you may have learned about personal space, "the mobile area around an individual of which he or she feels ownership and control" (Worchel, Cooper, & Goethals, 1991, p. 517). We seem to have a "bubble" of area around ourselves that we consider our own and wish to keep inviolate. We tend to feel uncomfortable when people get too close and violate our personal space. McBride, King, and James (1965) demonstrated this notion of discomfort, as they found that people's galvanic skin response readings were altered, a sign of stress, when their personal space was invaded.

Felipe Russo and Sommer (1966) conducted the classic experimental investigation of personal space violation. They observed students seated alone at large tables in a university library over a 30-minute period. In their control condition, no violation of personal space occurred; the experimenters merely watched to see what percentage of students remained during the time period. As you can see from Figure 8-6, most of the control students tended to stay at the table for the full 30 minutes. In Felipe Russo and Sommer's intermediate condition (Conditions II–V in Figure 8-6), a confederate of the experimenter took a seat at the table where a student was seated. The confederate sat in various positions at the table, but never directly next to the student. Figure 8-6 shows that a slightly higher percentage of students left in these conditions. In the personal-space violation condition (Condition I in Figure 8-6), the confederate sat at the chair immediately next to the student, despite the fact that no one else was seated at the table. It seems clear from Figure 8-6 that students probably felt uncomfortable in this situation as they left the table in much higher percentages than in the other conditions.

1. **Multiple Independent Groups Design.**   As you have probably discerned, Felipe Russo and Sommer's (1966) experiment used the multiple independent groups design. The IV was the type of personal-space invasion and had three levels (control, intermediate, and extreme). The DV is not totally clear from Figure 8-6, as both

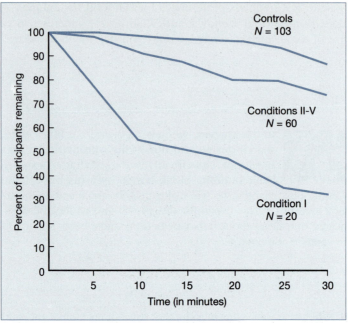

FIGURE 8-6   RESULTS FROM FELIPE RUSSO AND SOMMER (1966)

Source: From "Invasion of Personal Space" by N. J. Felipe Russo and R. Sommers, 1966,
Social Problems, 14, pp. 206–214. ©1966 by the Society for the Study of Social Problems.
Used with permission of publisher and authors.

percentage of students leaving and time of leaving are graphed. Either could serve
as a DV. For your hands-on activity with the multiple independent groups design,
you should replicate Felipe Russo and Sommer's classic experiment. We have purposely not provided all the details of their experiment so that you can make some
decisions on your own.

Psychological Detective

What types of decisions must
you make before beginning this
hands-on activity? In particular,
pay attention to operational definitions of your IV and DV. Write your definitions of those variables before reading
further. What about confounding variables? Do you see any that would be
problematical? List and explain any you
come up with.

How will you manipulate your IV? This will depend on the types of tables that
your library contains. You must be careful that your confederates (or fellow experimenters) use the same definition of intermediate and extreme personal-space violations. For example, at a table with three chairs on each side, what constitutes an intermediate violation? How close should the violator sit in the extreme condition?
You must define your IV manipulations carefully before beginning the project.

At the same time, you must choose your DV before beginning. Time is a good choice for your DV because it has more "room" for variability than merely leaving (a yes-no variable). You may wish to shorten the time period from 30 minutes to 10 and simply time how quickly the student leaves. If the student does not leave in the 10-minute period, simply record 10 minutes and go to the next condition.

The most obvious confounding variable is sex—of both the student *and* the violator. Think for a moment about all the various combinations: female student-female violator; female student-male violator; male student-female violator; male student-male violator. The sexual and personality dynamics of each of these combinations are different. You must think about how you wish to control this factor before beginning!

When you complete your data gathering, you should have a set of times for students in the three different conditions. Use a one-way ANOVA for independent groups to analyze your data. Remember that a significant F ratio will not provide the full set of answers you need about the results—post hoc analyses will be necessary. Were you able to replicate Felipe Russo and Sommer's (1966) results?

2. **Multiple Correlated Groups Design.**   To use a correlated groups design, you need to have natural sets, matched sets, or repeated measures. Because you are measuring the reactions of unaware student participants, you cannot gather any information directly from them. Therefore, you can rule out using natural or matched sets (unless you match solely on visible characteristics). This leaves you with the option of repeated measures. One potential problem that may have struck you in the previous activity revolves around the participants—were they equal when we began? Perhaps some people perceive personal-space invasions more keenly and would leave with less provocation. It is impossible to know, but using repeated measures would allow us to avoid that problem.

To use repeated measures, you will need to replicate the Felipe Russo and Sommer experiment with an important difference. Each student will participate in all three conditions. This necessity will probably require a little more effort on your part because you may have to "chase" the participants around the library if they change tables after having their personal space invaded.

Psychological Detective

How would order effects (see Chapter 4) be important in this experiment? Write an answer before you go on.

If you use the same order of conditions for all participants, you might find an order effect rather than the effect of the IV. Therefore, you should randomly choose the order in which each participant experiences the three conditions. Order effects can be particularly troublesome in repeated measures experiments because experiencing one treatment level can affect the participants' reaction to a different level. Imagine, for example, using a large, medium, and low level of reinforcement. If the low level is experienced first, it may be quite reinforcing. However, if a low level is experienced after a high or medium level, that low level may be interpreted almost as a punishment! Remember to use the counterbalancing techniques presented in Chapter 4 so that you will equalize the order effects across participants.

If a participant leaves the library before you can run all three conditions, you will have to delete that participant's data. (Remember from the ethical guidelines that participants may choose to discontinue their participation at any time. This is especially true in naturalistic research such as this when they are unaware that they are in an experiment.)

After you have collected the data, you will use a one-way ANOVA for correlated groups for analysis. The intriguing question is whether the results differ from those in the previous hands-on activity (or from Felipe Russo and Sommer's original experiment). Sometimes we find interesting differences when we conduct the same research with both independent groups and correlated groups.

Designing, Conducting, Analyzing, and Interpreting Experiments with Multiple Independent Variables

EXPERIMENTAL DESIGN: DOUBLING THE BASIC BUILDING BLOCK

This chapter will continue building on the experimental design material that we first encountered in Chapter 7. We start with our basic building block design (from Chapter 7) and enlarge it further from Chapter 8. We will see many familiar concepts from the two previous chapters, as well as from earlier in the text (e.g., IVs, DVs, extraneous variables, control, and so on). So you can expect some of this chapter to be a review of familiar concepts. However, we will apply those concepts in a new and different framework—the factorial experimental design.

Let's return to our analogy for experimental design that we first saw in Chapter 7—that of building objects with Lego or Tinkertoys. Chapters 7 and 8 have presented the beginner's set and a slightly larger version of that beginner's set, respectively. Now, with the factorial design, we will encounter the top-of-the-line, advanced set that has all the possible options. When you bought the largest set of building materials, you could build anything from very simple objects to extremely complicated structures; the same is true of experimental design. Using a factorial design gives us the power we need to devise an investigation of several **factors** in a single experiment. Factorial designs are the lifeblood of experimental psychology because they allow us to look at combinations of IVs at the same time, a situation that is quite similar to the real world. A factorial design is more like the real world because there are probably few situations in which your behavior is affected by only a single factor at a time. Imagine trying to isolate only one factor that affected your ACT or SAT scores! What about intelligence, motivation, courses you had taken, 8:00 on Saturday morning, health, and so on?

Factors Synonymous with IVs.

In Chapter 8 we used another analogy for our experimental designs—we compared the two-group design to a house, the multiple-group design to an apartment building, and the factorial design to a skyscraper. The idea behind this analogy was not to frighten you into worrying about how complex factorial designs are, but instead to make two points. First, as we have already mentioned, even complex designs are based on principles that you encountered previously with simple designs. As you move from building a house to a skyscraper, most of the principles of building remain the same—they are merely used on a larger scale. This formula is true also for experimental design: Although we will be dealing with more complex designs in this chapter, you already have the majority of the background you need from Chapters 7 and 8. Second, just as building larger buildings gives you more decisions and options, designing larger experiments gives you more decisions and options. Decisions, of course, imply responsibility. You will have to take on additional responsibility with a factorial design. Rather than planning an experiment with only one IV, you will be planning for two or three (or possibly even more) IVs. Additional IVs mean that you have more factors to choose and control. By taking on additional responsibilities, you also gain additional information. By moving from a one-IV experiment to a two-IV experiment, you will gain information about a second IV *and* the interaction between the two IVs. We will discuss interactions in depth soon. Let's examine the factorial design first.

THE FACTORIAL DESIGN

In this chapter, we will expand the basic two-group design by doubling it. Look back at Figure 7-2 (p. 206) and imagine what would happen if you doubled it. Of course, one possible result of doubling Figure 7-2 would be a design that we have already covered in Chapter 8—a multiple-group design with four levels. That design would result in an experiment similar to the continuing research problem of Chapter 8 if we planned an experiment contrasting the effects of four different texts rather than three. However, this type of doubling would be an extension rather than an expansion. We would take one IV with two levels (old text and new text) in Chapter 7 and extend it from two to four levels.

Psychological Detective

What would an *expansion* (rather than an extension) of Fig- ure 7-2 look like? Draw a diagram of this experiment before moving on.

Does your drawing resemble Figure 9-1? Contrast Figure 9-1 with Figures 8-2 and 8-3. Do you see the difference? To what can you attribute this difference? The answer is found in the next section.

FIGURE 9-1   SIMPLEST POSSIBLE FACTORIAL DESIGN (2 × 2)

Factor A (first IV)

	Level A1	Level A2
Level B1	A1B1	A2B1
Level B2	A1B2	A2B2

Factor B (second IV)

Independent variables Stimuli or aspects of the environment that are directly manipulated by the experimenter to determine their influences on behavior.

Factorial design An experimental design with more than one IV.

How Many IVs? For two chapters the first question we have faced when considering the choice of experimental designs has dealt with how many IVs our experiment will have. Nothing has changed in Chapter 9—we still begin with "How many **independent variables** will I use in my experiment?" (see Figure 9-2). For the first time, though, we have a different answer. We are moving into more complex designs that use at least two IVs. We refer to any design that uses at least two IVs as a **factorial design.** The factorial design gets its name because we refer to each IV as a factor; multiple IVs, then, yield a factorial design. Theoretically, there is no limit to the number of IVs that can be used in an experiment. Practically speaking, however, it is unlikely that you would want to design an experiment with more than two or three IVs. After that point, the increased complexity is such that it would tax your ability to conduct the experiment or your skill to interpret the results. Hence, we will use experimental designs with two IVs to illustrate our points, although we will give you an illustration of a design with three IVs toward the end of the chapter. Real-life detectives are often faced with complex cases that are similar to factorial designs. Imagine that you are a detective confronted with several suspects and that you are faced with evaluating the means, motive, and opportunity for each suspect. Can you see how such a situation is analogous to a factorial design?

How Many Groups or Levels? In looking at Figure 9-2 you will notice that this question that we asked in both Chapters 7 and 8 does not appear on the relevant portion of the flowchart. The reason for its absence is simple: Once you have two (or more) IVs, you will use a factorial design. The number of levels for each factor is unimportant at this point.

Let's return to Figure 9-1 for a moment. Do you see how it represents 2 two-group designs stacked on top of each other? That is what we meant earlier by doubling or expanding the two-group design. If we take 2 two-group designs and combine them, we end up with the design pictured in Figure 9-1, which has two IVs, each with two levels. This figure represents the simplest possible factorial design, which is known as a "2 × 2" design. This 2 × 2 shorthand notation tells us that we are dealing with a design that has two factors (IVs) because there are two digits given and that each of the two factors has two levels because each digit shown is a 2. Finally, when we complete the implied multiplication, this notation also tells us how many unique treatment combinations (or groups) our experiment requires. A 2 × 2 design requires four treatment combinations (two times two), whereas a 3 × 3 design requires nine treatment combinations.

Figure 9-1 shows an additional design notation. Various factors are often designated by letters, so that the first factor is labeled Factor A, the second as Factor B, and so on. The levels within a factor are often designated by the letter that corresponds to the factor and a number to differentiate the different levels. Thus, the two levels within the first factor would be labeled A1 and A2. If the factor has more than two levels, we continue numbering them in similar fashion until we reach the last level (e.g., A1, A2, A3 . . . An), where n represents the number of levels of the factor.

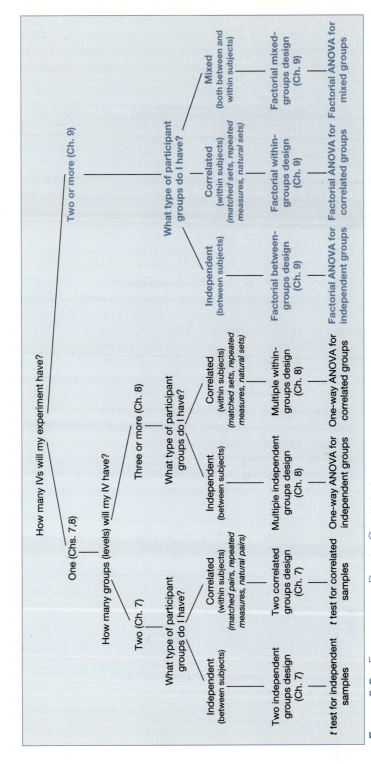

FIGURE 9-2 EXPERIMENTAL DESIGN QUESTIONS

279

What might such a 2 × 2 design look like in real life? To begin answering this question, refer to Figure 7-2, where we diagrammed the two-group experiment of Nancy Cathey (1992), in which she compared the performance of rats receiving caffeine to rats that received no caffeine.

Psychological Detective

How could you expand Cathey's experiment so that it becomes a 2 × 2 factorial design? Write your answer and draw a diagram of it before proceeding.

First, we hope you conceptualized a design like that shown in Figure 9-3. The first IV (A) should be caffeine, with the two levels representing the experimental group (receiving caffeine) and the control group (not receiving caffeine). The second IV (B) could be any number of variables, as long as the two groups differ on that IV. For example, let's say that you are interested in determining whether the effects of caffeine vary due to the rats' age. Therefore, your second IV (a measured rather than manipulated IV) would be the age of the rats, with your two groups composed of young versus old rats. This particular experimental design is shown in Figure 9-3. Four treatment groups are required, one for each possible combination of the two levels of the two treatments. Thus, we would have a group of young rats that receives caffeine, a group of young rats that does not receive caffeine, a group of old rats that receives caffeine, and a group of old rats that does not receive caffeine.

We hope that it is clear to you that this 2 × 2 design is composed of 2 two-group designs. One two-group design is used to contrast the effects of caffeine, and the second two-group design is used to contrast the effects of age. At this point, you might ask, "Wouldn't it be simpler to run two separate experiments rather than combining

FIGURE 9-3 EXPANSION OF CATHEY'S CAFFEINE STUDY

Factor A (caffeine)

		Caffeine	No caffeine
Factor B (age)	Young	young rats receiving caffeine	young rats receiving no caffeine
	Old	old rats receiving caffeine	old rats receiving no caffeine

them both into one experiment?" Although it might be somewhat easier to run two experiments, there are two disadvantages of conducting separate experiments. First, it is not as time efficient as running one experiment. Even if you ran the same number of participants through the experiment(s), two experiments will simply take longer to complete than one; there are fewer details to deal with in one experiment than in two. Imagine how inefficient it would be for a detective to complete an investigation of one suspect before even beginning the investigation of a second suspect! Second, by running two experiments, you would lose the advantage that you gain by conducting a factorial experiment—the interaction.

When we jointly combine two IVs in one experiment, we get all the information we would get from two experiments, plus a bonus. In this example, we will still determine the solitary effect of caffeine *and* the solitary effect of age. In a factorial experiment, these outcomes are termed the **main effects.** The bonus that we get from a factorial experiment is the **interaction** of the two IVs. We will discuss interactions at length later in the chapter, but let us provide you a preview at this point. Suppose we ran the caffeine-age study and found the results shown in Figure 9-4.

Main effect Refers to the sole effect of one IV in a factorial design.

Interaction The joint, simultaneous effect on the DV of more than one IV.

definition

Psychological Detective

Can you interpret the main effects shown in Figure 9-4? Did caffeine have any effect? Did age have any effect? Study the graph and think about these questions. Write answers about both main effects before you read any further.

FIGURE 9-4   HYPOTHETICAL RESULTS OF CAFFEINE-AGE EXPERIMENT

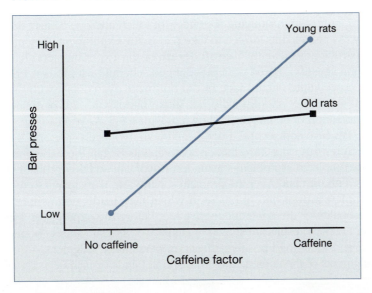

It does appear that caffeine had an effect. Both groups of rats (young and old) seem to increase the number of bar presses when they ingested caffeine (notice how the lines for both groups go up as they move from left [no caffeine] to right [caffeine]). On the other hand, age seems to have made no difference in the number of bar presses. It appears that both young rats and old rats made approximately equal numbers of presses. If you average the two points on the young rats' line and average the two points on the old rats' line, the two means would be virtually identical.

What you see graphically portrayed in Figure 9-4 is an interaction effect. We find significant interactions when the effects of one IV change as the other IV changes. Another common way of describing interactions is that the effects of one IV depend on the particular level of another IV. If these descriptions are difficult for you to understand, perhaps the example of Figure 9-4 will help. As you look at Figure 9-4, ask yourself whether the effects of caffeine are the same for both groups of rats. Although the performance of both groups increases under the influence of caffeine, it is clear that this effect is much more pronounced for the young rats, who press very little without caffeine but press like crazy when they are under the influence of caffeine. On the other hand, the older rats respond in similar fashions both with and without caffeine, although they do respond slightly more when they have caffeine. This difference for older rats might not even be significant. If you were describing these results to someone, would it be correct to say only that caffeine increases bar-press performance in rats? Or should you note that the effect of caffeine seems to vary as a function of the age of the rats—that caffeine greatly facilitates the bar-press performance in young rats but has only a small or nonexistent effect for older rats? It is apparent that the second conclusion, though more complex, paints a much clearer picture of the results. Thus, it seems that the effects of caffeine depend on the age of the rats; the effect of one IV depends on the specific level of the other IV. We will return to interactions later in this chapter to make certain that you understand them fully.

Let's look at an actual student example of a factorial design. Moira McGovern and Julie Fischer (1993), of the University of San Francisco, in CA, were interested in studying the effects of touch and eye contact on personality. As participants arrived to take part in the experiment, they met another participant (actually a **confederate** of the experimenters) leaving the testing situation. Based on a prearranged schedule with the experimenters, the confederate either made or did not make eye contact with the participant and either shook or did not shake hands with the participant. This combination of treatments is shown in Figure 9-5. As you can see, there are two IVs (eye contact and touch), each with two levels (present or absent).

After this brief introduction, participants began the experiment. They first completed a problem-solving test (involving addition problems), which was a **sham task.** After the problem-solving test, participants were asked to complete a brief questionnaire in which they made judgments about the personality of the confederate they met before the experiment. McGovern and Fischer's results are shown in Figure 9-6. As you can see, both eye contact and touch had positive effects on personality judgments—personality judgments of the confederates who shook hands or made eye contact were

Confederate
A person who appears to experimental participants to be just another participant in the experiment but who is actually fulfilling a specific role assigned by the experimenter.

Sham task
A task given to experimental participants by an experimenter to disguise the true purpose of the experiment.

definition

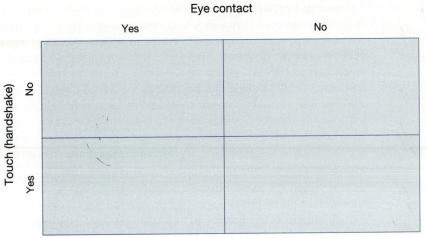

FIGURE 9-5   DIAGRAM OF MCGOVERN & FISCHER'S (1993) EXPERIMENT

Source: Adapted from M. E. McGovern and J. M. Fischer, *Positive judgments of personality as a function of touch and eye contact* April, 1993. Presented at the Western Psychology Conference for Undergraduate Research, Santa Clara, CA.

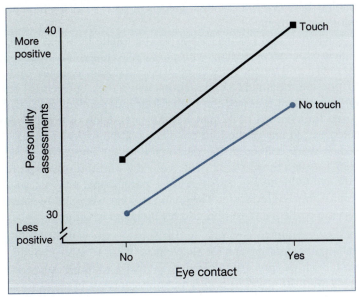

FIGURE 9-6   RESULTS FROM MCGOVERN & FISCHER'S (1993) EXPERIMENT

Source: Adapted from M. E. McGovern and J. M. Fischer, *Positive judgments of personality as a function of touch and eye contact* April, 1993. Presented at the Western Psychology Conference for Undergraduate Research, Santa Clara, CA.

more positive than for confederates who did not. Confederates who shook hands as well as made eye contact received the most positive assessments; those who neither shook hands nor made eye contact were rated lowest. Both of these main effects are relatively straightforward; there was no interaction between the two IVs.

definition

Independent groups Groups of participants that are formed by random assignment.

Correlated groups Groups of participants formed by matching, natural pairs, or repeated measures.

Mixed assignment A factorial design that has a mixture of independent groups for one IV and correlated groups for another IV. In larger factorial designs, at least one IV has independent groups and at least one has correlated groups. *(Also known as mixed groups.)*

Assigning Participants to Groups. As in Chapters 7 and 8, the matter of how we assign our research participants to groups is important. Again, we have two options for this assignment—**independent groups** or **correlated groups.** However, this question is not answered in such a simple manner as in the two-group and multiple-group designs, each of which had only one IV. Matters can become more complicated in a factorial design because we have two (or more) IVs to deal with. All IVs could have participants assigned randomly or in a correlated fashion, or we could have one IV with independent groups and one IV with correlated groups. We refer to this last possibility as **mixed assignment** (or mixed groups).

Random Assignment to Groups. Random assignment refers to a situation in which we assign our participants to groups in a nonsystematic way so that participants in one group are not tied, linked, or related to participants in other groups in any manner. Factorial designs in which *both* IVs involve random assignment are often labeled "totally between-groups designs" or "completely randomized designs" (see Figure 9-2). These labels should make sense from our discussion of between- and within-groups variance in Chapter 8. Between-groups variance refers to variability between independent groups of participants, which result from random assignment.

McGovern and Fischer (1993) used a totally between groups design for their experiment dealing with personality judgments as a function of eye contact and touch. Participants were randomly assigned to one of the four possible treatment combinations when they entered the lab. Thus, their experiment required the use of four independent groups of participants—they used four groups of 12 participants each. Each of the 48 participants could have taken part in any of the four conditions of the experiment.

After the data were collected, the personality judgments of the confederate were compared *between* those participants who did and did not experience eye contact with the confederate and *between* those participants who did and did not shake hands with the confederate. The comparisons were made between the groups because the participants were randomly assigned to groups.

Non-Random Assignment to Groups. In this section, we will deal with factorial designs in which participant groups for all IVs have been formed through non-random assignment. Such designs are referred to as totally within-groups (or subjects) designs. We may want to resort to non-random assignment in order to assure the equality of participant groups before we conduct the experiment. It is important to remember, particularly in research with small numbers of participants or with small IV effects, that random assignment cannot guarantee equality of groups. Let's take a brief look at the three methods of creating correlated groups.

1.   Matched Pairs or Sets. Matching can take place in either pairs or sets because factorial designs can use IVs with two or more levels. The more levels an IV has, the more work matching for that variable takes, simply because of having to form larger sets of participants that are equated on the matching variable. Also, the more precise the match that is necessary, the more difficult matching becomes. For example, matching on gender or educational level may be fairly simple. However, matching on college major or family background may be more difficult. Likewise, when more than one IV uses matching, the demand for a large number of a specific type of research participant may become overwhelming. For instance, using matched participants for both IVs in a 2 × 2 experiment requires four matched groups, a 2 × 3 requires six such groups, and a 3 × 3 design would necessitate nine matched groups. Imagine what would happen in an experiment with three IVs! For this reason, factorial designs that use matching for all IVs are relatively rare.

2. Repeated Measures. You will remember that a repeated measures design is one in which participants take part in all levels of an IV. In a completely within-group experiment using repeated measures, participants would take part fully and completely; that is, they would participate in every possible treatment combination. As you might imagine, this requirement often makes it difficult or impossible to conduct an experiment with repeated measures on each IV.

Psychological Detective

Would it have been possible to conduct McGovern and Fischer's (1993) experiment with repeated measures on both IVs? If it were possible, would it be wise to do so? Why or why not? Write your answers before continuing.

To answer the first question, you have to understand its implication. Look at Figure 9-5. To conduct this experiment using repeated measures on both IVs, each participant would experience each of the four possible conditions. Could a single participant experience a situation that involved meeting a stranger and receiving (1) neither a handshake nor eye contact, (2) a handshake but no eye contact, (3) eye contact but no handshake, and (4) both a handshake and eye contact? Certainly not all at once! For this experiment to use repeated measures fully, each participant would have to meet four different people and experience one of the four conditions listed earlier. So, yes, it would be *possible* to have repeated measures on both IVs.

Would it be wise to have repeated measures on both variables? "Being wise" is a little harder question to answer than "being possible" because it involves a value judgment. However, if you can think of a potential flaw in a design, then it is not wise to use that design. There is a fairly obvious potential flaw in using repeated measures on both factors in McGovern and Fischer's design. Imagine the multitude of factors that could enter into personality judgments of four different people other than whether they looked you in the eye or shook your hand. Isn't it logical to assume that physical appearance, sex, ethnic or racial identification, and many other factors might influence our personality judgments as much as (or more than) the IVs in the experiment? Much social psychology research exists to back that assumption. By needing a different confederate for each of the four treatment combinations, a high level of extraneous variation would be present in our experiment. Thus, our results would be unclear as to whether people made personality judgments based on physical contact, eye contact, their interaction, or a multitude of other factors.

Of course, not all factorial experiments would have these types of problems with using repeated measures. It is possible to design an experiment with multiple IVs in which you expose participants to all treatment combinations. As you have probably guessed by now, the smaller the design, the more feasible it is to include the same participants in all conditions of the experiment. Thus, a 2 × 2 design would be the most likely candidate for a totally repeated measures design.

3.   Natural Pairs or Sets. Using natural groups in a totally within-subject design would have the same difficulties as the matched pairs or sets variation of this design, but it would be even harder. If it would be difficult to form matched pairs or sets to participate in a factorial design, imagine how much harder it would be to find an adequate number of naturally linked participants. At least when we match participants, we usually have a large number to measure in our attempt to make matches. To use natural sets, we would have to find substantial numbers of natural groups. As we noted in Chapter 8, this approach is rarely used other than for animal littermates. We will not consider natural sets again in this chapter because of their infrequent use.

Let's examine a student research project that used a factorial design with a totally within subjects approach. Asmeret Hagos (1993), of the University of San Diego, in CA, was interested in the effects of word frequency and orthographic distinctiveness on memory for words. Word frequency (WF) refers to how often various words are seen in our language, whereas orthographic distinctiveness (OD) deals with the physical appearance or "shape" of a word. "Oddly shaped" words are high in orthographic distinctiveness, and words that are shaped like many other words are low on this variable. In Hagos's experiment, both WF and OD could be either high or low. Thus, the design was a 2 (high or low WF) × 2 (high or low OD) design (as in Figures 9-1 or 9-5). Remember, labeling a design a 2 × 2 means that it has two IVs, each with two levels. It is the two IVs that make the design a factorial. Participants in the experiment saw 20 words, 5 from each of the four possible treatment combinations (high WF–high OD, high WF–low OD, low WF–high OD, and low WF–low OD). The fact that participants saw words from *each* of the four treatment conditions means that repeated measures were used for both IVs; the participants saw both low- and high-frequency words and low and high orthographically distinct words. Hagos found a significant interaction between WF and OD such that frequency had little effect on recall of orthographically distinct words but had a strong effect on orthographically common words, with high-frequency words in this category being recalled more often than low-frequency words. Had Hagos conducted this experiment as two separate two-variable designs, we would never have gained the information about the interaction between WF and OD.

Mixed Assignment to Groups. We have the opportunity for a new type of group assignment that we have not encountered in the single-IV designs because factorial designs have at least two IVs. As we mentioned previously, mixed assignment designs involve a combination of random and non-random assignment, with at least one IV using each type of assignment to groups. In a two-IV factorial design, mixed assignment would involve one IV using random assignment and one IV using non-random assignment. In such designs, the use of repeated measures is probably more likely than other types of non-random assignment. What we often end up with in a *mixed factorial design* is two independent groups that are measured more than once. Such an experimental plan allows us to measure a difference between our groups and then determine whether that difference remains constant over time. Mixed designs combine the advantages of the two types of designs. The conservation of participants through the use of repeated measures for a between-subjects variable makes for a popular and powerful design.

Let's consider a student research example using a mixed design. Rebecca Pazdral (1993), of Mills College, in Oakland, CA, conducted a study to examine the effects of athleticism and physiological arousal on performance. Rebecca had 40 female college students (20 athletes and 20 nonathletes) play an electronic game (Simon) featuring increasingly complex patterns that players had to remember in order to perform well. After they had played the game, the students completed a 15-minute period of low-impact aerobic exercise; then the students played Simon again.

Psychological Detective

What are the two IVs in this experiment, and what are their respective levels? Which is the between-groups variable and which is the within-groups variable? How would you describe this experiment in shorthand notation? What is the DV in this experiment? Write your answers before continuing.

One IV is athleticism, with the levels of athlete and nonathlete. The second IV is physiological arousal, with the levels of normal arousal and arousal after 15 minutes of aerobic exercise. Athleticism is the between-groups variable because participants can take part in only one condition—you cannot be both an athlete and a nonathlete. Also, although athleticism is not randomly assigned, the two athleticism groups are independent—there is no relationship between a particular athlete and a particular nonathlete. Physiological arousal is the within-groups variable—students participated in both conditions of this variable, both before and after the exercise period. Because Pazdral's experiment had two IVs, both of which had two levels, her experiment would be a 2×2 design. Finally, the DV was the students' performance level on the Simon game. Athletes' and nonathletes' performance on the game was compared before and after the exercise period.

In her experiment Pazdral found evidence of an interaction between athleticism and arousal. Before the exercise period, the two groups did not perform differently on Simon. However, after the 15-minute period of exercise, the athletes performed better at Simon than did the nonathletes. Although you might not guess that athleticism would be a significant factor in playing an electronic game, it appears that conditioning might have made the athletes better prepared to deal with the physical effects of the exercise period. On the other hand, perhaps athletes differ from nonathletes in some other important way such as benefiting more from the single practice session. These two possible explanations should remind you to seek alternative explanations for your experimental results. Perhaps a follow-up experiment would help you find the correct hypothesis.

REVIEW SUMMARY

1. The plan by which psychologists guide their experiments is known as the **experimental design.**
2. If you have an experiment that consists of two (or more) IVs, you will use a **factorial design.**
3. The number of levels of each IV is not important in choosing the particular factorial design you will use.
4. Combining two IVs in an experiment allows you to test for **interactions**—that is, situations in which the effect of one IV depends on the specific level of another IV.
5. When you randomly assign research participants to their groups, you have **independent groups.** If all the IVs in your factorial design use independent groups, you are employing a **totally between-groups design.**
6. When you use matched pairs or sets, repeated measures, or natural pairs or sets, you have **correlated groups.** If all IVs in your experiment use correlated groups, you are using a **totally within groups design.**
7. **Mixed factorial designs** result from using both independent groups and correlated groups in a factorial design. At least one IV must use independent groups and at least one must use correlated groups.

STUDY BREAK

1. How is the two-group design related to the factorial design? Draw a picture as part of your answer.
2. Why should there be a practical limit to the number of IVs you could use in an experiment?
3. Matching
   1. mixed factorial design ℃
   2. totally between-groups 𝐴 design
   3. totally within-groups 𝐵 design

   A. fraternity members vs. nonmembers & men vs. women
   B. fraternity members matched for family income measured twice
   C. fraternity members vs. nonmembers measured twice

4. The simplest possible factorial design would have _____2_____ IV(s) and
_____4_____ total treatment group(s).

5. Devise an original example of a factorial design that uses mixed assignment to groups.

COMPARING THE FACTORIAL DESIGN TO TWO-GROUP AND MULTIPLE-GROUP DESIGNS

As we mentioned earlier, factorial designs are based on the basic building block designs we encountered in the two previous chapters. We create factorial designs by combining two of our basic building block designs into a single design. Again, detectives use basic investigative principles as their building blocks even in complex cases.

You may remember that we described two-group designs as being ideal for a preliminary investigation of a particular IV in a presence-absence format (refer back to Figure 7-2). In a similar fashion, 2 × 2 factorial designs may be used for preliminary investigations of two IVs. If you look at Figure 9-3, where we created a hypothetical expansion of Nancy Cathey's (1992) caffeine study, you can see that we used that design to make a preliminary investigation of caffeine (presence vs. absence) and age of the rats (young vs. old). When we completed this experiment, we would have information about whether caffeine and age have any effects on rats' performance. Suppose we wished to go further—what if we wanted to delve deeper into the effects of caffeine or age?

In Chapter 8 we found that the multiple-group design could be used to conduct more in-depth investigations of an IV that interests us. We took our basic two-group design and extended it to include more levels of our IV. We can make the same type of extension with factorial designs. Figure 9-7 shows you an extension of Figure 9-3 to include three levels of each IV, thus creating a 3 × 3 factorial design. Notice that Figure 9-7 is simply two three-level multiple-group designs combined into one design. From this hypothetical design, we would get much more specific information about the effects of caffeine because we used three different doses of caffeine rather than just its presence versus absence, as shown in Figure 9-3. Along the same line, we will get much more exact information about how rats' age affects their performance because we are using rats of three different ages instead of only young and old rats (as in Figure 9-3). Just as with the multiple-group design, there is no limit to the number of levels for any IV in a factorial design. Also, the number of levels of the IVs does not have to be equal. Thus, we could create 2 × 5 factorial designs, 2 × 3 factorial designs, 3 × 6 factorial designs, and so on.

To this point, our discussion of Figure 9-7 has not added anything that we couldn't obtain by conducting two separate experiments. Whether we conduct one factorial experiment or two single IV experiments, we will uncover information about the effects of our main effects or IVs. However, as we have already seen, the true advantage of factorial designs is their addition of interaction effects to the IV

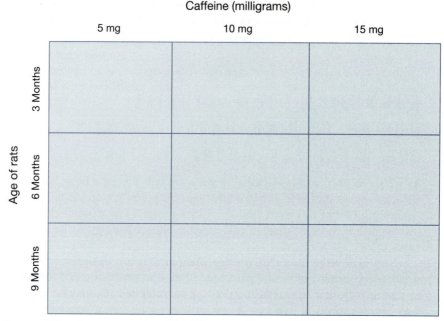

FIGURE 9-7 COMBINATION OF TWO MULTIPLE-GROUP DESIGNS

main effects. We have mentioned several times that interaction effects enable us to better understand the complexities of the world in which we live.

Unfortunately, we frequently come across students who are not interested in learning about complex relationships as characterized by interaction effects. Instead, they would prefer to conduct single-IV experiments because the results from such experiments are simpler to understand. We are not against simple research designs—they contribute a great deal to our ability to understand the world—but we are against the attitude that says, "I want to use simple research designs because they are easier." If your sole reason for choosing a research design is that it is simpler, we believe that you are making a choice for the wrong reason. Remember that we have repeatedly cautioned you to choose the simplest research design that will *adequately test your hypothesis*. It is possible that the simplest research design available will *not* adequately test your hypothesis. For example, if we already have a great deal of information about a particular IV, then a presence-versus-absence manipulation of that IV is probably too simple. By the same token, if we already know that a particular DV is caused by complex factors, then a simple design may not advance our knowledge any further. Let us provide you with an example in the following paragraph to illustrate what we're talking about.

Let's suppose that you wish to do some research on why college students make the grades that they do. In this research grades will be the DV, and you want to isolate the IV that causes those grades. One logical choice for a factor that causes grades is intelligence because it stands to reason that more intelligent students will make higher grades and less intelligent students will make lower grades. You know that you cannot give intelligence tests to a large number of college students, so you decide to use ACT or SAT scores as a very rough measure of intelligence. You choose a group of students with high ACT or SAT scores and a group of students with low ACT or SAT scores and compare their respective grades. Sure enough, you find that the students in the high group have higher GPAs than those in the low group. You are excited because your hypothesis has been confirmed. You write a report about your results and go on your merry way, telling everyone you meet that intelligence causes differences in college students' grades.

Psychological Detective

Is there anything wrong with the scenario we have just sketched for you? Do you see any specific flaws in the experiment itself? Do you see any flaws in the reasoning or in the original design? Record your ideas before reading any further.

Is the experiment described above flawed? Not really—there are no obvious violations of experimental guidelines nor any obvious extraneous variables. A better answer is that the original reasoning is flawed, or at least too simplistic.

Think about the original question for a moment. Do you believe that ACT or SAT scores can be used to explain everything there is to know about college students' grades? If you are like most students, your answer will be a resounding no. We all know students who entered college with low test scores, perhaps even on probation, but who have gone on to make good grades. On the other hand, we know students who entered with academic scholarships and who flunked out. Clearly, there must be more to grades than intelligence or whatever is measured by entrance exams. What about factors such as motivation and study skills? What about living in a dorm versus an apartment? What about being married versus being single? What about belonging to a sorority or fraternity versus being an independent? All these factors could contribute to some of the variability in GPAs that we observe among college students. Thus, if we decide to "put all our eggs in the basket" of entrance exam scores, we may be simplifying the question too much.

The problem with asking simple questions is that we get simple answers because that is all that is possible from the simple question. Again, there is nothing inherently wrong or bad about asking a simple question and getting a simple answer—*unless* we conclude that this simple answer tells us everything we need to know about our subject matter. Asking more complex questions may yield more complex answers, but those answers may give us a better idea of how the world actually works. Factorial designs give us the means of asking these more complex questions.

CHOOSING A FACTORIAL DESIGN

Three key considerations are important when you choose a particular factorial design. At the heart of the choice are your experimental questions; factorial designs provide considerable flexibility in devising an experiment to answer the questions you have. Second, it will not surprise you that you should consider issues of control in your design choice because experimental design is primarily concerned with the notion of control. Third, due to the wide degree of experimental choices possible with factorial designs, considerations of a practical nature are also important.

Experimental Questions. The number of questions we can ask in our experiment increases dramatically. Being able to ask additional questions is a great opportunity, but it also puts a burden on us. When we ask additional questions, we must make certain that the questions coordinate with each other. Just as many people would not want to wear clothes with colors that clash, we do not want to ask questions that "clash." By clashing questions, we refer to questions that do not make sense when put together. No doubt you have sat in class and heard a student ask a question that seemed totally "off the wall." The question seemed to have no relation to what was being covered in class. Experimental questions that have no relevance to each other may seem to clash when combined in the same experiment. For example, suppose you heard of a proposed experiment to find the effects of self-esteem and eye color on test performance. Does that planned experiment jar you somewhat? We hope it does. Does it make sense to combine self-esteem and eye color in an experiment? Does it make sense to examine the effects of eye color on test performance? This sounds like an IV that was thrown in simply because it could be. Could eye color be a logical IV? Perhaps it could in another situation. For example, eye color might well influence people's judgments of a target person's attractiveness or even of his or her intelligence. It seems unlikely, though, that eye color might affect one's test performance. We hope that "off the wall" combinations of IVs will be minimized by a review of the existing psychological literature. When you base your experimental questions on previous research and theory, the odds of using strange combinations of IVs is decreased.

Control Issues. We hope that by now you are able to anticipate the topic of discussion when you see the "Control Issues" heading. A glance at Figure 9-2 will remind you that we do need to consider independent versus correlated groups in factorial designs. A complicating factor for factorial designs is that you have to make this decision for each IV you include in your experiment.

Research psychologists typically assume that random assignment to groups will adequately equate the groups if you have approximately 10 participants per group. On the other hand, a correlated assignment scheme (matching or repeated measures) will provide you with greater assurance of the equality of the groups. We hope that by now you fully understand the reasoning behind these two approaches. If you need a review, look back to Chapters 7 and 8.

Principle of parsimony The belief that explanations of phenomena and events should remain simple until the simple explanations are no longer valid.

Practical Considerations. As IVs multiply in experimental designs, some of the practical issues involved become more complex. Often when students find that they can ask more than one question in an experiment, they go wild, adding IVs left and right, throwing in everything but the proverbial kitchen sink. Although curiosity is a commendable virtue, it is wise to keep your curiosity in check somewhat when designing an experiment. Remember the **principle of parsimony** that we encountered in Chapter 7: We are well advised to keep our experiment at the bare minimum necessary to answer the question(s) that most interest(s) us. We heard this principle cast in a slightly different light when a speaker was giving advice to graduate students about planning their theses and dissertations. This speaker advised students to follow the *KISS principle—Keep It Simple, Stupid.* This piece of advice was not given as an insult or meant condescendingly. The speaker merely realized that there seems to be a natural tendency to want to answer too many questions in one brilliantly conceived and wonderfully designed experiment.

With a two-group or multiple-group design, there is an obvious limitation on how many questions can be asked because of the single IV in those designs. However, with a factorial design, the sky seems to be the limit—you can use as many IVs with as many levels as you wish. However, you should always bear in mind that you are complicating matters when you add IVs and levels. Remember the two problems we mentioned earlier in the chapter. One complication occurs in actually conducting the experiment: More participants are required, more experimental sessions are necessary, you have more chances for things to go wrong, and so on. A second complication can occur in your data interpretation: Interactions between four, five, six, or more IVs become nearly impossible to interpret. It is probably this reason that explains why most factorial designs are limited to two or three IVs. Wise detectives limit their investigations to a few leads at a time rather than trying to simultaneously chase down every lead they get.

VARIATIONS ON FACTORIAL DESIGNS

In Chapters 7 and 8 we saw two variations that have carried with us to this chapter, comparing different amounts of an IV and using measured IVs. For factorial designs, we add to this list the use of more than two IVs.

Comparing Different Amounts of an IV. We have already mentioned this variation earlier in the chapter. When we created the hypothetical experiment diagrammed in Figure 9-7, we compared three different levels of caffeine exposure and three different ages of rats.

A caution is in order about adding levels to any IV in a factorial design. In the multiple-group design, when you used an additional level of your IV, you added only one group to your experiment. When you add a level to an IV in a factorial design, you add several groups to your experiment because each new level must be added under each level of your other independent variable(s). For example, expanding a 2 × 2 design to a 3 × 2 design requires 6 groups rather than 4. Enlarging a 2 × 2 × 2 design to a 3 × 2 × 2 design means using 12, rather than 8, groups. Adding levels in a factorial design increases groups in a multiplicative fashion.

Using Measured IVs. It will probably not surprise you to learn that we can use nonmanipulated IVs in factorial designs also. It is important to remember that using a measured rather than a manipulated IV results in **ex post facto research.** Without the con-

Ex post facto research A research approach in which the experimenter cannot directly manipulate the IV but can only classify, categorize, or measure the IV because it is predetermined in the participants (e.g., IV = sex).

definition

trol that comes from directly causing an IV to vary, we must exercise extreme caution in drawing conclusions from such studies. Still, ex post facto studies give us our only means of studying IVs such as sex or personality traits.

Because of the fact that factorial designs deal with more than one IV at a time, we can develop an experiment that uses one manipulated IV and one measured IV at the same time. Rebecca Pazdral's (1993) experiment, covered earlier in this chapter, was a good example of just such an experiment.

Psychological Detective

Go back and review Pazdral's experiment (on page 287). Which IV was manipulated and which was measured? Write your answers before reading further.

Remember that Pazdral studied the effects of athleticism and physiological arousal on performance by having groups of athletes and nonathletes play an electronic game before and after a 15-minute period of low-impact aerobic exercise. Rebecca could not manipulate the athleticism of her experimental participants; she selected students who were already athletes or nonathletes. However, she did manipulate the electronic-game playing. She controlled the fact that students played the game, then engaged in exercise, and then played the game again.

What are the implications for interpreting information from an experiment that uses both manipulated and measured IVs? We must still be cautious about interpreting information from the measured IV(s) because we did not cause the levels to vary. On the other hand, we are free to interpret information from manipulated IVs just as usual. Thus, Pazdral could be more certain about the results of electronic-game playing before and after aerobic exercise than she could about why the athletes outperformed the nonathletes at the electronic game.

Dealing with More than Two IVs. Designing an experiment with more than two IVs is probably the most important variation of the factorial design. In this section we will discuss the use of factorial designs with three IVs. Larger designs with more than three IVs would follow the same basic strategies that we outline here. Again, we must caution you against adding IVs to an experiment without a good reason.

Figure 9-8 depicts the simplest possible factorial design with three IVs (often referred to as a **three-way design**). As you can see, it is somewhat difficult to draw three-dimensional designs on a two-dimensional surface. This design has three IVs (A, B, and C), each with two levels. Thus, this design represents a 2 × 2 × 2 design. We could expand this design by adding levels to any of the IVs, but remember that the number of treatment combinations increases in a multiplicative rather than additive fashion.

Let's look at a hypothetical example of a three-way design. If you look back at Figure 9-3, you will remember that we conceptualized an ex-

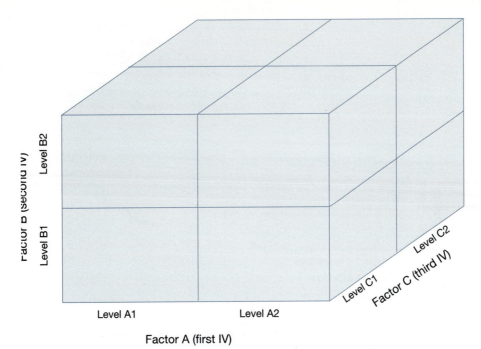

FIGURE 9-8   SIMPLEST POSSIBLE THREE-WAY FACTORIAL DESIGN (2 × 2 × 2)

tension of Nancy Cathey's (1992) caffeine study by adding a second IV, the age of the rats. Imagine that we were also interested in testing for the effects of the rats' sex, in testing whether male rats and female rats differ in their bar-press performance. This change would transform the design in Figure 9-3 to the design shown in Figure 9-9. We have "exploded" the design so that you can easily see each of the eight treatment combinations. Notice that there is a group of participants specified for each of those different treatment combinations.

Psychological Detective

Figure 9-9 specifies eight different combinations of treatments (the three IVs). Would this design require eight different groups of rats? Why or why not? Think carefully about your answer and write it down before moving on.

This design would require eight different groups of rats if it is planned as a totally between groups design. In that case, you would need to create eight different groups of rats through random assignment. The design would also require eight different groups if you used matched sets of rats. One possibility that would reduce

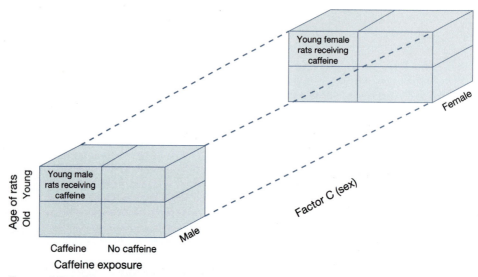

FIGURE 9-9   SECOND EXPANSION OF CATHEY'S (1992) CAFFEINE STUDY

the number of rats needed would be the use of repeated measures. Could any of the three IVs be used with repeated measures? Clearly, sex of the rats is out—a rat cannot be both male and female. Caffeine has the possibility of being used as a repeated measure, depending on how the caffeine is administered. In Cathey's original experiment, caffeine was given both pre- and postnatally. Such administration would rule out its use as a repeated measure. However, if you simply administered a dose of caffeine and then measured performance, the possibility of repeated measures does exist. It would also be possible to use age as a repeated measure if you were willing to wait on the young rats to age.

One more consideration is necessary before you could advocate the use of repeated measures—the DV. Can the DV be used more than once with the same rats? If we continue to use bar pressing as the DV, the answer would be no. We cannot train rats to bar press and later train them again, because they would already know how to bar press. If we switched to Cathey's other DV, maze performance, it would be possible to use repeated measures. Using repeated measures on maze performance would require two different but equal mazes, which should be possible to design.

Thus, the very long answer to a short question in the previous Psychological Detective section is "it depends." Although the design in Figure 9-9 specifies eight groups of rats, it does not necessarily specify eight *different* groups of rats. Our determination of the number of groups depends on whether we use independent groups or repeated measures.

One final point remains for us to cover about factorial designs with more than two IVs. We have mentioned interaction effects several times in this chapter. As we add IVs, we also add more interaction effects to our design. If we have three IVs—A, B, and C—we would obtain information about four interactions—AB, AC, BC, and ABC. To make these interactions more specific, let's use Figure 9-9 as our example. Given that our experiment diagrammed in Figure 9-9 has caffeine, age, and sex as IVs, our statistical tests will evaluate interactions for caffeine and age, caffeine and sex, age and sex, and for all three variables simultaneously (caffeine, age, and sex). You will find as many interaction effects as there are unique combinations of the treatments.

Psychological Detective

Imagine that you had an experiment with four IVs—A, B, C, and D. List all the possible interactions you would have.

Did you find that there are 11 possible interactions? Let's look at the possibilities:

Two-way (two IV) interactions: AB, AC, AD, BC, BD, CD
Three-way (three IV) interactions: ABC, ABD, ACD, BCD
Four-way (all four IVs) interactions: ABCD

The idea of evaluating 11 different interactions, including one with a possibility of all four variables interacting at once, may be challenging enough for you to understand why we suggest that you limit your experiments to no more than three IVs.

Review Summary

1. **Factorial designs** are created by combining two-group and/or multiple-group designs.
2. We use factorial designs to test the effects of more than one IV on a particular DV at the same time. These designs allow us to test under conditions that are more like the real world than dealing with only one variable at a time.
3. In choosing a particular factorial design, you must consider your experimental questions, issues of control, and practical matters.
4. In a factorial design, we can deal with different types or amounts of an IV or with measured IVs, just as we can with a two-group or multiple-group design.
5. Factorial designs may consist of three or more IVs, although the statistical interpretation of such designs becomes more complicated because of an increasing number of interactions.

Study Break

1. Why are factorial designs merely combinations of what you learned about in Chapters 7 and 8? Drawing a picture may help you here.

2. Suppose a friend told you about her 2 × 4 × 3 experimental design. Draw a diagram of this design. Explain the structure of this design.

3. Describe (a) totally between groups, (b) totally within groups, and (c) mixed groups-designs. How are they similar? How are they different?

4. Why should your experimental questions be your first consideration in choosing a factorial design?

5. Suppose you wish to test children from two different racial groups. You would be dealing with a(n) _____ IV.

6. Your friend who plans to take experimental psychology next term tells you that she is very excited about taking the class because she already has her experiment planned. She wants to test the effects of parental divorce, socioeconomic status, geographical area of residence, parental education, type of preschool attended, and parents' political preference on the sex-role development of children. What advice would you offer this friend?

STATISTICAL ANALYSIS: WHAT DO YOUR DATA SHOW? _____

We are certain that you know this by now, but we will remind you that experimental design and statistical analysis go hand in hand. You must plan your experiment carefully, choosing the experimental design that best enables you to ask your questions of interest. Having selected your experimental design from the list of choices we are presenting guarantees that you will be able to analyze your data with a standard statistical test. Thus, you will be spared the "experimental fate worse than death"—collecting your data and finding no test with which to analyze the data.

ANALYZING FACTORIAL DESIGNS

In this chapter we have covered designs with more than one IV. Depending on your statistics course, you may not have reached the point of analyzing data from these more complex designs. We analyze factorial designs with the same type of statistical test that we used for analyzing multiple-group designs—analysis of variance (ANOVA). As we mentioned in Chapter 8, we need to be able to distinguish among the various ANOVA approaches, so we often modify ANOVA with words that refer to the size of the design and how we assign participants to groups. Labels you may hear that refer to the size of the design include "factorial ANOVA" as a general term or "two-way ANOVA" or "three-way ANOVA" for designs with two or three IVs, respectively. Alternatively, the size of the design may be indicated as "X by Y," where X and Y represent the number of levels of the two factors, as we have noted several times in this chapter. Labels that describe how participants are assigned to groups might include "independent groups," "completely randomized," "completely between subjects," "completely between groups," "totally between subjects," or "totally between groups" for designs that use random assignment for all IVs. Designs that use matching or repeated measures may be called "randomized block," "completely within subjects," "completely within groups," "totally within subjects," or "totally within groups." Designs that use a mixture of between and within assignment procedures may be referred to as "mixed" or "split-plot factorial." As you can see, the labels for factorial designs can get quite long. Again, if you understand the principles behind the designs, the names are usually not difficult to interpret. For example, you might hear about a "three-way totally between groups" design or a "two-way mixed ANOVA."

Psychological Detective

Can you "decode" the two examples given in the previous sentence? What types of designs are indicated in these two cases? Write your answers before going further.

The design indicated by the "three-way totally between groups" label would include three IVs ("three-way") and would use random assignment of participants in all conditions. "Two-way mixed ANOVA" refers to an experiment with two IVs, one of which uses random assignment and one of which uses a correlated assignment technique (matching or repeated measures). Notice that these descriptions do not give us a full picture of the design because the numerical description was not given that would allow us to know how many levels each IV has. To get the fullest amount of information, a label such as "a 2 x 3 x 2 completely between groups design" is necessary. From this label, we know that there are three IVs, with two, three, and two levels respectively. We also know that participants were assigned to each of the IVs in a random manner. Notice how much experimental design information we can pack into a short descriptive label.

ANALYZING THE STATISTICAL EXAMPLE

In Chapter 8 we featured a hypothetical experiment to investigate the efficiency of different textbooks in teaching the introductory psychology course. That example used a multiple-group design because we compared three different texts to see how they affected students' performance. It should be clear to you that we must derive a new hypothetical experiment to use as an example in Chapter 9 because we are dealing with a new design.

Psychological Detective

How could we make a slight alteration in our introductory psychology textbook experiment of Chapter 8 in order to make it appropriate for use as an example in this chapter? Give this question some careful thought; write an answer before you read further. Make the alteration as simple as possible. To supplement your answer, draw a block diagram of your proposed experiment.

As is often the case when you are designing an experiment, there are many possible correct answers. The key feature that your altered experiment must contain is the *addition* of a second IV. Keeping the text difference as one IV and adding a second IV, your design should resemble Figure 9-1. Although you could have included more than two levels on either or both of your IVs, that would complicate the design. In asking you to keep your altered design simple, we also assumed you would not choose a three-IV design.

Our statistical example for this chapter will build on our example in Chapter 8. You will remember from Chapter 8 that we compared three different texts to determine whether the text made any difference in student quiz scores. Indeed, we did find that one of the texts led to better performance than the other two. Suppose that you adopted that particular text to use in your introductory class. It is now a year later and you receive a copy of a new book that looks even better to you than the book you're using now. As you did a year ago, you decide to test that impression by comparing the new book to the old book. However, the semester has already begun and you can't get enough copies of the new book in time to conduct the full experiment as you did earlier. Therefore, you decide to compare only portions of the books—you choose the chapters on biological bases of behavior and learning because your students often find those topics to be difficult. To get the best possible comparison between the two books, you also wish to compare the two different chapters of the books, using 10-point quizzes to measure your students' performance. Thus, you have designed a 2×2 experiment (see Figure 9-10) in which the two IVs are chapter (learning and biological bases) and type of book (old and new). You give the quizzes before you discuss the chapters in class so that you will have a true and fair test of the texts' information (and not your class presentation).

> **Treatment variability** Variability in DV scores that is due to the effects of the IV (*also known as between-groups variability*).
>
> **Error variability** Variability in DV scores that is due to factors other than the IV—individual differences, measurement error, and extraneous variation (*also known as within-groups variability*).

RATIONALE OF ANOVA

The rationale behind ANOVA for factorial designs is basically the same as we saw in Chapter 8, with one major modification. We still use ANOVA to partition the variability into two sources—**treatment variability** and **error variability.** However, with factorial designs, the sources of treat-

Textbook (Factor A)

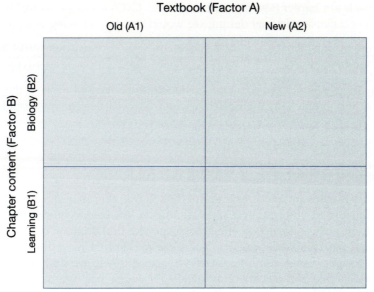

FIGURE 9-10 HYPOTHETICAL EXPERIMENT COMPARING TWO CHAPTERS FROM TWO BOOKS

ment variability increase. Instead of having one IV as the sole source of treatment variability, factorial designs have multiple IVs and their interactions as sources of treatment variability. Thus, rather than partitioning the variability as shown in Figure 8-4, we would divide the variability as shown in Figure 9-11. The actual distribution of the variance among the factors would depend, of course, on which effects were significant. If you used a factorial design with three IVs, the variability would be partitioned into even more components.

You might guess that we will add statistical formulas because we have added more components to the statistical analysis. You would be correct in this guess. You

FIGURE 9-11 PARTITIONING THE VARIABILITY IN A FACTORIAL DESIGN WITH TWO IVs

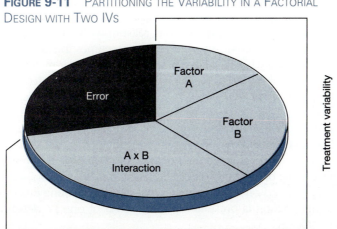

can turn back to Chapter 8 to review the general ANOVA equations for the one-IV situation. For a two-IV factorial design, we would use the following equations:

$$F_A = \frac{\text{IV A variability}}{\text{error variability}} \qquad F_B = \frac{\text{IV B variability}}{\text{error variability}} \qquad F_{A \times B} = \frac{\text{interaction variability}}{\text{error variability}}$$

These equations allow us to separately evaluate the effects of each of the two IVs as well as their interaction. If we used a larger factorial design, we would end up with an F ratio for each of the IVs and each interaction.

UNDERSTANDING INTERACTIONS

When two variables interact, their joint effect is one that may not be obvious or predictable from examining their separate effects. Let us cite one of the most famous examples of an interaction effect. Many people find drinking a glass or two of wine to be a pleasurable experience. Many people find taking a drive to be relaxing. What happens if we combine these two activities—do we end up with an extremely pleasurable and relaxing experience? Of course not. We may end up with deadly consequences. Interaction effects often occur with different drugs. Hence, you are often given very strict guidelines and warnings about combining various drugs. Combinations of drugs, in particular, are likely to have **synergistic effects**

Synergistic effects
Dramatic consequences that occur when you combine two or more substances, conditions, or organisms. The effects are greater than what is individually possible.

so that a joint effect occurs that is not predictable from either drug alone. You may have seen interaction or synergistic effects when two particular children are together. Separately, the children are calm and well behaved. However, when they are put together, watch out! Detectives are often faced with interaction effects in their work. A seemingly normal person, when confronted with a stressful day and an aggravating situation, may react violently. Neither the stress nor the aggravation alone would have led to a violent crime, but their combination could turn deadly.

Remember our earlier discussion of Figure 9-4 and the interaction pattern found there? In an experimental situation, we are concerned with how different levels of different IVs interact with respect to the DV. When we find a significant interaction, this means that the effects of the various IVs are not straightforward and simple. For this reason, we virtually ignore our IV main effects when we find a significant interaction. Sometimes interactions are difficult to interpret, particularly when we have more than two IVs or many levels of an IV. A strategy that often helps us make sense of an interaction is to graph it. By graphing your DV on the y axis and one IV on the x axis, you can depict your other IV with lines on the graph (see Chapter 6). By studying such a graph, you can usually deduce what happened to cause a significant interaction. For example, by examining Figure 9-4, you can see that the results for caffeine are not constant based on the age of the rats. Caffeine affected the behavior of young rats to a much greater degree than it affected the behavior of older rats. Thus, the effects of caffeine are not straightforward; they depend on whether you're talking about young rats or old rats. Remember that an interaction is present when the effect of one IV *depends on the specific level of the other IV.*

When you graph a significant interaction, you will often notice that the lines of the graph cross or converge. This pattern is a visual indication that the effects of one IV change as the second IV is varied. Nonsignificant interactions typically show lines that are close to parallel, as you saw in Figure 9-6. McGovern and Fischer (1993) found that both eye contact and touch made for more favorable personality judgments. However, there was no interaction between the two IVs. As we cover our statistical examples in the next few pages, we will pay special attention to the interaction effects.

INTERPRETATION: MAKING SENSE OF YOUR STATISTICS

Our statistical analyses of factorial designs will provide us more information than we got from two-group or multiple-group designs. The analyses are not necessarily more complicated than those we saw in Chapters 7 and 8, but they do provide more information because we have multiple IVs and interaction effects to analyze.

INTERPRETING COMPUTER STATISTICAL OUTPUT

As in Chapters 7 and 8, we will examine computer printouts from both SPSS and MYSTAT. If you look back at Figure 9-2, you will see that we have three different ANOVAs to cover, based on how we assign the participants to groups. We will deal with 2 x 2 analyses in these three different categories to fit our textbook-by-chapter experiment.

Two-Way ANOVA for Independent Samples. The two-way ANOVA for independent samples requires that we have two IVs (texts and chapters) with independent groups. To create this design we would use four different randomly assigned groups of students, one for each possible combination pictured in Figure 9-10. The DV scores (see Table 9-1) represent quiz scores on a 10-point quiz.

SPSS Results. The descriptive statistics are shown in Table 9-2a. You can see that the quizzes were rather difficult—perhaps because they were given before any classroom discussion of the material—because the mean for the "total population" (all 24 students) was 5.04. The means for the old texts and the new texts were 4.17 and 5.92, respectively; for the biology chapter and the learning chapter, the means were 4.25 and 5.83, respectively. The last set of descriptive statistics shows the combination of the two texts and the two chapters. Notice that the name of the IV is listed along with a number denoting the level of the IV (a key to those numbers appears at the top of the printout). Students taking the biology quiz after reading the old book averaged 4.33; those taking the same quiz after reading the new book averaged 4.17. For the learning chapter quiz, students using the old book had a mean of 4.00, whereas the students reading the new book averaged 7.67 on this

TABLE 9-1. HYPOTHETICAL QUIZ DATA FOR COMPARING TWO CHAPTERS FROM TWO BOOKS

Textbook

	Old	New	
Biology	5 6 1 2 5 7 $\bar{X} = 4.33$	4 3 5 2 6 5 $\bar{X} = 4.17$	Biology mean = 4.25
Learning	4 1 3 2 6 8 $\bar{X} = 4.00$	5 8 8 6 9 10 $\bar{X} = 7.67$	Learning mean = 5.83

Chapter content

Old mean = 4.17   New mean = 5.92

Total population mean = 5.04

quiz. Again, to make sure you entered the data correctly, you could check these means with a hand calculator in a matter of minutes.

The **source table** for the completely randomized factorial design appears in Table 9-2b. Above the table you see a label:

> QUIZSCOR
> BY   TEXT
>   CHAPTER

This label shows that the DV (QUIZSCOR) is being analyzed as a function of two IVs (TEXT and CHAPTER). In the body of the source table, we want to examine only the effects of those two IVs and their interaction. The remaining sources ("Main Effects," "2-Way Interactions," and "Explained") are redundant and can be ignored. One important item to note is that SPSS labels the error term as "Residual" in this printout. (If you need to review concepts like sum of squares or mean squares, you can refer back to Chapter 8.) When we examine the main effects, we find that TEXT produced an F ratio of 4.11, with a probability of chance of .06. The effect of CHAPTER shows an F ratio of 3.36, with a probability of .08. Can you verify these probabilities in the F table in the back of the book? You should find that the probability of each falls between the .05 and .10 levels in the table. Both of these IVs show **marginal significance,** which we usually attribute to probabilities of chance between 5% and 10%. Although marginal significance is not within the normal significance range, it is close

TABLE 9-2. SPSS OUTPUT FOR TWO-WAY ANOVA FOR INDEPENDENT SAMPLES

A. **KEY** Text: 1=old 2=new /
Chapter: 1=biology 2=learning

CELL MEANS

QUIZSCOR
BY TEXT
    CHAPTER

TOTAL POPULATION

    5.04
  (24)

TEXT
          1   2

    4.17   5.92
  (12)   (12)

CHAPTER

          1   2

    4.25   5.83
  (12)   (12)

                TEXT
CHAPTER   1   2

      1   4.33   4.17
              (6)   (6)

      2   4.00   7.67
              (6)   (6)

B.   ***ANALYSIS OF VARIANCE***

QUIZSCOR
by TEXT
    CHAPTER

Source of Variation	Sum of Squares	DF	Mean Square	F	Sig of F
Main Effects	33.417	2	16.708	3.734	.042
TEXT	18.375	1	18.375	4.106	.056
CHAPTER	15.042	1	15.042	3.361	.082
2-Way Interactions	22.042	1	22.042	4.926	.038
TEXT CHAPTER	22.042	1	22.042	4.926	.038
Explained	55.458	3	18.486	4.131	.020
Residual	89.500	20	4.475		
Total	144.958	23	6.303		

Type I error
Accepting the
experimental
hypothesis when the
null hypothesis is
true.

definition

enough that many experimenters discuss such results anyway. Keep in mind when you deal with higher and higher probabilities of chance that you are taking a greater risk of making a **Type I error** (see Chapter 6).

Our next step is to examine the interaction between the two IVs. Notice that we have one two-way interaction because we have just the two IVs. The interaction between TEXT and CHAPTER produced an *F* ratio of 4.93 and has $p < .04$, therefore denoting significance. Remember that a significant interaction renders the main effects meaningless because those main effects are qualified by the interaction and are not straightforward. Thus, to make sense out of these results, we must interpret the interaction. The first step in interpreting an interaction, remember, is to draw a graph of the results from the descriptive statistics. Figure 9-12 depicts this interaction.

MYSTAT Results. The descriptive statistics, obtained from MYSTAT's STATS routine, appear in Table 9-3A (see pp. 308—309). These were obtained from MYSTAT's STATS routine because descriptive statistics are not printed with the ANOVA program. We ran STATS four times to obtain this full complement of descriptives: once each for the total group, the TEXT groups, CHAPTER groups, and TEXT/CHAPTER combination groups. To help you interpret the statistics, we have labeled the printout for you: Text level 1 is old (o), Text level 2 is new (n), Chapter level 1 is biology (b), and Chapter level 2 is learning (l).

Table 9-3B shows you the source table from MYSTAT, which is highly similar to the SPSS source table in Table 9-2B. MYSTAT does not print the redundant

FIGURE 9-12   INTERACTION FOR TEXT AND CHAPTER EXPERIMENT

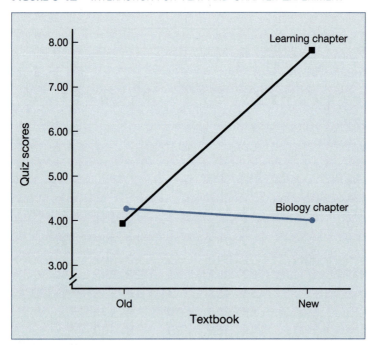

source information that appeared in the SPSS table. As you can see, the statistical results from MYSTAT match perfectly what appeared in the SPSS printout. Thus, we again see that TEXT and CHAPTER are marginally significant and the TEXT*CHAPTER interaction is significant ($p < .04$). Our interpretive procedure at this point mirrors what we wrote in the SPSS section, so we would graph the interaction (see Figure 9-12) and draw our conclusion from it.

Translating Statistics into Words. Remember that we are justified in drawing conclusions from our statistics *only if* we are certain that our experimental design and procedures had sufficient control to eliminate extraneous variables. Computers and statistical tests work only with the data you provide—they are not able to detect data from flawed experiments.

To interpret our statistics, let's return to the graph of our significant interaction (Figure 9-12).

Psychological Detective

Study Figure 9-12 carefully. What do you think caused the significant interaction? In other words, why do the results of one IV depend on the particular level of the second IV? Write your explanation in a sentence or two before proceeding.

You should remember that we described interactions as occurring when the lines on a graph cross or converge and that parallel lines indicate no interaction. The crossing lines of Figure 9-12, in conjunction with the low probability of chance for the interaction term, denote a significant interaction. When we examine the figure, the point that seems to differ most represents the scores on the learning quiz from the new text. This mean is considerably higher than the others. Thus, we would conclude that the learning chapter in the new text seems better in some way than the other chapters. Notice that our explanation of an interaction effect *must* include a reference to both IVs in order to make sense—the previous sentence mentions the *learning chapter* in the *new text*.

Psychological Detective

From looking at Figure 9-12, can you figure out why this interaction qualifies the marginally significant main effects? Write your answer before you read any further.

If we had drawn conclusions from the marginally significant main effects, we would have decided that students using the new text had marginally higher quiz

TABLE 9-3. MYSTAT OUTPUT FOR TWO-WAY ANOVA FOR INDEPENDENT SAMPLES

A. TOTAL
OBSERVATIONS: 24

QUIZSCOR

N OF CASES	24
MINIMUM	1.000
MAXIMUM	10.000
MEAN	5.042
STANDARD DEV	2.510

Descriptive Statistics for All Quizzes

THE FOLLOWING
RESULTS ARE FOR:
    TEXT   =   1.000
                    (old)

TOTAL
OBSERVATIONS: 12

QUIZSCOR

N OF CASES	12
MINIMUM	1.000
MAXIMUM	8.000
MEAN	4.167
STANDARD DEV	2.368

THE FOLLOWING
RESULTS ARE FOR:
    CHAPTER =   1.000
                    (biology)

TOTAL
OBSERVATIONS: 12

QUIZSCOR

N OF CASES	12
MINIMUM	1.000
MAXIMUM	7.000
MEAN	4.250
STANDARD DEV	1.865

THE FOLLOWING
RESULTS ARE FOR:
    TEXT   =   2.000
                    (new)

TOTAL
OBSERVATIONS: 12

QUIZSCOR

N OF CASES	12
MINIMUM	2.000
MAXIMUM	10.000
MEAN	5.917
STANDARD DEV	2.429

Descriptive Statistics for
Quizzes for the Two Texts

THE FOLLOWING
RESULTS ARE FOR:
    CHAPTER =   2.000
                    (learning)

TOTAL
OBSERVATIONS: 12

QUIZSCOR

N OF CASES	12
MINIMUM	1.000
MAXIMUM	10.000
MEAN	5.833
STANDARD DEV	2.887

Descriptive Statistics for Quizzes
Based on the Two Chapters

B. DEP VAR: QUIZSCOR   N: 24

ANALYSIS OF VARIANCE

SOURCE	SUM-OF-SQUARES	DF	MEAN-SQUARE	F-RATIO	P
TEXT	18.375	1	18.375	4.106	0.056
CHAPTER	15.042	1	15.042	3.361	0.082
TEXT* CHAPTER	22.042	1	22.042	4.926	0.038
ERROR	89.500	20	4.475		

```
THE FOLLOWING              THE FOLLOWING
RESULTS ARE FOR:           RESULTS ARE FOR:
     TEXT = 1.000 (o)           TEXT = 2.000 (n)
  CHAPTER = 1.000 (b)        CHAPTER = 1.000 (b)

TOTAL                      TOTAL
OBSERVATIONS:     6        OBSERVATIONS:     6

       QUIZSCOR                   QUIZSCOR

N OF CASES        6        N OF CASES        6
MINIMUM        1.000       MINIMUM        2.000
MAXIMUM        7.000       MAXIMUM        6.000
MEAN           4.333       MEAN           4.167
STANDARD                   STANDARD
  DEV          2.338         DEV          1.472


THE FOLLOWING              THE FOLLOWING
RESULTS ARE FOR:           RESULTS ARE FOR:
     TEXT = 1.000 (o)           TEXT = 2.000 (n)
  CHAPTER = 2.000 (l)        CHAPTER = 2.000 (l)

TOTAL                      TOTAL
OBSERVATIONS:     6        OBSERVATIONS:     6

       QUIZSCOR                   QUIZSCOR

N OF CASES        6        N OF CASES        6
MINIMUM        1.000       MINIMUM        5.000
MAXIMUM        8.000       MAXIMUM       10.000
MEAN           4.000       MEAN           7.667
STANDARD                   STANDARD
  DEV          2.608         DEV          1.862
```

Descriptive Statistics for Quizzes Based on the Combinations of
Two Texts and Two Chapters

means (5.92) than students using the old text (4.17). Also, we would have concluded that students taking the learning quiz had marginally higher scores (5.83) than students taking the biology quiz (4.25). When you look at Figure 9-12, does it appear that the new text actually leads to higher quiz scores? No, only the learning chapter in the new text has higher scores. Does it seem that the learning chapter leads to higher quiz scores than the biology chapter? No, only the new text's learning chapter is associated with higher quiz scores. If you attempt to interpret the main effects in a straightforward fashion when you have a significant interaction, you end up trying to make a gray situation into a black-and-white picture. In other words, you would be guilty of oversimplifying the results.

Our final step in interpreting the results is communicating our results to others. You will remember that we use a combination of statistical results and words to convey our findings in APA style. Here is one way you could present the results from this experiment:

> The effect of the texts on quiz scores was marginally significant, $\underline{F}(1, 20) = 4.11$, $\underline{p} = .056$. The chapter effect was also marginally significant, $\underline{F}(1, 20) = 3.36$, $\underline{p} = .082$. However, the main effects were qualified by a significant text by chapter interaction, $\underline{F}(1, 20) = 4.93$, $\underline{p} = .038$, $\eta^2 = .20$. The results of the interaction are graphed in Figure 1 [*See Figure 9-12 in this chapter*]. Visual inspection of the graph shows that quiz scores for the new text-learning chapter condition were higher than the other conditions.

Once again, our goal is to communicate our results clearly with the words alone. Although the concept of interactions is somewhat complicated for persons with no statistical background, we hope that an uninformed reader could understand our written explanation of the results. We want you to note two important points from this presentation of results. First, compared to the examples in Chapters 7 and 8, this written summary is longer. When you deal with factorial designs, you have more results to communicate, so your presentations will be longer. Second, although we presented the significance of the interaction and referred to its figure, we did not fully interpret the interaction. Results sections in experimental reports are only for presenting the results, not for full interpretation. As the APA *Publication Manual* notes in describing the results section, "Discussing the implications of the results is not appropriate here" (APA, 1994, p. 15).

Two-Way ANOVA for Correlated Samples. The two-way ANOVA for correlated samples requires that we have two IVs (texts and chapters) with correlated groups for both IVs. Most often these correlated groups would be formed by matching or the use of repeated measures. In our example of the text-chapter experiment, the first inclination is that repeated measures on both IVs would be quite simple—we would merely get one sample of students and have them take both quizzes from both texts.

Psychological Detective

Can you detect a flaw in the logic of having a single group of students taking all four quizzes as outlined in the previous sentence? Think carefully and write an answer before you go on.

If students read chapters about the identical topics and took a quiz on each text, an advantage for the second quiz on each topic would result. Specifically, when students took the second biology or learning quiz, they would have read *two* chapters about the same topic. On the other hand, when they took their first quiz on each topic, they would have read only one chapter on the topic. Clearly, repeated measures on the text variable would not be appropriate. Thus, for the text factor, we will form correlated groups by matching two groups of students. To ensure that intelligence and study habits are not extraneous variables, pairs of students will be matched on previous quiz scores. Then, we will randomly assign one member of each pair to the old text and one to the new text. To minimize our need for participants, we will use repeated measures on the chapter variable. Each student will read one text but take both quizzes from that text. Thus, our experimental design uses correlated groups for each IV, one formed through matching and one using repeated measures.

SPSS Results. SPSS's MANOVA procedure must be used because repeated measures are involved in this analysis. The means for this analysis appear in Table 9-4A. The information presented is relatively clear with one exception. As you can see, the means for each comparison are printed twice—once weighted and once unweighted. Typically, we look at the unweighted means; in this case, they are identical, so we can ignore the weighted information. Notice that only means are printed in this SPSS analysis. If you wanted further descriptive statistics such as standard deviations, you would need to use the DESCRIPTIVES procedure.

The source table for the two-way ANOVA with correlated groups appears in Table 9-4B. Notice that SPSS treats SUBJECTS (participants) as an IV. It is necessary to isolate this factor in order to "pull out" the variability due to the participants from the error term. The information presented for SUBJECTS is not important; we merely learn that different participants showed significant differences in their quiz scores— not a profound finding.

The remainder of the source table is relatively straightforward. The TEXT effect is significant at the .014 level and the CHAPTER effect is significant at the .023 level. However, both of those effects are rendered unimportant by the significant TEXT BY CHAPTER interaction (p = .008). Remember that this interaction effect signifies that the results of the IVs are not consistent across each other. To make sense of the interaction, we must plot the means for the text by chapter combinations. This interaction is again shown in Figure 9-12.

MYSTAT Results. To obtain descriptive statistics, we must use the STATS routine. Therefore, we would obtain the same information that we have seen previously in Table 9-3A. Because we have seen these results before, there is no need to review them again.

We saw in Chapter 8 that MYSTAT does not include statistical routines for ANOVA with correlated groups. However, if you include your participants (subjects) as a third IV, MYSTAT will perform the computations necessary for a two-way ANOVA for correlated groups, although the printout actually has three IVs (including subjects as a variable, just as with the SPSS analysis shown previously). The MYSTAT source table is shown in Table 9-5. As you can see, the SUBJECTS effect is significant, which merely demonstrates that students' quiz scores differed—again, not an important finding.

If we examine our main effects, we see that the TEXT effect ($p = .014$) and the CHAPTER effect ($p = .023$) are both significant. We must ignore these effects, though, because of the significant TEXT*CHAPTER interaction ($p = .008$). To interpret this interaction, we must plot the means on a graph (see Figure 9-12).

Translating Statistics into Words. One important lesson to learn from these different analyses of the same data deals with the power of designing experiments in different ways. For example, take a minute to compare the source tables for this analysis (Tables 9-4B and 9-5) to the source tables for the completely randomized analysis (Tables 9-2B and 9-3B). You will notice in the correlated samples design

TABLE 9-4. SPSS OUTPUT FOR TWO-WAY ANOVA FOR CORRELATED SAMPLES

A. Combined Observed Means for TEXT
Variable .. QUIZSCOR

TEXT		
Old	WGT.	4.16667
	UNWGT.	4.16667
New	WGT.	5.91667
	UNWGT.	5.91667

Combined Observed Means for CHAPTER
Variable .. QUIZSCOR

CHAPTER		
Biology	WGT.	4.25000
	UNWGT.	4.25000
Learning	WGT.	5.83333
	UNWGT.	5.83333

Combined Observed Means for TEXT BY CHAPTER
Variable .. QUIZSCOR

CHAPTER	TEXT	Old	New
Biology	WGT.	4.33333	4.16667
	UNWGT.	4.33333	4.16667
Learning	WGT.	4.00000	7.66667
	UNWGT.	4.00000	7.66667

B. ******************ANALYSIS OF VARIANCE

Tests of Significance for QUIZSCOR using
UNIQUE sums of squares

Source of Variation	SS	DF	MS	F	Sig of F
Error 1	35.29	15	2.35		
SUBJECTS	54.21	5	10.84	4.61	.010
TEXT	18.38	1	18.38	7.81	.014
CHAPTER	15.04	1	15.04	6.39	.023
TEXT BY CHAPTER	22.04	1	22.04	9.37	.008

TABLE 9-5. MYSTAT OUTPUT FOR TWO-WAY ANOVA FOR CORRELATED SAMPLES

DEP VAR:QUIZSCOR	N: 24				
ANALYSIS OF VARIANCE					
SOURCE	SUM-OF-SQUARES	DF	MEAN-SQUARE	F-RATIO	P
TEXT	18.375	1	18.375	7.810	0.014
CHAPTER	15.042	1	15.042	6.393	0.023
TEXT* CHAPTER	22.042	1	22.042	9.368	0.008
SUBJECTS	54.208	5	10.842	4.608	0.010
ERROR	35.292	15	2.353		

that the *F* ratios are larger and the probabilities are smaller for both the IVs and their interaction. In the previous chapters we told you that using correlated samples helps to reduce error variability by reducing some of the between-subject variability. The result is typically a stronger, more powerful test of the treatment effects, as is shown in this case.

To fully interpret the results of this experiment, we would need to make sense of the interaction shown in Figure 9-12. We will be briefer at this point because we have already carefully examined the interaction in the previous analysis section. Again, it is clear that the interaction occurred because students using the new text made higher quiz scores on the learning quiz. However, the effect was specific to that quiz on that text. The new text is not generally better because the biology quiz scores from the new text are not also higher. The learning material is not universally easier because the quiz scores on that topic from the old book are not higher. Thus, we must confine our conclusion to higher scores on that quiz from that text. Notice that explaining an interaction forces us to refer to both IVs in the same explanatory sentence—we can't ignore one IV to focus on the other.

Of course, we must still communicate our results to other parties using APA style. We rely on our standard combination of words and numbers for the summary of the results—words to explain and numbers to document the findings. One possible way of summarizing these results follows:

> Both the main effects of Text and Chapter were significant, $F(1, 15) = 7.81$, $p = .014$ and $F(1, 15) = 6.39$, $p = .023$, respectively. However, the interaction of Text and Chapter was also significant, $F(1, 15) = 9.37$, $p = .008$, $\eta^2 = .38$. This interaction appears in Figure 1 [*see Figure 9-12 in this chapter*]. Students taking the learning quiz from the new text scored considerably higher than students with any other combination of text and chapter.

You would provide a fuller explanation and interpretation of this interaction in the discussion section of your experimental report.

Two-Way ANOVA for Mixed Samples. The two-way ANOVA for mixed samples requires that we have two IVs (texts and chapters) with independent groups for one IV and correlated groups for the second IV. A logical way to create this design in our text-chapter experiment would be to use a different randomly assigned group of students for each text. Students using each text, however, would take both quizzes. Thus, text would use independent groups and constitute a between-subject variable whereas chapter would use repeated measures and be a within-subject variable. Looking at Figure 9-10 (p. 301), note that different students would use the two textbooks (across the top of the diagram) but would take both quizzes (looking down the diagram). The DV scores (see Table 9-1) still represent quiz scores on a 10-point quiz, but the same students produced the quiz scores for each quiz within the two books. This would be an efficient design because it would require fewer students to conduct the study and it would minimize the individual differences within the two quizzes.

SPSS Results. Again, the MANOVA procedure was used for this analysis. The descriptive statistics are shown in Table 9-6a. Although all possible means are not provided by MANOVA (e.g., for all participants or for old texts and new texts), these were obtained by running the DESCRIPTIVES program. We find an overall quiz score mean of 5.04, an old text mean quiz score of 4.17 and 5.92 for the new text, and mean scores of 4.25 on the biology chapter quiz and 5.83 on the learning chapter quiz. The four cell means are 4.33 for the old text-biology, 4.17 for the new text-biology, 4.00 for old text-learning, and 7.67 for new text-learning.

The SPSS source table is printed in two parts, both shown in Table 9-6b. As you can see from the headings, SPSS prints separate source tables for the between-subjects effects (independent groups) and for the within-subjects effects (repeated measures). The interaction is shown in the within-subjects table because it involves repeated measures across one of the variables involved.

Psychological Detective

Which IV is the between-subjects variable, and why? Which IV is the within-subjects variable, and why? Write your answers before you go on.

No, that wasn't a trick question—just a simple review query to make sure you're paying attention. The text is the between-subjects variable because different students use different texts. The chapter is the within-subjects variable because each student takes a quiz over both chapters (repeated measures).

The information for the text IV shows an *F* ratio of 2.70 and a probability of chance of .13—therefore, the text made no significant difference in the quiz scores. The chapter effect yields an *F* ratio of 7.02 with a probability of .024, a significant finding. However, we also notice that the text by chapter interaction is significant (.009), with an *F* ratio of 10.29. Because of this significant interaction, we will not interpret the significant chapter result. Once again, we need to graph the interaction in order to make sense of it (see Figure 9-12).

This pattern of results is different from either of the other two analyses in this chapter, again demonstrating the importance of experimental design in determining

TABLE 9-6. SPSS OUTPUT FOR TWO-WAY ANOVA FOR MIXED SAMPLES

A.

Variable	Mean	Std Dev	Minimum	Maximum	Valid N
QUIZSCOR	5.04	2.51	1	10	24

Variable	Mean	Std Dev	Minimum	Maximum	Valid N
OLD_TEXT	4.17	2.37	1	8	12
NEW_TEXT	5.92	2.43	2	10	12

Variable	Mean	Std Dev	Minimum	Maximum	Valid N
BIOLOGY	4.25	1.86	1	7	12
LEARNING	5.83	2.89	1	10	12

Cell Means and Standard Deviations
Variable .. BIOLOGY

FACTOR	CODE	Mean	Std. Dev.	N
TEXT	Old	4.333	2.338	6
TEXT	New	4.167	1.472	6
For entire sample		4.250	1.865	12

Variable .. LEARNING

FACTOR	CODE	Mean	Std. Dev.	N
TEXT	Old	4.000	2.608	6
TEXT	New	7.667	1.862	6
For entire sample		5.833	2.887	12

B. ***********************ANALYSIS OF VARIANCE

Tests of Between-Subject Effects.

Source of Variation	SS	DF	MS	F	Sig of F
WITHIN CELLS	68.08	10	6.81		
TEXT	18.37	1	18.37	2.70	.131

Tests involving 'Chapter' Within-Subject Effect.

Source of Variation	SS	DF	MS	F	Sig of F
WITHIN CELLS	21.42	10	2.14		
CHAPTER	15.04	1	15.04	7.02	.024
TEXT BY CHAPTER	22.04	1	22.04	10.29	.009

significance. Interestingly, the text effect was the weakest in this design. Kirk (1968) noted that tests of between-subjects factors are relatively weaker than tests of within-subjects factors in a split-plot design. The results of this analysis, when compared to the previous analysis, demonstrate that point.

MYSTAT Results. As mentioned previously in this chapter, we used the STATS routine to obtain descriptive statistics. The printout of this information appears in Table 9-3A.

As with the two-way ANOVA for correlated samples, MYSTAT does not include an analysis for a mixed factorial design. However, again MYSTAT can be "rigged" to provide such an analysis if we include participants (subjects) as a variable. As you will see, we will also have to do a small number of hand calculations after the MYSTAT analysis, but they are minor.

The source table for this MYSTAT analysis appears in Table 9-7A. The reason we still have some calculations to complete at this point is that MYSTAT treated our participants (subjects) as a variable, which we do not want to occur in this analysis. To create an error term for the between-groups IV (TEXT), we must add the sums of squares and degrees of freedom for the two sources that include variability due to the subject factor (SUBJ, TEXT*SUBJ). Deriving new values for the error sum of squares and degrees of freedom leads to a value for the error mean square (SS/df). With a new error mean square, we must also compute a new F ratio (MS$_{text}$/MS$_{error}$)

TABLE 9-7. MYSTAT OUTPUT FOR TWO-WAY ANOVA FOR MIXED SAMPLES

A. ANALYSIS OF VARIANCE

SOURCE	SUM-OF-SQUARES	DF	MEAN-SQUARE	F-RATIO	P
TEXT	18.375	1	18.375	8.580	0.015
SUBJECTS	54.208	5	10.842	5.062	0.014
TEXT*SUBJECTS	13.875	5	2.775	1.296	0.339
CHAPTER	15.042	1	15.042	7.023	0.024
CHAPTER*TEXT	22.042	1	22.042	10.292	0.009
ERROR	21.417	10	2.142		

B. ANALYSIS OF VARIANCE

SOURCE	SUM-OF-SQUARES	DF	MEAN-SQUARE	F-RATIO	P
TEXT	18.375	1	18.375	8.580 2.70	0.015 0.13
SUBJECTS	54.208 68.08	5 10	10.842 6.81	5.062	0.014
TEXT*SUBJECTS	13.875	5	2.775	1.296	0.339
CHAPTER	15.042	1	15.042	7.023	0.024
CHAPTER*TEXT	22.042	1	22.042	10.292	0.009
ERROR	21.417	10	2.142		

for the TEXT IV. As you can see, we have made the necessary computations in Table 9-7B. After all the calculations, we find that the F ratio for TEXT is 2.70, which has a probability of chance of .13, thus being nonsignificant. The CHAPTER IV shows significance (p = .024), but the interaction of CHAPTER*TEXT also is significant (p = .009), so the CHAPTER effect is essentially negated. To help us interpret the interaction, we graph it (see Figure 9-12).

Translating Statistics into Words. We have already completed some of our interpretation in our coverage of the statistical results. We know that the text effect was not significant and that the chapter variable was significant. However, because the interaction between text and chapter was significant, we ignore the chapter results and interpret the interaction.

Figure 9-12 shows that students who took the quiz about learning after reading the new text did better than when they took the biology quiz, and that their performance on the learning quiz was higher than that of the students who read the old text for both of their quizzes. How can we communicate these findings in APA format? Here's one possibility:

> Results from the mixed factorial ANOVA showed no effect of the text, $\underline{F}(1, 10)$ = 2.70, $\underline{p}$ = .13. The chapter effect was significant, $\underline{F}(1, 10)$ = 7.02, $\underline{p}$ = .024. This main effect, however, was qualified by a significant text by chapter interaction, $\underline{F}(1, 10)$ = 10.29, $\underline{p}$ = .009, η^2 = .51, which is shown in Figure 1 [*see Figure 9-12 in this chapter*]. This interaction shows that students who used the new text for the quiz on learning scored higher than they did on the biology quiz and higher than students who used the old text for both quizzes.

In the discussion section of your report, you would note that although the new book appears to be no better for the biology chapter, it appears to lead to higher scores on the learning chapter. Therefore, you should seriously consider switching texts and adopting the new book.

Psychological Detective

Note the high degree of similarity for the CHAPTER and INTERACTION effects in this mixed analysis and the completely within analysis in the previous section. Why do you think the probabilities of chance are within .001 in each case? Write an answer before continuing.

To answer this difficult question, you have to be able to see the similarities between these last two analyses. Although they may seem rather different, there is one great similarity between them. Both of these analyses, because of the underlying experimental designs, treat the CHAPTER and INTERACTION effects as within-groups effects. Thus, the two ANOVAs are essentially analyzing the same data in the same manner.

Reprinted from *The Chronicle of Higher Education*. By permission of Mischa Richter and Harald Bakken.

"On the other hand, if you're not interested in good and evil, this one would give you a good understanding of statistical probability."

A good background in statistics should help you from becoming this desperate.

As a final word about the analyses in this chapter, please remember that you cannot analyze the same data in several different manners in the real world of experimentation. We have used the same data for instructional purposes *and* to demonstrate how one experimental idea can be put in the context of several possible experimental designs.

Three-Way ANOVA for Independent Samples. As we have mentioned in this chapter, the possibilities for factorial designs are almost limitless when you consider that you can vary the number of IVs, vary the number of levels for each IV, and vary how participants are assigned to groups for each IV. Thus, there is no way that we could cover every possible type of factorial design in this chapter. We have concentrated on the simplest factorial designs (2 × 2) in order to provide you a basic introduction. However, before we leave factorial designs, we would like to give you an example of a factorial design involving three IVs. A three-way ANOVA for independent samples involves three IVs (thus the term three-way) that all deal with independent groups of participants. To implement this design, we will make one final alteration to our first text-chapter experiment in this chapter (using the factorial between-groups design). Imagine that you are talking to a faculty member who teaches at a different college—a school with open admissions (i.e., anyone who applies can get admitted). You attend a selective college (i.e., a school with stringent admissions policies) and wonder whether the type of college would make a difference in this comparison of texts and chapters. You enlist the faculty member's aid and set out to test this new question. Thus, your experimental design would now be a 2 × 2 × 2 (text by chapter by school) completely randomized design (all groups composed of different participants). The general design for this experiment is depicted in Figure 9-8 on page 295. The quiz scores of the students in the various treatment combinations are shown in Table 9-8.

TABLE 9-8. QUIZ SCORES FOR TEXT BY CHAPTER BY SCHOOL EXPERIMENT

		Selective School		Open Admissions School	
		Textbook		Textbook	
Chapter content		Old	New	Old	New
	Biology	5	4	5	4
		6	5	4	5
		1	5	6	2
		2	5	3	3
		5	6	7	4
		7	5	6	7
	Learning	6	5	6	5
		5	7	8	4
		4	7	7	5
		4	6	7	4
		6	8	9	5
		8	7	8	7

SPSS Results. The means for the variables and their combinations are shown in Table 9-9A. This table is somewhat complex—the means for the entire population and the three main effects appear in the first column, means for the three two-way interactions (TEXT by CHAPTER, TEXT by SCHOOL, CHAPTER by SCHOOL) are in the middle column, and the third column shows the means for the one three-way interaction (TEXT by CHAPTER by SCHOOL) or other descriptive statistics, you would need to run the DESCRIPTIVES process.

The source table for this analysis appears in Table 9-9B. As you can see, the table contains a wealth of information, neatly arranged by main effects, two-way interactions, and the three-way interaction. Remember we have talked many times about the notion that interactions qualify main effects. When we look at the three-way interaction, we find that it is not significant ($p = .24$). Had it been significant, all other effects (including the two-way interactions) would have been qualified. Examining the three two-way interactions, we find that two of them are not significant, TEXT by CHAPTER ($p = .55$) and CHAPTER by SCHOOL ($p = .84$). However, the TEXT by SCHOOL interaction does show significance ($p = .003$). Thus, the main effects of TEXT and SCHOOL are rendered meaningless—but they were not significant anyway ($p = .32$ and $.84$, respectively). The main effect of CHAPTER is significant ($p = .001$). We will interpret this main effect because it was not included in a significant interaction. Thus, we *can* interpret the effects of CHAPTER and the TEXT by SCHOOL interaction. To interpret this interaction, we must graph it (see Figure 9-13).

MYSTAT Results. By now we know that MYSTAT can reproduce SPSS's descriptive statistics with its STATS routine, so we will not use space repeating those means. The MYSTAT source table for this design appears in Table 9-10. As you can see, it

TABLE 9-9. SPSS Output for Three-Way ANOVA for Independent Samples

A.   **VARIABLE LABELS**Text: 1=old 2=new
                                                              CELL

```
        QUIZSCOR
BY   TEXT                                    CHAPTER
     CHAPTER                      TEXT           1              2
     SCHOOL
                                   1          4.75           6.50
TOTAL POPULATION                           (   12)         (   12)
                                   2          4.58           5.83
5.42                                       (   12)         (   12)
(    48)
```

```
TEXT                                          SCHOOL
        1             2          TEXT           1              2

      5.63          5.21           1          4.92           6.33
   (   24        (   24)                   (   12)         (   12)

CHAPTER                            2          5.83           4.58
        1             2                    (   12)         (   12)

      4.67          6.17                      SCHOOL
   (   24)        (   24)        CHAPTER        1              2

SCHOOL                             1          4.67           4.67
        1             2                    (   12)         (   12)

      5.38          5.46           2          6.08           6.25
   (   24)        (   24)                  (   12)         (   12)
```

B.   **ANALYSIS OF VARIANCE**

```
        QUIZSCOR
by  TEXT
    CHAPTER
    SCHOOL
```

Source of Variation	Sum of Squares	DF	Mean Square	F	Sig of F
Main Effects	29.167	3	9.722	4.667	.007
TEXT	2.083	1	2.083	1.000	.323
CHAPTER	27.000	1	27.000	12.960	.001
SCHOOL	.083	1	.083	.040	.842
2-Way Interactions	22.167	3	7.389	3.547	.023
TEXT CHAPTER	.750	1	.750	.360	.552
TEXT SCHOOL	21.333	1	21.333	10.240	.003
CHAPTER SCHOOL	.083	1	.083	.040	.842

Chapter: 1=biology 2=learning / School: 1=open 2=selective
M E A N S * * *

SCHOOL = 1

    CHAPTER
TEXT   1   2

    1   4.33   5.50
            (6)   (6)

    2   5.00   6.67
            (6)   (6)

SCHOOL = 2

    CHAPTER
TEXT   1   2

    1   5.17   7.50
            (6)   (6)

    2   4.17   5.00
            (6)   (6)

(*Source Table continues*)

Source of Variation	Sum of Squares	DF	Mean Square	F	Sig of F
3-Way Interactions	3.000	1	3.000	1.440	.237
TEXT CHAPTER SCHOOL	3.000	1	3.000	1.440	.237
Explained	54.333	7	7.762	3.726	.003
Residual	83.333	40	2.083		
Total	137.667	47	2.929		

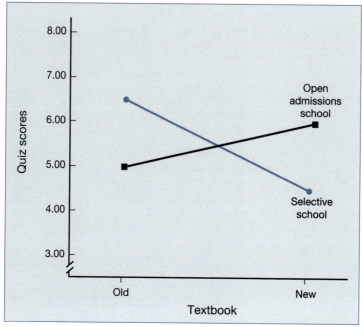

FIGURE 9-13   SIGNIFICANT TEXT BY SCHOOL INTERACTION FOR TEXT, CHAPTER, AND SCHOOL EXPERIMENT

is a virtual copy of the SPSS source table. We see the same significance for CHAPTER ($p = .001$) and for the TEXT*SCHOOL interaction ($p = .003$). Again, the graph of the interaction appears in Figure 9-13.

Translating Statistics into Words. We found a significant CHAPTER effect and a significant TEXT by SCHOOL interaction. All other main effects and interactions were not significant. When we look at the CHAPTER means, we find that mean scores for the biology quiz were 4.67, and for the learning quiz, 6.17. Therefore, we can conclude that students made significantly higher scores on the learning quiz.

The TEXT by SCHOOL interaction is graphed in Figure 9-13. Here we see a classic interaction pattern as the two lines cross.

Psychological Detective

Inspect Figure 9-13 closely. What occurred to cause a significant interaction? Write a short summary of your impressions before reading further.

From examining Figure 9-13 carefully, it appears that the preferred book varies by school. Students at the open admissions school scored higher on their quizzes

TABLE 9-10. MYSTAT OUTPUT FOR THREE-WAY ANOVA FOR INDEPENDENT SAMPLES

DEP VAR:QUIZSCOR   N: 48

ANALYSIS OF VARIANCE

SOURCE	SUM-OF-SQUARES	DF	MEAN-SQUARE	F-RATIO	P
TEXT	2.083	1	2.083	1.000	0.323
CHAPTER	27.000	1	27.000	12.960	0.001
SCHOOL	0.083	1	0.083	0.040	0.842
TEXT* CHAPTER	0.750	1	0.750	0.360	0.552
TEXT* SCHOOL	21.333	1	21.333	10.240	0.003
CHAPTER* SCHOOL	0.083	1	0.083	0.040	0.842
TEXT* CHAPTER* SCHOOL	3.000	1	3.000	1.440	0.237
ERROR	83.333	40	2.083		

when they used the new book. On the other hand, students at the selective admissions school performed better when they read the old text. Thus, the appropriate conclusion is that the best textbook you can use depends on the type of school at which you teach. This type of finding would help to confirm the notion that many faculty members have about certain texts—that they are written for a specific audience. A text used by students at Harvard, for example, may not be appropriate for students at less elite schools.

One last note about this design: We need to communicate our findings in APA style. You may shudder at the thought of writing such a large number of results in an APA format paragraph. Fortunately, with larger designs such as this, researchers often take a shortcut when writing their results. Here's an example of a short way to communicate these findings:

> The quiz scores were analyzed with a three-way randomized ANOVA, using text, chapter, and school as independent variables. Students scored higher on learning quizzes (M = 6.17) than on biology quizzes (M = 4.67), $F(1, 40)$ = 12.96, p = .001, η^2 = .24. The text by school interaction was significant, $F(1, 40)$ = 10.24, p = .003, η^2 = .20, and is graphed in Figure 1 [*see Figure 9-13 in the text*]. All other main effects, two-way interactions, and the three-way interaction were nonsignificant (all ps > .20).

As you can see, we spent the bulk of our commentary on our significant effects and summarized the five nonsignificant effects (two main effects, two two-way interactions, and the three-way interaction) in a single sentence. This type of coverage not only is economical but also focuses on the important findings—those that were significant.

There is one last point we would like to emphasize. Several times in this chapter we have alluded to the possibility of deriving complex results. In a three-factor

definition

Post hoc tests
Statistical comparisons that are made between group means after finding a significant *F* ratio.

experiment, you have a chance of finding a significant three-way interaction. Just to give you an idea of the complexity involved, we will show you an example of a student project that generated a significant three-way interaction. Pamela Elfenbaum and Lynda Sagrestano (1993), for Elfenbaum's honor's thesis at the University of California at Berkeley, conducted a study of men and women in power situations. They studied the effects of sex, power (defined as expertise on an issue), and groups' sex composition on various influence behaviors in the context of a two-person discussion of a controversial issue. Figure 9-14 shows their results for the DV of bullying. As you can see, novices (those with low expertise) tended not to try to influence through bullying, regardless of whether they were male or female *or* whether they were in a same-sex or mixed-sex dyad (pair). Experts tended to use the bullying strategy, but mostly in mixed-sex dyads. That is, male experts attempted to bully female novices and female experts attempted to bully male novices. You should also note that male experts tended to bully in both types of groups, but to a higher degree in mixed-sex dyads. Although these results are somewhat complex, they are certainly clear and understandable. But clearly, three-way interactions are not amenable to simple interpretations.

A FINAL NOTE

For simplicity's sake, all the analyses we have shown in this chapter have dealt with IVs that had only two levels. You remember from Chapter 8 that we often wish to

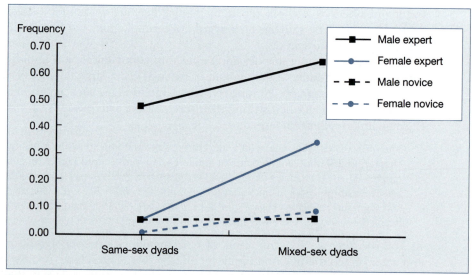

FIGURE 9-14 SIGNIFICANT THREE-WAY INTERACTION FROM ELFENBAUM AND SAGRESTANO (1993) Frequency of bullying is shown as a function of expert status, gender, and type of dyad.

Source: Figure 5 from "Influence Dynamics of Women and Men in Power Relationships" by P. D. Elfenbaum and L. M. Sagrestano, 1993. Paper presented to the American Psychological Society.

test IVs with more than two levels. In Figure 9-7 we showed you an example of a 3 × 3 design. This design had two IVs, each with three levels. Do you remember what happened in Chapter 8 when we found significance on an IV with three levels? To determine what caused the significant findings, we carried out **post hoc tests.** These tests that we calculated after finding a significant IV allowed us to determine which levels of that IV differed significantly.

Programmatic research A series of research experiments that deal with a related topic or question.

We hope that this issue has occurred to you at some point during this chapter. What do I do, in a factorial design, if an IV with more than two levels turns out to be significant? Assuming that this main effect is not qualified by an interaction, you would need to calculate a set of post hoc tests to determine exactly where the significance of that IV occurred.

THE CONTINUING RESEARCH PROBLEM

In Chapters 6 and 7 we began this section about our hypothetical continuing research problem. Our early interest was in determining whether an old textbook or a new textbook led to better student performance on quizzes. When we found that the new text was associated with higher scores, we enlarged our research question to include three different new texts (Chapter 8). Evidence showed that one of the three led to higher quiz scores, so we chose it to use in our introductory psychology course.

As you saw in Chapter 7, we began our research problem with a fairly simple question, and we got a fairly simple answer. However, that research led to a slightly more complex question, and so on. You should expect your research problems to show a similar pattern. Although you may start with a simple question and expect one experiment to provide all the answers, that is rarely the case. Keep your eyes open for new questions that arise after an experiment. Pursuing a line of **programmatic research** is challenging, invigorating, and interesting. Remember that pursuing such a line of research is how most famous psychologists have made names for themselves!

This chapter was more complicated than either Chapter 7 or Chapter 8. Let's review the steps we took in designing the experiments in this chapter. You may wish to refer to Figure 9-1 to follow each specific question.

1. After our preliminary research in Chapters 7 and 8, we decided to use two IVs (text, chapter) in these experiments. Each IV had two levels (text → old, new; chapter → learning, biological bases). This design allows us to determine the effects of the texts, the effects of the chapters, and the interaction between texts and chapters.

2. The DV was the score students made on each quiz.

3a. With large numbers of students, we randomly formed four groups of students, with each receiving one quiz from one text, resulting in a factorial between-groups design. We analyzed the quiz scores using a factorial ANOVA for independent groups and found that students performed best on quizzes on the learning chapter from the new text (see Figure 9-12).

3b. In a hypothetical situation when we had fewer students for the experiment, we used repeated measures on the chapter IV; that is, each student took both chapter quizzes. In addition, we formed matched pairs of students to control for intelligence and study habits, and we used these matched pairs for the text IV. Thus, this experiment used a factorial within-group design. We analyzed the data with a factorial ANOVA for correlated groups and found that students scored highest on quizzes from the new text's learning chapter (see Figure 9-12).

3c. In a third hypothetical situation, we had no previous quiz scores to form matched pairs. Thus, we randomly assigned students to the two text groups but did use repeated measures on the chapter IV so that students took both quizzes. This arrangement resulted in a factorial mixed-group design (one IV using independent groups, one using correlated groups). We analyzed the quiz scores with a factorial ANOVA for mixed groups and found the highest scores on the learning quizzes from the new text (see Figure 9-12).

4. We concluded that the new text would probably be the best choice for class. Although it seemed to make no difference for the biological bases quiz, students using the new text did perform better on the learning quizzes.

5. In our final experiment we added a third IV (school) to our design. This IV also had two levels (open vs. selective admission). This addition resulted in a $2 \times 2 \times 2$ completely between-subject design with text (old, new), chapter (biological bases, learning), and school (open, selective) as IVs. We analyzed quiz scores with a factorial ANOVA for independent groups and found that students made higher scores on learning quizzes than on the biological bases quizzes. The interaction between text and school was significant, with students at the open admissions school performing better on quizzes from the new text and selective admissions students doing better with the old text. Thus, the conclusion about which text is better depends on the type of school involved.

REVIEW SUMMARY

1. When you use an experimental design with two or more IVs and have only independent groups of participants, the proper statistical analysis is a factorial ANOVA for independent groups.

2. A factorial ANOVA for correlated groups is appropriate when your experimental design has two or more IVs and you used matched groups or repeated measures for all IVs.

3. If you have a design with two or more IVs and a mixture of independent and correlated groups for those IVs, you would use a factorial ANOVA for mixed groups to analyze your data.

4. ANOVA partitions the variability in the DV into separate sources for all IVs and their interactions and for error. F ratios show the ratio of the variation for the experimental effects to the error variation.

5. A significant F ratio for a main effect indicates that the particular IV caused a significant difference in the DV scores.

6. A significant interaction F ratio indicates that the two (or more) IVs involved had an interrelated effect on the DV scores. To make sense of an interaction, the DV scores should be graphed.

7. We use APA format to communicate our statistical results clearly and concisely. Proper format includes a written explanation of the findings documented with statistical results.

STUDY BREAK

1. You wish to compare the ACT or SAT scores of the freshman, sophomore, junior, and senior classes at your school as a function of sex. Draw a block diagram of this design. What design and statistical test would you use for this project?

2. You wonder whether test-taking practice and study courses can actually affect SAT or ACT scores. You recruit one group of students to help you. They take the test three times. Then you give them a study course for the test. They take an alternative form of the same test, also for three times. Thus, each student has taken two different tests three times (to study practice effects) and each student has taken the study course (to assess its effects). Draw a block diagram of this design. What design and statistical test would you use for this project?

3. You are interested in the same question as in Problem 2, but you recruit two groups of students to help you. One group takes the SAT or ACT three times; the other group has a study course and then takes the SAT or ACT three times. Draw a block diagram of this design. What design and statistical test would you use for this project?

4. What is an interaction effect? Why does a significant interaction render its associated main effects uninterpretable?

5. Suppose that in the hypothetical three-factor experiment presented earlier in this chapter, the three-way interaction was significant. Using Figure 9-13 as a starting point, show what the graph of such a significant interaction would look like. Draw a hypothetical example and write an interpretation of your hypothetical findings.

6. You wish to determine whether people's moods differ during the four seasons and by sex. What experimental design would you use for this research project? Why?

7. You choose to test people's preferences for fast food hamburgers based on three different restaurants (McDonald's, Burger King, Wendy's) and on three different age groups (children ages 4–12, college students, senior citizens). What experimental design would you use for this project? Why?

LOOKING AHEAD

In this chapter, we have learned about the most sophisticated of all experimental designs—the factorial designs that include multiple IVs. This completes a three-chapter section on experimental design, data analysis, and interpretation.

In the next chapter, we will look at two methods of evaluating our experiments. Our first concern will be with internal validity, where we ask questions about the soundness of our experiment. After satisfying that concern, we shift our attention to external validity, where we ask questions about applying our experimental findings to new situations and new groups.

HANDS-ON ACTIVITIES

In Chapter 8's hands-on activities we introduced the concept of personal space and asked you to replicate one of psychology's classic studies. You may remember that we cautioned you about a possible confounding problem in that study and urged you to control it. We were worried that the sex of the student and the confederate might interact in some way and cause you difficulty in your replication. Did you decide to control this confounding variable by holding it constant—say, by using only male-male pairs? Or did you attempt to balance this variable's effects in some way? Regardless of the control method you used, you were unable to assess the effects of student or confederate sex because you were using an experimental design with only one IV. Now that we have progressed to multiple-IV designs, we can conduct some original research to determine the effects of both student sex and confederate sex.

Two IVs

We wish to conduct an investigation of personal-space violation using the student participants' sex and the confederates' sex as IVs.

Psychological Detective

Draw a block diagram of this experiment. Which type of design (factorial between group, within group, or mixed) will be necessary? Give your answers before reading further.

Your block diagram should resemble Figure 9-1, with one factor being participant sex and the other confederate sex. The levels under each factor, of course, will be female and male. You will need to conduct this investigation with a factorial between-groups design because of the impossibility of using repeated measures with the measured IV of sex.

In order to maximize the personal-space violation, use only the extreme condition from Chapter 8—have the confederate sit immediately beside the student participant while there is no one else at the table. You will need confederates of both sexes to sit next to participants of both sexes. Use a 10-minute timing period and determine how quickly each student leaves the table, if at all. If the student does not leave, record 10 minutes and proceed to your next pairing. We recommend using at least 10 participants in each treatment group.

When you have gathered your data, you should have four groups of times, based on the combination of student participant and confederate sex (as in Figure 9-1). You will analyze your data with a factorial ANOVA for independent groups. You will probably find that some combinations of student sex and confederate sex lead to greater discomfort during personal space violation and, therefore, show very quick departures. Which combinations do you predict will lead to the greatest discomfort? Check these predictions after running the experiment.

Three IVs

In the previous experiment we recommended that you use only the most extreme personal space violation, that of sitting immediately beside the participant. If we add a third IV to the design, we can use all three personal-space conditions from Chapter 8—extreme, intermediate (sitting at the table but not immediately beside the participant), and control (no personal-space violation). This experiment's design will resemble Figure 9-8, with one exception.

Psychological Detective

How would you modify Figure 9-8 to accommodate this proposed experiment? Draw a diagram (with labels) of your answer before proceeding.

The difference of this proposed experiment with Figure 9-8 is that the proposed experiment is a $2 \times 2 \times 3$ experiment. Thus, Factor C (personal-space violation) in Figure 9-8 would have three levels (control, intermediate, extreme) rather than two. Factors A and B represent participant sex and confederate sex and would have two levels.

In order to make this proposed experiment economical, you may wish to make the personal space violation a repeated measure so that you need only 4 treatment groups measured three times each rather than 12 groups measured once. What do you think this experiment will demonstrate? We would not be surprised if you find some interesting interactions—some of the conditions that seemed quite uncomfortable in the previous experiment (using only the extreme personal-space violation) may not be so discomforting in less invasive conditions.

CHAPTER 10

How Good Is Your Experiment? Internal and External Validity

At this point in the text, we have covered all the basic information you need to know in order to conduct your research project. You know how to develop an experimental hypothesis (Chapter 2), how to choose your independent and dependent variables (Chapter 4), how to use control processes (Chapter 4), how to collect data and deal with your experimental participants (Chapter 5), and how to design, conduct, analyze, and interpret your experiment (Chapters 7 through 9). What is left to do? Well, you know that we are leading up to a chapter about writing your research report—we've referred to that several times. This chapter represents an important step you should take between the interpretation of your experimental data and writing your report. That step is evaluating your experiment.

An Introduction to Experiment Evaluation

When you evaluate your experiment, you should do so from two perspectives. First, you must evaluate the **internal validity** of your experiment. The question of internal validity revolves around **confounding** and **extraneous variables,** topics that we covered in Chapter 4. When you have an internally valid experiment, you are certain that your IV is responsible for the changes you observed in your DV. You have established a definite **cause-and-effect relationship,** knowing that the IV *caused* the change in the DV. For example, after many years of painstaking research, medical scientists know that cigarette smoking *causes* lung cancer. Although there are other variables that can also affect cancer, we know that smoking is a causative agent. Our goal as experimenters is to establish similar cause-and-effect relationships in psychology. To cite several such examples, we know that neurotransmitter imbalances can lead to behavioral abnormalities, reinforcement causes behavior to be repeated, multiple encodings of a stimulus item strengthen the memory for that item, intelligence is based on both biological and environmental factors, stress causes both positive and negative effects on our bodies and behavior, physical appearance affects our judgments of other people, and so on. In the case of other psychological concepts, we have not yet established definite cause-and-effect relationships, but we have developed hypotheses about such relationships. For example, when you studied abnormal behavior, you found that we have several theories about the etiology of most abnormal behaviors. Although definite cause-and-effect relationships are not established in such cases, researchers have several hypotheses that they are investigating. Experiments that are internally valid allow us to make statements such as "*X* causes *Y* to occur" with confidence.

The second type of evaluation that you must make of your experiment involves **external validity.** When you consider external validity, you are asking a question about **generalization.** The root word of *generalization* is "general." Of course, "general" is essentially the opposite of "specific." So, when we want to generalize our experimental results, we wish to move away from the specific to the more general. In essence, we would like to take our results beyond the narrow confines of our specific experiment. Imagine that you have conducted an experiment using 20 college students as your participants. Did your experimental question apply only to those 20 college students, or were you attempting to ask a general question that might be applicable to a larger group of students at your school, or to college students in general, or perhaps even to people in general? Few experimenters gather data that they intend to apply *only* to the participants they actually use in their experiments. Instead, they hope for general findings that will apply more broadly. When you examine different definitions of psychology, you find that many include a phrase about psychology being the "science of behavior." We don't think you've ever seen a definition that referred to the "science of blondes' behavior," or "the science of Californians' behavior," or "the science of children's behavior"—probably not even "the science of *human* behavior." Psychologists attempt to discover information that applies to everyone and everything. When we discover principles that apply broadly, then we have found behavior that is lawful. Finding such principles is a tall order, especially for a single experiment, but we keep this goal in mind as we do our research. We are ever mindful of the need and desire to extend our findings beyond our specific experiment.

> ## Generalization
> Applying the results from an experiment to a different situation or population.
>
> *definition*

Let us share with you a dilemma that this chapter posed for us. The dilemma revolved around where to put this chapter in the text. By placing it where we have, near the end of the book, you may get the idea that you need to worry about evaluating your experiment for internal and external validity only *after* you complete your experiment. Nothing could be farther from the truth. Rather, we hope that you are constantly evaluating your experiment. Much of what we have written for this chapter is designed to help you evaluate your experiment from Day 1—the day you first come up with an experimental idea. The information in this chapter dealing with internal validity enlarges on a topic that we have discussed several times throughout the text when we mentioned confounded experiments and extraneous variables and therefore would be appropriate to consult when designing your experiment. By the same token, researchers also take precautions when designing their experiments that will allow them to increase the generalizability of their final results. So, our dilemma was whether to place this chapter near the beginning of the book or near the back. We chose to put it near the back because you do need to step back to take another look at your experiment *after* you have completed collecting, analyzing, and interpreting your data. It is here that you are about to write your experimental report (see Chapter 12). Evaluating your experiment at this point gives you one last chance to check for any possible extraneous variables that may have occurred while you conducted your experiment. Also, at this point, you must decide how far you can legitimately generalize your results. Just as an artist steps back to scrutinize a painting or sculpture before unveiling it to the public, you have your last chance to detect any experimental flaws, no matter how minor they might be.

Another reason that we chose to place this chapter near the end of the text revolves around what you are likely to do with the information in this chapter in the future. Although we have written this chapter to help you evaluate your own research, it is a certainty that you will evaluate more studies conducted by other researchers than you will ever complete yourself. As you do a literature search for background information, you may look at hundreds of other articles. You will carefully scrutinize only a subset of those hundreds, but you will still read a good number of experimental articles. It is imperative that you are able to inspect those articles as closely as you would your own research project. You must be able to spot any flaws that might exist in these other studies because you will be basing your research on previous work of other researchers. If you base your study on research that has some flaw, your research may well end up being flawed. Let us give you an analogy. Suppose you were a medical doctor and needed to diagnose an illness in one of your patients. When you went to the lab, you accidentally picked up the lab reports for a different patient. How accurate would your diagnosis be for the original patient? Probably not very accurate! The parallel to designing your experiment is fairly close. If you begin your experiment with an incorrect premise or assumption, your experiment is probably doomed from its beginning. So, again, it is important to be able to evaluate other researchers' experiments before you begin your own.

If you are like many students, the last sentence of the previous paragraph may cause you some worry. You may wonder, "Who am *I* to be critiquing research conducted and published by psychologists?" If you find yourself saying something like this, you are selling yourself short. One of the behaviors our educational system fosters (sometimes too well) is respect for authorities. In school we learned that when we didn't have the answer for something, we could consult an authority. We could look up the answer in our book or in an encyclopedia, or we could ask a teacher. There is certainly nothing wrong with that approach—it helps make life much simpler. But this constant reliance on consulting authorities sometimes blinds us to the importance of questioning the answers we get (see our discussion of ways to acquire knowledge in Chapter 1). Although we are not encouraging you to become cynics about everything you hear, we do believe that it is important as well as valuable to carry around with you a little healthy skepticism. Thus, not only is it acceptable, but you are even encouraged to read research reports with a critical eye. *Do* think critically about the methods, the results, and the conclusions. *Do* question assumptions that researchers seem to make. *Do* wonder if there are other ways of defining and measuring the variables the experimenters used. In other words, don't merely be a passive recipient of experimental information—carefully sift it, weigh it, consider it before filing it away in your memory bank. Careful reading of and critical thinking about experimental reports has led many undergraduates (as well as graduate students and faculty members) to interesting and important research projects.

One final word before we begin our discussion of internal and external validity: We debated whether to use student research examples in this chapter and decided against it. Although we do not cite examples of experiments with problems in the chapter, using student examples while discussing potential problems might lead readers to draw inferences that we would not like. Thus, in the interest of preserving a high opinion of student research, you will find no student examples here.

INTERNAL VALIDITY: EVALUATING YOUR EXPERIMENT FROM THE INSIDE

In Chapter 4 we talked about the necessity for controlling extraneous variables in order to be able to reach a clear-cut conclusion from our experiment. It is only when we have designed our experiment in such a way to avoid the effects of potential extraneous variables that we can feel comfortable about making a cause-and-effect statement—that is, saying that Variable X (our IV) *caused* the change we observed in Variable Y (the DV). What we are trying to accomplish through our control techniques is to set up a buffer for our IV and DV so that they will not be affected by other variables. This reminds us of a cartoonlike toothpaste commercial we saw—perhaps you have seen it also. When the teeth brushed themselves with the particular brand of toothpaste being advertised, they developed a protective "invisible barrier" against tooth decay. In a similar fashion, our controls give our experiment a barrier against confounding (see Figure 10-1). In similar fashion, police detectives strive to make their case against a particular suspect airtight. If they have done their investigations well, the case against the accused should hold up flawlessly in court.

FIGURE 10-1 THE ROLE OF CONTROL PROCESSES IN PREVENTING EXPERIMENTAL CONFOUNDING

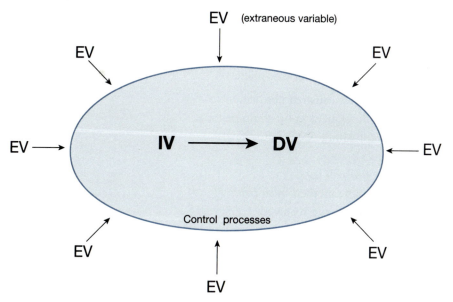

Dealing with the internal validity of an experiment is a funny process. We take many precautions aimed at increasing internal validity as we design and set up our experiment, but we usually specifically talk about internal validity only after we have completed our experiment. If this seems a little strange to you, don't be alarmed—it does seem odd at first. As we have told you previously in this chapter, internal validity revolves around the question of whether your IV actually created any change that you observe in your DV. As you can see in Figure 10-1, if you learned your lessons from Chapter 4 well and used adequate control techniques, your experiment should be free from confounding and you can, indeed, conclude that your IV caused the change in your DV. Let's review briefly.

Psychological Detective

Imagine that you have been given responsibility for conducting the famous Crest test—you are supposed to determine whether brushing with Crest toothpaste actually does reduce cavities. Your boss wants you to use an experimental group (Crest) and a control group (Brand X) in the experiment. Write down at least *five* potential extraneous variables for this experiment before reading further.

Although this exercise could easily have been an example dealing with confounding found in Chapter 4, it is also relevant to the issue of internal validity. If you fail to control an important extraneous variable, your experiment will not have internal validity. Were you able to list five possible extraneous variables? The list could be quite long; you may have thought of some possibilities that we didn't come up with. Remember, any factor that systematically differs between the two groups (other than the type of toothpaste) could be an extraneous variable and make it impossible to draw a definite conclusion about the effect of the toothpastes. Here's our (partial) list of possibilities:

number of times brushed per day

amount of time spent in brushing per day

how soon brushing occurs after meals

types of foods eaten

type of toothbrush used

dental genetics inherited from parents

degree of dental care received

different dentists' "operational definition" of what constitutes a cavity

whether the city's water is fluoridated

As we said, this list is not meant to be exhaustive—it merely gives you some ideas of factors that could be extraneous variables. To make certain you understand how an extraneous variable can undermine an experiment's internal validity, lets's use an example from the list above. In addition, we will discover why we take precautions aimed at internal validity *before* the experiment but assess the internal validity of an experiment *afterward*.

When you design the study, you want to make sure that children in the experimental and control groups brushed an equivalent number of times per day. Thus, you would instruct the parents to have their children brush after each meal. Your goal is to have all children brush three times a day. Suppose that you conducted the experiment and gathered your data. When you analyzed the data, you found that the experimental group (Crest) had significantly fewer cavities than the control group (Brand X). Your conclusion seems straightforward at this point: Brushing with Crest reduces cavities compared to brushing with Brand X. However, as you dig deeper into your data, you look at the questionnaire that you had the parents complete and find that children in the experimental group averaged 2.72 brushings a day compared to 1.98 times per day for the control group. Now it is obvious that your two groups differ on two factors—the type of toothpaste used *and* the number of brushings per day. Which factor is responsible for the lower number of cavities in the experimental group? It is impossible to tell! There is no statistical test that can separate these two confounded factors. So, you attempted to control the brushing factor before the experiment to assure internal validity. You could not assess your control technique until after the experiment, when you found out that your experiment was not internally valid. A word to the wise should be sufficient: Good experimental control leads to internally valid experiments.

THREATS TO INTERNAL VALIDITY

In this section we will alert you to several categories of factors that can cause problems with the internal validity of an experiment. These factors are details that you should attend to when planning and evaluating your own experiment and when scrutinizing research done by other investigators. This list is drawn largely from the work of Donald T. Campbell (1957) and his associates (Campbell & Stanley, 1966; Cook & Campbell, 1979).

History. We must beware of the possible extraneous variable of **history** in a repeated measures design (i.e., when experimental participants are measured more than once). We might administer the IV between the DV measurements (pretest, posttest), or we may be interested in the time course of the IV effect—how participants react to the IV over time. In this case, history refers to any significant event(s) other than the IV that occur between DV measurements. Campbell and Stanley (1966) cite the example of a 1940 experiment concerning informational propaganda. Attitudes were measured and then students read some Nazi propaganda. However, before the posttest was given, France fell to the Nazis. The subsequent attitude measurement was probably much more influenced by the historical event than

History A threat to internal validity; refers to events that occur between the DV measurements in a repeated measures design.

definition

by the propaganda. Obviously, this is an extreme example; historical events of this impact are rare. However, Campbell and Stanley also use the term to refer to less significant events that might occur during a lengthy experimental session. Noise or laughter or other similar events could occur during a session that might distract participants and cause them to react differently from participants who did not experience the same events. The distraction would then serve as an extraneous variable. One of our goals is to control or eliminate such distractions.

Maturation. This label seems to refer to experimental participants growing older during the course of an experiment, but that is somewhat misleading. Although true maturation is possible during a longitudinal study, Campbell (1957) used the term with a slightly different meaning. He did use **maturation** to refer to systematic time-related changes, but mostly of a shorter duration than we would typically expect. Campbell and Stanley (1966) gave examples of participants growing tired, hungry, or bored through the course of an experiment. As you can see, maturation would be possible in an experiment that extends over some amount of time. How much time must occur before maturational changes can take place could vary widely based on the experiment's demands on the participants, the topic of the experiment, or many participant variables (e.g., their motivation, how much sleep they got the night before, whether they have eaten recently, and so on). Maturational changes are more likely to occur in an experiment that uses repeated measures because experimental participants would be involved in the research for a longer period of time. You should attempt to safeguard against such changes if your experiment requires long sessions for your participants.

Testing. **Testing** is a definite threat to internal validity in repeated measures designs. As Campbell (1957) noted, if you take the same test more than once, scores on the second test may vary systematically from the first scores simply because you took the test a second time. This type of effect is often known as a **practice effect**—your score does not change because of anything you have done other than repeating the test.

For example, the people who run the testing services for the two major college entrance exams (ACT and SAT) acknowledge the existence of testing effects when they recommend that you take their tests two or three times in order to achieve your maximum possible score. It appears that there is some "learning to take a college entrance exam" behavior that contributes to your score on such tests. This factor is separate from what the test is designed to measure (your potential for doing college work). Thus, they are not surprised when your scores increase a little when you take the exam a second time; they actually expect an increase simply because you are familiar with the test and how it is given. However, two points about this specific testing effect are important to note. First, the effect is short-lived. You can expect to gain some points on a second (and perhaps third) attempt, but you will not continue to gain points indefinitely just from the practice of taking the test. If improvement was constant, students could "max out" their scores merely by taking the test many times. Second, the expected improvement is small. Both the ACT

Maturation
An internal validity threat; refers to changes in participants that occur over time during an experiment; could include actual physical maturation or tiredness, boredom, hunger, and so on.

Testing A threat to internal validity that occurs because measuring the DV causes a change in the DV.

Practice effect
A beneficial effect on a DV measurement caused by previous experience with the DV.

definition

administrators and the SAT administrators have a range of expected improvement that they consider normal. If you retake one of their tests and improve more than this normal range predicts, it is possible that your score will be questioned. You may be asked to provide documentation that accounts for your surprising improvement. If this documentation is not convincing, you may be asked to retake the test under their supervision. Unfortunately, the pressure to obtain scholarships (academic as well as athletic) has led some people to improve their scores through cheating or other unethical means.

In his discussion of testing effects, Campbell (1957) warned us against using **reactive measures** in our research. A measurement that is reactive changes the behavior in question simply by measuring it. This definition should sound somewhat familiar—remember **reactance (reactivity effect)** from Chapter 3? Let us refresh your memory with an example. One popular topic for social psychology research is attitude change. If you were going to conduct an experiment on attitudes and attitude change, how would you measure your participants' attitudes? If you are like most people, you probably responded "with an attitude questionnaire."

> **Reactive measures** DV measurements that actually change the DV being measured.
>
> **Reactance (reactivity effect)** The finding that participants respond differently when they know they are being observed.

Psychological Detective

Although questionnaires are commonly used to measure attitudes, they have a significant drawback. Can you figure out this drawback? Hint: This problem is particularly evident when you want to use an IV designed to change people's attitudes. Can you think of a means for overcoming this difficulty? Write your answers before moving on.

Many attitude questionnaires are reactive measures. If we ask you a number of questions about how you feel about people of different racial groups, or about women's rights, or about the President's job performance, you can probably figure out that an attitude is being measured. The problem with knowing that your attitude is being measured is that you can alter your answers on a questionnaire in any way you wish. For example, if I'm a woman administering a questionnaire to you, you may give answers that make you appear more sympathetic to women's issues. If I am of a different race than you, you may guard against giving answers that would make you look prejudiced. This type of problem is particularly acute if we use an experimental manipulation designed to change your attitude. If we give you a questionnaire about women's rights, then show you a pro–women's rights movie, then give you the questionnaire again, it doesn't take a rocket scientist to figure out that we're interested in finding out how the movie changed your attitude toward women's rights! What can you do?

Campbell (1957) advocated using **nonreactive measures** as much as possible. A nonreactive measure does not alter the participant's response by virtue of measuring it. Psychologists (and others) have devised many tools and techniques for nonreactive measures—one-way mirrors, hidden cameras and microphones, naturalistic observation, deception, and so on (see Chapter 3). If we are interested in your attitude about women's rights, perhaps we should see if you attend women's rights lectures or donate money to women's rights issues, ask you if you voted for a women's rights political candidate, or measure some other such behavior. In other words, if we can obtain some type of behavioral measure that is harder to fake than a questionnaire response, we may get a truer measure of your attitude. As a psychology student doing research, you should guard against using reactive measures, which are often appealing because they seem so easy to use.

Instrumentation (Instrument Decay). As with maturation, Campbell's category of instrumentation has a broader meaning than is implied by its name. Part of Campbell's (1957) description of **instrumentation** did refer to changes in measurement by various apparatuses, although his list now seems quite outdated (e.g., "the fatiguing of a spring scales, or the condensation of water vapor in a cloud chamber" [p. 299]). However, he also included human observers, judges, raters, and coders in this category. Thus, the broad definition of instrumentation refers to changes in measurement of the DV that are due to the measuring "device," whether that device is an actual piece of equipment or a human.

This measurement problem related to equipment is probably less of an issue today than it was in "the good old days." (By the way, "the good old days" is probably defined as whenever your professor was in school.) We're sure your instructor has a horror story about the time the equipment broke down in the middle of an important day of data collection. The reality of the situation is that even today equipment can break down or can develop flaws in measurement. You should always check out your equipment before using it to collect data each day. One of the drawbacks of modern equipment, such as computers, is that it may break down, but that fact will not be obvious to you. Although you can certainly tell whether or not a computer is working, you may not be able to tell if it appears to be working but actually has a bug or a virus. A careful experimenter checks out the equipment each day.

The same principle should govern your use of humans as monitors or scorers in your experiment. Often, you may serve as both the experimenter and the monitor or scorer for your experiment. This dual role places an extra obligation on you to be fair, impartial, and consistent in your behavior. In Chapter 4 we discussed the advantages of conducting a **double-blind experiment.** One of the major advantages of a double-blind situation is that you, as the experimenter, are able to remain neutral with respect to your different groups of experimental participants. For example, if you are scoring responses from your participants, you should have a set answer key with any judgment calls you might face worked out beforehand. So that you will not unconsciously favor one group over the other, you should score the responses blind as to which group a participant belongs to. If you have other persons scoring or monitoring your experiment, you should check their performance regularly to ensure that they remain consistent.

Statistical Regression. You may remember the concept of statistical regression from your statistics course. When you deal with extreme scores, it is likely that you will see regression to the mean. This merely means that if you remeasure participants who have extreme scores (either high or low), their subsequent scores are likely to regress or move toward the mean. The subsequent scores are still likely to be extreme in the same direction, but not as extreme. For example, if you made a very high A (or very low F) on the first exam, your second exam score will probably not be as high (or as low). If a 7′0″ basketball player has a son, the son will probably be tall but will probably be shorter than 7′0″. If a 4′6″ jockey has a son, the son will probably be short, but taller than 4′6″. When you have extreme scores, it is simply difficult to maintain that high degree of extremity over repeated measures.

How does **statistical regression** play a role in internal validity? It is fairly common to measure participants before an experiment in order to divide them into IV groups (based on whatever was measured). For example, imagine an experiment designed to test the effects of a study course for college entrance exams. As a preliminary measure, we give an ACT or SAT test to a large group of high school students. From this pool of students, we plan to select our experimental participants to take the study course. Which students are we likely to select? Why, of course, the ones who performed poorly on the test. After they take the study course, we have them retake the entrance exam. More than likely, we will find that their new scores are higher than the original scores. Why is this? Did the study course help the students improve their scores? It is certainly possible. However, isn't it also possible that regression toward the mean is at work? When you score near the low end of a test's possible score, there's not room to do much except improve. Sometimes it is difficult for people to see this point— they are convinced that the study course must be responsible for the improvement. To help illustrate the power of statistical regression, imagine a similar experiment performed with students who made the highest scores on the entrance exams. We want them to take our study course also. After our study course, we find that their second test scores are actually *lower* than the first set! Did our study course lower their scores? We certainly hope not. Having made an extremely high score on the first test, it is difficult to improve on the second.

The advice concerning statistical regression should be clear. If you select participants on the basis of extreme scores, you should beware of regression toward the mean as a possible explanation for higher or lower scores on a repeated (or similar) test.

Selection. It should come as no surprise to you that **selection** can serve as a threat to internal validity. We have discussed the problem of participant selection repeatedly in the last three chap-

Statistical regression A threat to internal validity that occurs when low scorers improve or high scorers fall on a second administration of a test due solely to statistical reasons.

Selection A threat to internal validity; if we choose participants in such a way that our groups are not equal before the experiment, we cannot be certain that our IV caused any difference we observe after the experiment.

definition

ters. Let us review briefly. Before we conduct our experiment, it is imperative that we can assume that our selected groups are equivalent. Starting with equal groups, we treat them identically except for the IV. Then if the groups are no longer equal after the experiment, we can assume that the IV caused that difference.

Suppose, however, that when we select our participants, we do so in such a way that the groups are not equal before the experiment. In such a case, differences that we observe between our groups after the experiment may actually reflect differences that existed *before* the experiment began. On the other hand, differences after the experiment may reflect differences that existed before the experiment *plus* a treatment effect. To avoid such a problem, you should use the control techniques mentioned in Chapter 4.

Be careful not to confuse the selection problem with assignment of participants to groups. Selection typically refers to using participants who are already assigned to a particular group by virtue of their group membership. Campbell and Stanley (1966) cite the example of comparing people who watched a particular TV program to those who did not. People who choose to watch a program or not to watch a program probably differ in ways other than the knowledge of the program content. For example, it is likely that there are differences in people who watch and those who do not watch soap operas that are unrelated to the actual content of the soap operas. Thus, using soap opera viewers and non–soap opera viewers as groups to study the impact of a particular soap opera episode dealing with rape is probably not the best way to study the impact of that episode.

Mortality. As you might guess, death is the original meaning of "mortality" in this context. In research that exposed animals to stress, chemicals, or other toxic agents, mortality could actually occur in significant numbers. Mortality could become a threat to internal validity if a treatment was so severe that significant numbers of animals in the treatment group died. Simply because they had survived, the remaining animals in the treatment group would probably be different in some way from the animals in the other groups. Although the other groups would still represent random samples, those in the particular treatment group would not.

In human research, **mortality** typically refers to experimental dropouts. Remember the ethical principle from Chapter 2 that gives participants the right to withdraw from an experiment at any point without penalty. A situation somewhat analogous to the animal example in the preceding paragraph could occur if many participants from one group withdraw from the experiment compared to small numbers from other groups. If such a differential dropout rate occurs, it is doubtful that the groups of participants would still be equal, as they were before the experiment began.

If your experiment contains a treatment condition that is unpleasant, demanding, or noxious in any way, you should pay careful attention to the dropout rate for the various groups. Differential dropout rates could also be a significant problem in research that spans a long time (weeks or months, for example). If one group shows a higher rate, your experiment may lack internal validity. One final word of caution: It is possible that groups in your experiment will not show different rates of dropping out

Mortality A threat to internal validity that can occur if experimental participants from different groups drop out of the experiment at different rates.

Reprinted with special permission of King Features Syndicate.

"Today is the final session of our lab on rats, and Willy, I don't think I have to remind you that this time if you eat yours, I'm not giving you another one."

We certainly hope that you never experience this type of mortality in your research!

but will have previously experienced different rates that helped compose the groups. Campbell (1957) cited the example of a very common experiment in educational settings, namely, making comparisons of different classes. Suppose we wish to determine whether our college's values-based education actually affects the values of the students. We choose a sample of freshmen and a sample of seniors and give them a questionnaire to measure their values in order to see whether their values are in line with our general education curriculum's values goals.

Psychological Detective

How might previous dropout rates damage the internal valid-   ity of this experiment? Write your answer before reading any further.

In this experiment it should not surprise you to find that the seniors' values are more in line with our college's stated values. Although this effect *could* be a result of taking our values-based curriculum, it could also represent the effect of mortality

Interactions with selection Threats to internal validity that can occur if there are systematic differences between or among selected treatment groups based on maturation, history, or instrumentation.

through dropouts. Most colleges bring in large numbers of freshmen and graduate only some percentage of those students a few years later. What type of student is more likely to leave? Probably students whose values are not in line with the college's values are more likely to drop out than those who agree with the college's values. Thus, when we assess seniors' values, we are measuring those students who did *not* drop out.

Interactions with Selection. In Chapter 9 we introduced factorial experiments and the related concepts of main effects and interactions. According to Campbell (1957; Cook & Campbell, 1979), the threats to internal validity we have discussed thus far function like main effects. In other words, they could have their extraneous effects separate and apart from other factors or variables. However, some of these threats to internal validity can also have interactive effects with the selection threat to produce other new threats. The chief culprits for interaction effects are selection-maturation, selection-history, and selection-instrumentation (Cook & Campbell, 1979).

These **interactions with selection** can occur when the groups we have selected show differences on another variable (i.e., maturation, history, or instrumentation) that vary systematically by groups. Let us give you an example for clarification. Suppose we are conducting a language development study in which we select our two groups from lower- and middle-class families. We wish to avoid selection as a threat to internal validity, so we pretest our children with a language test to ensure that our groups are equivalent beforehand. However, this pretesting could not account for the possibility that these two groups may show different maturation patterns, despite the fact that they are equal before the experiment begins. For example, if we look at children around the age of one, we may find that the two classes of children show no language differences. However, by age two, middle-class children might have larger vocabularies, talk more often, or have other linguistic advantages over lower-class children. Then if we look at children who are six, these linguistic advantages may disappear. If this were the case, comparing lower- and middle-class children's language proficiency at age two would show a selection-maturation interaction that would pose a threat to internal validity. Although one group of children would show an advantage over another group, the difference would not be a reliable, lasting difference. Therefore, any conclusion we reached that implied the permanence of such an effect would be invalid because the difference would have been based on different maturation schedules of the two groups.

As we said, similar interaction effects could occur between selection and history or between selection and instrumentation. A selection-history interaction that would jeopardize internal validity could occur if your different groups are chosen from different settings—for example, different countries, states, cities, or even schools within a city. This problem is especially acute in cross-cultural research (see Chapter 5). These different settings allow for different local histories (Cook & Campbell, 1979) that might affect the outcome variable(s). The selection and history are confounded together because the groups were selected on a basis that allows different histories. An example of a selection-instrumentation interaction (based on human "instrumentation") would be using different interpreters or scorers for participants that come from two different countries, assuming the IV was related to the country of origin.

Diffusion or Imitation of Treatments. **Diffusion or imitation of treatments** creates a problem with internal validity by negating or minimizing the difference between the groups in your experiment. This problem can occur easily if your treatment involves providing some information to participants in one group but not to participants in another group. If the informed participants communicate the vital information to the supposedly uninformed participants, then the two groups may behave in identical manners.

Psychological Detective

If these two groups behave identically, what experimental conclusion would you draw? What would be wrong with this conclusion? Write your answers before going further.

If the participants behave identically, the experimental outcome would indicate no difference between the groups based on the IV. The problem with this conclusion is that in truth, there would actually be no IV in the experiment because the IV was supposed to have been the difference in information between groups. It is typical for experimenters to request that participants not discuss details of the experiment until it is completed.

Experiments dealing with learning and memory are particularly susceptible to the imitation of treatments. For example, suppose we want to teach students in our classes a new, more effective study strategy. To simplify the experiment, we will use our 9:00 A.M. general psychology class as a control group and our 10:00 A.M. general psychology class as the experimental group. We teach the 9:00 A.M. class as usual, saying nothing to the students about how they should study for their quizzes and exams. In the 10:00 A.M. class, however, we teach our new study technique. After the first few quizzes and the first major exam, the students in the 10:00 A.M. class are so convinced of the effectiveness of their new study approach that they talk to their friends in the 9:00 A.M. class about it. Soon everyone in the 9:00 A.M. class knows about the new study technique and is also using it faithfully. At this point, we have the problem of treatment diffusion. Our participants in both groups are now using the same study strategy, which effectively no longer gives us an IV. This example deals with a between-subjects approach (different participants in each group). As you can well imagine, this problem is much more likely to occur in a within-subjects design using repeated measures. In such a design the participants would actually experience both (or all) levels of a particular IV. In this case, the participants would be free to use the strategy they

Diffusion or imitation of treatment A threat to internal validity that can occur if participants in one treatment group become familiar with the treatment of another group and copy that treatment.

definition

like the best, regardless of what you, as the experimenter, instructed them to do. It should be obvious that if you cannot guarantee control over the IV, the hope of having an experiment with internal validity is not strong.

Psychological Detective

 After discussing nine different threats to internal validity, we hope that you have been thinking about how to protect your experiment against these threats. Take a few moments to compose your thoughts about what measures you could take to "inoculate" your experiment against these problems. Record your answer before reading any further.

In the next section of this chapter we will provide several answers to this question.

REVIEW SUMMARY

1. For your experiment to have **internal validity,** it must be free from confounding due to extraneous variables.

2. There are nine specific threats to internal validity that we must guard against.

3. The **history** threat can occur if meaningful events that would affect the DV occur between two measurements of the DV (repeated measures).

4. The **maturation** threat may occur if experimental participants show some change due to time passage during an experiment.

5. The **testing** threat results if participants respond differently on the second measure of a DV simply because they have responded to the DV previously.

6. An **instrumentation** threat can refer to equipment changes or malfunctions *or* to human observers whose criteria change over time.

7. **Statistical regression** is a threat that can occur when participants are selected because of their extreme scores on some variable. Extreme scores are likely to regress toward the mean on a second measurement.

8. The **selection** threat results if we select groups of participants in such a way that our groups are not equal before the experiment.

9. **Mortality** becomes a threat if participants drop out of the experiment in different rates for different conditions.

10. **Interactions with selection** can occur for history, maturation, or instrumentation. If we select participants in such a way that they vary on these dimensions, then internal validity is threatened.

11. Diffusion or imitation of treatments is a threat if participants learn about treatments of other groups and copy them.

STUDY BREAK

1. Why is it important to evaluate your experiment for internal validity?

2. Match the internal validity threat with the appropriate situation.

1. history *b*
2. maturation *c*
3. testing *d*
4. instrumentation *a*

a. Your DV scorer gets sick and you recruit a new person to help you.
b. You are conducting an experiment on racial prejudice and a race riot occurs between tests.
c. Your participants grow bored and disinterested during your experimental sessions.
d. You use a before-and-after DV measurement and the participants remember some of their answers.

3. Match the threat to internal validity with the correct situation.

1. statistical regression *d*
2. mortality *a*
3. selection *b*
4. diffusion of treatments *c*

a. Many participants find one treatment condition very boring and quit.
b. You select males from lower-class homes and females from upper-class environments.
c. Students in your control group talk to students in the experimental group and imitate their treatment.
d. You select the worst students in the class and try a new tutoring strategy.

4. You want to compare the formal education of college students and senior citizens. You select a group of each type of participant and give each a written test of math, social studies, and grammatical information. What threat of internal validity appears likely in this situation? Why?

PROTECTING INTERNAL VALIDITY

How did you attempt to answer our query in the prior Psychological Detective section? There are two approaches you could take to fight the various threats to internal validity. In the first approach, you would attempt to answer the question nine different ways, giving one answer for each threat. Although this approach would be effective in controlling the threats, it would be time consuming and, perhaps, difficult to institute that many different controls simultaneously. We hope that the idea of the second approach occurred to you, even if you could not come up with a specific recommendation. How about controlling these threats through the use of experimental design? Detectives use standard "police procedures" to help them

Random assignment
A control technique that ensures that each participant has an equal chance of being assigned to any group in an experiment.

protect their cases; experimental design procedures can help us as psychological detectives.

In the three previous chapters we presented you with a variety of experimental designs, often noting various control aspects of those designs. However, we never mentioned the nine general threats to internal validity until this chapter. Can we apply experimental design to these problems? According to Campbell (1957) and Campbell and Stanley (1966), the answer is yes. Let's take a look at their recommendations.

Random Assignment. Although **random assignment** is not a specific experimental design, it is a technique that we can use within our experimental designs. Remember, with random assignment (see Chapter 4) we distribute the experimental participants into our various groups on a random (nonsystematic) basis. Thus, all participants have an equal chance of being assigned to *any* of our treatment groups. The purpose behind random assignment is to create different groups that are equated before beginning our experiment. According to Campbell and Stanley (1966, p. 25), "the most adequate all-purpose assurance of lack of initial biases between groups is randomization." Thus, random assignment can be a powerful tool. The only drawback to random assignment is that we cannot *guarantee* equality through its use.

One caution is in order at this point. Because *random* is a term used often in experimental design and methodology, it sometimes has slightly different meanings. For example, in Chapters 7, 8, and 9, we repeatedly referred to "independent" groups to describe groups of participants that were not correlated in any way (through matching, repeated measures, or natural pairs or sets). It is not unusual to see or hear such independent groups referred to as "random groups." Although this label makes sense because the groups are unrelated, it is also somewhat misleading. Try to remember back to Chapter 7 when we first talked about matching participants. At that point we stressed that after making your matched pairs of participants, you *randomly assigned* one member of each pair to each group. The same is true of naturally occurring pairs (or sets) of participants. These randomly assigned groups would clearly *not* be independent. Because of the power of random assignment to equate our groups, we must use it at every opportunity. Campbell and Stanley note that "within the limits of confidence stated by the tests of significance, randomization can suffice without the pretest" (1966, p. 25). Thus, according to Campbell and Stanley, it may not even be necessary to use matched groups because random assignment can be used to equate the groups.

Psychological Detective

What is the major exception to Campbell and Stanley's argument that randomization will create equal groups? Write your answer before reading further.

We hope that you remembered (from Chapters 7–9) that randomization is sup-posed to create equal groups *in the long run*. Therefore, you need to be aware of randomization's *possible* shortcoming if you conduct an experiment with small numbers of participants. Although randomization may create equal groups with few participants, we cannot be as confident about this possibility as when we use large groups.

Finally, you should remember from Chapter 4 that random assignment is *not* the same as **random selection.** Random assignment is related to the issue of inter-nal validity, whereas the notion of random selection is more involved with external validity, a topic we will consider later in this chapter.

Experimental Design. Campbell and Stanley (1966) reviewed six experimental designs and evaluated them in terms of controlling for internal validity. They rec-ommended three of the designs as being able to control the threats to internal va-lidity we have introduced in this chapter. Let's examine their three recommended designs.

The Pretest-Posttest Control Group Design. The pretest-posttest control group de-sign is diagrammed in Figure 10-2. As you can see, this design consists of two ran-domly assigned groups of participants, both of which are pretested, and one of which receives the IV.

The threats to internal validity that we summarized in this chapter are con-trolled by one of two mechanisms in this design. The random assignment of partici-pants to groups allows us to assume that the two groups are equated before the ex-periment, thus ruling out *selection* as a problem. Using a pretest and a posttest for *both* groups allows us to control the effects of *history, maturation,* and *testing* because they should affect both groups equally. If the control group shows a change between the pretests and posttests, then we know that some factor other than the IV is at work. *Regression toward the mean* is controlled as long as we assign our experimental and control groups from the same extreme pool of participants. If any of the *interactions with selection* occur, they should affect both groups equally, thus negating those effects on internal validity.

> **Random selection**
> Choosing participants from a population in such a way that all possible participants have an equal opportunity to be chosen.

FIGURE 10-2   THE PRETEST-POSTTEST CONTROL GROUP DESIGN

R	O_1		O_2	(control group)
R	O_3	X	O_4	(experimental group)

KEY:

R = Random assignment

O = Pretest or posttest observation or measurement

X = Experimental variable or event

Each row represents a different group of participants.

Left-to-right dimension represents passage of time.

Any letters vertical to each other occur simultaneously.

(Note: This key also applies to Figures 10-3, 10-5, and 10-6)

The other threats to internal validity are not controlled, but the pretest-posttest control group design does give us the ability to determine whether or not they were problematic in a given experiment. We can check to see whether *experimental mortality* was a problem or not because we measure both groups on two occasions. *Instrumentation* is measured if we are dealing with responses to a test, for example, but could still remain a problem if human interviewers or observers are used. There is simply no substitute for pre-training when you use humans to record or score data for you. Finally, *diffusion or imitation of treatments* could still remain a problem if participants from the control group (or different experimental groups) learn about the treatments for other groups. Again, though, you do have the control group as a "yardstick" to determine whether their scores increase or decrease in similar fashion to the experimental group's. If you see similar changes, you can suspect that internal validity controls may have failed.

The Solomon Four-Group Design. Figure 10-3 contains a diagram of the Solomon four-group design, first proposed by Solomon (1949). Notice that this design is identical to the pretest-posttest control group design with the first two groups but adds an additional two groups—thus gaining the name "four-group design." Because the Solomon four-group design has the same two groups as the pretest-posttest control group design, it has the same protection against the threats to internal validity. As you will see later in this chapter, the main advantage gained by adding the two additional groups relates to external validity.

FIGURE 10-3   THE SOLOMON FOUR GROUP-DESIGN   This design is used to protect internal validity.

$$
\begin{array}{lll}
R & O_1 & O_2 \\
R & O_3 \quad X & O_4 \\
R & & O_5 \\
R & \quad\;\; X & O_6
\end{array}
$$

One problem with the Solomon design revolves around statistical analysis of the data because there is no statistical test that can treat all six sets of data at the same time. Campbell and Stanley (1966) suggest treating the *posttest* scores as a factorial design, as shown in Figure 10-4. Unfortunately, this approach ignores all the pretest scores.

The Posttest-Only Control Group Design. Figure 10-5 shows the posttest-only control group design. As you can see by comparing Figure 10-5 to Figures 10-2 and 10-3, the posttest-only control group design is a copy of the pretest-posttest control group design but without the pretests included and is a copy of the two added groups in the Solomon four-group design. Does the lack of pretests render the posttest-only control group design less desirable than the other two designs that included them? No, because we can count on the random assignment to groups to equate the two groups. Thus, using random assignment of participants to groups and withholding the IV from one group to make it a control group is a powerful experimental design that controls the threats to internal validity we covered in this chapter.

FIGURE 10-4 FACTORIAL TREATMENT OF SOLOMON FOUR-GROUP DESIGN POSTTEST SCORES

	No IV	Receives IV
Pretested	O_2	O_4
Unpretested	O_5	O_6

Psychological Detective

After examining Figure 10-5, what type of design (from Chapters 7 through 9) does this appear to be? Write your answer before reading on.

We hope that you identified Figure 10-5 as the two-group design from Chapter 7. However, we must point out that it is *not* critical to have only two groups in this design. The posttest-only control group design could be extended by adding additional treatment groups, as shown in Figure 10-6. This extended design should

FIGURE 10-5 POSTTEST-ONLY CONTROL GROUP DESIGN   This is a powerful design for protecting internal validity.   .

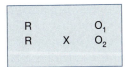

R O_1
R   X O_2

FIGURE 10-6 AN EXTENSION OF THE POSTTEST-ONLY CONTROL GROUP DESIGN
This design allows for testing multiple treatment groups.

R O_1
R X_1 O_2
R X_2 O_3
•   •   •
•   •   •
R X_n O_{n+1}

remind you of the multiple-group design from Chapter 8. Finally, we could create a factorial design from the posttest-only control group by combining two of these designs simultaneously so that we ended up with a block diagram similar to those from Chapter 9.

Psychological Detective

It should be clear that the posttest-only design is *not* defined by the number of groups. What is(are) the defining feature(s) of this design? Take a moment to study Figures 10-5 and 10-6 before recording your answer.

The two features that are necessary to "make" a posttest-only control group design are random assignment of participants to groups and the inclusion of a control (no treatment) group. These features allow the design to derive cause-and-effect statements by equating the groups before the experiment and controlling the threats to internal validity.

We hope you can appreciate the amount of control that can be gained by the two simple principles of random assignment and experimental design. Although these principles are simple, they are quite elegant in the power they bring to the experimental situation. You would be wise not to underestimate their importance.

THE BOTTOM LINE

How important is internal validity? It is only *the* most important property of any experiment. If you do not concern yourself with the internal validity of your experiment, you are "spinning your wheels" and wasting your time. Experiments are intended to derive cause-and-effect statements—to conclude that "*X* causes *Y* to occur." If you merely wish to learn something about the association of two variables, you can use one of the nonexperimental methods for acquiring data summarized in Chapter 3 or calculate a correlation coefficient. However, if you wish to investigate the cause(s) of a phenomenon, you must take care to control any extraneous variables that might affect your dependent variable. You cannot count on your statistical tests to provide the necessary control functions for you. Statistical tests merely analyze the numbers you bring to the test—they do not have the ability to remove confounding effects (or even to discern that confounding has occurred) in the data you bring.

One final caution is in order as we move toward the second major topic of this chapter: You must worry about internal validity before concerning yourself with external validity. An experiment without internal validity *cannot* have external validity.

Psychological Detective

Think about the previous sentence. Why can't you have an internally invalid experiment that is externally valid? Jot down your answer now.

If our experiment does not have internal validity, then we can place no confidence in its results. If you have results in which you have no confidence, why would you want to apply those results to a larger population? You must be confident that your experiment is internally valid before you look at generalizing your results. An internally valid experiment is not necessarily externally valid, but it has the potential to be.

REVIEW SUMMARY

1. One important control for internal validity is **random assignment of participants to groups.** This assures us that the groups are equated before beginning the experiment.

2. **Random selection** refers to choosing our participants from a population so that all potential participants could be chosen. Random selection is important to external validity.

3. The **pretest-posttest control group** design consists of two groups of participants that are randomly assigned to an experimental and control group, pretested and posttested, with the experimental group receiving the IV. This design controls for internal validity threats but has the problem of including a pretest.

4. The **Solomon four-group** design is a copy of the pretest-posttest control group design except that it adds two groups that are not pretested. This design also controls for internal validity tests but there is no statistical test that can be used to analyze all six sets of data.

5. The **posttest-only control group** design consists of two groups of participants that are randomly assigned to an experimental and control group with the experimental group receiving the IV treatment. Both groups are tested with a posttest. This design controls for internal validity threats and is free from other problems.

6. The posttest-only control group design can be extended to include additional treatment groups or additional IVs.

7. It is essential for an experiment to be internally valid. Otherwise, no conclusion can be drawn from the experiment.

Study Break

1. The two general methods that we use to protect the internal validity of our experiment are _____ _____ and _____ _____.

2. Why is it essential to use random assignment of our participants to their groups?

3. Distinguish between random assignment and random selection.

4. What is the drawback of using the pretest-posttest control group design to help with internal validity?

5. What is the drawback of using the Solomon four-group design as a control for internal validity?

6. Diagram the posttest-only control group design. Why is it a good choice for controlling internal validity?

7. Explain the following statement: An experiment cannot have external validity if it is not internally valid.

External Validity: Generalizing Your Experiment to the Outside

After you have satisfied yourself that your experiment (or an experiment that you are evaluating) is internally valid, then you can focus on its potential for external validity. As we mentioned earlier in this chapter, the question of external validity revolves around whether you can take the results of a particular experiment and generalize them beyond that original experiment. Generalization is an important aspect for any science—there are very few occasions when scientists wish to restrict their conclusions to only the relevant conditions of their original experiment. Although police detectives are usually interested in a specific culprit, they are also interested in developing criminal profiles that describe general traits of a specific type of offender (e.g., the profile of mass murderers or of child molesters).

There are three customary types of generalization in which we are interested. In **population generalization,** we are concerned about applying our findings to organisms beyond our actual experimental participants. When our students conduct research with fellow students from Emporia State University or Ouachita Baptist University as participants, they are not interested in applying their results only to students from their respective college. We doubt that many of you who do experimental projects will be trying to answer a question about your peers only at your school. Likewise, psychologists are not typically concerned with trying to discover truths about the humans or animals who actually compose the participants in their studies. Instead, in all cases we have just mentioned, the researchers (including you) are usually trying to discover general principles about behavior that are applicable to people or animals as a whole. Thus, we must concern ourselves with whether or not our results will apply to a larger group than our experimental participants.

Environmental generalization refers to the question of whether our experimental results will apply to situations that are different from that of our experiment. Again, it is doubtful that we are interested in finding results that are specific to the environment in which we tested our participants. Can we generalize our results from a college classroom or research lab in which we collected our data to other classrooms or labs or even the real-world environments in which behavior naturally occurs?

Finally, **temporal generalization** describes our desire that our research findings apply at all times and not to only a certain time period. For example, the discovery of seasonal affective disorder (depression only during winter months) is an exception to generalized information about depressive disorders. Can we be certain that research findings from the 1960s about gender differences are still applicable today? Such an issue raises thorny questions for the concept of temporal generalization.

We are forced to ask questions about the external validity of our research results because of the very property that we were concerned about in the first portion of this chapter—internal validity. To achieve a high degree of internal validity, researchers seek to exert control over a large number of factors. The best way to exert control over factors is to conduct your experiment in a lab (or similar setting) with participants who are highly similar.

definition

Environmental generalization
Applying the results from an experiment to a situation or environment that differs from that of the original experiment.

Temporal generalization
Applying the results from an experiment to a time that is different from that when the original experiment was conducted.

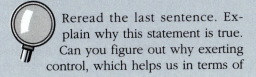

Psychological Detective

Reread the last sentence. Explain why this statement is true. Can you figure out why exerting control, which helps us in terms of internal validity, ends up weakening our external validity? Record your answers before moving on.

When we conduct our research in a laboratory, we can control many factors that might function as extraneous variables in the real world. For example, you can control factors such as temperature, lighting, outside noise, and so forth. In addition, you control the time at which your participants come to the experimental situation, as well as when and under what conditions they experience the IV. In short, the lab allows you to remove or hold constant the effects of many extraneous variables, which would be virtually impossible in the real world. In a similar fashion, using participants who are highly similar helps to reduce extraneous variation. For example, if you use only college students as participants, you will have an idea of their general reading ability if you have to compose a set of instructions for them to read. In the real world, potential participants would have a much wider range of reading abilities, thus adding extraneous variation to the experiment (see our discussion of nuisance variables in Chapter 4).

We hope that you can see that these advantages for internal validity become disadvantages for external validity. When we control so many factors so tightly, it is difficult to know if our results will apply to people or animals who are markedly different from our research participants and who encounter our research factors in the real world rather than in the artificial laboratory.

THREATS TO EXTERNAL VALIDITY (BASED ON METHODS)

Campbell has also written widely about factors relating to external validity. We will summarize four factors affecting external validity from Campbell and Stanley (1966).

Interaction of Testing and Treatment. When Campbell and Stanley (1966) rated the three experimental designs that we previously summarized (pretest-posttest control group, Solomon four-group, posttest-only control group) for internal validity, they also attempted to rate them concerning external validity (although that task is much more difficult). The **interaction of testing and treatment** is the most obvious threat to external validity, and it occurs for the pretest-posttest control group design (see Figure 10-2). External validity is threatened because both groups of participants are pretested and there is no control to determine whether the pretesting has an effect. As Solomon (1949) pointed out, "There is a great possibility that merely taking a pre-test changes the subjects' attitudes toward the training procedures" (p. 141).

Imagine that you are working on an experiment dealing with prejudice, specifically anti-Semitism. You decide to pretest your participants by giving them an anti-Semitism scale before showing them the movie *Schindler's List*. Does it seem likely that these people's reaction to the movie will be different from that of a group of people who were *not* pretested? This is the essence of an interaction between testing and treatment—because of a pretest, your participants' reaction to the treatment will be different. The pretest has a sensitizing effect on your participants; it is somewhat like giving a giant hint about the experiment's purpose before beginning the experiment. The pretesting effect is particularly troublesome for experiments that deal with attitudes and attitude change. This testing and treatment interaction is the reason that nonpretesting designs such as the posttest-only control group design were developed. Also, although the Solomon four-group design does incorporate pretests for two groups, it includes no pretesting of the remaining two groups, thus allowing for a measurement of any pretesting effect.

Interaction of Selection and Treatment. You will remember earlier in the chapter we covered "interactions with selection" as a threat to internal validity. In those cases, selection potentially interacted with other

Interaction of testing and treatment A threat to external validity that occurs when a pretest sensitizes participants to the treatment yet to come.

threats to internal validity such as history, maturation, and instrumentation. In this instance, however, the threat to external validity consists of an interaction between selection and treatments.

An **interaction of selection and treatments** occurs when the effects that you demonstrate hold true only for the particular groups that you selected for your experiment. Campbell and Stanley (1966) note that the threat of a selection by treatment interaction becomes greater as it becomes more difficult to find participants for your experiment. As it becomes harder to get participants, it becomes more likely that the participants you do locate will be unique and not representative of the general population.

One of your authors ran into a selection and treatment interaction when he was attempting to complete his doctoral dissertation, in which he was testing a particular explanation of a common and easy-to-find phenomenon. He had to conduct his experiment during summer school because he ran short of time. When he analyzed the data, the supposedly easy-to-find phenomenon was not evidenced by the statistics. Rather than concluding that the phenomenon did not exist (contrary to *much* published evidence), he decided that this finding was a result of a selection-treatment interaction. When he conducted his experiment a second time during the regular semester, the ubiquitous effect was found. It appears that for some reason, the summer school students were a unique population.

Reactive Arrangements. Reactive arrangements revolve around the artificial atmosphere of many psychological experiments. Because of our desire for control, we may create a highly contrived situation in a laboratory in which we attempt to measure a real-world behavior. There are some cases in which this type of arrangement is probably a dismal failure. As you saw in Chapter 4, experimental participants, particularly humans, seek clues about their environments. They may react to our experimental manipulations, but also to subtle cues that they find in the experimental situation. As Campbell and Stanley remarked, "The play-acting, outguessing, up-for-inspection, I'm-a-guinea-pig, or whatever attitudes so generated are unrepresentative of the school setting, and seem to be qualifiers of the effect of *X*, seriously hampering generalization" (1966, p. 20). Although their comment was directed at educational research, if we substitute "real world" for "school setting," the quote remains valid. Thus, **reactive arrangements** refer to those conditions of an experimental setting (other than the IV) that alter our participants' behavior. We cannot be sure that the behaviors we observe in the experiment will generalize outside that setting because these artificial conditions do not exist in the real world.

In Chapter 3 we mentioned a series of studies that are usually cited as being classic examples of reactive arrangements, the Hawthorne studies. You recall that productivity of a subset of plant workers was studied over a period of time. This subset of workers tended to increase productivity regardless of the changes instituted in their environment. One of the representative experiments dealt with the level of illumination in a work area. A control group worked in a room with 10 foot-candles of light while the experimental group's illumination began at 10 foot-candles and

Interaction of selection and treatment A threat to external validity that can occur when a treatment effect is found only for a specific sample of participants.

Reactive arrangements A threat to external validity caused by an experimental situation that alters participants' behavior, regardless of the IV involved.

definition

Demand characteristics
Cues from an experiment that give a participant some idea about the experimental hypothesis.

Multiple treatment interference A threat to external validity that occurs when a set of findings results only when participants experience multiple treatments in the same experiment.

was gradually decreased 1 foot-candle at a time until it reached 3 foot-candles. At this point, "the operatives protested, saying that they were hardly able to see what they were doing, and the production rate decreased. The operatives could and did maintain their efficiency to this point in spite of the discomfort and handicap of insufficient illumination" (Roethlisberger & Dickson, 1939, p. 17).

In Chapter 4 we introduced the concept of **demand characteristics.** According to Orne (1962), demand characteristics can convey the experimental hypothesis to the participants and give them clues about how to behave. You (or your friends) may have experienced something similar to demand characteristics if you are a psychology major. When you tell people you are a psychology major, a common response is "Are you going to psychoanalyze me?" Rather than responding to *you,* they are responding to the demand characteristics of a psychology major.

Orne believes that it is impossible to design an experiment without demand characteristics. He also believes that demand characteristics make generalizations difficult because it is not clear from a set of research findings whether the participants are responding to an experiment's IV, its demand characteristics, or both. It seems that reactive arrangements tend to increase demand characteristics, thus creating further difficulties with generalization.

Multiple Treatment Interference. As you can probably guess from the name of this threat to external validity, **multiple treatment interference** can occur only in experiments that involve presenting more than one treatment to the same participants, known as repeated measures designs. The potential problem that arises in repeated measures designs is that the findings we obtain may be specific to situations in which the experimental participants experience these multiple treatments. If they receive only one treatment, then the experimental results are different.

Campbell and Stanley (1966) cite Ebbinghaus's memory work as an example of multiple treatment interference. Ebbinghaus was a pioneer in the field of verbal learning, conducting many experiments of learning lists of nonsense syllables by serving as his own experimental participant. He is responsible for giving us early versions of many common learning phenomena such as learning and forgetting curves. However, as it turns out, some of Ebbinghaus's findings are specific to people who have learned a large number of lists of nonsense syllables and do not apply to people learning a single list of nonsense syllables. Thus, Ebbinghaus's results show a clear failure to generalize, based on the concept of multiple treatment interference.

Psychological Detective

In Chapter 8 we discussed the multiple-group design. Under what condition is multiple treatment interference a concern in the multiple-group design? When should you not worry about multiple treatment interference in the multiple-group design? Write an answer before you proceed.

By definition, multiple treatment interference can occur only when participants experience more than one treatment. Experiencing more than one treatment occurs in the multiple-group design *if* you use repeated measures. However, the remaining variations on the multiple-group design would not allow for multiple treatment interference. Independent groups, matched sets, or natural sets require using different participants in each group.

This ends the list of four threats to external validity summarized by Campbell and Stanley (1966). Let's take a brief look at five additional threats to external validity that are based on our experimental participants.

THREATS TO EXTERNAL VALIDITY (BASED ON OUR PARTICIPANTS)

We must always remember that our experimental participants are unique individuals just as the detective must remember that fact about each criminal. Certain unique traits may get in the way of our ability (or the detective's ability) to draw general conclusions.

The Infamous White Rat. Way back in 1950 (before one of your authors was even born), Frank Beach sounded the alarm about a distressing tendency he saw in **comparative psychology.** By charting the publication trends in that field from 1911 to 1947, he found that more and more articles were being published but fewer species were being studied. The Norway rat became a popular research animal in the 1920s and began to dominate research in the 1930s. Beach examined 613 research articles and found that 50% of them dealt with the rat, despite the fact that the Norway rat represented only .001% of all living creatures that could be studied.

Psychological Detective

Why should Beach's data give us reason for concern regarding external validity? Write two reasons before reading further.

There are two obvious concerns with external validity that arise from Beach's data. First, if you are interested in the behavior of subhumans, generalizing from rats to all other animals may be a stretch. Second, if you are interested in generalizing from animal to human behavior, there are certainly closer approximations to humans than rats in the animal kingdom.

The Ubiquitous College Student. We hope that you have had occasion to conduct a literature search at this point in your course. If you have, you should have noticed that experimental

Comparative psychology The study of behavior in different species, including humans.

First published in *APA Monitor.* Reprinted by Warren A. Street.

"There's always an oddball subject that screws up your data."

Sometimes it's hard to tell which participants are more numerous in psychology experiments—lab rats or college students!

definition

Convenience sampling A researcher's sampling of participants based on ease of locating the participants; often does not involve true random selection.

articles contain a subjects subsection within the methods section. Two momentary asides here: (1) The label "subjects" is to be replaced with "participants" according to the fourth edition of APA's *Publication Manual.* (2) You previously encountered the methods section in Chapter 5. We will put all the pieces of an experimental article together in Chapter 12.

If your literature search involved human participants, you probably noticed that college students very likely served as participants in the research you reviewed. There is a simple explanation for this fact. Psychology departments that support animal research typically have animal lab facilities—often colonies of rats, as we saw in the preceding section. Psychologists who want to conduct human research have no such labs filled with participants, of course, so they turn to a ready, convenient source of human participants—students in introductory psychology courses (a technique referred to as **convenience sampling**). Often students may be required to fulfill a certain number of hours of experimental participation in order to pass their introductory class. As well as providing a healthy supply of participants for psychology experiments, this requirement is rationalized as being an educational experience for the students. Such requirements have generated heated debates, some of which have focused on ethics. You will note in the ethical principles covered in Chapter 2 that coercion is not acceptable in finding experimental participants.

We are including this section not to focus on the ethics of using students as research participants but, rather, to focus on the implications of this reliance. Sears (1986) raised this very issue with regard to social psychology. He pointed out that early social psychologists studied a variety of types of participants, including populations as diverse as radio listeners, voters, soldiers, veterans, residents of housing projects, industrial workers, union members, and PTA members. However, by the 1960s psychology had become entrenched in using laboratory experiments with college students as participants.

Is it a problem to rely almost exclusively on college students? Clearly, such reliance is similar to the reliance on the white rat by animal researchers. Sears (1986) cited evidence concerning the differences between adolescents and adults and between college students and other late adolescents. He worried that several notable social psychology findings may be the product of using college students as participants rather than the larger population in general.

Psychological Detective

Reread the last sentence. Can you identify Sears's position as consistent with one of Campbell and Stanley's threats to external validity we discussed previously? Write an answer (and your rationale for the answer) before you read more.

Sears's hypothesis that some social psychology findings may be specific to college students fits into Campbell and Stanley's selection by treatment interaction. If Sears is correct, then a specific treatment might "work" only for college students. On the other hand, a particular IV might have a stronger (or weaker effect) for college students than for the general population.

As an example, Sears mentioned that much of social psychology revolves around attitudes and attitude change—research often shows that people's attitudes are easily changed. However, developmental research shows that the attitudes of late adolescents and young adults are less crystallized than those of older adults. Thus, we have to wonder whether people's attitudes really are easily changed or whether this finding is merely an artifact of the population that is most often studied—the college student.

Although Sears concentrated on social psychology findings, it does not take much thought to see how similar problems might exist in other traditional research areas of psychology. For example, because college students are both students and above average in intelligence, might their learning and memory processes be a poor representation of those processes in the general population? Motivational patterns in adolescents are certainly different in some ways from those processes in adults. The stresses affecting college students differ from those facing adults—might the coping processes be different also? We know that some mental illnesses are age related and therefore strike older or younger people more often. Overall, we should be careful in generalizing to the general population from results derived only from college students.

The "Opposite" or "Weaker" or "Inferior" or "Second" Sex. All four derogatory labels—"opposite," "weaker," "inferior," and "second"—have been applied to women at various points in time. As you took your school's required history, literature, and humanities classes, you probably noticed that famous women were in short supply. For many years (some would argue even now), women were simply not given the same opportunities as men in many situations.

This supposed inferiority of women carried over into psychological theories. For example, Freud's theories are biased toward men—remember castration anxiety and the Oedipus complex? The "parallel" concepts for women of penis envy and the Electra complex seem almost to be afterthoughts. The concept of penis envy, supposedly part of equating Freud's theory for women and men, has been attacked repeatedly by feminists. Erik Erikson's theory of psychosocial crises was labeled the "Eight Stages of Man." Not only did the name not acknowledge women, neither did the stages. Many women have not identified with Erikson's stages to the extent that men have. As Carol Tavris (1992) eloquently points out about developmental theories, "Theorists writing on adult development assumed that adults were male. Healthy 'adults' follow a single line from childhood to old age, a steady path of school, career, marriage, advancement, a child or two, retirement, and wisdom—in that order" (p. 37).

Tavris's thesis is that "despite women's gains in many fields in the last twenty years, the fundamental belief in the normalcy of men, and the corresponding abnormality of women, has remained virtually untouched" (p. 17). Tavris's ideas confront us with an interesting question: Are we developing a body of knowledge that pertains to all organisms, regardless of sex? One detail we mentioned about APA style in Chapter 5 and will emphasize in Chapter 12 is its requirement of nonsexist language in writing. Words carry hidden meaning, and sexist writing may lead to generalizations that are unwarranted. As psychology students, you should definitely be attuned to this issue. Surveys of psychology undergraduates across the country estimate that almost three quarters of all psychology majors are women. You may even encounter difficulty finding male participants for your future experiments. Without adequate male representation, the generality of your findings could be questioned.

Again, a word of caution is in order. When we generalize our findings, we typically generalize them to as large a segment of the population as we can. Beware of drawing sexist conclusions from your research.

Even the Rats and Students Were White. This section's heading is an adaptation of the title of Robert Guthrie's thought-provoking book *Even the Rat Was White* (1976). In the book, Guthrie chronicles many of the "scientific" attempts to measure and categorize African-Americans as inferior to Caucasians, such as anthropometric measurements (e.g., skull size and cranial capacity), mental testing, and the eugenics movement (improvement of heredity through genetic control).

Some psychology students may believe that there were no African-American pioneers in psychology. That assumption is far from the truth. Guthrie (1976) provides a list of the 32 African-Americans who earned doctorates in psychology and educational psychology in American universities between 1920 and 1950. He provides brief background and career sketches for 20 of these individuals. Let us give you a glimpse of two of these persons. Guthrie devotes a chapter to Francis Cecil Sumner, whom he labels the "Father of black American psychology" (p. 175). Sumner, born in Pine Bluff, Arkansas, was the first African-American to earn a Ph.D. in psychology in the Western Hemisphere. He earned his degree from Clark University in June 1920. His chief instructor was G. Stanley Hall; he also took courses from E. G. Boring. Sumner's dissertation title was "Psychoanalysis of Freud and Adler," which was later published in *Pedagogical Seminary* (later renamed the *Journal of Genetic Psychology*). Sumner went on to teaching positions at Wilberforce University and West Virginia Collegiate Institute. In 1928 he accepted a position at Howard University, becoming chair of the newly established department of psychology in 1930. Under Sumner's leadership Howard became one of the major producers of African-American Ph.D.s in psychology. He remained at Howard until his death in 1954.

Ruth Winifred Howard was the first African-American woman to earn a doctorate in psychology, from the University of Minnesota in 1934. (Inez Beverly Prosser had earned a Ph.D. in educational psychology from the University of Cincinnati one year earlier.) Howard's dissertation, "A Study of the Development of Triplets," was one of the first studies to deal with a sizable group of triplets. She completed a clinical internship at the Illinois Institute for Juvenile Research and spent her career in private practice in clinical psychology.

Just as history has failed to record the accomplishments of many women throughout time, it has largely ignored the accomplishments of African-Americans and other minority groups. Jones (1994) has pointed out the inherent duality of being an African American—that one is separately considered an African and an American. Other writers have made similar points about and pointed out problems for members of other minority groups—for example Marín (1994) for Hispanics, Lee and Hall (1994) for Asians, and Bennett (1994) for American Indians. According to Lonner and Malpass (1994b), projections indicate that in the next century the United States will be 24% Hispanic, 15% African-American, and 12% Asian. Thus, Caucasians will be in a minority for the first time in U.S. history. When we conduct research and make generalizations, we should be cautious that we do not exclude minority groups from our considerations.

Even the Rats, Students, and Minorities Were American. Although experimental psychology's early roots are based in Europe, this aspect of the discipline quickly became Americanized, largely due to the influence of John B. Watson's behaviorism. For many years the study of human behavior was actually the study of *American* behavior. However, in the mid-1960s this imbalanced situation slowly began to change as psychologists started taking culture and ethnicity more seriously (Lonner & Malpass, 1994a). We mentioned this new emphasis on ethnicity in the previous section and wish to introduce the notion of culture in this section.

The field of **cross-cultural psychology** has evolved from those changes that began in the 1960s. Today you can find text-

Cross-cultural psychology
The study of psychological principles in a variety of cultures to determine the limitations and the generality of those principles.

definition

Ethnocentric
Describes a belief or statement that is biased toward the individual's ethnic group.

books and courses devoted to this topic. We introduced you to cross-cultural research in Chapter 5. Because cross-cultural psychology "is primarily concerned with testing possible limitations to knowledge by studying people of different cultures" (Matsumoto, 1994, p. 15), it is closely intertwined with external validity. In fact, cross-cultural psychology tests the very limits of external validity. It asks the question of how far a set of experimental findings can be extended to other cultures. If our psychology is made up of findings that are applicable only to Americans, then we should not claim that we know everything there is to know about *human* behavior! Making an **ethnocentric** claim such as that is akin to American professional baseball claiming to play the *World* Series. What about the professional teams in Japan and other countries? Similarly, we shouldn't study maternal behaviors in the United States and claim that we know everything there is to know about mothering. Again, a word to the wise: Let's be careful about making grandiose claims about external validity when we don't have all the data. With our shrinking world of today, it is becoming easier and easier to conduct true cross-cultural research. Both the Lonner and Malpass (1994) book and the Matsumoto (1994) book will give you some good ideas about behavioral differences that exist as a function of culture.

THE DEVIL'S ADVOCATE: IS EXTERNAL VALIDITY ALWAYS NECESSARY?

Several years ago Douglas Mook (1983) published a thought-provoking article entitled "In Defense of External Invalidity." In this article Mook attacked the idea that all experiments should be designed to generalize to the real world. He maintained that such generalization is not always intended or meaningful.

Mook cited as an example Harlow's work with baby rhesus monkeys and their wire mesh and terrycloth surrogate mothers. As you no doubt remember, the baby monkeys received nourishment from the mesh mothers and warmth and contact from the cloth mothers. Later, when faced with a threatening situation, the baby monkeys ran to the cloth mothers for comfort. As virtually all introductory psychology students learn, Harlow's work has been used to support the importance of contact comfort for the development of attachment. Was Harlow's research strong in external validity? Hardly! Harlow's monkeys could scarcely be considered representative of the monkey population because they were born in the lab and orphaned. Was the experimental setting lifelike? Hardly! How many baby monkeys (or human infants) will ever be faced with a choice between a wire or cloth "mother"?

Did these shortcomings in external validity negate Harlow's findings? As Mook pointed out, that depends on the conclusion that Harlow wished to draw. What if Harlow's conclusion had been "Wild monkeys in the jungle probably would choose terry-cloth over wire mothers, too, if offered the choice" (Mook, 1983, p. 381)? Clearly, this conclusion could not be supported from Harlow's research because of the external validity problems mentioned in the previous paragraph.

On the other hand, Harlow could conclude that his experiment supported a theory of contact comfort for mother-infant attachment over a nourishment-based (drive reduction) theory. Is there a problem with this conclusion? No, because Harlow did not attempt a generalization—he merely drew a conclusion about a theory, based on a prediction from that theory. Mook argues that our concern with external validity is necessary only when we are trying to "predict real-life behavior in the real world" (p. 381). However, there are reasons to conduct research that do not involve trying to predict behavior in the real world. Mook points out four alternative goals of research that do not stress external validity. First, we may merely want to find out if something *can* happen (not whether it usually happens). Second, we may be predicting from the real world to the lab—seeing a phenomenon in the real world, we think it will operate in a certain manner in the lab. Third, if we can demonstrate that a phenomenon occurs in a lab's unnatural setting, the validity of the phenomenon may actually be strengthened. Finally, we may study phenomena in the lab that don't even have a real-world analogy.

We do not mean to undermine the importance of external validity by presenting Mook's arguments. However, it is important to know that not all psychologists worship at the shrine of external validity. Being concerned with real-world applications is certainly important, but (unlike internal validity) it is not an absolute necessity for every experiment. By the same token, the detective does not attempt to generate a generalized criminal profile for each crime that is committed.

The Bottom Line

Psychological Detective

Just as with internal validity, we have looked at nine different threats to external validity. We hope you have been considering these threats in light of your potential experiment. What can you do in an attempt to avoid external validity problems? Write an answer before you go on.

This is probably the most difficult Psychological Detective question of this chapter; there is a sense in which this question is a trick. It *may* be impossible to conduct a single experiment that has perfect external validity. If you attempted to devise an experiment that answered every threat to external validity that we listed, you might be old and gray before you completed the experiment. Imagine trying to find a pool of human experimental participants that would satisfy sex, race, ethnicity, and cultural generalizability. You would need to find large numbers of participants from around the world—clearly an impossible situation.

Does the dismal conclusion of the previous paragraph mean that we should merely throw up our hands and quit? Are we justified in ignoring the problem of

Replication
An additional scientific study that is conducted in exactly the same manner as the original research project.

Replication with extension
An experiment that seeks to confirm (replicate) a previous finding but does so in a different setting or with different participants or under different conditions.

external validity? Of course not! The important question becomes one of what steps we can take to maximize our chances of achieving external validity. First, we recommend that you pay particular attention to the first four external validity threats that we listed. To a large extent, you do have control over interactions of testing or selection and treatment, reactive arrangements, and multiple treatment interference. Careful experimental planning can usually allow you to avoid problems with those factors.

If you can control the methodological threats to external validity, that leaves you with the participant-related threats. It is unrealistic to expect any one experiment to be able to include all the various participants we would need to generalize our results across the world's population. Campbell and Stanley (1966) wrote that "the problems of external validity are not logically solvable in any neat, conclusive way" (p. 17). What is the solution?

It seems logical that the solution must involve an approach we discussed in Chapter 1—**replication.** When we replicate an experimental finding, we are able to place more confidence in that result. As we begin to see the same result time after time, we become more comfortable with the idea that it is a predictable, regularly occurring result. However, it is shortsighted for us to continually test the same types of participants in every experiment we conduct, whether those participants are white rats or white American college students. Thus, we need to go beyond replication to experiments that involve replication with extension.

In a **replication with extension** experiment, we retest for a particular experimental finding, but we do so in a slightly (or even radically) different context. For example, if we think we know a great deal about how American college students learn lists of nonsense syllables, we should not try to generalize those results to all humans. Instead, we should broaden our participant population. Do the same rules apply when we test elderly people, children, and less-educated people? Do the same findings occur when we test Hispanic-Americans, Asian-Americans, and African-Americans? Are the results similar in Japan, China, Peru, Australia, and so on? When we begin to collect data from experiments as indicated by the previous three sentences, then we truly start learning whether or not our findings are generally applicable.

There is another advantage to experiments that utilize replication with extension. Many times pure replication experiments are frowned on. Journals rarely, if ever, publish a straight replication study. Most undergraduates who complete required experimental projects are told that their projects must be original, that the project cannot be a replication study. Often, a replication with extension involves enough new work and produces enough new information that it will be acceptable either for a class requirement or for publication—or for both if you're extremely fortunate!

So what is the bottom line? We believe it is unrealistic to expect every (or any) experiment to be applicable to the entire world of animals or people. That type of external validity is probably a myth that exists only in fairy tales. However, we also believe that you should strive to make your experiment as externally valid as possible. That is, when you have choices, opt for the choices that will increase the external validity of your findings.

REVIEW SUMMARY

1. If your experiment is internally valid, then you can worry about **external validity,** which deals with applying your findings to new groups **(population generalization),** new situations **(environmental generalization),** and new times **(temporal generalization).** There are many threats to external validity.

2. The **interaction of testing and treatment** threat can occur if you pretest your participants and the pretest changes their reaction to the posttest.

3. The **interaction of selection and treatment** threat occurs if your findings apply only to the groups you selected for your experiment.

4. **Reactive arrangements** can threaten external validity if the experimental situation changes our participants' behavior.

5. **Multiple treatment interference** may threaten external validity if participants experience more than one treatment and this multiple participation causes a change in behavior.

6. Experimental psychology has been criticized for using only a narrow slice of possible types of participants in research. Animal research is particularly imbalanced by its overuse of rats as participants.

7. Human research has tended to focus on white, American college students as participants. Many theories seem to be aimed heavily or exclusively at men.

8. For reasons of external validity, there is currently a greater focus on research involving participants from the general population, women, ethnic minorities, and other cultures.

9. There are occasional instances when the external validity question is not relevant to research.

10. It is nearly impossible to devise a single experiment that can answer all questions about external validity. Conducting experiments that involve replication with extension is a good way to simultaneously increase external validity and gather new information.

STUDY BREAK

1. What is external validity? Why is it important to psychology?

2. Distinguish among population, environmental, and temporal generalization.

3. Why should we be concerned about trying to use different types of participants (such as minorities and people who are not college students) in psychology studies?

4. What is cross-cultural psychology? Why is it of particular relevance to this section of the chapter?

5. Match the external validity threat with the proper description.

1. testing-treatment interaction
2. selection-treatment interaction
3. reactive arrangements
4. multiple treatment interference

a. An effect occurs only if participants experience all the experiment's treatment conditions

b. Women, but not men, demonstrate an experimental effect.

c. Only participants who are pretested demonstrate an experimental effect.

d. Demand characteristics provide cues to the participants about how they should respond.

6. Why does Mook argue that external validity is not always necessary?

7. Why is the notion of external validity for a single experiment virtually impossible to achieve?

LOOKING AHEAD

At this point in the text you have learned how to complete the majority of the steps that are necessary to complete a psychological experiment. In this chapter you have learned how to evaluate your experiment's internal and external validity. Before we move on to completing your experimental report, we will look at some alternative research approaches that you may need to use sometime.

HANDS-ON ACTIVITIES

1. **Finding and Identifying Internal Validity Threats.**   Go to your college's library and find 10 experimental journal articles that are in your area of research interest. Read the method sections of those articles carefully. Note which threats to internal validity occurred in each experiment and the manner in which the researchers controlled for each threat. Can you find any threats that you believe the researchers may have missed? Prepare to give a 3-5 minute oral presentation to your class about the threat that you found most often in your research area.

2. **Protecting Internal Validity.**   Review your 10 journal articles from Activity 1 again. How many of the experiments used random assignment as a control technique? If random assignment was not used, what control was used in its place? How many of the 10 articles used the (1) pretest-posttest control group design, (2) Solomon four-group design, or (3) posttest-only control group design? Which design was the most popular? As you read the articles, can you determine why that design was most often used?

3. **Looking for Methodological External Validity Threats.**   In this chapter we summarized four threats to external validity based on the methodology of an exper-

iment. Again using your 10 experiments from Activity 1, can you find any evidence that experimenters guarded against these four threats in their experiments? If you find such examples, list the particular threat and the method used to guard against it. When you do not find such precautions, recommend at least one appropriate course of action for each experiment.

4. **Looking for Generalization beyond Participants.**   Go to your library and find 10 studies that used rats and 10 studies that used college students as participants. Read the discussion sections of these articles, looking for claims about generalizability. Do researchers tend to generalize beyond their particular research participants in either specific or implied manners? If so, do they provide any rationale for doing so? If not, do they mention why their conclusions are limited?

5. **Erroneous Generalization Concerning Sex, Race, or Culture.**   Find a book or summary of research concerning sex, race, or culture. Look for information concerning a particular research finding that was once thought to apply to everyone but that was later found to be specific to a specific sexual, racial, or cultural group. What implications did or could this faulty generalization have?

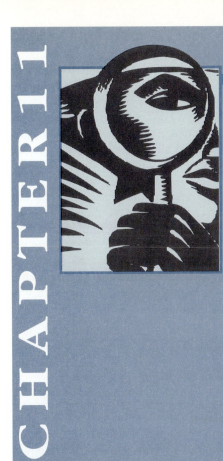

Alternative Research Approaches

Single-case experimental design
An experiment that consists of one participant (*also known as N = 1 designs*).

Case study approach
An observational technique in which we compile a record of observations about a single participant.

In Chapter 3 we learned about various nonexperimental methods of acquiring information. In the last four chapters, we learned about several different experimental designs (Chapters 7–9) and how to evaluate an experiment that used one of those designs (Chapter 10). Given that we have covered both nonexperimental methods *and* experimental designs, you probably think that we have exhausted all the methods psychologists use. Almost, but not quite! In this chapter we will cover three additional approaches to gathering information that psychologists sometimes use. If these methods were not covered in the chapters on nonexperimental and experimental approaches, then where does that leave them? These approaches exist somewhat in limbo—if we drew a continuum line with nonexperimental at one end and experimental at the other, these approaches would fall somewhere toward the experimental end. As we talk about these three approaches—single-case designs, quasi-experimental designs, and qualitative research—we will point out in more detail why these approaches seem neither fish nor fowl.

SINGLE-CASE EXPERIMENTAL DESIGNS

In the case of **single-case experimental designs** (also known as *N* = 1 designs), the name says it all. This term simply refers to an experimental design with one participant. This approach, of course, is quite similar to the detective's strategy of pursuing a single suspect.

Psychological Detective

The *N* = 1 approach probably sounds familiar to you. What data-gathering approach have we studied that involves one participant? Write your answer before reading further.

We hope you remember the **case study approach** from Chapter 3. In a case study, we conduct an intense observation of a single individual and compile a record of those observations. As we noted in Chapter 3, case studies are often used in clinical settings. If you have taken an abnormal psychology course, you probably remember reading case studies of people with various disorders. The case study is an excellent descriptive technique—if you read about an individual with a mental disorder, you get a vivid picture of what that disorder is like. However, a case study is *merely* a descriptive or observational approach; no variables are manipulated or controlled, observations are simply recorded. Thus, case studies do *not* allow us to draw cause-and-effect conclusions.

You will remember that we must institute control over the variables in an experiment in order to derive cause-and-effect statements. In a single-case design, we institute controls just as in a typical experiment—the only difference is that our experiment deals with only one participant. We hope that the single-case design raises many questions for you. After all, it does go against the grain of some principles we have developed thus far. Let's take a quick look at this design's history and uses, which will help you understand its importance.

HISTORY OF SINGLE-CASE DESIGNS

The single-case experimental design has quite an illustrious past in experimental psychology (Hersen, 1982; Hersen & Barlow, 1976). In the 1860s Fechner explored sensory processes through the use of psychophysical methods. Fechner developed two concepts that you probably remember from your introductory psychology course: sensory thresholds and the just noticeable difference (jnd). Fechner conducted his work on an in-depth basis with a series of individuals. Wundt's pioneering work with introspection was done with highly trained individual participants. Ebbinghaus conducted perhaps the most famous examples of single-case designs in our discipline. You may remember from Chapter 10 that Ebbinghaus was the pioneer in the field of verbal learning and memory. His research was somewhat unique, not that he used the single-case design, but that he was the single participant in those designs. According to Dukes (1965), Ebbinghaus learned about 2,000 lists of nonsense syllables in his research over many years. Dukes provides several other examples of famous single-case designs with which you are probably familiar, such as Cannon's study of stomach contractions and hunger, Watson and Rayner's study of Little Albert's learned fears, and several researchers' work with language learning in individual apes.

Other than the ape-language studies, all these single-case design examples date to the 1800s and early 1900s. Dukes (1965) found 246 single-case examples in the literature between 1939 and 1963. Clearly, there are fewer examples of single-case designs than group designs in the literature. Why is the difference so great? Hersen (1982) attributes the preference for group designs over single-case designs to statistical innovations made by Fisher. Sir Ronald A. Fisher was a pioneer of many statistical approaches and techniques. Most importantly for this discussion, in the 1920s, he developed ANOVA (Spatz, 1993), which we covered in some detail in Chapters 8 and 9. Combined with Gossett's early 1900s development of a test to accompany the t distribution (see Chapter 7), Fisher's work gave researchers a set of inferential statistical methods with which to analyze sets of data and draw conclusions. You may have taken these tests for granted, assuming that they had been around forever, but this is not the case. As these methods became popular and accessible to more researchers, the use of single-case designs declined. In today's research world, statistical analyses of incredibly complex designs can be completed in minutes (or even seconds) on computers that you can hold in your hand. The ease of these calculations has probably contributed to the popularity of group designs over single-case designs.

Tom Cheney

"Sooner or later he'll learn that when he presses the bar, he'll receive a salary."

Much psychological knowledge has been gained from single-case designs.

USES OF SINGLE-CASE DESIGNS

There is still a group of researchers who use single-case designs. Founded by B. F. Skinner, the **experimental analysis of behavior** approach still employs this technique. Skinner summarized his philosophy in this manner: "Instead of studying a thousand rats for one hour each, or a hundred rats for ten hours each, the investigator is likely to study one rat for a thousand hours" (1966, p. 21). The Society for the Experimental Analysis of Behavior was formed and began publishing its own journals, the *Journal of the Experimental Analysis of Behavior* (in 1958) and the *Journal of Applied Behavior Analysis* (in 1968). Thus, single-case designs are still used today. However, the number of users is small in comparison to group designs, as you could guess with only two journal titles devoted to this approach.

One question that might occur to you is "Why use a single-case design in the first place?" Dukes (1965) provided a number of convincing arguments for and situations that require single-case designs. Let's look at several. First, a sample of one is all you can manage if that sample exhausts the population. If you have access to a participant that is unique, you simply cannot find other participants. Of course, this example is perhaps closer to a case study than to an experiment because there would be no larger population to which you could generalize your findings. Second, if you can assume perfect generalizability, then a sample of one

Experimental analysis of behavior A research approach popularized by B. F. Skinner in which a single participant is studied.

definition

is appropriate. If there is only inconsequential variability between members of the population on a particular variable, then measuring one participant should be sufficient. Third, a single-case design would be most appropriate when a single *negative* instance would refute a theory or assumed universal relationship. If the scientific community believes that "all gaxes are male," then finding one female gax invalidates the thesis. Fourth, you may simply have limitations on your opportunity to observe a particular behavior. Behaviors that are real-world (i.e., nonlaboratory behaviors) in nature may be so rare that you can locate only one participant who exhibits the behavior. Dukes used examples of people who exhibit multiple personality disorder (again, close to a case study), who feel no pain, or who are totally color blind. You may remember reading about H.M. when you studied memory in introductory psychology. Because of surgery for epilepsy that removed part of his brain, H.M. could no longer form new long-term memories. Researchers have studied H.M. endlessly for clues about how the brain forms new memories (Corkin, 1984). Fifth, when research is extremely time consuming and expensive, requires extensive training, or is quite difficult to control, an investigator may choose to study only one participant. The studies in which researchers have attempted to teach apes to communicate through sign language, plastic symbols, or computers would fall into this category. Thus, it does seem that there are valid instances in which a single-case design would be totally appropriate.

> **Baseline** A measurement of a behavior that is made under normal conditions (i.e., no IV is present); a control condition.

GENERAL PROCEDURES OF SINGLE-CASE DESIGNS

Hersen (1982) lists three procedures that are characteristic of single-case designs: repeated measures, baseline measurement, and changing one variable at a time. Let's see why each of these procedures is important.

Repeated Measures. When we deal with many participants, we often measure them only once and then average all our observations. However, when you are dealing with only one participant, it is important to make sure that the behavior you are measuring is consistent. Thus, you would repeatedly measure the participant's behavior. Control during the measurement process is extremely important. Hersen and Barlow (1976) note that the procedures for measurement "must be clearly specified, observable, public, and replicable in all respects" (p. 71). In addition, these repeated measurements "must be done under exacting and totally standardized conditions with respect to measurement devices used, personnel involved, time or times of day measurements are recorded, instructions to the subject, and the specific environmental conditions" (Hersen & Barlow, 1976, p. 71). Thus, conducting a single-case design does *not* remove the experimenter's need to control factors as carefully as possible.

Baseline Measurement. In most single-case designs the initial experimental period is devoted to determining the **baseline** level of behavior. In essence, baseline

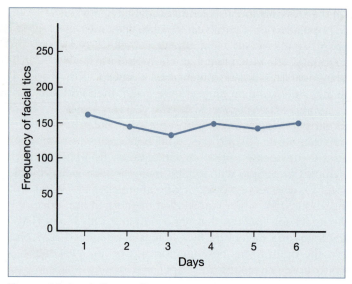

FIGURE 11-1   A STABLE BASELINE   Hypothetical data for mean number of facial tics averaged over three daily 15-minute videotaped sessions.

Source: Figure 3-1 from *Single-Case Experimental Designs: Strategies for Studying Behavioral Change* (p. 77) by M. Hersen and D. H. Barlow, 1976, New York: Pergamon Press. Used with permission of the publisher.

measurement serves as the control condition against which to compare the behavior as affected by the IV. When you are collecting baseline data, you hope to find a stable pattern of behavior so that you can more easily see any change that occurs in the behavior after your intervention (IV). Barlow and Hersen (1973) recommended that you collect *at least* three observations during the baseline period in order to establish a trend in the data. Although you may not achieve a stable measurement, the more observations you have, the more confident you can be that you have determined the general trend of the observations. Figure 11-1 depicts a hypothetical stable baseline presented by Hersen and Barlow (1976). Notice that they have increased their odds of finding a stable pattern by collecting data three times per day and averaging those data for the daily entry.

Changing One Variable at a Time.   In a single-case design it is vital that as the experimenter, you change only one variable at a time when you move from one phase of the experiment to the next.

Psychological Detective

Why would it be important to change only one variable at a time in a single-case design? Write an answer before you read further.

We hope that the answer to this question came easily. Changing one variable at a time is a basic experimental control procedure that we have stressed many times. If you allow two variables to change simultaneously, then you have a confounded experiment and cannot tell which variable has caused the change in behavior that you observe. This situation is exactly the same in a single-case design. If you record your baseline measurement, change several aspects of the participant's environment, then observe the behavior again, you have no way of knowing which changed aspect affected the behavior.

STATISTICS AND SINGLE-CASE DESIGNS

Traditionally, researchers have not computed statistical analyses of results from single-case designs. Not only has the development of statistical tests for such designs lagged behind multiple-case analyses, but there is also controversy about *whether* statistical analyses of single-case designs are even appropriate (Kazdin, 1976). Both Kazdin (1976) and Hersen (1982) summarized the arguments concerning statistical analyses. Let's take a quick look at this controversy.

The Case against Statistical Analysis. As we mentioned, tradition and history say that statistical analyses are not necessary in single-case designs. The tradition has been to visually inspect ("eyeball") the data to determine whether or not change has taken place. Researchers who hold this position believe that treatments that do not produce visually apparent effects are either weak or ineffective. Skinner (1966) wrote that "rate of responding and changes in rate can be directly observed . . . [and] statistical methods are unnecessary" (p. 20).

Because many single-case studies involve clinical treatments, another argument against statistical analysis is that statistical significance is not always the same as clinical significance. A statistical demonstration of change may not be satisfying for practical application. "For example, an autistic child may hit himself in the head 100 times an hour. Treatment may reduce this to 50 times per hour. Even though change has been achieved, a much larger change is needed to eliminate behavior" (Kazdin, 1984, p. 89).

Finally, to the prostatistics folks who argue that statistical analyses may help find effects that visual inspection would not (see next section), the antistatistics camp makes the point that such subtle effects may not be replicable (Kazdin, 1976). As you learned in the previous chapter, if you cannot replicate a result, it has no external validity.

The Case for Statistical Analysis. The argument for using statistical analyses of single-case designs revolves primarily around increased accuracy of conclusions. Jones, Vaught, and Weinrott (1977) have provided the most persuasive appeal for such analyses. They reviewed a number of studies published in the *Journal of Applied Behavior Analysis* that used visual inspection of data to draw conclusions. Jones et al. found that analyses of these data showed that sometimes conclusions drawn from visual inspections were correct and that sometimes the conclusions were incorrect. In the latter category, both Type I and Type II errors (see Chapter 6) occurred. In other words, some analyses showed *no* effect when the researchers had said there was an effect and some analyses showed significant effects when the researchers had said there were none. Kazdin (1976) points out that statistical analyses are particularly likely to uncover findings that do not show up in visual inspection when a stable baseline is not established, new areas of research are being investigated, or testing is done in the real world, which tends to increase extraneous variation.

As you can tell, there is no clear-cut answer concerning the use of statistics with single-case designs. Most researchers probably make their decision in such a situation based on a combination of personal preference, the audience for the information, and potential journal editors. Covering the various tests used to analyze single-case designs is beyond the scope of this text. Adaptations of *t* tests and ANOVA have been used, but these have suffered some problems with assumptions of the tests (Kazdin, 1976). For further information about such tests, see Kazdin (1976).

REPRESENTATIVE SINGLE-CASE DESIGNS

Researchers use a set of standard notation for single-case designs that makes the information easier to present and conceptualize. In this notation, **A** refers to the baseline measurement and **B** refers to the measurement during or after treatment. We read the notation for single-case designs in a left-to-right fashion to denote the passage of time.

A-B Design. In the **A-B design,** the simplest of the single-case designs, we make a baseline measurement, apply an IV, and then take a second measurement. We compare the B measurement to the A measurement in order to determine whether a change has occurred. Remember that A and B should represent several observations of the same behavior if we follow Barlow and Hersen's (1973) admonition. This design should remind you of a pretest-posttest design except for the absence of a control group. In the A-B design, the participant's A measurement serves as the control for the B measurement.

Hersen (1982) rates the A-B design as one of the weakest for inferring causality and notes that it is often deemed correlational.

Psychological Detective

Why do you think the A-B design is weak concerning causality? Think about this for a few moments and write your conclusion before continuing.

The A-B design is poor for determining causality because of many of the threats to internal validity that we reviewed in Chapter 10. It is possible that another factor could vary along with the treatment. This possibility is especially strong for extraneous variables that could be linked to time passage, such as history, maturation, and instrumentation. If such a factor varied across time with the IV, then any change in B could be due to either the treatment or the extraneous factor. Because there is no control group, we cannot rule out the extraneous variable as a causative factor.

Psychological Detective

Can you think of a solution to the causality problem inherent in the A-B design? Remember that you cannot add a control group or participants because this is a single-case design. Therefore, any control must occur with the single participant. Jot down any ideas you have before reading further.

The solution to this causality problem requires us to examine our next single-case design.

A-B-A Design. In the **A-B-A design,** the treatment phase is followed by a return to the baseline condition. If a change in behavior during B is actually due to the experimental treatment, the change should disappear when B is removed and you return to the baseline condition. If, on the other hand, a change in B was due to some extraneous variable, the change will not disappear when B is removed. Thus, the A-B-A design does provide for a causal relationship to be drawn.

> **A-B-A-B design**
> The most preferred single-case design consisting of a baseline, treatment, posttest, return to baseline, repeated treatment, and second posttest. This design gives the best chance of isolating causation.

Psychological Detective

There is one glaring drawback to the A-B-A design. Think about the implications of conducting a baseline-treatment-baseline experiment. Can you spot the drawback? How would you remedy this problem? Record your answers before moving forward.

If you end your experiment on a B phase, this leaves the participant in a baseline condition. If the treatment is a beneficial one, the participant is "left hanging" without the treatment. The solution to this problem requires us to examine another single-case design.

A-B-A-B Design. As you can figure out by now, the **A-B-A-B design** begins with a baseline period followed by treatment, baseline, and treatment periods consecutively. This design adds a final treatment period to the A-B-A design, thereby completing the experimental cycle with the participant in a treatment phase. Hersen and Barlow (1976) point out that this design gives two transitions (B to A and A to B) that can demonstrate the effect of the treatment variable. Thus, our ability to draw a cause-and-effect conclusion is strengthened.

Hall et al. (1971) used the A-B-A-B design in a special education setting. A 10-year-old boy (Johnny) continually talked out in class and disrupted the class, which led other children to imitate him. The researchers had the teacher measure Johnny's baseline talking-out behavior (A) for five 15-minute sessions under normal conditions. In implementing the treatment (B), the teacher ignored the talking out and paid more attention to Johnny's productive behavior (attention was contingent on the desired behavior), again for five 15-minute sessions. The teacher then repeated the A and B phases. Results from this study are shown in Figure 11-2. This graph shows us several things. First, it is clear that visual inspection of these results is enough to convince us of the efficacy of the treatment—the difference between baseline and treatment conditions is dramatic. Second, it is apparent that the treatment did work. When the teacher stopped attending to Johnny's talking-out behavior and paid attention to his productive behavior, the talking out decreased substantially. Third, we can determine that the increased productive behavior was

FIGURE 11-2   TALKING-OUT BEHAVIOR IN A MENTALLY RETARDED STUDENT   A record of talking-out behavior of an educable mentally retarded student. Baseline$_1$—before experimental conditions. Contingent Attention$_1$—systematic ignoring of talking out and increased teacher attention to appropriate behavior. Baseline$_2$—reinstatement of teacher attention to talking-out behavior. Contingent Attention$_2$—return to systematic ignoring of talking out and increased attention to appropriate behavior.

Source: Figure 2 from "The Teacher as Observer and Experimenter in the Modification of Disrupting and Talking-out Behaviors" by R. V. Hall, R. Fox, D. Willard, L. Goldsmith, M. Emerson, M. Owen, F. Davis, and E. Porcia, 1971, *Journal of Applied Behavior Analysis, 4,* p. 143.

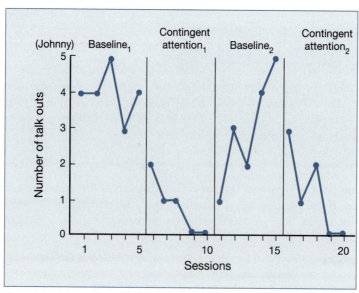

caused by the contingent attention because of the rapid increase in talking out when the attention was removed (see Baseline$_2$ on the graph).

Design and the Real World. From the preceding sections it should be clear that the A-B-A-B design is the preferred design for single-case research. However, we must ask whether typical practice actually follows the recommended path. Hersen and Barlow (1976) acknowledge that the A-B design is often used despite its shortcomings in terms of demonstrating causality. The main reason the A-B design is used concerns either the inability or undesirability to return to the baseline in the third stage. In the real world, perfect experimental design cannot always be used. We must simply accept that our ability to draw definitive conclusions in such instances is limited. Let's look at three common situations that preclude using a design other than the A-B design.

First, it may be impractical to reverse a treatment, which is typical in many field experiments. Campbell (1969) urged politicians to conduct social reforms as experiments: "We propose to initiate Policy A on an experimental basis. If after five years there has been no significant improvement, we will shift to Policy B" (p. 410). Political realities, of course, would not allow social change to be conducted experimentally. Campbell (1969) provides a good example of this problem. In 1955 Connecticut experienced a record number of traffic fatalities. The governor instituted a speeding crackdown in 1956, and traffic fatalities fell by more than 12%. Once this result occurred, it would have been politically stupid for the governor to announce, "We wish to determine whether the speeding crackdown actually caused the drop in auto deaths. Therefore, in 1957, we will relax our enforcement of speeding laws to find out whether fatalities increase once again." Yet this is what would be necessary in order to rule out rival hypotheses and draw a definitive cause-and-effect statement.

Second, it may be unethical to reverse a treatment. Lang and Melamed (1969) worked with a 9-month-old boy who had begun vomiting after meals when he was about 6 months old. Dietary changes had been implemented, medical tests had been conducted, exploratory surgery had been performed, but no organic cause could be found. The boy weighed 9 pounds, 4 ounces at birth, had gained to 17 pounds at six months of age, but weighed only 12 pounds at nine months. The child was being fed through a nose tube and was in critical condition (see Figure 11-3a). Lang and Melamed instituted a treatment consisting of brief and repeated shocks applied to the boy's leg at the first signs of vomiting and ending when vomiting ceased. By the third treatment session, one or two brief shocks were enough to stop the vomiting. By the fourth day of treatment, vomiting stopped, so treatment was discontinued. Two days later, some vomiting occurred, so the procedure was reinstated for three sessions. Five days later, the child was dismissed from the hospital (see Figure 11-3b). A month later he weighed 21 pounds and five months later weighed over 26 pounds, with no recurrence of vomiting. Although this treatment bears some resemblance to an A-B-A-B design (because of the brief relapse), the additional session was not originally intended and was *not* conducted as an intentional removal of B to chart a new baseline—the researchers believed that the problem had been cured at the point treatment was discontinued. We feel certain that you can see why ethical considerations would dictate an A-B design in this instance rather than the more experimentally rigorous A-B-A-B design.

Finally, it may be impossible to reverse a treatment if learning takes place dur-

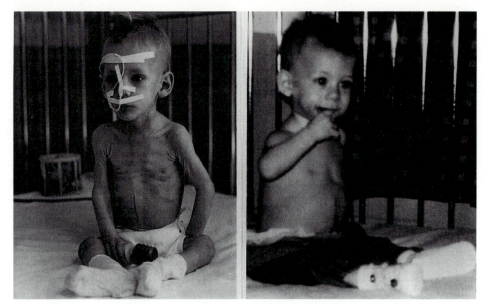

FIGURE 11-3 NINE-MONTH-OLD BOY HOSPITALIZED FOR FREQUENT VOMITING (A) BEFORE TREATMENT AND (B) AFTER TREATMENT (13 DAYS LATER)   The photograph at the left was taken during the observation period just prior to treatment. (It clearly illustrates the patient s debilitated condition—the lack of body fat, skin hanging in loose folds. The tape around the face holds tubing for the nasogastric pump. The photograph at the right was taken on the day of discharge from the hospital, 13 days after the first photo. The 26% increase in body weight already attained is easily seen in the full, more infantlike face, the rounded arms, and more substantial trunk.)

Source: Figure 1 from "Avoidance Conditioning Therapy of an Infant with Chronic Ruminative Vomiting" by P. J. Lang and B. G. Melamed, 1969, *Journal of Abnormal Psychology, 74,* pp. 1–8.

ing the treatment. Erica Berry, Michele Doty, Patricia Garcia, Jenni Mettler, and Tina Miller, students at the University of the Pacific, used an A-B design to teach a 3-year-old autistic child self-dressing skills (1993). The experimenters wanted to teach the child to put on and take off his shoes and socks. They used the operant procedures of shaping and reinforcement while working with the child for several weeks. The baseline (Pre) and posttest (Post) behavior measures are shown in Figure 11-4. As you can see, visual inspection of these data is convincing.

Psychological Detective

Why did Berry et al. (1993) *not* use the A-B-A-B design in this experiment? Write an answer before going on.

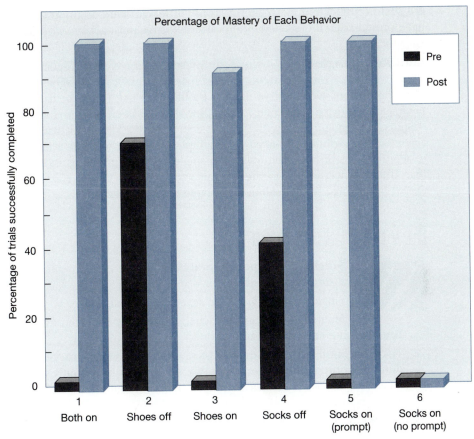

FIGURE 11-4 TEACHING AN AUTISTIC CHILD TO PUT ON OR TAKE OFF HIS SHOES AND SOCKS

Source: Figure 1 from "Teaching Self-dressing Skills to an Autistic Child Using Behavior Modification and Home Based Intervention" by E. Berry, M. Doty, P. Garcia, J. Mettler, and T. Miller, 1993. Paper presented at the Western Psychology Conference for Undergraduates, Santa Clara, CA. Used with permission of the authors.

Because the student experimenters had successfully taught the child how to put on and take off his shoes and socks, they could not "undo" this learning and return to the baseline condition. They could have put shoes and socks in front of the boy to see whether he would put them on without direction to do so, but that was not their target behavior. The original goal was to teach him to put on or take off his shoes and socks when told to do so. Having learned this behavior, the boy could not return to the baseline.

The bottom line to this section is that you as an experimenter may find yourself caught in the middle. On the one hand, you have the knowledge of proper experimental design and what is necessary to yield cause-and-effect explanations. On the other hand, you have the realities of applied situations. The best rule of thumb for such situations is that you should use the most stringent experimental design you can, but you should not give up on an important project if you can't use the absolute best design that exists. As a psychological detective, you have an edge on the real-life detective, who cannot apply a design even as rigorous as those we have presented in this section. The police detective must always work on a solution after the fact.

Additional Single-Case Designs. In presenting the A-B, A-B-A, and A-B-A-B designs, we have merely scratched the surface of single-case designs. We have covered the designs we think you might be likely to use in the near future. As you have seen from our references, entire books have been written about single-case designs. Hersen and Barlow (1976) also cover many additional variations on single-case designs, including designs with multiple baselines, multiple schedules, and interactions. Thus, if you ever envision a single-case design that is more complicated than the ones we have presented in this text, we refer you to Hersen and Barlow (1976) or a similar book dealing with single-case designs.

REVIEW SUMMARY

1. **Single-case experimental designs** are experiments that deal with a single participant.
2. Single-case designs have several legitimate uses.
3. Single-case designs are characterized by repeated measures, **baseline** measurement, and changing one variable at a time.
4. There is controversy over the use of statistics and single-case designs. The traditional approach has been to draw conclusions by visually examining the data. Proponents of statistical analysis maintain that analysis yields more correct conclusions.
5. The **A-B-A-B** single-case design allows you the best chance to draw a cause-and-effect conclusion regarding a treatment. Realities of the real world often force the use of **A-B** designs, which are particularly prone to alternative explanations.

STUDY BREAK

1. Why does history show single-case designs to be quite popular in psychology's early years but less popular today?
2. How can a single-case design be used to disprove a theory?
3. To come up with a comparison in the single-case design, we first measure behavior before the treatment during the _____ period. To get a stable measurement, we should make at least _____ observations.
4. Summarize two arguments for *and* two arguments against statistical analysis of single-case designs.
5. Match the design with the appropriate characteristic:
   1. A-B
   2. A-B-A
   3. A-B-A-B

   a. leaves the participant in a baseline phase
   b. best single-case design for determining cause-and-effect relationships
   c. has many threats to internal validity

6. Why might you be forced to use an A-B single-case design in the real world? Give an original example of such a situation.

Quasi-experimental research design
A design used when you cannot randomly assign your experimental participants to the groups but do manipulate an IV and measure a DV.

definition

QUASI-EXPERIMENTAL DESIGNS

In the previous section of the chapter, we discussed a research design that, other than its number of participants, resembles ones we covered previously. In this section we will deal with designs that are virtually identical to true experimental designs with the exception of random assignment of participants to groups. When we are able to manipulate an IV and measure a DV but *cannot* randomly assign our participants to groups, we must use a **quasi-experimental design.** Similarly, police detectives are sometimes faced with situations in which they must build their case on circumstantial evidence rather than using direct evidence.

Psychological Detective

What problem results when we cannot randomly assign research participants to groups? Do we have the same problem if we cannot randomly select our participants? Think carefully and write an answer before reading further.

Not being able to randomly assign our participants to their groups has the effect of violating an important assumption that allows us to draw cause-and-effect conclusions from our experiments—the assumption of equal groups before the experiment. Even if we can randomly select participants from a larger group, we cannot make cause-and-effect statements without random assignment. As Campbell and Stanley (1966) pointed out, the assumption of random assignment has been an important part of statistics and experimental design since the time of Fisher. If we unknowingly began an experiment with unequal groups and our statistics showed a difference after the experiment, we would make a Type I error (see Chapter 6) by concluding that the IV caused the difference that was actually present from the outset. Clearly, this would be problematical.

It is likely that our description of quasi-experimental design reminds you of the ex post facto study we mentioned in Chapter 3. Some writers categorize ex post facto and quasi-experimental designs together and some separately. We will draw a small, but significant, distinction between the two. Remember in Chapter 3 we described the ex post facto study as having an IV that had already occurred, that we could not manipulate. Thus, if we wish to study sex differences on mathematics or English achievement, we are studying the IV of biological sex, which we cannot control or manipulate. Of course, because the IV is a preexisting condition, we also cannot randomly assign our participants to groups.

On the other hand, in a quasi-experimental design, our participants belong to preexisting groups that we cannot randomly assign, but we *do* have control over the IV—we can administer it when and to whom we wish. Thus, we could choose our participants on the basis of sex and *then* have some of them participate in a workshop designed to improve their math or English achievement. In this case, the workshop (or lack thereof) would serve as the IV for the preexisting groups of boys and girls. Obviously, random assignment is impossible in this case. Quasi-experimental designs are a step closer to true experimental designs than ex post facto studies because you, as the experimenter, are able to exert control over the IV and its administration. Being able to administer your own IV is preferable to having nature administer it for you, at least in terms of control.

The basic rationale for using quasi-experimental designs is the same as that for ex post facto studies—your inability to assign participants at random. According to Hedrick, Bickman, and Rog (1993), "A quasi-experimental design is not the method of choice, but rather a fallback strategy for situations in which random assignment is not possible" (p. 62). When dealing with selection variables that do not allow for random assignment, we have the choice of using a quasi-experimental design or simply ignoring an important or interesting experimental question. Rather than letting such questions go unasked, researchers resort to quasi-experimental research.

HISTORY OF QUASI-EXPERIMENTAL DESIGNS

It is difficult to trace the history of quasi-experimental designs. Although McGuigan (1960) did not include the term in the first edition of his classic experimental psychology text, Campbell and Stanley (1966) used it in the title of their 1963 guide to experimental design. However, there is little doubt that researchers were tackling quasi-experimental design problems long before Campbell and Stanley's published work. Cook and Campbell (1979) noted that some researchers were writing about quasi-experiments in the 1950s, although the term did not originate until later. It is likely that Campbell and Stanley (1966) and Cook and Campbell (1979) are responsible for elevating quasi-experimental work to the respectable position it holds today.

USES OF QUASI-EXPERIMENTAL DESIGNS

Hedrick et al. (1993) have listed several specific situations that require quasi-experimental designs. Let's take a quick look at their list. First, there are many variables that simply make random assignment impossible. If we wish to study participants from certain groups (e.g., based on sex, age, or previous life experiences), we must use quasi-experimental designs. Second, when you wish to evaluate an ongoing or already completed program or intervention (a retrospective study), you would need to use a quasi-experimental design. Because the program began before you decided to evaluate it, you were unable to use control procedures from the outset. Third, studies of social conditions demand quasi-experimental designs. You would not study the effects of poverty, race, unemployment, or other such social factors through random assignment. Fourth, it is sometimes the case that random assignment is not possible because of expense, time, or monitoring difficulties. For example, if you conducted a cross-cultural research project involving participants from several different countries, it would be nearly impossible to guarantee that the same random assignment procedures were used in each setting. Fifth, the ethics of an experimental situation, particularly with psychological research, may necessitate quasi-experimentation. For example, if you are conducting a research program to evaluate a certain treatment, you must worry about the ethics of withholding that treatment from people who could benefit from it. As you will see, quasi-experimentation provides a design that will work in such situations to remove this ethical dilemma.

Nonequivalent group design
A design involving two or more groups that are not randomly assigned; a comparison group (no treatment) is compared to one or more treatment groups.

definition

Representative Quasi-experimental Designs

Unlike the single-case design, we did not include sections covering general procedures and statistics of quasi-experimental designs. It is difficult to derive general principles because the representative designs we are about to introduce are so varied in nature. The use of statistics for quasi-experimental designs is not an issue because quasi-experimental designs resemble true experiments other than the random assignment problem. Thus, the traditional statistical tests used with true experiments are also used for quasi-experiments.

Nonequivalent Group Design. The **nonequivalent group design** (Campbell & Stanley, 1966) is shown in Figure 11-5.

Psychological Detective

The nonequivalent group design should remind you of a design that we covered in Chapter 10. Which design does it resemble? How is it different? What is the implication of this difference? Write answers to these questions before you read further.

If you flip back to Figure 10-2, you will see that the nonequivalent group design bears a distinct resemblance to the pretest-posttest control group design. However, the nonequivalent group design is missing the Rs in front of the two groups;

```
O₁              O₂        (comparison group)
O₁        X     O₂        (treatment group)

KEY:
R = Random assignment
O = Pretest or posttest observation or measurement
X = Experimental variable or event
Each row represents a different group of participants.
Left-to-right dimension represents passage of time.
Any letters vertical to each other occur simultaneously.
Note: This key also applies to Figures 11-8 and 11-11.
```

FIGURE 11-5   THE NONEQUIVALENT GROUP DESIGN

random assignment is *not* used in creating the groups. The lack of random assignment means that our groups may differ before the experiment—thus the name *nonequivalent group* design.

You also will notice that the two groups are labeled as the comparison group (rather than control group) and the treatment group (rather than experimental group) (from Hedrick et al., 1993). The "treatment" to "experimental" change is not particularly important; those terms could be used interchangeably. However, changing the name from "control" to "comparison" group is an important and meaningful change. In the nonequivalent group design, this group serves as the comparison to the treatment group but cannot truly be called a control group because of the lack of random assignment.

It is possible to extend the nonequivalent group design to include more than one treatment group if you wish to contrast two or more treatment groups with your comparison group. The key to the nonequivalent group design is creating a good comparison group. As far as is possible, we attempt to create an equal group through our selection criteria rather than through random assignment.

> Examples of procedures for creating such a group include using members of a waiting list for a program/service; using people who did not volunteer for a program, but were eligible; using students in classes that will receive the curriculum (treatment) at a later date; and matching individual characteristics. (Hedrick et al., 1993, p. 59)

Geronimus (1991) provides a good example of creating a strong comparison group. She and her colleagues completed several studies of long-term outcomes for teen mothers. As you are probably aware, the stereotypical outcome for teen mothers is quite dismal—the age of mother correlates with negative factors such as poverty, dropout rates, and infant mortality. However, Geronimus believed that family factors such as socioeconomic status might be better predictors of these negative outcomes than the actual teen pregnancy. Random assignment for research on this topic would be impossible—you could not randomly assign teenage girls to become pregnant or not. Thus, quasi-experimentation was necessary. In looking for a comparison group that would be as similar as possible, Geronimus decided to use the teenage mothers' sisters who did not become pregnant until later in life. Thus, although the assignment to groups was not random, the groups were presumably very near to equivalence, particularly with respect to family background factors. Interestingly enough, when family background was controlled in this manner, many of the negative outcomes associated with teen pregnancy disappeared. For example, there was no longer any difference in the dropout rates of the two groups. "For indicators of infant health and children's sociocognitive development, at times the trends reversed direction (i.e., controlling for family background, the teen birth group did *better* than the postponers)" (Geronimus, 1991, p. 465).

In Geronimus's research, the "pretest" consisted of finding two women from the same family, one who first became pregnant as a teenager and one who did not get pregnant until after age 20. In this case the groups may still have been nonequivalent, but they were highly equivalent on family background. Sometimes it is impossible or undesirable to begin with equivalent groups, and the pretest serves much like a baseline measure for comparison with the posttest. In this type of situation, the label "nonequivalent groups" seems quite appropriate.

Ticia Casanova, a student at Mills College, used a nonequivalent group design in her research project (1993). She assessed students' attitudes toward the disabled and formed two groups, one with positive attitudes and one with negative attitudes. Thus, the groups were nonequivalent before the experiment began. The IV in Casanova's experiment consisted of watching an impartial video about the controversy over the Jerry Lewis Muscular Dystrophy Association telethon. (Lewis has been accused of evoking negative attitudes toward the disabled in order to raise more money.) After watching the video, Casanova remeasured the students' attitudes toward the disabled. She found that students who started with negative attitudes did not change their attitudes but that those who began the experiment with positive attitudes showed even more positive attitudes afterward. Because the two groups began the experiment as nonequivalent, the appropriate question after the experiment was *not* whether a difference existed, but whether the difference was the same as before the experiment (see Figure 11-6A) or whether the difference

FIGURE 11-6   *Two Possible Outcomes in a Nonequivalent Group Design*

Source: Thomas D. Cook and Donald T. Campbell, *Quasi-Experimentation: Design and Analysis.* Copyright ©1979 by Houghton-Mifflin Company. Reprinted by permission.

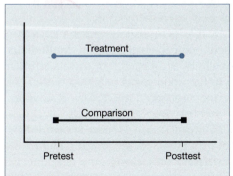

A. No effect of IV   B. Positive effect of IV

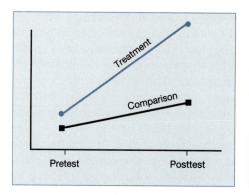
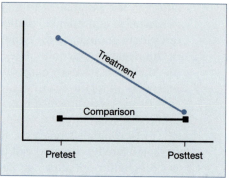
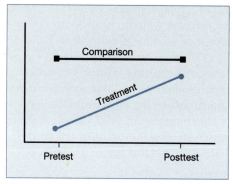
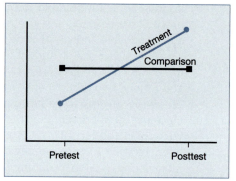

FIGURE 11-7   SEVERAL POSSIBLE OUTCOMES IN A NONEQUIVALENT GROUP DESIGN

Source: Thomas D. Cook and Donald T. Campbell, *Quasi-Experimentation: Design and Analysis.* Copyright ©1979 by Houghton-Mifflin and Company. Reprinted by permission.

had changed in some way. In Casanova's experiment the difference between the two groups had grown larger (as in Figure 11-6B), thus supporting the hypothesis that the IV had an effect on attitudes toward the disabled. Of course, there are several other possible outcomes that would also show some effect of the IV. More of Cook and Campbell's (1979) hypothetical outcomes are shown in Figure 11-7.

Thus far, our discussion of this design has seemed similar to that of true experimental designs. What is different about quasi-experimental designs? The most important point to remember is that quasi-experimental designs are more plagued by threats to internal validity. Because you have not used random assignment, your interpretation of the findings must be cautious. Cook and Campbell (1979) isolated four threats to internal validity that are not controlled in the nonequivalent group design. We will list these only briefly because they appeared previously in Chapter 10. First, **maturation** is a potential problem. Because the groups begin as unequal, there is a greater potential that results such as those shown in Figure 11-6b might be due to differential maturation of the groups rather than to the IV. Second, we must consider **instrumentation** in the nonequivalent group design. For example, if we demonstrate nonequivalence of our participants by using a scale during the pretest, we must worry about whether

Maturation
An internal validity threat; refers to changes in participants that occur over time during an experiment; could include actual physical maturation or tiredness, boredom, hunger, and so on.

definition

the scale is uniform—are the units of measurement equal through-out the scale? **Statistical regression** is the third internal validity threat present in the nonequivalent group design. Regression is particularly likely to be a problem if we select extreme scorers on the basis of our pretest. Finally, we must consider the threat to in-ternal validity of an **interaction between selection and (local) history.** If some local event differentially affected our treatment and comparison groups, we would have a problem.

In conclusion, the nonequivalent group design is a strong quasi-experimental design. Its strength lies in the fact that "it pro-vides an approximation to the experimental design and that, with care, it can support causal inference" (Hedrick et al., 1993, p. 62). However, we must be aware that the threat of confounds is high-er than for the experimental designs. Hedrick et al. (1993) warn that "throughout both the planning and execution phases of an applied research project, researchers must keep their eyes open to identify potential rival explanations for their results" (p. 64). Often researchers who use quasi-experimental designs must ad-dress potential rival hypotheses in their research reports.

Interrupted Time-Series Design. Another quasi-experimental design, the **interrupted time-series design,** involves measuring a group of participants repeatedly over time (the time-series), in-troducing a treatment (the interruption), and measuring the par-ticipants repeatedly again (more of the time-series). Look at Fig-ure 11-8 to see a graphic portrayal of an interrupted time-series design. We should make an important point about Figure 11-8: There is nothing magical about using five observations before (O_1-O_5) and after (O_6-O_{10}) the treatment. Any number of obser-vations large enough to establish a pattern can be used (Camp-bell & Stanley [1966] show four before and after; Cook & Camp-bell [1979] show five; Hedrick et al. [1993] show six before and five after). As you can probably guess, the idea behind an inter-rupted time-series design is to look for changes in the trend of the data before and after the treatment is applied. Thus, the inter-rupted time-series design is similar to an A-B design. A change in trend could be shown by a change in the *level* of the behavior (see Figure 11-9a), a change in the *rate* (slope) of the pattern of behavior (see Figure 11-9b), or both (see Figure 11-9c).

Interrupted time-series designs have been used for quite some time. Campbell and Stanley (1966) referred to their use in much of the classical research of nineteenth-century biology and physical science. Cook and

---

definition

Instrumentation A threat to internal validity that occurs if the equipment or human measuring the DV changes its measuring criterion over time.

Statistical regression A threat to internal validity that occurs when low scorers improve or high scorers fall on a second administration of a test due solely to statistical reasons.

Selection-history interaction A threat to internal validity that can occur if there are systematic differences in the histories (backgrounds) of selected treatment groups.

Interrupted time-series design A quasi-experimental design involving a single group of participants that includes repeated pre-treatment measures, an applied treatment, and repeated posttreatment measures.

FIGURE 11-8 AN INTERRUPTED TIME-SERIES DESIGN

| O_1 | O_2 | O_3 | O_4 | O_5 | X | O_6 | O_7 | O_8 | O_9 | O_{10} |

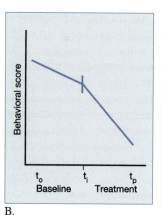

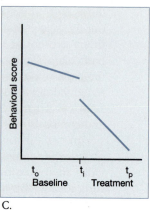

FIGURE 11-9   POTENTIAL CHANGES IN TREND IN A TIME-SERIES DESIGN   A. Change in level, no change in rate. B. No change in level, change in rate. C. Change in level, change in rate.

Source: Portions of Figure 1 from "Time-Series Analysis in Operant Research" by R. R. Jones, R. S. Vaught, and M. Weinrott, 1977, *Journal of Applied Behavior Analysis, 10,* pp. 151–166.

Campbell (1979) cited a representative 1924 study dealing with the effects of moving from a 10-hour to an 8-hour workday in London. Hedrick and Shipman (1988) used an interrupted time-series design to assess the impact of the 1981 Omnibus Budget Reconciliation Act (OBRA) that tightened the eligibility requirements for AFDC (Aid to Families with Dependent Children) assistance. As you can see in Figure 11-10, the immediate impact of this legislation was to lessen the number of cases handled by about 200,000. However, the number of cases after the change continued to climb at about the same slope it had before the change. Thus, the tightened eligibility requirements seemed to lower the *level* of the caseload but not its *rate.*

Psychological Detective

Review the threats to internal validity summarized in Chapter 10. Which threat would seem to create the greatest potential prob-lem for the interrupted time-series design? Why? Jot down your answers before going further.

History A threat to internal validity; refers to events that occur between the DV measurements in a repeated measures design.

According to Cook and Campbell (1979), the main threat to most interrupted time-series designs is **history.** One of the primary features of the interrupted time-series design is the passage of time to allow for many different measurements. This time passage raises the possibility that changes in behavior could be due to some important event other than the treatment. Because of the time taken by repeated measurements, another potential threat to internal validity is maturation. However, the repeated pretesting does allow for the assessment of any maturational trends; thus

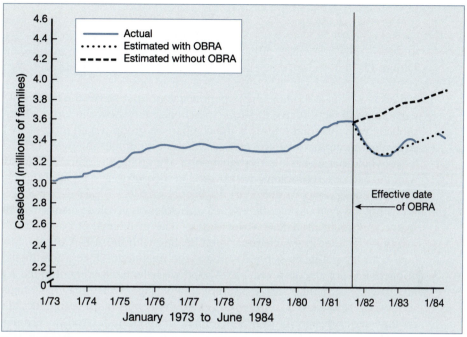

FIGURE 11-10   IMPACT OF TIGHTENED AFDC REQUIREMENTS ON CASELOAD

Source: T. E. Hedrick and S. L. Shipman, "Multiple Questions Require Multiple Designs: An Evaluation of the 1981 Changes to the AFDC Program," *Evaluation Review* (vol. 12), p. 438. Copyright ©1988 by Sage Publications, Inc. Reprinted by permission of Sage Publications, Inc.

if scores change at the same rate before and after the treatment, the change is due to maturation. Instrumentation could be a problem if record keeping or scoring procedures were changed over the course of time. Such a change, of course, would violate the principles of control in any experiment, not just an interrupted time-series design.

Although the interrupted time-series design can control for some of the internal validity threats, we still face the potential problem of history. This threat to internal validity is usually handled in one of three manners. First, Cook and Campbell (1979) advise frequent testing intervals. For example, if you test participants on a weekly rather than monthly, quarterly, or yearly basis, the probability of a major event occurring during the time period between the last pretest and the treatment is low. In addition, if you keep careful records of any possible effect-causing events during the quasi-experiment, it would be a simple matter to discern whether any fell at the critical period when you administered the treatment. This first approach to controlling history is probably the most widely used because of its ease and the drawbacks of the other two solutions to be covered next.

A second solution to the history threat is to include a comparison (control) group that does not receive the treatment. Such a design appears in Figure 11-11. As you can see, the comparison group receives the same number of measurements at the same times as the treatment (experimental) group. Thus, if any important histor-

| O_1 | O_2 | O_3 | O_4 | O_5 | X | O_6 | O_7 | O_8 | O_9 | O_{10} |
| O_1 | O_2 | O_3 | O_4 | O_5 | | O_6 | O_7 | O_8 | O_9 | O_{10} |

FIGURE 11-11   AN INTERRUPTED TIME-SERIES DESIGN WITH CONTROL GROUP

ical event occurs at the time the experimental group receives the treatment, the comparison group would have the same experience and show the same effect. The only problem with this solution is that the comparison group would most likely be a nonequivalent group because the groups were not randomly assigned. This nonequivalence would put us back in the situation of attempting to control for that difference, with the associated problems we covered in the previous section of this chapter.

The third possible solution to the history problem is probably the best solution but is not always possible. In essence, this solution involves using an A-B-A format within the interrupted time-series design. The problems, of course, are those we mentioned earlier in the chapter when dealing with the A-B-A design. Most importantly, it may not be possible to "undo" the treatment. Once a treatment has been applied, it is not always reversible. Also, if we halt an experiment in the A stage, we are leaving our participants in a nontreatment stage, which may have negative consequences. Hedrick et al. (1993) presented the results of an unintentional interrupted time-series design in an A-B-A format. In 1966 the federal government passed the Highway Safety Act, including a provision that mandated helmets for motorcyclists. However, in the late 1970s states began to repeal helmet laws because of pressure concerning individuals' freedom of choice. Thus, if we examine motorcycle fatality rates over many years, we have an A (no restrictions)-B (helmet laws)-A (fewer restrictions) format for an interrupted time-series design. Figure 11-12 shows the graph Hedrick et al. (1993) presented. Because of the drop in fatalities after the law was passed and the rise in fatalities after the repeal of the law in some states, it seems straightforward to derive a cause-and-effect relationship from these data. Although this type of design allows for a convincing conclusion, again we must point out that the circumstances that created it are unusual and would be difficult, if not impossible, to recreate in many typical quasi-experimental situations.

In summary, the interrupted time-series design has the ability to uncover cause-and-effect relationships. You must be especially careful of history effects when using this design; however, frequent testing helps reduce this threat. The interrupted time-series design is particularly helpful when dealing with applied types of problems such as therapeutic treatment or in educational settings.

REVIEW SUMMARY

1. **Quasi-experimental designs** are identical to true experimental designs except that participants are not randomly assigned to groups. Thus, our research groups may not be equal before the experiment, causing problems in drawing clear conclusions.

2. Unlike ex post facto designs, we are able to control the IV in a quasi-experimental design.

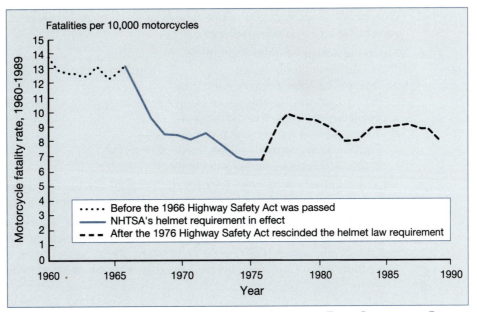

FIGURE 11-12   EFFECTS OF MANDATORY HELMET LAWS AND THEIR SUBSEQUENT REPEAL ON MOTORCYCLE FATALITIES

Source: Motorcycle Helmet Laws Save Lives and Reduce Costs to Society (GAO/RCED-91-170, July), Washington, DC.

3. There are many situations where the impossibility of random assignment makes quasi-experimentation necessary.

4. The **nonequivalent group design** involves comparing two groups—one receiving the IV and a comparison group that does not receive the IV. The groups are nonequivalent because of the lack of random assignment.

5. In the nonequivalent group design, it is imperative to select a comparison group that is as similar as possible to the treatment group.

6. **Maturation, instrumentation, statistical regression,** and **selection-history interactions** are all threats to internal validity in the nonequivalent group design.

7. An **interrupted time-series design** involves measuring participants several times, introducing an IV, and then measuring the participants several more times.

8. **History** is the main threat to internal validity in the interrupted time-series design. It can be controlled by testing frequently, including a comparison group, or removing the treatment after it has been applied (if possible).

STUDY BREAK

1. Differentiate between experimental designs, quasi-experimental designs, and ex post facto designs.

2. Give two reasons why you might choose to use a quasi-experimental design rather than an experimental design.

3. Match the design with the appropriate characteristics:

   BCF   1. Nonequivalent group design   2. Interrupted time-series design ADE

   a. typically has one group of participants 2
   b. has two groups of participants 1
   c. involves pretesting of participants 1
   d. does not involve pretesting participants 2
   e. is prone to the internal validity threat of history 2
   f. is prone to several internal validity threats 1

4. What was the key to Geronimus's research that allowed her to conclude that the effects of teenage pregnancy are not as negative as typically thought?

5. We summarized two interrupted time-series analyses in the text—one dealing with changing AFDC requirements (Figure 11-10) and one dealing with changing motorcycle helmet laws (Figure 11-12). Why are we more certain about our conclusion in the case of the helmet laws than with the AFDC requirements?

QUALITATIVE RESEARCH

We end this chapter with a brief look at the topic of **qualitative research.** In many ways this topic is reminiscent of Chapter 3, in which we introduced methods of gathering information through means other than experimentation. You will remember that we categorized the techniques in Chapter 3 as lacking the ability to provide cause-and-effect relationships between variables. In recent years there has been a renewal of interest in qualitative techniques as researchers have broadened their areas of inquiry. There is currently a tension between the traditional experimental approaches of empiricism and rationalism and the newer postmodern approaches.

As you have seen throughout this text, traditional experimentation assumes lawfulness and predictability and uses control processes and statistical tests in its search for truth. This approach is often referred to as **logical positivism.** On the other hand, postmodern approaches stress that truth may not be absolute. Truth can be relative, situational, contextual, or even changeable. Qualitative research approaches fit well within the postmodern category.

What *is* qualitative research? Strauss and Corbin (1990) refer to it as

> any kind of research that produces findings not arrived at by means of statistical procedures or other means of quantification. It can refer to research about persons' lives, stories, behavior, but also about organization functioning, social movements, or interactional relationships. (p. 17)

Qualitative research is known by many names and approaches. Packer and Addison (1989) refer to the interpretive approach and to hermeneutic (interpreting) investigations. Glesne and Peshkin (1992) summarize infor-

definition

Qualitative research Research approaches that rely less on control and statistical analysis and more on insight and understanding of the subject matter.

Logical positivism A research approach based on the collection and analysis of empirical data, which are used to derive conclusions.

mation about ethnography, case study, phenomenology, educational criticism, ecological psychology, symbolic interactionism, and cognitive anthropology.

Quantitative research tends to focus on determining cause-and-effect relationships, whereas qualitative research focuses more on deriving meaning from the relationships that are observed. Table 11-1 presents Glesne and Peshkin's comparison between the traits of quantitative research and the traits of qualitative research.

Psychological Detective

Compare the three *purposes* of each research approach in Table 11-1. We have spent virtually all our time in this book stressing the quantitative approach to research. Can you generate a description of qualitative research from the information we gave you previously and the purposes in Table 11-1? Write a short description of qualitative research (in your own words) before you read further.

TABLE 11-1. COMPARISONS BETWEEN QUANTITATIVE AND QUALITATIVE RESEARCH MODES

QUANTITATIVE MODE	QUALITATIVE MODE
Assumptions	
Social facts have an objective reality	Reality is socially constructed
Primacy of method	Primacy of subject matter
Variables can be identified and relationships measured	Variables are complex, interwoven, and difficult to measure
Etic (outsider's point of view)	Emic (insider's point of view)
Purpose	
Generalizability	Contextualization
Prediction	Interpretation
Causal explanations	Understanding actors' perspectives
Approach	
Begins with hypotheses and theories	Ends with hypotheses and grounded theory
Manipulation and control	Emergence and portrayal
Uses formal instruments	Researcher as instrument
Experimentation	Naturalistic
Deductive	Inductive
Component analysis	Searches for patterns
Seeks consensus, the norm	Seeks pluralism, complexity
Reduces data to numerical indices	Makes minor use of numerical indices
Researcher Role	
Detachment and impartiality	Personal involvement and partiality
Objective portrayal	Empathic understanding

Source: From *Becoming Qualitative Researchers* by Corrine Glesne and Alan Peshkin. Copyright ©1992 by Longman Publishers. Reprinted with permission.

This assignment is a difficult one—in fact, many full-fledged qualitative researchers might have difficulty with this task. A simplified description of qualitative research is that the qualitative researcher is more interested in setting the stage and telling the story of a phenomenon than in dissecting it piece by piece in an experiment. Thus, qualitative researchers focus more on the big picture of a behavior or an event than the microscopic examinations that characterize quantitative research. Qualitative researchers attempt to understand the worldview and world constructions of their *others* (Glesne and Peshkin's term for participants or subjects). "The researcher becomes the main research instrument as he or she observes, asks questions, and interacts with research participants" (Glesne & Peshkin, 1992, p. 6). Creswell (1994) provides an excellent example of the similarities and differences between quantitative and qualitative research, as well as demonstrating how the two approaches could be used to tackle similar questions.

You might ask why we are covering qualitative research at this point in the text given that we have already devoted an entire chapter to nonexperimental approaches to gathering data. First, the recent upsurge of interest in qualitative methods has led to a large number of new writings on this topic. Second, these new writings have yielded some methodological approaches that are also new relative to the material we covered in Chapter 3. Finally, these new approaches are making important contributions to our knowledge in diverse and nontraditional areas. For example, Packer and Addison (1989) provide accounts of investigations into physician socialization, moral conflicts and actions, change in therapy, and the textual unconscious. Let's examine three qualitative approaches.

ETHNOGRAPHY

Ethnography
A qualitative research approach that involves becoming a part of the culture you study.

Glesne and Peshkin (1992) favor using **ethnography,** which is based on the anthropological tradition of research. In the ethnographic approach, you would spend a long time becoming immersed in the "culture" of the population being studied. We enclosed the word *culture* in quotation marks in the previous sentence because we do not refer to culture only in the cross-cultural sense of the word (e.g., different tribes, countries, or continents). For example, you might wish to study an inner-city ghetto or a teenage gang using this approach. As a researcher, you would become immersed in this culture for a long period of time, and you would gather data primarily through participant observation (see Chapter 3) and interviewing. Rather than *studying* people from the outside, you *learn from* people by becoming a part of them. This approach is quite similar to that of the detective going undercover and infiltrating a group of suspects.

Psychological Detective

Why would long-term immersion in a different culture be important to the ethnographic approach? Write an answer before you read any further.

As we noted in Chapter 3, when you become immersed in a culture that is different from your own, one important key to gathering information is establishing rapport with the people you are studying. Without a good relationship, you may not be trusted and may be unable to gather any information or you may end up gathering information that is falsified for your "benefit."

Glesne and Peshkin (1992) differentiate between two types of participant observation depending on the degree of participation. The "observer as participant" refers to a researcher who primarily observes a situation but who interacts with the others. They use the example of Peshkin's semester-long study of a fundamentalist Christian school in which the researchers predominantly sat in the back of the classroom and took notes, with little interaction. On the other hand, the "participant as observer" refers to the researcher who becomes a part of the culture by working and interacting extensively with the others. Glesne spent a year in St. Vincent, where she socialized, assisted in farm work, and even became an intermediary with governmental agricultural agencies. There is a cost-benefit relationship with these two approaches: The more immersed in a culture you become, the more you stand to learn about it. However, you stand to lose your objectivity about a culture as you become more immersed in it. You can probably understand why strict experimentalists, by placing a premium on objectivity and control, shy away from ethnographic research.

CLINICAL PERSPECTIVE

Although some people categorize the **clinical perspective** or model as a subcategory of the ethnographic approach, Schein (1987) argues convincingly that the clinical model should be considered separately. There are several key differences between the two approaches:

- A client typically chooses the clinician, whereas the ethnographer chooses the others to be studied.
- Unlike ethnographers, clinicians cannot be unobtrusive because they have been asked to participate in the situation.
- Although the ethnographer can remain a passive observer, clinicians must intervene in the situation.
- The ethnographer's goal is understanding, whereas the clinician's goal is helping.

Thus, the ethnographer is content to be inside a system enough to develop a full understanding of the dynamics and interaction patterns. On the other hand, the clinician wishes not only to develop this understanding but also to change the dynamics and interaction patterns. Often the clinician deals with only a narrow slice of the whole, wanting to get an in-depth understanding of the problem area. The ethnographer, however, wants to develop a broad picture of the entire behavioral and interpersonal spectrum. The clinical approach is related to the detective who attempts to generate a psychological profile of a particular suspect.

An important question, of course, relating to both ethnography and the clinical perspective is how researchers scientifically

Clinical perspective
A qualitative research approach aimed at understanding and correcting a particular behavioral problem.

definition

validate what they have found. According to Schein (1987), the key for ethnographers is replication—if another ethnographer studies the same culture, will the conclusions be the same? On the other hand, for clinicians the key to validity is being able to predict the results of a given intervention. If you think about the meaning of this phrase, it should be clear that being able to predict the results of an intervention is very similar to having a cause-and-effect situation. Simply showing improvement is not enough to validate a clinical approach because, for example, we know that spontaneous cures or improvement are often shown.

GROUNDED THEORY

Grounded theory
A qualitative research approach that attempts to develop theories of understanding based on data from the real world.

Strauss and Corbin (1990) favor the **grounded theory** approach to qualitative research. The primary tools of discovery are interviews and observations, as with ethnography and the clinical perspective. However, grounded theory goes beyond the descriptive and interpretive goals of these two approaches and is aimed at building theories. The ultimate goal of this approach is to derive theories that are grounded in (based on) reality. A grounded theory is one that is uncovered, developed, and conditionally confirmed through collecting and making sense of data related to the issue at hand. The hope is that such theories will lead to a better understanding of the phenomenon of interest and to ideas for exerting some control over the phenomenon. Although grounded theory is designed to be a precise and rigorous process, creativity is also an important part of that process in that the researcher needs to ask innovative questions and come up with unique formulations of the data—"to create new order out of the old" (Strauss & Corbin, 1990, p. 27). The grounded theory approach is reminiscent of a detective's attempt to build a theory about why certain types of crimes are committed. For example, by interviewing a number of arsonists, you might develop a theory about why arson takes place.

Open coding
The process of describing your data through means such as examination, comparison, conceptualization, and categorization.

Axial coding
The process of rearranging your data after open coding so that new relationships are formed between concepts.

Strauss and Corbin (1990) do not advocate using grounded theory for all types of questions. In fact, they maintain that certain types of questions support certain types of research.

> For instance, if someone wanted to know whether one drug is more effective than another, then a double blind clinical trial would be more appropriate than a grounded theory study. However, if someone wanted to know what it was like to be a participant in a drug study, then he or she might sensibly engage in a grounded theory project or some other type of qualitative study. (Strauss & Corbin, 1990, p. 37)

Selective coding
The process of selecting your main phenomenon (core category) around which all other phenomena (subsidiary categories) are grouped, arranging the groupings, studying the results, and rearranging where necessary.

The use of literature also differs in the grounded theory approach. Strauss and Corbin recommend *against* knowing the research literature too well before a study because knowing the categories, classifications, and conclusions of previous researchers may constrain your creativity in finding new formulations. On the other hand, nontechnical materials such as let-

definition

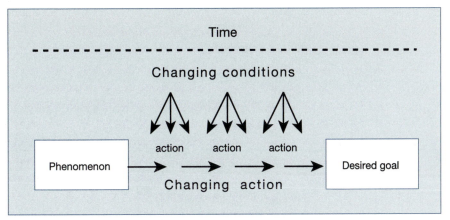

FIGURE 11-13   A PROCESS DIAGRAM

Source: A. Strauss and J. Corbin, *Basics of Qualitative Research: Grounded Theory Procedures and Techniques,* p. 145, Copyright ©1990 by Sage Publications, Inc. Reprinted by permission of Sage Publications, Inc.

ters, diaries, newspapers, biographies, and videotapes are essential to grounded theory studies, serving as primary sources.

The heart of the grounded theory approach occurs in its use of coding, which is analogous to data analysis in quantitative approaches. There are three different types of coding used in a more-or-less sequential manner (Strauss & Corbin, 1990). **Open coding** is much like the description goal of science. During open coding the researcher labels and categorizes the phenomena being studied. **Axial coding** involves finding links between categories and subcategories from open coding. The final process, **selective coding,** entails identifying a core category and relating the subsidiary categories to this core. From this last type of coding the grounded theory researcher moves toward developing a model of **process** or of a **transactional system,** which essentially tells the story of the outcome of the research. Process refers to a linking of actions and interactions that result in some outcome (see Figure 11-13 for a hypothetical process diagram). A transactional system is grounded theory's analytical method that allows an examination of the interactions of different events. The transactional system is depicted in a **conditional matrix** such as that shown in Figure 11-14. In the conditional matrix, the factors that are most pertinent to an event are shown at the interior, whereas the least important factors appear on the exterior. Once the coding is completed and a model of process or a transactional system developed, the grounded theory procedure is complete. It then remains for the researcher to write a report about the findings (often a book rather than a journal article). Subsequent grounded theory research projects tend to focus on different cultures. Comparisons between the original project and subsequent projects shed light on whether the original project has generalizability to other cultures or whether it is specific only to the culture studied.

Process The manner in which actions and interactions occur in a sequence or series.

Transactional system An analysis of how actions and interactions relate to their conditions and consequences.

Conditional matrix A diagram that helps the researcher consider the conditions and consequences related to the phenomenon under study.

definition

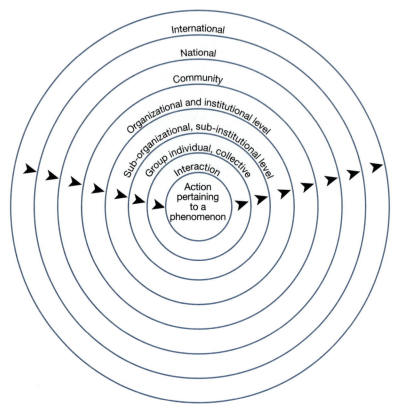

FIGURE 11-14   A TRANSACTIONAL SYSTEM CONDITIONAL MATRIX

Source: A. Strauss and J. Corbin, *Basics of Qualitative Research: Grounded Theory Procedures and Techniques,* p. 163. Copyright ©1990 by Sage Publications, Inc. Reprinted by permission of Sage Publications, Inc.

ALTERNATIVE RESEARCH APPROACHES: THE BOTTOM LINE

In this chapter we have briefly examined some innovative approaches to research that do not fit the traditional experimental mold. Although they do not use traditional methods of control, they do share the same goal—developing explanations for behavior. We hope that you have read this chapter and interpreted its cautions carefully. These methods vary considerably in their degree of approximation to experimentation; some are rather close, some seem much more descriptive. You must bear in mind that these alternative strategies all share one additional feature: They are questionable in terms of deriving cause-and-effect explanations for the behaviors being studied. Any conclusions you derive from one of these alternative approaches must be drawn in a tentative manner until additional replications increase your confidence in those conclusions.

REVIEW SUMMARY

1. **Qualitative research** is more concerned with relationships between variables and the "big picture" behind situations than it is with statistical analyses of minute aspects of a situation.

2. **Ethnography** is based on the anthropological research approach of living in and becoming part of a culture. This immersion in a culture provides the researcher with unique insights about the culture and how it functions.

3. The **clinical perspective** is similar to the ethnographic approach, although the clinician takes a more intrusive and intervening role. The goal of the clinician is also typically narrower than that of the ethnographer—the clinician endeavors to understand the problematic situation but not necessarily the entire system.

4. **Grounded theory** strives to develop theories about phenomena that are based on preexisting data within a system rather than artificially creating data from that system.

5. **Qualitative research** techniques are similar to descriptive techniques and thus suffer from difficulty in ascertaining cause-and-effect relationships.

STUDY BREAK

1. How does qualitative research differ from single-case and quasi-experimental designs?

2. Match the qualitative approach with the proper characteristics:
   1. Ethnography   2. Clinical perspective   3. Grounded theory
   a. uses coding for data analysis
   b. similar to an anthropological analysis
   c. researcher is more active than passive
   d. prediction of results is used to assess validation
   e. likely to use participant observation approach
   f. primarily interested in actions and interactions

LOOKING AHEAD

We have now completed our coverage of the various research approaches. We have tried to give you a complete picture of the different approaches along with their advantages and disadvantages. In the future, it will be your task to choose a research approach to fit your particular research question.

As we move to the final chapter in the text, we look at the culmination of any research effort—a final written report. In this chapter we will pull together the various aspects of writing in APA style we have previewed during the book and complete our coverage of this type of writing.

H A N D S - O N   A C T I V I T I E S

1. **Using a Single-Case Design.**   Single-case designs are often used in behavior modification settings. According to Weiten and Lloyd (1994), "Behavior modification is a systematic approach to changing behavior through the application of the principles of conditioning" (p. 126). Typically, behavior modification involves a trainer or therapist who attempts to change the behavior of a single participant. A variation on this approach is self-modification, in which an individual serves as his or her own trainer. Self-modification gives you an excellent opportunity to apply the single-case design. For this activity, you will need to follow the following steps.

   A. **Specify a target behavior.**   Choose a behavior you would like to change in some way. Be sure you pick a specific behavior such as "arguing with people" rather than "being disagreeable" so that you can easily measure the behavior. People often attempt to break themselves of bad habits through self-modification programs, so smoking, losing weight, biting your fingernails, or some similar behavior would be a good choice. On the other hand, you may wish to increase an infrequent behavior such as studying or listening to classical music.

   B. **Gather baseline data.**   As you saw in this chapter, you must know the level of the behavior before you intervene. Spend at least a few days measuring the rate of the behavior you wish to change. Also, as you monitor your behavior, try to discover any conditions that tend to lead to that behavior and any consequences that might help control it.

   C. **Design a program.**   The program you design will depend on whether you are attempting to increase or decrease a behavior. If you wish to increase a behavior, you may focus more on reinforcement, whereas punishment may be more useful for decreasing behaviors. For example, if you study an extra hour, you may wish to reward yourself by watching your favorite TV show. On the other hand, you might wear a rubber band around your wrist and pop yourself each time you find yourself biting your fingernails.

   D. **Execute and evaluate your program.**   Of course, after you have designed your program, you must put it into effect. Continue to monitor your behavior so that you can keep records to compare the before and after levels. It is often helpful to make a written contract with yourself (or others) that you will actually carry out your program—increasing your commitment is a powerful incentive.

   E. **End your program.**   At some point you will probably want to wean yourself away from your reinforcer(s) or punisher(s) to determine whether you have really learned the new behavior. This step, of course, is analogous to returning to the baseline condition. Be prepared to reinstitute your program if you find yourself slipping back to your old habits.

   For further information about self-modification programs, consult Weiten and Lloyd (1994), Watson and Tharp (1993), or a similar book.

2. **Finding Quasi-experimental Studies (I).**   In this chapter we contrasted the nonequivalent group design to ex post facto studies. Think about how these two designs would handle the independent variable of sex differently. Go to the library

and search the literature for two articles that use sex as a variable—be sure to find one ex post facto study and one using the nonequivalent group design. Contrast how the two studies deal with sex: How are they similar? How are they different?

3. **Finding Quasi-experimental Studies (II).**   In Activity 2 we did not ask you to find an interrupted time-series design that used sex as a variable. Can you figure out why we did not? Go to your library and find an article that uses the interrupted time-series design. Draw a diagram of your article in the fashion of Figure 11-8, labeling each O and X. What were the independent and dependent variables in your study?

4. **Designing Qualitative Research.**   Pick a psychological topic of interest to you that could be studied in an experimental *or* qualitative manner (e.g., the development of caretaker-offspring attachment). Write brief paragraphs describing how each different method (experimental, ethnography, clinical perspective, and grounded theory) would approach this topic through research. Do you think that different methods would be likely to yield different types of information? If so, give examples. If not, explain why not.

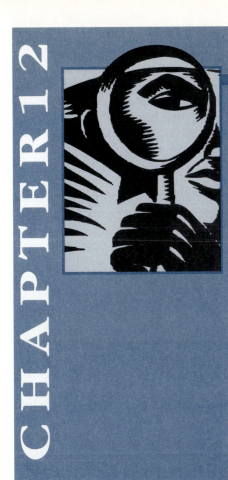

CHAPTER 12

Assembling the Research Report

The final step in the scientific process is communicating your results to other people who are interested in your research topic. As you have seen in numerous police shows, detectives have to spend time writing their reports also. Their purpose is no different from ours—communicating what has happened to a particular audience. We have given you instruction about writing and organizing various parts of a manuscript in **APA format** throughout several chapters of the text. In this chapter we will pull those pieces together and add the components that we have not yet covered. We will use a student research project as our example, tracing it from the research through the manuscript preparation to publication. In Chapter 7 we introduced Nancy Cathey's (1992) research project concerning the effects of caffeine on rats' learning and performance. What we didn't tell you then was that Nancy presented her research at the 1992 Southwestern Psychological Association meeting in Austin, Texas, and won the Undergraduate Poster Competition there. After revising her paper several times under the watchful eyes of your text authors, she eventually published the research (Cathey, Smith, & Davis, 1993). We include this research as an example not to intimidate you, but to show you what is possible at the undergraduate level.

However, before we get started, we need to make an important point: This chapter is not meant to substitute for the *Publication Manual of the American Psychological Association* (APA, 1994). There is simply no way for us to condense a 368-page book into a single chapter for this text. You should buy a *Publication Manual (PM)* and think of it as an investment in your future. As well as using it in this class, you will use it when you write term papers in other psychology classes and for any writing you will do if you go to graduate school in psychology. In addition, other academic disciplines are beginning to adopt APA style for their writing assignments. One of your authors has had colleagues in education, political science, and speech pathology borrow his *PM* for pointers on formatting and style.

APA Format Revisited and Extended

We first introduced APA format in Chapter 5. You can remind yourself of the major components of an APA format paper by looking at the list in Chapter 5. Let's review the components we covered already and then move on to the remaining elements. Keep in mind as you read these sections that you will find information that can help you write your paper at some future point, so it is likely that you will return to this chapter. By learning what is necessary for you to include as you write a manuscript, you will also get pointers about what you should look for as you read the different sections of journal articles. We believe that knowing how an article is written will help you better understand how to read an article and to extract the critical information from that article.

As we look at the various sections of the APA format paper, we will refer to the Cathey, Smith, and Davis manuscript as an example (Figures 12-1–

APA format
Accepted American Psychological Association (APA) form for preparing reports of psychological research.

definition

12-10 and Figure 12-13; M indicates manuscript, the number after M represents page order). In addition, you can refer to the published article (Cathey, Smith, & Davis, 1993) that is displayed in Figures 12-11, 12-12, 12-14, and 12-15 (JA indicates journal article) to see how a submitted manuscript is formatted as a journal article.

TITLE PAGE

The **title page** includes the **manuscript page header** and page number, the title, the author's or authors' name(s) and affiliation(s), and the **running head.** As you can see in Figure 12-1, Cathey used the same phrase for her manuscript page header and the running head. Although the same phrase is often a logical choice for both elements, APA style does not mandate it. The manuscript page header simply consists of the first two or three words of your title, whereas the running head is an abbreviated title that should not exceed 50 characters. Thus, the manuscript page header may not make sense, but the running head should communicate information about the contents of your manuscript because it would actually be printed with a published article (see Figure 12-14).

   You should be especially careful when you choose a title for your paper. Although it is often tempting to compose a title that is cute or catchy, such titles are often failures in communicating anything about the article's content. Keep in mind that more people will read your title than any other part of your manuscript, and they will use your title to decide whether to read the entire paper. Cathey's title is brief enough to fit APA's guidelines (10–12 words) and it fully communicates that the paper deals with how rats' bar-pressing and maze behaviors are affected by caffeine.

definition

Title page The first page of an APA format paper. It includes the manuscript page header, the running head, the manuscript's title, and name(s) of the author(s) and their affiliation(s).

Manuscript page header The first two or three words of the report's title. Appears five spaces to the left of the page number on each page of the research report.

Running head A condensed title that is printed at the top of alternate pages of a published article.

FIGURE 12-1 (M1)

Effects of Caffeine   1

Running head: EFFECTS OF CAFFEINE

Effects of Caffeine on Rats' Barpress and Maze Performance

Nancy R. Cathey and Randolph A. Smith

Ouachita Baptist University

Stephen F. Davis

Emporia State University

Abstract A brief description of the research that is presented in an APA format paper.

You will note that Cathey's final manuscript included two additional authors compared to her original paper. As we noted in Chapter 5, authors are listed in order of the importance of their contributions. The project was Cathey's idea for her experimental psychology course, so she was the primary author. Smith was the professor of her class and helped her develop her ideas, supervised the research project, assisted in the statistical analysis and interpretation, and participated with Cathey in co-writing the manuscript for submission. Davis, being at a different school, served as an outside consultant by providing background literature relevant to this research, giving procedural and design advice before the project began, and editing the written manuscript. Thus, although the research originated and was presented at a convention as a student project, by the time it was published, it had become a team effort among three people. Sometimes it is difficult to decide whether an individual merits being listed as an author on a publication. According to the *PM*, "Authorship encompasses not only those who do the actual writing but also those who have made substantial scientific contributions to a study" (APA, 1994, p. 4). This guideline is somewhat vague and results in people having to make "judgment calls" about authorship.

Finally, note that Davis's name and affiliation appear on separate lines from Cathey and Smith's in Figure 12-1. This separate listing is necessary for authors with different affiliations. The *PM* contains information about the title page on pages 7–8 and 248–250.

ABSTRACT

You can see the **abstract** of the manuscript in Figure 12-2. As we noted in Chapter 5, the abstract is important because if the title is appealing, people will read the abstract to learn more about your research. The *PM* states that an abstract for an experimental study should contain information about the problem, participants, experimental method, findings, and conclusions.

FIGURE 12-2 (M2)

Effects of Caffeine   2

Abstract

The effects of caffeine ingestion on rats were tested through barpress and maze performance. Four adult male and 4 adult female rats were bred, yielding 39 offspring (18 control, 21 experimental). The experimental pups received .50 mg/ml of caffeine in drinking water throughout gestation, weaning, and early adulthood; the control group received plain tap water. At 21 days of age the pups began barpress and maze learning. The subjects were allowed a total of 8 min for each test on alternate days. The results were characterized by the presence of several reliable caffeine X trials interactions. Inspection of the interactions prompted the generalization that although caffeine may facilitate performance early in training, it hinders performance on later trials.

Psychological Detective

Can you find information about each of the five topics (problem, participants, method, findings, conclusion) in the Abstract in Fig- ure 12-1B? Read it carefully and write a brief informative summary of each topic before going further.

Here's where we found the relevant information:

Problem—line 1
Participants—line 2
Experimental Method—lines 3—6
Findings—lines 6-7
Conclusions—lines 7-8

Did you find all the necessary information? Writing a good abstract is challenging because of the large amount of information that must be covered in little space. You can find more information about abstract on pages 8–11 and 250 of the *PM*.

INTRODUCTION

Figures 12-3 and 12-4 (first half) contain the manuscript's **intro-duction section.** Consistent with our Chapter 5 analogy, this introduction is "funnel-shaped." The first paragraph is broad, establishing caffeine as the variable of interest and demonstrating the scope of caffeine use. The second paragraph provides basic background information about why it is important to study the behavioral effects of caffeine. The third paragraph begins to narrow the funnel. Here, you read about some specific effects and dosage details of relevance to this research project. The fourth paragraph focuses on specific outcome behaviors that are relevant to the DVs of this experiment and on the time course of caffeine's effects. Finally, the last paragraph lays out the specific thesis of this research. Thus, the **thesis statement** (see Chapter 5) does not always occur in the first paragraph of the introduction. The *PM* provides more information concerning introductions on pages 11–12.

Psychological Detective

Can you identify the thesis state-ment in the last paragraph? Record your answer before reading fur-ther.

Effects of Caffeine on Rats' Barpress and Maze Performance

Caffeine, a methylxanthine, is a widely used central nervous system stimulant. Surveys report that 62% of Americans ingest at least 5 mg/kg per day from drinking coffee alone (West, Sobotka, Brodie, Beier, & O'Donnell, 1986). When other sources are taken into account, it can be said that Americans consume approximately 45 million pounds of caffeine every year (Stanwood, 1990). Despite its widespread use, caffeine may have potentially detrimental effects. For example, caffeine is a possible risk factor when it is consumed in coffee by pregnant women (Gullberg, Ferrell, & Christensen, 1986). In a 1980 position statement, the Food and Drug Administration advised pregnant women to eliminate their consumption of caffeine-containing products.

The teratogenic effects of caffeine on the developing human fetus are of particular interest because "caffeine easily crosses the placental barrier and its clearance is substantially delayed in pregnancy" (Glavin & Krueger, 1985, p. 29). Prenatal administration of caffeine to rats has been shown to negatively affect mortality rate, locomotor activity, metabolic processes, immune and endocrine functions, and neurological processes (Finn & Holtzman, 1986; Gullberg et al., 1986; West et al., 1986). Moreover, caffeine also may increase the frequency of self-injurious behavior in rats (Mueller, Saboda, Palmour, & Nyhan, 1982).

Research (e.g., Silinsky, 1989) shows that caffeine exerts its action by blocking the presynaptic activity of adenosine, a neurotransmitter that blocks the release of the excitatory neurotransmitter glutamate. Thus, caffeine ingestion results in an increase in the release of glutamate and leads to central nervous system arousal. Low doses of caffeine increase arousal and improve task performance, but with higher doses, anxiety and insomnia are prevalent (Glavin & Krueger, 1985). Although prenatal caffeine administration was employed in most of the studies cited here, the behavioral effects occurred postnatally, when the rats were no longer exposed to the chemical.

Research shows that the effects of caffeine vary across time and dosage. For example, caffeine may reduce within-session decrements in ambulation and rearing in adult rats, especially during the second hour of a session (Loke & Meliska, 1984). Changes in behavior across sessions

FIGURE 12-3 (M3)

The last sentence-and-a-half forms the thesis statement for Cathey's manuscript. Beginning with "it was hypothesized that a caffeine group," you see the specific predictions made for the performance of the two groups of rats.

Note that every fact-based statement is supported by a **citation** to a **reference.** If you wish to locate one of the references cited, you can find the necessary information in the **reference section** at the end of the paper (see Figure 12-10). As we

Effects of Caffeine   4

also have been noted. Tight circling increased and then decreased in frequency in adult rats (Mueller et al., 1982). Holloway and Thor (1982) found that locomotor activity increased consistently for the first several days of testing and then decreased rapidly after an average of 14 days. They concluded that rat pups respond to increasing doses of caffeine in a curvilinear fashion, such that an initial increase in activity is followed by a decrease.

In light of these observations, we exposed rats to caffeine throughout gestation, weaning, and early adulthood to measure the drug's effect on the acquisition of behaviors requiring locomotor activity. On the basis of previous activity data showing a curvilinear function relating activity and trials in caffeine-exposed animals (e.g., Holloway & Thor, 1982; Muller et al., 1982), it was hypothesized that a caffeine group would display high levels of maze and barpress performance in early trials, followed by a decline as training continued. On the other hand, a noncaffeine control group was expected to continue to increase in performance throughout training.

Method

Subjects

Four adult male and 4 adult female rats were randomly selected from the colony maintained at Ouachita Baptist University. These rats were randomly assigned to 4 male-female breeding pairs. The breeding pairs were housed together for 7 days and then separated. Pups were separated from the dams at 21 days of age and housed separately. The 39 pups delivered to the 4 dams (18 control, 21 experimental) served as subjects.

Apparatus

A Lafayette operant conditioning chamber (Model 84012) was used for barpress training. A modified Hampton Court maze (69.5 X 84.5 cm; alleys were 8.3 cm wide with 14.6-cm-high walls) with 11 choice points was used for all maze training.

Procedure

Upon formation, the breeding pairs were randomly assigned to the experimental (caffeine) or control (no caffeine) condition. Pairs in the experimental condition received .50 mg/ml caffeine in plain tap water, while controls received plain tap water. Solutions were presented in 250-ml

FIGURE 12-4 (M4)

showed you in Chapter 5, APA format uses a simple method of citing only the author(s) and date in the text. When a citation includes three to five authors, each author's last name is included in the first citation, with subsequent citations using only the first author's name, followed by et al. (Latin for "and others") and the date. As shown in the first and second paragraphs of the introduction, this rule creates the following citations:

Citation A notation in text that a particular reference was used. The citation provides the name(s) of the author(s) and date of the work's publication.

Reference A full bibliographic record of any work cited in the text of a psychological paper.

Reference section A complete listing of all the references cited in a psychological paper.

definition

Gullberg, Ferrell, & Christensen, 1986 *(first citation)*
Gullberg et al., 1986 *(second citation)*

If a citation includes six or more authors, *all* citations (including the first) consist of the first author's last name followed by et al. and the date. However, in the reference section, all names are included. The *PM* provides more information about reference citations in text on pages 168–174.

METHOD

You will find Cathey's **method section** in Figures 12-4 (last half) and 12-5 (first half). This method section has the typical three subsections that you saw in Chapter 5.

Participants (Subjects). The **participants subsection** enumerates and describes the experimental participants. Because Cathey's paper was written and published before the latest edition of the *PM,* the term *subjects* was used rather than *participants.* It appears from the *PM* that it may be permissible to use "subjects" when referring to animals (see page 14 of the *PM*). Because animals do not voluntarily participate in an experiment, we believe that using *subjects* would be appropriate. Only time (or your instructor) will tell which term becomes used for animals in experiments.

Notice that the experimental animals, the selection procedures, and housing conditions are described in sufficient detail to allow a replication of the study. See pages 13–14 of the *PM* for more information about this subsection.

Apparatus. Remember that the **apparatus subsection** can have various names depending on what you use in your particular experiment. Cathey used one piece of standard laboratory equipment (a Skinner box) that is described by manufacturer and model number. In addition, she used a customized piece of equipment (a maze) that is described in as much detail as necessary to provide the reader with a good idea of its features. As we told you in Chapter 5, metric measurements and abbreviations are used. See pages 105–111 of the *PM* for information on APA's metrication policy and list of accepted metric abbreviations.

In labeling this section you should choose the term that best describes the elements you used in conducting your experiment. Cathey chose "Apparatus" because she used laboratory equipment in her research. If you use items such as slides, pictures, videotapes, or paper-and-pencil tests that are not standardized, you would probably want to label this section **Materials.** If your "equipment" consists of standardized psychological testing materials, then the label of **Testing Instruments** would be appropriate. If your experiment entailed the use of more than one category, then you should combine the relevant names when labeling this subsection. The *PM* contains a short section concerning this subsection on page 14.

Method section
Second major section of the APA format paper. Contains information about the participants, the apparatus, materials, and testing instrument(s), and the procedures used in the experiment.

Participants subsection First subsection of the method section. Provides full information about the participants in the study.

Apparatus subsection Second subsection of the method section. When appropriate, contains information about the equipment used in the experiment.

Materials subsection Second subsection of the method section. When appropriate, contains information about materials other than equipment used in the experiment.

Testing instrument(s) subsection Second subsection of the method section. When appropriate, contains information about standardized tests used in the experiment.

definition

Procedure. Your primary goal in the **procedure subsection** is to describe how you conducted your experiment. Enough information should be given to allow a replication of your method, but unnecessary details should not be included (e.g., note that times were recorded with a stopwatch—the brand and model number would be overkill).

Procedure subsection Third subsection of the method section. Provides a step-by-step account of what the participants and experimenter did during the experiment.

FIGURE 12-5 (M5)

Effects of Caffeine 5

graduated drinking tubes and were the only available liquid throughout the experiment. Lights in the room were on a 12:12-h light-dark cycle. Beginning with Day 15 of gestation, the cages were checked daily for births; new litters were considered born the previous day. As soon as they were detected, pups were marked with a permanent marker for identification. Litters were checked daily for mortalities; one pup from the caffeine group died after birth. There were no visible differences in weight between either the dams or pups of the two groups.

At 21 days of age, the pups were weaned and began a series of tests on the barpress and maze tasks for food reinforcement. The subjects were food deprived for an average of 7 h (range, 6-8 h) prior to experimental testing. Otherwise food and fluids, which corresponded to those consumed by the respective dams, were freely available.

When the subjects were in the operant conditioning chamber, under conditions of continuous reinforcement, barpresses within an 8-min period were recorded. In the maze, the percent complete and actual time of completion were recorded, with an 8-min limit. Subjects alternated tasks each day until 8 sessions of each task had been completed (16 days).

Results

Percent of Maze Completion

Analysis of variance (ANOVA) of the percent of maze completion scores yielded a significant trials effect [$F(7, 259) = 19.64$, $p < .001$]. As can be seen from Figure 1, subjects completed a higher percentage of the maze across trials. The presence of a significant drug X trials interaction [$F(7, 259) = 2.75$, $p < .01$] indicated that statements concerning the trials effect must be considered in light of whether the subjects were caffeine exposed or not. A series of simple main effects analyses comparing the caffeine and the noncaffeine subjects on each trial was employed to probe the interaction. The results of these analyses indicated that the caffeine subjects completed a higher percentage of the maze on Trials 1 and 2 [$F(1, 301) = 8.56$, $p < .01$, and $F(1, 301) = 8.80$, $p < .01$, respectively].

Time of Maze Completion

The time of completion ANOVA yielded significance for the trials effect [$F(7, 259) = 28.59$, $p < .001$] and the drug X trials interaction [$F(7, 259) = 2.93$, $p < .01$]. As can be seen

Critical details are pertinent points that would need to be copied in a replication study. We believe that the following details are critical:

random assignment

.50-mg/ml caffeine concentration

no other liquids were available during the experiment

12:12 light-dark cycle

method of determining age of new pups

age at testing

food deprivation before testing

continuous reinforcement in the Skinner box

eight-minute testing periods

sequence of testing periods

Did we leave out any details that you included? If so, reread the procedure subsection to see whether your detail is absolutely necessary. For example, did you list the 250-ml drinking tubes as critical? Although it is desirable to measure the amount of water ingested, that measurement could be made from a variety of containers.

The procedure subsection is typically the longest of the three components of the method section. Its length will vary depending on how complex your experiment is. To read more about the procedure subsection, check pages 14-15 of the *PM*.

RESULTS

We introduced the format for the **results section** in Chapter 7 and reinforced those ideas in Chapters 8 and 9 when we discussed the notion of translating statistics into words. We do not use the word *translating* lightly—to some people, statistics resembles a foreign language. It is your job in the results section to decode the meaning of your numbers into words for the reader. At the same time you must provide the factual, numerical basis to back your decoding. The presentation of statistical results is covered on pages 15–18 and 111–119 of the *PM*. Figures 12-5 (second half) and 12-6 (first half) contain Cathey's results section. In Figure 12-12, you will notice that the results and discussion sections were combined into one section in the published journal article. This combination is common for certain journals or for shorter experimental articles. It is likely that your instructor will want you to keep your sections separate.

Results section
Third major section of the APA format paper. Contains information about the statistical findings from the experiment.

definition

from Figure 2, subjects generally took less time to complete the maze across trials. The results of simple main effects analyses indicated that the caffeine and noncaffeine groups differed on Trials 4 and 7 [$F(1, 301)$ = 4.86, p < .05, and $F(1, 301)$ = 4.01, p < .05, respectively]. The groups were marginally different on Trials 5 and 6 [$F(1, 301)$ = 3.38, p < .07 and $F(1, 301)$ = 3.66, p < .06, respectively]. Figure 2 shows that the noncaffeine group was slower on Trial 4 but faster on Trials 5, 6, and 7.

Barpress

As with the maze data, the barpress ANOVA yielded significance for the trials effect [$F(7, 259)$ = 74.68, p < .001] and drug X trials interaction [$F(7, 259)$ = 15.02, p < .001]. Figure 3 shows that the number of barpresses increased reliably from the beginning to the end of testing. Simple main effects analyses indicated that the groups differed marginally on Trial 3 [$F(1, 301)$ = 3.56, p < .07] and reliably on Trials 4-8 [smallest $F(1, 301)$ = 5.36, p < .05]. In these instances, the noncaffeine animals made more barpresses than did the caffeine animals.

Discussion

In the present study, we investigated the relationship between caffeine and the performance of learned behaviors requiring activity. Previous research on the effects of caffeine on locomotor activities has shown an initial facilitation of the behavior followed by a decrement; the present data are similar to those results. For maze running, caffeine facilitated early performance but hindered or had no effect on later performance. For barpressing, caffeine resulted in reduced behavior across trials. Caffeine subjects completed a higher percentage of the maze during the first two trials (see Figure 1) and completed the maze in less time on Trial 4, but took more time on Trials 5-7 (see Figure 2). Caffeine subjects also produced fewer barpresses on Trials 3-8.

These results are consistent with previous research dealing with locomotor activity, in that caffeine's effects were beneficial (or less of a hindrance) on early trials. As trials continued, the performance of caffeine subjects tended to level off, whereas the performance of noncaffeine subjects continued to improve toward a higher asymptotic level. Thus, it appears that caffeine produces beneficial effects on early trials but that caffeine produces deficits with extended testing.

The question of whether the caffeine-related decrements occurred because of prenatal or

FIGURE 12-6 (M6)

Inferential Statistics. As you write the results section, you should assume that your reader has a good understanding of statistics. Therefore, you do not review basic concepts such as how the null hypothesis is rejected. The most important information to report is the specific findings from your inferential statistics. In Cathey's paper, you see numerous examples of how to report results from factorial ANOVAs (F tests; see Chapter 9 for review).

Psychological Detective

Why did Cathey use a factorial ANOVA to analyze her data? What was or were her IV(s)? What was or were her DV(s)? Write your answers before reading further.

First, you should remember from Chapter 9 that a factorial ANOVA is used when you have more than one IV—thus, you should look for more than one IV in Cathey's experiment. The main focus of the experiment was caffeine, so one IV was drug (caffeine vs. no caffeine). You read in the procedure subsection that each task was tested over eight sessions, so the second IV was trials (Days 1–8).

Also in the Procedure subsection, you found out that two tasks were used—bar pressing and maze running. Bar pressing was measured by the number of presses in eight minutes; maze running was measured by percentage of completion and time of completion (both with an eight-minute limit). Therefore, three DVs were used: number of bar presses, percentage of maze completed, and maze completion time. To allow readers to process the information easily, Cathey's results section was divided into three subsections, one for each DV.

In presenting inferential statistical results, you must present the test that was used, the degrees of freedom for the test, the test statistics, and the probability level. In looking at Cathey's results, the first line provides us a good example:

Analysis of variance (ANOVA) of the percent of maze completion scores yielded a significant trials effect [$F(7, 259) = 19.64$, $p < .001$].

Notice that the statistical findings at the end of the sentence give us all four pieces of information: an F test (analysis of variance) was used, there were 7 and 259 degrees of freedom, the calculated test value was 19.64, and the probability of chance was less than one in a thousand. The same type of information is presented for findings relevant to the experimental hypothesis even if you do not find statistical significance. Although information from different test statistics will be presented in a slightly different fashion, these four basic pieces of information are always necessary. We presented a set of t test results in Chapter 7 that you can refer to. You can find examples of how to present other statistical test results on page 113 of the *PM*.

Descriptive Statistics. In order to give a full picture of the data, it is customary to present descriptive statistics in addition to the inferential statistics. Means and standard deviations typically allow readers to get a good feel for the data. With a small number of groups, you can present the descriptive statistics in the text, as we showed you in Chapter 7. On the other hand, with many groups, it may be more efficient and clearer to present the descriptive statistics in either a table or a figure, which we will discuss next.

Complementary Information. In presenting your results, you must first decide how best to give the reader the necessary information. If your statistical information is relatively simple, merely reporting your findings in words and numbers is usually adequate. For more complex analyses or results, you may wish to include tables or figures to further explicate your words and numbers.

Figures. Because all three of Cathey's DVs showed significant interactions, she used **figures** to clarify the presentation of results. The three figures appear in Figure 12-7. Figures can take the form of graphs (line, bar, circle or pie, scatter, or pictorial graphs), charts, dot maps, drawings, or photographs.

FIGURE 12-7 (M11, M12, M13)

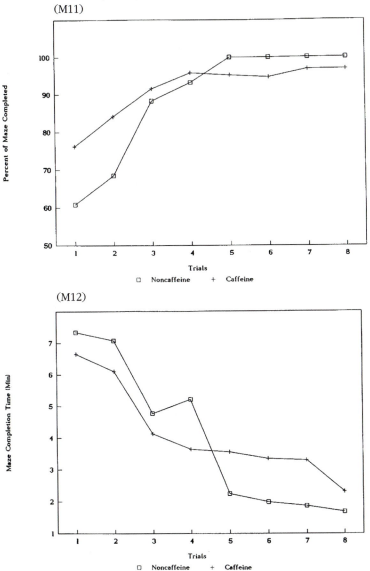

Figure 12-7 (continued)

(M13)

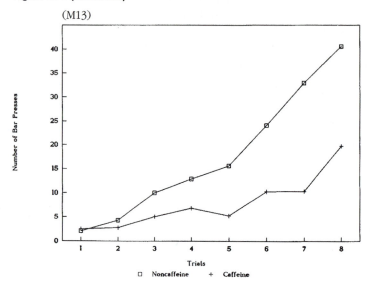

The *PM* presents information regarding figures on pages 141–163. As you can guess from the number of pages devoted to figures, they can be complex to deal with. However, the vast majority of the *PM* information about figures involves preparing figures for publication. Because you will probably be submitting your research paper as a class requirement, your instructor may not be a stickler for enforcing every APA requirement on figures you submit with your paper. For example, you can see from Figure 12-8 that **figure captions** appear on a separate page in a manuscript prepared for publication. Your instructor may choose to have you put your caption on the page with each figure.

Figure caption A descriptive label for a particular figure.

It is likely that the majority of figures you use will be line graphs (see Chapter 6) that depict findings similar to Cathey's. Line graphs are particularly good for showing interaction patterns. Fortunately, a number of good software programs for graphing exist that you might have access to. For example, the graphs in Figure 12-7 were made using Lotus123; the same graphs were used eventually in the published article. For your class project, ask your instructor about his or her preference as to how you should produce a figure. Regardless of how you create your figures,

FIGURE 12-8 (M10)

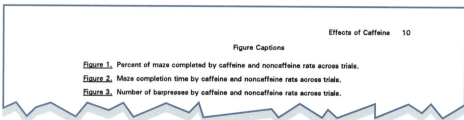

one rule is constant: Be certain that you refer to your figures in the text at an appropriate place. This reference will cue the reader to look at the figure in order to process its meaning.

Tables. A **table** consists of a display of data, usually in numerical form. Tables are an alternative to presenting data in pictorial form as a figure. To use a table, your data display should be large enough that it would be difficult or confusing to present it in the text.

Table A chart containing an array of descriptive statistics.

definition

    You often have to decide between using a table or a figure to present your data. Notice that Cathey presented her data only with figures rather than tables. We have adapted the data from her Figure 1 (Percent of maze completion) into the format that you see in Table 12-1. The advantage of the table over the figure is that standard deviations can be included in the table. The advantage of the figure over the table is accessibility—the data, particularly the significant interaction, seem easier to understand and conceptualize in the pictorial presentation. Based on these advantages, the figure seemed a better choice in this situation. For your experimental report, your decision may be different.

TABLE 12-1. MAZE COMPLETION DATA FROM CATHEY, SMITH, AND DAVIS (1993)

PERCENT OF MAZE COMPLETED BY CAFFEINE AND NONCAFFEINE RATS ACROSS TRIALS

| | TRIAL | | | | | | | |
SUBJECTS	1*	2*	3	4	5	6	7	8
Caffeine								
M	76.2	84.1	91.5	95.8	95.2	94.7	96.8	96.8
SD	25.7	19.1	16.4	11.9	10.8	14.3	10.0	9.9
Noncaffeine								
M	60.8	68.5	88.3	93.2	100.0	100.0	100.0	100.0
SD	34.5	25.0	18.1	14.8	0.0	0.0	0.0	0.0

*$p < .01$.

    Again, APA presents many guidelines for developing tables (see pages 120–141 of the *PM*). You should check with your instructor to find out which guidelines you must follow in your paper. Because a table is typically generated directly in your word-processing program (or on your typewriter), you may find a table easier to produce than a figure. However, your choice of a table versus a figure should be made on the quality of information provided to the reader rather than on ease of production. Again, if you use a table in your paper, be sure to refer to it at the appropriate point.

Psychological Detective

Can you think of a specific situation in which you would prefer a table over a figure? Write an answer before reading further.

The most obvious answer to this question is a situation in which you have a large number of means to present but for which there is not a significant interaction. We hope that a comparison of Figure 12-7 (M11) and Table 12-1 convinced you of the benefit of a figure for portraying interactions.

DISCUSSION

You can find Cathey's **discussion section** in Figures 12-6 (second half, p. 417) and 12-9. According to the *PM* (APA, 1994, p. 19), you should be guided by three questions in the discussion section:

- *What have I contributed here?*
- *How has my study helped to resolve the original problem?*
- *What conclusions and theoretical implications can I draw from my study?*

Typically, authors answer these three questions by (1) briefly restating their findings, (2) comparing and contrasting their findings to previous research cited in the introduction, and (3) giving their interpretation of their findings. Writing the discussion section is covered in pages 18–19 of the *PM*.

Restating Results. Your first task in the discussion section is to recap your results as briefly as possible. Typically, you will summarize only your significant findings, unless a null finding is particularly meaningful. If you conducted a large study with many outcomes, you may wish to feature only the most important findings at this point—typically those that have some bearing on your experimental hypothesis.

This summary ensures that the reader has extracted the most important information from your results section.

If you examine the three paragraphs of Cathey's discussion section, you will find that each paragraph uses one of the three techniques listed just before this section. In the first paragraph, the information from the results section is summarized in four sentences. The results from each DV are mentioned in a sentence or two, depending on the complexity and number of significant findings. As you look at the specific four sentences in Figure 12-6, notice that the first two refer to the main effects of caffeine on maze running and bar pressing. The final two sentences describe the significant interactions that were found.

Comparing Results to Previous Research. It is important for you to evaluate how your results "stack up" against previous findings in your area

Discussion section
Fourth major section of the APA format paper. Contains a summary of the experiment's results, a comparison of those results to previous research, and the conclusion(s) from the experiment.

FIGURE 12-9 (M7)

Effects of Caffeine   7

postnatal caffeine exposure is unanswered. Although the subjects in this study may have been affected prenatally by caffeine, they also continued to ingest caffeine postnatally. An extension of this research would be to test the maze and barpress performance of separate groups of animals exposed to caffeine prenatally and postnatally.

of research summarized in your introduction. The previous research studies will be related to, but not the same as, your experiment. Typically, you will have made a prediction before the experiment about your expected findings based on your survey of previous research. You should tell the reader how accurate your predictions were. This information will help the reader in drawing conclusions. For example, if you correctly predicted your results from previous research, the previous research and your study are both validated. On the other hand, if your prediction is not borne out, some doubt is cast—either your research or the previous research may be flawed in some way.

Looking at the second paragraph of Cathey's discussion section, you will see the comparison to previous research findings. In this case, the previous research studies were related to Cathey's study because they dealt with locomotor activity. On the other hand, these studies were different because they did not specifically measure bar pressing or maze running. Caffeine seemed to produce an immediate facilitative effect followed by a leveling-off or a decrement in performance in both the previous research and in Cathey's study.

Interpreting the Results. This portion of the discussion section gives you more of a free hand to engage in conjecture and speculation than any other portion of the experimental writeup. It is here that you draw the "bottom line" to your study: What is your overall conclusion? What are the implications of your results for any psychological theories? How can your results be applied in various settings—the laboratory, the real world, our body of psychological knowledge? What new research should grow out of this study? As you can see, there are a variety of questions you can address in your discussion section. Not all these questions are appropriate for every study—pick the ones that are most important for your particular experiment.

The interpretation of Cathey's results is contained in the last sentence of the discussion section s second paragraph. The similarity of the previous research findings and the findings from this study led to a general statement about caffeine's initial beneficial effects followed by a later deficit.

The final paragraph of Cathey's manuscript includes a question about the results and a direction for future research. Because the rats ingested the caffeine both before and after birth, it was not clear exactly when caffeine caused the performance deficits. The final sentence of the manuscript provided an experimental question for the future. Indeed, this question did lead to further research. O'Loughlin, Graves, Davis, and Smith (1993) conducted just such a study as mentioned in Cathey's manuscript. These researchers found that rats exposed to caffeine on a pre- and postnatal basis had higher rates of bar pressing than rats that were exposed to caffeine only after birth, implying that postnatal caffeine exposure causes the deficits noted. You may wish to mentally file this example away for future reference. As you read discussion sections of published articles, you might find ideas for your own research projects.

REFERENCES

It is your responsibility for two reasons to provide a complete list of accurate references to any published works that you cite in your research report. First, you must

Plagiarism Using someone else's work without giving credit to the original source.

give credit to the original author(s) for any ideas and information that you got from reading other works. If you take exact wordings, paraphrases, or even ideas from an author without giving credit for that source, you are guilty of **plagiarism** (see Chapter 2). Second, you are providing a historical account of the sources you consulted in the event that a reader wishes to read them in their entirety. Have you ever worked on a term paper and "lost" a good source that you had read because you didn't write down all the necessary bibliographic information and couldn't find it again? Most of us have had this experience, and it is quite frustrating. You can prevent that frustrating experience by providing your reader with a complete and accurate reference list. The *PM* describes the reference list section on page 20 and provides general pointers about the list as well as examples of APA format for 77 different types of sources on pages 174–222.

Before going further, we need to distinguish between a reference list and a bibliography that you might have learned about in English classes. The reference list is *not* a list of every source that you read when you were writing your introduction and planning your experiment. The only references that you list are those from which you actually obtained information and cited somewhere in your paper. If you do not cite a particular source, it should not be referenced.

The list of references begins on a new page after the end of your discussion section. You will find Cathey's references in Figure 12-10. As we have previously mentioned, this manuscript was originally written under the guidelines of the third edition of the *PM* (APA, 1983). One of the major changes from the third to fourth editions of the *PM* was in the format of the references (see Chapter 5). This change was made to make referencing an easier task in most word-processing programs. To avoid any confusion, we have changed the style of the references in Figure 12-10 from their original third edition format to the correct format of the fourth edition.

Psychological Detective

Look at Figure 12-10. All the references except one have the same format. Can you find the one that is different? Once you have found it, can you decipher why it is different from the others? Record your answer before reading further.

The different reference is the second one in the list—the Food and Drug Administration's *Report on Caffeine*. This booklet reference is formatted in the style for a book; the remaining references are formatted in the style for journal articles.

As you look at a reference, you will find that the information about author(s) and date is listed first. This location makes it easy for the reader to see an author and date citation in your text and then to find the corresponding reference in your reference list. The reference list is alphabetized by the surname of the first author. If you have more than one article by the same authors, you alphabetize by the name

Effects of Caffeine   8

References

Finn, I. F., & Holtzman, S. G. (1986). Tolerance to caffeine-induced stimulation of locomotor activity in rats. Journal of Pharmacology and Experimental Therapeutics, 238, 542-546.

Food and Drug Administration. (1980, September). Report on caffeine [Brochure]. Washington, DC: U.S. Department of Health and Human Services.

Glavin, G. B., & Krueger, H. (1985). Effects of prenatal caffeine administration on offspring mortality, open-field behavior and adult gastric ulcer susceptibility. Neurobehavioral Toxicology and Teratology, 7, 29-32.

Gullberg, E. I., Ferrell, F., & Christensen, H. D. (1986). Effects of postnatal caffeine exposure through dam's milk upon weanling rats. Pharmacology, Biochemistry, and Behavior, 24, 1695-1701.

Holloway, W. R., & Thor, D. (1982). Caffeine sensitivity in the neonatal rat. Neurobehavioral Toxicology and Teratology, 4, 331-333.

Loke, W. H., & Meliska, C. J. (1984). Effects of caffeine and nicotine on open-field exploration. Psychological Reports, 55, 447-451.

Mueller, K., Saboda, S., Palmour, R., & Nyhan, W. L. (1982). Self-injurious behavior produced in rats by daily caffeine and continuous amphetamine. Pharmacology, Biochemistry, and Behavior, 17, 613-617.

Silinsky, E. M. (1989). Adenosine derivatives and neuronal function. Seminars in the Neurosciences, 1, 155-165.

Stanwood, L. (1990). C is for coffee, chocolate, cola and...caffeine. Current Health 2, 13, 11-13.

West, G. L., Sobotka, T. J., Brodie, R. E., Beier, J. M., & O'Donnell, J. W. (1986). Postnatal neurobehavioral development in rats exposed in utero to caffeine. Neurobehavioral Toxicology and Teratology, 8, 29-43.

FIGURE 12-10 (M8)

of the second author. If the author information for two or more articles is identical, the references are arranged by date, with the earliest article listed first. If the author information and dates are identical, alphabetize by the first main word of the title, and add lowercase letters (*a, b,* etc.) to the date to differentiate the articles (see Chapter 5).

The title of the scholarly work is the next piece of information, followed by supplementary information that helps a reader locate that work. As you can see, the supplementary information differs depending on the particular type of reference you are using. Let's take a look at the general format for the three different types of references you are most likely to use in your papers.

Periodical Articles. Examples of 23 different types of references to periodicals are shown on pages 194–201 of the *PM*. Your most typical use of periodicals will be to reference articles in journals. The general format for periodicals is as follows (example adapted from APA, 1994, p. 182):

> Author, A. A., Author, B. B., & Author, C. C. (date). Title of article. <u>Title of Periodical, vol,</u> ppp–ppp.

For examples, you can examine all the references in Figure 12-10 except the second one (Food and Drug Administration). The last names and initials of *all* authors are given in the same order as in the journal article. You will remember that earlier in this chapter we mentioned using et al. for multiple-author works earlier in this chapter. You do not use et al. in the reference list—all authors are listed. The date refers to the year in which the particular journal issue containing the article was published. Be careful here—you may need to look at the front of the journal to get this information.

The title of the article is typed with *only* the first word capitalized and is *not* underlined. If the article title includes a colon, capitalize the first word after the colon also. In addition, any words that are normally capitalized (e.g., names, states, organizations, or test names) are capitalized.

The journal title, on the other hand, is typed with all primary words capitalized—words such as *a, and,* and *the* are not capitalized unless they are the first word or follow a colon. The journal title *is* underlined, as is the volume number of the journal that immediately follows the journal title. Only the volume number is typed—it is not preceded by Vol. or V. It is often the case that volumes of journals also have issue numbers. For example, volume 50 represents the 1995 issues of *American Psychologist;* each month's issue is represented by its own number. Thus, the January 1995 issue would be represented by Volume 50, Number 1, and so on. Most journals use continuous pagination throughout a volume. That is, the first issue of a new volume begins on page one and the pages run continuously until the next volume, which begins with page one. In this case, the issue number is not needed to find the referenced article and does not appear in the reference. A few journals, however, begin each issue with page one. If this is the case, then the issue number is necessary to find the article and is included in the reference. This reference format follows (example adapted from APA, 1994, p. 182):

> Author, A. A., Author, B. B., & Author, C. C. (date). Title of article. <u>Title of Periodical, vol</u> (n), ppp–ppp.

Notice that the issue number (n) is placed within parentheses and is *not* underlined. Finally, the inclusive page numbers of the article are given—numbers only, no p. or pp. preceding.

Books. The *PM* provides 12 examples of references to books on pages 201–204. This category consists of references to entire books rather than to chapters in edited books. The general format for book references is (example adapted from APA, 1994, p. 182):

> Author, A. A. (date). <u>Title of work.</u> Location: Publisher.

We have used a one-author example here, but don't be misled by it. All authors' names and initials are included, just as in the journal examples given previously. Use the date of the original publication of the book, which is usually found at the front of the book facing the title page.

The book's title is formatted in a combination of the styles seen earlier for article titles and journal titles. It follows the style for an article title in terms of capitalization—only the first word (and first word after a colon or normally capitalized words) are capitalized. However, like a journal title, the book's title is underlined.

The location and the name of the publisher are provided in the last portion of the reference. If the city, such as New York, is well known for publishing (see p. 176 of the *PM* for a complete list), it can be typed alone. Otherwise, the city and state (two-letter postal abbreviation) or country must be provided. Many publishers now have offices in several locations—typically the first location listed would be the one referenced. The name of the publisher is given in a brief form, omitting "superfluous terms, such as *Publishers, Co.,* or *Inc.,* which are not required to identify the publisher" (APA, 1994, p. 188). Many times you will find that a corporate author and publisher are the same, as with the *PM*. In such a case, rather than repeat the author information for the publisher, you simply type "Author" after the location (e.g., see the reference to the *PM* in the reference list for this book).

The only example of a book reference in Cathey's manuscript is the brochure published by the Food and Drug Administration. You see that "[Brochure]" was included in the reference to distinguish it from a book. Otherwise, the reference format is identical.

Chapters from Edited Books. Most edited books contain chapters that are written by different authors. The type of reference we are about to present allows you to cite information from a chapter within such a book. The *PM* gives eight examples of such references on pages 204–207. The general format of such a reference is (example adapted from APA, 1994, p. 182):

Author, A. A., & Author, B. B. (date). Title of chapter. In C. C. Editor, D. D.

Editor, & E. E. Editor (Eds.), Title of book (pp. nnn-nnn). Location: Publisher.

As you can see, this type of reference is much like a journal article reference combined with a book reference. This example includes two authors and three editors, but any number of either is possible. You would provide the information concerning author(s) and date as we have previously discussed. The title of the chapter refers to the specific smaller work within the larger book. The chapter title is capitalized in the same manner as a journal article title—capitalize only the first word, first word after a colon, and words that are normally capitalized.

All the editors' names are listed. Notice that the initials and surnames are *not* reversed. After a comma, the book's title is listed, with capitalization in the same fashion as mentioned previously for a book title. The inclusive pages of the chapter are given parenthetically after the book's title to make it easier for the reader to locate the specific chapter in the book. Finally, the location and publisher information are included as for any book.

Cathey's manuscript includes no examples of chapters in edited books. The following example is for a chapter that we cited in Chapter 11 of this text:

Hersen, M. (1982). Single-case experimental designs. In A. S. Bellack, M. Hersen, & A. E. Kazdin (Eds.), <u>International handbook of behavior modification and therapy</u> (pp. 167–203). New York: Plenum Press.

Other References. Although we expect that most of your references will be to periodicals, books, and chapters in edited books, the *PM* has almost 40 examples of other types of references you might use. These other references include technical and research reports, proceedings of meetings and symposia, doctoral dissertations and master's theses, unpublished works and publications of limited circulation, reviews, audiovisual media, and electronic media. No matter what type of material you wish to reference, the *PM* will have a format for you.

A Disclaimer. As we previously noted, the third edition of the *PM* (APA, 1983) used a different reference format. Although all the information included was the same, the appearance of the references was different. If you look at a reference in Figure 12-10, you will see that the initial line of each reference is indented and subsequent lines begin at the left margin. However, when references are printed in journal articles (see Figure 12-15), this margin situation is reversed—the first line begins at the left margin and subsequent lines are indented (referred to as a "hanging indent"). With this formatting, the first authors' names stand out and are easier to locate. Under the old *PM* guidelines, manuscript references were formatted as they are in publication. This formatting was more difficult to use with some word-processors, so the new format was developed for the current edition of the *PM* (APA, 1994).

We give you this explanation to alert you to the possibility that your instructor may require you to format your references as they would have been under the *PM*'s third edition guidelines. "Students should note that a hanging indent may be the format preferred by their university, as the paper will be prepared as a *final* copy" (APA, 1994, p. 251). Appendix A of the current *PM* addresses "Material Other Than Journal Articles" and includes a section on "Theses, Dissertations, and Student Papers." This section acknowledges that different departments and instructors may make variations in APA format for their purposes—strict APA format is intended primarily for submitting articles for publication.

Psychological Detective

Can you figure out why an APA formatted manuscript and a published article (or final copy) might differ in appearance? Jot down your idea(s) before going further.

APA format is intended to help journal editors and publishers produce a product more easily. On the other hand, in a published article or final copy, the appearance of the document is the more important goal. Instructors have a difficult dilemma deciding whether to require strict APA format or to require a more aesthetically appealing product. You can compare the figures in this chapter to note several format differences between a student paper and a published journal article.

FIGURE 12-11 (JA1)

Source: From "Effects of Caffeine on Rats' Barpress and Maze Performance" by N. R. Cathey, R. A. Smith, and S. F. Davis, 1993, *Bulletin of the Psychonomic Society, 31,* pp. 49–52. Used with permission of the publisher.

Bulletin of the Psychonomic Society
1993, 31 (1), 49-52

Effects of caffeine on rats' barpress and maze performance

NANCY R. CATHEY and RANDOLPH A. SMITH
Ouachita Baptist University, Arkadelphia, Arkansas

and

STEPHEN F. DAVIS
Emporia State University, Emporia, Kansas

The effects of caffeine ingestion on rats were tested through barpress and maze performance. Four adult male and 4 adult female rats were bred, yielding 39 offspring (18 control, 21 experimental). The experimental pups received .50 mg/ml of caffeine in drinking water throughout gestation, weaning, and early adulthood; the control group received plain tap water. At 21 days of age, the pups began barpress and maze learning. The subjects were allowed a total of 8 min for each test on alternate days. The results were characterized by the presence of several reliable caffeine × trials interactions. Inspection of the interactions prompted the generalization that although caffeine may facilitate performance early in training, it hinders performance on later trials.

Caffeine, a methylxanthine, is a widely used central nervous system stimulant. Surveys report that 62% of Americans ingest at least 5 mg/kg per day from drinking coffee alone (West, Sobotka, Brodie, Beier, & O'Donnell, 1986). When other sources are taken into account, it can be said that Americans consume approximately 45 million pounds of caffeine every year (Stanwood, 1990). Despite its widespread use, caffeine may have potentially detrimental effects. For example, caffeine is a possible risk factor when it is consumed in coffee by pregnant women (Gullberg, Ferrell, & Christensen, 1986). In a 1980 position statement, the Food and Drug Administration advised pregnant women to eliminate their consumption of caffeine-containing products.

The teratogenic effects of caffeine on the developing human fetus are of particular interest because "caffeine easily crosses the placental barrier and its clearance is substantially delayed in pregnancy" (Glavin & Krueger, 1985, p. 29). Prenatal administration of caffeine to rats has been shown to negatively affect mortality rate, locomotor activity, metabolic processes, immune and endocrine functions, and neurological processes (Finn & Holtzman, 1986; Gullberg et al., 1986; West et al., 1986). Moreover, caffeine also may increase the frequency of self-injurious behavior in rats (Mueller, Saboda, Palmour, & Nyhan, 1982).

Research (e.g., Silinsky, 1989) shows that caffeine exerts its action by blocking the presynaptic activity of adenosine, a neurotransmitter that blocks the release of the excitatory neurotransmitter glutamate. Thus, caffeine ingestion results in an increase in the release of glutamate and leads to central nervous system arousal. Low doses of caffeine increase arousal and improve task performance, but with higher doses, anxiety and insomnia are prevalent (Glavin & Krueger, 1985). Although prenatal caffeine administration was employed in most of the studies cited here, the behavioral effects occurred postnatally, when the rats were no longer exposed to the chemical.

Research shows that the effects of caffeine vary across time and dosage. For example, caffeine may reduce within-session decrements in ambulation and rearing in adult rats, especially during the second hour of a session (Loke & Meliska, 1984). Changes in behavior across sessions also have been noted. Tight circling increased and then decreased in frequency in adult rats (Mueller et al., 1982). Holloway and Thor (1982) found that locomotor activity increased consistently for the first several days of testing and then decreased rapidly after an average of 14 days. They concluded that rat pups respond to increasing doses of caffeine in a curvilinear fashion, such that an initial increase in activity is followed by a decrease.

In light of these observations, we exposed rats to caffeine throughout gestation, weaning, and early adulthood to measure the drug's effect on the acquisition of behaviors requiring locomotor activity. On the basis of previous activity data showing a curvilinear function relating activity and trials in caffeine-exposed animals (e.g., Holloway & Thor, 1982; Mueller et al., 1982), it was hypothesized that a caffeine group would display high levels of maze and barpress performance in early trials, followed by a decline as training continued. On the other hand, a non-

This paper was presented at the 1992 meeting of the Southwestern Psychological Association, Austin, TX. Requests for reprints should be sent to R. A. Smith, Department of Psychology, Ouachita Baptist University, Arkadelphia, AR 71998-0001.

50   CATHEY, SMITH, AND DAVIS

caffeine control group was expected to continue to increase in performance throughout training.

METHOD

Subjects

Four adult male and 4 adult female rats were randomly selected from the colony maintained at Ouachita Baptist University. These rats were randomly assigned to 4 male–female breeding pairs. The breeding pairs were housed together for 7 days and then separated. The pups were separated from the dams at 21 days of age and housed separately. The 39 pups delivered to the 4 dams (18 control, 21 experimental) served as the subjects.

Apparatus

A Lafayette operant conditioning chamber (Model 84012) was used for barpress training. A modified Hampton Court maze (69.5 × 84.5 cm; alleys were 8.3 cm wide with 14.6-cm-high walls) with 11 choice points was used for all maze training.

Procedure

Upon formation, the breeding pairs were randomly assigned to the experimental (caffeine) or control (no caffeine) condition. Pairs in the experimental condition received .50 mg/ml caffeine in plain tap water, while controls received plain tap water. Solutions were presented in 250-ml graduated drinking tubes and were the only available liquid throughout the experiment. Lights in the room were on a 12:12-h light:dark cycle. Beginning with Day 15 of gestation, the cages were checked daily for births; new litters were considered born the previous day. As soon as they were detected, pups were marked with a permanent marker for identification. Litters were checked daily for mortalities; one pup from the caffeine group died after birth. There were no visible differences in weight between either the dams or the pups of the two groups.

At 21 days of age, the pups were weaned and began a series of tests on the barpress and maze tasks for food reinforcement. The subjects were food deprived for an average of 7 h (range, 6–8 h) prior to experimental testing. Otherwise food and fluids, which corresponded to those consumed by the respective dams, were freely available.

When the subjects were in the operant conditioning chamber, under conditions of continuous reinforcement, barpresses within an 8-min period were recorded. In the maze, the percent complete and actual time of completion were recorded, with an 8-min limit. The subjects alternated tasks each day until 8 sessions of each task had been completed (16 days).

RESULTS AND DISCUSSION

Percent of Maze Completion

Analysis of variance (ANOVA) of the percent of maze completion scores yielded a significant trials effect $[F(7,259) = 19.64, p < .001]$. As can be seen from Figure 1, subjects completed a higher percentage of the maze across trials. The presence of a significant drug × trials interaction $[F(7,259) = 2.75, p < .01]$ indicated that statements concerning the trials effect must be considered in light of whether the subjects were caffeine exposed or not. A series of simple main effects analyses comparing the caffeine and the noncaffeine subjects on each trial was employed to probe the interaction. The results of these analyses indicated that the caffeine subjects completed a higher percentage of the maze on Trials 1 and 2 $[F(1,301) = 8.56, p < .01, \text{ and } F(1,301) = 8.80, p < .01, \text{ respectively}]$.

Time of Maze Completion

The time of completion ANOVA yielded significance for the trials effect $[F(7,259) = 28.59, p < .001]$ and for the drug × trials interaction $[F(7,259) = 2.93, p < .01]$. As can be seen from Figure 2, subjects generally took less time to complete the maze across trials. The results of simple main effects analyses indicated that the caffeine and noncaffeine groups differed on Trials 4 and 7 $[F(1,301) = 4.86, p < .05, \text{ and } F(1,301) = 4.01, p < .05, \text{ respectively}]$. The groups were marginally different on Trials 5 and 6 $[F(1,301) = 3.38, p < .07, \text{ and } F(1,301) = 3.66, p < .06, \text{ respectively}]$. Figure 2 shows that the noncaffeine group was slower on Trial 4 but faster on Trials 5, 6, and 7.

Barpress

As with the maze data, the barpress ANOVA yielded significance for the trials effect $[F(7,259) = 74.68, p < .001]$ and the drug × trials interaction $[F(7,259) = 15.02, p < .001]$. Figure 3 shows that the number of barpresses increased reliably from the beginning to the end of testing. Simple main effects analyses indicated that the groups differed marginally on Trial 3 $[F(1,301) = 3.56, p < .07]$ and reliably on Trials 4–8 [smallest $F(1,301) = 5.36, p < .05$]. In these instances, the noncaffeine animals made more barpresses than did the caffeine animals.

In the present study, we investigated the relationship between caffeine and the performance of learned behaviors requiring activity. Previous research on the effects of caffeine on locomotor activities has shown an initial facilitation of the behavior followed by a decrement; the present data are similar to those results. For maze running, caffeine facilitated early performance but hindered or had no effect on later conditioning. For barpressing, caffeine resulted in reduced behavior across trials. Caffeine subjects completed a higher percentage of the maze during the first two trials (see Figure 1) and completed the maze in less time on Trial 4, but took more time on Trials 5–7 (see Figure 2). Caffeine subjects also produced fewer barpresses on Trials 3–8.

These results are consistent with previous research dealing with locomotor activity, in that caffeine's effects were beneficial (or less of a hindrance) on early trials. As trials continued, the performance of the caffeine subjects tended to level off, whereas the performance of noncaffeine subjects continued to improve toward a higher asymptotic level. Thus, it appears that caffeine produces beneficial effects on early trials but that caffeine produces deficits with extended testing.

The question of whether the caffeine-related decrements occurred because of prenatal or postnatal caffeine exposure is unanswered. Although the subjects in this study may have been affected prenatally by caffeine, they also continued to ingest caffeine postnatally. An extension of this research would be to test the maze and barpress performance of separate groups of animals exposed to caffeine prenatally and postnatally.

FIGURE 12-12 (JA2)

AUTHOR NOTE

Your manuscript may or may not have an author note, depending on your instructor's preferences. If you do use an author note, begin it on a new page. As you can see from Cathey's author note in Figure 12-13, the fact of a prior presentation of the data is acknowledged and a name and address is provided for readers to contact for information or copies of the paper. Other information that might be included would be an acknowledgment of persons who helped the author(s) or sources of financial support that made the study possible. The *PM* provides information about the author note on pages 21, 164–166, and 252–253.

Effects of Caffeine   9

Author Note

This paper was presented at the 1992 meeting of the Southwestern Psychological Association, Austin, TX.

Requests for reprints should be sent to R. A. Smith, Department of Psychology, Ouachita Baptist University, Arkadelphia, AR 71998-0001.

FIGURE 12-13 (M9)

FIGURE 12-14 (JA3)

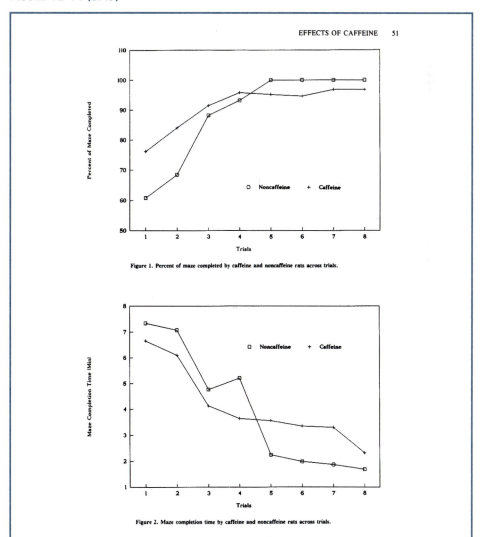

EFFECTS OF CAFFEINE   51

Figure 1. Percent of maze completed by caffeine and noncaffeine rats across trials.

Figure 2. Maze completion time by caffeine and noncaffeine rats across trials.

52   CATHEY, SMITH, AND DAVIS

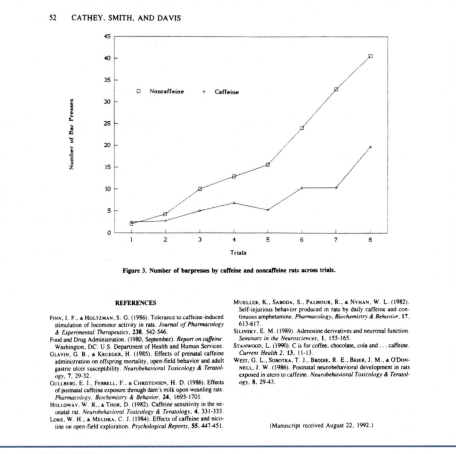

Figure 3. Number of barpresses by caffeine and noncaffeine rats across trials.

REFERENCES

Finn, I. F., & Holtzman, S. G. (1986). Tolerance to caffeine-induced stimulation of locomotor activity in rats. *Journal of Pharmacology & Experimental Therapeutics, 238,* 542-546.

Food and Drug Administration. (1980, September). *Report on caffeine.* Washington, DC: U.S. Department of Health and Human Services.

Glavin, G. B., & Krueger, H. (1985). Effects of prenatal caffeine administration on offspring mortality, open-field behavior and adult gastric ulcer susceptibility. *Neurobehavioral Toxicology & Teratology, 7,* 29-32.

Gullberg, E. I., Ferrell, F., & Christensen, H. D. (1986). Effects of postnatal caffeine exposure through dam's milk upon weanling rats. *Pharmacology, Biochemistry & Behavior, 24,* 1695-1701.

Holloway, W. R., & Thor, D. (1982). Caffeine sensitivity in the neonatal rat. *Neurobehavioral Toxicology & Teratology, 4,* 331-333.

Loke, W. H., & Meliska, C. J. (1984). Effects of caffeine and nicotine on open-field exploration. *Psychological Reports, 55,* 447-451.

Mueller, K., Saboda, S., Palmour, R., & Nyhan, W. L. (1982). Self-injurious behavior produced in rats by daily caffeine and continuous amphetamine. *Pharmacology, Biochemistry & Behavior, 17,* 613-617.

Silinsky, E. M. (1989). Adenosine derivatives and neuronal function. *Seminars in the Neurosciences, 1,* 155-165.

Stanwood, L. (1990). C is for coffee, chocolate, cola and ... caffeine. *Current Health 2, 13,* 11-13.

West, G. L., Sobotka, T. J., Brodie, R. E., Beier, J. M., & O'Donnell, J. W. (1986). Postnatal neurobehavioral development in rats exposed in utero to caffeine. *Neurobehavioral Toxicology & Teratology, 8,* 29-43.

(Manuscript received August 22, 1992.)

FIGURE 12-15 (JA4)

REVIEW SUMMARY

1. Psychologists use **APA style** to ensure uniformity of research reports.
2. The **title page** of a manuscript includes a **manuscript page header** and page number, the **running head,** the title, and author information.
3. The **abstract** is a brief summary of the contents of the research report.
4. The **introduction section** includes a thesis statement, literature review, and statement of the experimental hypothesis.
5. The **method section** contains a thorough description of the participants **(participants subsection),** the objects used in the experiment **(apparatus, materials,** or **testing instruments subsection),** and what took place during the study **(procedure subsection).**

6. The **results section** presents inferential and descriptive statistics to describe the experimental outcomes. **Figures** or **tables** may be used to complement the statistical information.

7. In the **discussion section,** the researcher draws conclusions from the experiment by summarizing the results, comparing the results to previous research, and interpreting the results.

8. The **reference list** provides bibliographic information for any works cited in the paper. APA format includes different reference formats for periodical articles, books, chapters from edited books, and a host of other sources.

9. The **author note** allows the author to thank people for their help, cite a previous presentation of the findings, and designate a contact person for information about the experiment.

STUDY BREAK

1. Why is the abstract the most widely read section of most research reports?

2. How is the introduction section similar to what is found in a typical term paper? How is it different?

3. List three different purposes of the method section. Which do you think is most important? Why?

4. We draw conclusions with _____ statistics and create a picture of our data with _____ statistics.

5. Could you use figures or tables as your sole information in a results section? Why or why not?

6. Some people believe that the discussion section is the most important section of an experiment report. Do you agree? Why or why not?

7. Why is the reference for a chapter from an edited book more complex than the reference for either a journal article or a book?

8. Matching:
   1. Title Page
   2. Abstract
   3. Introduction
   4. Method
   5. Results
   6. Discussion
   7. References
   8. Author Note

   a. presents statistical findings
   b. a short summary of the article
   c. includes full address of author
   d. reports the "bottom line" of the experiment
   e. includes manuscript page header and running head
   f. bibliographic information
   g. reviews previous research
   h. tells how the experiment was conducted

WRITING IN APA STYLE

We hope that you were a good student in your English composition classes because good writing is quite important in writing your research report. As we noted in Chapter 5, we do not want to attempt to teach writing, but we do want to provide some pointers you may find helpful. The topic of Chapter 2 in the *PM* is "Expression of Ideas." You should read that chapter carefully. In the next sections we will give you some general and specific guidelines that will assist you in writing your research report. As you will see, there are some differences between APA style and the way you learned to write in English classes. Scientific writing style is different in many ways from creative writing.

GENERAL GUIDELINES

The main objective of scientific writing is clear communication. It is your job to communicate your ideas as clearly as possible to the reader. The *PM* provides you with several hints about how to accomplish this goal. Be sure to read pages 23–31 in the *PM* to supplement the following information.

Orderly Presentation of Ideas. The key idea here is continuity. From the beginning of your research report to the end, you are writing a continuous idea or thought in which you tell the reader about your experiment. Do you remember sitting in class and getting lost in a lecture because you couldn't tell where the teacher was going (or where the teacher had been)? Those little side excursions in a lecture ("chasing rabbits") may be a delightful diversion in class, but they do tend to make you lose track of where you're going. Don't detour as you write your manuscript. Get on track and stay there with singlemindedness of purpose.

From Sidney Harris.

"In the social sciences we hardly use numbers, but we can write long, complicated sentences."

We hope you recognize that both statements in this cartoon are incorrect. In psychology, we *do* use numbers and we work hard at communicating clearly.

Smoothness of Expression. Writing in a continuous fashion will greatly aid your smoothness of expression. Creative writing is often not smooth because it uses literary devices to create tension or to conceal plot lines or to hide a surprise for later. Remember that scientific writing's goal is communication rather than escape and entertainment. One of the best things you can do to make your writing smooth is to work on transition sentences when you shift from one topic to another. Try to avoid abrupt shifts that make readers feel they have run into a wall.

Economy of Expression. Again, with your primary goal being communication, it is important to be direct and to the point in your writing. When journal editors work on submitted manuscripts, they have only a limited number of pages available for the journal to be published. Thus, it is to their advantage to have manuscripts that are short and communicative rather than long and unclear. Some people are surprised to find out that you can often shorten your writing and make it clearer at the same time. The *PM* specifically advises you to avoid jargon, wordiness, and redundancy. Also, you should not repeat yourself. (Yes, that second sentence was there on purpose—did you catch the unnecessary repetition?)

Precision and Clarity. We encourage you to work on becoming a wordsmith rather than a wordmonger. As you probably know, a smith is someone who works with a particular material (e.g., a tinsmith, a goldsmith). A wordsmith works carefully with words, whereas a wordmonger uses words carelessly. Make sure the words you use fit the exact purpose and meaning that you have in mind. One of the major problems many of us have with writing is that we write in the same manner that we speak. Ambiguities may occur in speech, but we often clarify matters because we can interact with the speaker. Interaction is not possible when reading a text passage. Therefore, choose your words carefully so that you truly do say what you mean. Such clarity rarely occurs on a first attempt at writing—be sure that you reread and edit everything you write.

Strategies to Improve Writing Style. The *PM* (APA, 1994, p. 31) suggests three approaches to becoming a more effective writer.

1. Write from an outline. If you have a "road map" for your writing, you are more likely to arrive at your destination in a timely fashion.

2. Write your first draft, put it away, and read it after a delay. If you attempt to cram your writing into a short time period, you will have difficulty editing your writing because you are likely to have the same thoughts you had a few minutes earlier. By giving yourself a time break, you are more likely to see the things you missed the first time—and it will be easier to think of ways to correct the problems.

3. Ask someone to evaluate your writing. It is usually quite helpful to have at least one other person read your papers before you submit them. It is easier for someone who is unfamiliar with the work to spot inconsistencies, weaknesses, ambiguities, and other flaws in your writing. Some instructors offer to critique rough drafts of your work—you should always take advantage of such an offer. Ask classmates to critique your writing and offer to do the same for them. You may learn a great deal both from their critique and from reading and critiquing someone else's writing.

GRAMMATICAL GUIDELINES

The *PM* covers a variety of guidelines about grammar on pages 31–60. Most of these guidelines are standard conventions of grammar that you learned in grammar classes. We urge you to review these pages to ensure that you remember this information. Rather than turning this book into a grammar handbook at this point, we will cover only those conventions that are specific to APA style or with which students seem to have difficulty.

Passive Voice. According to the *PM,* you should use active voice rather than passive voice in writing your research report. In passive voice, the true object of the verb becomes the subject of the sentence and the true subject becomes the object (Bellquist, 1993). Passive voice often appears in methods sections because it is used easily to avoid personalizing that section. Let us give an example to clarify:

> After viewing the slides, a recall test was given to participants.

This sentence is not direct and active; rather, it is indirect and passive. The test should be the object of the sentence, not the subject. Who did the acting? Presumably the experimenter did, but the experimenter is not even present in this sentence.

Psychological Detective

Reread the passive voice sentence. Can you recast it in active voice? Write a new sentence before reading further.

Actually, there are several ways you could change this sentence to make it active, depending on whether you want to include the experimenter or not. You could write:

> I gave the participants a recall test after they viewed the slides.

If you have coauthors for your experiment, the sentence could become this:

> We gave the participants a recall test after they viewed the slides.

Although many experimenters seem to be uncomfortable using first person (I, we), the *PM* specifically permits it. If you still wish to avoid first person, you could write:

> The participants took a recall test after viewing the slides.

In each of these sample sentences, you now have actors acting (active voice) rather than having something done to them (passive voice).

That versus Which. Clauses beginning with *that* are termed restrictive clauses and should be essential to the meaning of the sentence. On the other hand, clauses beginning with *which* can be either restrictive or nonrestrictive (simply adding additional information). In APA style, you should confine yourself to using *which* for nonrestrictive clauses only. Thus, *that* and *which* should not be used interchangeably. Using *which* is similar to making an "oh, by the way" addition to your sentence. To further help you distinguish the difference, remember that nonrestrictive clauses should be set off with commas. Let's look at some examples:

The stimulus items *that* were not recalled were the more difficult items.

The phrase "that were not recalled" is essential to the sentence's meaning. Imagine the sentence without that phrase—it would make no sense.

The stimulus items, *which* were nouns, were shown with a slide projector.

The phrase "which were nouns" is not essential to the meaning of this sentence. If we delete this phrase, the sentence retains its original meaning. The phrase does add some additional information about the stimulus items, but this information could be included elsewhere.

Words with Temporal Meaning. The words *since* and *while* can cause difficulty in scientific writing because they have more than one meaning in everyday usage. *Since* is often used interchangeably with *because,* and *while* is used to substitute for *although.* Some grammar stylebooks allow these multiple uses. APA style, however, does not. You should use *since* and *while* only for temporal purposes—in other words, to make time comparisons. Thus, *while* should be used to denote events that occur at the same time, and *since* should be used to denote that time has passed. Again, here are some examples:

Many different IQ tests have been developed *since* Binet's original version.

Note that here *since* refers to time that has occurred after Binet's test.

Since the XYZ group scored higher, we concluded that they learned the material better.

This use of *since* is incorrect—you should substitute *because* in its place.

While the participants were studying the verbal items, music was played.

Note that *while* in this sentence tells you that studying and music playing occurred simultaneously.

While some psychologists believe in Skinner's ideas, many others have rejected his beliefs.

This use of *while* is incorrect—nothing is occurring at the same time. Instead, a contrast is being drawn. You should substitute *although* in this sentence.

Bias in Language. We hope you remember that we stressed the use of **unbiased language** in Chapter 5. We believe that this type of writing is important in helping maintain a neutral (unbiased) approach to science. Thus, we wish to remind you of the need for removing biased terms from your writing. The *PM* (APA, 1994, pp. 47-50) gives three guidelines that may be helpful in reducing bias in writing.

> **definition**
>
> **Unbiased language** Language that does not display bias toward an individual or group.

- Describe at the appropriate level of specificity. In other words, you should describe persons as specifically as you can. When we use broad terms to describe people, we are more likely to include people who should not be included. For example, "Japanese-Americans" is more specific than "Asian-Americans."

- Be sensitive to labels. When we use stereotyped labels, we are likely using terms that contain bias. Basically, we should refer to groups as they wish to be referred to rather than imposing our own labels on them. When at all possible, it is better to avoid labels. As the *PM* points out, "people diagnosed with schizophrenia" is both more accurate and more preferred than "schizophrenics" (APA, 1994, p. 48).

- Acknowledge participation. This guideline is generally aimed at experiments using human participants, although it would not hurt us to keep it in mind for animal studies also. The general idea of this guideline is to make sure you remember that the participants in your experiment are individuals. This idea formed the rationale for changing the label subjects to the label "participants." Using active rather than passive voice also helps to personalize your participants.

A Disclaimer. Please remember that we could not possibly squeeze all the grammar guidelines from the *PM* into this section. Again, we chose to highlight the few that we did because they may differ from what you learned in English classes or because we know that students (and professors) tend to have trouble with these points of grammar and usage. We did *not* leave out the others because they are unimportant or even less important. We urge you to read pages 31-60 in the *PM* to review your knowledge of grammar.

APA Editorial Style

Chapter 3 of the *PM* addresses APA editorial style on pages 61-234—virtually half the book. This chapter gives writers a style guide to follow that will help create uniformity in writings by different authors in different publications. We have already covered the most important aspects of APA editorial style in this chapter and others—levels of headings, metrication, statistical copy in text, tables, figures, reference citations in text, and reference lists.

In addition to the important aspects of APA editorial style we have covered to this point, you should be aware that the *PM* gives you guidance on issues such as punctuation, spelling, capitalization, italics, abbreviations, seriation, quotations, numbers, footnotes, appendixes, and references to legal materials. Again, we do not have the space it would take to address every possible concern in this chapter. When you have questions about any of these matters, consult Chapter 3 in the *PM*.

PREPARING YOUR MANUSCRIPT

Chapter 4 of the *PM* (pp. 235–272) provides the guidelines you need in order to actually type your experimental paper. This chapter is probably one of the most-used chapters in the *PM* because it includes three examples of sample papers (pp. 258–272). These sample papers include notations of specific *PM* sections for each important component of the paper. We hope that the combination of the sample manuscript in this chapter and the sample papers in the *PM* make typing your paper a relatively simple matter.

Chapter 4 of the *PM* is primarily a reference chapter much like Chapter 3. You should consult it whenever you have a question about typing a specific portion of your manuscript. Let us provide you a short list of the highlights of the typing instructions:

- *Line Spacing.* Double-space everything everywhere.

- *Margins.* Use at least 1" margins on all sides. Keep in mind that for the top margin, this margin refers to the point at which the text begins rather than the manuscript page header and number. Thus, you can set the top margin in your word processor to less than 1" so that the text begins at least 1" down from the top of the paper.

- *Lines.* Set your word processor to left justification. Your paper should have a ragged right edge throughout (i.e., the right margin should not line up down the page). Do *not* divide or hyphenate words between lines.

- *Pages.* Number all pages (including the title page; excepting figures) consecutively. The following sections should begin on new pages: title page, abstract, introduction (remember *not* to label it "Introduction"), references, appendixes, author note, footnotes, tables (a separate page for each), figure captions, figures (each on a separate page).

- *Word Spacing.* Space once after all punctuation, including plus and minus signs in equations. There is no spacing before or after hyphens (-) or dashes (— or -). Type a hyphen to denote a negative value; in this case, use a space before the hyphen but not after.

- *Quotations.* Quotations that are shorter than 40 words are enclosed in double quotation marks (") and are written as part of the text. Longer quotations are blocked (indented) from the left margin—be sure to double-space them.

This list of highlights is not comprehensive. If you have questions about other matters as you type your manuscript, consult Chapter 4 of the *PM*.

REVIEW SUMMARY

1. The primary goal of scientific writing is clear communication.
2. Goals that aid in clear communication are orderly presentation of ideas, smoothness of expression, economy of expression, and a striving for precision and clarity.
3. To improve your writing style you should write from an outline, put away your first draft before editing it, and have someone evaluate your writing.
4. You should use active voice whenever possible in writing your research report.
5. *That* should be used only with restrictive clauses, which include information that is essential to the meaning of a sentence. *Which* should be used in nonrestrictive clauses, which add information but are not essential to a sentence's meaning.
6. *Since* should not be used to substitute for *because,* nor should *while* substitute for *although.* Both *since* and *while* should be used only for temporal (time-related) meaning.
7. Psychologists strive to use nonbiased language in their writing.
8. APA style includes guidelines on diverse matters such as punctuation, capitalization, quotations, numbers, appendixes, typing guidelines, and so on.
9. The *Publication Manual of the American Psychological Association* (APA, 1994) is the stylebook for psychological writing. It contains a wealth of information about the writing process.

STUDY BREAK

1. What would be wrong with writing your research paper in the style of Twain, Hemingway, or Faulkner? Be as specific as possible in your answer.
2. What are the three strategies to improve your writing style? As you list each strategy, also tell what you would have to change about your writing style to incorporate the strategy.
3. Change each of the following sentences in passive voice to active voice:
   An experiment was conducted by Jones (1995).
   The participants were seated in desks around the room.
   The stimulus items were projected from the rear of the cubicle.
   A significant interaction was found.
4. Choose the correct sentence from each pair below. Add punctuation if necessary. Justify your answers:
   a. The participants which were older were tested first.
      The participants that were older were tested first.
   b. The room which was a classroom was used for testing.
      The room that was a classroom was used for testing.
   c. The ANOVA which was analyzed on a computer was significant.
      The ANOVA that was analyzed on a computer was significant.

5. Decide whether each sentence below is correct or incorrect. If it is incorrect, correct it.

Since you are the oldest, you should go first.

Since I began that class I have learned much about statistics.

While we are watching TV, we can also study.

While you are older than me, I should still go first.

6. Try to use unbiased language to express each phrase:

Orientals —   elderly —

mankind —   girls and men —

mothering —   chairman —

homosexuals —   depressives —

7. Correct the following incorrect expressions:

a+b=c   trial - by - trial

- 1   Enter: Your name

Looking Ahead

At this point we have reached the end of this text—there is no Chapter 13 to look ahead to. We do, however, look ahead to your research career. Perhaps your research career will be nonexistent; you may not be required to design, plan, and conduct an experiment as part of this course or another course. In this case, we hope you have learned something about research that will make you a critical consumer of research information in the future. Perhaps your research career will entail only one study—the one you conduct for this course. We believe this book will prove helpful for you in that endeavor. Finally, perhaps some of you now envision an ongoing research career for yourselves. We hope this book has opened your eyes to the powerful possibilities of experimental research in psychology and that you are eager to follow that path in future.

Regardless of what your future plans regarding research are, we hope we have made you think, challenged you to work, helped you contemplate conducting research, and perhaps entertained and amused you a little along the way. All of you will be faced with research in some fashion in your futures. We wish you luck as you begin your journey.

Hands-On Activities

1. **Analyzing Your Roles as a Writer.**   This activity is designed for the entire class and is based on an idea shared by our friend and colleague Randall Wight. One of the difficulties students have in writing APA format papers is failing to realize that you must play a different role as you write each of the different sections of an APA format paper. Below is a list of sections and roles. Match each role with a particular section. Develop a list of three traits that would help you write in each of the roles. Compare your matches with those of the entire class—did your choices match? Once the class agrees on the correct matches, generate a classwide

list of the helpful traits for each section. This list will provide you with some cues that may be helpful for you as you write your research report.

SECTIONS	ROLES
Abstract	Statistician
Introduction	Journalist
Method	Obsessive-Compulsive
Results	Scientist
Discussion	Historian, Theoretician
References	Salesperson

2. **An Experimental Article Jigsaw Puzzle.**   This activity is based on a journal article by Ault (1991). To carry out this activity you will need to pair up with another student. Each of you should make two copies of a different journal article (make sure it has several paragraphs under each heading). Cut one copy into pieces so that each piece contains one paragraph and so that all the headings are removed. Scramble the paragraphs and give them to your partner. The task is to attempt to (1) put each paragraph under the correct heading and (2) put the paragraphs in order within each heading. This task will help acquaint you with the contents of each section in a way that reading a text cannot.

3. **Construct a Reference List.**   Imagine that you have cited the sources below in your introduction. Now you are ready to make your reference list. Using APA format, construct a reference list for these sources.

Source 1: This textbook

Source 2: The journal article shown below

Journal of Experimental Psychology: General
1995, Vol. 124, No. 2, 181–206

Causal Models and the Acquisition of Category Structure

Michael R. Waldmann
Max Planck Institute
for Psychological Research

Keith J. Holyoak and Angela Fratianne
University of California,
Los Angeles

Source 3: The book shown below

Library of Congress Cataloging-in-Publication Data

Rollins, Joan H.
    Women's minds/women's bodies : the psychology of women in a
biosocial context / Joan Rollins.
      p.   cm.
    Includes bibliographical references and index.
    ISBN 0-13-720343-8
    1. Women—Psychology. 2. Mind and body. I. Title.
HQ1206.R64 1996   95-26469
                              CIP

Senior editor: Heidi Freund
Editorial assistant: Jeffrey Arkin
Marketing manager: Michael Alread
Editorial/production supervision: Bob Moschetto
Senior managing editor: Bonnie Biller
Cover design: Bruce Kenselaar
Manufacturing buyer: Tricia Kenny

ISBN 0-13-720343-8

Prentice-Hall International (UK) Limited, *London*
Prentice-Hall of Australia Pty. Limited, *Sydney*
Prentice-Hall Canada Inc., *Toronto*
Prentice-Hall Hispanoamericana, S.A., *Mexico*
Prentice-Hall of India Private Limited, *New Delhi*
Prentice-Hall of Japan, Inc., *Tokyo*
Simon & Schuster Asia Pte. Ltd., *Singapore*
Editora Prentice-Hall do Brasil, Ltda., *Rio de Janeiro*

Source 4: The circled chapter from the book shown on these two pages.

Library of Congress Cataloging-in-Publication Data
Classic and contemporary readings in social psychology / [edited by]
  Erik J. Coats, Robert S. Feldman.
     p.   cm.
    Includes bibliographical references.
    ISBN 0-13-190216-4
    1. Social psychology.   I. Coats, Erik J., 1968–   II. Feldman,
Robert S. (Robert Stephen), 1947–
    HM251.C597   1996
    302—dc20   95-20433
                                                  CIP

Acquisitions editor: Heidi Freund
Production supervisor: Andrew Roney
Buyer: Tricia Kenny
Interior design: Lisa Jones

Credits and copyright acknowledgments
appear on pp. 259–260, which constitute
an extension of the copyright page.

 Copyright © 1996 by Prentice-Hall, Inc.
Simon & Schuster / A Viacom Company
Upper Saddle River, New Jersey 07458

Printed in the United States of America
10 9 8 7 6 5 4 3 2 1

ISBN 0-13-190216-4

Prentice-Hall International (UK) Limited, *London*
Prentice-Hall of Australia Pty. Limited, *Sydney*
Prentice-Hall Canada Inc., *Toronto*
Prentice-Hall Hispanoamericana, S.A., *Mexico*
Prentice-Hall of India Private Limited, *New Delhi*
Prentice-Hall of Japan, Inc., *Tokyo*
Simon & Schuster Asia Pte. Ltd., *Singapore*
Editora Prentice-Hall do Brasil, Ltda., *Rio de Janeiro*

CONTENTS

Appendix A

Statistical Tables

Table A-1. The *t* Distribution*

df	α Levels for Two-Tailed Test					
	.20	.10	.05	.02	.01	.001
	α Levels for One-Tailed Test					
	.10	.05	.025	.01	.005	.0005
1	3.078	6.314	12.706	31.821	63.657	636.619
2	1.886	2.920	4.303	6.965	9.925	31.598
3	1.638	2.353	3.182	4.541	5.841	12.924
4	1.533	2.132	2.776	3.747	4.604	8.610
5	1.476	2.015	2.571	3.365	4.032	6.869
6	1.440	1.943	2.447	3.143	3.707	5.959
7	1.415	1.895	2.365	2.998	3.499	5.408
8	1.397	1.860	2.306	2.896	3.355	5.041
9	1.383	1.833	2.262	2.821	3.250	4.781
10	1.372	1.812	2.228	2.764	3.169	4.587
11	1.363	1.796	2.201	2.718	3.106	4.437
12	1.356	1.782	2.179	2.681	3.055	4.318
13	1.350	1.771	2.160	2.650	3.012	4.221
14	1.345	1.761	2.145	2.624	2.977	4.140
15	1.341	1.753	2.131	2.602	2.947	4.073
16	1.337	1.746	2.120	2.583	2.921	4.015
17	1.333	1.740	2.110	2.567	2.898	3.965
18	1.330	1.734	2.101	2.552	2.878	3.922
19	1.328	1.729	2.093	2.539	2.861	3.883
20	1.325	1.725	2.086	2.528	2.845	3.850
21	1.323	1.721	2.080	2.518	2.831	3.819
22	1.321	1.717	2.074	2.508	2.819	3.792
23	1.319	1.714	2.069	2.500	2.807	3.767
24	1.318	1.711	2.064	2.492	2.797	3.745
25	1.316	1.708	2.060	2.485	2.787	3.725
26	1.315	1.706	2.056	2.479	2.779	3.707
27	1.314	1.703	2.052	2.473	2.771	3.690
28	1.313	1.701	2.048	2.467	2.763	3.674
29	1.311	1.699	2.045	2.462	2.756	3.659
30	1.310	1.697	2.042	2.457	2.750	3.646
40	1.303	1.684	2.021	2.423	2.704	3.551
60	1.296	1.671	2.000	2.390	2.660	3.460
120	1.289	1.658	1.980	2.358	2.617	3.373
∞	1.282	1.645	1.960	2.326	2.576	3.291

*To be significant the *t* obtained from the data must be equal to or larger than the value shown in the table.

Source: Table A-1 is taken from Table III of Fisher and Yates, *Statistical Tables for Biological, Agricultural and Medical Research*. Published by Longman Group UK Ltd., 1974. We are grateful to the Longman Group UK Ltd., on behalf of the literary Executor of the late Sir Ronald A. Fisher, F.R.S. and Dr. Frank Yates F.R.S for permission to reproduce Table III from *Statistical Tables for Biological, Agricultural and Medical Research* 61E (1974).

TABLE A-2. THE F DISTRIBUTION*

.05 (ROMAN) AND .01 (BOLDFACE) α LEVELS FOR THE DISTRIBUTION OF F

DEGREES OF FREEDOM (FOR THE NUMERATOR)

Each cell shows the .05 level (roman) / .01 level (boldface). Rows are Degrees of freedom (for the denominator).

df	1	2	3	4	5	6	7	8	9	10	11	12	14	16	20	24	30	40	50	75	100	200	500	∞
1	161 / **4,052**	200 / **4,999**	216 / **5,403**	225 / **5,625**	230 / **5,764**	234 / **5,859**	237 / **5,928**	239 / **5,981**	241 / **6,022**	242 / **6,056**	243 / **6,082**	244 / **6,106**	245 / **6,142**	246 / **6,169**	248 / **6,208**	249 / **6,234**	250 / **6,258**	251 / **6,286**	252 / **6,302**	253 / **6,323**	253 / **6,334**	254 / **6,352**	254 / **6,361**	254 / **6,366**
2	18.51 / **98.49**	19.00 / **99.00**	19.16 / **99.17**	19.25 / **99.25**	19.30 / **99.30**	19.33 / **99.33**	19.36 / **99.34**	19.37 / **99.36**	19.38 / **99.38**	19.39 / **99.40**	19.40 / **99.41**	19.41 / **99.42**	19.42 / **99.43**	19.43 / **99.44**	19.44 / **99.45**	19.45 / **99.46**	19.46 / **99.47**	19.47 / **99.48**	19.47 / **99.48**	19.48 / **99.49**	19.49 / **99.49**	19.49 / **99.49**	19.50 / **99.50**	19.50 / **99.50**
3	10.13 / **34.12**	9.55 / **30.82**	9.28 / **29.46**	9.12 / **28.71**	9.01 / **28.24**	8.94 / **27.91**	8.88 / **27.67**	8.84 / **27.49**	8.81 / **27.34**	8.78 / **27.23**	8.76 / **27.13**	8.74 / **27.05**	8.71 / **26.92**	8.69 / **26.83**	8.66 / **26.69**	8.64 / **26.60**	8.62 / **26.50**	8.60 / **26.41**	8.58 / **26.35**	8.57 / **26.27**	8.56 / **26.23**	8.54 / **26.18**	8.54 / **26.14**	8.53 / **26.12**
4	7.71 / **21.20**	6.94 / **18.00**	6.59 / **16.69**	6.39 / **15.98**	6.26 / **15.52**	6.16 / **15.21**	6.09 / **14.98**	6.04 / **14.80**	6.00 / **14.66**	5.96 / **14.54**	5.93 / **14.45**	5.91 / **14.37**	5.87 / **14.24**	5.84 / **14.15**	5.80 / **14.02**	5.77 / **13.93**	5.74 / **13.83**	5.71 / **13.74**	5.70 / **13.69**	5.68 / **13.61**	5.66 / **13.57**	5.65 / **13.52**	5.64 / **13.48**	5.63 / **13.46**
5	6.61 / **16.26**	5.79 / **13.27**	5.41 / **12.06**	5.19 / **11.39**	5.05 / **10.97**	4.95 / **10.67**	4.88 / **10.45**	4.82 / **10.27**	4.78 / **10.15**	4.74 / **10.05**	4.70 / **9.96**	4.68 / **9.89**	4.64 / **9.77**	4.60 / **9.68**	4.56 / **9.55**	4.53 / **9.47**	4.50 / **9.38**	4.46 / **9.29**	4.44 / **9.24**	4.42 / **9.17**	4.40 / **9.13**	4.38 / **9.07**	4.37 / **9.04**	4.36 / **9.02**
6	5.99 / **13.74**	5.14 / **10.92**	4.76 / **9.78**	4.53 / **9.15**	4.39 / **8.75**	4.28 / **8.47**	4.21 / **8.26**	4.15 / **8.10**	4.10 / **7.98**	4.06 / **7.87**	4.03 / **7.79**	4.00 / **7.72**	3.96 / **7.60**	3.92 / **7.52**	3.87 / **7.39**	3.84 / **7.31**	3.81 / **7.23**	3.77 / **7.14**	3.75 / **7.09**	3.72 / **7.02**	3.71 / **6.99**	3.69 / **6.94**	3.68 / **6.90**	3.67 / **6.88**
7	5.59 / **12.25**	4.74 / **9.55**	4.35 / **8.45**	4.12 / **7.85**	3.97 / **7.46**	3.87 / **7.19**	3.79 / **7.00**	3.73 / **6.84**	3.68 / **6.71**	3.63 / **6.62**	3.60 / **6.54**	3.57 / **6.47**	3.52 / **6.35**	3.49 / **6.27**	3.44 / **6.15**	3.41 / **6.07**	3.38 / **5.98**	3.34 / **5.90**	3.32 / **5.85**	3.29 / **5.78**	3.28 / **5.75**	3.25 / **5.70**	3.24 / **5.67**	3.23 / **5.65**
8	5.32 / **11.26**	4.46 / **8.65**	4.07 / **7.59**	3.84 / **7.01**	3.69 / **6.63**	3.58 / **6.37**	3.50 / **6.19**	3.44 / **6.03**	3.39 / **5.91**	3.34 / **5.82**	3.31 / **5.74**	3.28 / **5.67**	3.23 / **5.56**	3.20 / **5.48**	3.15 / **5.36**	3.12 / **5.28**	3.08 / **5.20**	3.05 / **5.11**	3.03 / **5.06**	3.00 / **5.00**	2.98 / **4.96**	2.96 / **4.91**	2.94 / **4.88**	2.93 / **4.86**
9	5.12 / **10.56**	4.26 / **8.02**	3.86 / **6.99**	3.63 / **6.42**	3.48 / **6.06**	3.37 / **5.80**	3.29 / **5.62**	3.23 / **5.47**	3.18 / **5.35**	3.13 / **5.26**	3.10 / **5.18**	3.07 / **5.11**	3.02 / **5.00**	2.98 / **4.92**	2.93 / **4.80**	2.90 / **4.73**	2.86 / **4.64**	2.82 / **4.56**	2.80 / **4.51**	2.77 / **4.45**	2.76 / **4.41**	2.73 / **4.36**	2.72 / **4.33**	2.71 / **4.31**
10	4.96 / **10.04**	4.10 / **7.56**	3.71 / **6.55**	3.48 / **5.99**	3.33 / **5.64**	3.22 / **5.39**	3.14 / **5.21**	3.07 / **5.06**	3.02 / **4.95**	2.97 / **4.85**	2.94 / **4.78**	2.91 / **4.71**	2.86 / **4.60**	2.82 / **4.52**	2.77 / **4.41**	2.74 / **4.33**	2.70 / **4.25**	2.67 / **4.17**	2.64 / **4.12**	2.61 / **4.05**	2.59 / **4.01**	2.56 / **3.96**	2.55 / **3.93**	2.54 / **3.91**
11	4.84 / **9.65**	3.98 / **7.20**	3.59 / **6.22**	3.36 / **5.67**	3.20 / **5.32**	3.09 / **5.07**	3.01 / **4.88**	2.95 / **4.74**	2.90 / **4.63**	2.86 / **4.54**	2.82 / **4.46**	2.79 / **4.40**	2.74 / **4.29**	2.70 / **4.21**	2.65 / **4.10**	2.61 / **4.02**	2.57 / **3.94**	2.53 / **3.86**	2.50 / **3.80**	2.47 / **3.74**	2.45 / **3.70**	2.42 / **3.66**	2.41 / **3.62**	2.40 / **3.60**
12	4.75 / **9.33**	3.88 / **6.93**	3.49 / **5.95**	3.26 / **5.41**	3.11 / **5.06**	3.00 / **4.82**	2.92 / **4.65**	2.85 / **4.50**	2.80 / **4.39**	2.76 / **4.30**	2.72 / **4.22**	2.69 / **4.16**	2.64 / **4.05**	2.60 / **3.98**	2.54 / **3.86**	2.50 / **3.78**	2.46 / **3.70**	2.42 / **3.61**	2.40 / **3.56**	2.36 / **3.49**	2.35 / **3.46**	2.32 / **3.41**	2.31 / **3.38**	2.30 / **3.36**
13	4.67 / **9.07**	3.80 / **6.70**	3.41 / **5.74**	3.18 / **5.20**	3.02 / **4.86**	2.92 / **4.62**	2.84 / **4.44**	2.77 / **4.30**	2.72 / **4.19**	2.67 / **4.10**	2.63 / **4.02**	2.60 / **3.96**	2.55 / **3.85**	2.51 / **3.78**	2.46 / **3.67**	2.42 / **3.59**	2.38 / **3.51**	2.34 / **3.42**	2.32 / **3.37**	2.28 / **3.30**	2.26 / **3.27**	2.24 / **3.21**	2.22 / **3.18**	2.21 / **3.16**

*To be significant the F obtained from the data must be equal to or larger than the value shown in the table.

Source: *Statistical Methods* (6th ed.) by G. W. Snedecor and W. G. Cochran, 1967, Ames, Iowa: Iowa State University Press. Used by permission of the Iowa State University Press.

DEGREES OF FREEDOM (FOR THE NUMERATOR)

	1	2	3	4	5	6	7	8	9	10	11	12	14	16	20	24	30	40	50	75	100	200	500	∞
14	4.60	3.74	3.34	3.11	2.96	2.85	2.77	2.70	2.65	2.60	2.56	2.53	2.48	2.44	2.39	2.35	2.31	2.27	2.24	2.21	2.19	2.16	2.14	2.13
	8.86	**6.51**	**5.56**	**5.03**	**4.69**	**4.46**	**4.28**	**4.14**	**4.03**	**3.94**	**3.86**	**3.80**	**3.70**	**3.62**	**3.51**	**3.43**	**3.34**	**3.26**	**3.21**	**3.14**	**3.11**	**3.06**	**3.02**	**3.00**
15	4.54	3.68	3.29	3.06	2.90	2.79	2.70	2.64	2.59	2.55	2.51	2.48	2.43	2.39	2.33	2.29	2.25	2.21	2.18	2.15	2.12	2.10	2.08	2.07
	8.68	**6.36**	**5.42**	**4.89**	**4.56**	**4.32**	**4.14**	**4.00**	**3.89**	**3.80**	**3.73**	**3.67**	**3.56**	**3.48**	**3.36**	**3.29**	**3.20**	**3.12**	**3.07**	**3.00**	**2.97**	**2.92**	**2.89**	**2.87**
16	4.49	3.63	3.24	3.01	2.85	2.74	2.66	2.59	2.54	2.49	2.45	2.42	2.37	2.33	2.28	2.24	2.20	2.16	2.13	2.09	2.07	2.04	2.02	2.01
	8.53	**6.23**	**5.29**	**4.77**	**4.44**	**4.20**	**4.03**	**3.89**	**3.78**	**3.69**	**3.61**	**3.55**	**3.45**	**3.37**	**3.25**	**3.18**	**3.10**	**3.01**	**2.96**	**2.89**	**2.86**	**2.80**	**2.77**	**2.75**
17	4.45	3.59	3.20	2.96	2.81	2.70	2.62	2.55	2.50	2.45	2.41	2.38	2.33	2.29	2.23	2.19	2.15	2.11	2.08	2.04	2.02	1.99	1.97	1.96
	8.40	**6.11**	**5.18**	**4.67**	**4.34**	**4.10**	**3.93**	**3.79**	**3.68**	**3.59**	**3.52**	**3.45**	**3.35**	**3.27**	**3.16**	**3.08**	**3.00**	**2.92**	**2.86**	**2.79**	**2.76**	**2.70**	**2.67**	**2.65**
18	4.41	3.55	3.16	2.93	2.77	2.66	2.58	2.51	2.46	2.41	2.37	2.34	2.29	2.25	2.19	2.15	2.11	2.07	2.04	2.00	1.89	1.95	1.93	1.92
	8.28	**6.01**	**5.09**	**4.58**	**4.25**	**4.01**	**3.85**	**3.71**	**3.60**	**3.51**	**3.44**	**3.37**	**3.27**	**3.19**	**3.07**	**3.00**	**2.91**	**2.83**	**2.78**	**2.71**	**2.68**	**2.62**	**2.59**	**2.57**
19	4.38	3.52	3.13	2.90	2.74	2.63	2.55	2.48	2.43	2.38	2.34	2.31	2.26	2.21	2.15	2.11	2.07	2.02	2.00	1.96	1.94	1.91	1.90	1.88
	8.18	**5.93**	**5.01**	**4.50**	**4.17**	**3.94**	**3.77**	**3.63**	**3.52**	**3.43**	**3.36**	**3.30**	**3.19**	**3.12**	**3.00**	**2.92**	**2.84**	**2.76**	**2.70**	**2.63**	**2.60**	**2.54**	**2.51**	**2.49**
20	4.35	3.49	3.10	2.87	2.71	2.60	2.52	2.45	2.40	2.35	2.31	2.28	2.23	2.18	2.12	2.08	2.04	1.99	1.96	1.92	1.90	1.87	1.85	1.84
	8.10	**5.85**	**4.94**	**4.43**	**4.10**	**3.87**	**3.71**	**3.56**	**3.45**	**3.37**	**3.30**	**3.23**	**3.13**	**3.05**	**2.94**	**2.86**	**2.77**	**2.69**	**2.63**	**2.56**	**2.53**	**2.47**	**2.44**	**2.42**
21	4.32	3.47	3.07	2.84	2.68	2.57	2.49	2.42	2.37	2.32	2.28	2.25	2.20	2.15	2.09	2.05	2.00	1.96	1.93	1.89	1.87	1.84	1.82	1.81
	8.02	**5.78**	**4.87**	**4.37**	**4.04**	**3.81**	**3.65**	**3.51**	**3.40**	**3.31**	**3.24**	**3.17**	**3.07**	**2.99**	**2.88**	**2.80**	**2.72**	**2.63**	**2.58**	**2.51**	**2.47**	**2.42**	**2.38**	**2.36**
22	4.30	3.44	3.05	2.82	2.66	2.55	2.47	2.40	2.35	2.30	2.26	2.23	2.18	2.13	2.07	2.03	1.98	1.93	1.91	1.87	1.84	1.81	1.80	1.78
	7.94	**5.72**	**4.82**	**4.31**	**3.99**	**3.76**	**3.59**	**3.45**	**3.35**	**3.26**	**3.18**	**3.12**	**3.02**	**2.94**	**2.83**	**2.75**	**2.67**	**2.58**	**2.53**	**2.46**	**2.42**	**2.37**	**2.33**	**2.31**
23	4.28	3.42	3.03	2.80	2.64	2.53	2.45	2.38	2.32	2.28	2.24	2.20	2.14	2.10	2.04	2.00	1.96	1.31	1.89	1.84	1.82	1.79	1.77	1.76
	7.88	**5.66**	**4.76**	**4.26**	**3.94**	**3.71**	**3.54**	**3.41**	**3.30**	**3.21**	**3.14**	**3.07**	**2.97**	**2.89**	**2.78**	**2.70**	**2.62**	**2.53**	**2.48**	**2.41**	**2.37**	**2.32**	**2.28**	**2.26**
24	4.26	3.40	3.01	2.78	2.62	2.51	2.43	2.36	2.30	2.26	2.22	2.18	2.13	2.09	2.02	1.98	1.94	1.89	1.86	1.82	1.80	1.76	1.74	1.73
	7.82	**5.61**	**4.72**	**4.22**	**3.90**	**3.67**	**3.50**	**3.36**	**3.25**	**3.17**	**3.09**	**3.03**	**2.93**	**2.85**	**2.74**	**2.66**	**2.58**	**2.49**	**2.44**	**2.36**	**2.33**	**2.27**	**2.23**	**2.21**
25	4.24	3.38	2.99	2.76	2.60	2.49	2.41	2.34	2.28	2.24	2.20	2.16	2.11	2.06	2.00	1.96	1.92	1.87	1.84	1.80	1.77	1.74	1.72	1.71
	7.77	**5.57**	**4.68**	**4.18**	**3.86**	**3.63**	**3.46**	**3.32**	**3.21**	**3.13**	**3.05**	**2.99**	**2.89**	**2.81**	**2.70**	**2.62**	**2.54**	**2.45**	**2.40**	**2.32**	**2.29**	**2.23**	**2.19**	**2.17**
26	4.22	3.37	2.98	2.74	2.59	2.47	2.39	2.32	2.27	2.22	2.18	2.15	2.10	2.05	1.99	1.95	1.90	1.85	1.82	1.78	1.76	1.72	1.70	1.69
	7.72	**5.53**	**4.64**	**4.14**	**3.82**	**3.59**	**3.42**	**3.29**	**3.17**	**3.09**	**3.02**	**2.96**	**2.86**	**2.77**	**2.66**	**2.58**	**2.50**	**2.41**	**2.36**	**2.28**	**2.25**	**2.19**	**2.15**	**2.13**
27	4.21	3.35	2.96	2.73	2.57	2.46	2.37	2.30	2.25	2.20	2.16	2.13	2.08	2.03	1.97	1.93	1.88	1.84	1.80	1.76	1.74	1.71	1.68	1.67
	7.68	**5.49**	**4.60**	**4.11**	**3.79**	**3.56**	**3.39**	**3.26**	**3.14**	**3.06**	**2.98**	**2.93**	**2.83**	**2.74**	**2.63**	**2.55**	**2.47**	**2.38**	**2.33**	**2.25**	**2.21**	**2.16**	**2.12**	**2.10**
28	4.20	3.34	2.95	2.71	2.56	2.44	2.36	2.29	2.24	2.19	2.15	2.12	2.06	2.02	1.96	1.91	1.87	1.81	1.78	1.75	1.72	1.69	1.67	1.65
	7.64	**5.45**	**4.57**	**4.07**	**3.46**	**3.53**	**3.36**	**3.23**	**3.11**	**3.03**	**2.95**	**2.90**	**2.80**	**2.71**	**2.60**	**2.52**	**2.44**	**2.35**	**2.30**	**2.22**	**2.18**	**2.13**	**2.09**	**2.06**
29	4.18	3.33	2.93	2.70	2.54	2.43	2.35	2.28	2.22	2.18	2.14	2.10	2.05	2.00	1.94	1.90	1.85	1.80	1.77	1.73	1.71	1.68	1.65	1.64
	7.60	**5.42**	**4.54**	**4.04**	**3.73**	**3.50**	**3.33**	**3.20**	**3.08**	**3.00**	**2.92**	**2.87**	**2.77**	**2.68**	**2.57**	**2.49**	**2.41**	**2.32**	**2.27**	**2.19**	**2.15**	**2.10**	**2.06**	**2.03**

Degrees of freedom (for the denominator)

TABLE A-2 (continued)

DEGREES OF FREEDOM (FOR THE NUMERATOR)

Degrees of freedom (for the denominator)

	1	2	3	4	5	6	7	8	9	10	11	12	14	16	20	24	30	40	50	75	100	200	500	∞
30	4.17 **7.56**	3.32 **5.39**	2.92 **4.51**	2.69 **4.02**	2.53 **3.70**	2.42 **3.47**	2.34 **3.30**	2.27 **3.17**	2.21 **3.06**	2.16 **2.98**	2.12 **2.90**	2.09 **2.84**	2.04 **2.74**	1.99 **2.66**	1.93 **2.55**	1.89 **2.47**	1.84 **2.38**	1.79 **2.29**	1.76 **2.24**	1.72 **2.16**	1.69 **2.13**	1.66 **2.07**	1.64 **2.03**	1.62 **2.01**
32	4.15 **7.50**	3.30 **5.34**	2.90 **4.46**	2.67 **3.97**	2.51 **3.66**	2.40 **3.42**	2.32 **3.25**	2.25 **3.12**	2.19 **3.01**	2.14 **2.94**	2.10 **2.86**	2.07 **2.80**	2.02 **2.70**	1.97 **2.62**	1.91 **2.51**	1.86 **2.42**	1.82 **2.34**	1.76 **2.25**	1.74 **2.20**	1.69 **2.12**	1.67 **2.08**	1.64 **2.02**	1.61 **1.98**	1.59 **1.96**
34	4.13 **7.44**	3.28 **5.29**	2.88 **4.42**	2.65 **3.93**	2.49 **3.61**	2.38 **3.38**	2.30 **3.21**	2.23 **3.08**	2.17 **2.97**	2.12 **2.89**	2.08 **2.82**	2.05 **2.76**	2.00 **2.66**	1.95 **2.58**	1.89 **2.47**	1.84 **2.38**	1.80 **2.30**	1.74 **2.21**	1.71 **2.15**	1.67 **2.08**	1.64 **2.04**	1.61 **1.98**	1.59 **1.94**	1.57 **1.91**
36	4.11 **7.39**	3.26 **5.25**	2.86 **4.38**	2.63 **3.89**	2.48 **3.58**	2.36 **3.35**	2.28 **3.18**	2.21 **3.04**	2.15 **2.94**	2.10 **2.86**	2.06 **2.78**	2.03 **2.72**	1.98 **2.62**	1.93 **2.54**	1.87 **2.43**	1.82 **2.35**	1.78 **2.26**	1.72 **2.17**	1.69 **2.12**	1.65 **2.04**	1.62 **2.00**	1.59 **1.94**	1.56 **1.90**	1.55 **1.87**
38	4.10 **7.35**	3.25 **5.21**	2.85 **4.34**	2.62 **3.86**	2.46 **3.54**	2.35 **3.32**	2.26 **3.15**	2.19 **3.02**	2.14 **2.91**	2.09 **2.82**	2.05 **2.75**	2.02 **2.69**	1.96 **2.59**	1.92 **2.51**	1.85 **2.40**	1.80 **2.32**	1.76 **2.22**	1.71 **2.14**	1.67 **2.08**	1.63 **2.00**	1.60 **1.97**	1.57 **1.90**	1.54 **1.86**	1.53 **1.84**
40	4.08 **7.31**	3.23 **5.18**	2.84 **4.31**	2.61 **3.83**	2.45 **3.51**	2.34 **3.29**	2.25 **3.12**	2.18 **2.99**	2.12 **2.88**	2.07 **2.80**	2.04 **2.73**	2.00 **2.66**	1.95 **2.56**	1.90 **2.49**	1.84 **2.37**	1.79 **2.29**	1.74 **2.20**	1.69 **2.11**	1.66 **2.05**	1.61 **1.97**	1.59 **1.94**	1.55 **1.88**	1.53 **1.84**	1.51 **1.81**
42	4.07 **7.27**	3.22 **5.15**	2.83 **4.29**	2.59 **3.80**	2.44 **3.49**	2.32 **3.26**	2.24 **3.10**	2.17 **2.96**	2.11 **2.86**	2.06 **2.77**	2.02 **2.70**	1.99 **2.64**	1.94 **2.54**	1.89 **2.46**	1.82 **2.35**	1.78 **2.26**	1.73 **2.17**	1.68 **2.08**	1.64 **2.02**	1.60 **1.94**	1.57 **1.91**	1.54 **1.85**	1.51 **1.80**	1.49 **1.78**
44	4.06 **7.24**	3.21 **5.12**	2.82 **4.26**	2.58 **3.78**	2.43 **3.46**	2.31 **3.24**	2.23 **3.07**	2.16 **2.94**	2.10 **2.84**	2.05 **2.75**	2.01 **2.68**	1.98 **2.62**	1.92 **2.52**	1.88 **2.44**	1.81 **2.32**	1.76 **2.24**	1.72 **2.15**	1.66 **2.06**	1.63 **2.00**	1.58 **1.92**	1.56 **1.88**	1.52 **1.82**	1.50 **1.78**	1.48 **1.75**
46	4.05 **7.21**	3.20 **5.10**	2.81 **4.24**	2.57 **3.76**	2.42 **3.44**	2.30 **3.22**	2.22 **3.05**	2.14 **2.92**	2.09 **2.82**	2.04 **2.73**	2.00 **2.66**	1.97 **2.60**	1.91 **2.50**	1.87 **2.42**	1.80 **2.30**	1.75 **2.22**	1.71 **2.13**	1.65 **2.04**	1.62 **1.98**	1.57 **1.90**	1.54 **1.86**	1.51 **1.80**	1.48 **1.76**	1.46 **1.72**
48	4.04 **7.19**	3.19 **5.08**	2.80 **4.22**	2.56 **3.74**	2.41 **3.42**	2.30 **3.20**	2.21 **3.04**	2.14 **2.90**	2.08 **2.80**	2.03 **2.71**	1.99 **2.64**	1.96 **2.58**	1.90 **2.48**	1.86 **2.40**	1.79 **2.28**	1.74 **2.20**	1.70 **2.11**	1.64 **2.02**	1.61 **1.96**	1.56 **1.88**	1.53 **1.84**	1.50 **1.78**	1.47 **1.73**	1.45 **1.70**
50	4.03 **7.17**	3.18 **5.06**	2.79 **4.20**	2.56 **3.72**	2.40 **3.41**	2.29 **3.18**	2.20 **3.02**	2.13 **2.88**	2.07 **2.78**	2.02 **2.70**	1.98 **2.62**	1.95 **2.56**	1.90 **2.46**	1.85 **2.39**	1.78 **2.26**	1.74 **2.18**	1.69 **2.10**	1.63 **2.00**	1.60 **1.94**	1.55 **1.86**	1.52 **1.82**	1.48 **1.76**	1.46 **1.71**	1.44 **1.68**
55	4.02 **7.12**	3.17 **5.01**	2.78 **4.16**	2.54 **3.68**	2.38 **3.37**	2.27 **3.15**	2.18 **2.98**	2.11 **2.85**	2.05 **2.75**	2.00 **2.66**	1.97 **2.59**	1.93 **2.53**	1.88 **2.43**	1.83 **2.35**	1.76 **2.23**	1.72 **2.15**	1.67 **2.06**	1.61 **1.96**	1.58 **1.90**	1.52 **1.82**	1.50 **1.78**	1.46 **1.71**	1.43 **1.66**	1.41 **1.64**
60	4.00 **7.08**	3.15 **4.98**	2.76 **4.13**	2.52 **3.65**	2.37 **3.34**	2.25 **3.12**	2.17 **2.95**	2.10 **2.82**	2.04 **2.72**	1.99 **2.63**	1.95 **2.56**	1.92 **2.50**	1.86 **2.40**	1.81 **2.32**	1.75 **2.20**	1.70 **2.12**	1.65 **2.03**	1.59 **1.93**	1.56 **1.87**	1.50 **1.79**	1.48 **1.74**	1.44 **1.68**	1.41 **1.63**	1.39 **1.60**
65	3.99 **7.04**	3.14 **4.95**	2.75 **4.10**	2.51 **3.62**	2.36 **3.31**	2.24 **3.09**	2.15 **2.93**	2.08 **2.79**	2.02 **2.70**	1.98 **2.61**	1.94 **2.54**	1.90 **2.47**	1.85 **2.37**	1.80 **2.30**	1.73 **2.18**	1.68 **2.09**	1.63 **2.00**	1.57 **1.90**	1.54 **1.84**	1.49 **1.76**	1.46 **1.71**	1.42 **1.64**	1.39 **1.60**	1.37 **1.56**
70	3.98 **7.01**	3.13 **4.92**	2.74 **4.08**	2.50 **3.60**	2.35 **3.29**	2.23 **3.07**	2.14 **2.91**	2.07 **2.77**	2.01 **2.67**	1.97 **2.59**	1.93 **2.51**	1.89 **2.45**	1.84 **2.35**	1.79 **2.28**	1.72 **2.15**	1.67 **2.07**	1.62 **1.98**	1.56 **1.88**	1.53 **1.82**	1.47 **1.74**	1.45 **1.69**	1.40 **1.62**	1.37 **1.56**	1.35 **1.53**
80	3.96 **6.96**	3.11 **4.88**	2.72 **4.04**	2.48 **3.56**	2.33 **3.25**	2.21 **3.04**	2.12 **2.87**	2.05 **2.74**	1.99 **2.64**	1.95 **2.55**	1.91 **2.48**	1.88 **2.41**	1.82 **2.32**	1.77 **2.24**	1.70 **2.11**	1.65 **2.03**	1.60 **1.94**	1.54 **1.84**	1.51 **1.78**	1.45 **1.70**	1.42 **1.65**	1.38 **1.57**	1.35 **1.52**	1.32 **1.49**

TABLE A-2 (continued)

	DEGREES OF FREEDOM (FOR THE NUMERATOR)																						
Degrees of freedom (for the denominator)	1	2	3	4	5	6	7	8	9	10	11	12	14	16	20	24	30	40	50	75	100	200	500	∞
100	3.94 **6.90**	3.09 **4.82**	2.70 **3.98**	2.46 **3.51**	2.30 **3.20**	2.19 **2.99**	2.10 **2.82**	2.03 **2.69**	1.97 **2.59**	1.92 **2.51**	1.88 **2.43**	1.85 **2.36**	1.79 **2.26**	1.75 **2.19**	1.68 **2.06**	1.63 **1.98**	1.57 **1.89**	1.51 **1.79**	1.48 **1.73**	1.42 **1.64**	1.39 **1.59**	1.34 **1.51**	1.30 **1.46**	1.28 **1.43**
125	3.92 **6.84**	3.07 **4.78**	2.68 **3.94**	2.44 **3.47**	2.29 **3.17**	2.17 **2.95**	2.08 **2.79**	2.01 **2.65**	1.95 **2.56**	1.90 **2.47**	1.86 **2.40**	1.83 **2.33**	1.77 **2.23**	1.72 **2.15**	1.65 **2.03**	1.60 **1.94**	1.55 **1.85**	1.49 **1.75**	1.45 **1.68**	1.39 **1.59**	1.36 **1.54**	1.31 **1.46**	1.27 **1.40**	1.25 **1.37**
150	3.91 **6.81**	3.06 **4.75**	2.67 **3.91**	2.43 **3.44**	2.27 **3.14**	2.16 **2.92**	2.07 **2.76**	2.00 **2.62**	1.94 **2.53**	1.89 **2.44**	1.85 **2.37**	1.82 **2.30**	1.76 **2.20**	1.71 **2.12**	1.64 **2.00**	1.59 **1.91**	1.54 **1.83**	1.47 **1.72**	1.44 **1.66**	1.37 **1.56**	1.34 **1.51**	1.29 **1.43**	1.25 **1.37**	1.22 **1.33**
200	3.89 **6.76**	3.04 **4.71**	2.65 **3.88**	2.41 **3.41**	2.26 **3.11**	2.14 **2.90**	2.05 **2.73**	1.98 **2.60**	1.92 **2.50**	1.87 **2.41**	1.83 **2.34**	1.80 **2.28**	1.74 **2.17**	1.69 **2.09**	1.62 **1.97**	1.57 **1.88**	1.52 **1.79**	1.45 **1.69**	1.42 **1.62**	1.35 **1.53**	1.32 **1.48**	1.26 **1.39**	1.22 **1.33**	1.19 **1.28**
400	3.86 **6.70**	3.02 **4.66**	2.62 **3.83**	2.39 **3.36**	2.23 **3.06**	2.12 **2.85**	2.03 **2.69**	1.96 **2.55**	1.90 **2.46**	1.85 **2.37**	1.81 **2.29**	1.78 **2.23**	1.72 **2.12**	1.67 **2.04**	1.60 **1.92**	1.54 **1.84**	1.49 **1.74**	1.42 **1.64**	1.38 **1.57**	1.32 **1.47**	1.28 **1.42**	1.22 **1.32**	1.16 **1.24**	1.13 **1.19**
1000	3.85 **6.66**	3.00 **4.62**	2.61 **3.80**	2.38 **3.34**	2.22 **3.04**	2.10 **2.82**	2.02 **2.66**	1.95 **2.53**	1.89 **2.43**	1.84 **2.34**	1.80 **2.26**	1.76 **2.20**	1.70 **2.09**	1.65 **2.01**	1.58 **1.89**	1.53 **1.81**	1.47 **1.71**	1.41 **1.61**	1.36 **1.54**	1.30 **1.44**	1.26 **1.38**	1.19 **1.28**	1.13 **1.19**	1.08 **1.11**
∞	3.84 **6.64**	2.99 **4.60**	2.60 **3.78**	2.37 **3.32**	2.21 **3.02**	2.09 **2.80**	2.01 **2.64**	1.94 **2.51**	1.88 **2.41**	1.83 **2.32**	1.79 **2.24**	1.75 **2.18**	1.69 **2.07**	1.64 **1.99**	1.57 **1.87**	1.52 **1.79**	1.46 **1.69**	1.40 **1.59**	1.35 **1.52**	1.28 **1.41**	1.24 **1.36**	1.17 **1.25**	1.11 **1.15**	1.00 **1.00**

Appendix B

Study Break Answers

CHAPTER 1

STUDY BREAK   **PAGE 12**

1. tenacity

2. credibility

3. Your perception that the world may be altered and your knowledge base would not be accurate.

4. 1-C;   2-D;   3-A;   4-B;   5-E

5. The "self-correcting nature of science" refers to the fact that because scientific findings are open to public scrutiny, they can be replicated. Replications will reveal any errors and faulty logic.

6. Control can refer to (a) the procedures that are used to account for the effects of unwanted factors and (b) the direct manipulation of factors of major interest in an experiment.

7. The experimenter attempts to establish a cause-and-effect relationship between the IV that is manipulated and the DV that is recorded.

STUDY BREAK   **PAGE 21**

1. The steps involved in the research process include the following:

    Problem.   You detect a gap in the knowledge base.

    Literature Review.   Consulting previous reports determines what has been found in the research area of interest.

    Theoretical Considerations.   The literature review highlights theories that point to relevant research projects.

    Hypothesis.   The literature review also highlights hypotheses (statements of the relationship between variables in more restricted domains of the research area). Such hypotheses will assist in the development of the experimental hypothesis—the predicted outcome of your research project.

    Experimental Design.   You develop the general plan for conducting the research project.

    Conduct the Experiment.   You conduct the research project according to the experimental design.

    Data Analysis and Statistical Decisions.   Based upon the statistical analysis, you decide whether the independent variable exerted a significant effect upon the dependent variable.

    Decisions in Terms of Past Research and Theory.   The statistical results guide decisions concerning the relationship of the present research project to past research and theoretical considerations.

Preparation of the Research Report.   You prepare a research report describing the rationale, conduct, and results of the experiment according to accepted American Psychological Association (APA) format.

Sharing Your Results: Presentation and Publication.   You share your research report with professional colleagues at a professional society meeting and/or by publication in a professional journal.

Finding a New Problem.   Your research results highlight another gap in our knowledge base and the research process begins again.

2.   Theories attempt to organize a general body of scientific data and point the way to new research. The hypothesis attempts to state specific IV-DV relationships within a selected portion of the larger, more comprehensive theory.

3.   The research or experimental hypothesis is the experimenter's predicted outcome or answer to the research project.

4.   experimental design

5.   The reasons for taking a research methods or experimental psychology course include that they

   a. assist you in other psychology courses

   b. enable you to conduct a research project after graduation

   c. assist you in getting into graduate school

   d. help you to become a knowledgeable consumer of psychological research

STUDY BREAK   PAGE 43

1.   1-C;   2-A;   3-D;   4-B;   5-G;   6-F;   7-E

2.   testable; likelihood of success

3.   *Nonsystematic sources* of research ideas include those instances or occurrences that make us believe that the research idea was unplanned. These types of research ideas are shown through "inspiration," "serendipity," and "everyday occurrences." *Systematic sources* of research ideas are carefully organized and logically thought out. This source of research ideas may be found in "past research," "theory," and "classroom lectures."

4.   The steps involved in conducting a search of the literature include:

   a. *Selection of Index Terms.* Select relevant terms for your area of interest from the *Thesaurus of Psychological Index Terms.*

   b. *Computerized Search of the Literature.* Use the selected index terms to access a computerized database, such as PsycLIT, of articles published from 1974 to the present.

   c. *Manual Search of the Literature.* Use index terms to access pre-1974 publications in *Psychological Abstracts.*

   d. *Obtaining Relevant Publications.* Use a combination of reading and notetaking, photocopying, interlibrary loan, and writing for reprints to obtain needed materials.

CHAPTER 2

e. *Integrating the Results of the Literature Search.* Develop a plan that will facilitate the integration of the literature you gathered.

5. Requesting a reprint brings you in direct contact with the author and allows you to request additional, related papers.

6. Synthetic statements are used in the experimental hypothesis because they can be either true or false.

7. General implication form presents the experimental hypothesis as an "if . . . then" statement where the if portion of the statement refers to the IV manipulation and the then portion of the statement refers to the predicted changes in the DV.

8. The "principle of falsifiability" refers to the fact that when an experiment does not turn out as expected, this result is seen as evidence that the experimental hypothesis is false.

9. inductive, deductive

10. directional, nondirectional

STUDY BREAK   PAGE 61

1. The atrocities of World War II where prisoners of war were unwillingly subjected to experiments using drugs, viruses, and toxic agents. The Tuskegee syphilis study examined the course of untreated syphilis in a group of men who did not realize they were being studied. Milgram's research on obedience studied the reaction to demands from an authority in participants who were being deceived.

2. The Nuremberg Code stressed the need to

   1. obtain participants' consent to participate in research
   2. inform participants about the nature of the research project
   3. avoid risks where possible
   4. protect participants against risks
   5. conduct research using qualified personnel

3. Deception may be needed if the results of a research project would be biased or contaminated by the participants knowing the nature of the experiment. A more general statement on the informed consent document in conjunction with a clear indication that the participants may terminate the project at any time might be used. Complete debriefing should follow the experiment.

4. Participants "at risk" are placed under some emotional or physical risk by virtue of their participation in the research project. Participants "at minimal risk" will not experience harmful effects by participating in the research project.

5. Aronson and Carlsmith (1968) indicate that the effective debriefing session should do the following:

     a. Establish the researcher's credibility as a scientist.

     b. Reassure the participants that it was natural to be deceived if deception was used.

     c. Not proceed too fast.

     d. Be sensitive to the discomfort felt by the participants.

     e. Be respectful of all guarantees of confidentiality and anonymity.

They also suggest that the experimenter not try to satisfy debriefing by sending a written explanation at a later time.

6. The guidelines for the ethical use of animals in research involve attention to each of the following:

    I. *Justification of Research.* The research should have a clear scientific purpose.

    II. *Personnel.* Only trained personnel who are familiar with the animal care guidelines should be involved with the research. All procedures must conform to appropriate federal guidelines.

    III. *Care and Housing of Animals.* Animal housing areas must comply with current regulations.

    IV. *Acquisition of Animals.* If animals are not bred in the laboratory, they must be acquired in a lawful, humane manner.

    V. *Experimental Procedures.* "Humane consideration for the well-being of the animal should be incorporated into the design and conduct of all procedures involving animals, while keeping in mind the primary goal of experimental procedures—the acquisition of sound, replicable data."

    VI. *Field Research.* Field research must be approved by the appropriate review board. Investigators should take special precautions to disturb their research population(s) and the environment as little as possible.

    VII. *Educational Use of Animals.* The educational use of animals must be approved by the appropriate review board. Instruction in the ethics of animal research is encouraged.

7. The IRB is the Institutional Review Board. The typical IRB at a college or university is composed of faculty members from a variety of disciplines, members from the community, and a veterinarian if animal proposals are considered. The IRB examines proposed procedures, questionnaires, the informed consent document, debriefing plans, the use of pain in animals, and proposed procedures for animal disposal.

8. The experimenter is responsible for the ethical conduct of the research project *and* the ethical presentation of the research results.

9. *Plagiarism* refers to the use of someone else's work without giving credit to the original author. *Fabrication of data* involves the creation of fictitious research data. Pressures for job security (tenure), salary increases, and ego involvement in the research are factors that might lead to such unethical behaviors.

CHAPTER 3

STUDY BREAK   **PAGE 80**

1. The reactance or reactivity effect refers to the biasing or influencing of the participants' scores or responses because they know they are being observed. Archival research avoids the reactance effect because the researcher does not observe the participants and the data of interest are recorded before they are used in the research project.

2. The problems specifically associated with archival research include (a) not knowing who the participants are; (b) selective deposit, wherein participants provide only certain types of data and omit others; and (c) survival of the records. Archival research, like the other descriptive methods, is not able to establish cause-and-effect statements.

3. 1-C;   2-A;   3-D;   4-E;   5-B

4. Situation sampling and time sampling are used to provide greater generality for the research project.

5. a. nominal   b. ratio   c. ordinal   d. nominal
   e. ratio   f. ordinal

6. The extent to which two observers agree is called interobserver reliability. It is calculated by dividing the number of times the observers agree by the number of opportunities for agreement and multiplying by 100. These calculations result in the percent agreement.

7. A positive correlation indicates that as one variable increases, the second variable also increases. A negative correlation indicates that as one variable increases, the other variable decreases. A zero correlation indicates that there is no lawful relation between the changes in one variable and the changes in the second variable.

8. An ex post facto study is one in which the experimenter is not able to directly manipulate the IV of interest. The effects of the IV have already taken place and the experimenter must study them "after the fact."

STUDY BREAK   **PAGE 95**

1. population; sample

2. Random sampling occurs when every member of the population has an equal chance of being selected. Random sampling with replacement occurs when the chosen items are returned to the population and can be selected on future occasions. When random sampling without replacement is used, the chosen item is not returned to the population.

3. When stratified random sampling is used, group homogeneity is increased. The more homogeneous the sample, the less chances there are for nuisance variables to operate. The less the chance for nuisance variables to operate, the smaller the within-group variability.

4. 1-D;   2-F;   3-G;   4-C;   5-A;   6-E;   7-B

5. The steps involved in developing a good survey include (a) determining *how* the information you seek is to be obtained and what type of instrument will you use, (b) determining the nature of the questions that will be used, (c) writing the items for your survey, (d) pilot testing your survey or questionnaire, (e) considering what demographic data are desired, and (f) specifying the procedures that will be followed in administering the survey or questionnaire.

6. The low return rate of mail surveys can be increased by (a) including a letter that clearly summarizes the nature and importance with the initial mailing (a self-addressed, prepaid return envelope should be included with the initial mailing) and (b) sending additional mailings at two- to three-week intervals.

7. The use of personal interviews is declining because (a) the expense involved in conducting them has increased greatly, (b) the fact that an individual administers the surveys increases the possibility for bias, and (c) the appeal of going from door to door is decreasing because of unavailability of respondents and high crime rates in large metropolitan areas.

8. Achievement tests are used to assess an individual's level of mastery or competence. Aptitude tests are used to assess an individual's skills or abilities.

9. The single-strata research approach attempts to secure research data from a single, specified segment of the population of interest. The cross-sectional research approach involves the comparison of two or more groups of participants during the same, rather limited, time span. The longitudinal research approach involves gathering information from a group of participants over an extended period of time.

CHAPTER 4

STUDY BREAK   PAGE 113

1. variable

2. 1-E;   2-C;   3-A;   4-F;   5-B;   6-D

3. The four ways to measure or record the DV include (a) correctness (correct or incorrect, as on a test question), (b) rate or frequency, (c) degree or amount, and (d) latency or duration.

4. You should record more than one DV if the additional DVs add meaningful information.

5. Nuisance variables are either characteristics of the participants or unintended influences of the experimental situation that cause variability within the groups to increase. Confounders are extraneous variables that influence the experiment in the same manner as IVs; they influence differences between groups. Because you cannot tell whether the results of an experiment are attributable to the IV or to a confounder (when it is present), confounders are more damaging to an experiment.

STUDY BREAK   PAGE 127

1. 1-C;   2-A;   3-B;   4-E;   5-D

2. Because all participants have an equal chance of being selected for each group in an experiment, any unique characteristics associated with the participants should be equally distributed across all groups in the experiment.

3. When within-subject counterbalancing is employed, each participant experiences more than one sequence of IV presentations. When within-group counterbalancing is employed, each participant experiences a different sequence of IV presentations.

4. *n!* refers to factoring or breaking a number into its component parts and then multiplying these component parts. *n!* can be used to determine the number of sequences required for complete counterbalancing: $4! = 4 \times 3 \times 2 \times 1 = 24$.

5. The requirements for complete counterbalancing are that (a) each participant must receive each treatment an equal number of times, (b) each treatment must appear an equal number of times at each testing or practice session, and (c) each treatment must precede and follow each of the other treatments an equal number of times.

6. The incomplete counterbalancing procedure refers to the use of some, but not all, of the possible sequences of treatment administration.

7. Carryover refers to the situation where the effects of one treatment persist to influence the participant's response on the next treatment. Differential carryover occurs when the response to one treatment depends on *which* treatment precedes it.

STUDY BREAK   PAGE 136

1. The experimenter's physiological characteristics, psychological characteristics, and personal expectancies for the outcome of the experiment can operate as extraneous variables and influence the responses of the participants.

2. 1-C;   2-A;   3-B;   4-E;   5-D

3. A Rosenthal effect is created when the experimenter expects the participants in a research project to behave in a certain manner. These experimenter expectancies influence the experimenter's behavior toward the participants, which in turn influences the participants to behave in the manner expected.

4. Automated equipment and instruments to present instructions and record data are frequently used to control for experimenter expectancies because they help minimize experimenter contact with the participants. By minimizing contact with the participants, the experimenter is less likely to influence the outcome of the experiment.

5. Most participants in a psychological research project want to participate in accordance with the experimenter's desires; that is, they want to be good participants. If demand characteristics are present, they may serve as cues for "good participant" behaviors.

6. nay-saying

CHAPTER 5

STUDY BREAK   PAGE **146**

1. Once a precedent or established pattern for using a particular type of research participant is begun, it is likely that that type of participant will be used in experiments in the research area in question.

2. White rats and college students are the favorite participants in psychological research because of precedent and availability. An established pattern of research with these two populations has been established, and they are easy to obtain.

3. The cost for testing each participant (finances), the time it will take to test each participant (time), the sheer number of participants that are available (availability), and the amount of variability we expect to observe within the groups are factors that influence the number of participants used in a research project.

4. By indicating how many participants were used in previous, successful experiments, the literature review can help guide the researcher's choice of number of participants.

5. The experimenter must be careful not to become a slave to elaborate pieces of equipment. If this situation occurs, then it is likely that the equipment may begin dictating the type of research that is conducted and/or the type of DV that is recorded.

STUDY BREAK   PAGE **152**

1. An emic is a culture-specific finding, whereas an etic is a universal truth or principle.

2. The goal of cross-cultural research is to determine if research findings are culture specific. This goal is incompatible with ethnocentrism because ethnocentrism views other cultures as an extension of that culture. Hence, according to an ethnocentric view, there is no need for cross-cultural research.

3. Culture can influence the choice of the research problem, the nature of the experimental hypothesis, selection of the IV(s), selection of the DV(s), selection of participants, sampling procedures, and the type of questionnaire that is used.

4. The tendency of a specific culture to respond in a certain manner is a cultural response set. The cultural response set must be acknowledged as a potential confounder and appropriate control procedures implemented to deal with it.

STUDY BREAK   PAGE **166**

1. "APA Format" refers to the accepted, standard form for preparing the results of psychological research that has been adopted by the American Psychological Association. APA format was developed in order to bring standardization and uniformness to the publication of research in the field of psychology.

2. 1-C;   2-E;   3-B;   4-D;   5-F;   6-A

3. The abstract is a one-paragraph description of the research that has been conducted. It should include a description of the intent and conduct (methodology) of the project, results, and implications.

4. "Avoiding bias in your language" means that you should not state or imply a bias toward or against an individual or group in the preparation of an APA format paper.

5. The method section contains specific information about the number and type of participants used in the research project, the apparatus or testing instruments that were employed, and the procedure used to test the participants. The method section is purposely intended to be this specific in order to allow other researchers to replicate the research project.

STUDY BREAK   PAGE 186

1. 1-G;   2-E;   3-A;   4-C;   5-B;   6-F;   7-D

2. mode, median

3. Because the three measures of central tendency (mean, median, and mode) are identical in a normal distribution, any one of them would serve as a representative measure of central tendency.

4. A pie chart is used when the researcher wants to depict percentages that total 100. The histogram is used to when we wish to present frequencies of a quantitative variable per category.

5. The ordinate is the vertical axis; it should be approximately two-thirds the size of the abscissa (horizontal axis). The DV is plotted on the ordinate, whereas the IV is plotted on the abscissa.

6. Because it takes into account only the highest and lowest scores and disregards the distribution of scores in between, the range does not convey much information.

7. Variance is a single number that represents the entire variability in a distribution of scores. The greater the variance, the larger the standard deviation.

8. Because the percentage of scores occurring between the mean and any standard deviation (e.g., +1, +2, −1, −2) away from the mean is constant, standard deviation scores from one distribution can be compared with standard deviation scores from other distributions.

STUDY BREAK   PAGE 199

1. 1-F;   2-H;   3-I;   4-B;   5-D;   6-C;   7-G;   8-E;   9-A

2. A positive correlation indicates that as one variable increases, the other variable under consideration also increases, whereas a perfect positive correlation indicates that for every unit of increase in one variable there is a corresponding increase of one unit in the other variable.

3. A zero correlation indicates that changes in one variable are not systematically related to changes in the other variable.

CHAPTER 6 *(vertical side tab)*

4. When two independent groups are being compared, the *t* test compares the difference between the means of the two groups to the amount of variability (error) that exists within the two groups. Because the groups are assumed to be equivalent at the start of the experiment, larger *t* values indicate greater influence of the IV.

5. "Level of significance" refers to the point at which the experimenter feels that a result occurs rarely by chance. If an experimental result occurs rarely by chance, we conclude that it is significant. Although the experimenter arbitrarily sets the level of significance, tradition has established the .05 level as an accepted level of significance.

6. Because researchers don't always know how a research project is going to turn out, it is safer to state a nondirectional hypothesis and use a two-tail test. If a directional hypothesis is stated and the results turn out differently, then the researcher is forced to reject the experimental hypothesis even though differences may exist between the groups.

CHAPTER 7

STUDY BREAK   PAGE 212

1. We cannot conduct a valid experiment with only one group because we have to have a second group for comparison purposes. We cannot tell whether our IV has any effect if we cannot compare the experimental group to a control group.

2. levels

3. Independent groups consist of participants who are totally unrelated to each other. Correlated groups are composed of pairs of participants who have some relationship to each other because (a) they have some natural relationship (natural pairs), (b) are matched with each other (matched pairs), or (c) are the same participants (repeated measures).

4. 1-D;   2-A;   3-B;   4-C

5. We must be cautious about the use of random assignment when we have small numbers of participants because the groups may end up being unequal before the experiment.

6. If your experiment could use either independent or correlated groups, you would most likely base your decision on the number of participants available to you. We often use correlated groups when we have a small number of participants so that we can be more confident about the equality of our groups. If you have many potential participants, independent groups will typically be equal.

STUDY BREAK   PAGE 219

1. It is important for our groups to be equal before the experiment so that any difference we detect in our DV can be attributed to the IV.

2. between-groups variability; error variability

3. Correlated groups have the advantages of ensuring equality of the participants before the experiment and of reducing error variability. Independent groups

are advantageous in that they are simpler than correlated groups and that they can be used in experimental situations that preclude correlated groups.

4. Many different answers are possible to the question about comparing differing amounts of an IV. Some representative examples include amount of study time or amount of reinforcement in a learning experiment, amount of pay or bonus on job performance, and length of therapy to treat a particular problem. As long as you chose a single IV and varied its amount (rather than presence vs. absence), your answer should be correct.

5. Again, many different answers are possible. Some possible answers include different types of life experiences, different majors, different musical preferences, and different hometowns. As long as you chose two levels of an IV that *cannot* be manipulated, your answer is correct.

STUDY BREAK   PAGE 232

1. To compare the stereotyping of a group of female executives to the stereotyping of a group of male executives, you would use a *t* test for independent samples because males and females represent independent groups.

2. To compare the stereotyping of a group of male executives before and after the ERA, you would use a *t* test for correlated samples because this represents repeated measures.

3. We usually look for descriptive statistics first on a computer printout because this information helps us understand how the groups performed on the DV.

4. homogeneity of variance; heterogeneity of variance

5. words; numbers (statistical information)

6. Group A scored significantly higher than Group B.

7. Research is a cyclical, ongoing process because each experiment typically raises new questions. A multitude of examples of cyclical research could be given. For example, you might test a new antihyperactivity drug against a control group. If the drug is helpful, then you would need additional research to determine the most effective dosage. In the future, you would want to test this drug against new drugs that arrive on the market.

STUDY BREAK   PAGE 250

1. The two-group design is the building block for the multiple-group design because the multiple-group design essentially takes a two-group design and adds more groups to it. Thus, the multiple-group design is similar to changing a two-group design into a three-group design (or larger).

2. one; three

3. A multiple-group design allows you to ask and answer more questions than does a two-group design. You may be able to run only one experiment instead of two or three. Therefore, the multiple-group design is more efficient than the two-group design—you can save time, effort, participants, and so on.

CHAPTER 8

4. There are many correct answers to this question. If you chose an IV that has more than two levels, your answer should be correct. For example, if you wished to test attendance in college students as a function of classification, you would use a multiple-group design with four groups (freshmen, sophomores, juniors, seniors).

5. Matched sets, repeated measures, and natural sets are all considered correlated groups because participants in such groups are related in some way.

6. There is no real limit on the number of groups in a multiple-group design. Practically speaking, it is rare to see more than four or five groups for a particular IV.

7. How many groups are required to adequately test your experimental hypothesis? Will you learn something important if you include more levels of your IV?

8. provide more control than independent groups designs

9. Practical considerations are more difficult in multiple correlated groups designs because there are simply more "equated" participants with which to deal. In repeated measures, participants must take part in more experimental sessions. Matched sets must include three (or more) matched participants. Natural sets require larger sets of participants.

10. To compare personality traits of firstborn, lastborn, and only children, we would use a multiple independent groups design (unless you matched participants on some variable). Repeated measures and natural sets are impossible (can you figure out why?). This would represent an ex post facto study because you cannot manipulate an individual's birth order.

STUDY BREAK   **PAGE 270**

1.   CLASSIFICATION

Freshman	Sophomore	Junior	Senior

This experiment would require a multiple independent groups design with four groups. The necessary statistical test would be a one-way ANOVA for independent groups (students could not be in more than one classification simultaneously).

2.   ACT/SAT ATTEMPTS

1st Attempt	2nd Attempt	3rd Attempt

This question requires a multiple correlated groups design with three groups. The proper statistical test would be a one-way ANOVA for correlated groups because each student takes the test three times (repeated measures).

3. Because we have more than two groups, it is necessary to compute post hoc tests to tell which groups are significantly different from the others.

4. between groups; within groups

5. Given the statistical information shown, we can conclude that students perform differently on their three attempts at taking the ACT or SAT (i.e., there is a statistically significant difference).

6. To draw a full and complete conclusion from Question 5, you would need the results from post hoc tests comparing the three means. With this information you could conclude whether students improve over time in taking the entrance exam.

7. It was important to have the information from Chapter 7's continuing research problem so that we could begin a follow-up experiment with the knowledge that the new text is a good text for class use. The follow-up experiment, then, can compare the good text to two other potential texts.

8. It depends. Do you want to measure the same people's moods across the four seasons (multiple correlated groups design) or four different groups of people in the four seasons (multiple independent groups)? Either approach is possible. Can you justify your answer? If you chose multiple correlated groups, your rationale should revolve around control issues. You should measure a large number of participants if you chose multiple independent groups.

9. It depends. Do you want the same people to eat at all four restaurants (multiple correlated groups) or to survey different people at each restaurant (multiple independent groups)? You could run the experiment either way. The rationale for your choice should be similar to that summarized in the answer to Question 8.

STUDY BREAK   PAGE 288

CHAPTER 9

1. The two-group design is related to the factorial design because it forms the underlying basis of a factorial design. For example, a 2 × 2 factorial design is simply two two-group designs combined (see the shaded section below).

2. There is a practical limit to the number of IVs you can use in an experiment so that you will be able to interpret the results easily. Interactions involving many variables can be quite difficult to understand.

3. 1-C;   2-A;   3-B

4. two; four

5. Numerous correct answers are possible. Your answer should consist of an experiment with two IVs. One IV should be a between-subjects variable (no relationship between participants); one should be a within-subjects variable (repeated measures, matching, or natural groups). For example, you might assign students to either a group that takes an ACT or SAT preparation course or does not take such a course (between subjects). Each group would take the ACT or SAT twice (repeated measures).

STUDY BREAK   PAGE 297

1. Factorial designs are combinations of the designs in Chapters 7 and 8 because a factorial design results from adding two (or more) simple designs (one IV each) together into a single design with two (or more) IVs; (e.g., see Figure 9-7).

2. A 2 × 4 × 3 experimental design consists of three IVs; one has two levels, one has four levels, and one has three levels:

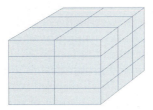

3. Totally between-groups designs use independent groups of participants for each IV. Totally within-groups designs use correlated groups of participants for all IVs. Mixed-groups designs have at least one IV that uses independent groups of participants and one that uses correlated groups. These designs are similar in that they are all factorial designs. They differ, of course, in the way that the experimenter assigns participants to groups.

4. Your experimental questions should be your first consideration in choosing a factorial design because the number of questions you ask will determine how many IVs your experiment will have.

5. measured

6. Your friend has listed six IVs that she wishes to include in her experiment. This is too ambitious for a beginning project, and the results could be incredibly difficult to interpret because of the many potential interactions.

STUDY BREAK   PAGE 327

1. Your experimental design has two IVs, classification and sex. Both are between-subject variables because a participant cannot be in more than one group. You would use the factorial between-group design and test the data with a factorial ANOVA for independent groups. Your block diagram would look like the following:

	Male	Female
Freshman		
Sophomore		
Junior		
Senior		

2. This experimental design has two IVs: test-taking practice and study course. Both are within-subject variables because each participant takes the tests repeatedly and takes the study course. You would use the factorial within-

group design and use a factorial ANOVA for correlated groups to analyze the data. Your block diagram would be the following:

No study course			
With study course			

                                         1st try   2nd try   3rd try

3. Again, you still have two IVs: the practice and the course. However, the study course is now a between-subject variable because some participants take it and some do not. Test-taking practice is a within-subject variable because each participant takes the test three times (repeated measures). Thus, you have factorial mixed-group design and would use a factorial ANOVA for mixed groups. Your block diagram would be the same as the one shown for Question 2—only the assignment of participants to groups differs.

4. An interaction effect is the simultaneous effect of two IVs in such a way that the effects of one IV depend on the particular level of the second IV. A significant interaction overrides any main effects because the interaction changes the meaning of the significant main effect.

5. Many different answers are possible. For the hypothetical experiment to have a significant three-way interaction, the different chapters would also be drawn into the interaction. Thus, your hypothetical graph should have four lines drawn on it—one for the biology chapter at the open admissions school, one for the learning chapter at the open admissions school, one for the biology chapter at the selective admissions school, and one for the learning chapter at the selective admissions school. Also, the four lines should not be parallel.

    One possible answer is shown in the graph below. In this example, the best quiz performance depends on the text, the chapter, and the school. For the learning chapter, there is really no difference based on either the particular text or the particular school. However, for the biology chapter, the old text is better at the selective admissions school, whereas the new text is better at the open admissions school.

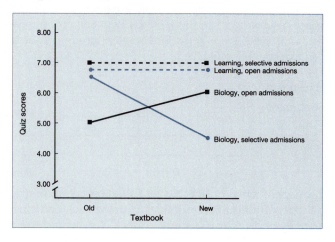

Against: Treatments should produce effects that are visually apparent. Clinical significance is more important than statistical significance.

5. 1-C;   2-A;   3-B

6. You might be forced to use an A-B single-case design in the real world because it can be impractical or unethical to reverse a treatment. Many examples are possible. Suppose you work with an individual who suffers from anorexia or bulimia. You institute a treatment and the individual shows marked improvement. However, you fear that removing the treatment could result in a recurrence of the problem.

STUDY BREAK   PAGE 395

1. Experimental designs involve manipulation of IVs, control of extraneous variables, and measurement of DVs so that cause-and-effect relationships can be determined. Ex post facto designs involve IVs that have already occurred or that are predetermined, such as sex. Quasi-experimental designs involve manipulating IVs with groups of participants that are predetermined, such as causing something to vary between men and women.

2. You might choose to use a quasi-experimental design rather than an experimental design in a situation when random assignment is impossible or if you wish to evaluate an ongoing program.

3. 1-B, C, F   2-A, D,* E

   *Figure 11-8 gives the impression that the interrupted time-series design includes pretesting—in some cases, it may actually be pretesting. In many situations that use this design, however, the observations before the treatment are not true pretests because they were not made with an experiment in mind; rather, they may often simply represent data that were already available (e.g., sales records). This is a fine distinction, and it could easily be argued that both designs actually include pretesting.

4. The key element in Geronimus's research that allowed a more positive conclusion about teen pregnancy was the realization that finding a true control group would be impossible; hence the need for a strong comparison group.

5. We are more certain about our conclusion in the helmet law case because it simulated an A-B-A design, whereas the AFDC study was only an A-B design. If we can return to the baseline condition, we usually get a better reading of our results.

STUDY BREAK   PAGE 403

1. Qualitative research differs from single-case and quasi-experimental designs primarily because these two designs are examples of quantitative approaches despite the fact that they do not allow for the best possible control.

2. 1-B, E   2-C, D   3-A, F

CHAPTER 12

Study Break   page 433

1. The abstract is the most widely read section of most research reports because it is published in *Psychological Abstracts* and computerized indices such as PsycLIT.

2. The introduction is similar to a typical term paper because it summarizes a body of knowledge about a relatively narrow topic. It is different from a term paper because it provides a rationale and lead-in to a particular experiment.

3. The method section is designed to describe (a) the research participants, (b) the equipment or materials used in the research, and (c) the manner in which the experiment was conducted. Although all this information is important, the procedures are probably the most important because they allow other researchers to replicate the study. If different participants or equipment (materials) are used, external validity would simply be increased.

4. inferential; descriptive

5. No, you could not use figures or tables as your sole information in a results section. Figures and tables are meant to supplement descriptive and inferential statistics, not to replace them.

6. Although this answer involves opinion, you can make a strong argument that the discussion section is the most important section because it summarizes the experiment's evidence, ties that evidence into previous findings, and draws an overall conclusion.

7. The reference for a chapter from an edited book is more complex than a journal article or book reference because such a reference must include information about both the chapter *and* the book.

8. 1-E   2-B   3-G   4-H   5-A   6-D   7-F   8-C

Study Break   page 440

1. You should not write your research paper in the style of a famous writer because your primary goal is communication rather than entertainment.

2. Three strategies used to improve writing style are (a) write from an outline, (b) write a draft and put it away for some time before rereading it, and (c) have another person read and evaluate your writing. You will have to answer for yourself what you need to change about your writing in order to incorporate these suggestions.

3. Jones (1995) conducted an experiment.

   The participants sat in desks around the room.

   I (or *"The experimenter"*) projected the stimulus items from the rear of the cubicle.

   I found a significant interaction. *or* The data showed a significant interaction.

4. **a.** The participants that were older were tested first. (It is important to distinguish the older participants from the younger.)

    b. The room, which was a classroom, was used for testing. (The notation that the room is a classroom is probably merely a side comment that is not vital in describing the room.)

    c. The ANOVA, which was analyzed on a computer, was significant. (The fact that the analysis was done on a computer should make no difference in its outcome.)

5. Because you are the oldest, you should go first. *Since* was incorrect because a justification was implied rather than a time reference.

Since I began that class I have learned much about statistics. Correct because *since* denotes something has happened after beginning the class.

While we are watching TV, we can also study. Correct because *while* denoted that watching TV and studying will occur at the same time.

Although you are older than me, I should still go first. *While* was incorrect because a contrast was implied rather than a time reference.

6.

Orientals—Asians	elderly—elderly people (or use specific age range)
mankind—humankind or humans	
mothering—parenting	girls and men—women and men
homosexuals—lesbian, gay	chairman—chair
	depressives—depressed patients

7.

a + b = c	trial-by-trial
–1	Enter: Your name

References

American Psychological Association. (1982). *Ethical principles in the conduct of research with human participants.* Washington, DC: Author.

American Psychological Association. (1983). *Publication manual of the American Psychological Association* (3rd ed.). Washington, DC: Author.

American Psychological Association. (1992). *Guidelines for ethical conduct in the care and use of animals.* Washington, DC: Author.

American Psychological Association. (1994). *Publication manual of the American Psychological Association* (4th ed.). Washington, DC: Author.

Anastasi, A. (1988). *Psychological testing* (6th ed.). New York: Macmillan.

Arb, J. D., Wood, K., & O'Loughlin, J. (1994, February). *Effects of cadmium exposure on shock-elicited aggression responding.* Paper presented at the annual Great Plains Students Psychology Convention, Kansas City, MO.

Aronson, E., & Carlsmith, J. M. (1968). Experimentation in social psychology. In G. Lindzey and E. Aronson (Eds.), *The handbook of social psychology* (2nd ed.). Reading, MA: Addison-Wesley.

Ault, R. L. (1991). What goes where? An activity to teach the organization of journal articles. *Teaching of Psychology, 18,* 45–46.

Barlow, D. H., & Hersen, M. (1973). Single-case experimental designs. *Archives of General Psychiatry, 29,* 319–325.

Baumrind, D. (1964). Some thoughts on the ethics of research: After reading Milgram's "Behavioral Study of Obedience." *American Psychologist, 19,* 421–423.

Beach, F. A. (1950). The snark was a boojum. *American Psychologist, 5,* 115–124.

Bellquist, J. E. (1993). *A guide to grammar and usage for psychology and related fields.* Hillsdale, NJ: Erlbaum.

Bender, K., Benkert, J., Ceresa, S., Costa, M. A., Foreman, C., Hinders, T., Kadochnikora, N., Seymore, K., & Thompson, T. (1993, April). *The effect of medication management training on self-administration, evaluation of medication side effects, and symptom recognition, and coping skills in chronic mentally ill outpatients.* Paper presented at the Western Psychology Conference for Undergraduate Research, Santa Clara, CA.

Benjamin, L. T., Jr. (1992, April). *Health, Happiness, and Success: The popular psychology magazine of the 1920s.* Paper presented at the annual meeting of the Eastern Psychological Association, Boston, MA.

Bennett, S. K. (1994). The American Indian: A psychological overview. In W. J. Lonner & R. Malpass (Eds.), *Psychology and culture* (pp. 35–39). Boston: Allyn and Bacon.

Berry, E., Doty, M., Garcia, P., Mettler, J., & Miller, T. (1993, April). *Teaching self-dressing skills to an autistic child using behavior modification and home based intervention*. Paper presented at the Western Psychology Conference for Undergraduates, Santa Clara, CA.

Blumenthal, A. L. (1991). The intrepid Joseph Jastrow. In G. A. Kimble, M. Wertheimer, & C. L. White (Eds.), *Portraits of pioneers in psychology* (pp. 75–87). Washington, DC: American Psychological Association.

Boring, E. G. (1950). *A history of modern psychology* (2nd ed.). New York: Appleton-Century-Crofts.

Bridgman, P. W. (1927). *The logic of modern physics*. New York: Macmillan.

Broad, W. J. (1980). Imbroglio at Yale (I): Emergence of a fraud. *Science, 210,* 38–41.

Burns, R. A., & Gordon, W. U. (1988). Some further observations on serial enumeration and categorical flexibility. *Animal Learning & Behavior, 16,* 425–428.

Burns, R. A., & Sanders, R. E. (1987). Concurrent counting of two and three events in a serial anticipation paradigm. *Bulletin of the Psychonomic Society, 25,* 479–481.

Campbell, D. T. (1957). Factors relevant to the validity of experiments in social settings. *Psychological Bulletin, 54,* 297–312.

Campbell, D. T. (1969). Reforms as experiments. *American Psychologist, 24,* 409–429.

Campbell, D. T., & Stanley, J. C. (1966). *Experimental and quasi-experimental designs for research*. Boston: Houghton Mifflin.

Casanova, T. (1993, April). *Attitudes towards the disabled and need for cognition as predictors of attitude polarization*. Paper presented at the Western Psychology Conference for Undergraduate Research, Santa Clara, CA.

Cathey, N. R. (1992, April). *Effects of caffeine on rats' bar press and maze performance*. Poster presented at Southwestern Psychological Association, Austin, TX.

Cathey, N. R., Smith, R. A., & Davis, S. F. (1993). Effects of caffeine on rats' barpress and maze performance. *Bulletin of the Psychonomic Society, 31,* 49–52.

Cohen, J. (1977). *Statistical power analysis for the behavioral sciences* (rev. ed.). New York: Academic Press.

Collins, N. L., & Read, S. J. (1990). Adult attachment, working models, and relationship quality in dating couples. *Journal of Personality and Social Psychology, 58,* 644–663.

Cook, T. D., & Campbell, D. T. (1979). *Quasi-experimentation: Design & analysis issues for field settings*. Boston: Houghton Mifflin.

Corkin, S. (1984). Lasting consequences of bilateral medial temporal lobectomy: Clinical course and experimental findings in H.M. *Seminars in Neurology, 4,* 249–259.

Creswell, J. W. (1994). *Research design: Qualitative and quantitative approaches*. Thousand Oaks, CA: Sage.

Darley, J. M., & Latan, B. (1968). Bystander intervention in emergencies: Diffusion of responsibility. *Journal of Personality and Social Psychology, 8,* 377–383.

Davis, S. F., Armstrong, S.L.W., & Huss, M. T. (1993). Shock-elicited aggression is influenced by lead and/or alcohol exposure. *Bulletin of the Psychonomic Society, 31,* 451–453.

Davis, S. F., Grover, C. A., & Erickson, C. A. (1987). A comparison of the aversiveness of denatonium saccharide and quinine in humans. *Bulletin of the Psychonomic Society, 25,* 462-463.

Davis, S. F., Grover, C. A., Erickson, C. A., Miller, L. A., & Bowman, J. A. (1987). Analyzing the aversiveness of denatonium saccharide. *Perceptual and Motor Skills, 64,* 1215-1222.

Department of Psychology, Bishop's University. *Plagiarism pamphlet.* Supplied December 23, 1994.

Dickens, D., Ishigame, A., Subacz, D., Sponsel, S., Strader, M., & Foy, J. (1992). The interaction of source and post-event misinformation on the accuracy of eyewitness testimony. *Modern Psychological Studies, 1,* 14-19.

Dukes, W. F. (1965). *N* = 1. *Psychological Bulletin, 64,* 74-79.

Elfenbaum, P. D., & Sagrestano, L. M. (1993, June). *Influence dynamics of women and men in power relationships.* Poster presented at the American Psychological Society, Chicago, IL.

Feist, P. S. (1993, May). *Effects of style of dress on witness credibility.* Paper presented at the annual meeting of the Midwestern Psychological Association, Chicago, IL.

Felipe Russo, N. J., & Sommer, R. (1966). Invasion of personal space. *Social Problems, 14,* 206-214.

Festinger, L. (1957). *A theory of cognitive dissonance.* Stanford, CA: Stanford University Press.

Fowler, M., & Mashburn, K. (1993, November). *Preferences in art due to media types and styles.* Paper presented at the annual meeting of the Association for Psychological and Educational Research in Kansas, Topeka, KS.

Geronimus, A. T. (1991). Teenage childbearing and social and reproductive disadvantage: The evolution of complex questions and the demise of simple answers. *Family Relations, 40,* 463-471.

Glesne, C., & Peshkin, A. (1992). *Becoming qualitative researchers: An introduction.* White Plains, NY: Longman.

Grunchla, L., Hegarty, M. R., Himmegar, A., Hollett, R., & Hostetter, M. (1993, May). *Don't touch that dial: How common auditory backgrounds affect students' reading comprehension.* Psi Chi poster presented at the annual meeting of the Midwestern Psychological Association, Chicago, IL.

Guerin, B. (1986). Mere presence effects in humans: A review. *Journal of Personality and Social Psychology, 22,* 38-77.

Gussman, K., & Harder, D. (1990). Offspring personality and perceptions of parental use of reward and punishment. *Psychological Reports, 67,* 923-930.

Guthrie, R. V. (1976). *Even the rat was white: A historical view of psychology.* New York: Harper & Row.

Hagos, A. (1993, April). *Effects of orthographic distinctiveness and word frequency on memory.* Presented at the Western Psychology Conference for Undergraduate Research, Santa Clara, CA.

Hall, R. V., Fox, R., Willard, D., Goldsmith, L., Emerson, M., Owen, M., Davis, F., & Porcia, E. (1971). The teacher as observer and experimenter in the modification of disputing and talking-out behaviors. *Journal of Applied Behavior Analysis, 4,* 141-149.

Hayes, K. M., Miller, H. R., & Davis, S. F. (1993). *Examining the relationship between interpersonal flexibility, self-esteem, and death anxiety.* Paper presented at the annual meeting of the Southwestern Psychological Association, Corpus Christi, TX.

Hedrick, T. E., Bickman, L., & Rog, D. J. (1993). *Applied research design: A practical guide.* Newbury Park, CA: Sage.

Hedrick, T. E., & Shipman, S. L. (1988). Multiple questions require multiple designs: An evaluation of the 1981 changes to the AFDC program. *Evaluation Review, 12,* 427–448.

Helmreich, R., & Stapp, J. (1974). Short form of the Texas Social Behavior Inventory (TSBI), an objective measure of self-esteem. *Bulletin of the Psychonomic Society, 4,* 473–475.

Hersen, M. (1982). Single-case experimental designs. In A. S. Bellack, M. Hersen, & A. E. Kazdin (Eds.), *International handbook of behavior modification and therapy* (pp. 167–203). New York: Plenum Press.

Hersen, M., & Barlow, D. H. (1976). *Single-case experimental designs: Strategies for studying behavioral change.* New York: Pergamon Press.

Hinkley, R. H., & Kohut, A. (1993). Polling and democracy in the former USSR and Eastern Europe. *The Public Perspective, 4*(6), 14–18.

Hurt, L. E., Palmer, S. J., Sereg, M. L., & Stephens, L. J. (1993, May). *Analysis of voter reactions to marital infidelity of political candidates: The role of voter political ideology, candidate party affiliation, and gender.* Paper presented at the annual meeting of the Midwestern Psychological Association, Chicago, IL.

Jagels, C. T. (1993, April). *Adjustment to college as a function of extraversion-introversion.* Paper presented at the Western Psychology Conference for Undergraduate Research, Santa Clara, CA.

Johnson, R., & Branscum, E. (1993, April). *Habituation in open field behavior of the rat: Relevance of fractal dimensions to behavioral measures.* Presented at the Western Psychology Conference for Undergraduate Research, Santa Clara, CA.

Jones, J. H. (1981). *Bad blood: The Tuskegee syphilis experiment.* New York: Free Press.

Jones, J. M. (1994). The African American: A duality dilemma? In W. J. Lonner & R. Malpass (Eds.), *Psychology and culture* (pp. 17–21). Boston: Allyn and Bacon.

Jones, R. R., Vaught, R. S., & Weinrott, M. (1977). Time-series analysis in operant research. *Journal of Applied Behavior Analysis, 10,* 151–166.

Kalat, J. (1992). *Biological psychology* (4th ed.). Belmont, CA: Wadsworth.

Kazdin, A. E. (1976). Statistical analyses for single-case experimental designs. In M. Hersen & D. H. Barlow (Eds.), *Single-case experimental designs: Strategies for studying behavioral change* (pp. 265–316). New York: Pergamon Press.

Kazdin, A. E. (1984). *Behavior modification in applied settings* (3rd ed.). Homewood, IL: Dorsey Press.

Keith-Spiegel, P. (1991). *The complete guide to graduate school admission: Psychology and related fields.* Hillsdale, NJ: Erlbaum.

Keppel, G., Saufley, W. H., Jr., & Tokunaga, H. (1992). *Introduction to design & analysis: A student's handbook* (2nd ed.). New York: W. H. Freeman.

Kimmel, A. J. (1988). *Ethics and values in applied social research.* Beverly Hills, CA: Sage.

Kirk, R. E. (1968). *Experimental design: Procedures for the behavioral sciences.* Belmont, CA: Brooks/Cole.

Kirk, R. E. (1996, April). *Practical significance: A concept whose time has come.* Southwestern Psychological Association presidential address, Houston, TX.

Koestler, A. (1964). *The act of creation.* New York: Macmillan.

Krantz, D. S., Glass, D. C., & Snyder, M. L. (1974). Helplessness, stress level, and the coronary-prone behavior pattern. *Journal of Experimental Social Psychology, 10,* 284-300.

Lang, P. J., & Melamed, B. G. (1969). Avoidance conditioning therapy of an infant with chronic ruminative vomiting. *Journal of Abnormal Psychology, 74,* 1-8.

Langley, W. M., Theis, J., Davis, S. F., Richard, M. M., & Grover, C. A. (1987). Effects of denatonium saccharide on the drinking behavior of the grasshopper mouse (*Onychomys leucogaster*). *Bulletin of the Psychonomic Society, 25,* 17-19.

Lawson, T. J. 1995. An advisor update: Gaining admission into graduate programs in psychology. *Teaching of Psychology, 22,* 225—227.

Lee, D. J., & Hall, C.C.I. (1994). Being Asian in North America. In W. J. Lonner & R. Malpass (Eds.), *Psychology and culture* (pp. 29-33). Boston: Allyn and Bacon.

Loftus, E. F. (1979). *Eyewitness testimony.* Cambridge, MA: Harvard University Press.

Lonner, W. J., & Malpass, R. (1994a). Preface. In W. J. Lonner & R. Malpass (Eds.), *Psychology and culture* (pp. ix-xiii). Boston: Allyn and Bacon.

Lonner, W. J., & Malpass, R. (1994b). When psychology and culture meet: An introduction to cross-cultural psychology. In W. J. Lonner & R. Malpass (Eds.), *Psychology and culture* (pp. 1-12). Boston: Allyn and Bacon.

Losch, M. E., & Cacioppo, J. T. (1990). Cognitive dissonance may enhance sympathetic tonus, but attitudes are changed to reduce negative affect rather than arousal. *Journal of Experimental Social Psychology, 26,* 289-304.

Mack, D., & Rainey, D. (1990). Female applicants' grooming and personnel selection. *Journal of Social Behavior and Personality, 5,* 399-407.

Maggio, R. (1991). *The bias-free word finder: A dictionary of nondiscriminatory language.* Boston: Beacon Press.

Mahoney, M. J. (1987). Scientific publication and knowledge politics. *Journal of Social Behavior and Personality, 2,* 165-176.

Marín, G. (1994). The experience of being a Hispanic in the United States. In W. J. Lonner & R. Malpass (Eds.), *Psychology and culture* (pp. 23-27). Boston: Allyn and Bacon.

Martin, K., Farruggia, S., & Yeske, K. (1993, May). *The effects of stress on reported state and trait anxiety.* Psi Chi paper presented at the annual meeting of the Midwestern Psychological Association, Chicago, IL.

Matsumoto, D. (1994). *People: Psychology from a cultural perspective.* Pacific Grove, CA: Brooks/Cole.

McBride, G., King, M. G., & James, J. W. (1965). Social proximity effects on galvanic skin responses in adult humans. *Journal of Psychology, 61,* 153-157.

McGovern, M. E., & Fischer, J. M. (1993, April). *Positive judgments of personality as a function of touch and eye contact*. Presented at the Western Psychology Conference for Undergraduate Research, Santa Clara, CA.

McGuigan, F. J. (1960). *Experimental psychology*. Englewood Cliffs, NJ: Prentice Hall.

McInerny, R. M. (1970). *A history of Western philosophy*. Notre Dame, IN: University of Notre Dame Press.

McNeal, T. (1994, April). *Does dream recall increase with length of sleep?* Paper presented at the Arkansas Symposium for Psychology Students, Magnolia, AR.

Medewar, P. B. (1979). *Advice to a young scientist*. New York: Harper & Row.

Messina, J. (1993, April). *Opiate withdrawal in infant guinea pigs*. Paper presented at the annual meeting of the Eastern Psychological Association.

Meyer, C. L. (1993, June). *Offspring self-esteem and perceptions of parental discipline*. Paper presented at the annual meeting of the American Psychological Society, Chicago, IL.

Milgram, S. (1963). Behavioral study of obedience. *Journal of Abnormal and Social Psychology, 67,* 371-378.

Milgram, S. (1964). Issues in the study of obedience: A reply to Baumrind. *American Psychologist, 19,* 848-852.

Miller, H. B., & Williams, W. H. (1983). *Ethics and animals*. Clifton, NJ: Humana Press.

Miller, N. E. (1985). The value of behavioral research on animals. *American Psychologist, 40,* 423-440.

Mills, B. S. (1993, March). *A develop-mental study of celebrity effectiveness in advertising for pre-adolescent children*. Paper presented at the annual Great Plains Students' Psychology Convention, Maryville, MO.

Mook, D. G. (1983). In defense of external invalidity. *American Psychologist, 38,* 379-387.

Mooney, R. L. (1950). *Mooney problem check list*. New York: The Psychological Corporation.

Nash, S. M. (1983). *The relationship between early ethanol exposure and adult taste preference*. Paper submitted for J. P. Guilford/Psi Chi undergraduate research competition.

Norusis, M. J. (1988). *SPSS-X introductory statistics guide*. Chicago, IL: SPSS Inc.

O'Loughlin, J., Graves, J. C., Davis, S. F., & Smith, R. A. (1993). Caffeine exposure affects barpressing. *Bulletin of the Psychonomic Society, 31,* 321-322.

Orne, M. T. (1962). On the social psychology of the psychological experiment: With particular reference to demand characteristics and their implications. *American Psychologist, 17,* 776-783.

Packer, M. J., & Addison, R. B. (Eds.). (1989). *Entering the circle: Hermeneutic investigation in psychology*. Albany, NY: SUNY Press.

Pazdral, R. K. (1993, April). *Performance as a function of physiological arousal: Athletic versus non-athletic persons*. Presented at the Western Psychology Conference for Undergraduate Research, Santa Clara, CA.

Plair, S. (1994, April). *Reactions to first intercourse: Differences in self-reported responses by gender*. Paper presented at the Arkansas Symposium for Psychology Students, Magnolia, AR.

Purdy, J. E., Reinehr, R. C., & Swartz, J. D. (1989). Graduate admissions criteria of leading psychology departments. *American Psychologist, 44,* 960–961.

Reagan, T. (1983). *The case for animal rights.* Berkeley, CA: University of California Press.

Reid, D. W., & Ware, E. E. (1973). Multidimensionality of internal-external control: Implications for past and future research. *Canadian Journal of Behavioural Research, 5,* 264–271.

Roethlisberger, F. J., & Dickson, W. J. (1939). *Management and the worker.* Cambridge, MA: Harvard University Press.

Rosenthal, R. (1966). *Experimenter effects in behavioral research.* New York: Appleton-Century-Crofts.

Rosenthal, R. (1976). *Experimenter effects in behavioral research* (enlarged ed.). New York: Irvington Press.

Rosenthal, R. (1977). Biasing effects of experimenters. *ETC: A review of general semantics, 34,* 253–264.

Rosenthal, R. (1985). From unconscious experimenter bias to teacher expectancy effects. In J. B. Dusek (Ed.), *Teacher expectancies.* Hillsdale, NJ: Lawrence Erlbaum Associates.

Rosenthal, R., & Fode, K. L. (1963). The effect of experimenter bias on the performance of the albino rat. *Behavioral Science, 8,* 183–189.

Rosenthal, R., & Jacobson, L. (1968). *Psychodynamics in the classroom.* New York: Holt.

Rosenthal, R., & Rosnow, R. L. (1984). *Essentials of behavioral research.* New York: McGraw-Hill.

Rosenthal, R., & Rosnow, R. (1991). *Essentials of behavioral research* (2nd ed.). New York: McGraw-Hill.

Sanford, K. (1993, April). *Correlates of adult romantic attachment style.* Presented at the Western Psychology Conference for Undergraduate Research, Santa Clara, CA.

Sasson, R., & Nelson, T. M. (1969). The human experimental subject in context. *Canadian Psychologist, 10,* 409–437.

Schein, E. H. (1987). *The clinical perspective in fieldwork.* Newbury Park, CA: Sage.

Schmeising, A. K., & Englert, N. E. (1993, May). *The detrimental effects of noise on social interaction.* Paper presented at the annual meeting of the Midwestern Psychological Association, Chicago, IL.

Schultz, D. P., & Schultz, S. E. (1992). *A history of modern psychology* (5th ed.). Fort Worth, TX: Harcourt Brace Jovanovich.

Sears, D. O. (1986). College sophomores in the laboratory: Influences of a narrow data base on social psychology's view of human nature. *Journal of Personality and Social Psychology, 51,* 515–530.

Singer, P. (1975). *Animal liberation.* New York: Random House.

Skinner, B. F. (1961). *Cumulative record* (Expanded edition). New York: Appleton-Century-Crofts.

Skinner, B. F. (1966). Operant behavior. In W. K. Honig (Ed.), *Operant behavior: Areas of research and application* (pp. 12–32). New York: Appleton-Century-Crofts.

Small, W. S. (1901). An experimental study of the mental processes of the rat. *American Journal of Psychology, 11,* 133–165.

Smith, R. A. (1985). Advising beginning psychology majors for graduate school. *Teaching of Psychology, 12,* 194–198.

Solomon, R. L. (1949). An extension of control group design. *Psychological Bulletin, 46,* 137–150.

Spatz, C. (1993). *Basic statistics: Tales of distributions* (5th ed.). Pacific Grove, CA: Brooks/Cole.

Steele, C. M., Southwick, L. L., & Critchlow, B. (1981). Dissonance and alcohol: Drinking your troubles away. *Journal of Personality and Social Psychology, 41,* 831–846.

Strauss, A., & Corbin, J. (1990). *Basics of qualitative research: Grounded theory procedures and techniques.* Newbury Park, CA: Sage.

Tarpy, R. M. (1982). *Principles of animal learning and motivation.* Glenview, IL: Scott, Foresman and Co.

Tavris, C. (1992). *The mismeasure of woman.* New York: Touchstone.

Templer, D. I. (1970). The construction and validation of a death anxiety scale. *Journal of General Psychology, 82,* 165–177.

Van Dyke, M. (1993, June). *Gender differences in mate preference.* Paper presented at the annual meeting of the American Psychological Society, Chicago, IL.

Vitacco, M., & Schmidt, S. (1993, May). *Self-esteem and death anxiety in middle-aged blue collar and college-aged males.* Paper presented at the annual meeting of the Midwestern Psychological Association, Chicago, IL.

Walker, A., Jr. (Ed.). (1994). *Thesaurus of psychological index terms.* Washington, DC: American Psychological Association.

Waterman, R. (1993, February). *Video games and mental rotation.* Paper presented at the annual Texas Christian University Psi Chi Convention, Fort Worth, TX.

Watson, D. L., & Tharp, R. G. (1993). *Self-directed behavior: Self-modification for personal adjustment* (6th ed.). Pacific Grove, CA: Brooks/Cole.

Weinberg, R. A. (1989). Intelligence and IQ: Landmark issues and great debates. *American Psychologist, 44,* 98–104.

Weintraub, D., Higgins, M., Beishline, M., Matchinsky, D., & Pierce, M. (1994, November). *Do impostors really hold irrational beliefs?* Paper presented at the annual meeting of the Association for Psychological and Educational Research in Kansas, Lawrence, KS.

Weiss, J., Gilbert, K., Giordano, P., & Davis, S. F. (1993). Academic dishonesty, Type A behavior, and classroom orientation. *Bulletin of the Psychonomic Society, 31,* 101–102.

Weiten, W., & Lloyd, M. A. (1994). *Psychology applied to modern life: Adjustment in the 90s* (4th ed.). Pacific Grove, CA: Brooks/Cole.

Worchel, S., Cooper, J., & Goethals, G. R. (1991). *Understanding social psychology* (5th ed.). Pacific Grove, CA: Brooks/Cole.

Yarbrough, L. (1993, April). *Effects of color on mail survey response rate.* Presented at the Arkansas Symposium for Psychology Students, Magnolia, AR.

Zajonc, R. B. (1965). Social facilitation. *Science, 149,* 269–274.

Index

Name

Subject